# Effective Training

JAMES W. THACKER  UNIVERSITY OF WINDSOR

P. NICK BLANCHARD  EASTERN MICHIGAN UNIVERSITY

PEARSON

Prentice
Hall

Toronto

**Library and Archives Canada Cataloguing in Publication**

Thacker, James W.
    Effective training / James W. Thacker, P. Nick Blanchard.

Includes index.
American eds. had authors in reverse order.
ISBN 0-13-127175-X

I. Blanchard, P. Nick  II. Blanchard, P. Nick  Effective training.
III. Title.

HF5549.5.T7T43 2006      658.3'124      C2005-902007-5

ISBN 0-13-127175-X

Vice-President, Editorial Director: Michael J. Young
Editor-in-Chief: Gary Bennett
Sponsoring Editor: Lori Will
Executive Marketing Manager: Cas Shields
Associate Editor: Eleanor MacKay
Production Editor: Cheryl Jackson
Copy Editor: Ron Jacques
Proofreader: Dawn Hunter
Production Coordinator: Andrea Falkenberg
Manufacturing Coordinator: Susan Johnson
Page Layout: Laser Words
Permissions Manager: Susan Wallace-Cox
Permissions Researcher: Amanda McCormick
Art Director: Mary Opper
Cover Image: Getty Images

1 2 3 4 5    10 09 08 07 06

Printed and bound in United States of America.

This book is dedicated with love and thanks to my wife and best friend, Gabrielle, without whose encouragement and participation this book could not have been written.

J. T.

This one's for Mom and Dad.

N. B.

# BRIEF CONTENTS

# CONTENTS

## Chapter 5   Traditional Training Methods   157

## Chapter 8   Evaluation of Training   261

# FOREWORD

## HR in a New Economy

We are on the threshold of change at least as radical as the industrial revolution. Today, in the early 21st century, with respect to knowledge management, we are as advanced as industrial management was in the early 20th century. In what *The Economist* terms, "a survey of the near future," Peter Drucker, the famous management guru, argues that where, in the past, we have been used to measuring our success through making things, the basis for success in the next society is knowledge—what we know and how we use it.[1] Changing demographics and the growth in knowledge work mean that the assumptions still held by many HR professionals about the nature of the workforce no longer hold. In the near future, most workers will no longer be full-time employees and knowledge workers will dominate the total work force. Yesterday's reality was characterized by stability, growth, monopolistic markets, and predictable technology. The next society will be a knowledge society characterized by "borderlessness," increased opportunity, and instability.

As the importance of knowledge and its application to organizational innovations increases, the good news is that HR professionals are in a position as never before—to play a vital role in organization effectiveness. The problem is the gap between promise and delivery.

Where is HRM today? Most of what constitutes the field of HRM is based on thinking developed through industrial management in the past decades and many HRM texts still reflect this traditional world. It is not surprising that studies indicate most HR practitioners do not consult academic research, and are frustrated at the lack of application and current relevance of what they do take the time to read. A hopeful sign is that the importance of HR knowledge is increasingly recognized by tomorrow's generation. In a recent (2001) survey of HRPAO members, almost three-quarters of HR professionals with less than 12 years experience reported that specialist education had played a highly significant role in their career progression.[2]

The development of the HR field is also demonstrated in the increasing recognition of a national Certified Human Resources Professional (CHRP) designation across Canada, characterized by a mix of HR knowledge and applied professional competencies. Students of HRM seeking the knowledge and application base necessary for achieving this designation and success in the profession will find the new Pearson HR Series an essential element of this goal.

## The Pearson HR Series

The Pearson HR series is designed for today's HR students, instructors, and professionals who need access to HR knowledge reflecting current realities (rather than yesterday's tradition) in a usable and applied format that considers the time pressures within which they must succeed. Some of the key characteristics of the series are:

- an emphasis on practicality
- ease of use and flexibility
- **incorporation of the CCHRA Required Professional Capabilities for Entry Level Practitioners and Experienced Professionals**

---

[1]Drucker, P. F., 2001. The Next Society, Special Survey in *The Economist*, 3 Nov., 2001, 1-20.

[2]Templer, A.J. and Belcourt, M. 2001. *HRPAO Professional Standards Education Survey*. HRPAO, Toronto.

- guidelines for fostering leadership and strategic vision
- guidelines for evaluating your organization's effectiveness
- a focus on innovations in HRM

The HR series intends to match all the key knowledge requirements of professional certification, but to do this with an eye to the evolving nature of these requirements. While on a march towards a knowledge economy, a qualified workforce equipped with the necessary skills for present and future endeavours remains a critical source of organizational growth and prosperity in Canada. In this context of change and ever-increasing competency demands I am delighted to introduce our new training and development text, which clearly addresses the fundamental contribution of a qualified and skilled workforce to organization effectiveness.

## Effective Training

*Effective Training* by Jim Thacker and Nick Blanchard presents a carefully reasoned and comprehensive analysis of human resources development within the framework of a strategic approach that is fully integrated into and supportive of organization strategy. Thacker and Blanchard argue that an effective human resource development process is one that requires close management control and commitment, but is also dependent on employee involvement and participation for its success.

This text is organized in a way that ensures students find useful information that they can apply to the world of work quickly and easily. It recognizes the changing reality of knowledge work and competencies in Canada today and, hence, the need for students to question and think about what they read. The authors use strategic models to introduce each stage of the training development process: needs assessment, design, development, implementation, and evaluation. The final chapters examine special training topics that include orientation, diversity, and team training as well as management development.

**The CCHRA Required Professional Capabilities.** Throughout its development, the authors have specifically incorporated into the text all of the key *Entry-Level* Required Professional Capabilities (RPCs) for ***Organizational Learning, Development and Training*** as outlined by the Canadian Council of Human Resources Associations (CCHRA), and the majority of the *Experienced Professional-Level* RPCs. A listing of these RPCs is included in the form of an appendix as a guide for those students seeking their CHRP accreditation. You can find a complete list of the Required Professional Capabiliies at **www.cchra-ccarh.ca/parc/en/section_3/ss33e.asp.**

The real strength of *Effective Training* stems from authors who have a thorough grasp of the essential foundational, social, and psychological principles of learning and who are continuously informed of the practical applications those principles have in the world of work. The authors have combined in-depth coverage of theory with numerous practical applications. These applications include: scenarios that demonstrate training in action, real-world examples, and training for small businesses. Practitioners themselves will be particularly pleased with the comprehensive Fabrics Inc. case in Chapters 3, 4, and 8, which guides the reader through all the steps of an actual training process using the authors' strategic HR development model. Finally, each chapter has a wealth of end-of-chapter material, which includes current cases, critical thinking questions, implications for practice, and web research exercises that will appeal to students and HR professionals alike.

Dr. Andrew Templer
Odette School of Business
University of Windsor
2005-03-12

# PREFACE

We created the idea for this book while fishing on a beautiful lake in northern Manitoba. Both of us were teaching a human resource development course and were unsatisfied with the texts available at the time. Our main concern was that we really needed two texts for the course, one providing the theory and scholarship surrounding the learning–teaching experience and one providing the application and "how to" part of the experience. This text is full of examples to provide the trainee with a clear understanding of the theory and conceptual framework we provide. An added case called Fabrics Inc. takes the reader through what actually occurs in the development of a training program. The case is developed step-by-step from needs analysis through design and evaluation. For example, in Chapter 3, the needs analysis process used in Fabrics Inc. is detailed so the trainee sees what is actually done. Then it is picked up again at the end of the design chapter and again the trainee is brought through the process to the end of design. This approach gives the trainee a real understanding of the things that need to be done and how they are actually done.

We continue to differ from other training books in that we place training activities in the context of organizational strategy. Whether you are a manager or a training practitioner, this book will be of both conceptual and practical value for developing training programs that meet strategic and tactical needs. At the same time, an overarching model of the training process will guide you step-by-step through the training procedures, from initial needs analysis through the evaluation of training's effectiveness. As human resource competencies become a significant competitive advantage, the pace and intensity of organizational training increases dramatically. Human resource development or "performance improvement" departments must demonstrate that their programs enhance competencies that are of strategic value. As a company's strategies change, the types of management competencies and styles need to change as well, and human resource development is responsible for this alignment. We address these and related issues because we believe that effective training practices are determined by the organizational context in which they occur.

## UNIQUE CHARACTERISTICS OF THIS BOOK

This book differs from others on the same topic in a number of ways. For example we:

- Integrate training into the strategic planning process.
- Show the important relationship between organizational development practitioners and trainers.
- Provide an overarching model of the training process, with a more detailed model of each phase of the process, making it easy to see how each phase connects to achieve the training objectives.
- Provide an understanding of training and its implementation as it relates to the small business.
- Integrate learning and design theory into the development of training so the reader understands how theory helps design effective training.
- Describe the step-by-step process of developing an actual training package as we move through each of the training process stages from needs analysis through the evaluation.

- Provide numerous examples of actual training situations in Canadian companies to highlight aspects of the training process.
- Provide a step-by-step process for developing learning objectives with many examples of good and bad objectives.
- Use a contingency approach, identifying alternative approaches to the training process and the associated strengths and limitations, rather than a "one best way."
- Incorporate a micro theory of design into the design of training.
- Provide a comprehensive case in Chapter 1 that is applicable throughout the text and is often referred to in the remaining chapters.

Other aspects of the text that we believe are important are:

- Learning objectives at the beginning of each chapter
- Definitions of terms in the margin
- Case at the beginning of each chapter, sometimes split with its follow-up at the end of the chapter
- Questions, cases, and exercises at the end of each chapter
- Section at the end of each chapter called Implications for Practice, which highlights important practical issues
- An instructor's manual with sample syllabi, answers to questions at the end of the chapters, and a test bank of questions
- PowerPoint slides of all tables and figures

Learning objectives provide trainees with an understanding of what the training is trying to accomplish, so they are an important part of the training process. Better learning is achieved if, at the beginning of training, people know where they should focus their attention. Therefore, at the beginning of each chapter we identify its learning objectives, stating what the reader should be capable of doing after completing the chapter. (The value of learning objectives and the characteristics of good objectives are discussed in depth in Chapter 4.)

Following the learning objectives is a case example to stimulate the reader to think about the issues that will be raised in the chapter. Throughout the chapter we refer back to the case to make specific points, asking the reader relevant questions about the case. Some of the cases are presented in totality at the beginning of the chapter; others are split into two parts, the first part stopping at a critical point, and the rest presented at the end of the chapter, so the reader can see how the issues were handled or what consequences resulted from the actions taken.

At the end of each chapter are discussion questions, cases, and exercises to enhance understanding. The instructor's manual provides more information about this material and offers additional ideas for teaching. It also includes sample course outlines and a test bank.

There is also a section called Implications for Practice at the end of each chapter, which provides a focus on the practical aspects to consider in development of training.

Another important difference in this book is the overarching model of the training process and its sub-processes. This model provides an understanding of the logical sequencing of training activities, from needs analysis to implementation and evaluation. The model demonstrates training as a system and how each of its processes is interconnected. Thus each phase of the training process (i.e., needs assessment, design, development, implementation, and evaluation) is covered in its own chapter. These chapters begin with a description of the types of input needed to complete that phase and the types of output produced. The bulk of each chapter provides a step-by-step description of how the input is transformed into the output. The output from one phase then becomes the input for the next.

For ease of reading we have not used the he/she convention when the context of the material requires a gender reference. Instead we alternate the use of gender throughout the text.

Most training books focus on large organizations that have access to many resources, ignoring the smaller companies with more limited resources. We address the training issues faced by smaller businesses in two ways. First, the contingency approach provides alternative activities and procedures, some of them compatible with limited resources. Throughout the book we address the applicability of various approaches to the smaller business. Second, many of the chapters include sections directed specifically at the small business. These sections provide possible alternatives and describe what some small businesses are actually doing in these areas. Unfortunately, the literature on small business training practices is relatively sparse. If you know of successful small business practices, we would love to hear about them and include them in subsequent editions.

We know that we failed to locate many of the excellent teaching techniques, exercises, and research applications that are available. Our goal is to improve this book continually so that it makes learning and teaching the joy that it can be. To that end we ask you to contact us with your thoughts, applications, exercises, and so on with the idea of sharing them. **You can reach us at jwt@uwindsor.ca or Nick.Blanchard@emich.edu.** Of course, any contributions will be acknowledged or cited as appropriate in future editions of this book.

## ORGANIZATION AND PLAN OF THE BOOK

We begin with an overview of training and a definition of key terms. The first chapter also discusses training's role in the organization, how training fits into the human resources (HR) function, and how the training function fits into the structure of large and small companies. We also discuss strategic planning and the roles human resources and HRD play in this process. Here we show how input from the human resources function in general and the human resource development function in particular can influence strategic direction. We then proceed to discuss how these functions develop internal strategies and tactics to support the company's strategic plan. Throughout the text, we often refer back to this chapter to demonstrate how strategic issues drive human resource development decisions. We also provide an important link between organizational development (OD) practitioners and trainers, showing how the competencies of each of these disciplines complement and support the objectives of the other. In the remaining chapters we use an OD philosophy to address ways in which the training process and outcomes can be integrated into other organizational systems. This integration of the training process into a systems perspective provides the reader with an understanding of where training fits in the organization and how it operates.

The case example provides a discussion point for many of the topics in this and subsequent chapters, allowing the trainee to walk through a case from the beginning of the strategic plan to the development of training.

Chapter 2 provides the theoretical and conceptual framework for understanding the training process. It begins with a short discussion of the practical application of theory. A model of the factors that determine performance (motivation, knowledge, skills, abilities, and environment) is followed by a review of theories of motivation and learning. These theories are discussed in terms of their application to training. Then there is a discussion of resistance to learning and applications of adult learning theory to overcoming this resistance. The chapter concludes with a discussion of individual trainee differences and offers training alternatives that can address such differences. The concepts and principles developed here are referred to throughout many of the following chapters, tying particular practices to the theoretical rationale for those practices.

Chapter 3 addresses the first phase of the training model presented in Chapter 1: needs analysis. An expanded graphic of this phase is presented and discussed at the outset so the reader will understand the organization of the chapter. The philosophy of needs analysis is discussed in terms of both its proactive use (as related to the strategic plan) and its reactive use (to deal with immediate concerns and changing conditions). The relationship between these two approaches is also explored. The steps involved in the needs analysis are discussed, along with the sources from which data can be gathered and to set training priorities. The chapter ends with an example of a real training process for Fabrics Inc., walking the trainee through the needs analysis as it is actually done for the company.

Chapter 4 begins with the second phase of the training model: training design. The outcomes of the needs assessment phase are shown as inputs to this phase. Then the chapter identifies the activities conducted in the design phase of training. First is the development of the training/learning objectives. Here a formula for development of learning objectives is provided along with numerous examples of effective objectives. Next we deal with the identification of organizational constraints on training and factors that will facilitate learning. The learning facilitation factors focus separately on the trainee and the training design. Following that, we discuss factors that facilitate the transfer of learning back to the trainee's job. These factors are broken down into training design factors and organizational systems factors back on the job. Next we discuss a micro theory of design and demonstrate how it helps in the design of a training program. We also integrate Social Learning Theory with the micro theory of design, showing how they are related. At the end of the chapter, Fabrics Inc. is revisited and the process of design is examined step-by-step.

Chapter 5 provides information on traditional methods of training such as Cases and Simulations through to on-the-job training. The various training methods are described, along with their strengths and limitations, using learning theory as a framework for this discussion. Included here are the relative costs; trainer versus trainee control over what is learned and how; effectiveness at developing knowledge, skills, or changing attitudes; and issues related to training group size and individual differences. Included in the discussion of each method is the practical application—how to use the method effectively.

Chapter 6 covers all the same issues covered in the previous chapter but for computer-based training methods. It also covers the various methods of delivery.

Chapter 7 begins with a summary table of the various methods' effectiveness in meeting knowledge, skill, and attitude change objectives. From there, it is divided into two parts: development and implementation of training. For development we again provide a model to follow through the process, examining the inputs (from the design phase) through to the outputs. Here we provide some forms that you might use, tables that provide step-by-step procedures for developing aspects of training, issues to consider in developing training using different methods, and so forth.

Then the model for implementation is provided, the outputs from the development becoming the inputs for the implementation. Here we follow the process of putting on the training and what needs to be done to assure success. Again the focus is on practical applications, beginning with hints to assist trainers in effective use of the lecture method. Then there is a practical guide related to aspects to consider in the implementation of training, including a dry run and pilot program. Finally we address some of the critical issues related to transfer of training.

Chapter 8 begins with the model for evaluation and addresses the issues and activities involved in the evaluation phase of the overarching training model. While various evaluation issues are discussed in each phase of the training model, we provide the bulk of the information at this point in the book (after development and implementation). However, we stress the importance of incorporating appropriate evaluation activities into each of the other phases of the model. Chapter 8 provides guidance and actual examples of the various types of evaluation that can be used. At the end of the chapter we revisit Fabrics Inc. to provide the process that takes place at this stage of training. Here, we provide actual evaluation forms that are used to test employees from Fabrics inc. at the end of training.

Chapter 9 contains two parts. First, the focus is on four special training topics: orientation, diversity, sexual harassment, and team training. In-depth discussion is provided, covering what organizations are doing in these areas and why it is important. Finally, a number of other special training topics are addressed in terms of their importance and what various organizations are doing in that area.

Chapter 10 begins with a general overview of a manager's job, and then discusses the types of competencies needed by managers. This discussion includes the conceptual, technical, and interpersonal knowledge and skills, as well as personal traits or styles. In addition to the traditional listing of various types of management development programs that address these areas of competency, the capacity of our readers is enhanced through a model that allows the training professional to determine what competencies a manager in a particular organization needs. The model integrates the competitive strategy, organizational structure, and technology literature into a continuum that describes the organizational context in which managers must operate. This context determines the relative value to the company that various managerial competencies and characteristics (such as style) are likely to provide. This chapter also discusses three important areas of managerial knowledge and competency: understanding of the organizational context, self-awareness and diagnostic skills, and adaptability. The special issues related to training top executives are also discussed. The chapter includes a discussion of the special needs of technical managers.

## ACKNOWLEDGMENTS

In a boat in northern Manitoba on a quiet sunny day, while we were catching our share of walleye, we conceived writing this book. From that time until now, many people helped make this book possible, and we are grateful to them. Of course, any errors or omissions are ultimately ours, and we bear responsibility for them.

The people at Pearson Education Canada were very helpful. Thanks to James Bosma, Acquisitions Editior, for working so hard and long to get the project off the ground. It did take a while. Special thanks to Eleanor MacKay, Associate Editor, whose advice, help, and most of all patience with us, were ultimately responsible for its final form. Thanks to Cheryl Jackson, production editor, for her timely feedback and assistance in turning our manuscript into this textbook.

Particular thanks to Ron Jacques, Dawn Hunter, Andrea Falkenberg, and Michelle Bellemare for their efforts related to copy editing, proofreading, production, and design. Having written a few textbooks we are aware that all editors, coordinators, and designers are not created equal, and, in Ron, Dawn, Andrea, and Michelle, we have good ones. We appreciate their diligence and skills. Thanks also to those anonymous yet most important people in editorial and production who create the final images, text, and layout that make reading and learning a pleasure. Thanks to Gabrielle Thacker, who is able to detect the errors that everyone else misses. Also thanks to JoAnn Foote, for her timely assistance in seeing that our ideas were expressed in the active voice.

We would like to acknowledge the contributions of both the academics and practitioners who shared their insights with us. Specifically, we would like to thank Mitchell Fields, University of Windsor; and Greg Huszczo and Rick Camp, both with Eastern Michigan University. Thanks go to Lee Sanborn of Ford Motor Company for providing information and access to portions of Ford's Production Systems training. Nina Adams helped us understand what virtual reality and multimedia mean in the world of computer training and we thank her. Thanks also to the folks at Simulearn who provided us with a unique experience in leadership training via computer simulation.

And of course a special thanks as well to the reviewers of earlier drafts of the book. Their feedback has really made a difference in the shaping of the book. They are Sean Burke, College of the North Atlantic; Jerome Collins, St. Clair College of Applied Arts and Technology; Wenlu Feng, Centennial College; Carolyn Gaunt, Cambrian College; Christine Jackson, Carleton University; Suzanne Kavanagh, George Brown College; Douglas LaPorte, George Brown College; Barbara Lipton, Seneca College; Carmen Mihai, Lakehead University; David Morrison, Durham College; Maureen Nummelin, Conestoga College and Carol Ann Samhaber, Algonquin College. We want them to know they were a real help, and it is much appreciated.

## ABOUT THE AUTHORS

*James Thacker*

Jim Thacker received an undergraduate degree in psychology from the University of Winnipeg in Winnipeg, Manitoba, and his doctorate in Industrial and Organizational psychology from Wayne State University. He is currently a professor at the University of Windsor's Odette School of Business. His research has been published in both academic (*Journal of Applied Psychology, Personnel Psychology, Academy of Management Journal*) and practitioner (*Journal of Managerial Psychology, The Human Resource Consultation: An International Journal*) journals. He co-authored the first Canadian edition of the text *Managing Human Resources* with Wayne Cascio, published in 1994, and with Nick Blanchard, co-authored *Effective Training: Systems Strategies and Practices*, published in 1999 and 2004.

He has been a consultant and trainer in the private sector (Michigan Bell, Ford, Hiram Walker's, Navistar, H.J. Heinz) and public sector (Revenue Canada, CanAm Friendship Center). Prior to obtaining his doctorate, Jim worked for a gas utility as a tradesman and served as vice-president of his local union (Oil, Chemical, and Atomic Workers) for a number of years. This firsthand experience as a tradesman and union official combined with his consulting and academic credentials provides Jim with a unique combination of perspectives and skills.

*Nick Blanchard*

Nick Blanchard completed his undergraduate studies in psychology at UCLA, his masters at San Diego State University, and his doctorate in industrial and organizational psychology at Wayne State University. He is a professor at Eastern Michigan University, where he has also served as Dean, Associate Dean and Head of the Management Department. His writings appear in both scholarly and applied publications. His earlier training texts, *Toward a More Organizationally Effective Training Strategy and Practice*, in 1986, and *Effective Training: Systems Strategies and Practices*, in 1999 and 2004, were published by Prentice Hall, New York. Dr. Blanchard served as consultant and trainer to many organizations including Bethlehem Steel, DaimlerChrysler Corporation, Domtar Gypsum, Ford Motor Company, and various local and state government agencies.

# TRAINING IN ORGANIZATIONS

*The conventional definition of management is getting work done through people, but real management is developing people through work . . .*

Agha Hasan Abedi, President, Bank Credit and Commerce International, Luxembourg

## CHAPTER OBJECTIVES

After reading this chapter, you should be able to:

- Describe the components of a general open systems model and how an open systems model applies to the training unit of an organization.

- List and describe interrelationships among the five phases of the training process model.

- Describe four challenges/opportunities for training in Canada.

- Describe the strategic planning process and the relationship of HR and HRD in both shaping and implementing the strategy.

- Describe the benefits of integrating organizational development and training principles.

- Describe the differences in how small and larger businesses might implement strategic planning and the training process model.

# CASE

## Taking Charge at Domtar: What It Takes for a Turnaround

Domtar, headquartered in Montreal, is the third-largest producer of uncoated freesheet paper in North America. In the decade prior to 1996 Domtar had one of the worst financial records in the pulp and paper industry. In 1996, Domtar was a bureaucratic and hierarchical organization with no clear goal. Half of its business was in "trouble areas." Moreover, the company did not have the critical mass to compete with the larger names in the field. The balance sheet was in bad shape and the company did not have Investment Grade Status on its long-term debt.

In July of 1996, Raymond Royer was named the President and Chief Executive Officer. This was quite a surprise, because although Royer had been successful at Bombardier, he had no knowledge of the pulp and paper industry. Many believed that to be successful at Domtar, you needed to know the industry.

Royer did understand that to be effective in any competitive industry, an organization needed to have a strategic direction and specific goals. He decided to focus on two goals: return on investment and customer service. Royer told Domtar executives that in order to survive, they needed to participate in the consolidation of the industry and increase its critical mass. The goal was to become a preferred supplier. The competitive strategy had to focus on being innovative in product design, high in product quality, and unique in customer service. At the same time, however, it had to do everything to keep costs down.

When Royer took over at Domtar, he explained to the executive team that there were three pillars to the company: "customers, shareholders, and ourselves." He noted that it is only "ourselves" that are able to have any impact on changing the company. He backed up his words with action by hiring the Kaizen guru from Bombardier. Kaizen, a process of getting employees involved by using their expertise in the development of new and more effective ways of doing things, had been very effective at Bombardier. Royer saw no reason why it would not be successful at Domtar. Royer also knew that for the new strategic direction and focus to be successful, everyone needed to both understand the changes being proposed and have the skills to achieve them. The success of any change process requires extensive training; therefore, training became a key part of Royer's strategy for Domtar.

This last point reflects the belief that it is the employees' competencies that make the difference. The "Domtar Difference," as it is called, is reflected in the statement "tapping the intelligence of the experts, our employees." But employees must be motivated to become involved in developing new ways of doing things. Thus Domtar needed to provide employees with incentives for change, new skills, and a different attitude toward work. One tactic for accomplishing this was the introduction of Kaizen.

Training at Domtar went beyond the traditional job training necessary to do the job effectively and included training in customer service and Kaizen. This is reflected in Domtar's mission, which is

- To meet the ever-changing needs of our customers,

- To provide shareholders with attractive returns, and

- To create an environment in which shared human values and personal commitment prevail.

In this regard, a performance management system was put in place to provide a mechanism for employees to know how effective they are. This process laid the groundwork for successfully attaining such objectives as improving employee performance, communicating the Domtar values, clarifying individual roles, and fostering better communication between employees and managers. Tied to this were performance incentives that rewarded employees with opportunities to share in the profits of the company.

Has Royer been successful with his approach? First-quarter net earnings in 1998 were $17 million, compared with a net loss of $12 million for the same time period in 1997, his first year in office. In 2002, third-quarter earnings were $59 million, and totalled $141 million for the year. That is not all. Recall his goal of return on equity for shareholders? Domtar has once again been included on the Dow Jones sustainability index. Domtar has been on this list since the list's inception in 1999 and is the only pulp and paper company in North America to be part of this index. To be on the list, a company must demonstrate an approach that "aims to create long-term shareholder value by embracing opportunities and managing risks that arise from economic, environmental, and social developments." Based on this, it could be said that Royer has been successful. In 2003, Paperloop, the pulp and paper industry's international research and information service, named Royer Global CEO of the Year.

He has not done all this through sound management policies alone. Some shrewd joint ventures and acquisitions helped Domtar become more competitive and improve their credit rating on their long-term debt, returning it to "investment grade." However, joint ventures and acquisitions bring additional challenges of integrating the new companies into the "Domtar way." Again, this requires training.

For example, when Domtar purchased the Ashdown Mill in Arkansas, the management team met with employees to set the climate for change. The plan was that within 14 months, all mill employees would complete a two-day training program designed to help them understand the Domtar culture and how to service customers. A manager always started the "one-day customer-focus" training, thus emphasizing the importance of the training. This manager returned again at lunch to answer any questions as the training proceeded. In addition, each supervisor received skill training on how to address employee issues effectively. How successful has all this training been? Employee Randy Gerber says the training "allows us to realize that to be successful, we must share human values and integrate them into our daily activities." The training shows that "the company is committed to the program." Tammy Waters, a Communications Coordinator, says the training "impacts the mill in many ways . . . for Ashdown employees it has become a way of life."

The same process takes place in Domtar's joint ventures. In northern Ontario, Domtar owns a 45 percent interest in a mill with the Cree of James Bay who own 55 percent. Despite its minority interest in the joint venture, training is an important part of Domtar involvement. Skills training still takes place on-site, but all management and teamwork training is done at Domtar's head office in Montreal.

Royer's ability to get employees to buy into this new way of doing business was necessary for the organization to succeed. Paperloop's Editorial Director for News Products, Will Mies, in describing why Royer was chosen for the award, stated: "We polled a large number of respected security analysts, investment officers, and portfolio managers, as well as our own staff of editors, analysts, and economists to determine a worthy winner this year. Raymond Royer emerged a clear favourite, with voters citing, in particular, his talent for turnaround, outstanding financial management, and consistently excellent merger, acquisition, and consolidation moves, as well as his ability to integrate acquired businesses through a management system that engages employees." Of course, that last part, "a management system that engages employees," could be said to be the key without which most of the rest would not work very well. That requires training.

Swift, A. Royer's Domtar turnaround. (2003, Oct. 6). *Financial Post*, p. FP3; Allen, B. (2003). The Domtar difference. www.pimaweb.org/conferences/june2003/BuddyAllen.pdf; Anonymous (2001, Jan.) Partnership between Domtar and Cree First Nations brings results. www.diversityupdate.com; Richard Descarries (2004), Manager, Corporate Communications and External Relations, Domtar; Personal communication. "Sharing Expertise: Domtar Forges business Partnerships with First Nations," April 2001, written for www.domtar.com. Reprinted with permission from Domtar.

# OVERVIEW OF TRAINING

The foundation material for the rest of the book is contained in this chapter. The chapter covers a broad set of fairly complicated organizational processes that provides the organizational context for training activities. Thus, we believe it is useful to give an overview of how this chapter is organized before you begin your discovery of the exciting world of training. We begin with an overview of what an effective training unit should accomplish in an organization, including our model of the training process. We then describe some of the challenges and opportunities facing training units in Canada. Because effective training is so closely tied to the strategic direction of the organization, we offer some basics of strategic planning and how the human resource (HR) unit and the training unit engage in that process. While training is the practice of improving the performance of individuals, organizational development (OD) is the practice of improving the organization's performance. Because OD is closely tied to both strategic planning and training, we review OD principles to show how OD and training are mutually beneficial processes. We then integrate all the material by describing how the training unit's strategy is shaped by the strategies adopted by the organization and the human resources unit. As a conclusion to this, we provide some examples of training unit strategic choices.

Training provides employees with the knowledge and skills to perform more effectively, thus preparing them to meet the inevitable changes that occur in their jobs. However, training is only an opportunity for learning. What is learned depends on many factors, such as the design and implementation of training, the motivation and learning style of the trainees, and the learning climate of the organization.

Training is also part of an integrated system in which performance is measured against criteria (best practices benchmarks) that are tied to strategic objectives. Training is used extensively to help employees understand how they are able to assist in meeting corporate objectives. Clearly, Domtar knows that. Recall that when Domtar purchased the Ashdown Mill, training was an immediate focus. Within 14 months all mill employees completed a two-day training program so they would understand Domtar's culture and know how to service customers in the appropriate

Domtar
*www.domtar.com*

manner. The importance of the training was reflected in always having a manager kick it off and later return to answer questions about the training.

# TRAINING AS AN OPEN SYSTEM

Figure 1-1 shows the general systems model used to describe business organizations.[1] This is an **open systems model**. Open systems have a dynamic relationship with their environment, while closed systems do not interact with their environment.

**Open Systems Model** a model that depicts the dynamic relationship an organization has with its environment.

As Figure 1-1 indicates, the system is open to influences from its environment and, in fact, depends on the environment for the input that keeps the system active. The environmental inputs are transformed into outputs by the system's processes. Outputs flow out to the environment and may or may not influence future inputs into the system.

A system, such as a business, must be responsive to the needs and demands of its environment because the environment provides the input needed for the system to replenish itself. For example, if a business is responsive to the needs of society by providing valued goods and services (output), it receives valued input from society in the form of financial and goodwill credits. The business uses these inputs to continue operating. If the business does not provide sufficient value to its environment, it will fail because the environment will not provide the necessary input for the system to replenish itself.

Many open systems exist as part of another open system and are therefore called subsystems of that larger system. For example, a product assembly system is a subsystem of a manufacturing system, which itself is a subsystem of the company, which is a subsystem of the industry, and so on. Training can be seen as a subsystem within the larger system of HR, which is a subsystem of the company. Figure 1-2 illustrates some of the exchanges that take place between the training system and the larger organizational system. The organization's mission, strategies, and resources all represent sources of input into the training subsystem. Of course, if the training department is part of a larger HR function, then these inputs would be filtered through that system. The organization provides inputs to the training subsystem such as organizational and employee needs, training budgets, staff, equipment, and so forth. This input is transformed through training processes into usable output for the organization (improved knowledge, skills, and attitudes [KSAs]; job performance;

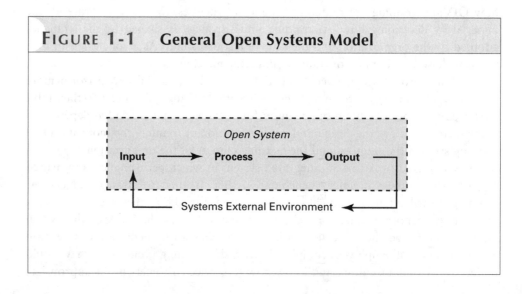

## FIGURE 1-1    General Open Systems Model

and so on). The open systems model illustrates how interconnected training activities are with what is happening in the organization as a whole. The bottom line here is that the organization invests money in the training function, for which it expects a favourable return. Periodically, the organization will examine the returns from training and determine whether the training system is working properly and what further investment is appropriate. Training in Action 1-1 demonstrates the consequences of a poor match between the training system and the organizational environment.

## Training in Action 1-1

### *Team Building Sizzles Then Fizzles*

The director of a city utilities department felt that creating employee problem-solving teams would improve the quality of operations and the efficiency of the department. All employees were provided the opportunity to participate in team-building and problem-solving training. About 60 percent of the employees, including the director and his management group, signed up for the training. Three-hour training sessions took place once a week for ten weeks. Working on a common process within their department, employees were grouped into teams for three weeks of team-building training and seven weeks of problem-solving training.

At the beginning of the problem-solving training, each team identified a problem in its area of operation. Each team then worked through the problem as they progressed though each step of the training. The team members were delighted

to be learning new skills while working on a real problem. By the end of training, each group actually solved, or made significant progress toward solving, the problem it was working on. Evaluations taken at the conclusion of training indicated that trainees enjoyed the training and understood the steps, tools, and techniques of team building and problem solving. The director was pleased with the results and submitted a report documenting the successes of the training to the city manager.

Follow-up evaluation conducted six months later showed only one team still in operation. The other teams fell apart for various reasons, such as excessive workloads, little recognition being given when problems were solved, non-trained employees resisting making changes in work processes, or teams being ridiculed by those who had not participated in training.

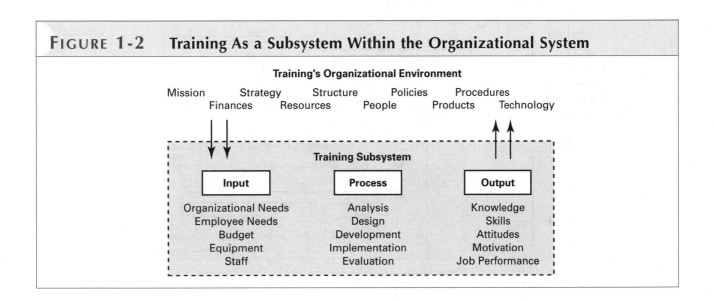

### FIGURE 1-2    Training As a Subsystem Within the Organizational System

# A TRAINING PROCESS MODEL

As shown in the open systems model, training is a process of transforming organizational inputs into output that meets organizational needs. Training is not just running training programs. Viewing training as simply a program or set of programs is too short-sighted. Training should be viewed as a set of integrated processes in which organizational and employee needs are analyzed and responded to in a rational, logical, and strategic manner. When training is conducted in this manner, the organization will improve, the value of the training unit will increase, and further investment in training is likely to occur. Our model of training processes, depicted in Figure 1-3, reflects this approach.

Figure 1-3 is merely an overview of the process. A more detailed figure for each phase is provided at the beginning of each relevant chapter, with the input and output of each process described in considerably more detail. For now, we will briefly describe the phases and their inputs and outputs.

The training process begins with some type of triggering event. The **triggering event** is the recognition that **actual organizational performance (AOP)** is less than the **expected organizational performance (EOP)**. For example, the expected quality level (EOP) for the department is three rejects per thousand. An examination of the data for last month indicates the quality level (AOP) is 17 rejects per thousand. This difference would trigger an analysis of why the number of rejects is so high.

**Analysis Phase** An effective business is one that is able to scan its environment and determine the products and services it can provide to meet customer or market needs. Similarly, an effective training system begins with a determination of customer needs in the needs analysis phase. In this case, the customer is the organization. These

**Triggering Event** the identification of a potential organizational performance gap.

**Actual Organizational Performance (AOP)** the level of performance that is actually occurring in the department or unit.

**Expected Organizational Performance (EOP)** the level of performance that is expected to be occurring in the department or unit.

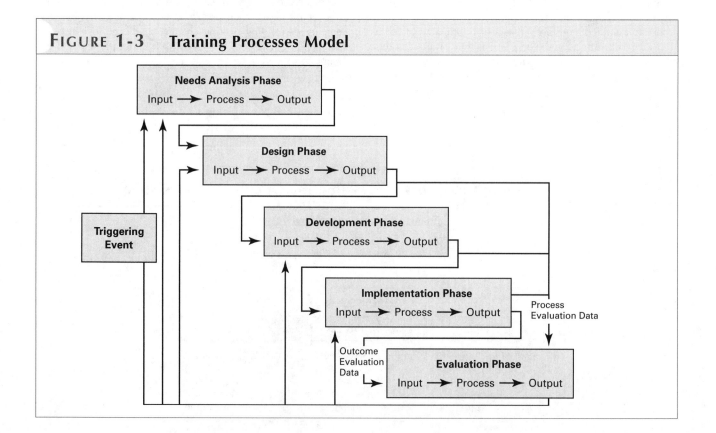

## FIGURE 1-3    Training Processes Model

needs show up as a **performance gap** when AOP is less than EOP. Things such as profitability shortfalls, low levels of customer satisfaction, or excessive scrap are all examples of a performance gap. Another type of performance gap is future-oriented. Here, the company is likely to perform poorly in the future unless changes are made. For example, if an organization wanted to install computer-based equipment in six months but employees were not computer literate, then it is expected that in the future there will be a performance gap.

Once a performance gap exists, the cause must be determined. The cause may be inadequate knowledge, skills, or attitudes (KSAs) of employees. If so, then training becomes a solution to this problem. Because not all performance problems are a result of KSA deficiencies, those problems for which training would be beneficial must be sifted from those for which training would not help. Other reasons why a performance gap will exist include motivation issues or faulty equipment, and these require a different solution.

This process of data gathering and causal analysis to determine which performance problems should be addressed by training is the analysis phase of the training process. It will be discussed in great detail in Chapter 3.

## Design Phase

In addition to the training needs identified in the training needs analysis (TNA), additional inputs to the **design phase** are developed from the organizational and operational analyses. An important output from the design phase is the development of **training objectives** that will provide direction in terms of who/what will be trained and how. These objectives specify the employee and organizational outcomes that should be achieved as a result of training.

The second part of the design process is identifying the factors needed in the training program to facilitate learning and its transfer back to the job, including identifying alternative methods of instruction. The training objectives also become inputs to the evaluation phase. The evaluation process begins after identifying evaluation objectives and it is conducted concurrently with the other phases of the training system. However, for convenience, we discuss evaluation after discussing all the other phases of the training process.

## Development Phase

**Program development** is the process of formulating an instructional strategy to meet a set of training objectives. The instructional strategy consists of the order, timing, and combination of elements to be used in the training program. Inputs into this phase are provided by the design phase and include the alternative instructional methods and the information relating to learning facilitation and transfer. Outputs are specific content, instructional methods, materials, equipment and media, manuals, and facilities integrated into a training plan designed to achieve the training objectives. These outputs of the development phase serve as inputs to the implementation phase.

## Implementation Phase

All the aspects of the training program come together during the **implementation phase**; however, it is a mistake to assume that everything will happen as planned. Therefore, it is useful to conduct a dry run and even a pilot of the program.

## Evaluation Phase

Although we discuss this phase of the model last, it actually begins during the development phase. Recall that evaluation objectives are an output of the design phase. These outputs become inputs to the **evaluation phase**. Another input is the organizational constraints. Time, money, and staff all affect how training is evaluated. Two types of evaluation are useful. First, **process evaluation** determines how well a particular process achieved its objectives (i.e., outputs). In other words, did the trainer follow the exact training process suggested? For example, if role-plays

**Performance Gap** exists when the actual level of performance is less than the expected level of performance.

**Design Phase** a systematic process for determining training objectives and the most effective method(s) to use (given organizational constraints) to achieve the objectives.

**Training Objectives** output from the design that identifies specifically the type of training outputs that will be expected.

**Program Development** putting together all the relevant material for the training.

**Implementation Phase** dry run, pilot testing and the actual training.

**Evaluation Phase** determining the success of the training based on the training objectives.
**Process Evaluation** examination of the way training was conducted to determine whether it met the expectations based on the design.

were in the design, were they used properly? Collecting and analyzing process data can provide early warning of potential problems in the training program.

**Outcome Evaluation**
measuring the value of training outcomes.

**Outcome evaluation**, the second type, is the evaluation conducted at the end of training to determine the effects of training on the trainee, the job, and the organization. This type of evaluation uses the training objectives as the standard. Outcome evaluation can also be used to improve training processes. Outcome evaluation data by themselves do not provide enough information for program improvement, but in combination with process evaluation data, they serve as a powerful tool for improving programs. For example, if one or more objectives are not achieved, the training process evaluation data can then be used to identify problems in the process and corrective action can be taken.

This text will take you through the complete training process as it would be conducted under ideal conditions. Unfortunately, most organizations do not operate in ideal conditions. Insufficient financial resources, time, and training professionals represent just a few of the challenges faced by most companies. Recognizing these limitations, we provide variations to the ideal training practices and systems that, although not ideal, do a reasonable job of accomplishing training objectives. Of course, these shortcuts exact a price, and we identify the major consequences associated with various alternatives. Thus we try to provide both "ideal" and more-practical approaches to implementing the training processes. Nonetheless, even in less-than-ideal conditions, all of the training processes are critical to the success of training. Although less-than-ideal methods may be used to carry out the training processes, elimination of one or more of the processes places the entire effort at grave risk.

# TRAINING IN CANADA: OPPORTUNITIES AND CHALLENGES

Canadian Council for Human Resource Associations in Canada
*www.cchra-ccarh.ca*

In the United States, as the new millennium unfolded, never was the belief in training as a tool for organizational success stronger. In 2002, U.S. training budgets for companies with 100 or more employees totalled more than $60 billion despite continued economic decline.[2] Unfortunately this is not the case in Canada. One report notes that the amount of money spent on training in Canada has been stagnant since the early 1990s.[3] This is further substantiated in a study conducted by the American Society for Training and Development (ASTD). In 1999, ASTD reported that organizations in European countries averaged $960 per employee for training. In the United States the amount was $650 per employee and in Canada $530 per employee.[4] So, Canada continues to lag behind the United States and other nations in the amount invested in training,[5] which in the long run can seriously affect its competitive position. This occurs in spite of evidence that shows that companies investing more in training produce improved financial results in terms of higher net sales per employee, gross profits per employee, and ratio of market to book value.[6]

Not all Canadian organizations are operating this way. Domtar, for example, considers training a very important part of their operation and spends about 4 percent of their annual salary costs on training. To put this in perspective, a study looking at Ontario and Quebec organizations' training budgets noted that the amount spent was generally less than 1.5 percent of annual salary costs in Quebec and less than 1 percent in Ontario.[7]

Is the money Domtar spends on training worth it? Using the Kaizen approach, employees developed a new way of cutting trees into planks. The result was fewer wood chips to transport and more logs produced per tree. Since 1997, it is estimated that Kaizen has saved Domtar about $230 million in production costs. Two of their mills are among the lowest cost mills in North America.

It is not just large organizations that see the value of spending lots of money on training. Scepter Manufacturing is a plastic supplier operating in Ontario. At one point, the company's training budget totalled $6000 and covered about 150 employees. A change in company strategy necessitated training all employees in various new technical areas and cross-training in other jobs within their work area. Performance measured after the training and the implementation of new systems indicated scrap was reduced by 50 percent and defective parts were reduced from 5 percent to 0.1 percent. Was training worth it? "Yes," said the plant manager, who indicated that the training budget increased to $60 000.[8] Although it is complex and time consuming to document how developing new employee skills results in increased operational profitability, the Scepter example shows it is both feasible and practical to do so. Chapter 8 provides the details for documenting and evaluating training results.

It is clear that there are many opportunities for training departments to assist companies in becoming more competitive. However, as with most opportunities, some risk is also involved. Training departments face a broad array of challenges, a sampling of which are described next.

## CHANGING DEMOGRAPHICS

In the last half of the twentieth century, major shifts occurred in Canadian demographics. These will dramatically affect businesses in the next 10 to 20 years. Principal among these demographic shifts are the following:

- An aging population,
- Reduced birth rates,
- Increased diversity of ethnic and cultural makeup, and
- Different values held by newer generations of employees.

These changes suggest that most companies now, or in the near future, face a severe shortage of skilled employees. Older workers retire, but fewer younger workers with the appropriate knowledge and skills are available to take their place.

Companies need to find opportunities to maintain and develop the competency levels of existing employees and ensure that new employees have the appropriate competencies. Training is one tool for these tasks.

Generation X and Y employees demand a more balanced lifestyle than did their predecessors, and their leverage with employers has never been greater. Training must assist in the reshaping of organizations and jobs to meet these lifestyle demands. The advancement of technology allows many employees to work outside company walls. This requires new workflow systems and management processes in which all employees must learn to operate. The increased diversity of the workforce will increase the demands on training to provide a workplace that is supportive of diversity while maintaining operational effectiveness. Companies must address the challenges of changing demographics, in part through their training function.

## KNOWLEDGE WORKERS

The first decade of the twenty-first century has seen the value of products and services determined more by the knowledge of the workforce and less by physical labour. This trend began with widespread use of personal computers in the mid-1980s and led to a "new economy." High-performing organizations have management that is both willing and determined to ensure that their employees are better trained because of economic pressures and consumer demands for higher-quality products and services. These demands require more effective and efficient job and workflow designs staffed with employees who are more knowledgeable, are committed to quality, show good judgment, and demonstrate multiple competencies. These changes create higher knowledge and competency requirements at every level in the organization. Training must address these needs because the demand for people holding these competencies is much larger than the supply.

Tied to the increased level of knowledge expected of all workers is the speed with which knowledge is acquired. In today's competitive business environment most companies have minimized the time it takes to move a product from the idea stage to the market place. This, however, puts great strains on the ability of the knowledge workers to be up to speed on the new products. The smart companies are now making "time to knowledge" as important as "time to market." One way they are accomplishing this is by getting the training department involved early in the product development stage. Innovative knowledge-delivery systems and increased breadth of training opportunities are other ways in which companies are creating more-knowledgeable workers more quickly.

The increased knowledge of the workforce is a double-edged sword for unions. On the one hand, union leadership demands that employers provide training for the rank and file to keep them up-to-date with modern operating methods. On the other hand, union leadership also understands that more-knowledgeable workers improve the efficiency of the company, resulting in reductions in the size of the bargaining unit. In Canada, unionization in the private sector has dropped to about 18 percent.[9] A major challenge for the future is finding a way for both the company and the union to prosper under intensely competitive conditions where a knowledgeable workforce is a competitive advantage.

## TRAINING AS CONTINUOUS IMPROVEMENT

Training must be seen as an integral part of the organization's performance improvement system. If not, it will continue to be seen as a cost centre, providing less-valued contributions to the organization. Training was a critical part of Domtar's change process. It assisted in educating employees regarding the mission, strategy, and objectives of the organization, and how these objectives translated to each employee's job behaviours. Experienced trainers know that effective training is structured as a continuous performance improvement process that is integrated with other systems and business strategies, just as at Domtar. Although a number of models exist for continuous improvement, common to them all are the following:

- Identification of performance improvement opportunities and analysis of what caused the opportunity to exist (gap analysis);

- Identification of alternative solutions to the opportunity and selection of the most beneficial solution. A training program is one of many possible performance improvement solutions;

- Design and implementation of the solution (training, if it is one of the selected solutions); and

- Evaluation of results that determines what further actions are taken.

Each of the above steps matches up well when placed against the training process model. That is because effective training is a continuous performance improvement process that does not stop and start with each program. The training function in organizations continuously searches for performance improvement opportunities, develops and implements solutions, and evaluates the effectiveness of the solutions.

# QUALITY

Quality improvement is a key component of most continuous improvement processes. High-quality products and services are necessary to stay in business in today's competitive markets and thus have high priority for most businesses. This is especially true for businesses that provide products or services directly to other businesses. Typically, these companies must demonstrate the quality of their products through quality systems developed by the purchasing company or by some globally accepted agency. For example, Ford, GM, and DaimlerChrysler impose their quality systems on suppliers. **ISO 9000**, though not universally adopted, is an example of a quality system adopted by companies across the globe. **ISO 9000** is a set of worldwide standards to ensure consistency in product quality by all companies that become certified. The International Organization for Standardization (ISO) in Geneva, Switzerland, developed the standards. To become certified a company must successfully complete the following five stages:[10]

**ISO 9000** A set of worldwide standards, developed by the International Organization for Standardization in Geneva, to ensure consistency in product quality.

1. Preaudit: assessing how you are doing now;

2. Process mapping: documenting the way things are done;

3. Change: developing processes to improve the way things are done to reach a desired level of quality;

4. Training: training in the new processes; and

5. Postaudit: assessing how well you are doing after the changes and continuing the improvement process.

Training is important in the ISO certification process, but it does not stop there. Training is required on a continuous basis even after certification is granted, since continuing audits ensure company compliance with the standards.

One outcome of the ISO process is better-trained personnel. Companies with ISO certification also find improved efficiency and internal communication, cost reductions, and improved ability to document quality-control processes to their customers.[11] Glen Black, President of the Process Quality Association in Canada, compared ISO-certified with non-certified companies. He found that certified companies are six times less likely to experience bankruptcy, average 76 percent lower warranty costs in customer-discovered defects, and allow 36 percent less bureaucracy within their company structure.[12] A cost comes with achieving these benefits, however. Once the company makes the decision to seek certification, it must be prepared to engage in a substantial amount of training, which can be costly. Furthermore, training is only one part of the overall cost, so each business must determine whether the costs of ISO certification are justified by the benefits.

# IMPORTANT CONCEPTS AND MEANINGS

The literature in training and development, as in other professional disciplines, is continually evolving. As a result, you will often find different meanings attached to the same terms. Thus, it is important for us to be clear about the terms and concepts we are using. It is also useful for you, the reader, to have a good understanding of how terms are commonly used in the field and how they will be used throughout the text.

The basic terms and concepts used throughout the book are defined in the following sections. Other terms will be defined as they occur in the text.

# LEARNING

Definitions for learning found in the literature vary according to the theoretical background of the authors. Unless otherwise indicated, the term **learning** in this text means a relatively permanent change in cognition (i.e., understanding and thinking) that results from experience and that directly influences behaviour. This definition, of course, reflects our own theoretical assumptions. We will discuss this definition and others at length in Chapter 2.

# KSAs

What is learned can be separated into different categories. Again, how these categories are defined differs according to the source. Traditionally, organizational psychologists used the categories "knowledge, skills, and abilities" (KSAs) to label the different types of learning outcomes. However, the term "abilities" is not typically defined much differently from the definitions given to skills and knowledge. Abilities, for example, are defined as "general capacities related to performing a set of tasks that are developed over time as a result of heredity and experience."[13] Skills are defined as "general capacities to perform a set of tasks developed as a result of training and experience."[14] The only difference seems to be whether heredity is involved. To our knowledge, the existing scientific evidence suggests that skills are influenced by heredity as well as by experience. Some authors make a distinction by categorizing skills as being psychomotor (behavioural) in nature, while abilities are categorized as cognitive. However, the definition of abilities does not differ from the most commonly accepted definition of knowledge, which covers both the facts people learn and the strategies they learn for using those facts, all cognitive in nature. Although some would argue that abilities are still distinguishable from knowledge and skills, we believe the distinction to be of minimal value. Conversely, attitudes are relatively easy to distinguish from knowledge or skills. In addition, it is scientifically well established that attitudes influence behaviour and that they are learned.[15] Thus, to our way of thinking, attitudes must be part of any holistic attempt to describe learning/training outcomes.

In this text, the initialism **KSAs** refers to the learning outcomes of knowledge, skills, and attitudes.

## Knowledge

**Knowledge**. **Knowledge** is an organized body of facts, principles, procedures, and information acquired over the years.[16] It is the precursor to learning skills.

## Skills

**Skills.** We use Dunnette's definition of **skill** as "the capacities needed to perform a set of tasks that are developed as a result of training and experience."[17] A person's skills are reflected by how well she is able to carry out specific actions such as operating a piece of equipment, communicating effectively, or implementing a business strategy. Skills are dependent on knowledge; the person must know *what* to do and *when* to do it. However, a gap separates knowing those things from actually being able to *do* them. A skill is a proficiency at doing something; it is beyond just knowing how to do it.

## Attitudes

**Attitudes**. **Attitudes** are employee beliefs and opinions that support or inhibit behaviour.[18] In a training context, you are concerned about employees' attitudes in relation to their learning of the training material and their job performance. The beliefs and opinions the person holds about objects or events (such as management, union, empowerment, and training) create positive or negative feelings about those objects and events. Thus, changing a person's beliefs or opinions can change the desirability of the

---

**Learning** a relatively permanent change in cognition (i.e., understanding and thinking) that results from experience and that directly influences behaviour.

**KSAs** an initialism that refers to the learning outcomes of knowledge, skills, and attitudes.

**Knowledge** an organized body of facts, principles, procedures, and information that has been acquired over the years.

**Skills** the capacities needed to perform a set of tasks that are developed as a result of training and experience.

**Attitudes** employee beliefs and opinions that support or inhibit behaviour.

object or event. For example, if an employee has positive feelings about a supervisor, those positive feelings are likely to become associated with the employee's job. If the employee learns from a co-worker that the supervisor said negative things about her, job satisfaction is likely to be reduced, even though nothing about the job itself actually changed. What changed is the employee's belief about the supervisor's opinion of her.

Attitudes are important to training because they affect motivation. **Motivation** is reflected in the goals people choose to pursue and the effort they use in achieving those goals. Goals and effort are influenced by how the person feels about things related to the goal (i.e., attitudes). Since a person's attitude influences behaviour, attitudes that motivate employees to perform or learn more effectively need to be addressed through training. Do you think Domtar employees immediately embraced the new way of doing business? Were they anxious to get involved in making the company more profitable before the training and other changes were implemented? Highly unlikely. That is why it is important to address attitudes as well as skills in a training program.

Consider Lockheed Corporation. Concerned about the security of their products and product development processes, they realized they needed either to significantly increase the current security force, which was costly, or include security in the job descriptions of all employees. Lockheed chose the latter approach, implementing security awareness training and annual security refresher training. The sessions were designed to change employees' attitudes about their jobs. Employees saw workplace

**Motivation** the goals a person chooses to pursue and the effort they use in achieving those goals.

## Training in Action 1-2

### *Training Needs in the Student Registration Office*

The offices of the President and Provost at a large university were receiving many complaints about the registration office being unresponsive to student problems during registration for classes. The Director of Registration felt that, because of the high turnover in customer service representatives (CSRs) who handled student problems, most CSRs did not know the proper procedure. The director wanted to initiate training in registration procedures immediately and called in a consultant to assist in developing and conducting the training.

After listening to the director's description of what was wanted, the consultant said, "You're probably right. Of course, we could conduct a training needs analysis to clarify the exact nature of the performance problem." The director was concerned about the time required for a needs analysis and wanted to get training started right away. However, in agreeing that the needs analysis would determine specific problem areas, the director said, "Okay, do the analysis, but let's get started on training right away. I want them to know exactly what they are supposed to do."

The needs analysis revealed the steps and procedures that an effective CSR was required to complete in dealing with an unhappy customer. For example, one of the first steps was for the CSR to identify and clarify the customer's problem, and to acknowledge the feelings the customer was displaying (e.g., anger or frustration) in a friendly and empathetic manner.

Once these feelings had been acknowledged, the CSR was to determine the exact nature of the customer's problem through non-evaluative questioning (i.e., determining the facts without placing blame for outcomes).

Interviews with the CSRs established that they all knew the correct procedure and most could quote it word for word. However, observation of the CSRs at work showed marked differences in how the procedure was carried out. Further analysis of each CSR's skills in performing these tasks revealed that the primary causes of unsatisfactory performance were low skill levels and inappropriate attitudes. Even though nearly everyone "knew" what to do, some were not good at doing it. Others did not believe it was important to follow every step. One CSR said, "Hey, if they get their problem solved, what do they care if I acknowledged their feelings?"

Certainly training was required in this case, but not the "knowledge" training the registration director thought was necessary. For those CSRs who lacked the behavioural skill to carry out the procedures, demonstrations and practice sessions with immediate feedback were provided. For those CSRs who had the skill but did not understand the importance of all the procedures, training sessions were conducted in which the CSRs re-evaluated their attitudes through various educational and experiential activities.

security as part of their individual responsibility rather than as the responsibility of the security department alone. Five years after the start of the program, the number of reports of "suspicious incidents" increased by 700 percent.[19] Training in Action 1-2 illustrates the importance of examining not only attitudes but also knowledge and skills when designing training programs.

# COMPETENCIES

**Competency** the integrated set of knowledge, skills, and attitudes that are required for a person to be successful in performing a group of related tasks.

A **competency** is a set of knowledge, skills, and attitudes that enable a person to be successful at a number of similar tasks. In the broadest sense, a job is broken down into a set of tasks, and the competencies required to perform the job are determined through an analysis of these tasks. A competency is more than just KSAs; it is the ability to integrate and use the KSAs to perform a task successfully. A carpenter, for example, has knowledge about different types of wood, tools and their uses, and types of finishes that can be applied to wood. This knowledge alone will not make that person a good carpenter. The carpenter may also possess a set of skills such as cutting, shaping, joining, and finishing. These skills alone will not make a good carpenter. The carpenter may love working with wood, place a high value on quality, and find great satisfaction working on the details of planning a project. These attitudes alone will not make a good carpenter. It is the combination of these KSAs and others such as hand-eye coordination, visual acuity, patience, and judgment that allow the carpenter to become proficient. To be successful at carpentry, or any other occupation, a person must acquire multiple competencies. A trainer can identify the key KSAs that make a master performer successful at a given job and then group these KSAs into appropriate clusters. This provides a broad set of competencies required for the job. Linking these competencies to a set of behaviours that allow trainers to "know it when they see it" provides a valuable tool for hiring, training, and determining pay rates for the job. We spend a great deal of time discussing KSAs because they are the foundation of competencies. Competencies are useful for understanding how the KSAs combine to influence job performance. The KSAs determine what types of training will improve competencies and thus lead to improved job performance.

# TRAINING, DEVELOPMENT, AND EDUCATION

**Training** the systematic process of providing an opportunity to learn KSAs for current or future jobs.

**Development** the learning of KSAs.

The terms *training, development*, and *education* are used in different ways by various authors. Here, the terms *training* and *development* refer to distinct, but related, aspects of learning. Training is a set of activities, whereas development is the desired outcome of those activities. **Training** is the systematic process of providing an opportunity to learn KSAs for current or future jobs; **development** refers to the learning of KSAs. In other words, training provides the opportunity for learning, and development is the result of learning. "Training departments" and "management training" are now called Human Resource Development (HRD) departments and Management Development, respectively. The change in terminology reflects the change from a focus on the process (training) to a focus on the outcome (development).

**Education** training that is more general in nature, not specific to a job.

**Education** is typically differentiated from training and development by the types of KSAs developed, which are more general in nature. While training is typically focused on job-specific KSAs, education focuses on more-general KSAs related to, but not specifically tailored to, a person's career or job.

# THE ROLE OF HRD IN THE ORGANIZATION

The role of the HRD department is to improve the organization's effectiveness by providing employees with the KSAs that will enhance their current or future job performance. At the same time, effective training must address the personal needs of employees and help them to learn, grow, and cope with the issues that are important to them. Focusing on KSAs that do not meet the needs of the organization is not productive. Likewise, unless the new KSAs are seen as relevant and important by the employees, they won't transfer back to the employee's job, thus wasting company resources. Truly effective training strategies and practices simultaneously meet the needs of the organization while responding to the needs of individual employees. The most effective way of ensuring training dollars are put to the best use is to align training activities to the company's strategic plan. An understanding of some basic strategic planning processes will help you see how HRD and strategic planning are intertwined.

Human Resources and Skills Development Canada (HRSDC) *www.hrsdc.gc.ca/en/ home.shtml*

## STRATEGIC PLANNING AND HRD

Formalized **strategic planning** is a proactive process used to decide how best to meet the demands of the environment in the near- (e.g., next year or two) and long-term (e.g., next 5 to 10 years). A **proactive strategy** requires a more formalized process typically involving sophisticated analytical and decision-making tools. It is proactive because it is a deliberate process for determining how the organization should respond to the anticipated business environment. Its purpose is to create a good fit between the organization and its future environment.

However, strategy can also develop in a more reactive fashion, responding to short-term business conditions. In a **reactive strategy**, less formal analysis and planning occur and more attention is focused on the immediate future. Many suggest that both reactive and proactive strategies are necessary for an organization to be effective.[20] The formalized (proactive) process uses a best guess about what the future will bring; the day-to-day (reactive) operations confront what that future has actually brought. A strategic plan that positions the firm for long-term expectations but is modified by the firm's experience as it moves forward is preferable to either a rigidly held long-term plan or reacting only to short-term experience.

**Strategic Planning** a proactive process used to decide how best to meet the demands of the environment.

**Proactive Strategy** the long-term plans for achieving the organization's goals and objectives given the future expectations in the environment.

**Reactive Strategy** the plans for achieving the organization's immediate goals and objectives in response to current environmental conditions.

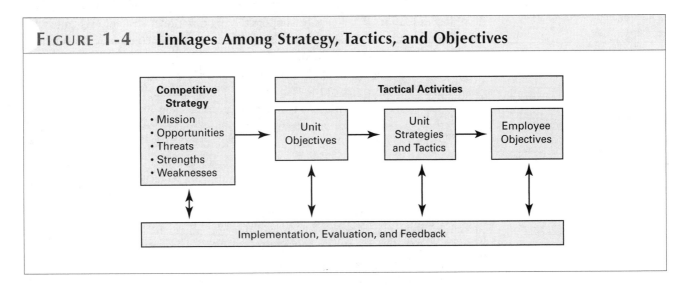

## FIGURE 1-4 Linkages Among Strategy, Tactics, and Objectives

The strategy an organization develops provides direction to its individual units (departments). The units develop or are given objectives that will help accomplish the strategy. To accomplish their objectives, the units then develop their own strategies and tactics. Individuals within the unit are given or develop objectives that will help achieve the unit's objectives through the chosen tactics. Thus, when viewed from the HR unit, the strategy provides general direction that leads to the objectives for HR. These objectives require supporting tactics that lead individuals to achieve a set of objectives (see Figure 1-4). In this way, plans providing direction for fulfilling the organization's mission are developed and coordinated throughout the organization. As you can see, the planning of strategy occurs throughout the organization, with each higher level of the organization providing direction to the lower levels. The process of developing strategic plans is similar whether the strategy is being developed for the entire organization or for some subunit. What differs is the type of information that is collected and analyzed in developing the strategy and the level of detail provided in directing actions.

In the Domtar case, do you think the HRD department needed to be involved in shaping the strategy? Quite likely. Strategy development depended heavily on the competencies of upper management and executive personnel. Without knowing the current capabilities of these individuals, the company does not know whether it has the capabilities to implement the strategy successfully. HRD can and should be involved with strategic planning at the following three levels: organizational strategy, HR strategy (tactics), and HRD strategy (more tactics).

At the organizational level, HRD can contribute to the shaping of the organization's strategy, though this role may not be obvious. In the Domtar case, it became clear that no one had the knowledge and skills to implement a Kaizen approach to quality management. So, what are the alternatives? Hire people from the outside? Train high-potential insiders? The answers to these questions help define the objectives and tactics used in pursuing the organization's competitive strategy.

The second strategic role for HRD is influencing the organization's HR strategy. The **HR strategy** is one level below the organization's strategy and is the set of tactics HR will use to support the competitive strategy. In the Domtar case, the HR strategy was to provide employees with the skills they needed to be more innovative and effective. Kaizen training was used to accomplish this. However, this requires identifying who will train the workforce in Kaizen, and this is where the HR strategy provides the direction to the HRD strategy. It is the place at which two-way communication between the HR and HRD managers is vital.

The third strategic role for the HRD function is developing and implementing its own strategy. **HRD strategy** is the set of tactics used to support the achievement of the HR strategies that are developed to support the organizational strategy. When viewed from an organizational level, HR and HRD strategies are tactics containing considerably more detail about actions to be taken than is provided in the organizational strategy.

In the Domtar case, the HRD manager must provide the HR manager with an assessment of the feasibility of the HR strategy. This is accomplished by assessing the Domtar employees to determine whether there are sufficient numbers possessing the KSAs to train the rest of the employees in Kaizen methods. If there are not enough (or any) with the skills, then Domtar may want to select those whom they believe are not only able to learn Kaizen but also able to teach it to others. Alternatively, it may be better to outsource the training. Before committing to either strategy, the HRD manager must determine the probable cost and time parameters of each strategy, and then consult with the HR manager to make sure the HRD strategies fit within the constraints of the organization. Of course, this and other HR programs will depend on an up-to-date Human Resource Information System (HRIS) that provides accurate and meaningful data necessary for HR planning.

**HR Strategy** the set of tactics HR will use to support the competitive strategy.

**HRD Strategy** the set of tactics HRD will use to support the HR strategy.

Let's take a look at the challenges that HR and HRD faced in moving forward with the Kaizen strategy. How does Domtar determine the competencies of its executives? Assuming they conduct a needs analysis, how will they store and review the information? Clearly, the development of the HRIS is an important first step. If they decide to develop their current executives, should the executive development programs be centralized at corporate HR or decentralized to the regions and divisions? Should they be developed in-house or outsourced to firms specializing in executive development? How does executive development fit into the culture of the organization? The answers to these kinds of questions provide additional content to the HRD strategy.

A scan of the HRD departments across a wide variety of companies would reveal many similarities. However, many differences exist among organizations in terms of how much training is provided, who gets trained in what areas, and who provides the training. Some companies' approaches to HRD help them achieve their objectives, while the approaches of other companies hinder this. To understand why similar approaches to HRD might lead one company to be successful and another unsuccessful, or why different approaches by two companies can each be successful, a critical examination of the relationship of HRD activities to the strategy of the company must be completed. Different strategies and strategic planning processes have different HRD implications, as the following discussion will explain. Some additional discussion of competitive strategy is provided in the management development chapter.

Strategies define how the organization will go about accomplishing its mission. Definitions of **organizational strategy** all include the following elements:

Strategies attempt to optimize the match between the organization's mission, what is occurring or is projected to occur in the external environment, and the organization's internal operations.

Strategies include

1. setting short- and long-term business objectives for the organization,

2. setting courses of action necessary to achieve those objectives, and

3. allocating the resources needed to carry out those actions.

## STRATEGIC CHOICES FOR DEALING WITH THE EXTERNAL ENVIRONMENT

The literature dealing with strategy contains a great many categorizations and terms that refer to different types and levels of an external strategy. For simplicity we choose one, competitive strategy, to demonstrate the relationship among organizational strategy, HR, and HRD. What most companies call their **competitive strategy** concerns positioning themselves in the marketplace. This, their most important strategy, includes the set of interrelated internal and external choices the company makes to improve or retain its competitive position. Competitive strategy also provides the added benefit of a documented relationship to many aspects of managerial and organizational behaviour.[21]

Two competitive positioning strategies illustrate a continuum of possible competitive strategies: market leader and cost leader. These two extremes clearly illustrate the implications for developing HR and HRD strategies that are consistent with the competitive strategy.

**Market leader** organizations, also called prospectors[22] and innovators,[23] find and exploit new product and market opportunities. Success depends on their capacity to survey a wide range of environmental conditions, trends, and events, and to move

**Organizational Strategy** An organization's attempt to optimize the match between its mission, what is occurring (or is projected to occur) in the external environment, and the organization's internal operations.

**Competitive Strategy** the plans that focus on the position the organization wishes to take in the marketplace.

**Market Leader** a strategy with the goal of finding and exploiting new product and market opportunities.

quickly into windows of opportunity. Market leaders typically use multiple technologies capable of being used in many different ways.

The **cost leader**,[24] also referred to as the defender,[25] represents the opposite end of the continuum. Its main goal is to be the low-cost provider in the industry. Success depends on pricing competitiveness and having a product that is acceptable to (but not necessarily the best in) the market. Success is achieved by producing a standardized product or service efficiently, by using economies of scale, by using low-cost labour, and by introducing innovative production methods.

# INTERNAL ALIGNMENT WITH STRATEGIC DIRECTION

Once a company has chosen a competitive (external) strategy, it needs to align the internal environment with that strategy. To accomplish this the company needs an **internal strategy** to address how the organization must change in order to carry out the competitive strategy. The two key factors in the internal strategy are the organization's core technology (how the principal products or services are created) and its structure (e.g., division of labour, policies, procedures).

Technology is how the work gets done in the organization. Each unit in the organization uses technology to accomplish its tasks. **Core technology** refers to the main activities associated with producing the organization's principal products and services. Technology can be categorized a number of ways.[26] Taking some liberties with these approaches, we use a simple continuum of "routine" to "non-routine" technologies. At one end, the **routine technology** label is applied to tasks with outcomes that (1) are highly predictable, (2) demonstrate few problems, and (3) use well-structured and well-defined solutions when problems do occur. High-volume assembly lines, such as in a garment factory or some automobile plants, are examples of routine technology. Such operations consist of highly specialized tasks and well-defined rules for coordinating activities. Decisions are usually top-down and highly formalized, leaving little discretion to the line employee. Routine technology is most often seen in the cost-leader strategy. Even though the initial infrastructure required to put this technology in place can be expensive, its efficiency in high-volume production provides low production cost per unit.

A task using **non-routine technology** is characterized by (1) results that are difficult to predict, (2) problems that occur often and unexpectedly, and (3) solutions to problems that are not readily available and need to be developed on a case-by-case basis. With this type of technology, management needs to provide lower-level managers and line employees with more decision-making authority to meet the challenges encountered. This responsibility, of course, means the firm needs employees with a higher level of KSAs. This technology also requires greater task interdependence, which increases the need for coordination and integration. Managers and workers need decision-making authority within their own areas, but their activities must also be coordinated with the activities of others. Thus, employees must be given clear goals and parameters for their work outcomes but also be allowed to determine the best way to meet them. This type of technology is more typical of market leader strategies in which the development and production of new products is key. The cost of the non-routine technology may be high, but new products may command high prices in the marketplace. Leading-edge software and computer chip developers, such as Microsoft and Intel, are examples of such companies.

Structural implications of strategy also must be addressed. The organization's structure refers to how a firm is organized (how labour is divided) as well as to the policies and procedures used for coordinating its various activities. Although there

**Cost Leader** a strategy with the goal of being the low-cost provider in the industry.

**Internal Strategy** the plan for changing the organization to align it with its competitive strategy.

**Core Technology** the main activities associated with producing the organization's principal products and services.

**Routine Technology** tasks with outcomes that are highly predictable, demonstrate few problems, and use well-structured, well-defined solutions when problems do occur.

**Non-routine Technology** tasks with outcomes that are difficult to predict, where problems occur often and unexpectedly, and solutions are not readily available but need to be developed on a case-by-case basis.

are many structural components, we will examine only these three: organizational design, decision-making autonomy, and division of labour.

Organizations must be designed to ensure the effective operation of the core technology. **Organizational design** refers to the number and formality of rules, policies, and procedures created to direct employee behaviour. An organization's design can lie somewhere on a continuum ranging from mechanistic to organic.[27] A highly **mechanistic design** reflects an organization with highly defined tasks, rigid and detailed procedures, high reliance on authority, and vertical communication channels. A highly **organic design** reflects an organization that has flexibility in its rules and procedures, loosely defined tasks, high reliance on expertise, and horizontal communication channels. Few organizations operate on the extremes of this continuum, but most lean more toward one end or the other.

The organic design places more emphasis on KSAs, whereas the mechanistic focuses more on technical and financial systems and resources. In the mechanistic design, employees' technical and interpersonal skills and behaviours are prescribed. In the organic design, these skills and behaviours are permitted to evolve (within broad parameters) in order to supplement and complement the unit's technology. As you might suspect, the organic design is most appropriate for non-routine technologies, whereas the mechanistic design is more appropriate for routine technologies.[28]

**Decision autonomy** is the amount of authority given to employees in deciding how to complete a task and the degree to which they are able to influence goals and strategies for their work unit.[29] Individual or small group decision-making autonomy is a function of whether decisions are centralized or decentralized. Cost efficiencies are associated with more centralization, whereas flexibility/adaptability is associated with decentralization.[30] Thus, centralized structures are more appropriate for cost leader strategies and decentralization for market leaders.

**Division of labour** is the way in which the work is divided and organized. One way in which labour is divided is between line (those working directly with the core technology) and staff (everyone else); another is between management and labour. Some organizations divide themselves by products, others by customers or geography. Some divide the work into functional areas, while others organize work around the processes in their core technology. Even though these divisions are important, we focus on the degree of specialization of duties and responsibilities within the organization. We place organizations on a continuum from narrowly defined (specialized) to generally defined duties and responsibilities. The more narrow the duties and responsibilities, the more centralized the decision-making and the more mechanistic the organization will be. This results from the need to coordinate extensively the activities of employees whose scope of responsibility is fairly narrow. In organizations with duties and responsibilities that are more broadly defined, a more organic and decentralized structure is appropriate. This allows employees to coordinate their activities less formally and provides more flexibility and adaptability for the organization. Again, you can see the close relationship between an organization's core technology and how labour is divided.

**Organizational Design** the number and formality of rules, policies, and procedures created to direct employee behaviour.

**Mechanistic Design** an organization with highly defined tasks, rigid and detailed procedures, high reliance on authority, and vertical communication channels.

**Organic Design** an organization that has flexibility in its rules and procedures, loosely defined tasks, high reliance on expertise, and horizontal communication channels.

**Decision Autonomy** the level of freedom to make decisions.

**Division of Labour** the way in which work is organized and divided.

# ROLE OF HR IN SUPPORTING STRATEGIC PLAN

The HR function must support and enhance the organization's corporate strategy. This is accomplished by making sure the various components in the HR system—such as staffing, human resource planning, performance appraisal, compensation, health and safety, employee and union relations, and, of course, training—are aligned with the strategic plan. Each of these systems influences the organization. Integrated

International Association of Human Resources Information and Management *www.ihrim.org*

under the HR umbrella, they can enhance the organization's ability to mobilize the necessary human resources to carry out a competitive strategy.

Why should companies invest in developing a strategic HR management capability? The evidence indicates that firms that do so will significantly increase the market value of the firm.[31] Data collected from more than 2400 firms show that firms with HR systems that achieve operational excellence and are aligned with the firm's strategic goals improve their market value by about 20 percent. This evidence suggests that investing in HR excellence and bringing HR systems into alignment with business strategies leads to competitive advantage.

In addition to contributing to the development of the organization's competitive strategy, HR activities must support those strategies once they are adopted. Decisions about competitive strategy need to be reflected in HR strategy, and vice versa. For example, if the company's operations are labour-intensive and a strong union consistently demands high wages and restrictive work rules, it would be foolish to adopt a cost leader strategy without addressing these issues first. Similarly, once the company makes the decision to adopt a cost leader strategy, HR must develop its own strategies for supporting cost leadership. Let's assume a cost leader strategy requires a change in production technology (e.g., more automation); this change could be accomplished only if HR is capable of staffing the new technology. HR's input into the strategy formulation process might be the identification of what it would take to staff the proposed technology and the likelihood of being able to do so. Failure to address the HR side of the strategy could lead to the purchase and installation of a new technology that, among other things, is too costly to staff, creates labour conflict, produces conflicts in the existing culture, or requires lengthy training, thus delaying the implementation of the technology. Might any of these things happen at Domtar?

# ROLE OF **HRD** IN SUPPORTING THE STRATEGIC PLAN

Professional Assessment Resource Centre Required Professional Capabilities
*www.cchra-ccarh.ca/parc/en/section_3/ss33e.asp*

Throughout this text, we emphasize that HRD is in the business of supporting the organization's strategies, goals, and objectives. In this supporting role, HRD contributes to the organization's competitive position in the following ways:

- By ensuring employees have the necessary competencies to meet strategic performance demands,

- By identifying and assisting in the removal of barriers to desired performance, and

- By providing key information related to the development of competitive strategies.

The last point, "providing key information," involves many issues. HRD needs to provide an assessment of employees' strengths and weaknesses relative to the competitive strategy. Unfortunately, many organizations do not think of HRD in this strategic sense. Product innovation or cost leadership strategies are often formulated with little consideration of employee capabilities, and it is only after implementation problems surface that HRD considerations may arise. These problems often result in costly delays in implementing the strategy, perhaps even dooming the strategy to failure. Assuming the competitive strategy requires increasing the competencies of employees, the various methods of approaching this task would need to be examined. From this evaluation, HRD could make an estimate of how long it will take before employees are ready to implement the strategy and the amount of resources required. This information is provided to the strategic planning group to determine the cost/benefit of the strategy.

Hiring from outside the organization is another way of improving the competency base of the organization. In this approach, competencies are imported through recruitment and hiring. Even here, however, HRD needs to be involved in orientation and any other new employee training. Adding competencies through new hires implies current employees would be terminated or reassigned. The implication of this approach must be considered and factored into the strategy feasibility equation. If termination or reassignment becomes part of the internal strategy, training will likely be necessary. Reassigned employees will require training in their new duties and responsibilities. Some form of outplacement training may be needed for those terminated.

We are not suggesting that HR issues should be the only, or most important, influence on the strategic direction taken by an organization. However, they should be part of the equation. The relative importance of strategic variables such as technology, financial assets, product, and human resources varies from one context to the next. Likewise, the importance of HRD issues to competitive strategy depends on how central employee expertise is to the business success and the value of using current employees compared with acquiring new ones.

# OD, STRATEGY, AND TRAINING

The planning and implementation of strategy involves change—both in the way the organization interacts with its external environment and in how it manages its internal operations. **Organizational development** (OD) is the field of study that deals with creating and implementing planned change. This is why it is important HRD understands OD principles.

OD provides a research base and set of techniques related to organizational improvement and managing change. As the organization's objectives and strategies change, the KSAs required of employees change as well. However, it is not enough simply to provide new KSAs. The organization's systems and procedures must change to support the use of the new KSAs if the desired change in performance is to occur. In the Domtar case, what types of systems and procedures needed to change to make the new strategy successful? The reward system? The way Domtar is organized? The HRD process? The field of OD provides processes for identifying when systems and procedures need to change and how to manage the change. So, let's examine the strategic planning process and the ways HRD and OD can support each other in the implementation of a strategic plan.

**Organizational Development**
the field of study that deals with creating and implementing planned change.

## OD AND STRATEGY

Whether an organization's strategies are developed proactively, reactively, or both, they require support from the internal systems. Organizational change is an inherent part of the processes of developing and implementing strategy. Organizations must resolve the following three core issues in developing and implementing strategy:[32]

1.  *Technical design issues.* These issues arise in relation to how the product or service will be determined, created, and delivered.

2.  *Cultural/ideological issues.* These issues relate to the shared beliefs and values that employees need to hold for the strategy to be implemented effectively.

3.  *Political issues.* These issues occur as a result of shifting power and resources within the organization as the strategy is pursued.

These three issues determine the organization's ability to achieve its objectives. In developing strategy, decisions such as what products to develop, how to manufacture them, and what marketing techniques to use will signal shifts in organizational values, power, and resources. These issues will need to be managed effectively to create support for, rather than resistance to, the strategic plan. The field of organizational development can offer a great deal to help organizations manage change effectively. Use of OD techniques provides methods for change to occur in an objective, goal-directed manner that addresses both the needs of the organization and the employees affected by the change. OD uses an open system, planned change process that is rooted in the behavioural sciences and aimed at enhancing organizational and employee effectiveness. A model of a generic planned change process is provided in Table 1-1.

The strategic planning process, if done properly, is an OD approach to change. The first step, establishing a compelling need for change, occurs in strategic planning during the environmental scanning phase. The need for change is made apparent when the strategic planners identify the threats and opportunities in the external environment and compare that information with what the organization is currently doing. A need for change is established when a gap exists between what the organization is doing and what the external environment requires (or will require). Next, the company's business objectives are set (step 2 in the change model). The company's current strengths and weaknesses are analyzed to determine what internal changes are necessary (step 3). This information provides the compelling need for internal change, and internal strategic objectives are developed for these areas. The rest of the steps in the OD model concern the development of tactical activities to achieve the strategic objectives.

## Levels of Internal Change and Resistance

Whenever internal change is planned, the plan should address the following three levels in the organization:

1. *The organization itself:* The way the organization is put together (i.e., what we call structure and design) must be examined to ensure that work is allocated appropriately and organizational systems are supportive of the change. This level of analysis identifies how labour is to be divided and what rules and procedures will govern operations.

2. *Groups and their interrelationships:* The way work is performed in the organizational units (i.e., the sociotechnical systems) and how the outputs of the various units are integrated are the focus of this level of analysis. The issues here concern the design of jobs within units of the organization and the interrelationships of the jobs to one another.

3. *Individuals within groups:* The changes in performance that will be required of employees must be identified and mechanisms—facilities, machines, equipment, and KSAs—put into place to enable the desired performance to occur.

### TABLE 1-1    Steps in a Generic Planned Change Model

1. A compelling need for change is established.
2. Goals are developed and agreed to by the concerned parties.
3. The cause of the need for change is determined.
4. Alternative approaches for addressing the cause are identified and evaluated.
5. An approach to addressing the cause is selected.
6. The approach is carried out.
7. The results of the approach are evaluated.
8. The results are fed back to the organization.
   - If results are favourable, go to step 9.
   - If results are unfavourable, go back to step 4.
9. The change becomes internalized. The changes made become routine and the normal way the organization conducts its business.

Resistance to change is a common occurrence. Without sufficient motivation to change, resistance is natural. Change requires effort, new learning, and possible shifts of resources and outcomes. Often, those satisfied with the status quo can create enough resistance to derail the change effort, even to the point that the business fails. A major factor in this resistance is the failure of the change process to address all three levels of change. For example, instituting a work-team system in the organization without addressing the performance-appraisal system will naturally cause resistance to the new approach. People may ask, "Why should we work as a team if we're getting evaluated as individuals?"

Achieving successful change at one level, then, requires analysis and possibly interventions at all three levels. Consider the impact of a change in the organizational structure. Work would be allocated differently, so that some units might get work they have not done before while others might have certain jobs taken away. The affected units would need to change their work processes because they would have different amounts or types of work to do. These changes would require OD interventions at the group level. Here, the OD practitioner is involved in the design or redesign of jobs and work systems and the associated interpersonal relationships. In addition, changes in how these work groups interact with others would be required, because they would now be producing something different. Employee resistance to new procedures would need to be addressed as jobs are being redesigned. At the individual level, employees would also need to acquire the knowledge and skills necessary to perform their redesigned jobs.

You might think that these three levels of change are intertwined only if the change occurs at the organizational level. However, they are integrated no matter where the initial change takes place, which is why it is important to take a systems perspective. Let's say you want employees to increase their skill at integrating quality control (QC) into their production work. Of course, training at the individual level is an issue. Is it the only issue for the change to be successful? Even if employees' KSAs are developed, the job itself and the organizational systems must support using the KSAs. The company will need to ensure that the design of the job supports the performance desired from its employees. For example, the equipment and tools might need to be changed. If employees feel that QC is just a way for management to eliminate their jobs, they may resist this intervention, and providing new KSAs will not be enough. Work group norms (i.e., attitudes) will need to be changed to be consistent with QC objectives. At the organizational level, reward and appraisal systems would need to support the desired performance outcomes and work procedures. If the focus of the appraisal system does not assess the quality of the employees' work, but only the quantity produced, employees would not be likely to sacrifice quantity for quality. The appraisal system needs to reflect the importance of quality as well as quantity. The point is that the components of the organization (structure and design, jobs and employees) are interdependent, and changes in one need to be addressed as part of the overall change effort. The training needs analysis process (Chapter 3) provides a model for determining not only what training is needed but also what other changes are necessary to support the training.

Another important point is that most change carries with it the need for changing employees' attitudes. It is the central focus in overcoming resistance to change. It is most effectively accomplished through involving employees in the change process and through education and training. Involving employees develops commitment to the change for several reasons:

- They are intimately familiar with the current system and can make valuable contributions to the change effort, increasing its chances of success.

- They become knowledgeable about what will happen as a result of the change (reducing fear of the unknown).

- They are acting in a way that is supportive of the change by being part of the process, and their beliefs about the change become more positive.

Educating employees about the need for change also affects attitudes by allowing employees to understand the consequences of not changing and the benefits that change can bring. Training allows employees to develop the knowledge and skills to be successful under the new conditions.

## TRAINING AND OD

Using OD's principles of change management will increase the probability that your organization's strategic plans will be effectively implemented. But training also focuses on change, so principles of change are applicable to training efforts as well. By including an analysis of organizational problems as an integral part of the training needs analysis, the organization ends up not only with training programs that address critical competencies but also an increased awareness of what problems need to be solved by other means. Trainers also use organizational information to design better programs so that application problems are included in the training rather than becoming surprises after training begins.

Despite the seemingly obvious advantages of collaboration between OD and training professionals, a gulf sometimes seems to separate the two. Consider the following examples:[33]

- An executive complains that his training and OD people cannot seem to work together.

- Training staff complains at length about a manager they consider unreasonable and attributes her faults to her background in OD.

- A training staff member objects strongly when told that training needs analysis data could be used to identify performance problem solutions other than training.

Table 1-2 provides some insight as to why conflict such as in the preceding examples exists. OD practitioners are typically strategic, and executives are usually their clients. Trainers are typically tactical, and their clients are lower in the hierarchy (see Figure 1-1 for differences between strategy and tactics). It is the nature of the OD practice to challenge assumptions underlying organizational practices. Trainers typically take organizational procedures and practices as givens, trying to make people more effective within those practices. For example, suppose the needs analysis data show that the problems in a work unit are a result of its manager acting inconsistently and arbitrarily. More OD professionals than training professionals would be willing to be guided by the data and confront the manager. Training professionals may be willing to say that no employee training needs were identified but less likely to tell the manager that his or her behaviour needs to change. OD professionals, however, are much more likely to get tagged with the "analysis paralysis" label than are trainers, who are seen as "doers." Yet as Table 1-2 suggests, each would benefit by working closely with the other because one's apparent weakness is the other's strength.

## TABLE 1-2 Differences Between OD Practitioners and Trainers

| Issue | OD Practitioner | Trainer |
|---|---|---|
| **Role** | Strategic | Tactical |
| **Client** | Top management | Middle- to lower-level management |
| **Response to problems with organizational politics, structure, etc.** | Challenge and confront | Work around or within the system |
| **Organizational perception** | Overly analytical | Gets things done |

**Why Trainers Need OD Competencies** Trainers can benefit from using OD if only because its planning procedures help to clarify what is needed in a given organizational situation. We believe that training programs will also benefit from the application of many other elements from the field of OD. OD's emphasis on participative approaches to problem solving suggests that training is better when trainees take an active role in selecting their training opportunities and in the training itself. When trainees are involved in the planning stages, they are less likely to demonstrate resistance. This learner-focused orientation opens communication channels and results in higher levels of motivation during the training program. A participative orientation also ties line managers directly to the training process by involving them in assessing their employees' needs, developing the training, and developing support systems for applying the training back on the job.

In the training needs analysis and training design chapters, we emphasize an open systems approach. The needs analysis chapter focuses on understanding training needs in the context of organizational systems. The design chapter emphasizes connections between the training program and other organizational systems. These connections help to ensure transfer of the training to the job. Many trainers told us of their frustrations when trainees were excited about what they learned, but at the conclusion of training nothing changed. The design chapter describes why this can happen and how to avoid this type of training disaster.

**Why OD Professionals Need Training Competencies** Although generally successful, OD has experienced some glaring failures, many of which could have been avoided with more attention to training principles.[34] Earlier, we identified the types of training required as a prerequisite or supplement to various OD techniques. OD interventions nearly always involve groups of employees in structured activities such as planning, problem solving, and intergroup conflict management. It is naive to assume that one can bring people together to solve new problems, in new relationships, in new situations, with new processes, without prior training. These employees need to

- Have a common KSA base in these areas,

- Understand group dynamics and be skilled at working in groups, and

- Understand and be skilled at using a common problem-solving model.

If OD practitioners are not skilled in designing and implementing training programs, they must develop collaborative relationships with trainers who are. Such collaboration provides an excellent opportunity for involving internal training resources in change efforts. It is especially helpful when an OD consultant, familiar with good training practices, is retained from outside the organization. When HRD and OD work together in a collaborative fashion, they will go a long way toward defusing any conflict between external consultants and the HR function.

If OD is to be a long-term effort, the change must be institutionalized into the way the company does business. In one study only about one-third of the OD efforts examined lasted more than five years.[35] This finding indicates that training is a critical component to institutionalizing the change. Three situations are identified as key times for training:

1. When the OD process is started, training is needed to provide education about the change process and to provide the necessary KSAs.

2. After the process has been in place for a while, some retraining or upgrading of KSAs is required to sustain the process.

3. As new employees enter the organization, they need an understanding of the process and the KSAs.

Although most organizations provide the initial training, few conduct follow-up training or modify their new-employee training to include the new process and the related KSAs.

# PUTTING IT ALL TOGETHER

Recall from Figure 1-1 that it is not enough for the organization to develop competitive strategies—these strategies must be followed with action. The strategies are implemented through a tactical action plan consisting of the actions required and the unit(s) responsible for those actions. The process begins with assigning objectives to the different work units of the organization. The units must then develop strategies and implementation tactics to achieve the objectives. Eventually, they are translated into individual employee objectives. The objectives for the HRD unit, as for all functional areas, must be tied directly to organizational strategies. Of course, for HRD these will be filtered through the strategies the HR unit developed to achieve its objectives.

## DEVELOPING AN HRD STRATEGY

Society for Human Resource Management
*www.shrm.org*

Without a strategic plan, training is likely to be managed in a haphazard manner, its resources underutilized, and its full strategic value not realized. At the most basic level, the training function must make strategic decisions about where it will focus its resources and energies. It also depends in part on the environment in which training operates, the resources available (financial, material, and personnel), and the core competencies contained within the training function. Analysis of these areas leads to strategic decisions about the technology that should be used to develop necessary employee competencies. The organization and its HR unit form the bulk of HRD's environment. Thus, in developing an HRD strategy, these areas must be analyzed. How to conduct this analysis and sources from which data can be obtained are detailed in Chapter 3. For now we will provide some examples of how HR and HRD strategy might be developed, based on the competitive strategy of the organization.

**Organizational and HR Strategy** Since the market leader strategy depends on innovation, employee knowledge and skills are critically important. Highly skilled and knowledgeable people must be hired and developed. They need to work under a structure that allows them latitude in how they go about their work. Reward and feedback systems must focus on long-term rather than short-term performance. Some amount of failure must be expected as employees try out new ideas. The failure of an experiment can be positive if it brings the organization closer to realizing its objectives through the learning that occurs. If failure is punished, employees will be reluctant to attempt new things. Hewlett-Packard, Raytheon, and PepsiCo illustrate this philosophy by selecting highly trained and skilled employees, being committed to their long-term development, and developing systems that evaluate and reward employees for their contributions to the company's objectives.[36] HRD in the market leader organization must adopt a strategy that builds on the already high level of competency brought into the organization.

Cost leader organizations, in contrast, emphasize tight fiscal and management controls. Because their leadership position is dependent on their ability to produce high volumes at low cost, efficiency and productivity are critical. Strategies for reducing costs include reducing the number of employees, reducing wages and salaries, using part-time and contract labour, and improving work methods. Conforming to standardized procedures is emphasized in these organizations, and training helps to ensure conformance. On-the-job training (OJT) techniques are used more frequently for line employees. It is only at the middle-management levels and above that more autonomous decision-making occurs and that higher-level competencies are emphasized. In these organizations, training is more likely to be focused on management.

## Integrating HRD and OD Activities

Most organizations' competitive strategy calls for some type of performance improvement, both for the organization as a whole and for individuals. Perhaps the most effective way to ensure the seamless implementation of performance improvement plans is to integrate HRD and OD. Trainers and OD professionals have legitimate differences in the nature of the change they are responsible for, but their interests are intimately connected. Each can provide valuable service to the other. Nonetheless, as we noted, they are often at odds with each other. One reason for the division between them is that companies typically organize around their different functional activities, and OD and HRD departments are often separated.[37] This separation increases the differences in perspective, role, value of service, clients, and so on. An obvious solution is to house them together in something like a performance improvement department within HR. This would be an example of a structural change to align the organization's internal structure with its strategic direction.

Of course, this type of organizational change effort will require attention to critical change management issues. For example, such a department would need different measures of success than either currently uses. Success could be measured by contribution to business results, rather than by the number of bodies passing through training courses or the number of teams built and facilitated by OD staff. This overarching goal would require trainers to identify system deficiencies that are likely to interfere with training, and OD staff to identify KSA deficiencies that are likely to interfere with system changes.

Companies such as Andersen Consulting-Education, AT&T, and Universal Card Service made these changes and improved their business operations.[38] These companies found that integrating OD and training activities requires sponsorship from the top HR and other executives. One way toward full-scale integration of these activities is to develop pilot collaborations focusing on a particular business problem. This approach allows staff from each discipline to learn more about how the other operates and where the synergy exists. In addition, the HR executive needs to encourage people in both disciplines to learn as much as possible about the other. Another process that should lead to better integration of training and OD activities is having the staff in both areas work together to identify barriers to collaboration and identify ways to remove those barriers. This activity not only creates familiarity but also uses the OD principle of involving those affected by the change in the change process. By integrating the two activities, the organization also has the potential benefit of cross-functional training, increasing the KSAs of both groups. At Domtar, Claude Belley is the Senior Vice-President of Human Resources and Organizational Development. Do you think he understands the importance of this type of integration? Might this have contributed to Domtar's success?

## Some Strategic Training Alternatives

One strategic decision the HRD department needs to make is whether training is developed in-house or not. Organizations in a stable environment where training needs do not change rapidly often choose to do most of the training themselves. This strategy is most appropriate for cost leaders.

| TABLE 1-3    Questions to Assess Training Provider Capabilities |
| --- |
| What is their background (education, experience, etc.)? |
| Have they ever provided these particular training programs or services before? |
| Have they conducted formal evaluations of their results? If so, what have been the results? |
| Can they give you the names of people in these companies who could speak knowledgeably about the trainer's products and services? |
| Can they give you names of those who were recipients of the service and those who brought the training provider into the organization and oversaw the training or the service? |
| Can they provide an outline of their approach or process? How do they go about developing a program, delivering training, or providing a training service? |
| If they are providing training previously developed, can they show you materials, such as hand-outs, exercises, and videos? |
| If these materials are not specific to your organization, how will they alter them to make them appropriate for your situation? |

Using outside vendors is a strategy appropriate for larger organizations whose training needs vary dramatically over short periods of time. Thus, market leaders and those HRD departments that operate in uncertain environments will find many advantages in this strategy, as will small businesses.

In these situations, the training function's role is to select and manage training suppliers. Suppliers may be training firms, consultants, professional seminars, college/university courses, and increasingly, professional training offered through universities. The core competencies required of the HRD function using this strategy revolve around the selection and management of training providers. As a large number of firms and individuals offer training services, the manager must carefully screen potential providers. Obviously, cost is one factor to consider. Typically, the low-cost providers are those who recently entered the field. However, the fact that a provider is more expensive or experienced does not mean its quality is higher. Within your budgetary limits, the primary criterion should be the ability to provide the desired KSAs to your employees. Some key questions for making this determination are listed in Table 1-3. Of course, this list is not sufficient to evaluate the provider fully, but it provides a good start for making comparisons.

**Small Business** an organization that has fewer than 100 employees.

We identified just a few of the myriad HR and HRD strategy implications. The most important point is for you to understand that the organization's competitive strategy and the supporting HR strategies determine HRD's strategic direction.

## Focus on Small Business

Most business texts, especially those covering human resource management (HRM), focus on medium-to-large-sized businesses for a number of reasons, including

- Research typically requires a larger sample size;
- Larger firms have the budgets to support research;
- Policies and procedures are more formalized and thus easier to track; and

- Techniques described in HR texts usually require a formal HR function containing multiple areas of specialization, such as compensation, HRD, selection, and so on.

When small businesses are overlooked, a major component of the economic engine that runs North America is ignored.[39] For Canadian organizations, the definition for small business is generally accepted as fewer than 100 employees. Statistics Canada indicates that these small firms make up about 98 percent of the Canadian economy.[40] Therefore, increasing the effectiveness of small, entrepreneurial firms through relevant research is important. We generally use the term **small business** here to refer to organizations with fewer than 100 employees, but we on occasion use examples with about 150 employees. Larger companies that employ fewer than 500 people are considered to be medium-sized.

The model of the training process that we present is applicable to both large and small businesses, but the ways in which it is implemented can differ dramatically with the size of the company. One difference is the number of employees who need to be trained. Because larger companies train greater numbers of employees, they must use a more systematic and controlled method of determining what training needs exist. In smaller companies, the owner or president can have a close working knowledge of each employee and his or her training needs. Another difference is in developing training programs. The smaller business can easily determine what types of training are more or less important to the company's objectives and can design training accordingly. In larger companies, again, a more systematic and formal approach is needed because the firm's strategies and objectives are more complex. In larger companies, economies of scale can be obtained if common training needs across the workforce are identified, thus reducing the per-person cost of training. However, a more rigorous approach to identifying needs is required because more employees are involved.

Another difference between large and small companies is that small companies can use less-costly and less-formalized methods for evaluating training because the results are more easily observed. Throughout the following chapters, where applicable, we will have a Focus on Small Business section. Here we will identify strategies and practices that might be more appropriate for the smaller business. Where research results are applicable, we highlight their implications. When research is not available, we offer logic and applied examples.

## Summary

Training faces increasing demands to demonstrate results in terms of return on investment. With these demands come increased opportunities for the training function to influence the direction and operations of the company. Changing demographics, steadily increasing market competitiveness, high demand for and short supply of knowledge workers, and customer demands for high-quality products and services all challenge companies and their training departments.

Important concepts and terms in the field of training were defined and discussed including learning, knowledge, skills, and attitudes. Also how attitudes affect motivation (and in turn affect behaviour) was explained. Though differing opinions exist in the field of training about what constitutes training versus development and education, training in this text will be considered to be the experiences provided to people that enable them to learn job-related KSAs. Education will be considered to be the experiences that enable people to learn more general KSAs that are related to, but not specifically tailored to, a person's job. Development will be considered to be the learning that occurs as a result of training or education.

Evidence is accumulating that those companies that spend more on training are achieving better financial results. Improved operating methods (such as ISO 9000) and increasing employee competencies are also resulting in declining union membership. This trend places the leadership of unions in the dilemma of demanding increased training for their membership to ensure job security, while at the same time recognizing that higher-skilled employees allow the company to do more with fewer people.

Training needs to use the organization's strategy as a guide in the development of training. Two market strategies—market leader and cost leader—provide clear differences in how the organization is structured are presented and demonstrate how these different strategies lead to different training needs. Each results in different implications for how HR goes about its business. The HR department needs to be involved in the strategic planning process by providing information about workforce readiness to meet alternative strategic directions. HR also provides input in relation to managing change arising from new strategic directions. From this and other information, a strategic direction is determined.

HR and HRD need to develop their own strategies to support the overall strategic plan. It is HRD's responsibility to focus on what changes in KSAs are required to meet the strategic objectives. HRD also needs to partner with other parts of the organization to identify any other roadblocks to achieving employee performance objectives and assist in removing them.

The choice of strategic direction will also help determine the way HRD is structured. Cost leader organizations operate in a stable environment and training can generally be centralized. Market leaders, conversely, operate in an uncertain environment and the HRD department needs to be more decentralized.

Training is more than a program of providing KSAs to employees; it is an organizational change effort. As such, the OD techniques are useful tools for trainers. Similarly, OD efforts often require training, so training skills are useful for OD technicians. To be more effective, these two groups should consider working closely together and using each other's capabilities.

Effective training occurs as a set of phase(s) in which each phase acquires input, engages in a set of processes, and produces output needed for subsequent phases. The training process model provides a visual understanding of how the phases relate to each other. Although the model shows the phases occurring as sequential steps (needs analysis, design, development, implementation, and evaluation), in fact these phases occur in a dynamic fashion with feedback from one phase leading to the next phase as well as recycling through some aspects of the previous phase.

## Implications for Practice

**1.** An open systems view of training is useful because it helps us understand why it is important to examine the organization as well as the individual when trying to improve an individual's behaviour.

**2.** Training in organizations is more critical than ever before because of changing demographics, a focus on continuous improvement (especially quality), and increasing skill requirements for many jobs.

**3.** Training is a continuous improvement process, focused on individuals, consisting of five interrelated phases.

**4.** The involvement of HR and HRD in the development of the organization's strategic plans improves the likelihood of successful implementation by providing a thorough analysis of current employees' potential for meeting the objectives.

**5.** The training unit needs to develop its own strategies in alignment with those of the HR unit and the organization as a whole.

**6.** Training needs to be thought of as an organizational intervention, not just a program to provide employees with new skills. Without such a focus, many skills will not easily transfer to the job.

**7.** HR can learn a great deal from OD people and vice versa. Integrating the two can result in higher levels of organizational and individual performance.

**8.** Small businesses need to utilize strategic planning and the training process model, though the implementation will be different due to size and resources.

## Key Terms

## Questions for Review

1.  Describe the relationship between the HR and the HRD functions in a large organization. How might a small organization handle the responsibilities of these two areas?

2.  What factors might inhibit HRD managers from developing a strategic planning approach to training? How might these factors be overcome?

3.  Consider the following problem-solving model. Based on the discussion in this chapter, describe how the training process model is or is not consistent with this model.

**Problem-Solving Process**

- Define and understand the problem.

- Determine the cause of the problem.

- Identify potential solutions to the problem.

- Select the solution that provides the most benefits for the least cost.

- Develop an action plan for putting the solution in place.

- Implement the solution.

- Evaluate and, if necessary, modify the solution.

## Exercises

1.  Review the material in Training in Action 1-2. Assume you were hired to develop a training program for these CSRs. Write down the four most important knowledge, skills, or attitudes that you believe your training design must address and your reasoning for selecting these. If done as a group exercise, allow each member of the group to share the KSAs they

identified as well as their reasoning. Then, reach a group consensus as to the four most important KSAs and your rationale for including each KSA. Each group will then report to the rest of the class.

2.  In small groups, discuss the training responsibilities of supervisors and managers who are not part of

the HRD department. Prepare a list of what those responsibilities might be and a rationale for your choices.

3. Identify two organizations with different environments and core technologies. Describe what these differences are. Indicate how the HRD strategies of these companies might be similar or different. Provide a rationale for your conclusions based on concepts in the chapter.

4. Conduct an interview with a small business owner or manager. Get a good understanding of how he or she approaches training in their company. What differences do you see between how this company approaches training and what was described in this chapter? What are the reasons for this difference?

## Web Research

Each year a number of companies are identified as the "Best Canadian Companies to work for." Go on the Web and find a company that has made a recent list. See if there is information on their training. Also, using a Web search engine, find any articles that have been written about this company that are related to its training (in *The Globe, National Post, Canadian Business, HR reporter*, etc.). Write a short report on your findings.

## CASE ANALYSIS

1. How did Domtar's strategies align with its mission? Explain your answer.

2. Thinking back to the Domtar case, which of the two competitive strategies described in the chapter do you think they were closer to? Explain your answer and describe what that meant for HR and HRD.

3. Given the difficulty of organizational change, what factors can you suggest contributed to the success at Domtar? How did Domtar's management at all levels contribute to reducing resistance to change? What else might they have done?

4. What were the major HRD challenges associated with Domtar's acquisitions and joint partnerships? How were these challenges addressed and what were the risks associated with these approaches?

5. Take the critical facts in the Domtar case and place them into the appropriate phases of the training model presented in the chapter. Begin with the triggering event and provide a rationale for why each fact belongs in the phase in which you have placed it.

# 2

# LEARNING MOTIVATION AND PERFORMANCE

*The secret of education lies in respecting the pupil . . .*
Ralph Waldo Emerson

## CHAPTER OBJECTIVES

After reading this chapter, you should be able to:

- Explain why it is important to understand theory.

- Identify the major factors that determine human performance and their relevance to training.

- Describe the cognitive and behavioural approaches to learning and their contradictory implications for instructional practices.

- Identify a learning theory that integrates cognitive and behaviourist perspectives and describe how its processes and components relate to training.

- Describe the causes of resistance to learning.

- Explain the effect of group dynamics on learning and the transfer of training.

- Explain why different people need different training methods to learn the same things.

- Identify the characteristics of training design that motivate learning and accommodate trainee differences.

# CASE

Claudia, a successful 33-year-old corporate marketing executive, found herself in the mountains of Alberta preparing to climb a rope ladder attached to a tree. When she reached the top of the ladder, she would fall off backward. It wouldn't be an accident. No, she wasn't suicidal or deranged. She was participating in an executive development program called Wilderness Training Lab.

At the corporate office in Winnipeg, she was known as an independent, smart, and tenacious businesswoman. She quickly moved up the corporate ladder from Product Research Assistant to Brand Manager. Claudia had a reputation for micromanaging her subordinates and being a loner. When asked about these issues, Claudia replied, "When I was in college, I had a lot of group projects. At first I went along with group decisions and trusted others to do a good job, even though I felt anxious about putting my grade in the hands of someone else. It seemed to be a good way to get along in the group. Those projects received mediocre grades, and I'm only satisfied with being the best. Then I started to take over the leadership of every group I was in. I developed the plan, decided who would do what and what the timelines were, and always took on the most difficult and complex parts myself, all the time making sure the others were doing what they were assigned. From then on my group projects always got an 'A' I carried those lessons with me into the workplace and I've had good success here too. Maybe it rubs some people the wrong way, but it works for me. The only trouble I'm having is keeping up with all my projects. Some of the other brand managers want to work with me on joint projects, but I do not have time. Besides, they probably just want me to do their work for them or steal my ideas. The VP of Marketing will be retiring soon and only one of the seven Brand Managers will get that job. What's in it for me if I collaborate with them? Let each of us sink or swim on our own merits."

A few months ago, the VP of Marketing, Sandy Cines, discussed career plans with Claudia. Sandy had always praised and encouraged Claudia's work, but this time he was a little reserved. He suggested, in rather strong terms, that she attend a Wilderness Executive Development Program. Claudia hesitated because of her workload and upcoming deadlines. Sandy said, "Well, I'll leave the decision up to you. The Director of Training and I have looked at your strengths and what you'll need for the next level as an executive. Technically you're very strong, but more important at the next level is building good interpersonal relationships. The Training Director recommended this program for you, but, as I said, I'll leave the decision up to you."

Claudia wondered what he thought was wrong with her interpersonal relationships. She had great relationships with customers, with outside vendors, and in her personal life. Relationships with her subordinates and peers needed to be different. She needed to be firmer and less flexible with them, did she not? She did not think she had bad relationships with her subordinates or peers. They never complained to her. However, Claudia decided it was pretty clear that Sandy wanted her to attend the Wilderness program.

In Alberta, she found a diverse group of men and women executives from all over North America. Many confided that their organizations had sent them to "learn how to be more effective in groups." Most of them indicated they were interested and eager but a little nervous about what was expected of them. They soon found out. They were divided into groups of ten and taken out on the "course."

The first training exercise was climbing the "trust ladder." Doug, the Program Director, explained that the group members would have to rely on each other quite a bit during the coming week. To demonstrate that the group could be trusted, each person was to climb to the top of the ladder and fall backward into the group, who would catch the person in a proper manner. Doug showed them how. After everyone had completed the exercise, they discussed risk taking, building and trusting one's support systems, being part of a support system, and communicating one's needs. Then came more challenging exercises, such as building and using rope bridges to cross a stream, white-water rafting, and—the most physically challenging of all—scaling a four-metre wall. The front of the wall was sheer and smooth. A platform on which two people could stand at about waist level with the top of the wall, and from which extended a ladder to the ground, was on the other side.

Everyone had to scale the wall and no one could stand on the platform until he or she had scaled the wall. It was a timed event, and the groups were in competition with one another. The first thing a group had to do was develop a plan. Strong and tall people were needed to boost the others to a point where they could pull themselves over. Some stood on the platform and helped those who were not strong enough to pull themselves over. It was clear the first people over also had to be strong. Another problem was the last person over. Everyone, except the last pair, would have "spotters" in case of a fall. Also the last person would have no one left to boost him or her to the top. Someone would have to act as a human rope, hanging down from the top so the last person could climb up the person and over the wall. Therefore, the last person would have to be light but strong enough to boost the second-to-last person up and to climb over the human rope. In order to determine the order, the group members needed to share with one another their strengths and weaknesses. Claudia wanted to be the last person so she could make sure everyone was doing what they were supposed to, and also because, as the last person over the wall, she would represent the group's successful completion of this exercise. Two of the strongest men in the group confessed to having injuries that would hamper them. Claudia realized that her tennis elbow would be a great liability. When it came to her turn to discuss her strengths and weaknesses, she was honest about her injury and indicated she would fit best somewhere in the middle where many people could help her.

When Claudia's turn to climb came, she called out to those on top what to expect—where she couldn't put much strain and how she would indicate that someone was pulling too hard. Then she was being pushed up with spotters all around her, and the next thing she knew she was over the wall.

Later, when the members discussed the event, Claudia asked what impact her limitations caused in the group. Those who had been pullers replied, "None." They said they knew what to do, because she had told them about her problem ahead of time.

While getting packed to go home, Claudia thought about how much she had learned about herself and her relationship to other people, especially at work. She recognized that she generally failed to trust others to do their part and so she was not being as effective as she could be. Her success came at a high price because of the extra workload she imposed on herself. In addition, she wondered, "What is the price my subordinates pay? How have my actions affected their attitudes and performance? Do I need to be so competitive with my peers? Is that behaviour really in my or my company's best interests?" She knew she would have a lot to think about on the trip home.

# A FEW WORDS ABOUT THEORY

Theories are speculative road maps for how things work. In fact, most of us develop our own theories to explain how the world around us works. The child yells, "I want an ice cream cone." He is told, "No, not until you ask properly." After a number of such incidents, the child begins to see that when he says "please" he is more successful than when he says "Gimme" or "I want." The child develops a theory of how to get things he wants; he must always say "please." "Good" theories assemble a number of facts, show the relationship among those facts, and develop a logical rationale for what is likely to be true, given those facts. From theory, predictions or hypotheses can be generated and tested. If the tests show the predictions are correct, the theory is supported. If the new facts are inconsistent with the predictions, the theory is revised or discarded. Suppose the child in the previous situation takes his theory to the extreme. When he says "please" but is denied his request, he continues to badger the person, saying "pleeeease, pleeease." If he soon finds this approach does not work, he may revise the theory. The new theory says "please" works more often than not, but if you have to say it over and over, it does not work. In fact, it makes the person annoyed. This process of developing, testing, and reformulating a theory is the basis of science. It is how new knowledge is created. A good theory is also practical because it

- explains facts as simply as possible,

- predicts future events, and

- provides information on what can be done to prevent undesirable things from happening.

**Theories** are abstractions that allow us to make sense out of a large number of facts related to an issue. Effective training practices are developed from theories and theoretical constructs that describe how learning occurs and what motivates people. This chapter is about theory and so it is necessarily somewhat abstract. Unfortunately, some people may see little value in wading through the complex logic and rationale of theories. It is easier to follow a set of instructions like a recipe. But, in training, as in business, a single recipe will not work. Recipes require standardized ingredients—businesses do not have standardized ingredients. Each organization is unique, with different missions, strategies, environments, technologies, and people.

**Theories** abstractions that allow us to make sense of a large number of facts related to an issue.

The interaction of these elements creates a different "chemistry" in each organization, thus making a "one best way for everyone" approach ineffective. Theories provide the guidelines, principles, and predictions that allow organizations to create the right recipe for their situation. Successful people in business pay attention to theory.

Firms in all industries from manufacturing to telecommunications, from energy production to health care (e.g., Ford, 3M, Microsoft, Motorola, Toshiba, Toyota, and Xerox), jumped ahead of the competition because they understood and applied theories. Some of these theories concern the product, others concern how the product is made, and still others how the firm is managed. Rather than copying others, these companies understood the underlying theories related to what they were trying to do and applied those theories to meeting their goals. As the quality guru W. E. Deming indicates, experience teaches nothing without theory.[1] He warns that unless you understand the theory behind someone's success, copying can lead to chaos.[2] A survey of *Fortune* 1000 companies engaged in programs to improve quality (e.g., total quality management ISO 9000) and involve employees in decision-making supports this view. The companies that applied the underlying models and theories correctly were getting the best results; those that simply put programs into place were getting the worst results.[3]

Consider pay systems. Suppose a company pays its employees on the basis of how much they produce (i.e., a piece-rate system). The company is successful and the employees make a high wage. You decide to institute the piece-rate system in your company. Will it work? It might, but it might not. Its success will depend on the total reward system, what the company is trying to accomplish, and what the employees value. For example, employees may turn out a high volume of the product but at the cost of many problems with quality. They may produce more than can be sold. Piece-rate systems can create a "norm" in the work group that prohibits them from producing more than a specified amount (to avoid increases in the product/money ratio or to protect slower workers). In other words, the differences in the people and work environments affect the success of the piece-rate system.

An understanding of motivational theory allows a manager to improve employee performance levels by applying the principles of motivation to his firm's unique circumstances. The same is true with training. Whether one company's training program will work in another's, will depend on the needs of the latter company, its employees, and the training system used. Copying without understanding is like taking someone else's prescription drugs. Even though they may have made someone else better, they could kill you.

What theories are important to the success of the training enterprise? If trainees do not learn, then training has failed. Theories of learning are certainly important. If trainees learn but do not try to transfer the learning to the job, then training has failed. Add theories of motivation to the list. If the trainees learn and try to transfer the learning to the job site, but obstacles in their work environment prevent them from making the transfer, then training again has failed. It failed because the changes in the work environment that needed to support the desired behaviour were not considered. Thus, in order to design and implement effective training programs, you need to understand how people learn, what motivates learning and performance, and how the learning and work environment affect motivation and performance. This chapter focuses on these topics. The theories, models, and concepts discussed here serve as a foundation for the rest of the book. We will refer to these theories and their implications for training throughout the text because they are related to each phase of the training process.

# UNDERSTANDING MOTIVATION AND PERFORMANCE

Your job performance and your behaviour in general are a function of what you know, what you are able to do, and what you believe (KSAs). If you do not have the KSAs, you cannot perform. However, additional factors are important in determining your performance. Figure 2-1 depicts a general **performance model**. This model indicates that a person's performance (P) depends on the interaction of motivation (M), KSAs, and environment (E). Motivation arises from your needs and beliefs about how best to satisfy those needs. Both motivation and KSAs are part of your memory and thinking systems (i.e., cognitive structure). **Environment** refers to the physical surroundings in which performance must occur, including barriers and aids to performance as well as objects and events (cues) that you might see as indicating that your performance will be rewarded or punished.

Think back to the Wilderness Training case. Which of Claudia's KSAs allowed her to reach her current position? Her boss felt she lacked the interpersonal skills necessary for developing good relationships. Did she lack these skills or was she not motivated to use them? Apparently she had the skills since she was able to develop good relationships with others with whom she was not working directly. The Training Director probably understood this fact, because he suggested the Wilderness Training rather than an interpersonal skill-building workshop. The Wilderness Training did not teach people how to develop good interpersonal relationships as much as it broke down barriers that prevented those relationships from developing. The program worked on the motivation and attitudes of the trainees. What barriers in Claudia's work environment might keep her from developing these relationships? How about the upcoming retirement of the VP and that open position? What criteria could be used in evaluating managers that would encourage them to develop positive relationships with peers and subordinates?

Each of the factors M, KSA, and E in Figure 2-1 can influence performance, but the combination of these factors determines the person's performance. The weakest factor, then, limits the likelihood of engaging in any activity. For instance, no matter how knowledgeable or skilled you are, if you are not motivated to perform the activity—or worse, are motivated to not perform it—then you will not. If the environment does not support the activity or blocks it, then it does not matter how

**Performance Model** a depiction of the inputs that need to be considered in determining performance levels.

**Environment** the physical surroundings in which performance must occur, including barriers and aids to performance as well as objects and events (cues) that you might see as indicating that your performance will be rewarded or punished.

## FIGURE 2-1   Factors Determining Human Performance

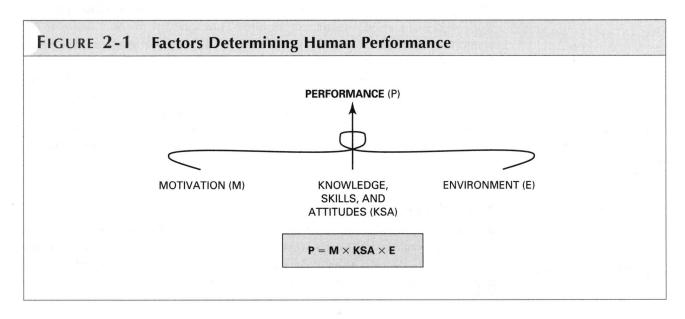

PERFORMANCE (P)

MOTIVATION (M)          KNOWLEDGE, SKILLS, AND ATTITUDES (KSA)          ENVIRONMENT (E)

$$P = M \times KSA \times E$$

motivated or knowledgeable you are—you will not do it. For example, if necessary tools are not working or equipment is missing, you won't attempt the activity. Likewise, if the environment is sending signals that your performance will be punished, you won't perform. In Claudia's case, she seemed to want to stay at work and not attend the training. However, her boss gave strong indications that staying would be viewed negatively. Her environment changed, signalling that old ways of performing would not be rewarded and new ways would.

This model in Figure 2-1 is important for determining employee training needs. It helps us understand whether poor job performance is a result of KSAs or other factors. It is also important in the design of training. When putting together the learning modules and training methods, the trainer must consider how they will affect the trainees' motivation to learn. Similarly, when selecting the training facility and materials, we must consider how they will interact with trainee motivation. When we ask trainees to use their new knowledge and skills back on the job, we must make sure the environment is supportive of this new way of performing. A deeper understanding of the three determinants of performance will increase your ability to design and implement effective training programs. First, we look at motivation, presenting the most prominent theories and clarifying their relationship to the training enterprise.

## MOTIVATION: WHY DO THEY ACT LIKE THAT?

**Motivation** the direction, persistence, and amount of effort expended by an individual to achieve a specified outcome.

Motivation is part of a person's cognitive structure and is not directly observable. Thus, it is typically defined in terms of its effects on behaviour, which are observable. Most of the scientific literature defines **motivation** as the direction, persistence, and amount of effort expended by an individual to achieve a specified outcome. In other words, the following factors reflect a person's motivation:

- What need(s) the person is trying to satisfy,

- What types of activity the person engages in to satisfy the need,

- How long the person engages in the activity, and

- How hard the person works at it.

Go back to Claudia's situation. What need is she is trying to satisfy: the growth need or the need to achieve and get ahead in the company? To answer this, look at the types of activities she is involved in. She takes on extra projects, volunteers to work on task forces, works late, and so forth. How long has she been doing it? For about two years. How hard does she work at it? Well, it seems pretty hard: She works 12-hour days and often goes in on Saturday.

Motivation is goal-directed and derived both from people's personal needs and from the decision processes used to satisfy those needs. Separate theories evolved to explain the relationship between needs and motivation, and between decision processes and motivation. Needs theories attempt to describe the types of needs people have, their relative importance, and how they are related to each other. Process theories attempt to describe and explain how a person's needs are translated into actions to satisfy the needs.

**Needs Theory** theories of motivation that explain the various types of human needs that are motivating.

**ERG Theory** a need theory of motivation taken from the work of Maslow describing three types of need: existence, relatedness, and growth.

**Existence Needs** physiological and security needs.

## Needs Theory
Our needs are the basis of our motivation and the reason for almost all of our activity. Understanding a person's needs helps you to understand his behaviour. From Maslow's early work,[4] Clayton Alderfrer developed a **needs theory** of motivation called **ERG theory**.[5] ERG is an initialism representing the three basic needs of the theory: existence, relatedness, and growth. **Existence needs** correspond to

Maslow's lower-order physiological and security needs. They are the immediate needs required to sustain life—needs for food, shelter, and the like—as well as the need for some security in the future for a safe and healthy life. **Relatedness needs** reflect people's need to be valued and accepted by others. Interpersonal relationships and group membership (work, family, friends, etc.) act to satisfy these needs. **Growth needs** include feelings of self-worth and competency and achieving our potential. Recognition, accomplishment, challenging opportunities, and a feeling of fulfillment are outcomes that can satisfy these needs. Even though some disagreement exists in the scientific community about the relationships among these needs and their relative importance at any given point in life, few dispute the idea that these needs exist for everyone.

> **Relatedness Needs** need to be valued and accepted by others.
>
> **Growth Needs** feelings of self-worth and competency and achieving our potential.

People work to satisfy their needs. Understanding the types and strengths of employee needs is important to the training process. It can help to identify some of the causes of poor performance and therefore determine training needs. Consider the employee who has strong relatedness needs but whose job is structured so that he must work alone most of the time. He may not be getting the required quality and quantity of work completed because he spends too much time socializing with others in the workplace. Additional technical KSAs will do little to improve his job performance. Performance improvement would more likely result from some other type of training (perhaps time management) or some non-training intervention (such as job redesign or counselling).

Website about ERG theory
*http://changingminds.org/ explanations/theories/ erg_theory.htm*

Understanding needs is also important in designing training programs and facilities. Trainers need to make sure that the environment and training methods—that is, how the training is conducted and where it takes place—meet the trainee's physical, relationship, and growth needs. We discuss these issues in depth in the chapters covering training design, development, and implementation. Think back to the Wilderness Training case to get a sense of how training methods, materials, and environment influence trainee motivation.

Although motivated to attend the training because of her boss's pressure, was Claudia motivated to learn when she first arrived, or was she skeptical about the value of the training? What if she had attended a series of lectures on the importance of developing strong interpersonal relationships instead of the outdoor group experiences? Would she have been as motivated to absorb the lessons and apply them to her work? How strong do you think Claudia's relatedness needs were? How effective would training be that focused on showing her how changing her behaviour would result in increased acceptance by her peers? It seems apparent that Claudia did have high growth needs. The outdoor training presented her with a series of physical and psychological challenges, fitting in with her growth needs and motivating her to become an involved participant in the training.

The few empirical studies conducted on this topic tend to support Alderfer's notion that people can experience needs in all three areas simultaneously.[6] The relative satisfaction level in each area determines the importance of the needs. Unsatisfied needs motivate us, and motivation decreases as needs in an area are satisfied. However, needs in these three basic areas tend to renew themselves; they can also expand. Although you may have a good job that provides you with food, shelter, and security, you may start to feel the need for better food, a larger and more comfortable home, a larger savings account, or an investment portfolio. Similarly, even though your relationships with family, friends, and co-workers may at first satisfy your relatedness needs, you may begin to feel that you would like the relationships to be better or closer, or that you want to develop additional relationships.

Sometimes our needs may conflict with one another, or one type of need may become more important than the others. Then we feel we must choose one over the other, which is what happened with Claudia. We cannot be sure how strong her relatedness needs are, but we do know that she saw them as conflicting with her ability to satisfy her growth needs at work. The Wilderness Training was designed to satisfy the trainees' needs for growth and relationships at the same time. Step by step, the training demonstrated how building strong interpersonal relationships could not only satisfy relationship needs but also make greater accomplishments possible.

This example illustrates a central point about motivating trainees to learn. The best training incorporates opportunities to satisfy all three categories of needs. The training facility and accommodations address, in part, existence needs. How much trainees learn is also dependent on the trainees' physical comfort, level of hunger, and so on. Demonstrating how the training will improve the trainee's competencies, and in turn increase job security and fulfill existence needs, will motivate the trainee. Building a network of positive relationships among trainees and between trainees and the trainer will address relatedness needs. Using methods that provide challenging experiences that lead to the attainment of the target KSAs will address growth needs. By having training address all levels of needs in some way, you can be assured that all trainees will find at least one need that requires satisfying. This will go a long way toward motivating all trainees because you offer something for everyone.

Needs theory leads to implications for the training process even after completion of the training. Trainers must make sure trainees are able to see how learning fulfills their needs. In Claudia's case, her boss provided some of that linkage when he told her how important relationship building is to her current and future job success (i.e., security needs). What could the trainers at the Wilderness Training Lab do to create these links? We discuss this issue more in the next section, since these links are the focus of the process theories.

**Process Theories** theories that describe how a person's needs translate into action.

## Process Theories

Needs are only part of the motivation equation. Deciding how to go about satisfying those needs is the other part. **Process theories** of motivation describe how a person's needs translate into action. Although many types of process theories exist, we will focus on the three with the most direct implications for training: classical conditioning, reinforcement theory, and expectancy theory.

**Classical Conditioning** the association of a generalized response to some signal in the environment.

### Classical Conditioning.

Classical conditioning is the association of a generalized response to some signal in the environment. It typically involves learning to emit a non-voluntary response to some signal that in the past did not produce that response. For example, when an optometrist examines your eyes, she may put you in front of a machine that blows a puff of air into your eye. This puff of air causes you to blink your eye. If a red light came on just before the puff of air, you would probably learn to associate the puff of air with the red light and begin blinking whenever the red light comes on. At that point, you learned to blink (generalized response) in response to the red light (signal).

The most widely known example of this type of learning involves Pavlov's dogs.[7] Pavlov was not studying learning; he was examining the physiology of digestion by measuring the amount of salivation produced by various substances placed on the tongues of dogs. As the story goes, Pavlov observed that the dogs began to salivate upon his entering the lab, thus playing havoc with his desire to determine the amount of saliva produced by various substances. He speculated that over time his entrance was followed so often with substances placed on the dogs' tongues that the dogs learned to salivate on his entrance.

Table 2-1 shows how the classical conditioning process works. Step 1 reflects the state of affairs before conditioning takes place. Certain factors in the environment (unconditioned stimuli) produce automatic responses (unconditioned responses) in animals and people. If we place an unconditioned stimulus such as meat powder on a dog's tongue, an unconditioned response would be the dog's salivation. That is, the

## TABLE 2-1    Classical Conditioning Process

| | | |
|---|---|---|
| **STEP 1 Unconditioned Stimulus**<br>(Meat powder) | $\longrightarrow$ | **Unconditioned Response**<br>(Salivation) |
| **STEP 2 Conditioned Stimulus paired**<br>**with Unconditioned Stimulus**<br>(Buzzer followed closely<br>in time, over many trials,<br>by meat powder) | $\longrightarrow$ | **Unconditioned Response**<br>(Salivation) |
| **STEP 3 Conditioned Stimulus**<br>(Buzzer alone) | $\longrightarrow$ | **Conditioned Response**<br>(Salivation) |

dog need not be trained (conditioned) to salivate when meat powder is put on its tongue. However, this salivation response does not occur with every stimulus that might be in the dog's environment, such as a buzzer. If, however, you sounded that buzzer just before putting meat powder on the dog's tongue, over a number of trials the buzzer would become a conditioned stimulus. The dog is learning (being conditioned) to associate the buzzer with the meat powder. However, you are still putting meat powder on the dog's tongue, so the salivation is really a response to the meat powder and remains an unconditioned response. This situation is reflected in step 2 of Table 2-1. In step 3, you stop putting meat powder on the dog's tongue after sounding the buzzer. If the dog salivates at the buzzer, you have created a conditioned response (salivation) to a conditioned stimulus (the buzzer). Continually sounding the buzzer without offering the meat powder will extinguish (remove) this response. Over time, the conditioned response gradually disappears. Through conditioning, a response to one stimulus can be transferred to another, unrelated stimulus.

Classical conditioning occurs frequently in the workplace, though it typically receives little attention. The noon whistle blows at the factory and the worker's digestive juices begin to flow. Sparks fly from the welding machine and your eyes blink, even though you are wearing goggles. As you will see later, this type of learning can have an impact on the learning environment.

*Reinforcement Theory*. **Reinforcement theory** is relatively simple on the surface but can be difficult to apply. It does not provide all the answers for how needs are translated into action; but its major points are essential for understanding human behaviour. The foundation for reinforcement theory comes from the work of E. L. Thorndike.[8] Thorndike's **law of effect** states that behaviour followed by satisfying experiences tends to be repeated, and behaviour followed by annoyance or dissatisfaction tends to be avoided. B. F. Skinner used this principle in developing the operant conditioning model and reinforcement theory.[9]

The basic components of learning in **operant conditioning** are illustrated in Figure 2-2. A person is faced with an object or event in the environment (stimulus) and behaves in a certain way (response). That behaviour results in an outcome (consequence) to the individual that is positive or negative. In the illustration, the man has seen a book of great interest (environmental stimulus) while on the way to work. He purchases the book and reads it (response) while continuing to walk to work. You can imagine the consequence. The environment provides stimuli that elicit behaviours and consequences that reinforce or punish them.

In similar situations, the consequences of past behaviour affect future behaviour. How will the man in Figure 2-2 respond to books while walking in the near future? Operant learning theory says the man will learn to avoid reading and walking. A person's motivation (i.e., direction, magnitude, and persistence of behaviour), then, is a

**Reinforcement Theory** A theory of motivation that uses the Law of Effect to predict behaviour.

**Law of Effect** behaviour followed by satisfying experiences tends to be repeated, and behaviour followed by annoyance or dissatisfaction tends to be avoided.

**Operant Conditioning** a type of learning where specific types of behaviour are reinforced.

## FIGURE 2-2  Behaviourist Model of Learning

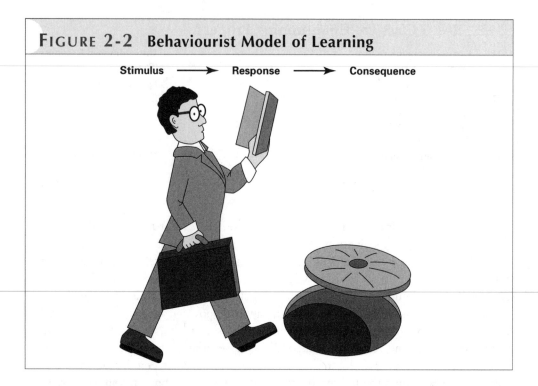

Stimulus ———→ Response ———→ Consequence

Website about behaviourism
*http://en.wikipedia.org/wiki/Behaviorism*

function of her reinforcement history. Unfortunately, reinforcement theory provides no explanation of the processes involved in storing, retrieving, or using the lessons of past reinforcement. The model leaves us wondering how future behaviour becomes influenced by previous reinforcement history. Nevertheless, the theory does convincingly predict the various effects on future behaviour caused by the consequences of past behaviour.

Skinner identified four types of consequences that can result from behaviour:

1. Positive reinforcement,

2. Negative reinforcement,

3. Punishment, and

4. Extinction.

When behaviour results in either positive or negative reinforcement, the likelihood is increased that the behaviour will occur in future similar circumstances. **Positive reinforcement** occurs when your behaviour results in something desirable happening to you—either tangible (such as receiving money), psychological (such as feeling pleasure), or some combination of the two. **Negative reinforcement** occurs when your behaviour results in removing something you find annoying, frustrating, or unpleasant. This "good" outcome increases your likelihood of repeating the behaviour. For example, if, when you have a headache, you take an Aspirin and the headache goes away, the "Aspirin-taking response" is negatively reinforced. Nothing is inherently desirable about taking the Aspirin; its reinforcing power comes from its ability to remove the pain. The environment or the person can provide both positive and negative reinforcement. For example, a person receives pay for his work. The environment provides the positive reinforcement (pay). When a person feels a sense of pride and accomplishment after completing a task, the person is positively reinforcing himself.

Your behaviour is punished when it results in something undesirable happening to you. **Punishment** decreases the likelihood of the response occurring in the

**Positive Reinforcement** behaviour that results in something desirable happening to you—it can be tangible, psychological, or some combination of the two.

**Negative Reinforcement** behaviour that results in removing something you find annoying, frustrating, or unpleasant.

**Punishment** behaviour that results in something undesirable happening to you—it can be tangible or psychological or both and can come from the environment or be self-administered.

future. Like reinforcement, punishment can be tangible, psychological, or both and can come from the environment or be self-administered. In Figure 2-2, the environment provides the punishment. However, when we do things that violate our personal values and beliefs and therefore experience negative feelings, we are self-punishing that behaviour. Punishment exists when you receive something unpleasant or when you lose something desirable. The latter form of punishment is called **extinction**. For example, you may buy books by a certain author because of the positive feelings you experience as you read them. However, while reading the last two books by this author, you did not experience those positive feelings. Therefore you stop buying this author's books. When the person's behaviour (like buying and reading the books) no longer produces the desired outcomes, the behaviour is less likely to occur in the future. Figure 2-3 depicts the various types of behavioural consequences.

**Extinction** a form of punishment in which you lose something desirable.

A few examples here should clear up any misunderstandings or confusion created by these definitions. First, think back to the Wilderness Training Lab case. What kind of reinforcement history did Claudia experience from working in groups? Her first group experiences in college resulted in the negative outcomes (for her) of mediocre grades. Since her cooperative behaviour in groups was punished, she stopped it. When she changed her behaviour to become more directive, monitoring and doing more of the important work, two consequences resulted: (1) she was positively reinforced by good grades; (2) she avoided the negative feelings of anxiety about having other group members not do their assignments well and the resulting mediocre grades. Her new group behaviour was both positively and negatively reinforced over a number of years. It is no wonder, then, that she continued to work in groups this way. Is it possible Claudia avoided working in groups with her peers because she couldn't control those groups in the same way she could her subordinates? The training she received provided her with new group situations in which she was positively reinforced (e.g., recognition, accomplishment) for using a new set of group behaviours.

In another example, after working for a few hours, Jon, a machinist, suddenly hears a loud unpleasant screeching noise coming from the exhaust fans near his work area. He finds the electrical switch and turns the fans off; he later switches them on

## FIGURE 2-3  Types of Consequences That May Follow Behaviour

|  | Desirable Consequences | Undesirable Consequences |
|---|---|---|
| Trainee Receives | Behaviour Positively Rainforced | Behaviour punished |
| Trainee Loses | Behaviour Punished (Extinction) | Behaviour Negatively Reinforced |

again, and they work for the rest of the day. The same thing happens the next two days. The fourth day, when he takes his break he shuts the fans off before the noise begins. When he returns from his break, he turns them on and they operate normally for the rest of the day. This behaviour becomes a daily habit with Jon. What Jon does not know is that plant maintenance repaired the fan the evening before he began his "shutting it off at the break" behaviour. Jon maintained his behaviour because it was negatively reinforcing. By "giving the fans a rest," he avoided the loud, unpleasant noise. As this worked every time, it was self-reinforcing. This is how superstitious behaviours develop.

**Reinforcement Versus Punishment.** Punishment can eliminate undesirable behaviour in the workplace. However, several problems make it undesirable as a management or training tool.

- It does not motivate people to do things, only not to do things. It does not indicate what the desired behaviour is, only what is not desired.

- If the undesired behaviour is punished only sometimes, people will learn the situations in which they can get away with it. The saying, "While the cat's away, the mice will play," neatly captures one problem with this technique; punishment requires constant vigilance on the part of a supervisor and encourages employee efforts to "beat the system."

- If a person's undesired behaviour is rewarding, the punishment must be severe enough to offset the behaviour's reinforcing properties. Escalating negative outcomes to employees raises ethical, moral, and commonsense objections.

- Someone must do the punishing. This person becomes someone to be avoided. Supervisors avoided by subordinates experience leadership problems.

Positive and negative reinforcement are better tools for motivating and especially for training employees. Negative reinforcement can cause the desired behaviour to become self-reinforcing, like Jon's turning off the fans. When the person continually performs the desired behaviour (avoiding the undesired behaviour), negative outcomes are avoided. If the desired behaviour is then also positively reinforced, the person not only avoids the negative outcome but also receives a positive outcome. As with Claudia in the opening case, the result is a strong maintenance of the behaviour.

With reinforcement, the person doing the reinforcing does not always need to be present for the desired behaviour to occur. The employee actively seeks to make the reinforcing agent (e.g., supervisor or trainer) aware of her behaviour. When punishment is used as the motivational or learning mechanism, the employee attempts to hide behaviour so as to avoid the consequences. Obviously, a trainer or supervisor's job is much easier when employees are attempting to communicate what they are doing rather than hiding it.

Thus, either positive or negative reinforcement is preferred over punishment as a strategy for motivating learning and behaviour change. Used in combination, positive and negative reinforcement appear more effective than either used alone.[10] For those interested in finding out more about how to implement positive, humanistic, and effective work environments, we would encourage you to read Dick Grote's *Discipline Without Punishment*.[11]

Reinforcement theory suggests that any training must be concerned not only with teaching the KSAs but also the consequences that are attached to the following:

- the learning process,
- the old way of doing the job, and
- the new way of doing the job.

These factors play a key role in determining how much is learned and how much is actually used back on the job.

As noted earlier, many unanswered questions arise when using reinforcement theory to describe the motivational process. Expectancy theory, however, provides some additional explanation and leads to many more implications for training.

*Expectancy Theory.* In 1964 Victor Vroom published a theory of work motivation called **expectancy theory**.[12] This theory describes the cognitive processes involved in deciding the best course of action for achieving our goals (i.e., satisfying our needs). A **cognitive process** is a mental activity such as information storage, retrieval, or use. Thinking and decision-making are cognitive processes. In its most basic form, expectancy theory proposes that a person's motivation can be explained by the relationship among three conceptually distinct elements:

**Expectancy Theory** theory of motivation that uses cognitive processes as a means of determining the best course of action for achieving our goals.

**Cognitive Process** a mental activity such as information storage, retrieval, or use. Thinking and decision-making are cognitive processes.

1. The level of success expected by the individual (e.g., how well she will be able to do what she set out to do), which is termed Expectancy 1,

2. The individual's beliefs about what the outcomes will be if she is successful. The expected outcomes and their likelihood of occurrence make up Expectancy 2, and

3. The individual's feelings about the various outcomes' positive or negative value. An outcome's subjective value is referred to as its **valence**.

**Valence** The attractiveness of outcomes to an individual.

In combination, these elements determine the individual's motivation (i.e., effort) to engage in a particular course of action. When situations allow different courses of action, as most do, the one with the highest motivation level is chosen. The motivation level for a particular course of action can be calculated mathematically with the following formula:

$$\text{Effort} = \text{Expectancy } 1_i \times \Sigma_{ij} \, (\text{Expectancy } 2_{ij} \times \text{Valence}_{ij})$$

Although this formula is useful for those conducting research on motivation, it is not particularly useful in the day-to-day activities of most people. It does, however, present some important implications for training and learning, which we discuss shortly.

To gain a better understanding of the expectancy theory framework, let's go back to Claudia at the point at which she was trying to decide whether to attend the executive development seminar as suggested by her boss. Today is the last day she can register for the seminar that starts in two weeks. She postponed the decision as long as possible and now must decide. She feels confident about her ability to complete this training successfully, but she holds some doubts about whether it will teach her anything useful about running her marketing operation or working more effectively in a group. She knows that during her week of training, the marketing strategies for five important accounts will arrive on her desk and she will need to review and finalize them before forwarding them to top management. They are due on the Wednesday following training. In addition, her normal work will continue to pile up. Claudia faces the choice between incompatible courses of action. Her cognitive processes, in expectancy theory terms, are illustrated in Figure 2-4.

Examining Claudia's situation in terms of expectancy theory, we see that her expectations of success (Expectancy 1) are high for both behaviours. The expectancy of 1.0 means she is 100 percent sure that she would successfully be able to complete either course of action. The Expectancy 2 links reflect the outcomes that Claudia anticipates if she successfully completes the seminar or stays at the office and completes her workload. If she turns down the training and stays on the job, she believes there is a 50 percent chance her boss will see her skills as inadequate. It would be higher, but she believes if she can do a superior job on these strategies, he will not think those relationship skills are so important. She believes it's 90 percent likely she

## FIGURE 2-4    Illustration of Expectancy Theory

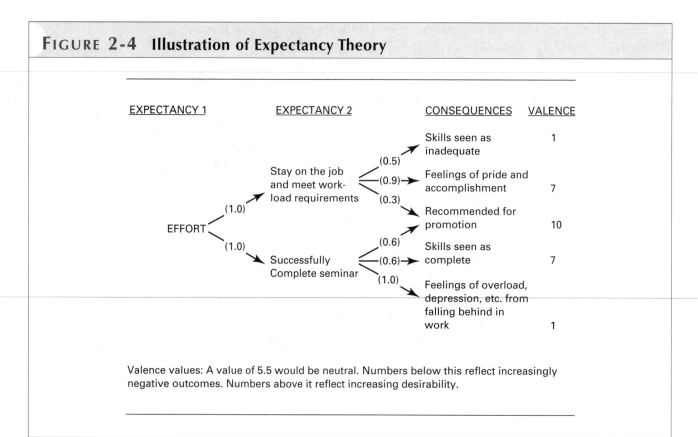

Valence values: A value of 5.5 would be neutral. Numbers below this reflect increasingly negative outcomes. Numbers above it reflect increasing desirability.

will have feelings of pride and accomplishment for getting all her work completed on time. However, if she turns down the training, she believes there is only a 30 percent chance her boss will recommend her for promotion.

Conversely, if she goes to the training, she believes the likelihood is 60 percent that her boss will evaluate her as having a more complete set of managerial skills. However, she will fall behind in her work, and it is a certainty (1.0) she will feel harried, overloaded, and depressed. Yet she sees the chances of being recommended for a promotion increasing to 60 percent if she goes to training. As the valences in Figure 2-4 show, she values her boss's recommendation for promotion the most. She views having her boss evaluate her skills as being inadequate and the feelings associated with being behind in her work as the least desirable of the outcomes. Use the formula to calculate Claudia's motivation. By multiplying each Expectancy 2 by its respective outcome valence, summing the values, and then multiplying the total by the Expectancy 1, we arrive at a force of 9.8 for non-attendance at the seminar.

Using the same procedure for the alternative goal—attending the seminar—we find a force of 11.2. Thus, for Claudia the motivation to stay at work is less than the motivation to attend the seminar. Even though the actual values of expectancies and valences are interesting from a scientific perspective, from a practical standpoint it is the relationships among the elements of the model that are useful. This example illustrates the cognitive processes that link a person's goals, possible courses of action, and likely outcomes. These connections determine the person's motivation and are what is missing from the reinforcement theory. Of course, we simplified the situation considerably from what Claudia would actually face in the real work setting. She had many other alternatives. She could delegate someone to cover most of the normal work coming across her desk (though she was not especially comfortable with delegating). She could arrange for the marketing strategies to be sent to her in Alberta in order to work on them at night, after training, and on the weekend. Each of these alternatives would present its own expected outcomes and associated valences.

Faced with the situation Claudia faced, what would you do? It is unlikely that you would place the same value (valence) on the outcomes or give them the same likelihood of occurring. You might identify more or fewer outcomes. One of the things that makes this theory so useful is that it takes into account the fact that people view the world differently and are motivated by different things.

Few people would consciously go through the formal math or mapping of expectancy theory, but it is interesting to note that most training programs that teach decision-making use a model similar to this one. More typically, we go through these processes unconsciously and in a less-systematic fashion. We choose a particular way of behaving because of our expectations about the costs and benefits of that action. Relationships between our past behaviour and its consequences are combined with current information to make inferences about the consequences of our future behaviour. Some implications for training become rather obvious here.

First, to be willing to try, a person must believe he or she stands a reasonable chance of being successful. Expectancy 1 exerts the most influence on our behaviour because we do not waste our time trying to do things we believe we cannot do. Sometimes this belief makes people reluctant to go to training, so trainers must demonstrate that success is likely for the participants. Second, and related to needs and reinforcement theory, trainers must make sure the right outcomes are attached to the successful completion of training. Trainees should be able to see clear connections between the content of training and important organizational and personal outcomes. Third, the training outcomes must be made as desirable as possible for the trainees rather than just for the organization, the supervisor, or the trainer.

# SELF-EFFICACY AND MOTIVATION

Feelings about our own competency are reflected in the concept of **self-efficacy**, which is one of the better-researched constructs related to motivation. High self-efficacy is associated with a belief that we can and will perform successfully. Individuals with low self-efficacy are preoccupied with concerns about failure.[13] Research supports the belief that the higher the self-efficacy, the better the performance.[14] Not only is performance better, but in difficult situations those with high self-efficacy also try harder, while those with low self-efficacy tend to reduce effort or give up.[15] In a training context, research shows that those with high self-efficacy beliefs are more motivated to learn and are more likely to transfer that learning.[16]

**Self-Efficacy** a belief about our ability to perform successfully.

Several factors combine to provide employees with an estimate of their ability to be successful:

- *Prior experience*: The person's past successes and failures and their consequences,
- *Behavioural models*: Successes and failures of others observed attempting the behaviour,
- *Others' feedback*: The encouragement or discouragement provided by others, and
- *Physical and emotional state*: The physical or emotional limitations believed to affect ability to perform.

Self-efficacy, therefore, plays a large role in the person's Expectancy 1 evaluation. The employee's feelings of self-efficacy are translated into behaviour. If success is expected, the employee works harder, longer, and more creatively in anticipation of the positive consequences of a successful effort. If failure is expected, the employee acts to minimize the negative consequences of failure. For example, withdrawing from the activity (refusing to try) moves the person away from proven failure to simply "I did not try." It also allows the person to say, "At least I did not put a lot of energy into it," or make some other rationalization. The point is that the employee's self-efficacy sets up the person's behaviour to fulfill the self-efficacy beliefs. In expectancy theory terms, if I do not believe I can successfully do something, I won't exert the effort to do it; instead, I'll do something else.

What can be done specifically to improve an individual's self-efficacy? The supervisor can provide the employee with confidence through persuasion. Convincing her that she is quite capable of succeeding in the training will help. Also, seeing others who are similar to the employee succeed will improve the employee's self-efficacy.

Training can improve self-efficacy either directly or indirectly as a by-product.[17] If the employee experiences low self-efficacy regarding his or her abilities to perform the job, but evidence indicates he or she possesses the requisite KSAs, a program of improving self-concept and confidence is needed. When low self-efficacy results from a true lack of required KSAs, attaining competency in these KSAs should increase the employee's self-efficacy, if the training allows the trainee to demonstrate mastery on a continuous basis. Trainers can also emphasize what the objectives are as well as the success of similar sets of trainees in the past.

Self-efficacy is very powerful in terms of facilitating trainee success. It seems to be a good predictor of both learning in the training environment and transfer of the behaviour to the job.[18] So, determining a trainee's self-efficacy before training and, if low, providing means to improve the trainee's self-efficacy would seem to be a worthwhile endeavour.

# UNDERSTANDING LEARNING

Theories of learning are important in the development of training. We examine the essential elements of learning theories and identify their relationship to training. Specific applications of the theories are provided in subsequent chapters.

Information on creativity and learning in non-profit settings *www.mapfornonprofits.org*

## WHAT IS LEARNING?

To understand the differences among learning theories, it helps to understand the difficulties of simply defining the concept of learning. Learning is not directly observable, but it is something that almost everyone says they experience. People can "feel" that they learned. It is clear from physiological evidence that learning is related to changes in the physical, neuronal structure of the brain and its related electrochemical functioning.[19] However, how or why these electrochemical changes take place is still unknown. Learning is closely tied to memory; whatever is learned must be retained if it is to be useful. Electrochemical changes created during learning apparently create a relatively permanent change in neural functioning that becomes what is commonly termed *memory*. Again, relatively few definitive answers exist about how or where learning is stored in the central nervous system.

<u>**Two Definitions of Learning**</u> Since we cannot observe learning, we must infer it occurs by looking at its observable effects. What things, influenced by learning, can we observe? The answer is the learner's behaviour. For instance, in school tests are given to determine what has been learned. The way questions are answered is the observable behaviour. In the workplace, your supervisor might look for ways you perform your job differently after training. Since learning is measured in terms of relatively permanent changes in behaviour, this becomes the operational definition of learning for many theorists. Behaviourists in particular adopt this definition.

Cognitive theorists, however, insist that even though learning can be inferred from behaviour, it is separate from the behaviour itself. By examining the ways in which people respond to information and the ways in which different types of behaviour are grouped or separated, they developed theories of how information is learned. For cognitive theorists, learning represents a change in the content, organization, and storage of information (see the section "Example of Cognitive Theory"). The term used to refer to the mental processing of information is **cognition**. For cognitive theorists, learning is defined as a relatively permanent change in cognition occurring as a result of experience. These theorists discuss learning in terms of mental infrastructures or schema rather than in terms of behaviour. Learning is seen as the building and reorganization of schema to make sense of new information. Bruner,[20] Gagné,[21] and Piaget[22] are among the cognitive theorists.

**Cognition** the mental processing of information.

<u>**Implications of Behaviourist Versus Cognitive Approaches**</u> At first, the differences in the definition of learning may not seem important. It may seem to be a simple difference of whether learning is synonymous with behaviour or with how information is processed, organized, and stored. However, these differences create widely different approaches to how education and training are conducted.

One obvious and important difference is where control of learning is believed to occur. The behaviourist approach suggests that the environment controls learning. Certain external stimuli are present, the person responds to them, and certain consequences result. It is the model of learning implied in Figure 2-2 (page 42) and discussed earlier as part of reinforcement theory. In the behaviourist approach, the trainer controls learning by controlling the stimuli and consequences that the learner experiences. The learner depends on the trainer to elicit the correct associations between stimulus and response. Note that this model does not include the brain or any mental activity. B. F. Skinner's explanation of learning perhaps clarifies why he was sometimes referred to as a radical behaviourist. He defined learning as "a relatively permanent change in behaviour in response to a particular stimulus or set of stimuli."[23] In other words, we perceive things a certain way because of the consequences of perceiving them that way. Learning occurs when new consequences are experienced.

In contrast, the cognitive approach suggests that the learner controls learning. Prospective learners come to training with their own set of goals and priorities. They possess a set of cognitive structures for understanding their environment and how it works. They even develop their own set of strategies about how to learn. The learners decide what is important to learn and go about learning by applying the strategies they developed and with which they feel comfortable. For cognitive theorists, the learner controls what is learned and how. The trainer and the learning environment facilitate that process to a greater or lesser degree. Adoption of one approach or the other leads to implications for how training is conducted and the atmosphere of the training environment. Table 2-2 lists some of the instructional implications of these two positions. For some learning situations, a behaviourist approach is better, and for others a cognitive approach works better.[24] We discuss this issue again later in the chapter.

## TABLE 2-2  Some Training Implications of Cognitive and Behaviourist Learning Theory

| Issue | Cognitive Approach | Behaviourist Approach |
|---|---|---|
| Learner's role | Active, self-directed, self-evaluating | Passive, dependent |
| Instructor's role | Facilitator, coordinator, and presenter | Director, monitor, and evaluator |
| Training content | Problem or task oriented | Subject oriented |
| Learner motivation | More internally motivated | More externally motivated |
| Training climate | Relaxed, mutually trustful respectful, and collaborative | Formal, authority oriented, judgmental and competitive |
| Instructional goals | Collaboratively developed | Developed by instructor |
| Instructional activities | Interactive, group, project oriented, and experiential | Directive, individual, and subject oriented |

**Accommodation** the process of changing our cognitive map of the world to correspond with our experience in it.

**Assimilation** the incorporation of new experience into our existing cognitive map.

*Example of Cognitive Theory.* Piaget identified two cognitive processes critical for learning: accommodation and assimilation. **Accommodation** is the process of changing our construction ("cognitive map") of the world to correspond with our experience in it. Piaget indicated that accommodation occurs through the creation of new categories, or schema, to accommodate experience that does not fit into existing categories. **Assimilation** is the incorporation of new experience into existing categories. In cognitive map terms, accommodation changes the map whereas assimilation fills in the detail. These two processes are most clearly evident in young children but exist in adults as well. Suppose Mike (age 8) is in the rear seat of the car with his younger brother Brandon (almost 2 and learning to talk) as Dad drives through some farmland. As they pass a pasture where horses are grazing, Mike points and says, "Look Brandon, horses." Brandon responds hesitantly, "Horsies?" Mike excitedly replies, "Yes, that's right, horsies!" Dad glances back and says, "Good work, Brandon, you now know a new word!" Brandon is pleased and repeats the word several times to himself. As they continue driving, they pass another pasture with cows grazing. Brandon yells, "Look Mike, horsies!" Mike or Dad is now faced with teaching Brandon the difference between horses and cows.

What is the learning process that took place? Brandon started out with no understanding of horse or cow. When presented with a new perceptual experience and a label, Brandon created a new cognitive category that might include the following parameters: large, four-legged, brown, moving thing with a tail. So, when Brandon saw the cows, they fit enough of the parameters that he attempted to assimilate this new experience into the category "horsies." If Mike and Dad do a good job of teaching Brandon the differences between horses and cows, he will learn to discriminate between these two and create a separate category for cows (accommodation). What he does not know yet is that later in life he will be taught to create new categories such as mammals and species and that both horses and cows are included in some categories but not in others.

The processes of assimilation and accommodation reflect the way we organize our experience and the meanings we attach to the world as we encounter it. Our behaviour depends on how we accommodated or assimilated previous stimuli.

## Integration of Cognitive and Behavioural Approaches We believe

that the cognitive and behavioural approaches must be integrated to provide a full definition of learning. **Learning**, as we use the term throughout this text, is defined as a relatively permanent change in cognition resulting from experience and directly influencing behaviour. A fairly obvious implication of this definition is that changes in cognition and related behaviour that result from things other than experience (e.g., effects of drugs, fatigue, and the like) would not be considered learning. The definition also implies that changes in cognition and behaviour that are short-lived have not been learned. For example, memorizing a phone number long enough to walk from the telephone directory to the phone and dial the number would not fit into our definition. However, learning the mnemonic techniques that allow you to do that would be learning, if they were retained over a relatively long period of time.

Learning, as defined here, is not dependent on behaviour. Relatively permanent cognitive changes (new KSAs) can occur in the absence of observable behaviour. However, only the learner would know whether the learning took place. For example, think of courses you took in which the material was presented in a lecture or audiovisual form. If it was effective, you changed your way of thinking about the topic or came to a deeper understanding of the material—even though you did nothing other than pay attention and think about what was presented. However, until you engage in some activity related to the topic, no one other than you would know that learning had taken place. This phenomenon could also happen with skills. Suppose you are a chef and you attend a seminar on preparing a dish. You observe the presenter enhancing the flavour of a dish using a technique of which you had no previous knowledge. You go back to your kitchen, try the technique, and are successful on the first try. You acquired the "flavouring" skill through observation rather than behaviour. However, you might not be sure you had acquired the skill until after you engaged in the behaviour. Additionally, the more you use the technique, the more permanent (i.e., resistant to forgetting) it would become. Thus, behaviour is both an important measure of and a means of learning.

Each of these two approaches produces valuable insights about learning. Learning theories that integrate the substantiated aspects of both approaches explain learning more completely than either one alone. We discuss such a theory next.

# SOCIAL LEARNING THEORY

Albert Bandura and his associates developed a model of learning known variously as observational learning, vicarious learning, and most often, social learning theory.[25] One of the theory's most important contributions to the science of learning was demonstrating that learning could occur without any overt behaviour by the learner. That is, the learner did not have to do anything except observe what was going on around her. No behaviour pattern was produced and no reinforcement given.

The basic premise of **Social Learning Theory** is that events and consequences in the learning situation are cognitively processed before they are learned or influence behaviour. The processing of information leads to learning and changes in behaviour. Certainly, the consequences of behaviour (reinforcement or punishment) influence the likelihood of that behaviour in the future, but they do so as a result of how they are perceived, interpreted, and stored in memory. Thus, a person can learn by observing the behaviour of others and the consequences that result. This theory contradicts the strict behaviourists, who claim that learning can occur only as a result of a person's own behaviour and its consequences. The cognitive processes that are a part of social learning theory are motivation, attention, retention, and to some extent behavioural reproduction. Figure 2-5 illustrates the relationships among these cognitive processes.

**Learning** a relatively permanent change in cognition resulting from experience and directly influencing behaviour.

**Social Learning Theory** A cognitive theory of learning that incorporates anticipatory learning.

# MOTIVATION

Although motivation was discussed at length earlier in this chapter, it is useful to see how it fits in with social learning theory. As the model indicates, motivation both influences and is influenced by the other processes. The learner's needs determine what things receive attention and are processed for retention. As depicted in the model, social learning theory incorporates the operant conditioning concept of behavioural consequences affecting the likelihood of future behaviour. However, whereas operant conditioning principles stipulate that the consequence can only be learned through the learner's behaviour—consequence pairings—social learning theory suggests that behavioural consequences can be acquired through anticipatory learning. **Anticipatory learning** occurs when a person learns what consequences are associated with a behaviour (or set of behaviours) without actually engaging in the behaviour and receiving the consequences. By observing someone else's behaviour, the observer can learn something about how to perform the behaviour and also something about the consequences of the behaviour. Thus, this theory provides a model for learning through observation alone. For this reason, it is often referred to as a theory of observational or vicarious learning. However, the model of learning processes illustrated in Figure 2-5 is more than just observational learning. It combines cognitive and behaviourist concepts into a comprehensive set of integrated processes that are applicable to all types of learning, providing another set of tools for designing and implementing training. Additional motivational issues are discussed later in the "Motivation to Learn" section.

**Anticipatory Learning** learning that occurs when a person finds out what consequences are associated with a behaviour (or set of behaviours) without actually engaging in the behaviour or receiving the consequences.

# ATTENTION

The learning process begins with the learner's **attention** becoming focused on particular objects and events in the environment (stimuli). Of the great multitude of objects and events in the typical environment, we notice many of them but pay attention only to some. The things we pay attention to are those that stand out for some reason (loud, bright, unusual, etc.) or those that we learn are important (e.g., lead to need satisfaction). This reaction is reflected in the fact that we are more likely to model the behaviour of

**Attention** getting the person to focus where you want her to.

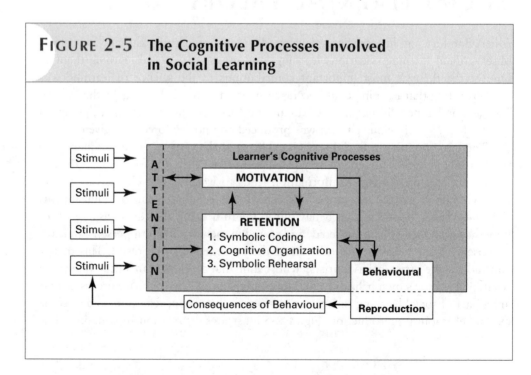

**FIGURE 2-5    The Cognitive Processes Involved in Social Learning**

someone who is spotlighted in some way (highly publicized, unusually attractive, popular, etc.) than of someone who is not. Similarly, we are more likely to model someone who seems to receive a lot of reinforcement than someone who receives little.

The concept of attention is important in training. Learning is improved by making key learning points stand out so that the trainees will focus attention on them. Eliminating extraneous objects, such as cell phones and beepers, keeps trainees from becoming distracted during training. Making learning exercises fun and interesting keeps attention focused on the learning topic. However, exercises that are fun but do not relate to the learning objectives draw attention away from what trainees are expected to learn, making the training less effective. The training design chapter addresses issues related to capturing trainee attention.

## RETENTION

Once attention is focused on an object or event, the incoming information is processed for possible **retention**. Some of the information will be retained and some will be lost. The more training is designed to facilitate the retention processes, the more learning will occur. The initial phase of retention is the translation of the information into symbols meaningful to the individual, a process called **symbolic coding**. It typically takes the form of reducing the external objects and events to internal images and verbal symbols. These symbols are then organized into the existing cognitive structure through associations with previously stored information. **Cognitive organization** can be facilitated in training by asking the trainees to provide examples of how the new information relates to what they already know. This exercise serves two purposes. It allows the trainee to code and store the information more easily, and it allows the trainer to see whether the desired associations are being made. The training design chapter also discusses other ways in which training can facilitate retention.

To facilitate the retention process, the learner should "practise" the learned material through **symbolic rehearsal**, which involves visualizing or imagining how the knowledge or skill will be used. If the focus is on skill building, the trainee imagines using the skills in different situations. This exercise is usually fairly easy to do because the skill helps to define the situations. When the focus of learning is knowledge, it is sometimes more difficult to imagine how it can or will be used. For example, think back to when you were learning the multiplication tables. Most of us memorized these through constant repetition over many months, and that repetition provided us with the experience of using multiplication to solve problems. Each year as we advanced to the next grade, we were given more multiplication problems to solve. In contrast, storing information without any associations with personal use—in other words, just memorizing—typically results in only short-term retention. Students who have ever crammed for an exam are probably familiar with this phenomenon. Thus, associating information with its uses enhances the storage and retrieval process. The symbolic rehearsal process can be thought of as mental practice. Observing others use the knowledge or skill provides additional opportunities for symbolic rehearsal because as you watch them you can put yourself in their place. Symbolic rehearsal also increases the ability to generalize learning to novel situations. The discussion on training design in Chapter 4 discusses other ways to enhance retention through symbolic rehearsal.

## BEHAVIOURAL REPRODUCTION

**Behavioural reproduction** is repeated practice. The more a person practises using new information, the more it is learned and retained. The effectiveness of practice depends on how the practice is designed and reinforced, as we will discuss in detail in

**Retention** the process of storing and being able to access what is learned.

**Symbolic Coding** the translation of the information into symbols meaningful to the individual.

**Cognitive Organization** the organizing of these symbols into the existing cognitive structure through associations with previously stored information.

**Symbolic Rehearsal** the visualization or imagining of how the knowledge or skill will be used.

**Behavioural Reproduction** repeated practice.

the training-design chapter. Figure 2-5 shows the behavioural reproduction process as being a part of both the learner's cognitive processes and the external environment. This duality reflects the fact that the person's cognitive processes initiate the behaviour—the person must retrieve the appropriate behaviour from storage and direct the body to perform the appropriate actions—and then the behaviour itself actually occurs in, and becomes part of, the environment.

We already spent considerable time discussing the importance of behavioural consequences. One additional point is worth making, however. If consequences are to affect behaviour, the individuals must be aware of these consequences. For example, assume a supervisor recommends an employee for a bonus but has not yet told the employee. Subjectively, for the employee it is not a consequence of behaviour, even though objectively it is. Even when aware of a consequence, the person may misinterpret its value. The supervisor who is disappointed in an employee's performance may sarcastically say, "Really nice job," but the employee may misinterpret this as giving praise. Thus, the person must be aware of and correctly interpret behavioural consequences if those consequences are going to have the desired effect. Effective training programs need to call attention to the desirable consequences of learning and of using the learning back on the job.

# RELATING INSTRUCTION TO LEARNING

Learning theory describes how individuals learn. Gagné and his associates suggest that effective instruction requires a "set of events" external to the learner, designed to facilitate the internal process of learning.[26] So what things (external events) are needed to facilitate the trainees' learning of a particular objective? Put another way, can the sequencing of events in a training process increase the likelihood that learning will occur?

**Micro Theory of Instructional Design** a guide for designing training.

The answer is yes. A particular order of presenting material will facilitate learning. Gagné and his associates provide a **Micro Theory of Instructional Design**, which is a guide for designing training. It is relevant for all three types of learning outcomes: cognitive knowledge, skill-based, and attitudinal. The theory provides nine steps (sets of events) to follow in developing training for a learning objective.[27] To be most effective, this "set of events" should be arranged in a specific order, as depicted in Table 2-3. Gagné and his associates do not indicate that the nine steps are necessary for every learning objective, or that the sequencing must be exactly as indicated. They say:

> [T]hese events of instruction do not invariably occur in this exact order, though this is the most probable order... by no means are all of these events provided for every lesson.... Their role is to stimulate internal information processes ... sometimes an event will be obvious to the learner and not needed... or provided by the learner themselves.... In using the checklist the designer asks, "Do these learners need support at this stage for learning this task?"[28]

Let's go through each of the events using a learning objective related to teaching apprentice electricians.[29] The learning objective is to determine the amperage of an appliance, given the watts and voltage. The first event, "gaining attention," is obtained by showing a short video in which a family is in a kitchen; the lights, radio, and toaster are all on. One of the children plugs in the blender and when she turns it on, the radio, lights, and toaster shut off. This gets everyone's attention (instructional event one). Now you ask, "What happened here?" When the answer is given (a fuse was blown), you discuss why it happened and move to the second event: "Inform the learner of the objective." The objective is to calculate the amperage of appliances in order to wire a room properly with the correct number and type of plugs based on what will be used in that room. The next event is "stimulate recall of prerequisites." Here, you would ask apprentices to recall the typical voltage in a house (it is 120 volts, but for ease of calculation here we will round to 100). You then ask, "Where is the wattage for appliances found?" The answer is on a label on the back or side of the

## TABLE 2-3  Gagné-Briggs Nine Events of Instruction

| Instructional Event | What is does . . . Gets trainee |
|---|---|
| Gaining attention | To focus on the trainer |
| Informing the trainee of the goal (objective) | To begin to focus on the goal |
| Stimulating recall of prior knowledge (learning) | To retrieve prior learning to working memory |
| Presenting the stimulus material | To selectively perceive important parts of training |
| Providing learning guidance | To consider how the new material fits into trainee's overall schema, and clarify where it belongs for ease of retrieval |
| Eliciting the performance | To do it |
| Providing feedback | To perform effectively by reinforcing correct responses and assisting when incorrect |
| Assessing performance | To attempt a number of similar problems to determine if the trainee has the concept |
| Enhancing retention and transfer | To do more complex and varied examples of the concept and assess the success |

Source: Gagné R. M., Briggs, L., & Wager, W. (1992). *Principles of Instructional Design.* Fort Worth: Harcourt Brace Jovanovich.

appliance. Then ask, "What is the purpose of fuses?" The answer is to prevent circuit overload. Finally, ask how their size is measured (amps).

"Presenting the stimulus" is done by providing the formula for determining amperage (amps = watts/volts). Given the wattage of the blender (1000 watts), you ask, "What is its amperage?" You may give a few more examples. Next, for the "provide learning guidance" event, you ask the apprentices to go back to the example at the beginning of the discussion. Tell them the kitchen was all wired to one typical 15-amp fuse, and ask, "Would the fuse have still blown if the toaster was not plugged in?" They cannot give the correct answer because they need more information, so you discuss the need to have the wattage of everything in the kitchen to determine the total amps. You then give the wattages to them (100-watt light, 1000-watt toaster, 10-watt radio) and ask for the amps generated for each.

For the next event, "eliciting performance," you provide the apprentices with the wattage of a number of appliances (refrigerator: 1000 watts, TV: 300 watts, space heater: 1400 watts, and so forth) and ask them to determine the amps each will require. To "provide feedback," you review the answers to the preceding questions and determine how well each apprentice understood the process. "Assessing performance" is done by providing the apprentices with a number of problems for which they need to calculate the amps of appliances. For the final event, "enhancing retention and transfer," you provide them with the problem of wiring a workshop. The appliances to be used in the workshop include a table saw, router, planer, drill press, sander, four lights, radio, electric heater, and so forth. You also give the wattage for each of the appliances. Then you ask them to indicate how many 15-amp circuits they would need to provide to be most efficient and what they would put on the same circuit.

Using the theory helps you create a setting in which learning is most likely. Table 2-4 provides another example.

## TABLE 2-4  Example of a Lesson in Problem Solving

Objective: Given a drawing of a plot of land, the trainee generates a plan for a sprinkler system that will cover at least 90% of the land, using the least amount of materials (PVC pipe and sprinkler heads).

| Event | Media | Prescription |
|---|---|---|
| 1. Gaining attention | Live instruction and overhead projector | Show pictures of sprinkler coverage of a rectangular plot of ground. One highly successful (90%) coverage, one unsuccessful (70% coverage), and one using too many sprinkler heads. Show these rapidly, inviting attention to their differences. |
| 2. Informing the learner of the objective | Same | The problem to be solved is to design the most efficient sprinkler system for a plot of ground—one that covers at least 90% and uses the least amount of pipe and sprinkler heads. |
| 3. Stimulating recall of requisites | Overhead projector | Have the learners recall applicable rules. Since the sprinkler heads they will use spray in circles and partial circles, rules to be recalled are (1) area of a circle, (2) area of quarter and half circles, (3) the area of rectangular areas, (4) the area of irregular shapes made by the intersection of circular arcs with straight sides. |
| 4. Presenting the stimulus material | Same | Restate the problem in general terms, and then add specific details: (a) rectangular lot 50 by 100 ft; (2) radius of the sprinklers, 5 ft; (3) water source in the center of the lot. |
| 5. Providing learning guidance | Same | The trainee will need to design tentative sprinkler layouts, draw them out, and calculate the relative efficiency of each. Guidance may be given by informing the learner of various options if it appears that rules are not being applied correctly. For example, "Could you get more efficient coverage in the corner by using a quarter-circle sprinkler head?" Or "It looks like you have a lot to overlap; are you allowing for a 10% noncoverage?" ask the learner what rule he is following for placing the sprinkler. |
| 6. Eliciting performance | | |
| 7. Providing feedback | Oral review by instructor | Confirm good moves, when in a suitable direction. If the learner doesn't see a possible solution, suggestions may be made. For example, "Why don't you draw four circles that barely touch, calculate the area, then draw a rectangle around the circles and calculate the area of coverage to see how much you have?" |

## TABLE 2-4 (Continued)

| Event | Media | Prescription |
|---|---|---|
| 8. Assessing performance | Instructor | Present a different problem using the same type of sprinkler, with different lot shape and size. Check the efficiency of the trainee's solution in terms of coverage and amount of materials used. |
| 9. Enhancing retention and transfer | Worksheet | Present several different problems varying in shape of lot, position of the water source, and area of sprinkler coverage. Assess the generalizability of trainee problem solving to these new situations. |

*Source:* Gagné, R. M., Briggs, L., & Wager, W. (1992). *Principles of Instructional Design.* Fort Worth: Harcourt Brace Jovanovich.

# WHY ARE THEY RESISTING AND WHAT CAN I DO ABOUT IT?

Learning, like eating, is one of the most fundamental processes of survival, yet trainers and managers continually complain about trainees who do not pay attention, are disruptive, and demonstrate a general resistance to learning new material.

Often, the older the trainees or the higher their education, the more resistant they are. If learning is a basic human process, why are so many complaints of this type made?

Viewing learning as a performance outcome is the first step to understanding **resistance to learning.** Most learning is not something that happens automatically or unconsciously. It is an activity we decide to do or not do. From the performance model discussed earlier (see Figure 2-1 on page 37), we know that learning performance is determined by a person's motivation, KSAs, and learning environment.

**Resistance to Learning** not wanting to go through the discomfort of change.

## MOTIVATION TO LEARN

Most trainees arrive at training with an elaborate and highly integrated **cognitive structure.** They already know a lot about themselves, their work, their company, and many other things.[30] The objective of training is to change some part of that cognitive structure so that the trainee's performance will be improved. Change creates anxiety, however, for the following reasons:

**Cognitive structure** The result of how we organize and classify what we learn in our mind.

| | |
|---|---|
| Fear of the unknown | "Right now I know how things work, but I do not know how this training will affect things." |
| Fear of incompetence | "I do not know whether I'll be able to learn this stuff." |
| Fear of losing rewards | "What will happen to my pay, status, and perqs, among other things?" |
| Fear of lost influence | "Will this training make me more or less valuable?" |
| Fear or lost investments | "I've spent a lot of time and energy learning to do it this way. Why change?" |

These concerns deal with the trainees' needs, their current competencies, and how training will change their current outcomes. Expectancy theory addresses these factors, and the trainees' motivation to learn will depend on the answers to these questions. To the degree that the answers indicate that learning is worth the effort, the individual will be motivated to learn.

Even when trainees acknowledge the value of the training, they may believe the effort required to master the learning is just not worthwhile. One example of this is the reluctance of many experienced managers to learn how to use computers. These managers are often bright and competent in other aspects of their jobs but continue in their old ways of communicating and calculating, even though they see that the computer could increase their capabilities. They already have well-developed cognitive structures regarding what they already know. It is just too difficult to change these cognitive structures and learn the new KSAs. The more difficult a task is, the greater the resistance is likely to be. The benefits of doing a difficult task must be much higher than the costs to induce the person to do it. Why is learning more difficult for those with more-extensive and -developed cognitive structures?

In Piaget's terms, the accommodation process (developing new cognitive categories) is the most difficult, while assimilation (adding new things to existing categories) is relatively easy. Accommodation requires a learner to create new categories that then need to be linked to other related categories. The more categories that exist and the more developed they are, the more difficult the learning. When assimilating, the learner simply adds new elements and rearranges associations among elements within a single category. When accommodating, not only must learners create a new category and place elements into that category, but they must also associate this category with other categories. The elements within those categories must be modified to create the network of associations that appropriately incorporates the new information.

This type of situation occurs whenever a company changes the paradigms it uses for conducting its business. For example, think about what supervisors face when companies move from a traditional, centralized, hierarchical, autocratic decision-making process to a flexible, team-based, more consensus-based, employee-involvement system. From their experience and training in the traditional system, the supervisors developed a cognitive structure for getting things done. They learned how to make all the decisions for their subordinates and developed a system for communicating those decisions and ensuring that they are carried out effectively. These strategies were probably reinforced over many years. A new piece of equipment or a change in the work process brings new procedures that are learned and assimilated into the supervisor's decision-making structure relatively easily. Under the new, team-based decision-making, however, the whole process of making decisions must be relearned because the underlying organizational assumptions have changed. For the supervisor, the focus is no longer on the quality of decisions but on the supervisor's ability to facilitate quality decisions by the team. Although some aspects of the supervisor's old decision-making process might still be useful, his cognitive structure must be changed to incorporate the new concepts, and the useful aspects of the old concepts must be reorganized and integrated with the new. For this reason, learning the new system will be more difficult for supervisors with a lot of experience than for a newly hired supervisor with little experience in the traditional system.

Resistance to learning also comes from defensiveness. The more experienced a person is, the more she has already learned, which means a more developed, integrated, and complex cognitive structure. A great deal of effort went into creating that cognitive structure. Training can, in a sense, be seen as an attack on a person's competence, especially if the training is mandatory. Trainees in this situation can also feel they are being told that the trainer knows more about how to run their area than they do. In these cases, the trainees are likely to try to show the trainer, and the other trainees, that the training or the trainer is inadequate or irrelevant or that their current KSAs are better than what training has to offer.

This generalization is not to say that older, more-experienced people cannot learn new things or discard old beliefs. They frequently do. As adults mature, they appear to go through periodic episodes of cognitive reorganization, in which concepts or principles of long standing are re-evaluated.[31] During these cognitive reorganizations, knowledge that is of little functional value is discarded and new KSAs are discovered and integrated into their cognitive structure, especially in times of transition such as job or career changes. For adults, the key factor in discarding old learning and acquiring new learning is its practical usefulness. Training that seems abstract, theoretical, or otherwise unrelated to doing the job will likely be ignored or resisted. Training that can demonstrate its value and practical utility will find trainees eager to learn.

# GROUP DYNAMICS

**Group dynamics**, and its impact on motivation, is another reason for trainees to resist learning new ways. The power and control of the group over its members was first noted in the Hawthorne studies of the 1920s and 1930s.[32] Even though members of the group were paid a piece rate, the output from members of the group was always within a certain number of units. Examination of this study revealed that the group set a standard, rewarded those who remained within the standard, and punished those who did much more or much less. Thus, the group norm of a certain number of units was generally followed.

The power of the group comes from rewards for members who follow group norms or punishment for those who do not. These rewards or punishments can be as simple as talking to (reward) or shunning (punishment) a group member. Punishment can also be severe, such as slashing tires or physically threatening those who do not comply. If you want to be a good group member, you must agree with and follow what the group decides is best. Consider the following scenario. Sarah arrives at the training centre early, excited to be attending a workshop on how to communicate with customers more effectively. Fellow trainees are talking among themselves, making fun of the training. One of them says, "They are going to tell us how to do our job; I bet the trainer has never even done our job, so how could he know?" Another responds, "Yeah, these workshops are put together by those who never worked in a real job, but at least we can enjoy this as a day off work." Then one turns to Sarah and says, "Hey, I see you managed to con your boss into sending you here for a rest too—good work." To be part of the "in group" Sarah will have to agree, and, as a result, will not likely participate in the training as much as she would want to. This behaviour will affect the amount she learns.

Say that in spite of her (and everyone else's) lack of participation in the workshop, Sarah did learn a few skills. Now she goes back to her workplace. There she hears co-workers comment, "Well did you enjoy your day off? Wasn't that training the stupidest stuff you have ever seen?" and "Can you imagine using that 'active listening' stuff on a real customer?" With such comments, what is the likelihood Sarah will want to try some of these new skills? Group dynamics is a powerful force that can drastically inhibit both learning and transfer of skills.[33]

Group dynamics can also be used to support high performance. The pyjama factory experiments of the late 1940s compared employees in two groups where change was necessary in how the jobs were done.[34] In one group employees were told about the

**Group Dynamics** the process whereby the group provides pressure for conformity to its expectations.

changes, and in the other the members provided input into the changes. The no-participation group showed a drop in productivity from the baseline, and the participation group showed an increase in productivity from the baseline. The most important factor in the difference was group norms that developed either to restrict output (no-participation group) or increase it (participation group). More recent research indicates that trainees' perception of their work groups' support for training is a strong predictor of the likelihood that trainees will transfer what they learned to the job.[35] The control the work group exerts over the individual member is a double-edged sword. It is a good thing if the norms are developed in line with the organizational goals. One way of developing these norms is to allow input from the work group on decisions that will affect them. The movement toward more teams and teamwork in organizations provides such opportunities, but in order to ensure the right norms are developed, these work groups need to be nurtured and made to feel valuable.[36]

# TRAINING THAT MOTIVATES ADULTS TO LEARN

Learning occurs quite frequently in adults when it appears to offer practical application immediately or in the near future.[37] For example, a study showed that IBM sales representatives averaged more than 1100 hours a year in "new learning episodes." (A new learning episode was defined as a deliberate attempt to gain and retain some significant knowledge or skill for problem solving or personal change.) Professors, by contrast, averaged slightly more time (1745 hours) on fewer episodes. Clearly, adults are not resistant to learning but they are sometimes resistant to training offered by their companies. Why?

## TRAINING RELEVANCE, VALUE, AND READINESS TO LEARN

Some of the most often mentioned reasons for adults engaging in new learning are problems on the job, job/occupational changes, home and personal responsibilities, and competency at some hobby or recreational activity. In the study mentioned previously, about two-thirds of the learning episodes were job-related. The need to know and the readiness to learn are critical aspects in the success of adult learning programs.[38] The need to know refers to the value of the knowledge to the learner. Adults most often seek to learn when the learning is life-, task-, or problem-centred.[39] Readiness to learn refers to the amount of prerequisite knowledge (KSAs) the trainee possesses and the trainee's belief in his or her ability to learn the material. This aspect is consistent with the principles of self-efficacy and expectancy theory. People's motivation to learn a particular knowledge or skill set is directly influenced by their belief that if they put forth the effort, they will be successful in their learning (Expectancy 1). Beyond this expectation, they must feel that the benefits of learning the KSAs outweigh the benefits of not learning them (Expectancy 2).

The challenge is to provide instruction in a context that overcomes the natural resistance of adult learners to changing their cognitive structures. Making the relevance and value of the learning clear, as it relates to the trainee and organizational goals, addresses one source of resistance to learning. Ensuring that the trainee believes she can successfully master the training content is another important motivator. Over time, adults may develop feelings of low self-efficacy in certain areas and feelings of high self-efficacy in others. For those with a low self-efficacy for learning in general or for the specific content area of the training, the trainer needs to change the self-efficacy beliefs so trainees are more willing to attempt new learning. Doing so requires a careful match between the trainee's characteristics (e.g., KSA level, learning-style preferences) and the design of the training. Trainers can overcome a significant type of resistance to learning by demonstrating that learning in the subject area can be as easy as in areas in which trainees have high self-efficacy.

## ALLOWING TRAINEES CONTROL OVER THEIR LEARNING

As we pointed out, trainees walk into training with well-developed cognitive maps that reflect their experiences. Since these experiences differ from person to person, any given training group is likely to differ considerably in the KSAs they possess and in their learning strategies. Trainees often view these differences as hindrances to their learning and resist training with others who are dissimilar. However, these differences can be viewed as a learning resource if the trainees are willing to share their experiences and strategies and if the training environment supports such an exchange. In fact, adult learners prefer sharing their learning experience with others if the environment is supportive. Even though adults prefer to plan their own learning projects and to adopt a self-directed approach to learning, this preference does not imply a desire to learn in isolation. Rather, it reflects a desire to set their own pace, establish their own structure for learning, and employ flexibility in the learning methods. More often than not, adults seek learning assistance from others. In short, they do not mind learning from others, but they want to maintain some control over the learning experience. These characteristics suggest that training that incorporates individualized components and also makes use of shared, relevant experiences will be most effective at overcoming resistance to learning.

Although it is true that many adults are able to learn new competencies even when they are not told the significance or usefulness of the training, they are much less likely to be able to apply these new competencies to their job. Research suggests that trainees receiving instruction on how to perform a set of skills show improved performance at the end of training but fail to use the skills on their own or to generalize the skill usage to similar situations.[40] Training that provides instruction on the "how to" and includes the "why and when" results in improved performance as well as continued use of the skill across appropriate situations.[41]

## INVOLVING TRAINEES IN THE PROCESS

Training, then, should take into account the motivational and cognitive processes that influence the trainee's readiness and willingness to learn. Many writers emphasize the importance of participation, choice, personal experiences, critical reflection, and critical thinking as key characteristics of adult learning.[42] Involving the trainees in the learning process from needs assessment to design and evaluation addresses many of these issues.

Involvement is a key part of overcoming resistance to change. You may remember, from the discussion of OD principles in Chapter 1, that involving those who are affected by change in planning and implementing the change creates a sense of ownership.

The result is increased commitment to the change as well as better implementation of the change. Supervisors, as well as trainees, should be involved in determining the training needs because both are affected by the change. Supervisors have a clearer understanding of why new KSAs are necessary, how they fit in with the overall plans for the work unit, and the consequences of their employees learning or not learning the new KSAs. The trainees, in turn, see what KSAs they need to improve and understand why those KSAs will be of value. Involving trainees in needs analysis and other parts of the training process will be discussed in more depth in relevant chapters.

# INDIVIDUAL DIFFERENCES RELATED TO LEARNING

Some interesting findings came from studies regarding the learning process for low-ability and high-ability individuals.[43] Goal setting as a motivational incentive does not always operate with the same magnitude for these two groups. When those with low ability are starting to learn a moderately difficult task, providing goals to them will inhibit, rather than enhance, learning. Although the same is true for high-ability individuals, it is not nearly as severe. High-ability individuals, it seems, have the extra cognitive capacity to focus on goals as well as the new learning in the early learning stage. This difference disappears as the task is learned, and then goal setting enhances performance of both low- and high-ability individuals. Even though a difference separates the two groups, results from this research suggest that overall, it is wise not to introduce goal setting as a motivational device early in the training process.

Although we indicated that it is desirable to consider diversity among trainees as an opportunity, this is true only up to a point. For example, trainees who are substantially less knowledgeable than others can create significant problems. They may not be able to keep up with the material, or if the material is presented at a slower pace, the more knowledgeable trainees are bored to tears. It is not only differences in KSAs that can create problems in a training group. A contingency approach to adult learning looks at the characteristics of trainees, such as those listed in Table 2-5, that suggest different approaches to training and development.[44]

The logic of using different approaches for trainees with different characteristics makes some sense, but research in most of these areas is sparse or nonexistent. Currently, research in the areas of resistance to change, absorption level, and topic interest provide some substantiation for providing different training designs to different populations. For example, those with low self-efficacy should have training that first addresses the self-efficacy issue; for those with a high sense of self-efficacy, this training would seem not only irrelevant but also

| TABLE 2-5 Dimensions for Trainee Assessment Prior to Training | |
|---|---|
| 1. Instrumentality | Desire for immediate applicability of the material to be learned |
| 2. Skepticism | Need for logic, evidence, and examples |
| 3. Resistance to change | Fear of unknown or personal consequences of change related to feelings about self-efficacy and locus of control orientation |
| 4. Attention span | Amount of time before attentiveness is substantially diminished |
| 5. Expectation level | Trainee's quality/quantity requirements of training |
| 6. Dominant needs | Intrinsic and extrinsic motivators that drive the trainee |
| 7. Absorption level | Pace at which trainee expects and can absorb new material |
| 8. Topical interest | Trainee's personal (job-relevant) interest in the material |

demeaning. Of course, providing different training designs becomes more complex and more costly for the organization.

Differences in learning characteristics can have important consequences for training; however, providing separate training sessions may not always be the most practical or cost-effective way to achieve the organization's HRD goals. Thus, training programs need to be designed to accommodate a sufficiently large group of trainees while at the same time considering individual differences. Training design issues are discussed in more detail in Chapter 5. However, training professionals should consider the following nine principles in developing training programs for their employees:[45]

1. Identify the types of individual learning strengths and problems, and tailor the training around them.

2. Align learning objectives to organizational goals.

3. Define program goals and objectives clearly at the start.

4. Engage the trainee, thus maximizing attention, expectations, and memory.

5. Use a systematic, logically connected sequencing of learning activities so that trainees master lower levels of learning before moving to higher levels.

6. Use a variety of training methods.

7. Use realistic job- or life-relevant training material.

8. Allow trainees to work together and share experiences.

9. Provide constant feedback and reinforcement while encouraging self-assessment.

The trainer can address the diversity of characteristics trainees bring to training within the context of a group-learning environment by applying these principles to training programs.

## Summary

An employee's performance is a function of motivation, KSAs, and the environment. To understand motivation we turned to two types of theories of motivation: need and process. Need theories, such as ERG, explain what it is that motivates an individual. Process theories, such as expectancy theory, explain how individuals are motivated.

Two historical approaches to understanding learning are the behaviourist perspective (Skinner) and the cognitive perspective (Piaget). To fully understand learning, we examine it from a more-integrated approach through Bandura's social learning theory. The behavioural approach (reinforcement theory) focuses on the importance of the environment, and the cognitive approach (accommodation/assimilation) emphasizes the notion that learning can take place without any behaviour being exhibited. Together they provide a more complete picture of the learning process than either can do alone. The process of learning provides the foundation for designing effective training. Gagné and colleagues provide this foundation with their theory of instructional design (nine events of instruction).

To motivate employees to learn, you must first realize they already know a great deal, possess highly integrative cognitive structures, and have been successful to date. A number of reasons explain why they are hesitant to learn more material, such as fear of the unknown or of not being successful at learning the new material. To motivate them, you need to make the training relevant and valuable, and be sure they are confident of being successful. Goal setting will increase motivation in the later parts of the training program but will interfere with learning in the early stages. Finally, trainee involvement with each phase of the training process will facilitate trainee interest and motivation in the training.

One final concern in making training relevant is the issue of individual differences. In general, we advise you to treat the diversity of individual characteristics in a training group as an opportunity. However, sometimes it will be best to develop separate training programs. Nine principles are offered for addressing individual differences in the design of training programs.

## Implications for Practice

**1.** There is no such thing as someone "not being motivated," unless they are dead. The person is always motivated but may not be motivated to do the things you want. Understanding theories of motivation can help a supervisor determine motivators and manipulate expectancies to increase the likelihood a person will behave in appropriate ways.

**2.** Understanding learning theory provides us with the ability to identify learning processes that are activated at various points in training. This provides us with a method for designing our training to increase the likelihood training will lead to learning.

**3.** Classical conditioning, because it is automatic, requires us to be diligent in setting up the surroundings for trainees. Providing an environment that leads to positive feelings will improve the likelihood that trainees will not be distracted by negative physiological symptoms.

**4.** Development of positive group pressures for learning and transfer of training is an effective method of improving the likelihood of success.

## Key Terms

Accommodation  *50*

Anticipatory learning  *52*

Assimilation  *50*

Attention  *52*

Behavioural reproduction  *53*

Classical conditioning  *40*

Cognition  *49*

Cognitive organization  *53*

Cognitive process  *45*

Cognitive structure  *57*

Environment  *37*

ERG theory  *38*

Existence needs  *38*

Expectancy theory  *45*

Extinction  *43*

Group dynamics  *59*

Growth needs  *39*

Law of effect  *41*

Learning  *51*

Micro Theory of Instructional Design  *54*

Motivation  *38*

Needs theory  *38*

Negative reinforcement  *42*

Operant conditioning  *41*

Performance model  *37*

Positive reinforcement  *42*

Process theories  *40*

Punishment  *42*

Reinforcement theory  *41*

Relatedness needs  *39*

Resistance to learning  *57*

Retention  *53*

Self-efficacy  *47*

Social learning theory  *51*

Symbolic coding  *53*

Symbolic rehearsal  *53*

Theories  *35*

Valence  *45*

## Questions for Review

1. Explain the behavioural and cognitive approaches to learning. Which is most relevant to training? Explain your answer.

2. You are a trainer explaining expectancy theory to a group of managers so they can better understand and deal with employee motivation problems. One of the managers says, "I do not have time for this theory stuff. I want real-world training that helps me in my job." How would you respond to the trainee? What is your rationale for your response?

3. List the nine events of instruction as outlined by Gagné-Briggs, and indicate how you would use them in a training situation.

4. Explain why different people need different training methods.

5. How does a work group exert control over the performance of a worker? Provide a rationale for why this "power" is a positive or negative thing.

6. How can training be designed to motivate learning and accommodate trainee differences?

## Exercises

1. The following steps provide practice in implementing a social learning strategy.
   a. Consult with a friend, co-worker, or fellow student to identify a target behaviour the person does not currently have but would like to have.
   b. Develop a social learning strategy for the person to acquire that behaviour.
   c. Implement the strategy.
   d. In small groups or with the whole class, describe what you tried to do and what happened.

2. In groups of four to six people, discuss the differences among you that would impact the kind of training you would prefer. Use Table 2-5 on page 62 to start your discussion, but do not limit it to only those characteristics. What accounts for the differences and similarities among your group members?

3. Observe an introductory course in computer programming. Then observe an introductory course in art or music. Which course uses a more behavioural and which a more cognitive approach to learning? If possible, interview the instructors to find out why they use the approach they do. Describe the match between the instructional approach and the subject matter.

4. Use the following to see how expectancy theory explains differences in student motivation.
   a. In a small group, discuss the most important outcome you want to achieve in this class (it may or may not be a letter grade). Have each person indicate how valuable that outcome is to him or her using a scale from 1 = "not at all desirable" to 10 = "extremely desirable."

   b. Ask a group member to describe his or her most important outcome; ask that person to indicate how motivated he or she is to achieve this outcome compared with the other things he or she wants to do this term (use a scale of 1 = "not at all motivated" to 10 = "extremely motivated").
   c. Then ask that same person to describe the things that must be done (performance level) in order to achieve that outcome.
   d. Next, ask the person to indicate the Expectancy 1 level (the belief that he or she will reach the performance level). Then ask the person to describe Expectancy 2 (the likelihood that successful performance will result in the outcome). Use probabilities (e.g., .1 = "very unlikely,".5 = "50% chance of happening,".9 = "very likely") to reflect expectancies.
   e. Now examine the expectancy linkages to see how well they conform to the person's level of motivation. Discuss any discrepancies and why they exist.

5. This exercise is for those who are working together on a project. Without conversation among members of your group, write a list of the group's norms for performance on the project. When you are done, indicate whether you follow each of the norms and why. Once everyone has finished the tasks above, collect all the responses and mix them up. Hand them out. Allow each person to read the responses they received and compile the responses on a flip chart. Once all responses have been read, discuss the implications of your group's perception of performance norms.

## Web Research

Look on the Web for learning theories that are not in the text. Find one and suggest how it could be used in training.

# CASE ANALYSIS

*Rick's New Job*

Rick recently received an MBA. In university, he was known as smart, hardworking, and friendly. His good grades landed him an internship with Peterson Paper Products to head up their sales department. Near the end of the internship Val Peterson, the President and founder of the company, asked Rick to meet him after work to discuss the future.

### Peterson Paper Products

Val Peterson founded Peterson Paper Products (PPP) 17 years ago. It purchases raw paper of varying grades and produces paper stock for business, personal stationery, and greeting cards. Its annual sales topped $15 million, and it employs 80 to 90 people, depending on demand. Sales gradually declined over the last two years after steady and sometimes spectacular growth during the previous seven years. Competition increased markedly over the last three years, and profit margins dwindled. Although PPP is known for the high quality of its products, consumers are shifting from premium-priced, high-quality products to products with higher overall value. Through all of these changes, PPP maintained a close-knit family culture. At least half of the employees have been with the company since the beginning or are friends or relatives of the Petersons or Mr. Ball, Val's partner.

Val Peterson, 53, holds the majority of stock in this privately held company that he founded. He began working summers in a paper company during high school. He supervised a shift at a paper plant while he went to college at night. After graduation, he worked at increasingly higher management levels, occasionally switching employers for a promotion. Eighteen years ago, he quit his vice-presidency with a major paper product manufacturer to start his own company. Employees see him as charismatic, even-tempered, and reasonable. He spends most of his time and energy on company business, putting in 12-hour days.

Rosie Peterson, 50, is Val's wife, and the Controller for the company. She holds 5 percent of the company stock. Rosie never went to college, and her accounting methods are rather primitive (all paper and pencil). Nonetheless, she is always on top of the financial picture and puts in nearly as many hours as Val. She exerts a great deal of influence in the operations and direction of PPP.

Walter Ball, 61, is both Mr. Peterson's friend and business partner. He owns 25 percent of the stock and has known Val since before the start of PPP. He is VP of Operations, which means he oversees the computer information systems that run the paper production process and handles the technical side of the business. He is not current on the latest computer or manufacturing technology, but he loves the paper business. He says he will probably retire at 65, but most say they will believe it when they see it.

Diane Able, 41, is the Customer Service Manager and is married to Steve Able, the Chief Engineer. Diane worked her way up in the company over the last ten years. She is often asked to assist Mr. Peterson with projects because of her commonsense, and he trusts her to keep information to herself.

### Rick's Offer

When Rick met Mr. Peterson to "discuss the future," he was nervous. He knew Mr. Peterson liked his work so far, but did not know if it was enough to extend his internship another six months. So far, he had worked with Mr. Peterson only on special projects and did not know the rest of the management group well. He was flabbergasted when Mr. Peterson said, "I was thinking that you might like to work here at PPP full-time and help us out with our sales department."

The two of them discussed the problems in the sales area and talked about what could be done to boost sales. Rick agreed to start the next Monday. During this conversation, Rosie walked in and suggested they all go out to dinner. At dinner, Rosie emphasized to Rick that PPP was a family operation, down-to-earth and informal. "You probably shouldn't try to change things too quickly," she warned. "People need time to get used to you. You have to remember, you're an outsider here and everyone else is an insider." Then Val moved the conversation back to what the future could be like at PPP.

### Rick's Awakening

The first few days at work, Rick spent time getting to know the plant and operations, meeting all the employees, and familiarizing himself with the problems in sales. He met with Val each morning and afternoon. He also met with the key managers, not only to introduce himself but also to convey his desire to work collaboratively with them in addressing the problems in sales. He was conscious not to flaunt his university education and to convey that he recognized he was a newcomer and had a lot to learn. In the middle of his second week, Val told him that his reception by the other employees was going very well. "Your enthusiasm and motivation seem to be contagious. Having you join us shows them that things need to change if we're going to reach our goals."

Rick noticed, however, that the managers always went out in groups, and he had not been invited along. Also he was not included in the informal discussion groups that formed periodically during the day. In fact, the conversation usually stopped when he approached. Everyone was friendly, he thought; maybe it would just take a little more time.

By his third week, Rick identified some of the problems in the sales department. Among the four salespeople, morale and productivity were moderate to low. He was unable to find any sales strategy, mission, or objectives. The records showed that Val was by far the leading salesperson. The others indicated that Mr. Peterson "always works with us very closely to make sure we do things right. If he senses there might be a problem, he steps in right away." After formulating a plan, Rick discussed it with Mr. Peterson. "First, I would like to institute weekly sales meetings so we keep everyone up-to-date. I also want to create a centralized sales database," he told him. Mr. Peterson smiled and agreed. Rick felt he was finally a manager. He did feel that he should have mentioned his idea for creating a sales department mission and strategy but recalled Rosie's caution about not moving too fast.

Rick discussed with Mr. Ball the possibility of using the centralized computer system to run word processing and spreadsheet software on terminals. Mr. Ball was concerned that outsiders could access the data in the spreadsheets. Anyway, he did not think the system could handle that task because its primary function was production. Puzzled, Rick asked if a PC could be allocated to him. Mr. Ball said that no one in the company had one.

"Well," Rick thought, "I'll just have to bring mine from home." The next Monday Rick walked through the office carrying his computer. Several of the other managers looked at him quizzically. Making light of it he said, "I'm not smart enough to keep everything in my head and I do not have enough time to write it all down on paper." As he was setting up the computer he got a call from Val. "Rick, that computer you brought in has caused a heck of a ruckus. Can you lie low with it until I get back late this afternoon?" Rick thought Val sounded strained but chalked it up to overwork.

Rick agreed and left the computer on his desk, partly assembled. Five minutes later, Rosie walked into his office.

"Do you think it's funny bringing that thing in here? What are you trying to prove—how backward we all are? How much better you are with your big initials behind your name? You're still an outsider here, buster, and do not forget it."

Rick tried to explain how much more productive the sales department would be and that he had tried to use the company's computer system. However, Rosie was not listening. "Did you think about checking with me before bringing that in? With Val or even Walter? Don't you think we have a right to know what you're bringing in here?" Rick knew argument would do no good, so he apologized for not checking with everyone first. He said he had a meeting with Val for later to talk about it. Rosie said, "Good, talk to Val, but don't think he calls all the shots here."

At the meeting with Val, Val agreed that the computer would certainly help solve the problems in sales. "But, you have to be sensitive to the feelings of Rosie and the other managers. It would be best if you did not use the computer for a while until things calm down."

The next day Walter walked into Rick's office. He told Rick he had moved far too fast with the computer. "That's not how it's done here, son. Maybe you're spending too much time listening to what Val says. He isn't really the one to talk to about these kinds of issues. Next time you just ask old Uncle Walter."

Without his computer, Rick spent the next few weeks building the database by hand and conducting sales meetings with his staff. He tried to set up meetings with Mr. Peterson, but Val was usually too busy. One day, Rick asked Diane Able about not being able to see Mr. Peterson and she said, "You know, you monopolized a lot of his time early on. Those of us who worked closely with him before you came were pushed aside so he could spend time with you. Now, it's your turn to wait."

"Are you the one who's been spending all the time with him?" Rick asked.

"Well, it's been me and some of the other managers. We've really been taking a beating in sales, so we need to figure out how to reduce our costs," Ms. Able answered.

A few weeks later, Rick was called in to Val's office. Val began, "Rick, you know we've been going through some bad times. We're reducing head count and I'm afraid you're one of the people we're going to let go. It has nothing to do with your work. You haven't really been here long enough to have either succeeded or failed. It's just that we had unrealistic expectations about how quickly things in sales would turn around. I feel terrible having to do this and I'll do everything I can to help you find another job."

After packing his things and loading up the car, Rick sat in his car and stared out the window. "Welcome to the real world," he thought to himself.

*(continued)*

## Case Questions

1. Why do you think Rick was let go? How does re-inforcement theory apply to this situation?

2. Explain Rosie and Walter's reaction to Rick's computer in terms of resistance to change. How might Rick have used the concepts in this chapter to approach the computer situation so as to gain acceptance?

3. Explain Rick's inability to "fit in" using social learning theory. Where did the breakdowns occur?

4. If Val hired you to develop a management training program for the senior managers at PPP, how would you go about designing the program? Provide appropriate theoretical rationale to support your position.

# 3

# NEEDS ANALYSIS

*If you don't know where you are going, any road will take you there.*

Lewis Carroll in *Alice's Adventures In Wonderland* (1865)

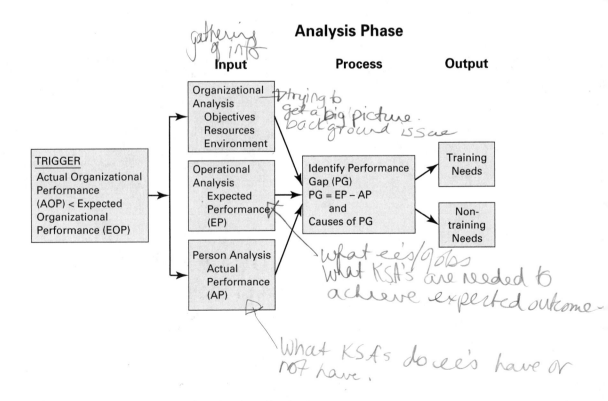

**Analysis Phase**

*gathering of info*

**Input**          **Process**          **Output**

Organizational
Analysis
  Objectives
  Resources
  Environment

*trying to get a big picture. background issue*

TRIGGER
Actual Organizational
Performance
(AOP) < Expected
Organizational
Performance (EOP)

Operational
Analysis
  Expected
  Performance
  (EP)

Identify Performance
Gap (PG)
PG = EP – AP
and
Causes of PG

Training
Needs

Non-
training
Needs

Person Analysis
  Actual
  Performance
  (AP)

*what ee's/jobs what KSA's are needed to achieve expected outcome.*

*What KSA's do ee's have or not have.*

## CHAPTER OBJECTIVES

After reading this chapter, you should be able to:

- Describe the purpose of a needs analysis.

- List and describe the steps in conducting a needs analysis.

- Explain what a competency is and why it is useful.

- List four contaminations of a criterion.

- Differentiate between proactive and reactive needs analysis and the situations favouring the use of one over the other.

- Outline the rationale for using performance appraisal information for a needs analysis and identify what type of performance appraisal method is appropriate.

- Describe the relationship between needs analysis and the design and evaluation of training.

## CASE

### Developing a Training Package at Westcan

Chris is a human resource manager at Westcan Hydraulics, and Irven, the VP of HR is her boss. One morning Irven called Chris into his office. "I just saw an old training film called *Meetings Bloody Meetings* starring John Cleese," he said. "It deals with effective ways of running meetings." Irven, a competent and well-liked engineer, had been promoted to Vice-President of HR three months earlier. Although he had no HR expertise, he had been an effective production manager, and the president of the company hoped that Irven would provide a measure of credibility to the HR department. In the past, employees saw the HR department as one that forced its silly ideas on the rest of the company with little understanding of how to make those ideas work.

"Well," said Chris "I. . . ."

"Oh, yes," Irven interjected, "I talked to a few managers this morning and they were enthusiastic about it. It's the first time I have ever seen managers enthusiastic about any type of training. Do we have such a training package available?"

"No, I do not believe so," Chris replied.

"Well," said Irven, "We need a one-day training session. It must be interesting, useful, and generalizable to all managers. Okay?" With that, Irven stood up, signalling that the meeting was over.

Chris went to work designing the training. She began by going to the local university and viewing the meetings film her boss had seen. After examining some books that dealt with meetings, she decided she had a good idea of what made meetings effective. She then called Larry, a friend at Satellite Systems, to see what he had.

He faxed over a copy of a lecture he had given on the do's and don'ts an effective meeting. It was nicely broken down into three parts: pre-meeting, meeting, and post-meeting. That information and a simulated meeting (to provide hands-on practice) could make up the one-day training program. Chris had never written a simulation and would need help. She put in a call to Karen; a subordinate who was fresh out of university, and had majored in HR. Karen would surely be able to help develop a simulation.

# WHY CONDUCT A TRAINING NEEDS ANALYSIS?

**Training Needs Analysis (TNA)** a systematic process for determining the cause of a performance gap.

What is wrong with the situation at Westcan? It is a scene that repeats itself in some form every day. The boss wants some training, and the HR manager complies. After all, the boss must know what kind of training the employees need. Right? Maybe not. Recall from Chapter 1 that a **training needs analysis** (TNA) is a systematic method for determining what caused performance to be less than expected or required. Performance improvement[1] is the focus of training. This is obvious when you turn to the beginning of the chapter and look at the analysis phase figure. Note the "trigger" for doing a needs analysis occurs when **actual organizational performance (AOP)** is less than **expected organizational performance (EOP)**. Is this the case at Westcan? Perhaps. In this situation, we might consider the VP's suggestion that there is a need for training the "trigger" to conduct a needs analysis. Are the performance levels in the organization's meetings less than expected? To answer this question, Chris would need to conduct a training needs analysis.

If AOP is less than EOP at Westcan, Chris needs to identify where differences exist in terms of the meetings held at Westcan. Once these are known, other questions need answering. How many meetings are ineffective? What is causing the problem? Is it the manager's knowledge of "how to run an effective meeting," or are other issues causing the meetings to be ineffective? How much do these managers already know about meetings, and how skilful are they at applying this knowledge? Chris needs to answer these and other questions by conducting a TNA before she begins to design the training program for effective meetings. Instead, Chris assumes she knows what managers require and begins to develop the training based on her assumptions without conducting a TNA to determine exactly what the deficiencies are. Think about this scenario as we examine the process of a TNA. Would you want to be in Chris's shoes? We refer back to this example throughout the chapter and at the end we give you the rest of the story.

A TNA is important because it helps determine whether training can correct the performance problem. In some cases, the TNA indicates that employees lack necessary KSAs to do the job and they require training. In other cases, employees have the KSAs to do the job, but there are roadblocks preventing effective performance. These obstacles need to be identified and removed. As a training professional, you will use the TNA to make sure you provide the right training to the right people. Chris at Westcan is overlooking a critical part of the training process by not completing a TNA. Instead, she is relying on what Irven says and jumping directly to the training-design phase. If Chris first conducted a TNA she could accomplish several important things:

- Increase the chances that the time and money spent on training is spent wisely,
- Determine the benchmark for evaluation of training,
- Increase the motivation of participants, and
- Align her training activities with the company's strategic plan.

Why spend thousands of dollars, or more, on a training program no one needs? With increased concern about costs in organizations today, it is important that all departments, including human resources, use resources wisely.

A TNA will provide a benchmark of the performance levels and KSAs trainees possess prior to training. These benchmarks will let you compare performance before and after training. This will allow you to demonstrate the cost savings or value added as a result of training.[2] More will be said about these evaluation issues in Chapter 8.

A TNA provides more than just evaluation measures. Using a TNA ensures your training focuses on KSAs the trainees really need. If trainees see the training as relevant, they are more likely to be interested in attending. Consider the employees who do not need the training but are sent by their supervisor anyway. Are they going to take the training seriously? Probably not. In fact, their lack of interest may be distracting to those who need and want the training. Worse, they may cause other trainees not to take the training seriously. The needs analysis also allows the trainer to begin by explaining how the training will be useful. A good TNA ensures that only those who need the training attend and provides the data to show trainees why the training will be useful to them.

As noted in Chapter 1, implementing a strategic plan requires careful analysis of the organization's human resource capabilities. A TNA is the process for determining

**Actual Organizational Performance (AOP)** the performance level of the organization, department, or unit.

**Expected Organizational Performance (EOP)** the performance level or goal that has been set and is expected of the organization, department, or unit.

Website on Determining Training Needs
*www.hr-guide.com/data/G510.htm*

the degree to which employees possess the necessary KSAs to carry out the strategies. Training can then be designed in alignment with this strategic plan. The TNA also provides HRD with information as to the relevance of training to the strategic plan. This information is helpful in determining which training needs are more important.

# WHEN TO CONDUCT A TRAINING NEEDS ANALYSIS

There are times when a TNA may not be necessary. For example, if the organization is trying to communicate a new vision or address legal concerns, it may be advisable to train all employees. Suppose the company has concerns regarding sexual harassment. Everyone should be aware of how seriously top management considers breaches of their "sexual harassment" policy. Here, company-wide training on the issue may be necessary. Sending everyone to a workshop on sexual harassment ensures that management's expectations regarding this issue are clear. It also demonstrates an employer's position on sexual harassment to the courts, should an employee consider a sexual harassment lawsuit.

Another situation in which a TNA might not be necessary is if a team requires team-building skills. In this instance, the goal of training is to build the dynamics of the team so that the members work together cohesively and effectively, as well as to provide the relevant KSAs. Everyone on the team must be part of the training, even though he or she may already possess many team KSAs.

For most types of training, however, a needs analysis is beneficial and will increase the relevance and effectiveness of training. For example, team building for teams that have been working together for a while would benefit from a TNA. In this case the needs analysis focus is on the team itself, not the individuals on the team. Only teams that demonstrate problems in effectiveness or cohesion would go through a TNA to determine if training is necessary. Teams already functioning effectively would not need to attend, so the overall cost of training is reduced.

**Organizational Analysis** an examination of an organization's strategy, its goals/objectives, and the systems and practices in place to determine how they affect employee performance.

**Operational Analysis** an examination of specific jobs to determine the requirements, in terms of the tasks required to be done, and the KSAs needed to do them, to get the job done. It is analogous to a job analysis.

**Person Analysis** an examination of the employees in the jobs to determine whether they have the required KSAs to perform at the expected level.

**Expected Performance (EP)** the level of performance expected in a particular job.

**Actual Performance (AP)** the actual level of performance by an individual in that job.

# THE TNA MODEL

Examine the model at the start of the chapter. The first part of the model indicates what triggers a TNA. When a key decision-maker suggests there is a performance problem that is occurring or may occur in the future, a TNA is triggered.

The next step in the TNA model is the input, which consists of an organizational analysis, an operational analysis, and a person analysis. The **organizational analysis** is an examination of an organization's strategy, its goals/objectives, and the systems and practices in place to determine how they affect employee performance. An **operational analysis** is the examination of specific jobs to determine the requirements, in terms of the tasks required to be done, and the KSAs needed to do them to get the job done. It is analogous to a job analysis or a task analysis as it is sometimes called. A **person analysis** is the examination of the employees in the jobs to determine whether they have the required KSAs to perform at the expected level.

In the process phase, the operational analysis provides information on expected performance. **Expected performance (EP)** is the level of performance expected in a particular job.

The person analysis provides information on actual performance. **Actual performance (AP)** is the current level of performance by an individual on a particular job. When actual performance is lower than expected performance, then a performance gap is identified. And as noted in the model, a **performance gap (PG)** is the difference between expected performance and actual performance.

The "output" phase is your conclusion as to whether the performance gap indicates either training or non-training needs, and in some cases, both. This will be explained later.

So, as you can see from the model, a TNA is conducted when a key decision-maker in the company notes that AOP is less than EOP (reactive TNA). Or she believes AOP will be less than EOP in the future (proactive TNA). A **reactive TNA** focuses on current performance problems. A **proactive TNA** focuses on anticipated or probable performance problems in the future. Let's look at an example of each.

A current performance gap triggers a reactive TNA. For example, if the expected number of widgets produced per week is 5000 and actual production is only 4300, you need to investigate this gap.

As an example of the proactive approach, consider an organization's decision to implement statistical process control (SPC) to improve the quality of its widgets. Sometime in the near future, the employees producing widgets will begin using SPC methods. Potential for a future PG exists if the employees do not have the appropriate KSAs. This potential gap triggers a proactive TNA to determine whether employees will be able to perform as needed when the organization implements SPC. You conduct an assessment of employees' capabilities regarding SPC and find they are not able to perform the arithmetic needed in the use of SPC. This PG will need to be addressed before SPC can be implemented. As this example illustrates, when you expect a performance gap to occur at some point in the future, you should conduct a proactive TNA to verify that the performance gap will exist and identify the specific KSAs that need to be developed.

A PG may occur for many reasons (see Figure 3-1), only one of which is a lack of KSAs. You need to conduct the TNA to discover why the performance gap exists and what can be done to correct it. Consider the problem at Bell Telephone Company a few years back. Sales revenue did not meet expected levels (AOP was less than EOP), triggering a TNA. The TNA identified that sales were indeed below expectations. The TNA narrowed the source of the less-than-expected sales to the installation and repair unit. Bell had hoped to increase revenue by having their installation and repair employees make sales pitches to customers for additional services when on a service call. However, data on sales indicated few such sales took place, so AP was less than EP. Note in Figure 3-1 that a number of possible causes of a PG are listed. If the cause is not a KSA deficiency, then some non-training solution is required to alleviate the PG.

What caused the PG? It was not a KSA deficiency. Installation and repair employees' performance was based on the time it took them to complete a call. They had a certain amount of time to complete each call. If they took longer than the time allotted for a number of calls, their performance was rated as below average. The time allotment was not changed, even though employees were now expected to stick around and try to sell Bell products and services. So, most employees simply did not spend any time selling. In this example reward/punishment incongruities were causing the PG. We return to examine Figure 3-1 in more detail later, but now let's examine where we look for discrepancies.

# WHERE TO LOOK FOR PERFORMANCE GAPS

There are numerous places to look for PGs. A company's archival data such as its profitability, market share, grievance levels, productivity, and quality measures provide

**Performance Gap (PG)** the difference between expected performance and actual performance.

**Reactive TNA** a TNA focusing on a performance problem in the present.

**Proactive TNA** a TNA focusing on an performance problem anticipated in the future.

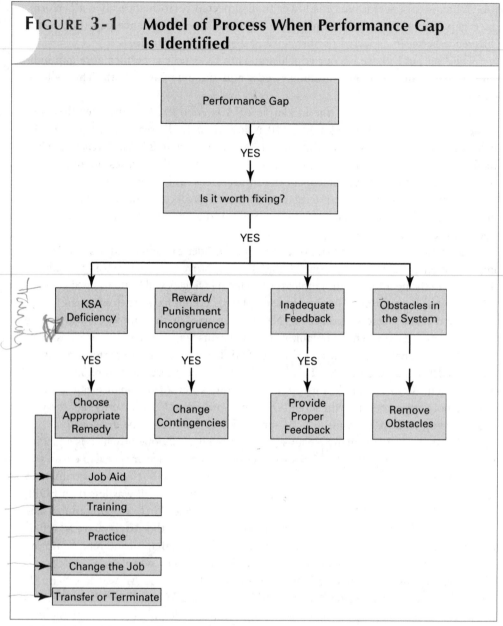

**FIGURE 3-1    Model of Process When Performance Gap Is Identified**

*Source:* Adapted from Michalak and Yager (1979).

indicators of how it is operating. These are included in Table 3-1, which provides a list of sources for gathering data related to potential discrepancies. Let's examine a few to see how the process works. The first data source, organizational goals and objectives and budgets, provides standards against which unit performance can be measured. Suppose, for example, the triggering event was a loss in profitability because of excessive costs related to warranty work. A reactive TNA is implemented and might lead you to examine the quality standard for rejects in the production department. The standard (EP) is less than one per thousand, but you see the actual performance (AP) is 12 per thousand.

The process is similar when you expect future performance to be less than what it should be. Here a proactive TNA is initiated. Suppose the company's new strategic plan indicates a substantial modernization of the plant, including new computerized machinery. There is no PG now, but the Plant Manager believes there will be when the new machinery arrives. This possible performance gap in the future prompts a

## TABLE 3-1 Recommended Data Sources for Locating Performance Gaps

| Sources of Data | Implications for Training Needs | Examples |
|---|---|---|
| 1. Organizational Goals | This source suggests where training emphasis should be placed. | Maintain a quality standard of no more than one reject per thousand. |
| Objectives and budget | This source provides information on both standards and direction. | Achieve a goal to become ISO certified and allow $90 000 to this effort. |
| 2. Labour Inventory | This source helps HRD identify where training is needed because of retirement turnover, age, etc. | Thirty percent of our truck drivers will retire over the next four years. |
| 3. Organizational Climate Indicators | These "quality of working life" indicators at the organization level provide indicators of organizational performance gaps. | |
| a. Labour–management data, strikes, lockouts, etc. | These indicators relate to work participation or productivity and are useful in discrepancy analysis and in helping management set a value on the behaviours it wishes to improve through training. | Seventy percent of the grievances are related to the behaviours of six supervisors. |
| b. Grievances | | |
| c. Turnover | | High absenteeism for clerical staff. |
| d. Absenteeism | | |
| e. Suggestions | | Accident rate for line workers increasing. |
| f. Productivity | | |
| g. Accidents | | |
| h. Short-term sickness | | |
| i. Attitude surveys | Surveys are good for locating discrepancies between organizational expectations and perceived results. | Line workers' attitude toward teamwork is poor. |
| 4. Analysis of Efficiency Indexes | | |
| a. Costs of labour | | Labour costs have increased by 8% in the last year. |
| b. Quality of product | | Number of rejects has increased by 30% since the new batch of workers began. |
| c. Waste | | Wasted steel has increased by 14% since the company began using part-time workers. |
| 5. Changes in System or Subsystem | New or changed equipment may require training. | The line has shut down about once per day since the new machinery was installed. |
| 6. MBO or Work Planning and Review systems | Provides actual baseline performance data on a continuous basis. From these measures the company is able to determine improvement or deterioration of performance. | |

*Source:* References for all at these methods can be found in M. Moore, P. Dutton (1978). Training Needs Analysis: Review Critique. *Academy of Management Review* 3 532–545.

"proactive" TNA. As part of this TNA, the HRD department will need to assess the employees' current level of KSAs for operating the new machinery. If these current KSAs are not sufficient, a performance gap exists for the future.

Number two, labour inventory, is also useful to determine performance gaps in the future and the types of training necessary to prevent such a performance gap from occurring. Knowing that a number of senior engineers are retiring over the next few years can trigger the HRD department to start training those in line for promotion to obtain some necessary skills. Not being aware of these retiring employees could lead to a performance gap because the company would lack enough senior engineers to manage the expected number of projects.

Finally, let's examine data source three: organizational climate indicators. Identification of high absenteeism in a particular area, or an increasing accident rate, provides you with early signs of problems. The quicker you are able to identify problems, the quicker you will be able to find and implement solutions. This is one secret to an effective HRD department. Cindy Baerman, the Human Resource Development Officer of Miller Brewing Company, provides an example for this. She began attending production meetings a few years back. She received funny looks, as the meetings were held to focus on production problems. Why would HRD want to be there? As Cindy pointed out, "What better place to learn of the type of performance problems the line manager is having?"[3] For her, the focus was on performance management. Being able to react quickly to maintain and improve performance is the first step in a continuous performance improvement framework, which is so important in today's environment.[4]

# THE FRAMEWORK FOR CONDUCTING A TNA

Once a trigger has set a TNA in motion the three levels of analysis—organizational operational, and person—need to be completed.[5] Let's examine each of these inputs in more detail.

## ORGANIZATIONAL ANALYSIS

An organizational analysis focuses on the strategies of the organization, the resources in the organization, the allocation of these resources,[6] and the total internal environment.[7] The internal environment includes an examination of structures, policies and procedures, job design, workflow processes, and other factors that facilitate or inhibit an employee's ability to meet job performance expectations.

An organizational analysis is necessary to help identify the cause of discrepancies and, specifically, to determine whether discrepancies are, in fact, correctable through training. According to Nancy Gordon, a TNA analyst at Bell Telephone, about 85 percent of all requests for training turned out to be related to issues that could not be addressed by training. They were, instead, incongruencies in the organizational environment that inhibited or prevented the appropriate work behaviours (see Training in Action 3-1).

An organizational analysis, then, should be able to provide information about the following:

- The mission and strategies of an organization,
- The resources and allocation of the resources, given the objectives,

- The factors in the internal environment that may be causing the problem, and
- The impact of the preceding factors on developing, providing, and transferring the KSAs to the job if training is the chosen solution to the PG.

<u>Mission and Strategies</u> As part of an organizational analysis, the examination of the mission and strategies helps the analyst place the training in a particular context. Consider the Windsor Ford Engine Plant mission statement: "Our mission is to continually improve our products and services to meet our customers' needs, allowing us to prosper as a business and provide a reasonable return to our stockholders." A strategy arising from that mission statement was to focus on the team approach for continuous improvement. Two types of training traditionally used to support this strategy are training in problem solving and negotiations. But what if the workers in the plant are offered training in traditional negotiations skills? Is this in line with the team approach? Perhaps not. Problem-solving training requires openness and trust to be effective. Traditional negotiations training often teaches that it is useful not to reveal all your information, but instead to hold back and attempt to get the best deal for yourself or your department that you can. To offer such training would at best not reinforce an environment of openness and trust and at worst would actually impede it.

## Training in Action 3-1

### *Incongruities in the Organizational Environment*

A bank manager decided that in order to increase profits, he would send all his tellers to a training workshop about the products and services the bank offered. He wanted the tellers to provide such information to customers who came into the bank, thinking that this would increase the number of products and services sold.

The manager developed a method of tracking the number of products and services sold so he could have a measure of the success of the training. After a time he noticed no increase in sales. Training did not result in an increase in sales. What went wrong?

Analysis revealed that when tellers returned from training, they also returned to the same appraisal system in place before the training. Performance assessment was based largely on the number of customers the teller was able to process. Why would a teller risk receiving a low performance rating in order to spend time telling customers about the products and services being offered by the bank?

*Source:* Adapted from Johnson, C. (1995). Making your training stick. *HR Magazine*, May, pp. 55–60.

A company's mission and strategies also indicate priorities for training. Training resources are always finite, so decisions must be made as to where to spend the training budget. If, for example, "Quality is job one" at Ford, the analyst knows that development of KSAs relating to quality should receive priority. Thinking back to the Westcan case, can you identify how that company's priorities would be related to the need for effective meetings?

*Capital Resources.* **Capital Resources** refer to a company's finances, equipment, and facilities. During strategic planning decisions are made as to where money should be spent. If a large expenditure is made on new equipment for the machinists, or toward becoming ISO 9000 certified, these strategic decisions will help determine the priorities for the HRD department. In the case of purchasing new equipment for machinists, HRD's priority would be the machinists' positions. You would need to assess the machinists' level of KSAs to determine whether they needed training to operate the new machinery. This decision to focus on the machinist is based on the financial

**Capital Resources** the holdings an organization has, such as property, equipment, finances, etc.

decisions made at the strategic level. Likewise, the strategic choice of becoming ISO 9000 certified should indicate to you that support in that area is needed. After all, significant company resources will be directed toward these strategic initiatives. If the employees are not able to operate the new equipment or engage in the tasks required for ISO certification, the money put toward those initiatives will be wasted.

Another concern for HRD is its own budget. Decisions about how to provide the required training are a function of the money HRD has available for training. Deciding whether to use external consultants or internal staff depends on a number of issues, not the least of which is cost. In the Westcan case, Chris decided to develop the training herself. Hiring a consultant to provide the training might get better results, but Chris would have to weigh that decision against other training needs at Westcan, given her limited budget.

**Human Resources** the level of KSAs employees working for the organization have.

*Human Resources.* The other area of resources that needs to be addressed is **human resources.** Examination of an organization's human resource KSAs takes place on two levels. They include a general strategic needs assessment and a more specific training needs assessment. First, at the strategic level, HRD provides top management with an assessment of the current employees' ability and potential to support various strategies. With this information, top management knows the capabilities of their employees and can factor those capabilities into their strategic decision-making. Heinz Canada's Leamington plant decided a number of years ago that their strategic plan was to improve their efficiency in producing ketchup. They wanted to purchase a state-of-the-art automated ketchup maker. The HRD department provided top management with information on the KSAs of the current workforce. This information indicated that no one had the skills necessary, and, in fact, many had reading difficulties, such that operating computer-controlled machinery might be a concern. Because the strategic planning group knew this information early in the strategic planning phase, they were able to make an informed decision about how to proceed. They considered the following choices:

- Abandon the idea of purchasing such equipment and consider alternative strategic plans.

- Hire employees who have the skills to operate such machinery.

- Train current employees to operate the machinery.

Heinz chose to move forward with the plan and train their current employees. Since they addressed the issue early, Heinz had plenty of time to train their employees.

HRD's strategic needs assessment is more proactive and provides a great deal of information about the capabilities of the workforce to carry out various strategic alternatives. This information helps decision makers decide which strategic alternatives will be followed. Once managers approve a strategic plan, HRD can focus on areas where priorities are identified from the strategic plan.

At the second level HRD focuses on those employees who are identified to be working in areas with performance gaps. This is really part of the person analysis, but an example will help to clarify the difference. In our earlier example, it would be the machinist who had to learn to use the new computerized machinery. What about in the Heinz example? Recall that none of the Heinz employees has the required KSAs to operate the new ketchup equipment. As a result, although they are effective employees at the present time, a performance gap will develop when the new equipment arrives. The HRD department's priority is to provide the employees with the requisite KSAs so that when the ketchup machine arrives, they will be able to operate it effectively.

**Organizational Environment**
how the organization is designed, including structures (e.g., organic or mechanistic) and designs (e.g., workflow, division of labour, pay systems, and reward policies).

*Organizational Environment.* Another key objective of the organizational analysis is to examine the organizational environment. The **organizational environment** is made up of various structures (e.g., mechanistic or organic) and designs (e.g., work-flow, division of labour, pay system, and reward policies). The environmental analysis determines how congruent these structures are with the performance objectives of the department or unit in which discrepancies have been identified. Identifying these incongruencies early and changing them will help to ensure that when training is complete, the new skills will transfer to the job.

Consider two organizations:

"Organization A" decides to adopt a more team-oriented approach. The company's mission and objectives reflect this recent change in company policy. Present procedures include the use of a suggestion box and provide rewards for individual suggestions for suggestions that improve company performance.

"Organization B's" mission and objectives can be summed up as "quality is most important." One of the organization's policies is that performance appraisals for first-line management provide a measure of how well these managers meet productivity quotas. However, the appraisals measure nothing related to quality of the product.

In the first scenario, do you believe the individual incentive system would re-inforce or hinder the team approach? If, after training and implementing the team approach, teams were not producing innovative ideas, would that mean the training was not effective? You cannot really tell. The skills may be learned but not transferred to the job. Consider the reward/punishment incongruence (see Figure 3-1) between rewarding for individual ideas (suggestion box) and instituting a team approach, which meant sharing ideas with the team. If I can get a reward for my idea by put-ting it in the suggestion box, why would I want to freely share it with the team? Identifying this incongruence and removing it before instituting the team approach would facilitate transfer of the training.

In the second scenario, would you expect training in quality issues to be effective, or is training even needed? Instead of training, it might be possible simply to redesign the performance appraisal to emphasize quality.

These examples illustrate the value of conducting an analysis of the organiza-tional environment as it relates to performance problems. Consider one other point. The analysis at the environmental level should not be conducted until you have an idea what jobs are targeted either for their performance problems or because of future changes. This targeting allows for a certain degree of focus when you are conducting the analysis; you gather data that are relevant only to those jobs. Otherwise, you may gather an enormous amount of information on jobs that may be irrelevant and there-fore waste valuable resources.

**Where to Collect Data**  Table 3-2 identifies potential individuals to be interviewed and points to raise with them. Once a performance gap is identified in a specific department or location, then the cause of the gap needs to be determined. You should not assume that training is required to alleviate the gap. Do not forget Nancy Gordon's words: "About 85 percent of training requests turn out to be solvable without training."

## OPERATIONAL ANALYSIS

When a PG is identified, an operational analysis is conducted in conjunction with the organizational analysis in order to fully understand the nature of the PG. The opera-tional analysis determines exactly what is required of employees in order for them to be effective. Techniques for obtaining task and KSA data are usually in the form of a job analysis. Table 3-3 shows sources for operational analysis data. The most frequently used process includes questioning employees doing the job and their supervisors. Let's now examine this process of analyzing a job and the issues to consider.

## TABLE 3-2  What Do You Ask and of Whom?

| What to Ask About | Whom to Ask |
|---|---|
| **Mission Goals and Objectives** | |
| What are the goals and objectives of the organization? | Top management |
| How much money has been allocated to any new initiatives? | Relevant department managers, supervisors, and incumbents |
| Is there general understanding of these objectives? | |
| **Social Influences** | |
| What is the general feeling in the organization regarding meeting goals and objectives? | Top management |
| What is the social pressure in your department regarding these goals and objectives, and regarding productivity? | Relevant department managers, supervisors, and incumbents |
| **Reward Systems** | |
| What are the rewards and how are they distributed? | Top management |
| Are there incentives, are they tied to the goals and objectives? | Relevant department managers, supervisors, and incumbents |
| What specifically do high performers get as rewards? | |
| **Job Design** | |
| How are the jobs organized? | Relevant supervisors and incumbents, perhaps relevant department managers |
| Where does their work/material/information come from, where do they send it when done? | |
| Does the design of the job in any way inhibit incumbents from being high performers? | |
| **Job Performance** | |
| How do employees know what level of performance is acceptable? | Relevant supervisors and incumbents |
| How do they find out if their level of performance is acceptable? | |
| Is there a formal feedback process (performance appraisal for example)? | |
| Are there opportunities for help if required? | |
| **Methods and Practices** | |
| What are the policies/procedures/rules in the organization? Which if any inhibit performance? | Relevant department managers, supervisors, and incumbents |

## TABLE 3-3 Recommended Data Sources for Operational Analysis

| Sources for Obtaining Job Data | Training Need Implications | Practical Concerns |
|---|---|---|
| 1. Job Descriptions | This source outlines the job's typical duties and responsibilities but is not meant to be all-inclusive. | Need to determine how developed. Often written up quickly by supervisor or incumbent with little understanding of what is required |
| 2. Job Specifications | These are specified tasks required for each job. More specific than job descriptions and may include judgments of required KSAs. | May be product of the job description and suffer from the same problems |
| 3. Performance Standards | This source provides objectives related to the tasks required and their standards in terms of performance. | Very useful if available, and accurate, but often organizations do not have formal performance standards |
| 4. Ask Questions About the Job<br>  a. Of the job holders<br>  b. Of the supervisor | Asking both job holder and relevant supervisors provides accurate data. | Must be done correctly to be of value |

**Analyzing the Job** HR employees need to know how to conduct an effective job analysis. More detail on how this is done can be found in many texts such as *Performance Management* by Das[8] and *Effective Training: Systems strategies and practices* by Blanchard and Thacker.[9] Here, we will provide a cursory examination of the process with emphasis on training.

*What Is the Job?* The first step is to determine exactly what job is going to be analyzed. In today's environment, a common job title can mask real differences in the tasks that are carried out. An extreme example is at Honda Canada Manufacturing, where everyone from line workers to top management has the job title of "Associate." Other organizations use the same job title for employees who do different tasks because they work in different departments and geographical locations.

As Table 3-3 indicates, data can be gathered from a number of sources. Job descriptions and specifications are one source of data for understanding the job and its basic requirements. If this information was gathered through a job analysis, you can be confident of its value. Even if it was not, it provides a basic understanding of the job and is useful before starting to ask questions of these employees.

When analyzing a job, the incumbent needs to provide relevant information about the job; after all, she is the expert regarding how the job is done. Data should also be gathered from the incumbents' supervisor because

- This information provides a different perspective and helps yield a well-rounded concept of exactly what is required; and

- When discrepancies are noted between what the supervisor and the incumbents say, an investigation into the reason for the discrepancy can provide useful information.

Earlier, we suggested that trainers need organizational development (OD) skills. In this instance, those skills provide an effective way of resolving differences between incumbents and supervisors regarding how the job should be performed. A more proactive approach is to avoid conflicting beliefs between subordinates and supervisors in the first place by implementing the **job expectation technique**.[10] This technique includes facilitating a meeting between subordinates and supervisors to discuss the job responsibilities of the subordinates. The goal here is to clarify job expectations. This process may sound simplistic, but it requires trust and respect between supervisors and their subordinates. In reality, many job incumbents learn about their job through working with other incumbents and through trial and error.

***What to Ask About.*** Several job analysis techniques are available for gathering information about a job. The two main categories are worker-oriented and task-oriented approaches. A **worker-oriented job analysis** focuses on the KSAs that are required on the job rather than on the tasks or behaviours. Incumbents are asked to rate how important a list of KSAs (e.g., far visual differentiation—the ability to differentiate details at distances beyond arms length—use of precision tools, use of measuring devices) is to the job. A drawback of this approach is that task statements are not available to show how the KSAs are linked to the tasks. This link is useful not only for justifying the KSA requirements but also for developing scenarios to be used in the actual training.

The **task-oriented job analysis**, as the name implies, identifies the various work activities (tasks) required to perform the job. After the tasks are identified, systematically examine these tasks to determine the KSAs necessary to perform these tasks. Now you have justification for the KSAs and potential ideas for developing training. That is why this approach is preferred for a TNA.

One example of the task-oriented approach is the **job-duty-task method** depicted in Figure 3-2. Note that the job is identified first, and then each of the duties is written out. The writing out of the duties provides a stimulus to generate tasks and subtasks for each of these duties. From the duties, you identify the relevant tasks and any subtasks each of these tasks might have. Once all the tasks are identified, identify the relevant KSAs required to perform each of these tasks. This provides the justification for requiring these KSAs. It is also possible to list all duties first, followed by tasks and subtasks for each duty, then go back and identify the KSAs for each of the tasks and subtasks. It is equally appropriate to go through each duty, determine the subtasks, and then identify the required KSAs before moving to the next duty.

Determining what the incumbents do in the job identifies the duties, tasks, and subtasks. This information is generally obtained by interviewing a number of incumbents and their supervisors. The list of tasks necessary to do the job is developed by systematically examining each duty and inquiring about the tasks. Identifying the required KSAs is done through examination of each task and asking the question, "What knowledge, skills, and attitudes are necessary to perform a particular task?"

Figure 3-3 depicts an example of a completed job-duty-task method for the job of a human resource professional.

Incumbents are a critical group for obtaining information about the job in a job analysis. But what if no incumbents are available? In today's environment of fast-changing technology, jobs are constantly changing. In some cases, new technology creates a job that requires skills distinctly different from the job it is replacing. In the example cited earlier in this chapter, management at the Heinz plant in Leamington ordered a state-of-the-art ketchup machine. Previously, ketchup was made with low-technology equipment. This new machine required new skills, so the question was: How do you perform a job analysis for a job that does not exist? Dr. Mitchell Fields

**Job Expectation Technique** method of clarifying job expectations for a particular position by having the supervisor meet with the incumbent for the sole purpose of clarifying for both exactly what is required on the job.

**Worker-Oriented Job Analysis** method of job analysis that focuses only on the KSAs required to get the job done.

**Task-Oriented Job Analysis** job analysis that determines the tasks necessary to do the job, then from these, determines the KSAs necessary to perform the tasks.

**Job-Duty-Task Method** a structured task-oriented job analysis method.

## FIGURE 3-2  Form for Recording Task Analysis Results Using the Job-Duty-Task Method of Job Analysis

Job Title: _____          Specific Duty: _____

| Tasks | Subtasks | Knowledge and Skills Required |
|---|---|---|
| | | _____ |
| 1. _____ | 1. _____ | _____ |
| | 2. _____ | _____ |
| | 3. _____ | _____ |
| 2. _____ | 1. _____ | _____ |
| | 2. _____ | _____ |
| | 3. _____ | _____ |
| 3. _____ | 1. _____ | _____ |
| | 2. _____ | _____ |

*Source:* Adapted from Mills, Pace, and Peterson (1988).

## FIGURE 3-3  Applying the Job-Duty-Task Method to the Job of Human Resource Professional

Job Title: HRD Professional _____          Specific Duty: Task Analysis _____

| Tasks | Subtasks | Knowledge and Skills Required |
|---|---|---|
| 1. List tasks | 1. Observe behaviour | List four characteristics of behaviour Classify behaviour |
| | 2. Select verb | Have knowledge of action verbs Have grammatical skills |
| | 3. Record behaviour | State so understood by others Record neatly |
| 2. List subtasks | 1. Observe behaviour | List all remaining acts Classify behaviour |
| | 2. Select verb | State correctly Have grammatical skill |
| | 3. Record behaviour | Record so it is neat and understood by others |
| 3. List knowledge | 1. State what must be known | Classify all information |
| | 2. Determine complexity of skill | Determine whether skills represent a series of acts that must be learned in a sequence |

*Source:* Adapted from Mills, Pace, and Peterson (1988).

## TABLE 3-4  Job Analysis When There Are No Incumbents

The H.J. Heinz Company in Leamington, Ontario, is unionized. The union contract stipulates that new jobs go to existing employees. The company was purchasing a new machine for making ketchup and wanted to be sure those selected for this new job would have the KSAs to do the job. A person analysis indicated most employees did not have much formal education and had very low reading levels. An operational analysis (job analysis) is necessary to determine future KSAs needed. But how do you do a job analysis when there are no incumbents, as the job does not exist? Dr. Fields outlines how he did the job analysis.

1. I contacted the manufacturer of the new equipment and asked if that or similar equipment was being used elsewhere, so that job analysis data could be obtained from another company. In this case, no other application existed.

2. I obtained specifications and operating manuals for the new machinery. The manuals were incomplete and difficult to understand. In fact, they were more complex than they needed to be. As a result, initially I thought a high level of reading comprehension would be necessary.

3. I interviewed engineers who were responsible for designing the new machinery. This is where I received important information as to its operation. However, the engineers tended to overestimate the level of aptitude required. They believed that operators would be making modifications to the programming software. Further discussions revealed that for the operator's job, reading requirements were minimal. Operating manuals were needed only for maintenance and repair.

4. I obtained blueprints and layouts of the physical equipment, as well as flowcharts of the operating software. This material indicated that the operators would be required to interface with a user-friendly, icon-driven software package (far less than the complex programming tasks envisioned by the engineers).

5. I identified two main tasks. First, the operators would be required to keep track of the mechanical operations of a number of different (but integrated) assembly operations. I determined, therefore, that mechanical aptitude was necessary. Second, the operators had to look at a two-dimensional VDT (video display terminal) and make decisions about the three-dimensional assembly-line operation. Having skill in spatial relations, therefore, would also be important.

6. On the basis of the skills identified, I suggested two subtests of the Differential Aptitude Test for use in selection of employees: mechanical comprehension and spatial relations tests. All operators were selected from current employees. The major advantage to these two tests is that reading level (which was determined not to be important) is not a factor.

was approached by Heinz Canada to assist in determining the selection and training requirements for the new job. Table 3-4 describes how Dr. Fields did this.

### What You Should Get from the Job Analysis (Expected Performance)  Using the task-oriented approach yields both the tasks and KSAs required to perform the job. KSAs are important, as it is the KSAs that need to be trained. But the tasks are also important for the following reasons:

- Identifying the expected behaviour that needs to be performed on the job and performance deficits,

- Developing actual training programs, and

- Making subsequent evaluations of the training.[11]

Knowing all the tasks that are necessary to be effective in a particular job provides justification for the KSAs employees are expected to have. In the ketchup machine example, the machine operator was required to watch a video display, which is two-dimensional, and make decisions about the assembly line, which is three-dimensional. This justifies the need for spatial relations.

A list of job-related tasks would also help develop training. Once the tasks to be performed are known, training that closely resembles the real job can be developed. Consider the job of a customer service representative. We determined one of the important tasks is to "deal with irate customers." We used this task to help develop role-plays that closely emulate the real job. Using real-task behaviours in training makes the training more relevant and interesting to trainees and assists in the transfer of training.

Finally, we can use task information to develop tests that are reflective not only of the training but also of the job. These tests can be used in the person analysis phase to identify those with training needs and can also serve to evaluate the effectiveness of training. Task identification leads to identification of the knowledge, skills, and attitudes necessary to do the job.

*Knowledge*. All jobs require some type of knowledge. The job analysis should provide a list of tasks that, when examined, will point to the knowledge requirements necessary to be successful. Going back to our customer service job, we find that knowledge of "steps in a conflict resolution model" would be important.

*Skill*. The job analysis should provide a list of all skills required to perform the job successfully. Consider again, our customer service representative's task of "dealing with an irate customer." This task requires conflict resolution skills. A completed job analysis will identify a complete list of required KSAs for the job, thus providing needs analysis with an understanding of all the job requirements.

*Attitude*. What are the attitudinal outcomes from the job analysis? Actually many job analysts do not incorporate attitudes into their model of job analysis.[12] The job analysis gives an understanding of the tasks that must be done. For each task required, knowledge and skills are inferred. But analysts stop here. We believe attitudes are important, and they are derived simply by asking the question, "Can you think of any attitudes or feelings a person could have that might facilitate or inhibit an employee from doing any part of this job well?"

What attitudes should a customer service representative have to be successful? Would a positive attitude toward helping people be useful? What about a job that requires working in teams? Here, a person should have a positive attitude toward the team approach or perhaps have a positive attitude toward working with others. Such data provide the analyst with information on what should be addressed in training. Just such an issue was of concern in the new Ford assembly plant (see Training in Action 3-2). In this instance the incumbents were unavailable because the plant was not yet open. So, the needs analysis was conducted using their supervisors, who were brought on board early to prepare the plant for opening.

## Competency Modelling Another approach to conducting an operational analysis is to identify key competencies of the job.

A **competency** is a cluster of related knowledge, skills, and attitudes that differentiate high performers from average performers.[13] Or, as the Alberta Public Service website reads, "Competencies provide a means of looking at those behaviours that differentiate the 'best from the rest.'[14] This definition is specific to North America. Other countries such as the United Kingdom and Australia define competencies as simply "what someone needs to be doing to be competent at their job."[15]

Some disagreement arises as to whether deriving competencies is a process different from job analysis. Some experts in the Human Resources field indicate the process is the same, but the majority suggests it is different.[16] To this majority, the major difference is that job analysis derives "tasks" or the "what" that is done on the job, leading to the determination of knowledge and skills but not attitudes. A competency-based approach focuses on all the characteristics that underlie successful performance, not just on the knowledge and skills derived from the tasks. Competencies place equal weight on attitudes, feelings, and motivation, as well as knowledge and skills. Since we incorporate attitudes into our job analysis model, we agree with both sets of experts. Although the data derived are somewhat different for competencies, the

**Competency** a cluster of related knowledge, skills, and attitudes that differentiate "high" performers from average performers.

## Training in Action 3-2

### *Changing Attitudes Toward the Team Approach*

The Ford production plants have moved toward a team approach. The team approach is part of the "Ford Production System." The Windsor Engine Plant was new, and there was an agreement with the Canadian Auto Workers (CAW) stipulating that employees from other plants had first choice of the new jobs.

Employees transferred from other plants for many reasons: cleaner plant, closer to home, old job being phased out. Few transferred to work in a team environment. In fact, it is well known that the CAW traditionally opposes such efforts. In the case of the Windsor Engine Plant they made an exception.

In a determination of the skills needed, it became evident that many of the employees would be older, and the concern was that they would be set in their ways and generally against the team approach. The training consisted of team skills such as communication skills, effective meeting skills, and problem-solving skills. Also, a component was added to influence attitudes toward the team approach.

This "component" consisted of an orientation to the team process. Modules were designed to show the advantages of teams for the company and workers. An exercise called "Best Job/Worst Job" allowed trainees to describe what they considered to be a "best job." Then trainees were asked to consider what teamwork provided in terms of what they would do. What trainees discovered was their own description of a "best job" looked quite similar to what their job would look like in a team environment. The training also provided a six-hour session on individual growth and self-fulfillment. It was assumed that helping employees to focus on these issues would improve their attitudes toward the team approach.

Did the training have a significant impact on attitudes? No one knows for sure. After all the time and money spent on the training, there was no formal evaluation of the process. This omission should not be a surprise, as you will see in Chapter 8 on evaluation.

Website on competency modeling for companies
*www.camdenconsulting.com/
index.cfm/Capabilities/
Competency_Modeling*

process for determining competencies is similar to the typical job analysis. Before discussing the how-to regarding competencies, let's look at the makeup of one.

Consider the competency "time management for a manager." Skills for this competency include delegating, prioritizing, and making to-do lists. The knowledge required is "knowledge of the value of a manager's time." For example, if the manager knew she was valued at $120 per hour, it would help her see the value of determining what she does and what she should delegate. Attitudes reflecting "I have no one I can trust to do this;" "I cannot say no;" "It is quicker if I do it myself;" all get in the way of effective delegation, which in turn affects time management.

***Why Competencies?*** When compared with KSAs, competencies exhibit the following characteristics:[17]

- They are more general in nature.
- They show a longer-term fit.
- They include knowledge, skills, feelings, and motivation.
- They tie into corporate goals.

Competencies tend to be of a more general nature and therefore applicable to a number of jobs. In some cases, competencies are applicable to everyone at a particular level no matter what department, such as all first-line supervisors, or even multiple levels of a job, such as all managers. Northern Telecom, for example, developed a set of competencies relevant to all their managers (see Training in Action 3-3). Note that for different levels of management, the competency remains the same, but the behaviours expected are different. In this way, the focus is always on the same set of key competencies but with a different behaviour, depending on the management level.

In today's environment jobs are always changing. Even shop-floor jobs are under constant change, in many cases requiring more decision-making and other new responsibilities. This constant evolving means the specifics obtained in job analysis can become dated. A more general focus of competencies is advantageous to such ever-changing jobs.

Using competencies makes it easier to identify the emotional aspects of work performance. For example, organizations increasingly focus on issues such as "meeting customer expectations." This area of the job, which requires dealing with people rather than producing goods, requires a broad view of good performance. Many argue that this broad view is easier to obtain using competency models.

Finally, in the process of developing the job competencies, a great deal of effort is made to understand the business context and competitive strategy. Competencies are then developed with a focus on these broader goals of the organization in conjunction with the specific job in question.[18]

## Training in Action 3-3

### Northern Telecom Has a List of Competencies That Are Relevant for All Levels of Managers

Northern Telecom developed a list of Core Values for the company.

Excellence: We have only one standard, excellent.

Teamwork: We share one vision and are a team.

Customers: We create superior value for our customers.

Commitment: We do what we say we do.

Innovation: We embrace change.

People: Our people are our strength.

Northern Telecom instituted a performance appraisal and development process based on the "People" value. In separate meetings with his or her supervisor each employee had the opportunity to work on the development of objectives and his or her own development. The common competencies that are applicable to all managers are defined differently at each level.

One of these competencies and the relevant descriptions is listed below.

| Competency | Demonstration of the Competency | | |
|---|---|---|---|
| | First level | Mid level | Senior level |
| Customer Orientation | Develops customer consciousness in others | Understands customer needs and translates to the goals of the organization | Establishes a relationship at the strategic level |
| | Communicates and resolves conflict | Fosters process improvement and change with linkages to customer groups | Gains trust of customers |
| | Ensures work (own and team) exceeds customer expectations | | Formulates strategies to meet identified and anticipated requirements |
| | | Instills and maintains customer focus of work unit | Is considered by customers to be an extension of the organization |

***What to Ask About.*** A number of methods have been used to develop competency models.[19] According to Maxine Dalton of the Centre for Creative Leadership, some are not very effective. She indicated that about 70 percent of competency models are just a list of positive attributes obtained in a half-day meeting with senior management.[20]

Generally, more methodologically sound procedures entail the following process:

- Meet with upper management to
  - Determine strategies, goals, specific challenges, or specific focus, and
  - Generate some tentative competencies.
- Identify specific jobs.
- Meet with high performers of those jobs and their supervisors to
  - Determine critical incidents that make "high performers" different from average performers,
  - Focus on the aspects that tie into the strategic direction of the company, and
  - Formulate some tentative competencies.
- Determine the competencies that overlap with upper-management competencies.
- Verify the preceding information with another group of high performers and their supervisors.
- Link this information to job analysis information obtained from the job to articulate specific KSAs that make up the competency.

Regarding the last point, competency models are more general and fit a number of jobs. Linking these competencies to the KSAs of the job will ensure that the competencies are not only valid but also able to stand up in court. This linkage also provides the information needed to develop training. Having the KSAs that make up the competency helps determine what the training should look like.

***Concerns About Competencies.*** When done correctly, a job analysis is scientific and defendable in court. It reflects what is required to do the job, making selection, training, and performance appraisal relevant and valid. To date, there have been no challenges to competency models, but they are not developed with the same rigor as a job analysis.[21] Also, as often occurs with new ideas, organizations develop competency models with little understanding of the process outlined above. Competency models, however, will continue to be developed, particularly for training and development, for the following reasons:

- Training based only on task analysis can become dated quickly as the nature of work undergoes constant dynamic change.

- Hourly paid employees are being expected to participate much more in decision making and ensuring customer satisfaction, rather than simply producing a product.

- Corporate downsizing is forcing a move away from tight job design to more flexible job design.

- Competencies help the HRD department focus its training.

This latter point is particularly important. Competencies are not only related to each managerial level in the organization but are also tied to the strategic direction of the organization. Furthermore, by definition, competencies are what separate high performers from others. With limited resources, decisions related to what needs to be provided in the way of management training is clear.

In very well run organizations the HR department has a Human Resource Information System (HRIS). This system provides information on individual managers in terms of what positions they have held, what training they have received, their performance levels related to the competencies, and, of specific interest to the HRD department, required competency training for managers. This system makes the task of identifying what training needs to be offered much easier. Examination of the HRIS tells the HRD manager how many need training in each of the competencies.

In summary, some concern that competencies are not developed with the rigour of job analysis may be raised, and the lack of specificity may not be able to stand court challenges when they occur. We argue that as with any tool, proper methodology will result in relevant and definable competencies. Organizations that determine they would like to use competencies should not abandon job analysis but should use this methodology to demonstrate the link between the relevant KSAs and key competencies of the job.

## Criteria Development

Criteria are measures of expected performance. The data gathered in the operational analysis describe what the expected performance is for the job. From this, ways to measure both the level of job performance and the employees' KSAs will have to be developed. Development of sound criteria is important, as they will be used not only to measure how employees are doing but also as a measure of training success. So, let's examine this issue of criteria development in more detail. Two critical components of good criteria measures are that they have both reliable and valid.

**Reliability** is the consistency of a measurement. It is often calculated using a correlation coefficient. It can be measured in the following two ways: across similar measures (split half reliability), and across time (test retest reliability).

For the **split half** method, let's assume that 100 multiple-choice questions are used to test students' knowledge of this course. To determine the reliability of the test, the instructor splits the test into two: even-numbered questions and odd-numbered questions. He considers them as separate tests, even though the 100 questions are given at the same time. Adding up the score of the odd-numbered and even-numbered questions provides two scores for each student. Correlating the two scores, the instructor determines how reliable the test is. A high correlation would suggest that the test is highly reliable.

In the **test retest** method, the instructor gives the test today and again in three days. He correlates student scores from the two time periods. Again, a high correlation between the two sets of scores would indicate a reliable test.

Highly reliable criteria measures are important. Consider a criterion for a machinist who has completed training. He must produce a shaft exactly four centimetres thick. A test is constructed requiring the trainee to produce a shaft with the correct specifications. To pass the test, the trainee must produce a shaft whose measurement can be off by no more than 2/1000ths of a centimetre. The evaluator measures the shaft with a micrometer (a measurement instrument able to detect differences in thousandths of centimetres). She finds it 1/1000ths of a centimetre too large. If she measured it tomorrow, she would find the same results. If another instructor measured it using the same procedure, he would find the same results. This criterion is highly reliable. If a ruler is used instead of a micrometer, the results may still be reliable but less so, because the less-accurate ruler makes judgment errors in reading the scale more likely. Developing well-designed instrumentation, therefore, is important to obtaining a reliable measure, whether it is for a machinist or a measure of interpersonal skills.

Although developing a reliable instrument is important, the reliability in the *use* of the instrument is of equal importance. Both the instrument and the procedure used in applying it affect the reliability of the results. Without training, the evaluator in the example above would not know how much to tighten the micrometer around the

**Criteria** standards from which decisions can be made.

**Reliability** the consistency of a measurement.

**Split Half Reliability** a measure of reliability that splits the test/scale in half and correlates the results of one half with the other.

**Test Retest Reliability** a measure of reliability that administers the same test/scale at two different times and correlates the results of the two times.

shaft before obtaining the measurement. If one evaluator tightened it as much as he could and another tightened it just until she felt the first sign of resistance, the difference in results could be more than the 2/1000ths of a centimetre tolerance allowed.

*Validity.* **Validity** is the degree to which a measurement actually measures what you say it is measuring. Compared with reliability, which is the consistency of a measure, validity is more difficult to assess. Consider the question, "Has training resulted in learning?" Learning is a physiological process that takes place in the brain. We are unable to assess this process directly, so we test individuals and, on the basis of their scores, we infer whether learning takes place. It is not a direct measure of the learning process but an inference based on behaviour.

To better understand the problems associated with validity, let's look at what we call the **ultimate criterion**.[22] The ultimate criterion is what we would like to be able to measure if it were possible to do so. It would include the exact indicators of the object being measured. However, we are never able to measure the ultimate criterion, because it is simply a theoretical construct. We must settle for what we are able to measure, which is the **actual criterion**.[23] Examining the relationship between the ultimate criterion and the actual criterion provides us with insight into the problems associated with criteria development. The actual criterion, what we settle for, can be thought of in terms of its relevance, deficiency, and contamination in relation to the ultimate criterion (see Figure 3-4).

*Criterion Relevancy.* **Criterion relevancy** is the portion of the actual criterion that overlaps the ultimate criterion (see Figure 3-4) and represents the validity of the actual criterion. However, given that we can never measure the ultimate criterion, an empirical measure of this validity (a correlation between the ultimate criterion and actual criterion) is not possible. This problem illustrates the need for logical and rational analysis in developing the actual criterion to obtain the best approximation of the ultimate criterion.

Let's look at an example in which training is designed to improve interpersonal relationships. Raters evaluate the learning by rating a trainee's behaviours in a scripted role-play. The degree to which the raters are trained, to which the scales to be used in rating are well developed, and to which examples of acceptable and less-acceptable behaviour are clear to the raters are all factors that contribute to the validity of the criterion (overlap of actual with ultimate). Since these will never match the ultimate criterion perfectly, deficiencies and contamination will always be factors. The more rigorous the development of criterion measures and processes, however, the more the actual criterion will approach the ultimate criterion.

**Validity** the degree to which a measurement actually measures what you say it is measuring.

**Ultimate Criterion** a theoretical construct denoting a true and exact measure of an object; which is impossible to obtain.

**Actual Criterion** a measure that we construct for measuring an object.

**Criterion Relevancy** the portion of the ultimate criterion that we are able to measure with our actual criterion.

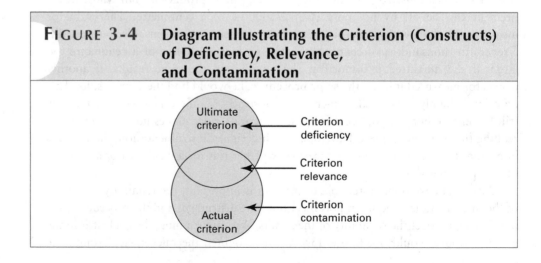

**FIGURE 3-4    Diagram Illustrating the Criterion (Constructs) of Deficiency, Relevance, and Contamination**

*Criterion Deficiency.* **Criterion deficiency** is the part of the ultimate criterion that we miss when we use the actual criterion, or the degree to which we are not measuring important aspects of performance. The factors that make up a trainee's ability to produce parts with a tolerance of a few thousandths of a centimetre are more complex than simply being able to do it under ideal testing conditions. Factors such as noise in the plant, climate in the plant, different types of parts that need to be machined, and supervisor-subordinate relationships contribute to making a machinist successful. Our measure of success (producing one part in a training room) will obviously be deficient when compared with an ultimate measure of a successful machinist, which takes into consideration all the above factors (the ultimate criterion).

*Criterion Contamination.* Just as any measure will miss some important aspects of true success (criterion deficiency), so too will it contain some part that measures aspects not related to the true measure of success (**criterion contamination**). This part of the actual criterion does not overlap with the ultimate criterion.[24]

The two main categories of contamination are error and bias. **Error** is random variation. It is, by definition, not correlated with anything, and therefore, not as great a concern as is bias. Error lowers validity but does not cause misrepresentation of the data unless the error is too large. Then, of course, error can be a problem. Poorly trained evaluators, poorly developed instruments, or other factors could also cause high error content.

When the contamination is **bias** rather than error, it means you are measuring something other than what you want to measure. A large amount of contamination will lead to erroneous conclusions about the object you are measuring. Four sources of such bias are opportunity bias, group characteristic bias, bias in ratings, and knowledge of predictor bias.[25]

When certain individuals have some advantage that provides them with a higher level of performance, irrespective of their own skill level, **opportunity bias** occurs. Suppose, for example, you wanted to know if knowledge gained during training predicted performance on the job. To do this, you would correlate the scores on the training exam with performance one year later. If the correlation is positive and strong, this suggests those scoring highest on the training test also produced the most product and best quality (i.e., a high correlation between success in training and overall performance after training). However, those who scored the highest in training received the newest machines to work on as a reward. The relationship between the two scores was contaminated by the fact that the better trainees received the better machines. These machines may have provided the opportunity for success.

If something about the group creates higher (or lower) performance, irrespective of an individual's capability, that is called **group characteristic bias**. For example, trainees who did well in training are placed with Supervisor A, who was progressive and participative in her approach. Those who did less well in training are placed with a more authoritarian supervisor who would "keep an eye on them." Once again, those who did better in training may produce more and better-quality products as a function of the climate created by Supervisor A, not the training they received.

**Bias in performance ratings** is another possible contaminant. Bias in performance ratings is that portion of the actual criterion not correlated with the ultimate criterion but correlated with variables used by raters in their subjective judgments. Supervisors often use subjective ratings in evaluations. These ratings can be tainted because even in areas where objective data are available, it may not reflect the actual skill level of the worker. Some workers have better territories (sales), better equipment (machinist), or a better environment (clean, well lit). In many cases, the supervisor does not take these differences into account when rating subordinates. One of the most frequent

---

**Criterion Deficiency** that portion of the ultimate criterion that is not measured by the actual criterion.

**Criterion Contamination** the portion of the actual criterion that is not related to the ultimate criterion (true performance).

**Error** the portion of the actual criterion that, although not correlated with the ultimate criterion, is also not correlated with other variables.

**Bias** the portion of the actual criterion that is not correlated with the ultimate criterion but is correlated with other variables.

**Opportunity Bias** the portion of the actual criterion not correlated with the ultimate criterion but correlated with variables beyond the control of the performer.

**Group Characteristic Bias** the portion of the actual criterion not correlated with the ultimate criterion but correlated with factors related to group membership.

**Bias in Performance Ratings** the portion of the actual criterion not correlated with the ultimate criterion but correlated with variables used by raters in their subjective judgments.

**Halo Effect** one dimension of performance influences all other dimensions.

biases in performance ratings is the **halo effect**. It is a powerful force in rating subordinates. It occurs when a supervisor rates a subordinate on all dimensions of performance on the basis of knowledge of only one dimension. For example, Susan is well organized, so she is rated as a great performer. Supervisors need to be trained to avoid these biases.

The final possible contaminant is **knowledge of predictor bias**. The criterion for success in training could be thought of as a predictor of later performance on the job; successful training should contribute to successful performance. But knowing each employee's success level in training could influence the supervisor's ratings at some time in the future.

**Knowledge of Predictor Bias** knowing how successful a person was in an earlier situation (test/training) influences how you rate the success of the person at a later time.

***Development of Criteria.*** It may seem that developing sound criteria is impossible. Not so. As we discussed previously, the operational analysis identifies the level of acceptable performance. From this analysis, criteria can be developed. Once criteria are established, the next step is to carefully develop instruments to measure the criteria. The instruments should leave as little as possible to the judgment of the rater.

Consider the job of internal auditor. One of the tasks identified from the operational analysis is "knowledge of which reference books to use for auditing problems." A part of the knowledge required, then, is to know what is contained in the various reference manuals. Training would require the trainee to learn what was contained in the various reference books. A criterion for success would be demonstrating this knowledge.

If you want to develop a reliable and valid measure of the criterion "understanding what is contained in the reference manuals," an excellent method would be a multiple-choice test of the material. The advantage of a well-designed multiple-choice test is that minimal judgment is necessary. So no matter who scores the test, the outcome will be the same, making it highly reliable. Taking care to choose a cross-section of questions from all the material will provide a level of validity. Given that well-designed multiple-choice tests can accurately measure any type of knowledge,[26] we strongly suggest their use when possible.

Developing sound criteria for skills is more difficult and may not be as reliable. However, instruments to measure skills, if carefully developed, can still meet reliability requirements. Some examples of such measuring instruments are presented in the discussion of evaluation in Chapter 8, under "Fabrics Inc."

In the internal auditor example above, an expected behaviour might be "calm an irate department head." The skill required to accomplish this behaviour could be "active listening." A measure of the criterion would be how a trainee behaves in a role-play situation in which the role-player becomes angry at something the auditor says.

In the case of measuring the criterion "calming an irate department head," it is critical to develop clear rules and examples of what is and is not acceptable. Also, it is important to train raters in the use of the rules and to provide examples. The more familiar the raters are with good, average, and poor responses, the more reliable the measure can be.

**Content Validity** use of an expert to determine that the outcome (e.g., test) is representative of the domain of information/situations it purports to represent.

Validity in such instances is called **content validity,** when an expert examines the criteria on the basis of her knowledge of the TNA.[27] It is important, therefore, to conduct a good TNA, for everything that follows from it (both training content and evaluation instruments) is based on that analysis.

The time and effort spent developing a sound criterion are critical to the training process. Once developed, the criterion is used to determine the

- Expected level of performance (operational analysis),
- Likelihood the incumbent can reach it (person analysis),

- Training needs for those who cannot reach it (a training objective), and

- Measure of training effectiveness (training success).

# PERSON ANALYSIS

The operational analysis determines the tasks (or competencies) and KSAs necessary to reach or exceed expected performance (EP). Conducting a person analysis will identify those incumbents who are not meeting the performance requirements and determine why. Here, each employee is examined to determine who does not have the necessary KSAs to meet performance expectations. Imagine that the expected organizational performance for a department that assembles widgets is five rejects per month. This department's actual organizational performance is 20 rejects per month. This triggers a TNA. The operational analysis identifies the KSAs necessary to build the widgets properly. A person analysis is conducted to determine which, if any, of the employees do not have these KSAs. Those employees will be sent to training. Recall from the training model that the formula for a performance gap is

Expected performance – Actual performance = Performance gap

A performance gap is most often thought of in the reactive sense, the difference between expected performance and actual performance. For example, assume the standard number of snowmobile trailers a "Builder Class 2" is expected to produce is 1.5 per day. For the last three weeks three employees in this class are averaging 0.6 trailers per day. The performance gap is 0.9 trailers per day.

In the proactive analysis, the expected organizational performance is what is needed in the future and actual organizational performance is the likely performance level with current KSAs. Suppose that the trailer manufacturer in the preceding example decides to purchase equipment that will bend the trailer frame to the correct shape, eliminating a number of welds. The engineering studies indicate that this change in production process will increase the "Builder Class 2" output to three trailers per day. At the present KSA level "Builder Class 2" employees are expected to produce 1.5 trailers per day. Here, the performance gap for the person is the "future" required performance level (three trailers per day) less their predicted performance level in the future, given their current level of KSAs. This PG will be 1.5 trailers per day. Will this require training on the new equipment? You do not know until you complete a TNA.

## <u>Where to Collect Data (Actual Performance)</u> Table 3-5 shows sources for person analysis information. We will discuss two of the more commonly used sources, performance appraisal and proficiency tests, in some detail. We will also address the less commonly used attitude survey.

*Performance Appraisal.* Supervisors are the ones who most often complete performance appraisals.[28] If supervisory ratings actually provided an accurate assessment of an employee's deficiencies, other assessment tools would hardly be necessary. But these ratings often suffer from a lack of reliability and validity for a number of reasons:

- Lack of supervisor training on how to use appraisals,

- Lack of opportunity for the supervisor to see substantial amounts of a subordinate's performance,

- Rater errors such as bias and halo and leniency effects, among others, and

- Poorly developed appraisals and appraisal processes.

## TABLE 3-5  Data Sources for Person Analysis

| Sources for Obtaining Data | Training Need Implications | Remarks |
|---|---|---|
| 1. Supervisor Performance Appraisals | Useful if done specifically for TNA. | Supervisor ratings often not just for TNA, and often not done well. |
| 2. Performance Data<br>a. Productivity<br>b. Absenteeism and tardiness<br>c. Accidents<br>d. Grievances<br>e. Waste<br>f. Product quality<br>g. Downtime<br>h. Customer complaints | | Useful, easy to analyze and quantify for the purposes of determining actual performance |
| 3. Observation—Work Sampling | More subjective technique but provides both employee behaviour and results of the behaviour. | This is done effectively in some situations such as customer service where employees know that the telephone calls employees answer from customers can be monitored |
| 4. Interviews/Questionnaires | Individual knows what he (she) needs training on. Also involvement in TNA motivates employees to learn. | Need to be sure employee believes it is in her best interest to be honest, otherwise she may not be forthcoming as you would like |
| 5. Proficiency Tests<br>a. Job knowledge | Can be tailor-made or standardized. | Care in the development of scoring keys is important and difficult to do if not trained in the process |
| b. Skills | Care must be taken so that they measure job related qualities. | |
| c. Achievement | | |
| 6. Attitude Surveys | Useful to determine morale, motivation, and satisfaction of employees. | Important to use well-developed scales |
| 7. Devised Situations | Certain knowledge, skills, and or attitudes are demonstrated in these techniques. | Useful but again care in development of scoring criteria is important |
| a. Role-play<br>b. Case study<br>c. Business games<br>d. In basket | | |

| TABLE 3-5 *(Continued)* | | |
| --- | --- | --- |
| *Sources for Obtaining Data* | *Training Need Implications* | *Remarks* |
| 8. Assessment Centres | Combination of several of the above techniques into an intensive assessment program. | Although expensive, these are very good as they use multiple raters and exercises to to assess employees. Also criteria for performance are well developed |
| 9. Coaching | Similar to interview, one to one. | Must choose coaches carefully and train them if you want them to be effective |
| 10. MBO or Work Planning | Provides actual performance data on a recurring basis related to individuals' goals. | Good process when implemented properly |

If appraisal instruments are developed properly and the process of completing them followed conscientiously, performance appraisals can be a valuable source of employee training needs. The literature, however, suggests this is not often the case.

Supervisor ratings provide less-than-accurate assessments of the incumbent's KSAs for both political and interpersonal reasons.[29] This inaccuracy is less likely to occur if performance appraisal information is gathered specifically for employee development, where the climate in the organization fosters such development.[30]

A number of things can be done to minimize problems with supervisor ratings, such as:

- Have the appraisal system be relevant to the job. Sometimes appraisals are too generic to be appropriate. Also, they need to be acceptable to both supervisor and employee.[31]

- Be sure the supervisor has access to relevant information to make accurate appraisals. As noted earlier, in some cases supervisors are not in contact with subordinates often enough on the job to be aware of their performance.[32]

- Provide incentives for supervisors to complete accurate ratings. One way to do this is to use the performance appraisal for the TNA only. As Murphy and Cleveland note:

  > It is likely that a supervisor experiences little conflict when information from a performance appraisal is being used for providing feedback to employees on their strengths and weaknesses and to recommend employees to training programs.[33]

One way you can obtain better ratings is to provide training on how to complete such appraisals. Training should address how to avoid various types of rater bias such as halo[34] and leniency[35] effects.

Another concern is that for some jobs, such as teaching and sales, supervisors do not often get to see the employee in action. Sometimes the supervisor is unfamiliar with the job details. Perhaps the best way to deal with these concerns is similar to the method suggested for dealing with gathering job analysis data: the more perspectives, the better the picture. For this reason, it is useful to consider additional potential raters of employee performance.

*Self-Ratings.* **Self-ratings** are a possibility for determining employee needs. Much of the research on self-ratings suggests that the individual tends to overrate her capabilities.

**Self-Ratings** performance appraisals completed by the ratee on him-/herself

However, evidence also indicates that the inflated ratings are a function of the rating instruments rather than the individual attempting to sound better.[36] Also, when self-raters understand the performance system, they are more likely to agree with supervisor ratings.[37] These findings suggest that self-ratings are accurate if subordinates are more involved in the development of the appraisal process.

McEnery and McEnery examined self-ratings and supervisory ratings gathered for a needs analysis related to training.[38] They noted that self-ratings were inflated but were also more discriminating in identifying different needs than were supervisory ratings. Furthermore, the results suggested that supervisory assessment of "subordinate needs" more closely resembled the needs of the raters themselves. More recent research noted that self-ratings actually have lower measurement errors than supervisor ratings on some performance dimensions.[39] In short, self-ratings are an important part of any needs assessment.

Generally, the more sources used to gather information, the higher the reliability and validity of the results. This tendency supports use of the **360-degree performance review** by which an employee rates himself on a number of dimensions and also receives ratings on these dimensions from his supervisor, peers, subordinates, and sometimes even customers.[40] This information is fed back to the individual. This broader view takes pressure off the supervisor, especially when others in the loop agree more with the supervisor than with the individual. Such data provide a springboard for dialogue between the supervisor and the subordinate regarding the subordinate's needs.

The advantages of this process are that the various groups see the person under different conditions, maintain different relationships with the individual, and also have different expectations regarding performance. Evidence indicates ratees find feedback from peers and subordinates particularly useful in planning their developmental goals.[41] And, as noted before, the more sources of such information, the better. The disadvantage of the 360-degree performance review is the amount of time it takes and the cost of implementation. If not properly integrated into the company's HR system, it can also lead to negative results.[42] So, in order for it to be effective, a supportive climate is necessary for development in general,[43] and as always, support from top management is helpful.

To summarize, performance assessments designed to focus on development are more likely to provide accurate data than are more generic or all-purpose appraisals. Also, to determine developmental needs, both supervisory ratings and self-ratings should be gathered. Both parties need to be involved in the assessment process. As McEnery and McEnery suggest, the supervisor provides a valuable perspective on the subordinate's needs. The subordinate gains insight into his needs through discussion with the supervisor. This process will also improve communication between the supervisor and the subordinate and will serve to improve the accuracy of the assessment. Three hundred sixty-degree feedback data are also very useful in determining an employee's needs. These data will allow for an examination of the performance from a broader perspective. It is important, however, that if 360-degree feedback is being used, it must be incorporated properly into the organization. Halton Healthcare Services uses 360-degree feedback as a developmental tool for improving their manager's skills (See Training in Action 3-4).

*Proficiency Tests.* Rather than rely on ratings of job performance, an alternative is to test the individual under controlled conditions. Proficiency tests can measure both knowledge (cognitive) and skill (behavioural).

**Cognitive tests** measure levels of knowledge. Plumbers need to understand government regulations for installing water and drainage systems in a house, supervisors need to understand the procedures for assigning overtime, and salespeople need to understand the procedures for accepting returned merchandise. Any job has a certain

**360-Degree Performance Review** performance appraisal that involves supervisor, peer, subordinate, and sometimes customer ratings.

**Cognitive Test** a test to measure knowledge.

## Training in Action 3-4

### 360-Degree Feedback at Halton Healthcare Services

After a merger of two hospitals on the outskirts of Toronto, HR Manager Bonnie Harrow realized there was a major task ahead: integrating the two sets of management groups and helping them to develop.

Ms Harrow decided that the starting point would be a developmentally oriented 360-degree review process of the 110 managers. Rather than trying to develop one, she decided to purchase one from Panoramic Feedback out of Toronto. She also decided to use an outside consultant to manage the process, in order to increase the comfort level of those participating.

The 360-degree process was to focus on how others in the workplace viewed managers. It was not linked to salary raises but was for developmental purposes only. Initially managers were hesitant about the process, never having experienced

so many others rating their performance. However, when the results came back, managers were anxious to see them. The data provided both positive areas and areas of concern for each manager. This balance made it easier for managers to accept the areas of concern. Managers were generally rated as technically competent, with teamwork and communication being the areas needing work.

Since teamwork and communication reflect the core values of the hospital, assistance for improving them is provided at Halton. The 360-degree feedback is ongoing, enabling managers to track improvements and/or lapses after being trained. As well, this ongoing feedback process provides an incentive to use the skills taught.

*Source:* Reprinted with permission of Panoramic Feedback.com.

amount of knowledge attached to it, and a test to measure that knowledge can be developed. Tests of knowledge can be paper-and-pencil. A concern of using such tests is they might reflect the reading level of the participant when reading is not an important skill for the job. If you are concerned about the knowledge level of incumbents and reading is not a required KSA, paper-and-pencil tests would not be appropriate. In such cases these tests could be given orally.

Paper-and-pencil tests offer a number of advantages, as they can be

- Given to large numbers of individuals at once,
- Scored easily, and
- Provide an effective method of determining areas in which there is a lack of knowledge.

The disadvantages include the following:

- Time and effort are required to develop a comprehensive test that is both reliable and valid; and
- If the test format is other than true-false or multiple choice, developing effective scoring keys takes a great deal of time.

**Behavioural tests** measure skills and are important means of determining an employee's training needs. Such tests can incorporate **work samples**, which are simply work situations designed to reflect what actually happens in the workplace. Standardized rating methods are developed so everyone is presented with the same situation and measured according to preset criteria. For example, a welder may be required to measure and cut three pieces of channel iron, then weld them at right angles to make a U; a salesclerk may be required to respond to an irate customer who provides standardized antagonistic responses to the salesclerk's handling of a situation; or a manager may be required to make a presentation to a boss on the advantages of going global. **Assessment centres** are an expansion of the work sample approach. They often involve a number of work samples and other tests along

**Behavioural Test** a test to measure behaviour.

**Work Sample** an actual part of a job is constructed as a test and measures of effectiveness are developed.

Halton Healthcare Servicies (360-degree performance review)
*www.haltonhealthcare.com*

**Assessment Centre** a method of testing that utilizes many types of tests (personality, simulations, cognitive) and multiple raters.

with a number of assessors who evaluate individuals in different situations. Although assessment centres are costly to develop and administer (they often require two to three days off-site), they provide a comprehensive analysis of needs, especially for managerial positions.

*Attitude Measures*. Attitudes are an important part of organizational effectiveness. If, for example, the team approach is an organizational objective, then attitudes toward this approach are important. Some organizations routinely conduct various attitude surveys. In such a situation, a scale related to the attitude toward teamwork could simply be included. If this practice does not exist, it might be useful to consider instituting one. At the very least, organizations could survey trainees before training to determine how they feel about teams and teamwork (if teamwork was a performance gap).

Developing attitude scales requires a great deal of skill; therefore it is much better to use well-developed scales found in the literature. Texts such as *Assessing Organizational Change*[44] and *The Experience of Work*[45] contain a number of attitudinal measures. Another source that publishes such scales is the Institute for Social Research at the University of Michigan.[46]

# GATHERING DATA FOR A TNA: FINAL THOUGHTS

For a conceptual understanding of the types of data required to conduct a TNA, it is useful to divide the TNA input phase into three distinct stages: organization, operation, and person. Practically, however, they are highly interrelated and often conducted at the same time. The sources for each of these analyses as found in Tables 3-1, 3-3, and 3-5, show a great deal of overlap. For example, if you were interviewing incumbents regarding operational analysis, you would at the same time obtain information regarding roadblocks to getting the job done, which is part of the organizational analysis. When you examine the performance data for the person analysis, it is useful to determine any structural reasons for the poor performance, which is part of the organizational analysis. This gathering of multiple levels of information at one time is again illustrated in the Fabrics Inc. example at the end of the chapter.

Once the operational analysis data determine the KSAs for the job, the person analysis will define whether each of the relevant employees possesses these KSAs. For those who do not, the PG between what is required and what the employee has, serves as the impetus for developing necessary training.

For the TNA to be effective, it is important that the employee development be of high concern to both the individual and the organization. This is more likely to occur when an organization does the following:

- Puts procedures in place that allow for developmental appraisals to take place regularly and separately from appraisals used for other personnel decisions,

- Allows the individual to provide input into the process through self-appraisal,

- Places a high value on developing subordinates by rewarding supervisors who spend time doing so, and

- Provides opportunities for employees to receive the training and mentoring necessary for development.

However, although having these procedures in place will serve the organization well, it is still not enough! Numerous stories recount supervisors who simply go through the motions of a performance appraisal and employee development, then get on with the "real work." Such attitudes on the part of supervisors are likely to undermine any employee development system. Subordinates' perceptions of the process must also be positive, and they must believe training will be useful in their development, particularly when self-assessment is being used in the TNA.[47]

Recall from the analysis phase of the training model that the organizational, operational, and person analysis are the inputs. The process is the identification of the gap, which is done by comparing the actual performance with the expected performance. The resulting discrepancies become the output of the TNA.

# OUTPUT OF TNA

As noted in the training model at the start of the chapter, outputs include both training and non-training needs. Training needs are dealt with by designing appropriate training programs, which are discussed in the next chapter. Here, we examine non-training needs.

## NON-TRAINING NEEDS

Non-training needs include those that show no KSA deficiency, as well as those characterized by a KSA deficiency but for which training is not the best solution. First, those that show no KSA deficiency, as depicted in Figure 3-1, near the beginning of this chapter.

### Non-training Needs That Have No KSA Deficiency These performance gaps are not a result of a lack of KSAs, but a result of

- Reward/punishment incongruencies,
- Inadequate or inappropriate feedback, and/or
- Obstacles in the system.

No amount of KSA development will improve performance in situations where these discrepancies exist. The causes of these performance gaps will be uncovered in the organizational and operational analysis.

*Reward/Punishment Incongruencies.* Can working at the expected level of performance be punishing? The answer is yes, it can. Consider Nancy, the employee who always has her work done on time and done well. The other three employees in the department often complete assignments late and their work tends to be done sloppily. Now the supervisor has a very difficult assignment that must be done in record time. Whoever gets the job will need to work late for the next few weeks. Who is assigned to the job? Nancy, of course. Nancy's reward for being a good performer is to get the difficult assignments that require staying late to complete. Soon Nancy catches on and begins acting more like the rest of the employees in her department. When Nancy is not working at the expected level, training her will not help. Her lower performance is not a KSA problem. So, is training going to help Nancy? No. Training her supervisor how to motivate all department employees might be useful. It would also be useful to have systems in place to motivate the supervisor to reward employees appropriately.

*Inadequate Feedback.* Another non-training need comes from employees not receiving appropriate feedback. Numerous examples tell of employees who believe they are good performers, but their supervisors believe otherwise. Supervisors generally dislike providing negative feedback.[48] In fact, some suggest that it is the most disliked of all managerial activities.[49] So they simply do not say anything to the employee. Once again, the problem is not a training issue for the subordinate, but it could be for the supervisor.

*Obstacles in the System.* Conditions in the workplace that obstruct the desired performance level are a third reason for deficiencies in performance. Receiving material too late, using worn-out machinery, and being constantly interrupted are but a few of the possibilities that could hinder performance. Once identified, these roadblocks need to be removed, a complex task that in some cases may require high-level support. Suppose a supervisor has too many reports to file each week and this responsibility takes away from the time needed to help subordinates. However, middle management needs these reports. The only way to reduce the amount of paperwork is to request that middle management reduce the number of reports they receive or find another way to generate them. This problem is not an easy one to solve, but as you can see, providing the supervisor with training related to helping subordinates will not solve the problem.

## Non-training Needs That Have a KSA Deficiency

Non-training needs where a KSA deficiency is present are also presented in Figure 3-1. Note that even when it is a KSA deficiency there are solutions other than training.[50]

**Job Aid** a set of instructions, diagrams, or other form of providing information that is available at the job site to provide guidance to the worker.

*Job Aids.* A **job aid** is a set of instructions, diagrams, or other form of providing information that is available at the job site. Its purpose is to provide guidance to the worker. A job aid is useful if the worker's task is complex, if it requires a number of steps, or if it is dangerous to forget a step. Airline pilots use job aids—a list of things they must do prior to takeoff—so they do not forget any of the steps required. Another example of a job aid would be a diagram. Rather than teaching someone a number of steps in wiring an automobile, a picture depicting where the wires should go should suffice.

*Practice.* For tasks that are important but are performed infrequently, employees can easily forget or become less proficient at them. For this reason, police officers are required to practise on the firing range each month. Schools conduct fire drills as practice for an important event that may never occur. In these cases, providing the practice is meant to prevent a performance gap. If a performance gap in an infrequently performed task is discovered, periodic practice sessions should be considered to ensure the gap does not continue to occur, particularly if its occurrence can have serious consequences.

*Changing the Job Itself.* This approach may seem extreme, but it is sometimes worth considering. A number of years ago, salespeople in automobile dealerships were completely responsible for the job of selling a car, from meeting the customer through to closing the deal. The most difficult part of selling is closing the deal, which requires certain KSAs that are difficult to impart through training. As a result, many car salespeople did not last long in the business. This deficiency led the dealers to change the job. They provided the salesperson with the skills to show the car, discuss various options, and negotiate to a certain extent. Then, when it came to closing the deal, the salesperson could send the customer to the sales manager. Thus, the job was changed so that the salesperson no longer needed to know how to close the deal.

## TRAINING NEEDS

For those performance gaps that result from the employees' lack of KSAs and for which training is a solution, list and describe the KSAs clearly and unambiguously. Use these KSAs to develop training objectives (discussed in detail in the next chapter).

# APPROACHES TO TNA

Now that we have examined the general approach of conducting a TNA, we examine more closely the distinction between proactive and reactive. The reactive approach is identical to what has been presented in the general approach. The proactive approach deserves the more detailed discussion below.

## PROACTIVE TNA

The proactive TNA focuses on future human resource requirements, whereas the reactive TNA focuses on current performance. Jobs are dynamic, always changing over time. Today, however, the changes in some jobs are much more dramatic than in the past. Employees need to be prepared for these changes. Employees may be performing just fine, but the changes coming down the pike will cause performance problems unless appropriate preparations are made. These are the situations in which the proactive TNA is used.

An effective, proactive procedure used for planning key promotions and transfers is succession planning. **Succession planning** is the identification and development of employees, perceived to be of high potential, to fill key positions in the company as they become vacant. The first step in the development of a succession plan is to identify key positions in the organization. These positions, if left vacant for any length of time, would negatively affect organizational functioning. In practice, these positions are often high-level management positions such as vice-president of finance or plant manager, but they could be at any level (e.g., moldmaker if the position is key to the operation and difficult to fill). Once the key positions are identified, employees with the potential to fill these key positions are identified. Then information is provided on employees' readiness to fill the position if it becomes vacant. Employee readiness, of course, is the difference between what is expected in the new job versus what the employee is currently capable of doing. Organizations with this type of system in place have a ready-made TNA.

When preparing employees for changes in their current jobs, it is important that the TNA identify the expected changes in performance. Once the performance expectations are determined, the new KSAs required for that job can then be identified. These future KSAs are compared with the incumbent's current KSAs, and any resulting discrepancies are addressed through training. Consider Heinz in Leamington, Ontario. When they determined that they would be moving to a high-tech ketchup machine, it was necessary to determine what KSAs would be necessary to operate it. Training in these KSAs occurred *before* the new equipment was in place.

<u>Organizational Analysis</u> The proactive approach starts with expected changes and any new objectives. As an analyst, try to determine the best fit between the organization's current internal environment (structures, policies, procedures, etc.) and future expectations and objectives. As an example, questions regarding the formal structure might include the following:

- Are pay practices congruent with the new direction taken by the company? Example: Would a strict hourly pay structure fit if the plan were to treat each department as entrepreneurial?

- Is the emphasis of the new priorities congruent with the performance appraisal system? Example: If the priority is quality, does the performance appraisal have a dimension to measure this?

**Succession Planning** a process of identifying and developing high-potential employees (often executives) for promotion to key positions.

Articles on Succession Planning
*www.chrs.net*

- Is the strategy congruent with the current practices? Example: The new strategy is to move to a more positive union-management relationship. Currently a policy does not allow any union business to be conducted on company time. Should this policy be revisited?

- Are enough employees available to accomplish the objective? Example: The plan is to improve quality to meet ISO 9000 standards, but employees are constantly rushed because of a lack of personnel. Does the company need to consider massive hiring or training of current employees?

Informal procedures might be evaluated with the following questions:

- Are norms in place that would restrict output?

- Will workers believe that changes in performance are required?

- What formal procedures are short-circuited by informal procedures, and what are the implications (perhaps the formal procedure is inappropriate)?

These questions need to be asked at all levels in the organization, but specifically at the departmental level where more meaningful data will be found. Often, those in higher levels of management take a different view of the impact of various policies on behaviour.

## Operational Analysis

**Strategic Job Analysis** job analysis that examines KSAs required for effective performance in a job as it is expected to exist in the future.

Job analysts gather information not only on what tasks are done but also on what tasks will be required in the future. **Strategic job analysis** is defined as the identification of the KSAs required for effective performance in a job as it is expected to exist in the future.[51] Data gathering is identical to that in traditional job analysis, with the addition of a section called "gather information on the future." For this section, it is necessary to look at changes in areas such as societal values, political and legal issues, economics, market, labour, and technology, as well as how those changes would affect the job in question. In this case, input from more than just incumbents and supervisors is necessary. Information from the following people is necessary:[52]

- At least one person involved in corporate strategy and closely tied to the job in question,

- Someone who is aware of how the competition structures the job (technologically and from a human resource standpoint),

- An efficiency expert (internal technology/communication expert),

- Someone who worked his way up through the job in question, and

- A forward-thinking incumbent (one willing to suggest new ideas).

This list is not exhaustive and serves only as a guide. Once these data are gathered, a revision of the tasks and KSAs based on these changes can be determined. The training function then uses this information, coupled with person analysis, to determine future training needs. The previous discussion about what to do if no job incumbents are available is helpful here. In reality, no job incumbents exist if the job will change in substantial ways.

At first this task may seem rather daunting; however, it does not need to be. The first step is to identify the critical jobs. For example, if the primary function of the organization is writing software, the computer programmers' job will be more critical to the effectiveness of the organization than the file clerk's and should be examined first. Likewise, if the organization is making parts for the automotive industry, mold-making might be a critical job.

## Person Analysis

Assessment of the person (for the required KSAs) is identical for the proactive or reactive TNA, so the information presented earlier on person analysis is applicable.

## REACTIVE VERSUS PROACTIVE

From a systems perspective, it makes sense that a proactive approach would be better than a reactive approach. Obviously, anticipating needs is better than waiting until they cause problems. Companies that integrate the training function with strategic objectives are more readily able to respond to the rapidly changing technology and business conditions that are an everyday part of corporate life.[53] However, even when operating proactively, the organization will at times need to react to changes in the environment. Strategic plans are not cast in concrete but must be adapted to current events. Using a combination of proactive and reactive strategies allows an organization to be most effective. It is, in fact, possible that a proactive approach is more important for market leader organizations than for cost leader organizations.[54] Market leaders need to be much more aware of their environment and anticipate how they will respond to that environment; otherwise they will not survive.[55] In reality, however, many organizations operate from a reactive perspective when it comes to training.

# TRAINING IN SMALL BUSINESS

Some suggest the small business is not simply a miniature large organization but a unique entity in itself.[56] So what is true for large organizations, in terms of HR practices, for example, may not be relevant for small ones. This assessment may be true, but many of the HR practices necessary to be effective are similar. In a small business, the HR procedures that management decides to implement are likely more important because errors in judgment that create challenges for large companies (such as the building of the Edsel car by Ford) could destroy a small business. Therefore, the proactive approach to training would seem to be more important for the small business. Furthermore, in smaller organizations it is easier to integrate a proactive approach because fewer employees are involved.

The top management of a small business is usually the owner, who is usually responsible for any training.[57] However, this person likely does not have any HR background and may not understand how a proactive approach to training can be advantageous.[58] In fact, much of the dissatisfaction with training in the small business sector is a function of the reactive approach, which responds to a crisis with a "quick fix." The small business owner/manager needs to realize that sound training practices tied to the strategic plan will pay off in the long run, as Metro Tool and Die discovered in our Focus on Small Business.

Other evidence indicates that more small manufacturing businesses are undertaking TNA. One reason for this is the wish to become ISO certified. David Alcock works for the Canadian Plastics Training Centre (CPTC) in Toronto, which provides training to many of the small mold-making companies in the region. He says that because of the investment required in becoming ISO certified, companies are requesting a TNA to obtain the maximum effect for their training dollars. He noted that in the last few years, more than half of the company's customers, many of which are small businesses, requested a TNA.

The time factor is always a concern for any business but particularly for small business. For small business, the TNA often seems a waste of time. Techniques can speed up the process of working through a TNA, but generally these techniques require a trained analyst in order to be effective.[59] Here are some tips for the small business HR person or manager to consider when faced with conducting a TNA:[60]

- Be clear on what is to be done;
- Examine existing available data;

## Focus on Small Business

### Training: Where Is the Return?

Metro Tool and Die of Mississauga, Ontario, has 42 employees, most of whom have little education or training. Mr. Panteno, the owner, was interested in improving the quality and efficiency of his shop. He contacted Fabian Hogan, a consultant with the Ontario Skills Development Ministry. After an assessment, Mr. Hogan suggested that all employees receive training in basic literacy skills, blueprint reading, and instrumentation die setup. Doing this would entail a considerable expense, but the consultant convinced Mr. Panteno that the investment was, in the long term, a good one. At 3:30 every day training sessions were held on company premises and company time. Was this commitment to training worthwhile? Since completion of the training, rejects dropped from 7500 per million to 325 per million. The company won the prestigious Xerox Quality Award in a worldwide competition. Metro recently provided one of its customers with a $9600 cost savings. In the owner's own words, "Training has paid for itself. There is no tool and die company like us. We are a small company using big-company tactics."

*Source*: Adapted from MacKinnon, D. J. (1992). Training days at Metro Tool, *Toronto Star*, April 22.

- Develop some ideas related to the issue and test them in the data gathering;
- Collapse the steps; and
- Use technology.

The most important thing is to clarify what type of performance gap is being dealt with, and then map out a plan of what to do for the TNA before venturing out to do it. Examine records, minutes, and any other documentation related to the gap. Determine who needs to be talked to and what questions will need to be asked. (A re-examination of Tables 3-1 and 3-2 might be helpful here.) Sometimes it is difficult to help employees understand exactly what is being sought.

Consider Fred, the only salesperson in the organization who consistently gets letters of praise from customers and high repeat business. When Fred is asked what he does that makes him so successful, his response is, "I do not know, I just treat them well." To explore this more, outline a scenario that you think might be correct. Such a scenario might look like this: When a customer comes in, Bill greets them by name, asks about the family, asks them questions about themselves, then asks what he can do for them today, and so forth. Once Fred hears the scenario, he can correct or amend it so the scenario fits what he actually does. You provided Fred with a template from which to provide information to you. Clearly, one way to speed up the process is to collapse the steps. For example, meet with everyone at once and give them a possible solution to the problem. Now ask for candid responses to questions such as, "Is this an adequate description of the problem? Is the proposed solution the best one? What would you do differently?" or "What would prevent the successful implementation of this solution?" Of course, it is necessary to be assured that everyone at the meeting is willing to be open and honest. Finally, the use of e-mail, discussion boards, and so forth, can help to gather information from a number of employees with minimum time spent actually meeting them. Place the problem or issue on a discussion board and ask for comments. Return to it from time to time to review comments and questions and pose new or follow-up questions. E-mail is also a way of soliciting input. Simply get a group on an e-mail list and conduct meetings using the technology.

Problems can arise when you do not do the full TNA, however, leading to less-than-ideal solutions. Still, the shortcut is better than not doing a TNA at all. Often the ramifications of not doing a TNA are time and money wasted on things unrelated to solving the problem. Even for a small business it is important to do something, rather than nothing, even if it is less than ideal.

## ASSISTANCE FOR SMALL BUSINESSES

In Canada, the Federal Business Development Bank (FBDB) assists small businesses in various ways, one of which is providing training seminars on topics important to them. The main problem with these resources is that many small businesses do not take advantage of them. Arnold Gavel, a small-business owner from Winnipeg, was being sued for wrongful dismissal. He was surprised that the terminated employee was able to sue. When asked if he had ever attended the various types of seminars offered by the FBDB, Arnold replied that he had seen advertisements for them but never thought they were of interest. Was one related to training managers how to discipline and discharge? Absolutely.

When the small business does not have time or expertise, government-sponsored consultants can provide support. Furthermore, in most universities, graduate students in psychology or business would welcome the opportunity to become involved. These individuals often operate under the watchful eye of highly trained professors and are willing to do the work at a fraction of the cost a professional would charge, simply for the experience. In fact, if the situation provided research possibilities, the project might be done for free. As well, many business schools have professional training consultants associated with their Continuing Education or Executive Education programs, who also provide seminars and/or consulting. For those who argue that small businesses simply cannot afford the time to do a comprehensive TNA, we argue the opposite; they cannot afford not to. It is better to do something rather than nothing.

## TNA AND DESIGN

We return now to the opening case, Westcan. Remember that Chris was all set to begin developing an "effective meeting" training program. As you read the rest of the case, think about the things you learned about conducting a TNA. Note that the TNA Westcan uses is much simpler and less formal than some we discussed. However, the value of doing the TNA is quite obvious.

The needs assessment shows that training was required at Westcan, but not the training Chris first imagined. Her problem was that she did not have enough information to understand the types of needs the managers had. Without this information, she began to design what she thought would be a good "effective meeting" training session. What would have happened if she had gone ahead with her original plan? After conducting the TNA, she is now in a much better position to design an appropriate training program. The next step is to develop a clear set of training objectives that will drive both the design and evaluation of training. The importance of sound training objectives cannot be overstressed. Chapter 4 provides a step-by-step procedure for developing these objectives and meshing them with training design issues and constraints.

Chris told Karen about the conversation with Irven and what she had put together. Chris said, "What remains is to develop the simulation. Can you help?"

"Sure," said Karen, "but it's too bad you are so far along. I may have been able to help you design the training."

Chris indicated she had not put a great deal of time into designing the training and was open to any suggestions.

Karen suggested that Chris consider doing a needs analysis. "In a way, you completed a partial operational analysis by determining what is required in running an effective meeting. What we do not know is where the managers are deficient; we call that a person analysis. One way to obtain that information is to ask the managers to describe how their meetings currently run and the areas they see as ineffective. Their answers should reflect the areas in which they are deficient. Also, by asking the managers what training they want, we could ensure the training was relevant. Another method would be to sit in and observe how they run their meetings. It would allow us to identify deficiencies they might be unaware of," said Karen. Karen noted that in her brief time at Westcan, it seemed that pre-meeting information was well distributed and understood, agendas were given, and notice of meetings always contained the relevant information.

"You might be right," said Chris. "I simply never thought of asking them." Together they developed a questionnaire asking questions related to effective meetings, such as "What would you like to see contained in a one-day effective meeting workshop?" and "How well do the meetings with your staff stay on track?" They also got permission to sit in on a number of meetings.

The returned surveys and meeting observations indicated most managers understood the rules of effective meetings. All had at one time or another attended a lecture or read material on running an effective meeting. The problem was that they had never been able to turn the knowledge into action. They knew what to do, just not how to do it. They wanted practice, with feedback from a professional. They also wanted the training to be for the exact teams they continually operated in, which required that management and non-management from a team attend the same training and learn the behaviours required for effective meetings together. After going through the TNA with Karen and documenting all the information, Chris said to Karen, "Well, it looks like the training I was going to provide was way off the mark compared with what we now know they need. I owe you a dinner."

## Summary

Training is a reasonable solution when a performance gap is caused by an employee's lack of KSAs. However, most problems identified by managers as requiring training actually do not require training. Most such problems are a function of a poor match between organizational structure (reward/punishment incongruities, inadequate feedback, or obstacles in the system) and performance expectations. A TNA will reveal the location and reason for the problem.

When a KSA deficiency creates a performance gap and training is required, the TNA ensures that the KSA deficiencies are identified. Training that is focused on these KSAs will be relevant and hence more motivating for the trainees. The likelihood is higher that training will be successful when a TNA is conducted because

- The appropriate KSAs required to do the job are identified (operational analysis);
- The KSAs of the employees in that job are determined (person analysis), so only those needing training are trained; and
- Roadblocks to transfer of the training are identified (organizational analysis) and removed.

The TNA consists of organizational, operational, and person analysis. The organizational analysis is designed to assess the capital resources, human resource availability, and the work environment. It is important to understand the amount and type of resources available and what type of environment the affected employees work in. Often, employees are not performing at the expected level for reasons other than a lack of KSAs. The organizational analysis identifies these reasons so they can be rectified. Even where KSAs are the problem, other remedies (job aids, practice, and so forth) can be considered before training.

The operational analysis provides information pertaining to the KSA requirements for the job in question. Observing the job, doing the job, and examining job descriptions and specifications are some of the ways of determining this information. The method most often used, however, is to ask incumbents and supervisors what is required in a systematic way.

The person analysis provides information as to each employee's specific level of competence regarding the KSA requirements. A number of methods can be used to determine competence levels, such as examining performance appraisals, testing, or simply asking employees where they encounter problems. Each of these approaches offers advantages, and the one you choose depends on factors such as time and availability.

There are two types of TNA: proactive and reactive. With proactive TNA, the focus is on planned changes to jobs and performance expectations. Typically these changes evolve from strategic planning but may occur from other processes as well. Because the proactive TNA anticipates future changes, it must also anticipate the KSAs required to meet or exceed performance expectations in the future. As a result, some of the types of information collected are different from that collected for the reactive TNA.

The reactive TNA is far more common and is a response to a current performance gap. Here, the TNA needs to be completed more quickly, because the gap is already affecting productivity. An effective organization uses both proactive and reactive types of TNA.

## Implications for Practice

**1.** Not all performance problems are training issues. Most performance problems turn out to be a function of other factors. Always do an analysis of the problem to determine the exact nature of the problem. Even when it is a training problem, this analysis is important.

**2.** Organizations that are proactive in their assessment of training needs are more likely to survive in today's environment than those that do not.

**3.** Even when KSAs are deficient, do not automatically decide on training. There are other mechanisms for dealing with these deficiencies—such as job aids—that may be less expensive.

**4.** When providing a new direction for the company, always examine the organizational structures and processes currently in place to ensure that they do not impede the change you are trying to implement.

**5.** If you are using a competency-based approach in your organization, spend time determining the required competencies using a systematic job analysis approach; do not just generate a list of things that sound nice to have.

## Key Terms

Actual criterion   *90*

Actual organizational performance (AOP)   *71*

Actual performance (AP)   *72*

Assessment centre   *98*

Behavioural test   *97*

Bias   *91*

Bias in performance ratings   *91*

Capital resources   *77*

Cognitive test   *97*

Competency   *85*

Content validity   *92*

Criteria   *89*

Criterion contamination   *91*

Criterion deficiency   *91*

Criterion relevancy   *90*

Error   *91*

Expected performance (EP)   *72*

Expected organizational performance (EOP)   *71*

Group characteristic bias   *91*

Halo effect   *92*

## Questions for Review

1. What is the purpose of a TNA? Is it always necessary?

2. What is the difference between proactive and reactive TNA? When is proactive better?

3. What are competencies, and why are they popular in training departments? How are competency models related to job analysis?

4. Describe how you would go about analyzing the future training needs of your university.

5. To obtain person analysis data, why not just use the performance appraisal completed by the supervisor? How can you obtain the best information possible if performance appraisal data must be used? How do self-ratings fit into this approach?

## Exercises

1. In a small group, analyze the job of "student." What are the duties and tasks required? From these tasks, list the KSAs that students need. Are any in your group deficient in any of these KSAs? Now identify and list the workshops offered to students to help them be successful. Are these relevant to the KSAs you identified? What additional programs would you recommend be offered?

2. Do the same job analysis for students in another field and compare it with yours. Are the KSAs the same for a student in science and arts? In law or engineering? What, if anything, is different?

3. Talk to someone you know who is currently working and see whether it would be possible to do a TNA on a particular job classification or on his or her job. Even interviewing only a few employees would provide enough information to give you an idea of how to conduct the TNA.

## Web Research

Conduct a search of the Internet to identify a needs analysis model that is different from the one presented in this chapter. Summarize the two models and describe how they differ. Provide a critical analysis of these differences.

## CASE ANALYSIS

Fred recently became a manager at a local hardware store that employs six managers and 55 non-management employees. As new, larger chains such as Home Depot come to the area, the owner is concerned about losing many of his customers because he cannot compete on the basis of price. The management team met and discussed its strategic response. The team determined that the hardware store would focus on particular items and make personalized service the cornerstone of its effort. Fred's responsibility was to train all non-management employees in good customer relations skills; for that he was given a budget of $70 000. Over the past six months, Fred has received a number of training brochures from outside organizations.

One of the brochures boasted, "Three-day workshop, $35 000. We will come in and train all your employees (maximum of 50 per session) so that any customer who comes to your store once will come again."

Another said, "One-day seminar on customer service skills. The best in the country. Only $8000 (maximum participants 70)."

A third said, "Customer satisfaction guaranteed on our customer satisfaction training for sales clerks. Three-day workshop, $25 000. Maximum participants 25 to allow for individual help."

Fred liked the third one because it provided personalized training. He called the company to talk about its offering. The consultant said that by keeping the number small, he would be able to provide actual work simulations for each of the trainees. He also indicated he would tailor the simulations to reflect the hardware store. Fred noted they would need two sessions and asked the consultant if he could take a few more per session to accommodate the 55 employees. The consultant agreed. The training went ahead, and the cost was under budget by $20 000.

### Case Questions

1. Do you agree with Fred's choice? Why?

2. What else might Fred do before choosing a training package? Describe your approach in some detail.

3. If training went ahead as indicated, how successful do you think it would be? Explain your answer using concepts from this chapter.

## The Training Program (Fabrics Inc.)

*[handwritten annotation: – No company direction on H.R. Systems → none in place → no performance appraisal]*

This section is the beginning of a step-by-step process for developing a training program for a small fabrications company. Here, we examine the TNA for the program, and in subsequent chapters we will continue the process through to the evaluation.

Fabrics Inc., once a small organization, recently experienced an incredible growth. What was, only two years ago, a business in which the owner was also the supervisor of 40 employees, is now a firm of more than 200 employees. The fast growth proved good for some, with the opportunity for advancement. The owner called a consultant to help him with a few problems that emerged with the fast growth. "I seem to have trouble keeping my mold-makers and some other key employees," he said. "They are in demand, and although I am competitive regarding money, I think the new supervisors are not treating them well. Also, I received some complaints from customers about the way supervisors talk to them. The supervisors were all promoted from within, without any formal training in supervising employees. They know their stuff regarding the work the employees are doing so they are able to help employees who are having problems, but they seem to get into arguments easily and I hear a lot of yelling going on in the plant. When we were smaller, I looked after the supervisory responsibilities myself and never found a reason to yell at the employees, so I think the supervisors need some training in effective ways to deal with employees. I only have nine supervisors—could you give them some sort of training to be better?"

The consultant responded, "If you want to be sure that we deal with the problem, it would be useful to determine what issues are creating the problems and, from that, recommend a course of action."

"Actually, I talked to a few other vendors and they indicate they have some traditional basic supervisor training packages that would fit our needs and, therefore, they could start right away. I really want this fixed fast," the owner said.

"Well, I can understand that, but you do want to be sure that the training you get is relevant to the problems you experienced; otherwise, it is a waste of money. How about I simply contract to do a training needs analysis and give you a report of the findings? Then, based on this information, you can decide whether any of the other vendors or the training I can provide best fits your needs in terms of relevancy and cost. That way, you are assured that any training you purchase will be relevant," said the consultant.

"How long would that take?" the owner asked.

"It requires that I talk to you in a bit more detail, and

also to those involved, some of the supervisors and sub-ordinates. If they are readily available I would be done this week, with a report going to you early next week," the consultant replied. The owner asked how much it would cost, and after negotiating for 15 minutes, agreed to the project, and they returned to the office to write up the contract for a needs analysis.

The interview with the owner (who was also the manager of all the first-line supervisors) was scheduled first and included an organizational and operational analysis. What follows is an edited version of the questions related to the organizational analysis.

### Direction of the Organization

Q: What is the mission of the company? What are the goals employees should be working for?

A: I do not really have time for that kind of stuff. I have to keep the organization running.

Q: If there is no mission, how do employees understand what the focus of their job should be?

A: They understand that they need to do their jobs.

Q: What about goals or objectives?

A: Again, I do not have the time for that and I have never needed such stuff in the past.

Q: That may be true, but you are much larger now and do need to communicate these things in some fashion. How do employees know what to focus on: quality, quantity, customer service, keeping costs down?

A: All of those things are important, but I get your point. I never actually indicated anything about this to them. I simply took it for granted that they understood it.

Q: What type of management style do you want super-visors to have, and how do you promote that?

A: I assumed that they would supervise like me. I always listened to them when they were workers. I believe in treating everyone with dignity and respect, and expect others to do the same. I do not have any method to transmit that except to follow my style.

### HR Systems

Q: What criteria are used to select, transfer, and pro-mote individuals?

A: I hired a firm to do all the hiring for me when I was expanding. Told them I wanted qualified workers. As for the promotion to supervisor, I picked the best workers.

Q: Best how? What criteria were you using?

A: Well, I picked those who were the hardest workers, the ones who always turned out the best work the fastest, and were always willing to work late to get the job done.

Q: Are there formal appraisal systems? If yes, what is the information used for promotion, bonuses, and so forth?

A: Do not have time for that. I believe that people gener-ally know when they are doing a good job. If they are not, I will not keep them.

### Job Design

Q: How are supervisors' jobs organized? Where do they get their information and where does it go?

A: Supervisors receive the orders for each day at the beginning of the day and then give it out to the rel-evant workers. They then keep track of it to see that it is done on time and out to the customer.

### Reward Systems

Q: What incentives are in place to encourage employees to work toward the success of the organization?

A: Well, I think I pay them well.

Q: Does everyone receive the same amount of pay?

A: At the present time, yes, because they are all rela-tively new supervisors. I do plan to give them raises based on how well they are performing.

Q: But you indicated that you do not really have a method of informing them what you are measuring them on. How are they to know what is important?

A: Well, I will tell them. I guess I need to be consider-ing that issue down the road.

### Performance

Q: How do the supervisors know what their role in the company is?

A: I told them they needed to supervise the employees and what that entailed.

Q: How do they find out how well they are doing in their job? Is there a formal feedback process?

A: I talk to them about how they are doing from time to time, but I get your point and will think about that.

Q: Are there opportunities for help if they are having problems?

A: Take this problem with the yelling and getting employees angry at them. I have talked to them about it and have offered to get them training.

Q: How do they feel about that?

A: Actually they thought it was great. As I said, none of these supervisors have had anything in the way of supervisory training.

### Methods and Practices

Q: What are the policies, procedures, and rules in the organization? In your view, how do they facilitate or inhibit performance?

A: I really do not think there is anything hindering their performance. I am always willing to help, but I also have work to do. That is why I promoted employees to supervisors, so I would not have to deal with that part of the business.

After gathering information on the organization, the consultant gathered operational analysis data from the manager (owner). The consultant used the method pro-vided in Figure 3-2. What follows is a portion of the completed form.

| Job Title: Supervisor | | Specific duty: be sure work is completed and sent to the customer on time |
| --- | --- | --- |
| **TASKS** | **SUBTASKS** | **KSAs** |
| Organize jobs in manner that ensures completion on time | Examine jobs and assess time required | Knowledge of types of jobs we get |
| | | Knowledge of times required for jobs to be completed |
| | Sort and give jobs to appropriate employees | Organization and prioritizing skills |
| | | Knowledge of employees' capabilities |
| Monitor progress of work | Talk to employees about their progress on jobs | Knowledge of proper feedback |
| | | Effective feedback skills |
| | | Helping attitude |
| | Examine specific job products during production to ensure quality | Knowledge of quality standards |
| | | Quality assessment skills |
| Listen effectively | Provide feedback to employees about performance | Knowledge of effective listening skills |
| | | Knowledge of conflict styles |
| | | Conflict resolution skills |
| | | Knowledge of proper feedback |
| | | Effective feedback skills |
| | | Positive attitude for treating employees with respect |

And so forth. . .

Next, the consultant met with the supervisors, first as a single group of nine to do an operational analysis, then individually to discuss individual performance. He chose to use a slightly different approach to the operational analysis because he expected they might have some problems working from the form used with the owner. The following excerpt comes from that interview.

To begin the meeting, the consultant said:

I am here to find out just what your job as supervisor entails. This step is the first in determining what training we can provide to make you more effective in your job. First, we need to know what it is you do on the job. So I am going to let you provide me with a list of the things you do on the job—the tasks. Let me give you an example of what I mean. For the job of a salesperson, I might be told a required task was to "sell printers." This description is too general to be useful, or you might say you must "introduce yourself to a new client," which is too specific. What we need is somewhere in between these two extremes, such as "make oral presentation to a small group of people." Are there any questions? OK, let's begin.

Q: Think of a typical Monday. What's the first thing you do when you arrive at work?

A: Check the answering machine.

Q: That is a little too specific. Why do you check the answering machine?

A: I need to return any important calls from suppliers or customers.

Q: What do these calls deal with?

A: Complaints usually, although some are checking on the status of their job.

Q: Anybody else do anything different from that?

A: No.

Q: What do you do next?

A: Examine the jobs that have come in and prioritize them based on their complexity and due date.

Q: The task, then, is organizing and prioritizing the new jobs you received. What next?

A: Meet with each subordinate, see how they are doing, and distribute the new work.

Q: Tell me what "see how they are doing" means.

A: I make sure they are on schedule with their work. I check their progress on the jobs they are working on.

Q: OK, so check on progress of subordinates is the task. What next?

A: After all the work is distributed I check to see what orders are due to be completed and sent out today.

Q: OK, but I guess that assumes everyone is on schedule. What do you do if someone is behind in their job?

A: Depends how far behind the job is. If it is serious, I may simply take the job away and give it to someone I think can do the job faster.

A: I do not do that. I find out what the problem is and help the person get back on track.

Q: So you spend some time training that person?

A: Well sort of. It is not formal training but I will see why the person is having problems and give some of my "tricks of the trade" to speed things up.

Q: Anybody deal with this issue differently?

A: I do not usually have the time to do any training. I will give it to someone who can do it, or in some cases just do the job myself. Sometimes that is faster. After all, we have all this useless paperwork that we have to do.

Q: I want to come back to the paperwork, but first, are you saying that no standard exists for dealing with employees who are having problems with particular jobs?

A: Sure there is. The boss expects us to train them, but with the pressure for production, we often do not have time to do that.

A: Well, I agree with that. Even though I do stop and spend time helping, I often feel the pressure to rush and probably do not do a good job of it. I do try and tell them what they need to do to improve in the particular area.

*Although the format used in the session starts first thing in the morning and continues through a typical day, clues often emerge as to other tasks that are done. The mentioning of "tell them what they need to do to improve" causes the consultant to focus on that task and what other tasks are related to it, because the owner did indicate providing feedback was an important task.*

Q: OK, let's look at the issue of telling them how to improve. We could think of that as giving feedback to employees. What other tasks require you to discuss things with subordinates?

A: We are supposed to deal with their concerns.

A: Yeah that's right, and also we are supposed to meet one-on-one with them and discuss their performance. Trouble is, these new employees are know-it-alls and not willing to listen.

A: You're right about that. On more than one occasion many of us resort to yelling at these guys to get them to respond.

A: Boy, is that ever true.

Q: What about the paperwork?

A: Well, it is stupid. A clerk could do it, but we are expected to do it. If we do not, then billing and other problems come up, so we have to do it or else.

A: Yeah, it takes away from us being out here where we are needed.

And so forth. . .

Other questions that might be asked:

What is the next thing you would do in the afternoon?

The next?

What is the last thing you do in the day?

That pretty much describes a typical day (Monday in this case). Is there anything you would do at the beginning of the week (Monday) that is not done at other times?

How about at the end of the week? Is there anything you do then that is not done during the rest of the week?

Is there anything that you do only once or twice a week that we missed?

Now think about the beginning of the month. What do you do at the beginning of the month that is not done at other times?

How about the end of the month?

Is there anything that is done only a few times a month that we might have missed?

The beginning of the year?

The end of the year?

Are there any tasks that we may have missed because they occur only once in a while?

*You will note that often it is necessary to redefine the task statements for the incumbent. This art comes with practice. The following list contains of some of the tasks and relevant KSAs obtained from the TNA.*

| TASKS | KSAS |
|---|---|
| Deal with customer complaints | Knowledge of effective listening processes |
| | Knowledge of conflict resolution strategies |
| | Listening skills |
| | Conflict resolution skills |
| Organize and prioritize jobs | Knowledge of types of jobs received |
| | Knowledge of time required for various jobs |
| | Organization and planning skills |

| | |
|---|---|
| Check on progress of subordinates' work and provide feedback on performance | Knowledge of proper feedback processes Communication skills |
| Deal with concerns of employees | Positive attitude toward treating employees with respect Knowledge of effective listening processes Knowledge of communication strategies Positive attitude toward helping employees |

Next, for the person analysis, individual meetings with supervisors were conducted, as well as one with the owner (supervisor of the supervisors). The questions came right from the job analysis and asked about the supervisors' knowledge of the areas identified, as well as the skills needed, and their attitudes toward issues identified as important in their job. The introduction to the interview was:

> From the interviews, I have listed a number of knowledge, skills, and attitudes that are necessary to be an effective supervisor here at Fabrics Inc. I would like to ask you how proficient you believe you are in each of them. By the way, do not feel bad if you have no understanding of many of these concepts; many do not. Remember, the information gathered will be used to determine how to help you be a better supervisor, so candid responses are encouraged. In terms of having knowledge of the following, indicate to me if you have no understanding, a very low level of understanding, some understanding, a fair amount of understanding, or complete understanding.

The results of the TNA identified a number of KSAs (training needs) that were deficient, as well as some non-training needs.

### Addressing Non-training Needs

The following non-training issues need to be addressed to help ensure supervisory training will be transferred to the job:

- Have owner (either with others or on his own) determine the goals and objectives of the company and which aspects of performance should be focused on.

- Set up a formal appraisal system where in one session the owner sits down with each supervisor to discuss performance and set objectives. In another session performance development is discussed.

- Use objectives set for the year and clarify how rewards (bonus, pay raises, and so forth) will be tied to the objectives.

- Set up similar sessions for supervisor and subordinates in terms of developmental performance review (at a minimum). Also, consider incentives based on performance appraisals.

- Hire someone to relieve the supervisors of some of their paperwork so they can spend more time on the floor.

And so forth. . .

### Training Needs

A number of training needs were evident from the needs analysis beyond what was indicated by the owner. Specific to those issues, however, supervisors were particularly candid in indicating they had never been exposed to any type of feedback or communication skills. They had no knowledge or skills in these areas. Attitudes in this area were mixed. Some believed that the best way to provide feedback is to "call it like it is." "Some of these guys are simply not willing to listen, and you need to be tough," was a typical comment from these supervisors. Others believed that treating subordinates the way you would like to be treated goes a long way in gaining their support and willingness to listen.

A partial list of training needs includes lack of knowledge and skill in:

Effective listening

Communication

Conflict resolution

Effective feedback

Employee performance measurement

Employee motivation... and so forth

At this point we will leave "the training program" with the needs identified. The next step is the design phase. We will return to Fabrics Inc. at the end of Chapter 4.

# 4

# TRAINING DESIGN

*If you're not sure where you are going, you're liable to end up someplace else.*
Robert Mager. (1975). *Preparing Instructional Objectives*. Pitman Learning: Belmont California

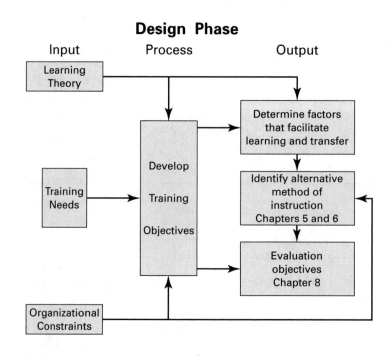

**Design Phase**

# CHAPTER OBJECTIVES

After reading this chapter, you should be able to:

- Identify three constraints an HRD department might face in the design of training, and what might be done to deal with each.

- Describe the purpose of learning objectives, the criteria for evaluating such objectives, and the advantages of developing these objectives.

- List the reasons that learning objectives are a benefit to the trainee, training designer, trainer, and training evaluator.

- Explain, using expectancy theory, how to motivate a trainee to attend training.

- Describe social learning theory and how it helps in the design of training.

- Explain what to include in training to facilitate transfer of training to the workplace.

- Identify the help that supervisors, peers, and trainers can provide back on the job to assist in the transfer of training.

- Explain the relationship between the Gagné-Briggs theory of instruction and social learning theory.

- Describe the advantages a small business has when considering the transfer of training.

# CASE

## *The Real World of Training... What Is Wrong Here?*

### CASE 1

A large government-operated training establishment offered a course in which trainees learned how to operate and repair a large, complex electronic system. The goal of the course was simple: to develop trainees' ability to operate and maintain the electronic system. It was impossible to provide every trainee with his or her own system on which to practise, but the instructor decided to increase the amount of troubleshooting experience by providing classroom exercises on troubleshooting. The instructor posed various problems for the trainees to solve. For a specific problem, such as a burned-out capacitor, he asked the trainees to identify the symptoms that would appear (e.g., the control board would not operate). After the training, the instructor was surprised to learn that many trainees were not doing well on the job. They seemed to be able to operate the equipment, but when it came to troubleshooting, they were not performing well.

### CASE 2

The chief instructor of a 32-week military course examined the grades of the last four groups that completed the course. He noted an unusual trend. Trainees did poorly on the first exam but then did considerably better on the second and third exams. Then the trainees did poorly on the fourth, but improved on the fifth and sixth. This trend continued throughout the 32 weeks, even for the brightest trainees. What was going on here?

The design phase of the training model at the start of the chapter provides an overview of the process we will follow in this chapter. We have the information obtained from the training needs analysis (TNA). This information, along with organizational constraints and learning theories, are the inputs into the design phase. These are used to determine the learning objectives, the process part of the model. There are three outputs. The first is to determine the factors that facilitate learning and transfer of training, which is what this chapter is about. The two other outputs that come from the design phase are

- Identifying the most appropriate method of instruction, given the learning objectives and our understanding of what facilitates learning and transfer, (Chapters 5, 6); and

- Determining the methods of evaluation given the learning objectives (Chapter 8).

As noted, this chapter is about design. Training needs, learning theories, and an understanding of the constraints placed on the HRD department are the inputs into the first step of the design phase—developing objectives. These objectives are then used to drive the design of training (content, methods, materials, etc.). Decisions about training design integrate what we know about *how* people learn (learning theory) with *what* they need to learn. From there, we develop the appropriate training. Of course, the plan must take into consideration any constraints (money, time, facilities, etc.) the organization may have. On the basis of all this information, a particular design is created, from which a training program is developed.

Suppose a HRD department completed a TNA and identified that supervisors need training in effective communication skills. The next decisions to be made include

- What method of training to use,

- How much time to allot for the training,

- How many trainees to train at the same time,

- Whether training is conducted on company time or overtime,

- Whether training is voluntary or mandatory, and

- Whether to use an on-site or off-site location for training.

Deciding these issues is to some extent based on organizational constraints. If the HRD department does not have the resources to develop the program, or supervisors cannot be off the job for more than a half-day, then these factors will help shape what the training will look like and how it will be offered.

# ORGANIZATIONAL CONSTRAINTS

In a perfect world, it would be possible to develop the perfect training program for every training need identified. For supervisors who need effective communication training, you could develop a two-week intensive training package using the most-effective methods with plenty of practice built in. Reality prevails, however, and the constraints around which training must be designed must be considered. Many of these constraints influence the type of training that can be offered. Table 4-1 provides a list of some of these constraints and various ways to approach training design based on these constraints. This list is not exhaustive and serves primarily as an example of the ways in which organizational constraints affect the methods and approaches used to meet the training needs. We discuss two major categories of constraints: organizational/environmental and trainee population. Each affects the issue of whether to train and the type of training that can be offered.

**TABLE 4-1  Some Organizational Constraints and Ways of Dealing with Them**

| Constraint | Suggestion for How to Handle |
|---|---|
| Need high level of simulation[a] because: | |
| Law (fire drills) | Incorporate longer lead times to prepare |
| Task is critical to the job (police firing a gun) | simulations/role-plays. |
| Mistakes are costly (airline pilot) | Purchase simulators. |
| Trainees vary in amount of experience | Consider modularization. |
| Trainees have large differences in ability levels | Use programmed instruction.[b] Have high level of trainer–trainee interaction. |
| Mix of employees and new hires trained on a new procedure | Consider different training programs because of possible negative transfer for employees but not for new hires. |
| Long lag between end of training and use of skill on the job | Distribute practice through the lag. Provide refresher material or models for the employees to follow. |
| Short lead time | Use external consultant or packaged training. |
| Bias against a type of training (e.g., role-play) | Develop proof of effectiveness into the training package. |
| | Use another method. |
| Few trainees available at any one time | Use programmed instruction.[b] |
| Small organization with limited funds | Hire consultant or purchase training. Join consortium. |

[a] This constraint results if you are forced to provide a more costly training program involving simulators or costly practice sessions and so forth.
[b] This method of instruction is discussed in Chapter 6 and provides self-paced learning.

# ORGANIZATIONAL/ENVIRONMENTAL CONSTRAINTS

Budgets are generally limited, so choices must be made about who gets trained and what type of training they receive. One way of making these decisions is to use the strategic direction of the organization to set priorities. The strategic planning process, when completed, provides a rationale for determining who gets how much of what kind of training. Recall the Domtar case presented in Chapter 1. The "Domtar difference" was "tapping the intelligence of the experts, our employees." The tactic for doing this was the introduction of Kaizen. Clearly, then, training dollars will be marked for such training given that it is a primary operating principle. The next decision is to determine whether Domtar plans to use internal resources for the training or hire outside consultants. Here, they decided to hire someone with the expertise and bring them in-house to oversee a major undertaking—the training of all employees in the Kaizen method.

Even if the organization does not have a clear strategic plan in place, having the top managers in HR develop their own mission and goals for the HR area is a good idea. This is accomplished by meeting with executives to discuss priorities. Such meetings help define HR priorities and determine how to put resources in line with the direction of the company. A side benefit is that the process may stimulate top management to engage in strategic planning.

The technological sophistication of the organization affects which type of training can be offered. If, as in the Domtar case, there are a number of locations and each location has access to computer networks or videoconferencing, this will help shape the type of training you can offer.

Decisions about training priorities must also follow the law. The federal government and every provincial and territorial government have health and safety regulations that mandate certain training requirements. A study of Canadian organizations revealed that about 9 percent of their training budgets were used for such mandated training. This was the fifth-largest amount out of 13 categories.[1] This type of training includes telling employees what hazardous waste they are exposed to, educating them about the risks, and providing them with the KSAs to handle the waste in a safe manner. Training in this and other safety areas should have high priority.

The Human Rights Commissions in Canada have in some instances ordered organizations to train employees on issues related to discrimination.[2] Some organizations may have diversity training in order to prevent discrimination from occurring, while others like Ernst and Young provide such training because they see it as producing a corporate advantage.[3] The legal issues and this type of training in general are discussed further in Chapter 9.

A certain portion of training budgets must go toward mandated training, taking money away from other possible training. We are not suggesting that this mandated training is in any way inappropriate or unnecessary, just that its effects on a fixed training budget may mean that other possible training activities are curtailed.

## Budgeting for Training

The budgeting process presented here is from the perspective of the HRD department that charges its customers (departments in the organization) for the services that HRD provides. Charging for services is occurring more frequently in organizations because HRD departments are being asked to justify their existence just like other departments. In fact, in some cases they are expected to market their training outside as well as inside the organization.[4] This budgeting process is, for the most part, similar to that used by an outside consultant bidding on a project. So, when providing estimates, it is necessary to understand that departments are competing for resources and that the estimate must be as accurate as possible. Otherwise the department could lose the training to an outside consultant or have the training put off until later.

Initial estimates can be difficult to determine accurately and various scenarios may need to be provided to the client. Since the estimate is often expected before a needs assessment is completed, several scenarios are helpful to decision-makers. Before a TNA, there is not really a clear idea of what, or how much, training is required. So how to start? Begin with the triggering event, as explained in Chapter 3. Provide budget estimates for different training scenarios or deal with this issue the way it was done in the Fabrics Inc. example presented at the end of Chapter 3. Recall that the consultant offered to do a TNA that would provide a clearer idea of what was required. The consultant offered to bid on the training, based on the TNA, like anyone else. This bid would be more accurate because the issues were identified and the amount of training required was clearer.

Once the length of training is determined, it is necessary to estimate the amount of time it will take to develop the training for delivery. The more accurate this estimate is, the more accurate the costing will be and the more credibility the department will have with clients. The length of the training program is a good guide for estimating the length of time to prepare. The ratio of preparation time to training days varies a great deal, however. It can range from 12:1, if much of the material is in some form of readiness, to 300:1, if it is computer-based training with little already prepared. In many cases, when training is requested, the client wants a proposed training solution and its associated costs quickly. To respond quickly, Brooke Broadbent, a training consultant, developed a method for estimating how long it will take to develop training. This guide is shown in Table 4-2. Depending on a number of factors,

## TABLE 4-2 Guide for Determining Time Required to Prepare Training

| Variables | Level of Effort for Design | | |
|---|---|---|---|
| | Low | Medium | High |
| **Who** | | | |
| 1. The designer's knowledge related to instructional design | Extensive knowledge and skills | Moderate knowledge and skills | Minimal knowledge and skills |
| 2. The designer's knowledge of the training subject matter | Extensive knowledge | Some knowledge | No knowledge |
| 3. The size and complexity of the target training group | Small, homogeneous | Medium, moderately complex | Large, complex |
| 4. The designer's and the client's track record for sticking to plans | Always stick | Sometimes stick | Never stick |
| **What** | | | |
| 5. The number of instruction modules | Few (5 modules) | Several (8 modules) | Many (12 modules) |
| 6. The elements included in the training materials | Participant materials only | An instructor manual and a participant manual | Both an instructor manual, a participant manual, and job aids |
| 7. The client's or organization's expectations regarding packaging | Minimal (produced in house) | Modest (desktop publishing) | Extensive (professionally produced) |
| 8. What is considered final product | Designer completes firstdraft; client rest | Designer completes up to pilot | Designer completes all drafts and finalizes after pilot |
| **How** | | | |
| 9. Data collection | A focus group made up of a few well informed people | A focus group and a few interviews | Several focus groups and several interviews |
| 10. The designer's interaction with the client | Deals directly with top decision maker | Deals with more than one level of decision makers | Deals with a complex labour management committee |
| 11. The client's level of involvement | Approves general direction and final draft | Reviews and approves approves key materials | Reviews and approves all materials |
| 12. The program's degree of interactivity | Minimal | Moderate | Extensive |

### Effort

| | Low | Medium | High |
|---|---|---|---|
| Totals | _____ × 1 = _____ | _____ × 2 = _____ | _____ × 3 = _____ |

Add the weighted totals from the high, medium, and low columns to get an estimate of the number of days it will take to develop 1 day of instructor-led training.

*Source:* Broadbent, B. (1998). The Training Formula. *Training & Development* 52:41–43.

including expertise in developing training, it is possible to make a rough calculation of the length of time it will take to develop the training. First, circle either low, medium, or high for each of the 12 variables related to the questions on who, when, and how. Then count up the number that were circled in each column and put that number at the bottom of the table. Now multiply as instructed in the table and add the totals from the three columns together. That is the approximate number of days it will take. Imagine calculating a bid on a one-day workshop on Effective Communication. Examining Table 4-2, you check "low" for all but the last factor (degree of interactivity). You rate "high" for this item because of the extensive interaction within the training program. Based on the table, the training will require 14 days to prepare $(11 \times 1) + (0 \times 2) + (1 \times 3)$. A simple calculation on overall cost could be done based on this information, but it might seem high to a client who does not know what is involved in the development of training. So it is useful to have some sort of breakdown as depicted in Table 4-3. With such estimates, it is a good idea to build in a contingency fund of about 10 percent, to help cover unforeseen costs. This portion is indicated under miscellaneous. The "rate" should include both the trainer's fee as well as overhead costs. In the example depicted in Table 4-3, if the training were presented only once, the cost of the total training package would be $15 400 plus the cost of the one-day training session. If it is to be offered ten times, then the total cost of the development can be amortized over the ten sessions, making its cost per session or per employee much less.

So far, we have only dealt with the developmental costs associated with training. Direct costs associated with delivering the training (trainer compensation, travel, facilities, food and beverages, and so forth), indirect costs, overhead costs, participant compensation, and evaluation costs must also be included to determine the total cost. For an example of a more inclusive estimate of the total costs associated with delivering a training program, see Table 4-4.

**Trainee Population** What if the TNA identifies two or more subgroups with the same learning objectives but different levels of KSAs? It is difficult to develop a single training program to meet all their needs. Going back to our supervisors who need the communication training, what if the TNA indicated that half of them previously received training in active listening and were reasonably proficient in it? The effective communication model we plan to use in the training of supervisors involves five steps, the first of which is active listening. The training could be designed in a modular manner to provide only the relevant modules to each subgroup. In our

## TABLE 4-3 Proposal for Developing a One-Day Workshop on Effective Communication

| Action | Time | Rate | Total |
|---|---|---|---|
| **Prepare** | | | |
| Interview relevant employees to determine issues and context to develop training | 1 day | $1 000 | $ 1 000 |
| Develop objectives and plan for developing training, including identifying appropriate strategies (methods) to be used in instruction; also development of evaluation objectives | 2.5 days | $1 000 | $ 2 500 |
| Develop training materials based on objectives | 8 days | $1 000 | $ 8 000 |
| Develop visual aids and evaluation material | 2.5 days | $1 000 | $ 2 500 |
| Miscellaneous | | | $ 1 400 |
| TOTAL | | | $15 400 |

## TABLE 4-4 Training Costs for Grievance-Reduction Training

**Developmental Costs**

| | |
|---|---|
| 1. 20 days of director's time at $50 000 per year | $  4 000 |
| 2. 5 days of trainer's time at $30 000 per year | $    600 |
| 3. Materials | $  1 000 |

**Direct Costs**

| | |
|---|---|
| 1. 5 days of trainer's time at $30 000 per year | $    600 |
| 2. Training facility rental for 5 days at $150 per day | $    750 |
| 3. Materials and equipment | $  2 000 |
| 4. Coffee, juice, and muffins | $    600 |

**Indirect Costs**

| | |
|---|---|
| 1. 1 day of trainer preparation at $30 000 per year | $    120 |
| 2. 3 days of administrative preparation at $20 000 per year | $    240 |

**Participant Compensation**

| | |
|---|---|
| 1. 30 supervisors attending 5-day workshop (average $35 000/yr.) | $ 21 000 |

**Evaluation Costs**

| | |
|---|---|
| 1. 6 days of evaluator's time at $30 000 per year | $    720 |
| 2. Materials | $    800 |
| **Total Training Costs** | **$32 430** |

*Note:* Calculations for the personnel costs are based on a 250-day work year.

supervisor example, the first module would be skill building in the active listening process, and only those not already proficient need attend. Then all of the supervisors would receive the effective communication training, with the understanding that all were proficient in the active listening portion of the model.

Sometimes the needs analysis identifies a wide variability in the KSAs of the target population. In this case, the training design could provide individualized instruction, accomplished through computer-based or video instruction, although both take a long time to develop. Another alternative would be to allow for small classes and a high level of interaction between the instructor and each trainee.

In some instances, trainees hold negative feelings about a particular training technique. If this attitude is known during the design stage, a different technique can be considered. Alternatively, the design could build in attitude-change modules at the beginning. We found, for example, that many managers do not want to role-play in training. We often hear arguments such as "This is silly," or "These never work." One way to handle this resistance is simply to call it something different. The term *play*, for some, suggests it is not serious learning. Sometimes when we present the technique, we suggest it is time for some "behavioural practice." This simple change in terms causes the exercise to be received more positively. The point here is that if, through the needs analysis, it is discovered that a particular method of training is disliked because of past experience or word of mouth, the training design should include a way of changing the perception or another method should be used.

Refer back to the design phase of the training model and note that with these two inputs—TNA and organizational constraints—we develop the learning objectives.

# DEVELOPING LEARNING OBJECTIVES

Based on the TNA, a number of KSAs that employees are deficient in are identified. The next step is to be sure training reflects the requirements outlined in the TNA.

**Learning Objectives** describe the KSAs that trainees are expected to acquire throughout the training program and the ways that learning will be demonstrated.

Information on training design *www.reproline.jhu.edu/ english/6read/6training/ Tngworks/designing.htm*

**Desired Outcome** Indicates what the trainee should learn in training.

**Conditions** Indicates under what conditions the desired outcome is expected to occur.

**Standards** Indicates the criteria that signify an acceptable outcome.

Developing learning objectives does this. **Learning objectives** refer to the KSAs that trainees are expected to acquire throughout the training program and the ways that learning will be demonstrated.

The TNA is a critical part of determining the learning objectives for training. To summarize briefly, integrating the organization, job, and person analyses results in the identification of performance deficiencies, their negative effect on organizational outcomes, and the identification of the cause of the deficiencies (i.e., motivation, KSAs, environment). With this information, determine what

- Performance deficiencies can and should be addressed by training, and
- KSAs need to be learned in order to change job behaviour so that the performance deficiencies are reduced or eliminated.

Learning objectives are statements about what is expected to be accomplished. A good objective has three components:[5]

1. **Desired outcome:** What should be expected to occur?
2. **Conditions:** Under what conditions is the outcome expected to occur?
3. **Standards:** What criteria signify that the outcome is acceptable?

It is difficult to write good learning objectives. Care must be taken to ensure that the three components are specified in unambiguous terms and the full range of expectations is addressed.

## WRITING A GOOD LEARNING OBJECTIVE

Learning can be observed only through its influence on behaviour. Thus, when writing a learning objective, think not only about what will be learned but also about how the learning will be demonstrated. Thus, clearly articulated learning objectives are a critical first step in developing an effective training program.

**<u>Desired Outcome: Behaviour</u>** The desired behaviour must be worded clearly and unambiguously. Anyone reading the objective should be able to understand what the learner will be required to demonstrate to indicate she learned the KSA. A learning objective that states "to understand fully how to splice electrical wire" is ambiguous. It fails to specify what the trainee will be able to do. What behaviour will indicate that the trainee "understands fully"? Recall what we said earlier—think not only about what will be learned but also about how the learning will be demonstrated. A clearer learning objective would be "will be able to splice electrical wires of any gauge." This statement indicates what the learner should be able to do at the end of training. Consider another example: "The trainee will demonstrate how to differentiate (by sorting into two piles) between computer chips that are within specification and those that are outside of specification." Here it is clear what is expected but not how the trainee is expected to differentiate between the computer chips.

**<u>Conditions</u>** Explaining the conditions under which the behaviour must occur further clarifies exactly what is required. In the preceding example, it is not clear how the trainee is to determine whether the computer chips are within specifications. Is it a visual examination or is a tester used? Providing the conditions makes the objective even clearer: "Using an ohmmeter and chart, the trainee will be able to differentiate (by sorting into two piles) between computer chips that are within specification and those that are outside of specification."

A description of the conditions (assistance or barriers) under which the desired behaviour will be performed should be provided. For example, the statement "Using an ohmmeter and chart" indicates the help that is provided. If the objective began with the phrase "Without the use of reference material," it is clear that the trainee must discriminate between the chips without using any aids.

Writing in conditions is necessary in some cases and not in others. In the following example, it is critical to know that the pie charts must be developed using a specific software package: "Present the results of an accounting problem in pie chart form, using the Harvard Graphics software." Conditions should be included only if they help clarify what is required.

**Standards** Standards are the criteria for success. Three potential standards are accuracy, quality, and speed. For example, a learning objective might define accuracy as "being able to take a reading off an altimeter with an error of no more than three metres." A quality standard might be indicated by the statement, "is within engineering specifications 99.9 percent of the time." Or, if speed is a critical concern, "will be completed in 15 minutes or less."

Here are a few examples of learning objectives for a telephone repairperson in training. The desired behaviour is **bolded**, the conditions are *italicized* and the standards are <u>underlined</u>.

> *Using a drop wire, bushing and connector, but without the use of a manual,* **the trainee will splice a drop wire** <u>according to the standards set out in the manual</u>.

> *Using a standard climbing harness and spikes,* **the trainee will climb a standard telephone pole** <u>within five minutes,</u> following all safety procedures.

> **The trainee will splice,** <u>according to code,</u> **six sets of wires** <u>in ten minutes</u> *while at the top of a telephone pole wearing all standard safety gear.*

## The Formula for Writing the Objective

The outcome specifies the type of behaviour; the conditions state the where, when, and what tools will be used, and standards describe the criteria for judging the adequacy of the behaviour. Remember that a learning objective should state clearly what must be accomplished by the training. Here are the steps to follow:

- Write out the "desired behaviour." Here, the verb needs to describe clearly what will be done: a "doing" verb, such as *count, place, install, list, solve, replace, sort, recite,* is used to indicate some action. Do not use the word *understand.* Always make sure the verb describes an action.

- Now add the conditions under which the behaviour must be done. This description encompasses the use or non-use of aids. So, "using an ohmmeter," "using reference material provided," "using a standard climbing harness and spikes," "while at the top of a telephone pole," "without the use of a manual," "without the use of a calculator" are all examples of conditions that would be expected in certain situations.

- Finally, it needs to be clear what standards for success will be used. How will the trainee know he successfully completed the training? What level of accuracy is required? Is quality or speed an important part of success? "According to code," "following all safety procedures," "within five minutes," "according to the manual" "within 15 minutes," "with no more than three errors," "obtaining a score of 80 percent" are all possible standards.

Now, to test whether the learning objective is effective, ask someone to read it and explain exactly what she believes a trainee needs to do, under what conditions, and how the trainee will know if she is successful. If the person can articulate these factors, the learning objective is a good one.

For some practice in this process, cover the right column of Table 4-5, and read the objective on the left side of the table. This is a poorly written objective. Improve this objective using the formula. Now check the right side for an example of how the objective can be improved. How did you do? Now do the remaining objectives, as this will provide good practice for writing effective objectives.

**Attitudes** Sometimes attitudes, as well as knowledge and skills, are the focus of training. "How do you write a learning objective for an attitude?" When the goal of training is attitude change, the focus of training activities is to provide the trainees with information that contradicts inappropriate attitudes and supports more appropriate attitudes. Thus, training does not focus on changing attitudes specifically, but rather on providing new knowledge. This new knowledge might consist of alternative views and information related to attitudes. Therefore, learning objectives for attitude change should focus on acquisition of the relevant information rather than on the resulting attitude change.

Consider training that is attempting to improve attitudes toward teamwork in a group of trainees who all scored below the midpoint on a TNA teamwork awareness survey. In this case the learning objective might read as follows: At the end of training,

## TABLE 4-5 Learning Objectives Improved

| Before | After |
|---|---|
| *Upon completion of training the trainee:* | *Upon completion of training the trainee:* |
| Will be able to apply theories of motivation to different situations. | After reading a scenario of an unmotivated student, and without the use of any outside material, identify orally to the class what you would do to motivate the student, and explain which theory you used and why. Trainee must identify at least three motivators and tie to correct theory. Must be correct on four of five scenarios. |
| Will be able to recognize and identify different personalities, and know how to motivate them. | Will be able to watch a fellow trainee role-play a situation and correctly explain in writing what type of personality is being exhibited and what to do to motivate him or her. Trainee must be 100 percent correct on the personality and identify at least two motivators. |
| Will understand what is necessary to have an effective team. | When asked, trainee must provide orally to the trainer five things that are necessary to have an effective team and be 100 percent correct. |
| Will have knowledge of three types of active listening, and be able to use the appropriate one in a particular situation. | Correctly identify in writing three types of active listening that were identified in training, when asked. |
| | In a role-play, respond verbally to an angry comment using one of the appropriate active listening types, then explain to the class which was used and why. |
| Will be able to say no to boss and peers when asked to do extra work. | In a role-play, respond correctly to the situation using one of the ways of saying "no" from the training manual, then explain to the class which you used and why with 100 percent accuracy. |

trainees will demonstrate an increased awareness of the positive aspects of teamwork (new knowledge) as demonstrated by a 50 percent improvement on the team awareness survey.

Recall that the reason we want to affect an attitude is to influence behaviour. In this example, we want trainees to have positive attitudes so that once they are back in the workplace, they will participate fully in team meetings.

# WHY USE LEARNING OBJECTIVES?

Developing good learning objectives takes time, effort, and careful thought. Why bother? Instead, spend that time constructively developing the actual training. In fact, some HRD specialists seriously question the value of specific learning objectives.[6] Some concerns about the use of objectives include the following:

- Waste of valuable time,

- Inhibited flexibility,

- Focus moved from other areas,

- Unrealistic for management training and other soft areas of training, and

- Not practical in today's workplace.

Regarding the first concern, the argument is that resources are often scarce and the time taken to develop the objectives takes away from more important endeavours. On the face of it, this generalization may be true, but the objectives guide the development of training and may even result in less time to develop the training because of the clear guidelines objectives provide. Go back and look at the objectives in Table 4-5. Note in the "After" column how much clearer the focus is regarding "what will be trained" as compared with the "Before" column.

Some suggest that objectives inhibit the trainer's flexibility to respond to trainee needs. The counterargument here is that a comprehensive TNA is designed to determine trainees' needs and the objectives focus specifically on those needs. They do, perhaps, inhibit the trainer's flexibility to go off on tangents that she might like to pursue, but adhering to a focused direction is a positive thing.

Moving the focus from other areas is again the point of having objectives. The idea is to keep the focus on the topics identified in the TNA.

Some suggest that concrete objectives are not possible in management training or areas such as time management or interpersonal skills.[7] Again, we argue that whatever the training, the goal is to achieve certain outcomes, and those outcomes need to be translated into objectives. With time management, for example, you want trainees to gain some cognitive knowledge about strategies for time management. The purpose is for them to develop skills to use in the workplace. Trainees must know the skills before they will transfer them into the workplace. So articulating an objective that states, "At the end of training, trainees will demonstrate time management skills by completing an 'in-basket exercise' within 45 minutes and be able to provide an appropriate time management rationale for each decision," makes perfect sense.

Finally, some say objectives have outlived their usefulness, and they are too specific for today's complex jobs.[8] They say we need to find methods that are better at determining what is required for effective performance. Although this reasoning may be true at a more macro level, the purpose of objectives as a guide for training development is still valid. The complexities of the job will surface during a TNA, but it is still necessary in any job to have competence in specific KSAs to be an effective performer.

The majority of HRD specialists agree that training objectives are important from the following stakeholders' perspectives:

- Trainee,
- Designer of training,
- Trainer, and
- Evaluator of training.

## THE TRAINEE

Trainees benefit from training objectives because the training objectives

- Reduce anxiety related to the unknown,
- Focus attention, and
- Increase the likelihood that the trainees will be successful in training.

High levels of anxiety can negatively affect learning.[9] Not knowing what to expect in a situation creates anxiety. Training objectives provide a clear understanding of what will be taking place over the training period. This reduces the anxiety felt from not knowing what to expect. The objectives also focus attention on relevant topics to be trained, which, recalling social learning theory in Chapter 2, is the important first step to learning. Thus, from a learning theory perspective, it is important to let the trainee know what the performance expectations are and be able to refer to them throughout the training. Also, as was indicated in the chapter on learning, this information will assist the learner both in focusing attention and cognitively organizing the new information.

Finally, learning objectives increase relevant learning[10] and the likelihood that trainees will be successful in training. This makes sense according to goal-setting research,[11] which indicates that when specific and challenging goals are set, the probability is higher that these goals will be achieved than when no goal is set or an instruction to "do the best you can" is given.[12] A goal is what a learning objective is.

## THE TRAINING DESIGNER

The learning objectives guide the designer of the training or the purchaser of a training package. The objectives directly translate the training needs into training outcomes. With clear objectives, training methods and content can be checked against the objectives to ensure that they are consistent. Furthermore, evidence shows that following learning objectives results in the development of better lesson plans.[13]

Suppose the designer is told to "design training to provide salespeople with skills in customer service." Does the designer design a course in interpersonal skills so salespeople learn how to be friendly and upbeat? Does the designer design a course in product knowledge so the salesperson can provide information about the various products and their features to customers? Does the designer design a course in technical expertise so salespeople can assist customers in getting the product to work effectively? Consider the learning objective that reads "After completing training, participants will, using paraphrasing or decoding and feedback (desired outcome), respond to an angry customer (conditions), suggesting two alternative remedies judged by the customer to be appropriate for resolving the problem (standard)." This learning objective provides a clear, unambiguous goal for the designer. The designer can then design a course in active listening (paraphrasing, decoding and feedback), with the focus on dealing with angry customers. Without that guidance, the training may not be designed appropriately.

## THE TRAINER

With clear learning objectives, the trainer can facilitate the learning process more effectively. Clear, specific objectives allow the trainer to more readily determine how well the trainees are progressing and thus make the appropriate adjustments. In addition, the trainer is able to highlight the relationship of particular segments of the training to the objectives. Some trainers may see objectives as infringing on their freedom to train the way they want to. It is probably for those trainers that objectives do the most good, keeping the trainer on the right track.

## TRAINING EVALUATOR

Evaluating training is much easier when objectives are used because these objectives define the behaviours expected at the end of training. With no clear indication of what training is supposed to accomplish, an evaluator has no way to assess whether the training was effective. It is analogous to the army sergeant who tells the private, "Dig a hole here." The private starts to dig and the sergeant walks away. After digging a few minutes, the private begins to worry because he knows he's in trouble. He doesn't know how deep the hole should be, how long, wide, or anything else. When the private sees the platoon leader walk by, he asks him, "How am I doing on this hole, sir?" The platoon leader, of course, says, "How should I know?" When good objectives are developed, the evaluator simply needs to assess whether the stated outcomes and standards are met.

# FACILITATION OF LEARNING: FOCUS ON THE TRAINEE

Recall from Figure 2-1 the factors influencing performance ($P = M \times KSA \times E$). Many issues exist within each of these factors that will make it easier or more difficult for the trainee to achieve the learning objectives.

## INDIVIDUAL DIFFERENCES IN KSAs

The TNA supplies not only information on the need for training but also on the trainees' readiness for such training. Let's take the example of employees recently hired or promoted. They were selected because of their KSAs, but they need some initial training to learn the specifics of this particular job at this company. Perfect selection techniques would ensure that those hired have the requisite KSAs to be successful in training, but few selection techniques are perfect. Even the best selection practices result in a certain number of individuals who are selected but subsequently are not successful. If these false positives—those predicted to be successful but are not—can somehow be identified in the TNA, the design of training might be able to address the issues that would prevent them from being successful.

For example, some who are identified as in need of training may not have the requisite KSAs to make use of the training methods and materials that would be effective for 90 percent of the other potential trainees. Providing a remedial training module for this group prior to the regular training may increase their likelihood of their successfully completing training.

The selection process sets minimum criteria (based on a job analysis) that individuals must meet in order to be selected. Even here, however, if all met those criteria, some individual differences in abilities would be evident. Some will show higher levels of the KSA in question, and others may not possess the minimum skills (e.g., false positive). Needs assessment data that show large differences among the potential trainees indicate that the training design must be adjusted to address the differences, which relates back to organizational constraints (Table 4-1). If the variance in KSAs is large, you need to consider a design that allows those with lower levels of the KSAs to "catch up." Otherwise, the training is demotivating by being too boring for some and too complex for others.

By not accounting for trainee differences, companies can be the losers. Bob Filipczak, Staff Editor for *Training* magazine, reports on an insurance company that hired a number of older workers for its call centre.[14] The company believed that an older voice could relate to older customers better. The older workers were sent through the company computer-training program. Many of them quit before completing training and those who did stay were substandard performers. The company decided it was simply a bad idea to hire older workers, as they were not capable of learning the new technology. After discussions with a consultant, the company decided to try again. This time, the training was extended. Trainers were able to work more closely with the older trainees. As a result, performance on the job after training was on par with the younger employees.

Just how important is the individual difference issue? Consider the following:

- Canada has the highest per capita immigration in the world.

- In 1997, only 18 percent of immigrants to Canada came from Europe and 3 percent from the United States.[15]

- In Canada, aboriginal unemployment is about 30 percent; both provincial and territorial and federal legislation encourages employers to hire them into the workforce.

- New technology and government legislation in Canada is making it easier for people with disabilities to enter the workforce.

These facts suggest a different workforce emerging in Canada. With this increase in diversity will come an increase in individual differences in more than just KSAs. Different cultures and ethnicities mean different ways of viewing the workplace and its norms and values. Care in the needs assessment to understand the special requirements of some individuals will help tremendously in designing a successful training program.

Individual differences in background and traits may result in differences in how people learn.[16] Note in Figure 4-1, that training design A produces better results for those at all levels of the particular trait, suggesting that training design A is the method of choice. In Figure 4-2, however, design A provides positive results for those high in the trait but not for those low in the trait. In contrast, training design B provides positive results for those low in the trait but not those high in the trait. Here, those low in the trait should receive training design B, whereas those high in the trait should receive training design A.

The individual difference issue is complex, and interactions are not easily generalizable to different situations.[17] It usually makes more sense to think of additional rather than different training for employees who differ in KSAs. When clear differences do exist in learning style preferences, two options are available. All trainees can receive the same training, but it needs to be designed to accommodate all trainees'

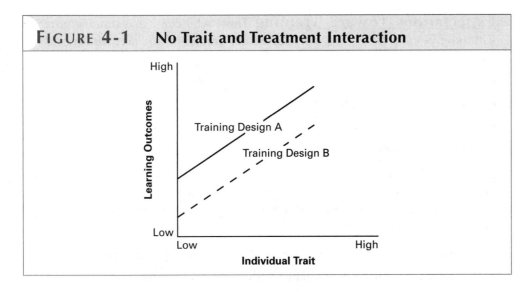

**FIGURE 4-1     No Trait and Treatment Interaction**

learning style preferences. In this situation, each learning topic would incorporate different methods of instruction. This method offers the advantage of covering the same learning point in different ways, thus facilitating the learning process for everyone. Disadvantages include increased time to complete training and higher costs to design than the time and costs involved in simply providing one mode of instruction. However, this expense must be weighed against the cost of putting people who are unable to learn the required KSAs through training.

An alternative is to create separate training programs designed around the learning style preferences of each group. Here, the training is tailored to the preference of the training group, but multiple training programs need to be designed, developed, and implemented. Time for everyone to complete training is minimized, but the cost of development remains high.

## MOTIVATION OF TRAINEE

As the performance formula ($P = M \times KSA \times E$) indicates, if motivation is lacking, no learning is likely to occur. Thus, training should be designed not only to provide KSAs but also to motivate trainees to learn those KSAs and apply them to their jobs.

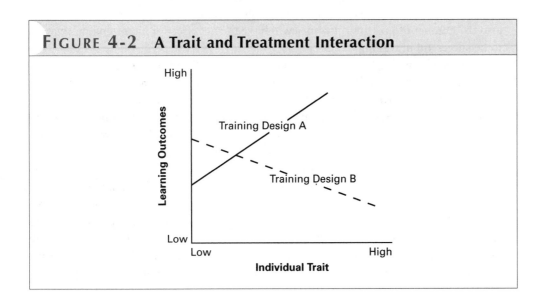

**FIGURE 4-2     A Trait and Treatment Interaction**

### Expectations Toward Training

Those who come to a training program with positive expectations are more successful. Trainees who agree with such statements as:

- "Even if I fail, this training will be a valuable experience."
- "I will get more from this training than most people."
- "I have a better chance of passing this training than most others."
- "If I have trouble during training, I will try harder."

are more likely to meet the objectives than those who do not.[18] Those with positive expectations are more motivated. If such expectations were determined during the needs assessment, an intervention could take place for those with unfavourable expectations. These interventions might include

- Showing the trainee that he or she has the ability to complete training,
- Clarifying the outcomes associated with completed training, and
- Showing that positive outcomes are more likely to occur if training is completed.

Evidence indicates that doing these things increases motivation to learn.[19]

Suppose one of your supervisors has poor relations with her subordinates. Sending her to training to provide her with better interpersonal skills is fruitless unless she sees the value in such training. If, in the TNA, it is determined that she has low expectations and sees no value in the training, she could be asked to attend a pre-training workshop. You design the workshop to show the advantages of a positive relationship between supervisors and subordinates. The workshop also previews the training, showing that participants can learn the skills if they put forth the effort. Attending such a pre-training workshop, the supervisor would more likely be motivated to learn the skills.

### Expectancy Theory Implications

Let's return to the intervention we suggested previously. We have trainees whom we believe have negative expectations regarding training. By intervening before training and providing the trainee with information that shows he or she can succeed in the training, we are influencing Expectancy 1 (E1, the belief that effort will lead to desired performance). By clarifying the positive outcomes of training, we assure the trainee is aware of all the positive outcomes of being successful in training. Finally, by showing that training increases the positive outcomes, we influence Expectancy 2 (E2, the belief that desired performance will lead to desired outcomes). Increasing the expectancies (1 and 2) and also the number of positive outcomes will have the net effect of increasing motivation to be successful in training.

No one consciously goes systematically through all the steps suggested in expectancy theory to make a decision, but unconsciously such a process does occur. Understanding the process helps to focus on an important process that influences motivation. An example will illustrate the point. A TNA in the area Bill supervises found lower than expected productivity. It was also found that Bill's subordinates were afraid to talk to him about problems they experienced doing their work. An interview with Bill revealed that he believed that the best way to supervise was to be tough. "If they are afraid of what I might do to them if they screw up, they will work harder," he said. Bill seemed to like the idea that subordinates were afraid of him. Based on this information, Bill was encouraged to attend a training workshop. The workshop covers active listening, effective feedback, and other skills designed to teach supervisors how to interact better with subordinates, peers, and superiors. Will he be motivated to learn these skills? Let's look inside Bill's head, as represented in Training in Action 4-1.

To answer the question of whether Bill will be motivated to learn, we need to examine the factors in expectancy theory. What does Bill consider to be possible outcomes of successful training, and what is the attractiveness (valence) of each of the outcomes? An examination of Training in Action 4-1 indicates he sees promotion as one outcome, and it is a fairly attractive outcome (7 on a 10-point scale). Less stress is another outcome, but that is not especially attractive (4 on a 10-point scale). Altogether Bill identified six outcomes that might occur if he is successful at training. If he is unsuccessful, he identifies three outcomes, and all three are attractive; the lowest being an 8 on a 10-point scale. Notice that Bill does not perceive that his training can have any impact on the productivity of his workgroup.

Now examine the likelihood that Bill believes that the outcomes he identified will actually occur (E2) if he is successful/unsuccessful in training. If successful in training (improves his interpersonal skills) the likelihood of him being promoted is low (0.2 or a 20 percent probability). The likelihood he will feel less stress is quite high at 0.8. All

# Training in Action 4-1

## *Analysis of Bill's Motivation*

What are the outcomes Bill sees and their attractiveness (valence) to him (on a scale of 1 to 10) if he is successful in training versus if he is unsuccessful?

| Outcomes If Successful | Valence | Outcomes if not Successful | Valence |
|---|---|---|---|
| Promotion | 7 | Does not have to change behaviour | 10 |
| Better at job | 8 | Employees still afraid of him | 8 |
| Less tension between Bill and subordinates | 6 | Not ridiculed by coworkers for being a nice guy | 9 |
| Less feeling of stress | 4 | | |
| Better relationship with union | 7 | | |
| Fewer grievances | 9 | | |

How likely is it that if Bill is successful or unsuccessful, these outcomes will actually occur (Expectancy 2)? These expectancies are based on Bill's belief that they will occur and range from 0.0 (not at all likely to occur) to 1.0 (guaranteed to occur).

| Outcomes If Successful | Exp 2 | Valence | Outcomes if Not Successful | Exp 2 | Valence |
|---|---|---|---|---|---|
| Promotion | .2 | 7 | Does not have to change behaviour | 1.0 | 10 |
| Better at job | .6 | 8 | Employees still afraid of him | 1.0 | 8 |
| Less tension between Bill and subordinates | .7 | 6 | Not ridiculed by coworkers for being a nice guy | 1.0 | 9 |
| Less feeling of stress | .8 | 4 | | | |
| Better relationship with union | .4 | 7 | | | |
| Fewer grievances | .6 | 9 | | | |

Finally, how likely does Bill think it is that he could learn the new skills if he really tried (Expectancy 1)? This likelihood is also expressed as a probability (0 to 1.0).

In this case, Bill believes the skills will be difficult for him to learn, and he also believes that "leopards cannot change their spots." Therefore, Bill believes that if he really tries, there is only a 0.5 chance he will be successful. On the other hand, if he does not try, he definitely (1.0) will not learn or change his behaviour.

others are somewhere in between. If he is unsuccessful (does not learn the new skills), the probability that he will not have to change his behaviour (he will behave in the same manner as before) is 1.0, or absolutely guaranteed. By not being successful in training, no one would expect him to change his behaviour. Similarly, because he has not changed his behaviour, employees will still be afraid of him (probability of 1.0); he will be the same old Bill, and his peers will not ridicule him. As for Bill's belief about his ability to complete training successfully, he believes that if he really tries, it (E1) is 0.5. If he does not try, he believes the likelihood of being unsuccessful is 1.0, or guaranteed to happen. Let's determine whether he is likely to try in training through the following calculations:

## Formula

$$E1[(E2_{outcome1} \times V_{outcome1}) + (E2_{outcome2} \times V_{outcome2}) + \cdots + (E2_{outcome6} \times V_{outcome6})]$$

where V is the valence, or attractiveness of the outcome.

## Will try in training

$$0.5[(0.2 \times 7) + (0.6 \times 8) + (0.7 \times 6) + (0.8 \times 4) + (0.4 \times 7) + (0.6 \times 9)] = 10.9$$

## Will not try in training

$$1.0[(1.0 \times 10) + (1.0 \times 8) + (1.0 \times 9)] = 27.0$$

Based on these calculations, it is clear that Bill will not try in the training. The motivation not to try is substantially higher than the motivation to try. What can be done to influence Bill to learn? A number of approaches can be taken. First, recall from Chapter 2 that expectancies are beliefs about the way things are. They can be influenced in a number of ways (e.g., past experience, communication from others). If Bill heard from other supervisors that the training was not difficult, he might change his belief about how difficult it would be to complete the training successfully (Expectancy 1). If Bill learned supervisors who were successful in training were promoted more often than others, this information would influence Bill's belief that if he completed training he would get promoted (Expectancy 2). If those who go to training generally receive higher pay raises and Bill is not aware of this fact, make him aware of the relationship between training and the raise (Expectancy 2). This relationship will add an additional positive outcome to Bill's calculations, with a high probability of occurring.

It is also possible that Bill did not consider some potentially positive outcomes such as "Improved productivity in his area," "Respect from upper management," "Better relationship with family and friends" (because he will be able to use the skills in his personal life as well), and "Better able to persuade others of his point of view." Once made aware of these outcomes, depending on their attractiveness, the motivation may be altered to try rather than not. For example, "Respect of upper management" might be a given (E2 = 1.0) for all those who successfully complete the training. If this outcome were highly attractive to Bill, it would go a long way toward changing the decision to "try."

Other ways to influence Bill's motivation to learn can focus on enhancing Expectancies 1 and 2 and clarifying the types of outcomes that will result from successful training. As Bill's supervisor, you could:[20]

- Discuss Bill's job performance and job-related goals and reach agreement that he needs to improve some set of KSAs in order to achieve those goals. Providing focus on goals presents specific outcomes the trainee may not have considered.

- Agree that this particular training program is the best alternative available for achieving the desired improvement (Expectancy 1).
- Agree that demonstrated improvement in the identified KSA area will result in desirable outcomes for him (Expectancy 2).

These steps should result in Bill's realizing the advantages of successful training and make his attitude more positive. In the design of training, therefore, it is important to include such pre-training interventions. An integral part of a training design might be working with the supervisors to ensure that the suggested discussions take place. In large organizations with well-organized human resource functions, the trainee-supervisor discussions might take place in the formal performance review. A portion of any thorough review is the developmental aspect, which is useful for the supervisor to use with subordinates in determining training needs and increasing the motivation to learn.

As noted earlier it is not likely anyone consciously goes through the expectancy model process. After all, many of the factors such as Expectancy 1 and 2, and valences are not known. But the model is still useful. It provides evidence of the complexity of the motivational process, and what factors to consider when meeting with a subordinate to discuss their development and motivate them to improve. Discussion regarding what his preferences are (outcomes), his belief in getting them (Expectancy 2), his belief in being able to perform at an expected level (Expectancy 1), and so forth, can assist in helping change the subordinate's perceptions and improve motivation, without resorting to the complex analysis above.

## Implications from Conditioning and Reinforcement (The Environment)

*Classical Conditioning*. Recall from Chapter 2 that classical conditioning takes place without awareness. We salivate when we smell something we like cooking because of prior learning. Emotional responses can be conditioned in a similar manner. A trainee who had bad experiences in school may feel anxious and even sick on entering a training room set up like a school classroom. Trainees who experience high stress in their jobs become conditioned to feel stressed when they arrive at work. Eventually, just seeing the building begins to create the stress because the two events are so often paired. Having someone in such an emotional state does not facilitate effective training, which might be a good reason to hold the training off-site for employees of this type. The point here is that some situations are associated with unpleasant emotional conditioned responses. Pleasant emotional responses are conditioned to other situations. When designing training, in most circumstances, you want to create situations that are pleasant. When the trainees are comfortable both physically and emotionally, they are better able to focus their attention on training. For these reasons, it is useful to know in advance as much about the trainee as possible.

*Operant Conditioning*. Recall from Chapter 2 that if a particular behaviour is immediately followed by a reward, that behaviour is likely to be repeated. Also, punishment that immediately follows a particular behaviour will decrease the likelihood of that behaviour continuing. The following are important points to consider in the design of effective training:

- Know the things your trainees will see as rewarding and those that will be seen as punishing.
- Plan to reward at lower levels for effort and higher levels for success using successive approximations.
- Use both tangible and intangible rewards. Do not underestimate the power of trainees learning how to self-reward. Sometimes trainers will give coupons to trainees as a recognition and reward for participating in training exercises.

These coupons are then redeemed at the end of the day for prizes such as books and/or other mementos related to the training.

- Do not forget that feedback is a reinforcer and key element in learning. Design feedback to show what the trainee did well and what needs improvement.

The following example illustrates these points.

Some trainees are reluctant to role-play. However, role-plays are one of the more effective methods for achieving behaviour change. If role-plays are incorporated into the training design, it is also important to design a procedure for ensuring that positive reinforcement rather than punishment follows. For example, the two trainers might first act out a simple role-play to demonstrate how it is done. After it is over, the trainers thank each other and point out some positive things that each did during the role-play. They might then indicate that they would like someone to volunteer to do another simple role-play, and when the trainee is finished the trainer and the other trainees applaud the efforts. Of course, this approach is successful only if the applause is seen as both real and reinforcing. You might then give the trainee feedback, highlighting the positive things done, and present the trainee with a "participation ticket" that can be exchanged later for a training memento.

**Goal Setting** Goal-setting research consistently demonstrates that specific, challenging goals result in higher motivation levels than do no goals or the goal of "do the best you can."[21] Specific goals direct the individual's energy and attention toward meeting the goal. A number of conditions related to goal setting affect performance:[22]

- Individuals who are given a specific, hard, or challenging goal perform better than those given specific easy goals, "do the best you can" goals, or no goals.

- Goals appear to result in more predictable effects when they are given in specific terms rather than as vague intentions.

- Goals must be matched to the ability of the individual so the person is likely to achieve it. Being able to achieve the goal is important for an individual's self-efficacy, for that is how individuals judge their ability to perform well on the tasks. For this reason, the analyst will need to design intermediate goals that reflect progress.

- Feedback concerning the degree to which the goal is being achieved is necessary for goal setting to have the desired effect.

- For goal setting to be effective, the individual needs to accept the goal that is set.

What is the application of this goal-setting research to training? Well, what better way to capture the interest and attention of trainees than to provide them with individual goals? Learning objectives, discussed earlier, are a form of goal setting and could provide challenging, specific goals. These goals provide the measuring stick against which trainees can evaluate their progress and from which they derive self-satisfaction as they progress.

So far, we have discussed getting and keeping trainees interested in the training. Now let us examine how to facilitate the learning process. In this regard, a number of important factors need to be addressed when you are designing a training program. These factors will be presented under two headings: facilitation of learning and facilitation of transfer. Facilitation of transfer, of course, also helps facilitation of learning.

# FACILITATION OF LEARNING: FOCUS ON TRAINING DESIGN

To develop effective training programs, it is important to understand learning theory, or more specifically, how individuals learn.[23] Among many learning theories, we choose to focus on social learning theory. This theory provides a broad understanding of the process of learning, yet is relatively easy to understand.

# SOCIAL LEARNING THEORY

Let's examine the parts of social learning theory as they relate to training. Specific training events that correspond to the specific learning processes are illustrated in Table 4-6.

Social learning Theory
(A. Bandura)
*http://tip.psychology.org/bandura.html*

### Attention/Expectancy Social learning theory (see Figure 2-5 on page 52) indicates that the trainee's motivation influences where attention is directed. Trainees attend to things in the environment that are most important to them. Thus, the environment and process should be structured so that the most important things are the learning events and materials. Attention distracters need to be removed and creature comforts attended to.

*Eliminating Distractions.* The room should be at a comfortable temperature, not too hot or too cold. People are generally comfortable at a temperature between 21 and 22 degrees Celsius, with a humidity level at about 50 percent. The walls should be a neutral but pleasant colour, free from distracting objects (e.g., posters, notices, and pictures unrelated to training). The room should be soundproof. The room should have no view to the outside, but if the room has windows, close the shades or curtains. Ideally, the learning facility will be away from the workplace so trainees can concentrate on learning rather than be sidetracked by what might be going on at work. If the training must be conducted at the work site, establish a rule that no interruptions are allowed (from bosses, subordinates, or others who "just need a few minutes with..."). This rule also means no phones, beepers, or other communication devices while training is being conducted. Since communicating with the work area can be important, the training facility should have a system for incoming messages that can be delivered to trainees during breaks and after completion of training.

The seating should be such that trainees will not become uncomfortable over a two-hour period, but not become so comfortable that they must fight off sleep. Choose comfortable, flexible, cloth-covered chairs with armrests. Trainees will also need a surface to place their training materials on and for writing.

Schedule training activities with the following rule in mind: "The brain can absorb only as much as the seat can endure." Breaks should be scheduled so that trainees do not have to sit for too long at one time. Provide refreshments if trainees are likely to be hungry at the start of or during training. A growling stomach is a significant force in taking the trainee's mind off the learning. Remember, food is a

## TABLE 4-6 Learning Processes and Corresponding Training Events

| | |
|---|---|
| **Attention/Expectancy** | Learning environment, pre-training communications, statement of objectives and process, highlighting of key learning points |
| **Retention** | |
| Activation of memory | Stimulation of prior related learning |
| Symbolic coding and cognitive organization | Presentation of various encoding schemes and cognitive images, associations with previously learned material, order of presentation during training |
| Symbolic rehearsal and cues for retrieval | Case studies, hypothetical scenarios, aids for transfer of learning (identical elements and principles) |
| **Behavioural Reproduction** | Active and guided practice (role-plays and simulations) |
| **Reinforcement** | Assessment and feedback (positive and/or negative) |

reinforcer, so it is important to create positive associations for training while keeping trainees attentive. If lunch is provided, it should be light and not contain large amounts of carbohydrates, which tend to make people drowsy. Also avoid turkey, because it is sleep inducing. Remember how you feel after a turkey dinner? Obviously, alcohol should be avoided.

***Attracting Attention***. The first steps in motivating the employees and setting their expectations are to notify them that they will be participating in the training, inform them of the nature of the training, and explain its job-related benefits. This communication should, at a minimum, indicate the learning objectives and agenda. State the objectives again at the outset of training, and review them at strategic points throughout. Reiterating the objectives helps to keep the focus of training on the desired outcomes and attention on the important training activities. However, it is not enough for the trainer simply to state the objectives from time to time. The trainees must accept those objectives. To this end, ask trainees to describe how accomplishing the objectives will lead to resolving job-related problems. This exercise not only focuses trainees' attention on the learning objectives but also builds commitment that will facilitate the transfer of new KSAs back to the job.

In addition to accepting the learning objectives, trainees must also feel that the objectives are achievable. This principle comes directly from both expectancy theory and goal setting. Here is how achievable goals can be designed into the training. At the start of training, the overall objective may seem difficult, if not impossible, to achieve. Point out that the overall objective is just the final step in a series of obtainable sub-objectives. Research on goal setting suggests that following these procedures will result in higher levels of trainee learning.[24] Suppose the overall objective of a one-day seminar was "to calm an irate customer, without giving in to his request, using the conflict resolution model." The thought of calming an irate customer using a method (conflict resolution model) that the trainees know nothing about could create a high level of anxiety. An intermediate objective that stated, "Respond to a single angry comment using active listening," does not seem as imposing and would provide a view of one of the steps toward reaching the overall objective.

Finally, the trainees' attention should be focused on the critical aspects of each step in the learning process. Techniques for highlighting the important points should be built into the learning activities so that the appropriate material is processed into permanently stored information.[25] The method of highlighting will vary according to the instructional method (e.g., case study, lecture). In the example of conflict resolution training discussed previously, suppose the training included a videotape of the correct steps. As the video progressed through the various stages of the conflict resolution model, these steps would flash on the bottom of the screen. This model begins with active listening, so as the video shows the person using active listening, "Active Listening" will be flashed on the bottom of the screen. This device would give the trainee an idea of how to perform each step and how the steps integrate into the total model.

## Retention

An individual goes through four stages in the process of retaining something she is taught:

1. Activation of memory,
2. Symbolic coding,
3. Cognitive organization, and
4. Symbolic rehearsal and cues for retrieval.

***Activation of Memory***. Information that is attended to is transformed into symbolically coded (typically as language) long-term memory. From there, it is called up when the appropriate cues are present.[26] Before the symbolic encoding process can begin, relevant prior learning must be stimulated, so connections between the new information and the old can be established. The trainer, through stimulating the recall of the relevant prerequisite learning, or prior supportive learning, can facilitate this process.

Assume the trainer wants the management trainees to learn the "relevant employee characteristics" for matching managerial behaviour to the needs of the subordinate. The trainer can stimulate the recall of the prerequisite learning by asking the trainees to "try to remember the names of the relevant employee characteristics and what things differentiate them from irrelevant characteristics." Recalling supportive, prior learning can be stimulated by asking the trainees to draw on related experience. In this case, the trainer might say, "Think back to employees you've dealt with in the past. How would you determine which of their characteristics would be relevant to the management style you adopt with them?" This activity would recall information supporting the new learning, providing a context for the new learning to occur.

*Symbolic Coding and Cognitive Organization.* Once the appropriate prior learning is recalled, the trainee is ready to encode the new information. The trainer can facilitate the encoding process through the technique of **guided discovery**. Typically, the trainer makes statements and then asks a question. Assume the trainees just watched a video of a supervisor and a subordinate discussing the subordinate's work performance. Following the video the trainer might say, "Remember, certain employee characteristics are more closely related to how the employee approaches the work situation. In the video, how did the employee approach the work situation and what characteristics are most likely to influence this approach?" The statement is intended to stimulate relevant prior learning and the question is designed to allow the trainee to discover the appropriate rule from the cues provided. The question should not contain all the information needed for the answer but should suggest a strategy for discovering the answer. The trainee develops a coding scheme that relates the new learning to prior learning by engaging in guided discovery.

> **Guided Discovery** a process of questioning that allows a trainee to discover rules and relationships which in turn develops a coding scheme for storing the new learning.

Encoding can be enhanced through the use of images, in addition to being coded as verbal propositions. When **symbolic coding** incorporates both verbal propositions and images, retention of the information is improved, probably because image retention and language retention occur through different cognitive channels.[27] The addition of visual material in support of the oral and written language increases the trainees' ability to remember the information.

> **Symbolic Coding** the translation of the information into symbols meaningful to the individual.

**Cognitive organization** is intimately tied to symbolic coding. The way information is organized during training and the prior learning that supports learning the new information shape the way the new information is organized into the cognitive structure. Likewise, the visual images used in training provide suggestions for how information fits together. When you develop the materials and the flow of a training program, you should make sure the new learning builds on relevant older learning. The flow of training should help the learner organize the new material by providing various organizational strategies.

> **Cognitive Organization** the organizing of these symbols into the existing cognitive structure through associations with previously stored information.

*Symbolic Rehearsal and Behavioural Reproduction.* Symbolic rehearsal and behavioural reproduction are types of practice. **Symbolic rehearsal** is practising symbolically, as when the trainer asks the trainees to imagine a hypothetical situation and discuss how they would behave. At this point, the trainees are not actually doing what they have learned to do—they are thinking, talking, or writing about it. Case studies provide one form of symbolic rehearsal. Trainees read about a situation and describe how they would handle the situation.

> **Symbolic Rehearsal** the visualization or imagining of how the knowledge or skill will be used.

**Behavioural reproduction** is the transformation of the learning into actual behaviour. Pilot training provides a clear example of the difference between these two types of practice. Pilots go through an extensive training process in learning how to fly a

> **Behavioural Reproduction** repeated practice.

new aircraft. They read manuals, attend lectures, watch videos, and engage in computer-assisted, self-paced learning modules. Once a sufficient amount of learning occurs, the pilot trainees demonstrate their knowledge of procedures through discussions with the trainer and one another about what they would do in specific situations. They are given written or visual scenarios and asked how they would respond. All of these activities are symbolic rehearsal. When trainees demonstrate sufficient cognitive command of the aircraft's systems, procedures, and capabilities, they are put into flight simulators, which allow them to practise flying the aircraft. After they demonstrate competence flying the aircraft in simulation, they fly the actual aircraft under the supervision of an experienced pilot. The simulation and supervised flights are behavioural reproduction activities.

# FACILITATION OF TRANSFER: FOCUS ON TRAINING DESIGN

**Transfer of Training** how much of what is learned transfers to the job.

**Positive Transfer** Indicates training resulted in a higher level of job performance

**Zero Transfer** Indicates training resulted in no difference in job performance

**Negative Transfer** Indicates training resulted in a lower level of job performance

**Transfer of training** refers to how much of what is learned in training transfers to the job. Training can result in the following transfer outcomes:[28]

- **Positive transfer:** A higher level of job performance,
- **Zero transfer:** No change in job performance, or
- **Negative transfer:** A lower level of job performance.

The goal is to have training result in positive transfer to the job.

Research into factors that influence transfer of training focuses on three areas: conditions of practice, identical elements, and stimulus variability. The research also provides evidence that the nature of feedback, the strategies used for retention, and goal setting can influence how well the training is transferred back to the job.

## CONDITIONS OF PRACTICE

Opportunities for trainees to practise can be designed in a number of ways. Each will facilitate the transfer of training more or less effectively depending on the nature of the KSAs to be learned.

**Spaced Practice** training is done with rest periods specifically designed into the program.

**Massed Practice** training is done all at once with no substantial rest periods.

### Massed Versus Spaced Practice

Which is more effective—having trainees practise continuously for four hours, for one hour on four different days, or for a half-hour on eight different days? Research demonstrated that material learned under the latter approach, **spaced practice**, is generally retained longer than is material learned under the first approach, **massed practice**.[29] This finding is one of the most replicated in psychological research,[30] and additional support was found for simple motor tasks in a recent meta-analytic review of the research.[31] However, spaced practice requires a longer training cycle and management generally resists it. Training departments need to become more creative in developing their training to allow for spaced practice. Instead of the traditional one-day workshop, eight one-hour sessions at the beginning of the workday might be possible. Instead of a five-day workshop, consider once a week for five weeks. This approach also gives trainees time to think about and even practise the knowledge or skill on their own.

Regarding more-complex tasks, the recent meta-analytic review is inconclusive. The value of using spaced practice for complex tasks is not as critical.[32] Tasks that are difficult and complex seem to be performed better when massed practice is provided first, followed by briefer sessions with more frequent rest intervals.[33]

## Whole Versus Part Learning

Which is better, **part learning** or **whole learning**? Whether trainees should learn parts of the task separately or learn the whole task all at once depends on whether the task can be logically divided into parts. In many cases, it is just too difficult to design part-task training.[34] Whole training devices are much easier because the design can be modelled after the real device (e.g., pilot training simulators). James Naylor suggests that even when the task can be divided into parts, the whole method is still preferred when

- The intelligence of the trainee is high,
- The training material is high in task organization but low in complexity, and
- Practice is spaced rather than massed.[35]

**Task organization** relates to the degree to which the tasks are interrelated (highly dependent on each other). For example, in driving a car, the steering, braking, and acceleration are highly interdependent when you are turning a corner (high organization). Starting a standard-shift car, however, requires a number of tasks that are not as highly organized (pushing in the clutch, putting the gear shift in neutral, placing the foot on accelerator, and turning the key to start). **Task complexity** relates to the level of difficulty of performing each task.[36]

In the design of training, it is often not practical to attempt to subdivide the task into meaningful parts. If it is possible to subdivide them, use the whole method if the task organization is high; use the part method if task organization is low.

As an example of high-task organization, imagine training a backhoe operator to dig a hole by first having her practise raising and lowering the boom, then moving the outer arm in and out, and finally moving the bucket. This sequence simply does not make sense. Ultimately the trainee has to learn how to open each of the valves concurrently and sequentially in the digging of a hole. An example of low-task organization is the maintenance of the backhoe. Here a number of tasks (check the teeth on the bucket, check the hydraulic oil, and inspect the boom for cracks) are not highly organized, so each could be taught separately.

A third option, **progressive part training**, can be used when tasks are not as clear in their organization. Consider the training of conflict resolution skills. Imagine that the model to be taught involves four steps (actively listen, indicate respect, be assertive, and provide information). These tasks are interdependent but might also be taught separately. In this case, a combination of the two types may make sense. First, the trainees learn and practise active listening; then active listening and indicating respect; then active listening, indicating respect, and being assertive; and finally, the whole model. In this way, the trainee learns each step but, at the same time, learns the integration of the adjoining step.

Whole, part, and a combination of the two (progressive part) learning are represented in the following diagram:

**Phases**

| Training Type | Phase 1 | Phase 2 | Phase 3 | Phase 4 | Phase 5 |
|---|---|---|---|---|---|
| Whole | A+B+C+D | A+B+C+D | A+B+C+D | A+B+C+D | A+B+C+D |
| Part | A | B | C | D | A+B+C+D |
| Progressive Part | A | A+B | A+B+C | A+B+C+D | A+B+C+D |

As mentioned previously, even though these different ways of training a task are potentially viable, for complex tasks the use of "whole learning" is preferred.

## Overlearning

**Overlearning** is the process of providing trainees with continued practice far beyond the point at which they perform the task successfully.[37] The more a task is overlearned, the greater the retention.[38]

---

**Part Learning** the task to be trained is broken down into parts that are learned separately before being put together and learned.

**Whole Learning** the task to be trained is kept intact and taught as a complete unit from the beginning.

**Task Organization** the degree to which tasks are interrelated.

**Task Complexity** the level of difficulty in performing a task.

**Progressive Part Training** a number of tasks are taught by teaching the first task, then the first and second task, then the first, second, and third task, etc., until the total activity has been taught.

**Overlearning** process of providing trainees with continued practice far beyond the point at which they perform the task successfully.

Overlearning is particularly valuable for tasks that are not used frequently or if the opportunity to practise them is limited. In a study of soldiers assembling and disassembling their weapons, the overlearning group received extra trials equal to the number of trials it took them to learn the task. The other group, called the refresher group, received the same extra number of trials as the overlearning group, but at a later date. The third group received no extra trials. The overlearning and refresher groups both outperformed the third group, but the overlearning group also retained more than the refresher group.[39] Even when material/skills are overlearned, however, it is important to put mechanisms in place to reinforce the use and practice of the learned behaviours on a continual basis, especially when it is a newly learned knowledge or skill.[40]

When trainees practise a skill beyond the ability to simply do the task, the responses become more automatic and eventually do not require thinking. For this reason, overlearning is most valuable for tasks performed in high-intensity or high-stress situations such as emergencies. For example, one trainee recalls that numerous times during initial pilot training in the air force, the instructor would pull back the throttle of the aircraft and yell, "Emergency!" He did it frequently, and soon the trainee discovered that thinking was not even required—the emergency procedures became automatic. This reflexive nature is important in a situation where correct responses are critical.

## MAXIMIZE SIMILARITY

**Identical Elements** having the training experience match the actual job experience as closely as possible.

Maximizing similarity is also known as **identical elements**. The more the elements in the training design are identical to the actual work setting, the more likely it is that transfer will occur.[41] Two areas of similarity are possible: the tasks to be performed, and the environment in which they are to be performed. How to increase similarity? A newscaster reading the news on television must use a teleprompter (the task) while someone is talking to him via an earphone (environment). After the basic skill is learned, to ensure transfer the trainees practise the skill in an environment similar to their actual workplace environment. A machinist is exposed to the background noise of the factory floor and the interruptions common to the job. The secretary is exposed to the office noise as well as the interruptions that occur in the office.

## VARY THE SITUATION

It is much easier to use the concept of identical elements for motor or technical skills, where most of the elements required for learning are in the job situation. When conceptual or administrative skills are required, as in management training, a great deal of variability often characterizes typical situations, and the use of identical elements simply is not effective. In such cases, the general principles approach is more useful.[42]

## GENERAL PRINCIPLES

For much of management training, it is impossible to provide specific training for what to do in every situation that might arise. It is necessary, therefore, to provide a framework or context for what is being taught, which is what strategic knowledge training attempts to do. Training through general principles will better equip trainees to handle novel situations.

Suppose that in teaching managers how to motivate employees, you tell them that praise is a good motivator. A manager goes back to the job and begins praising workers.

Some workers are not motivated and, in some cases, they even become less motivated. The manager is at a loss. If, however, the managers were taught some general principles about motivation, they would understand the responses they get and alter their own behaviour. The principles related to expectancy theory suggest that certain reinforcers are attractive to some and not to others. Furthermore, it indicates that praise must be a function of performance to be motivating. The manager could think through these principles and identify what change was required in order to motivate those not responding to the praise. For some of these employees, the attractive outcome may be for the manager to say nothing and stay away when they perform at an appropriate level.

# OTHER CONSIDERATIONS TO FACILITATE TRANSFER

### Knowledge of Results
Providing feedback (**knowledge of results**) to a trainee is important to learning and the transfer of training back to the job. Feedback performs three functions:[43]

1. It tells trainees whether their responses are correct, allowing for necessary adjustments in their behaviour.

2. It makes the learning more interesting, encouraging trainees to continue.

3. It leads to specific goals for maintaining or improving performance.

**Knowledge of Results** Providing trainees with knowledge of how they are doing.

When providing such feedback, it is better to indicate that the trainee can control the level of performance. Sometimes, inexperienced trainers will try to be supportive by suggesting that the task is difficult, so any problems in mastering it are understandable.[44] This approach reinforces low self-efficacy. Feedback indicating that a trainee can master the task improves a person's self-efficacy, and trainees with high self-efficacy tend to be more motivated and achieve more.[45]

Frequent opportunities to provide feedback should be part of the training design. Providing feedback takes a rather long time if the group is large because the trainer needs to get to all trainees and monitor improvements. To help overcome this problem, other trainees can be used to provide feedback. For example, three-person groups can be used in interpersonal skills training. One of the three acts as an observer of the behaviour and provides feedback to the person who is practising.

### Combination of Relapse Prevention and Goal Setting
A major reason training does not transfer to the job is that, once back on the job, the trainee faces many of the same pressures that caused reduced effectiveness in the first place. Marx[46] instituted a system of **relapse prevention** into his training, modelled after a successful approach to assisting addicts to resist returning to their addictive behaviour.[47] The strategy sensitizes trainees to the fact that relapse is likely, prepares them for it by having them identify high-risk situations that will result in relapse, and helps them develop coping strategies to prevent such a relapse.

**Relapse Prevention** process of helping training transfer to the job by preparing trainees for the problems associated with the transfer.

Goal setting has also been shown to increase the likelihood of transfer.[48] With goal setting, the trainees are required to meet with fellow trainees to discuss the goals and how they will accomplish them. Furthermore, trainees are required to keep a record of their goal accomplishments, return these records to the trainer, and promise to meet at a later date to discuss these accomplishments publicly. This public commitment, through documentation of behaviour, discussions with fellow trainees, and monitoring by trainers, further increases the likelihood of transfer.

Some evidence shows that relapse prevention without goal setting is not always successful,[49] so Marx incorporated both the goal setting and public commitment into his relapse prevention training.[50] This revised relapse prevention training includes the seven steps presented in Table 4-7.

## TABLE 4-7  Seven-Step Relapse-Prevention Training

| Step | Purpose |
|---|---|
| 1. Choose a skill to retain | Helps manager to identify and quantify the skill chosen. Goal setting and monitoring of the skill require clear definitions of the skills, so this is an important step and often requires help from the trainer. "Be nice to my employees" is not clear enough and needs to be revised to something more concrete such as "Provide praise to employees when they meet their quota." |
| 2. Set goals | Once a skill has been defined and quantified, then appropriate definitions of what a slip (warning that goal is in jeopardy) and relapse (more serious disengagement from goal) are. From this, goals are set as to what is desired. For example, the goal might be to praise at least five employees a minimum of once a day when they meet their quotas. Then define what a slip is: "Two consecutive days where five employees are not praised"; and what a relapse is: "A week where targeted behaviour is not met." |
| 3. Commit to retain the skill | Need to think about the reasons for maintaining the skill. Trainees write out advantages of maintaining the skills. |
| 4. Learn coping (relapse prevention) strategies | These strategies help increase awareness of potential trouble spots, how to respond emotionally and behaviourally, where to get help, and so forth. |
| 5. Identify likely circumstances for first relapse | Here the trainees are asked to think of a situation that would most likely cause them to slip back to old behaviour. Prepares them for when it really happens and provides a nice transition to the next step, which is practice. |
| 6. Practise coping (relapse prevention) strategies | With an understanding of what will cause a slip, trainees work in small groups practising (using role-plays and so forth) how to maintain the skill in such situations. |
| 7. Learn to monitor target skill | Develop feedback mechanisms to help you monitor the frequency of using the specified skill. Use of whiteboard in office or notepad where you can check off each time you use the skill. |

Source: Adapted from Marx, R. D. (1982). Relapse prevention for managerial training: A model for maintenance of behavior change. *Academy of Management Review* 7:433–41.

This combination of relapse prevention and goal setting is a powerful tool for encouraging transfer. The relapse part uses both cognitive and behavioural components to facilitate long-term maintenance of the newly learned behaviours.[51] Trainees leave the training expecting that relapse is a strong possibility, but possessing a repertoire of coping responses to deal with it. The addition of the goal setting and public commitment further provides an incentive for transfer. Recent research indicates this method is particularly effective where the climate for the transfer is not supportive.[52]

# FACILITATION OF TRANSFER: FOCUS ON ORGANIZATIONAL INTERVENTION

In Chapter 3, we noted that once a performance gap is identified, the next step is to determine how much of the gap is a function of inadequate KSAs, and how much from other factors. Remember what Nancy Gordon from Ameritech said: Many of these deficiencies are a function of organizational forces and not a lack of KSAs. Just as these forces can interfere with effective performance, they can also interfere with new learning and inhibit transfer. To increase the likelihood of transfer, therefore, it is useful to harness as much help as possible back on the job.

## SUPERVISOR SUPPORT

Supervisor support is one of the key determining factors for the transfer of training.[53] Supervisors need to understand the behaviours being trained and provide support for trainees who use these new behaviours back on the job. In addition, research indicates that transfer is more likely when supervisors provide trainees with desired outcomes upon successful completion of training.[54] These actions on the part of supervisors will go a long way toward facilitating transfer.

Supervisors can affect their employees' learning and transfer of training in other ways as well. If employees who are motivated to improve (involved in their own development) receive support from their supervisors for such developmental activity, this support enhances their motivation.[55] Also, motivation to learn can be enhanced when employees understand realistic information regarding the benefits of their development activities.[56] Two other factors that affect motivation to learn are the employee's perception of training relevance and reduction of negative side effects (like work that piles up) of attending training.[57] These two factors can also be controlled, to a great extent, by the supervisor.

## PEER SUPPORT

Research indicates peer support can also have a positive impact on transfer of training.[58] If the trainee is the only one from a department who receives training, peers back on the job may not understand how to provide social support. In some climates, this situation could result in pressure from more experienced peers to "forget all that stuff." With the right climate, however, peers can provide the proper support to use the training. What is the right climate? Learning must be considered an integral aspect of the organization's ongoing operation, becoming part of the employees' and managers' responsibilities. If everyone is involved in the learning process, it continues beyond the classroom. Most important, all employees must understand and support overall organizational objectives. By involving the entire workgroup in training, the resulting peer pressure will support company goals and objectives. With this type of climate, it is possible to use peer support in a more-formalized manner. Peers could be considered potential coaches. Although it is the supervisor who is generally thought of as a coach to help recently trained employees transfer their skills to the workplace, experienced peers can also take on this role.[59] The peers would receive training as coaches and be provided with specific checklists to evaluate trainees periodically on their performance. In addition, more experienced peers can serve as mentors, willing to answer questions and provide advice, guidance, and support to remedy the difficulties trainees may encounter in applying the new skills to the work situation.

We discuss strategies for dealing with different climates in a later section. For now, it is sufficient to note that it is the training department's responsibility to inform upper management of the advantages of creating such a climate if the goal is to encourage transfer of training.

## TRAINER SUPPORT

Conventional wisdom is that the trainer's job is done when training is over. More recent research, however, demonstrates the value of continued trainer involvement in the transfer of training. Trainees who commit to meet the trainer and other trainees at some later date to discuss transfer of training use the training more effectively.[60] Thus, value derives from the continued involvement of the trainer, who can be a useful resource in helping trainees work through any problems encountered in the workplace.

In this regard, one idea is to have trainers monitor trainees at some point after training to assess how they are doing and provide feedback.[61] The trainer sits in and observes the trainee in a situation where she is required to use the trained behaviour. To be effective, the **sit-in** must be

**Sit-In** a process to assist in transfer of training that involves the trainer observing job behaviours and providing feedback.

- Voluntary on the part of the trainee,
- Confidential between the trainer and trainee, and
- Used only for developmental purposes, not administrative.

During the sit-in, the trainer must not interrupt the interaction between the trainee and others and provide feedback only after the session is over. After all, "Who is better to be coaching the trainee on behaviours that were learned in training than the trainer?"[62]

Using the trainer in a follow-up to facilitate transfer of training might spread the trainers rather thin. However, it is important to consider the investment already made in training. If transfer does not occur, the investment is lost.

## REWARD SYSTEMS

As noted earlier, valued outcomes contingent upon successful training enhance training transfer.[63] Operant conditioning is a powerful regulator of behaviour. Employees are quite adept at determining which behaviours can get them in trouble, bring them rewards, or result in their being left alone. If trained behaviours are not reinforced, then the likelihood is small that such behaviours will be exhibited. Part of the trainer's responsibility is to work with the supervisor and other parts of the organization to align reward systems to support the behaviours learned in training.

## CLIMATE AND CULTURE

In a systems approach to training, as many forces as possible in the organization need to be focused on reinforcing the learned behaviours in order to ensure transfer. Although supervisors, peers, and reward systems all influence an organization's climate and culture, these factors need to be discussed in their own right.

## Climate

**Climate** Climate can influence the transfer of training.[64] Climate is generally conceptualized as the perception of salient characteristics of the organization.[65] Such salient characteristics as company policies, reward systems, and management behaviours are important in determining the organizational climate. Supervisor support and peer support are part of the total climate that will reinforce the use of the trained skills, but they alone do not make up an organization's climate. Other climate factors such as company policies and the attitudes reflected by upper management regarding training, if positive, will also support the transfer of training. Consider how trainees perceive training. If they believe adequate resources (time and money) went into the development of training, trainees are more motivated to attend and learn. The message here is that the company cares enough about this training to devote valued resources. If these characteristics do not describe the climate, it may be better to not offer training at all.[66] Cultivating such a supportive climate toward training is important and does facilitate transfer.[67]

Climate is related to and in many ways reflects the culture of an organization. When asked, "What is useful in promoting transfer of training?" HR specialists and supervisors responded that it is critical to have a culture that supports training.[68]

**Climate** the perception of salient characteristics of the organization such as company policies, reward systems, and behaviours of management.

# Training in Action 4-2

## *Helping to Ensure Transfer*

Dr. Richard Camp is a consultant to a number of organizations in Canada, the United States, and abroad. A few years back, an executive search firm hired him to train their employees on effective interviewing techniques, a key part of their job. Dr. Camp, in a meeting with their management, discussed the importance of approaching the training as an intervention and the need to consider a number of organizational factors to ensure the training transferred to the job. The client was spending a great deal of money on the training and was willing to do what was necessary to ensure transfer, which would be especially difficult because the international company is highly decentralized.

After a number of meetings with management, Dr. Camp designed a three-day workshop to provide the requested interview skills. The president and all of top management were the first to go through the training. This training not only provided them with the necessary skills but also garnered their support for the process throughout the organization. Dr. Camp then began training all of the other employees. To indicate the importance of the training to the trainees, at the beginning of the training he showed a video of the company president. In the video, the president indicated the importance of the training and how it would make them a more effective organization. Furthermore, a senior manager was also attending each training session and verbalized support for the training. This senior manager was also able to provide real-life examples of employees using old versus newly trained skills, as well as answer questions that arose about using the training back on the job. This reinforcement put the training in a real organizational context for the trainees.

In each local area, trainees identified as "stars" (those effectively using the process) were used as resource persons to facilitate transfer. After training, coaches were assigned to employees. Remember that everyone received the training, so experienced coaches were available. Dr. Camp developed a one-day workshop of refresher training and went to local offices to provide it. At the end of this training, Dr. Camp encouraged trainees to send him copies of the "outcome of an interview process" so he could provide them with feedback to again facilitate effective transfer to the job.

Dr. Camp then suggested the company develop a task force to examine how effective the transfer of training was and consider other steps that could be taken to ensure that trainees were transferring the new skills to the job. A representative of the task force began meeting with employees (while they were at different training sessions) to explore ways of facilitating the transfer. One of the ideas to come from these meetings was that each trainee team up with another who was at the training session. When they got back to their respective offices throughout the world, they would stay in contact, providing support, feedback, and ideas for dealing with obstacles to using the trained skills.

How successful was the training? Management determined some bottom-line results that suggest the training helped them be more profitable. Does everyone use the skills as effectively as they could? No, but the organization continues to work on ideas to encourage the transfer. Recently, the task force began discussing the possibility of videos and online information to introduce the skills and to reinforce the correct use of the skills.

**Culture** a pattern of basic assumptions invented, discovered, or developed by a group within the organization.

## Culture

Culture is defined as a pattern of basic assumptions invented, discovered, or developed by a group within the organization. It can be considered a set of shared understandings about the organization.[69] One type of culture—a continuous learning culture—evidenced by the shared understanding that learning is an important part of the job, shows a positive impact on the transfer of training.[70] A continuous learning culture is influenced by a variety of factors such as challenging jobs, social support (peer and supervisor), and developmental systems that allow employees the opportunity to learn continually and receive appropriate training.

## Influencing Climate and Culture

Given the importance of climate, what can be done if the climate is non-supportive or neutral regarding training? Changing climate and culture in an organization is a long and difficult process and must be done from the top. Issues related to the mismatch of the training goals and organizational climate and culture should surface in the organizational analysis part of the needs analysis. This information would then be provided to the top HR manager.

Evidence in North America indicates that the human resource department of organizations now carries more influence in organizational decision-making than in the past[71] and employees in these departments are better trained in human resource issues.[72] With this increased influence and training, HR professionals are responsible for helping the company leadership to understand and resolve conflicts between organizational strategies and objectives and the existing climate and culture. Training in Action 4-2 provides an example of things that, incorporated into the training process to facilitate transfer, help to change the learning climate and culture.

# DESIGN THEORY

**Design Theory** A guide that outlines the things you need to consider in putting a training program together to increase the likelihood that learning will occur.

Design theory provides guidance in the development of training through outlining a roadmap of what to do and why. In developing a training module, using the theory helps to ensure you are providing effective techniques to assist trainees in the learning of the material.

## GAGNÉ-BRIGGS THEORY

Conditions of Learning
(R. Gagné)
*http://tip.psychology.org/gagne.html*

The Gagné-Briggs theory of instructional design,[73] discussed in Chapter 2, is applicable to cognitive, behavioural, and attitudinal learning. As a micro theory, it provides a set of procedures to follow for each instructional event to enhance learning. The theory identifies nine events of instruction, which are tied to social learning theory (see Table 4-8). Note that the first event in the theory of instructional design is "attention," which parallels that of social learning theory. The next event, "informing of the objectives," further activates a process of getting the trainees' "attention" focused. Stimulating recall of prerequisite learning ties into activation of memory. Let's examine the nine events of instruction in more detail. As we do so, we will refer back to relevant sections of social learning theory for additional information.

### Gain Attention

Attention can be gained in a number of ways (raise voice, clap hands, or a comment such as "Now watch me carefully"), but is best when tied to the training at hand. If the training was in problem solving, for example, ask the question, "How do you go about solving a problem?" or "We have high absenteeism; what should we do about it?" These types of questions focus discussion on the types of problems trainees face and their typical problem-solving approaches. This initial focus leads nicely into the introduction of the problem-solving objectives. Another

## TABLE 4-8 Gagné-Briggs Nine Events of Instruction

| Instructional Event | Relation to Social Learning Theory |
|---|---|
| Gain attention | Attention |
| Inform the trainee of goal (objectives) | Attention |
| Stimulate recall of prior knowledge | Retention: Activation of memory |
| Present the material | Retention: Activation of memory/semantic coding/cognitive organization |
| Provide guidance for learning | Retention: Semantic coding/cognitive organization through guided discovery |
| | Retention: Symbolic rehearsal |
| Elicit performance (practice) | Behavioural reproduction |
| Provide informative feedback | Reinforcement |
| Assess performance | |
| Enhance retention and transfer | Reinforcement |

*Source:* Gagné, R. M., Briggs, L., & Wager. W., (1992). *Principles of Instructional Design.* Fort Worth: Harcourt Brace Jovanovich.

way to gain attention is to have the CEO/president welcome the trainees and indicate how important the training is to the future of the company. This approach was effective for the training developed by Dr. Camp in Training in Action 4-2. High-level support for training is always important, and when a key decision-maker takes time to convey this support, it is especially effective in getting trainees' attention.

## Inform the Learner of the Goal or Objective

We covered learning objectives and their importance in depth. Clearly, this step is important in getting the trainee focused and aware of not only what needs to be learned but also what will be required when training is complete. Also, it is useful to tie the training back to the job and how it will help trainees be better performers. Having done a TNA, this will be an easy task.

## Stimulate Recall of Prior Relevant Knowledge (Learning)

This step is important to ensure that the trainee has accessed the information/ knowledge necessary for the learning that is about to take place. At the moment of learning, all relevant prerequisite capabilities must be highly accessible to be part of the learning event.[74] Suppose "team problem solving" training is to be conducted. Previously, some brainstorming training and problem-definition training had been completed. Now trainees should be thinking about these topics so the previous learning will be accessible to the problem-solving training. Ask for an explanation of brainstorming from a trainee or focus a discussion on these two topics and show how they are related to the present learning task. Or simply review the two topics with a high level of participation from trainees.

## Present Material to Be Learned

Material is presented in a logical and understandable format. This point seems obvious, but recall that what the trainer may think obvious may not fit in the trainees' schema. To ensure understanding, the method of instruction should include a number of questions designed to elicit responses from trainees regarding their level of understanding. Highlight important points with verbal emphasis (raise voice, slow down presentation for effect). Use easel sheets with bold print to highlight important learning points. Also, eliciting examples from trainees serves to ensure trainees understand the material. The training in team problem solving should list the steps on an easel board for all to see, with sub-steps provided under each of the main headings. Some simple examples of problems and the procedure to solve them could be on a video for effect. The video could be stopped at each step to highlight the step and the preparation for the next step. These examples reflect ways in which the organization and presentation of material assist the trainee in their symbolic coding and cognitive organization.

## Provide Guidance for Learning

The key here is to guide the trainees to the appropriate answer/conclusion, not just to tell them the answer. Get trainees to examine the possibilities related to the topic, both right and wrong. When the solution is reached, the overall discussion will have helped trainees obtain an in-depth understanding of the topic. Provide them with a problem and ask for possible alternatives. For example, in problem-solving training, give trainees a problem such as "absenteeism is high" and ask them to "define the problem" (the first step in problem solving). This task gets trainees thinking and providing different perspectives. These different perspectives are shared and all can assess (depending on whether the response was correct) their own level of understanding. Providing numerous examples allows the trainees to see the generality of the material to many situations. Asking for their examples confirms that the material is being put in the correct context.

## Elicit the Performance

Here, trainees actually do it. For example, in the case of learning a problem-solving model, they now would work in teams to solve a real problem. The problem should be similar to or even the same problem they have been discussing all along. It should also be the simplest type of problem they are likely to come across. Until now, working through the solution was piecemeal; now, as a team, they do it as a whole integrated process without interaction with other teams or the trainer. Once successful, provide a more complex problem to solve—even suggest they use one they previously encountered in their workplace.

## Provide Feedback

Once the team completes a process, a feedback session as to how they did is essential. Feedback can be provided in numerous ways. Videotaping the session and going over it with the team (time-consuming), sitting in on parts of each meeting and providing feedback, or having another team watch and provide feedback are all methods used to provide feedback. The type you use will, to some extent, be a function of the time available and the number of trainees. Of course, designing a program in which training is spread over a number of weeks would allow for more individual feedback between training sessions, but the benefits must be weighed against the cost of trainer time. The important thing is that trainees know what they are doing right and wrong and are able to make corrections before training is complete.

## Assess Performance

The Gagné-Briggs theory indicates learning should be assessed after each topic is taught. So, after training on effective feedback skills and before moving to performance appraisal training, you need to assess the learning that took place regarding feedback skills. The assessment need not be formal, especially when a formal evaluation may be planned for the end of the training program. But some method of determining whether the trainees learned the material is necessary. Questioning (for cognitive knowledge) is one way to assess this. Asking trainees for a behavioural response (a skill) is also a form of assessment. This approach has two purposes: It confirms that learning took place and provides for additional practice at recalling the knowledge or performing the skill.

## Enhance Retention and Transfer

An important part of any training program is the transfer of the training to the job. Designing the program to facilitate retention and transfer is one of the more critical components of the training design. If the purpose of the training is cognitive knowledge, the opportunity for review (retrieval of the information) needs to be provided at spaced intervals after the training is complete. The same applies to skills. All of the support processes discussed earlier are relevant here. For an example of using the design theory to develop training, see Table 4-9 below.

# THE SMALL BUSINESS

Small businesses follow more sophisticated human resource policies today than in the 1980s.[75] In fact, a recent study suggests that many of their policies and practices are not much different from those of large businesses.[76] In another study, a comparison of small and large companies that implemented total quality management found that the small companies were equally involved in human resource activities such as training,

Zenon Environmental Inc. (small business with efficient HR management)
*www.zenonenv.com*

## TABLE 4-9  A Sample Training Design Using the Gagné-Briggs Model

| Event | Feedback Training |
|---|---|
| Gain attention | Ask trainees questions to initiate interest in topic of feedback: "Who has received constructive feedback that they actually appreciated?" If some have, ask them what it was about the feedback that made it better than other feedback they received. If no one has, ask what it was about previous feedback that made them not appreciate it. Have a brief discussion about what is wrong with the typical feedback we receive and what would make it better. |
| Inform of goal | Show objectives and discuss; tie to previous discussion. |
| Stimulate recall of prior knowledge | Ask, "How do you behave when you are trying to help someone versus when you are disciplining them?" "How do you behave toward someone you are trying to help (helping is what feedback is all about)?" Get trainees to verbalize things they do such as "provide it in private," "do it as soon as possible," and so forth, to put them in a helping frame of mind. Their "working memory" now has access to their rules for helping |
| Present material | Share a list of what makes for effective feedback—be specific, not general; be descriptive, not evaluative; and so forth. Present it on an easel sheet in bold. Provide examples for each item. |
| Provide guidance | Provide trainees with multiple examples (some good, some poor) and ask for input as to effectiveness. Give a handout sheet with a number of feedback statements and ask trainees to rate their effectiveness. In small groups have trainees discuss their results and come up with a group consensus as to which are good and which are not as good. Have them provide a rationale. Now go through each and ask trainees to discuss in terms of their responses. |
| Elicit performance | Performance here is knowledge about what is effective and not effective feedback. Ask trainees to form groups of three. Have one of the three teach the others the rules of effective feedback with examples. Then switch, so each trainee has the opportunity to show they know the information well enough to teach it to others and provide their own unique examples. |
| Provide feedback | The other two trainees receiving training complete an evaluation form giving feedback to the one doing the training. The trainer also goes around to each group and provides feedback. |
| Assess performance | Conduct a quiz that asks trainees to recall the rules for effective feedback. Go through a list of feedback examples (similar to the ones earlier) and indicate which are effective, which are not effective, and why they were not effective. |
| Enhance retention and transfer | Trainees will be back to learn the behavioural component of the training in a week. At this time, review will take place to facilitate retention. |

and equally successful in producing quality products.[77] This finding suggests small businesses are beginning to realize the importance of sound human resource practices. The major difference between small and large business is the impact successful training can have on the organization as a whole.

Much of what was discussed earlier is relevant for any size organization. Ensuring that employees are highly motivated to learn and presenting interesting and relevant training is the goal no matter what the size of the company. Again, the major problem in many training programs is not the learning of the skills but the transfer of these skills to the job. We believe that given the requirements necessary for transfer of training, the small business enjoys a definite advantage. We see that climate and a continuous learning culture go a long way toward ensuring the transfer of training. Although any organizational change is difficult, a small organization should be able to accomplish climate and culture change faster and more easily than a large one. Furthermore, in the small business, it should be easier to obtain and demonstrate top management's commitment. In many of the large company interventions conducted by the authors, top management provides written or verbal support for the intervention, but little else. Most of our dealings are with the human resource manager, rather than the CEO or president. Although we stress the continued involvement of upper management, we often have little interaction with top management once the intervention has begun. Top management typically feels they must spend their time on more important things.

In the small firm, it is often the CEO or owner who makes decisions about the type of training and development that will be provided.[78] Access to these individuals is much easier and provides a greater opportunity for you to influence them. Because of their greater involvement, they often develop a clearer understanding of their role in making training successful. An example of this involvement is shown in our Focus on Small Business.

Will the training in our Focus on Small Business transfer? According to the research, it stands a good chance. The fact that the organization is small enough that all could attend the same training at the same time and experience the same things will help the transfer process. This situation simply could not occur in a larger company.

## Focus on Small Business

### Real Support

The Sandwich Community Health Centre is a service-oriented organization with about 35 employees located in the community of Sandwich, Ontario. The Executive Director and Assistant Executive Director of the organization wanted to integrate the two areas of the organization (clinical and health promotion) as well as develop a team approach to much of the community care they offer. After a discussion of the issue, a consultant conducted a TNA and provided training on communication skills and conflict resolution.

Everyone attended training, even the Executive Director. This involvement by top management conveyed an important message about the importance of the training. Top management also insisted that the training be evaluated. Knowing that an assessment would be made at some future date kept everyone focused on the need to change. Finally, although no formal culture assessment was made, the interviews conducted in the TNA clearly indicated a climate of continuous learning.

# OUTCOMES OF DESIGN

As noted at the start of the chapter, it is necessary to understand the various factors that facilitate learning and transfer in order to develop effective training programs. This is one of the three outputs of the design phase. Table 4-10 provides a summary of some of these factors and how they are related to the theories of design presented earlier.

The other two outputs are the development of evaluation methods, presented in Chapter 8, and the identification of alternative methods of instruction, which are presented in Chapters 5 and 6.

**TABLE 4-10 Learning and Transfer Factors As Related to Social Learning Theory and Gagné-Briggs Theory of Design**

| | Social Learning Theory | Gagné-Briggs Nine Events of Instruction | Factors to Consider |
|---|---|---|---|
| **Pre-training** | **Attention/Expectancy** | | |
| | Influence expectations and attitudes of trainees | | Identify those with low expectations/poor attitudes and send to pre-training workshop to improve. |
| | | | Provide information to influence expectancies and identify positive outcomes of training. |
| | Demonstrate the need for training and set goals | | Perform needs analysis so only relevant trainees attend training. |
| | | | Discuss performance of trainee (at supervisory level) and set mutual goals based on future training. |
| | | | Distribute learning objectives prior to training. |
| **Training** | **Attention/Expectancy** | **Gain attention** | |
| Beginning | Create/reinforce positive attitude toward training | | Allow suitable time for instructor and trainee introductions and develop a relaxed atmosphere. |
| | | **Inform trainee of goals** | Allow for time to go through needs analysis, show learning objectives, and discuss usefulness |

*(continued)*

## TABLE 4-10  (Continued)

| | Social Learning Theory | Gagné-Briggs Nine Events of Instruction | Factors to Consider |
|---|---|---|---|
| | | | on the job; draw examples from trainees. |
| | Eliminate distractions | | Choose site where anxiety level will be low (see classical conditioning). |
| | | | Choose proper facilities. |
| During | **Retention** | | |
| | Make relevant | | Continue to focus on training objectives. |
| | | **Stimulate recall of prior knowledge** | Develop links between previous learning and the new learning (activation of memory). |
| | | **Present material** | Use multiple media and make interesting. |
| | | | Ask questions to obtain trainee involvement. |
| | Make interesting | **Provide guidance for learning** | Get trainees involved (symbolic rehearsal). |
| | | | Use relevant examples and offer many of them. |
| | **Behavioural Reproduction/ Reinforcement** Encourage learning | **Elicit performance** | Provide relevant practice process (including maximum similarity different and/or situations). |
| | | **Provide feedback** | Tell trainees how they are doing. |
| Ending | **Reinforcement** | | |
| | Ensure trainees see results of training | **Assess performance** | Provide time to examine objectives to determine what was accomplished. |
| | | | Provide time to evaluate performance level accomplished and provide feedback. |
| | Sensitize trainees to difficulty in transfer training | **Enhance retention and transfer** | Incorporate relapse prevention strategy. |
| | | | Establish trainer commitment to meet with trainees to facilitate transfer. |
| | | | Develop trainees' goals for transfer of training. |
| **Post-training** | **Reinforcement** | | |
| | Facilitate transfer | | Obtain support from supervisor/peers/trainer to help trainee in transferring the training to the work place. |
| | | | Ensure that reward systems are in line with newly trained behaviours. |

# CASE

## The Real World of Training... What Is Wrong Here?

Were you able to figure out what went wrong in the two cases at the beginning of the chapter? Both deal with the need to develop good training objectives.

## CASE 1

Recall the incidents discussed in Case 1 at the beginning of the chapter. Training in troubleshooting did not transfer well. What went wrong? Would more training help the employees become better trouble-shooters? Re-examine the training that took place. The instructor provided a problem, and the trainees indicated the symptoms that would result from the problem. This problem/symptom sequence was the exact opposite of what they would be required to do on the job, which involved seeing a symptom and then determining the problem. Had proper learning objectives been developed before the design of the training, the instructor would have realized this mistake. For example, consider the learning objective, "Upon describing what is wrong with the system (a symptom), the trainee will immediately be able to describe all the possible problems that might cause these symptoms." Had this objective been developed before training, the type of training required would have been more obvious.

## CASE 2

In Case 2, all the trainees followed a cycle of doing poorly on tests 1, 4, 7, 10, and 13, and much better on the other exams.

Further analysis revealed that the 32-week course was divided into five subsections, each of which had three tests. Also, a different instructor taught each subsection. On the very first test, the trainees did not know what to expect and so did poorly. Once they understood what to expect on the tests, they improved on the remaining two tests. When a new instructor arrived, they prepared as usual only to find the type of test had changed; once again they did poorly. When they understood what the new instructor wanted, they did better. It was "getting used to what the instructor wanted" that caused the cycle. Objectives were vague and trainees did not know what to expect. The chief instructor then developed learning objectives for all subsections, which provided guidance to both instructors and trainees as to what exams would be about. The problem disappeared.

*Source:* Mager, R. (1975). *Preparing Instructional Objectives.* Belmont, CA: Pitman Learning.

## Summary

In the design of training, a number of constraints need to be considered, such as how much time will be given to prepare and present training, how much of a priority it is, and how much money can be spent. These will all place constraints on the type of training offered. Once these questions are answered, it is necessary to determine the type of trainees, their current level of KSAs, their motivation to learn, and how homogeneous they will be as a group in terms of these factors. Answers to these questions will provide you with a framework that will be used to develop the objectives for training.

Learning objectives provide clear, unambiguous goals for the training. An effective objective contains three parts: (1) desired behaviours, or what the trainee is expected to be able to do; (2) conditions, or what help/environment trainees will have when performing the expected behaviour; and (3) standards, or what will be required to be successful. Learning objectives should be developed for reaction to training, learning, transfer to the job, and organizational outcomes. These objectives provide guidance for designing and developing the training. They also provide the trainer with clear instructions on what to train and how to do it. Finally, they inform the trainees about what to expect.

In the design of training, consider two aspects: learning and transfer. To facilitate learning, the design must address the motivation of the trainees and the environment in which training will take place. Social learning theory and the Gagné-Briggs micro theory of design provide a framework for setting up each instructional event in a manner that is most effective. To facilitate transfer, consider issues such as type of practice, whole or part learning, overlearning, and similarity to the job. Also, using a combination of goal setting and relapse prevention helps trainees transfer the KSAs to the job.

The support of the supervisor and peers in the work group is just as important to transfer, and sit-ins by the trainer will help too. Finally, congruent reward systems and a supportive climate/culture need to be present to ensure transfer.

This chapter sets the stage for showing the link between the learning objectives and the methods used to provide training. Understanding what makes a good learning objective and the groundwork in terms of what facilitates learning and transfer based on theory allow for an examination of the methods of training and the link between these methods and the learning objectives.

## Implications for Practice

**1.** The difficult task of developing learning objectives takes a great deal of time and effort. However, once developed they provide such clear and unambiguous direction for everyone concerned that they are well worth it.

**2.** It is critical to have the supervisors of trainees ready to support the trainees when they return from training. It is often during the first few days back on the job when all can be forgotten if the right support is not provided.

**3.** Pay close attention to the steps in Gagne's theory of instructional design when developing training. It will result in a higher likelihood that learning will occur.

**4.** The more the training replicates the job environment the higher the likelihood transfer of the training will take place.

## Key Terms

Behavioural reproduction    *137*

Climate    *145*

Cognitive organization    *137*

Conditions    *122*

Culture    *146*

Design theory    *146*

Desired outcome    *122*

Guided discovery    *137*

Identical elements    *140*

Knowledge of results    *141*

Learning objectives    *122*

Massed practice    *138*

Negative transfer    *138*

Overlearning    *139*

Part learning    *139*

Positive transfer    *138*

Progressive part training    *139*

Relapse prevention    *141*

Sit-in    *144*

Spaced practice    *138*

Standards    *122*

Symbolic coding    *137*

Symbolic rehearsal    *137*

Task complexity    *139*

Task organization    *139*

Transfer of training    *138*

Whole learning    *139*

Zero transfer    *138*

## Questions for Review

1. What is a learning objective? List and explain its three components.

2. What can be done long before the trainee attends training to ensure that the trainee will be motivated to learn?

3. How does knowledge of classical and operant conditioning assist you in designing effective training?

4. How would you present training material in a manner that facilitates retention?

5. If a particular task were critical to saving a life (police officer shooting a gun, pilot responding to an emergency), what factors would you build into the design of training to ensure that the behaviour was both learned and transferred to the workplace?

6. To help ensure transfer of training, what would you do outside the training itself? Who would you involve and how? What would you do about the organizational structure/environment?

7. Suppose you are designing a training program for a group of 40 employees. These employees come from a wide range of ethnic and cultural backgrounds and have different educational and experience backgrounds relative to the content area of the training. What training design features would you use to address these constraints?

8. Discuss the Gagné-Briggs theory of design and its relationship to social learning theory.

## Exercises

1. You perhaps already noted that the learning objectives at the beginning of each chapter do not completely follow the three criteria we identified. They all describe the outcome in behavioural terms but do not identify the conditions or standards, which vary with the instructor. Assume you will be the instructor for this chapter and rewrite each of the learning objectives at the beginning of the chapter in complete form. Your trainees are corporate HRD employees and you are training them on the contents of this chapter. Additionally, write an objective for each of the other types of training objectives (trainee reaction, transfer of training, organizational outcome).

2. What is your grade point average since you started your education at this institution? How hard do you work to maintain that average: 3 (very hard/hard), 2 (about average), 1 (enough to get by)? Now ask yourself why. Tie your answer into Expectancies 1 and 2 and the valence of outcomes. Break into groups that contain a mix of 1s, 2s, and 3s. Discuss what makes the person in your group a 3. Is it attractive outcomes (valence), confidence in ability (Expectancy 1), or belief that it will result in the positive outcomes desired? From that information, is there any way you believe you could influence the 2s or 1s to be more motivated? What would you try to influence? Explain your approach in terms of Expectancies 1 and 2. How does this process relate to trainee populations in the workplace?

## Web Research

Conduct an Internet search to identify two companies that provide training design consulting services. For each of them identify their design process. Compare and contrast each in terms of their approach.

## CASE ANALYSIS

1. Review the Domtar case from Chapter 1 and answer the following questions:

a. In the implementation of Kaizen, what groups of employees are likely to need training? How should the trainees be organized? Think of this issue from a training design perspective as well as a training content perspective.

b. For the type of training envisioned, what are the learning objectives? Write these objectives in complete form.

c. For each group of employees that will need training, what are the organizational constraints that need to be addressed in the design of the training? What design features should be used to address these constraints? Be sure to address both the learning and transfer of training issues.

2. How important is attitude change when Domtar purchases another company? What are some of the ways training could assist in changing attitudes?

## The Training Program (Fabrics Inc.)

This continues the description of the Fabrics Inc., training program begun in Chapter 3. Recall that Fabrics Inc. grew quickly and experienced problems with its supervisors. In Chapter 3, we described how the consultant completed a needs analysis. From this TNA, the consultant determined a number of areas in which supervisors could use training. A partial list included a lack of KSAs in the following areas:

Effective listening

Communication

Conflict resolution

Effective feedback

Measuring employee performance

Motivating employees

For the purpose of this exercise, we deal with only one, conflict resolution. The first step will be to develop the learning objectives.

### THE LEARNING OBJECTIVES

Some of the learning objectives are as follows:

- The trainee will, <u>with no errors,</u> **present in writing the four types of active listening, along with examples of each of the types,** *with no help from reference material.*

- *When, in a role-play, the trainee is presented with an angry comment,* **the trainee will respond** <u>immediately</u> **using one of the active listening types.** The trainee will **then explain orally the technique used and why,** *with no help from reference material.* <u>The trainee will be presented with five of these comments and be expected to correctly respond and explain a minimum of four.</u>

- The trainee will, <u>with 100 percent accuracy,</u> **provide in writing each step of the conflict resolution model, along with a relevant example,** *with no help from any reference material.*

- *In a role-play of an angry customer,* the trainee/employee **will show concern for the customer by listening and providing alternative solutions, using the steps in the conflict resolution model,** *with help from an easel sheet that has the steps listed on it.* <u>Trainee must use all the steps and two types of active listening in the role-play.</u>

- *After watching a role-play of an angry person and an employee using the conflict resolution model,* **the trainee will,** *without reference to material, immediately* **provide feedback as to the effectiveness of the person using the conflict resolution model.** <u>Trainee must identify four of the six errors.</u>

### DESIGN ISSUES

The conflict resolution model has four steps:

1. Use active listening,
2. Indicate respect,
3. Be assertive, and
4. Provide information.

One design consideration is related to the whole vs. part learning discussed earlier. Should we conduct the training, as a whole, each part separately first then all together, or progressive part? An examination of the model reveals that the first part, active listening is a complex task by itself,[79] and can be used independently of the rest of the model. The other three steps are not as complex, and are much more interrelated, so the decision is made to use a hybrid of the progressive part method. We will first train the active listening, then the whole model including active listening. In part/whole language this means we would teach step 1, then step 1 + 2 + 3 + 4.

For the module related to teaching active listening we want to begin by getting trainees' attention, as suggested by design theory. This can be accomplished by showing a video of two people in a heated argument and then asking; " Has that situation ever happened to you? Would you like to have a better way of responding in such a situation so tempers do not flare?" This would allow you to then introduce active listening. The next step in the theory is to inform of the goal. Presenting the learning objective related to active listening accomplishes this. The training would continue to be designed paying close attention to the steps in the design theory.

We will return to Fabrics Inc. in Chapter 8, to provide the process for preparing to evaluate the training there. We will not be covering Fabrics Inc. in Chapters 5, 6, and 7, where we discuss development and implementation of training.

# 5

## TRADITIONAL TRAINING METHODS

*If you would thoroughly know anything, teach it to others.*

Tryon Edwards (1809–1894)

## CHAPTER OBJECTIVES

After reading this chapter, you should be able to:

- Describe the purposes, procedures, strengths, and limitations of the following training methods:
    - Lectures, lecture/discussions, and demonstrations,
    - Games and simulations, and
    - On-the-job training (OJT).

- Describe the types of learning objectives for which each method is most suited.

- Identify the various audiovisual options and their strengths and weaknesses.

### CASE

### *Changing Managerial Attitudes About Problem-Solving Teams*

An automobile parts manufacturer planned to implement employee problem-solving teams. A training needs analysis of middle- and first-level managers conducted prior to implementation showed that managers were resistant to these proposed changes in the work design that would give hourly employees more authority in making decisions. Of the many reasons for this resistance, two of the most common statements were "These decisions are ones we are supposed to be making" and "This change will reduce the need for managers. Some of us will lose our jobs."

*(continued)*

Training provided to these managers was designed to give them the KSAs necessary to function in the new team-based system. There were sessions on problem solving, conflict resolution, and running effective meetings. These had a lecture component for knowledge and role-plays for skill development. Lectures/discussions addressed concerns about reducing managerial positions. For example, one lecture explained that the company did not intend to lay off or terminate any managers as a result of this change, but it would reduce the size of the managerial workforce through attrition. In the discussion that followed, managers were able to gain comfort about how these changes would affect their job security.

Another lecture/discussion focused on the change in duties and responsibilities of first-line managers. Supervisors would be given new duties and responsibilities, taking the place of those tasks transferred to the hourly employees who now composed the problem-solving teams. The new responsibilities included facilitating team problem solving and decision-making, serving as a liaison between the team and other parts of the organization, acquiring resources for the team, and doing long-range planning. These new responsibilities were incorporated into a new performance appraisal for first-line managers and the for-mer responsibilities that had been taken on by the teams were removed. During the discussion sessions following the lecture the managers expressed fears and concerns not covered in the lecture, such as how they were to acquire the new skills. The trainer was able to address these issues either directly, by indicating other parts of the training program that dealt with those issues, or by indicating a willingness to bring someone in to address the issues at the next session.

In summary, these lectures, discussions, and question periods made it clear to trainees that no manager would be terminated just because some of their current responsibilities were being transferred to the teams. Although the managers were losing some responsibilities, they were gaining others. Their performance reviews would be based on the new responsibilities. This shift made it clear that they needed to develop the KSAs necessary to carry out the new responsibilities.

As a result, the training managers' motivation to learn the new skills increased. Another important part of this training was to improve these managers' attitudes toward the team process. A subsequent survey of the managers showed a significantly more positive attitude toward the problem-solving team concept.

## OVERVIEW OF THE CHAPTER

RedR (traditional and new training)
*www.redr.ca*

This chapter provides a basic understanding of traditional training methods in terms of their strengths and limitations related to cost, suitable learning objectives, and other factors related to their effectiveness. In the next chapter, we will discuss the same issues as they relate to computer-based training. A summary of these two chapters will be presented in a table at the start of Chapter 7. Development and implementation of the training is discussed in Chapter 7.

## MATCHING METHODS WITH OUTCOMES

**Knowledge** an organized body of facts, principles, procedures, and information.

**Skills** the capacities needed to perform a set of tasks.

**Attitudes** employee beliefs and opinions that support or inhibit behaviour.

The material in this chapter and the next will provide the basic methods and delivery systems used in training. The designer of a training program needs to understand each of these in order to determine which is the best method to meet training objectives, considering the organizational constraints. Since instructional methods differ in their ability to influence knowledge, skills, and attitudes, the training designer must be able to evaluate a method's strengths and weaknesses in order to make good decisions about its use. Before moving into that discussion, a brief review of the KSA definitions might be helpful. Refer to the definitions in Chapter 1 for more detail. **Knowledge** is an organized body of facts, principles, procedures, and information. **Skills** are the capacities needed to perform a set of tasks. **Attitudes** are employee beliefs and opinions that support or inhibit behaviour.

Identify some of the knowledge, skill, and attitude objectives in the opening case. Many training programs set learning objectives in more than one area. This will usually require a combination of several methods into an integrated whole, because no single method can do everything well. For example, among the methods used in the opening case are lecture, lecture/discussion, and role-plays. Each method is used to accomplish different parts of the training objectives, but it is the combination of methods that allows the full set of training objectives to be achieved.

The various methods can be divided into cognitive and behavioural approaches. **Cognitive methods** provide verbal or written information, demonstrate relationships among concepts, or provide rules on how to do something. These methods stimulate learning through their impact on cognitive processes and are associated most closely with changes in knowledge and attitudes. Though these types of methods can influence skill development, it is not their strength. Conversely, **behavioural methods** allow the trainee to practise behaviour in a real or simulated fashion. They stimulate learning through behaviour and are best used for skill development and attitude change. Thus, either behavioural or cognitive learning methods can be used effectively to change attitudes, though they do so through different means.

**Cognitive Methods** provide verbal or written information, demonstrate relationships among concepts, or provide rules on how to do something.

**Behavioural Methods** allow the trainee to practise behaviour in a real or simulated fashion.

# LECTURES AND DEMONSTRATIONS

The lecture is one of the most frequently used and oldest forms of training. Nearly all training programs contain some lecture component and a great many provide some type of demonstration. Although they have similar characteristics, they are appropriate for different objectives. We will discuss the lecture first.

The lecture can be in printed or oral form. The oral lecture can be live or presented on video. In any form, the lecture is best used to present information designed to create understanding of a topic as well as to influence attitudes related to the topic. In its simplest form, the lecture is merely telling someone about something.[1] It is difficult to imagine training that does not use the lecture format to some extent. When the trainer begins a training session by telling the trainees the objectives, the agenda, and the process that will be used in training, the trainer is using the lecture method.

Several variations in the lecture format allow it to be more or less formal or interactive.[2] The clearest difference is the role that trainees are expected to play. The straight lecture does not include trainees interacting with the trainer. Adding discussion and a question-and-answer period invites the trainees to be more interactive in the learning process.

## STRAIGHT LECTURE/LECTURETTE

The **straight lecture** is a presentation of information by the trainer. The trainee's role is to try to absorb the information.[3] The lecture is typically thought of in terms of a lecturer speaking to a group (the trainees) about a topic. However, the lecture may also take the form of printed text, such as this book. The only differences between a straight lecture and the same material in print are the lecturer's control of the speed at which material is presented, the voice inflections, the body language used to emphasize points, and of course the visual image of the lecturer.

**Straight Lecture** a presentation of information that the trainee attempts to absorb.

A good lecture is well organized and begins with an introduction that lays out the purpose of the lecture and the order in which topics will be covered. If it is an oral lecture, the introduction should cover any rules about interrupting the lecture for questions and any opportunity for clarification. The main body of the lecture—the topic content—follows the introduction. These parts of the topic area should be logically sequenced so that trainees are prepared for each topic by the content of the preceding topics. The lecture should conclude with a summary of the main learning points or conclusions.

**Lecturette** has the same characteristics as the lecture but usually lasts less than 20 minutes.

Since lectures require long periods of trainee inactivity, a shorter version of a lecture, the **lecturette**, is often used. It has the same characteristics as the lecture but usually lasts less than 20 minutes if done orally. In print, the lecturette would be a shorter amount of printed text to read (e.g., this section on lecture/discussion compared with the whole chapter).

During an oral lecture or lecturette, the trainee listens, observes, and takes notes. Even when done well, it is not an especially effective technique for learning. However, it is useful when a large number of people must be given a specified set of information. The oral lecture should not contain too many learning points unless printed text accompanies the lecture, as trainees tend to forget information provided orally. A major concern about the straight lecture method is the inability to identify and correct misunderstandings.

When the only training objective is to acquire specific factual information, increased learning can often be achieved at less cost by putting the information into text. This way, employees can read or view the material at their leisure and lost productivity because of training is minimized. The added value provided by the oral lecture is the credibility the lecturer can give to the material by his or her personal presence and the attention commanded through presentation skills.

### How to Use the Straight Lecture Effectively
If an oral lecture is used, the trainer must be clear and articulate. He must be familiar with the use of a microphone if a large number of trainees will be present. Table 5-1 provides a number of common errors made by lecturers and ways to avoid them. Of course, these will also apply to the lecture/discussion method.

## DISCUSSION METHOD

**Lecture/Discussion Method** a lecturette that provides trainees with information that is supported, reinforced, and expanded on through interactions both among the trainees and between the trainees and the trainer.

The **lecture/discussion method** uses a lecturette to provide trainees with information that is supported, reinforced, and expanded on through interactions among the trainees and between the trainees and the trainer. This added communication has much greater power than the lecture. Trainers can achieve more complex learning objectives—such as problem solving—through the use of logically sequenced lecturettes followed by immediate discussion and questioning.

The lecture/discussion method provides a two-way flow of communication. Knowledge is communicated from trainer to trainees and communication from trainees back to the trainer conveys understanding. Verbal and nonverbal feedback from trainees enables the trainer to determine whether the material is understood. If not, the trainer may need to spend more time on this area or present the information again in a different manner.

Both the trainees and the trainer can ask questions. When the trainees volunteer questions, they demonstrate their thinking about the content of the lecture. A trainer who asks questions stimulates thinking about the key areas that are important to know. Questioning (by trainees or the trainer) and discussions are beneficial because they enhance understanding and keep trainees focused on the material. Furthermore, discussions allow the trainee to be actively engaged in the content of the lecture, an activity that improves recall and future use.

### How to Use the Lecture/Discussion Effectively
Training that requires trainees to understand and integrate material before moving forward also requires two-way communication. Two-way communication, including questioning, is accomplished through the lecture/discussion method.

## TABLE 5-1 Typical Lecture Presentation Errors and Ways to Avoid Them

| Errors | Ways to Avoid |
|---|---|
| Talking with back to trainees while writing on board or flip chart | Don't talk and write at the same time. Prepare flip charts ahead of time when possible. If considerable board work is required, use overhead transparencies. |
| Using highly technical words, unfamiliar jargon, or complex sentences | If technical words or jargon must be used, provide definitions. Simplify the language and sentences so the meaning is clear. Pilot test at least part of the lecture with an audience similar to the trainees. |
| Providing examples or asides without much relevance to the trainees | The lecturer need not provide all the examples. Ask trainees to provide some of the examples or illustrations. In preparing the lecture, go to the supervisors of the trainees to get examples that are relevant. |
| Reading rather than lecturing | Prepare an outline of points to be covered rather than a word-for-word script. Be familiar with each point on the outline so that you are able to talk about it without reference to notes. |
| Speaking in a monotone | Listen to TV and radio commentators, paying close attention to when and in what way they change their tone and the pitch of their voice. Practise fluctuating the tone and pitch of your voice on tape and in everyday conversation. Use pauses in your lecture so you can think about how you want to say something. |
| Making distracting gestures | Videotape a lecture you are giving and observe your gestures. If they are distracting or irritating to you, the trainees probably feel the same way. Some gestures are useful and keep trainee attention. Don't stand stiff as a board either. The gestures you use are habits and can be practised out or in. |
| Leaving projector on with no image or an irrelevant image | Get in the habit of glancing at the projected image as you are talking about the material it displays. When you are at the end of the material, you will see that it is time to turn the projector off or change the image. |
| Losing your place in the lecture | Not being able to find your place happens most frequently because your notes are too detailed. Another technique is to check off topics completed. |

*Questioning.* Questioning is a powerful tool for starting discussions and can help trainees discover for themselves the answers to questions asked. Questions also help the trainer determine whether trainees understand the information correctly and help create a common understanding. Trainers should be familiar with a number of question types. First, let us examine the closed vs. open-ended question.

The **closed-ended question** asks for a specific answer. "What are the five strategies for dealing with conflict?" "What is the next step in the procedure?" This type of question is useful to assess learning or review previous material.

The **open-ended question** requires no specific response. In this case, no answer is a wrong answer—you are seeking an opinion. "What do you think about this method of problem solving?" "How would you approach this issue?" "What did you learn from that exercise?" These types of questions are useful for obtaining trainee involvement, generating discussion, and demonstrating that the trainer is willing to listen to the trainees' point of view.

Both types are useful. Closed-ended questions are useful to regain control of the discussion or to assess understanding of specific points. Open-ended questions are useful to relax the trainees or explore their beliefs and opinions about issues.

**Closed-Ended Question** a question that asks for a specific answer.

**Open-Ended Question** a question that seeks an opinion and has no right or wrong answers.

The next two types are the overhead question and the direct question. **Overhead questions** are either open- or closed-ended, directed at the whole group rather than at one person in particular. They are non-threatening because they do not require any particular person to respond. This type of question is useful when trainees are highly involved and respond readily. If no one responds, tension can mount. Increased tension, however, is not always negative. Some trainers become anxious if their overhead question is not answered within 10 to 15 seconds. To relieve their tension, trainers answer the question themselves. Effective trainers understand that unanswered questions create tension in the trainees, which is a good thing because it helps to focus trainee attention on the material being presented. This topic is discussed further in the "Encouraging Trainees to Respond" section. When only a few trainees are answering the questions, and it is the same trainees over and over, it is wise to revert to the direct question.

The **direct question** is asked of a particular trainee. It is used to draw out non-participators and obtain differing points of view. As any trainer knows, a few trainees will often willingly answer any and all questions. If the same few trainees prevail over and over, many other trainees will tire of hearing from them and will withdraw. Keeping everyone involved in a discussion is an important skill required of an effective trainer. Most trainees begin responding to questions once they see that answering a question is a safe and rewarding experience.

Assume you are the trainer and a trainee asks you a question. Repeat the question so everyone can hear it and ask the trainee group to answer it. This is the **relay question** technique. For example, a trainee might ask, "How would this concept work in a unionized shop?" As the trainer you might respond, "An interesting issue. Does anyone have any ideas?" Redirecting questions to the trainee group allows you to hear the trainees' views and then reinforce appropriate responses. It can lead to interesting discussions about the issue, which may not otherwise come up.

The **reverse question** is similar, except that the question is stated back to the person who asked it. Again, as the trainer and responding to the same question, you might say, "Interesting question, Bill. Your area is unionized; how do you think it would work there?" Use this approach when you believe that the questioner really wants to provide an answer but is hesitant. This technique is also helpful to get a feeling for how deeply the trainee wants to delve into the question. Be careful in redirecting a question back to the questioner, however. If overused, it could inhibit trainees from asking a question for fear of having to answer it themselves.

***Encouraging Trainees to Respond.*** Asking questions is only half of the equation in an effective discussion. Trainees must also respond. Here are some tips on how to encourage responses:[4]

- Do not rush to fill the silence. Trainers tend to show less tolerance for silence than do trainees. Sometimes waiting them out will work. Remember, the trainees are just learning the material, and it may take them a bit of time to process through the material mentally to arrive at an answer with which they feel comfortable.

- Ask them to write out an answer. Say, "Pick up your pens and write down a few reasons why workers are not motivated." Then allow them time for this task. Trainees are much more willing to read what they write than answer off the top of their heads.[5] This method also allows the trainer to ask specific trainees to respond, as the pressure of the "unknown" question is alleviated. A variation is to ask trainees to share their responses with one or two other trainees and come up with a common answer. This technique further diffuses the accountability problem.

**Overhead Question** a question directed at the whole group rather than at one person in particular.

**Direct Question** a question asked of a particular trainee.

**Relay Question** a question from a trainee that the trainer redirects back to the trainee group.

**Reverse Question** a question that the trainer redirects to the trainee who asked it.

- Use the **guided discovery** method when faced with no response to a question. As the trainer you would not answer the question but would ask a new question that addresses much more basic material that the trainees should already understand. When the correct answer is given, move to a slightly more complex question. Each question is designed to bring the trainees closer to "discovering" the answer to the question themselves. It encourages trainees to respond because the questions are easy at the beginning and also the answer to the last helps to answer the next.

**Guided Discovery** when not getting an answer to a question, the trainer asks more basic questions, with each question designed to bring the trainees closer to "discovering" the answer to the original question.

## DEMONSTRATIONS

A **demonstration** is a visual display of how to do something or how something works. To be most effective, a demonstration should be integrated with the lecture/discussion method. Whether demonstrating how to do something or how something works, the principles of an effective demonstration are the same. The demonstration is most useful when your training objectives are to increase knowledge, technical skills, or interpersonal skills.

**Demonstration** a visual display of how to do something or how something works.

The most effective demonstrations provide each trainee with the resources and materials needed to perform the operations being demonstrated. Each trainee is then able to copy the demonstration process immediately after watching. As trainees are performing the demonstration, the trainer can move around the room giving feedback. Even having teams of four to five trainees sharing the demonstration materials provides opportunities for them to watch others and do it at least once themselves. While one trainee is performing the demonstration, fellow trainees can recall the steps in the sequence and provide feedback. This approach also presents opportunities for questions, instructor clarification, and group discussion, all of which contribute to a common understanding of what should be done, when, and why.

### How to Use the Demonstration Effectively
To conduct an effective demonstration, first prepare the lesson plan by breaking down the task to be performed into smaller, easily learned parts. Then sequentially organize the parts of the task and prepare an explanation for why each action is required. There are two main components to the demonstration—present and try out. The following steps are part of the "present" component. Complete each of the following steps for each part of the task:

- Tell the trainees what you will be doing so they understand what you will be showing them. This focuses their attention on the critical aspects of the task.

- Demonstrate the task, describing what you are doing while you are doing it.

- Explain why each part of the task should be performed in that way immediately after you demonstrate a part of the task.

Just as in the lecture, the level of involvement of the trainee can vary in a demonstration. As with the lecture, more trainee involvement leads to more learning. The following steps increase the value of the demonstration.

After the trainer completes the demonstration it is time for the trainee to "try out" the demonstration by doing the following:

- Ask the trainee to "talk through" the task before actually doing it.

- Give the trainee an opportunity to do the task and to describe what he or she is doing and why.

- Provide feedback, both positive and negative.
- Let the learner practise.

The temptation is not to spend much time on this process, as it seems so easy and obvious. However, it is important to remember that what is being demonstrated may be easy for someone who is familiar with it, but not for a novice.

## STRENGTHS AND LIMITATIONS OF LECTURES AND DEMONSTRATION

In examining the strengths and limitations of the various methods, we focus on four major issues:

1. The cost of both financial and other resources required to achieve the training objective(s),

2. The amount of control the trainer has over the material that will be covered,

3. The type(s) of learning objectives addressed, and

4. The ways in which the method activates different social learning theory processes.

**Costs** The financial costs typically associated with developing and implementing lectures, lecture/discussions, and demonstrations include the following:

- Development costs related to creating the content and organization of the training,
- Cost of ancillary materials to facilitate learning,
- Compensation of trainer and trainee time spent in training,
- Cost of the training facility for the program, and
- Travel, lodging, and food for the trainer and trainees.

In terms of development and delivery, printed lectures are the most time-efficient. Oral lectures followed by discussions and demonstrations require increasingly more time. Of course, the more questions, discussion, and participation allowed, the greater the amount of time required. If the training objective focuses on factual information, and interaction is not important, printed text, video lecture, or demonstration will be more efficient and equally effective. The advantage of the live lecture is that it guarantees that everyone is exposed to the information. Printed or video lectures rely on trainees following instructions.

## Control of Material and Process

Lectures, discussions, and demonstrations provide a high degree of trainer control over the training process and content. The material covered is predetermined by the trainer, as are the processes used to present the material. The trainees have little, if any, influence other than whatever involvement was allowed in the TNA and program design process. However, as the training becomes more interactive, trainees are able to exert more control. Trainee questions or answers to questions shape the content of what is covered. The group dynamics help to shape the processes used by the trainer in presenting the information.

For example, in lecture/discussions, the order in which issues arise is determined partly by the lecture content, the types of questions raised, and the results of the discussion sessions. Discussions can move into tangential areas not specifically addressed in the lecture material but which are of interest to the trainees. This is, in fact, what occurred in the opening case. Managers were concerned about a number of issues not specifically addressed by the training that had occurred so far. This was taking their attention away from the training at hand. Being able to address these concerns early on in training and provide the appropriate information helped to refocus attention on the training material.

**Learning Objectives (KSAs)** The lecture is most useful when trainees lack knowledge or have attitudes conflicting with the training objectives. The printed or video lecture is effective because it can be studied in more depth and retained to refresh learning over time. The lecture/discussion method is more effective than the straight lecture for learning higher-level knowledge such as concepts and principles. The lecture/discussion method is also more effective than the straight lecture at producing attitude changes. Since attitudes consist of a person's beliefs and feelings about an object or event, new learning can modify them. The lecture, especially combined with discussion, can change employee attitudes by providing new insights, facts, and understanding as illustrated in the opening case. Since lectures and discussions do not provide opportunities for behavioural reproduction, they should not be used for skill development objectives.

If the training objective is skill improvement, the demonstration may be appropriate. As training objectives often include both knowledge and skill development, it is likely that more than just a demonstration is needed. For example, the training objective may be to improve managers' ability to conduct effective meetings. First, the managers would need to know the components of effective meetings (facts) and when and how to use them (procedures). The lecture/discussion method may be appropriate to meet these objectives, but the skill development objectives should be addressed through methods that show trainees how to conduct meetings and allow them to practise these skills. The demonstration may also influence attitudes. For example, a new product demonstration is intended not only to show how the product works, but also to generate enthusiasm in the sales force about the product.

**Learning Process** In describing the effects of the various methods on learning processes, we return to social learning theory. Review these learning processes (attention, retention, and behavioural reproduction) by returning to Chapter 2 and specifically Figure 2-5 on page 52.

Lectures, lecture/discussions, and demonstrations can be good at capturing trainee attention, at least in the short term. They show some strength in the area of retention, especially discussions and demonstrations. Even though only demonstrations are good at facilitating behavioural reproduction, lectures and discussion can develop attitudes that are supportive of the desired behaviour.

Table 5-2 lists the basic components of the lecture/discussion, and, using social learning theory, indicates the learning process affected. Table 5-3 provides the same information for the demonstration.

*Attention.* Done properly, lectures and demonstrations attract and maintain the attention of trainees. In fact, of the three learning processes (attention, retention, and behavioural reproduction), attracting attention is what the lecture does best. Demonstrations, when combined with lecturettes, are better at covering all the learning processes than either is alone. It is easy to gain the attention of the trainees at the start, but trainees' attention wanders, especially in longer lectures and demonstrations. Thus, these methods have a limitation in this regard. Printed and video lectures offer the advantage that the trainee can put down the lecture when attention begins to wander and come back to it when in a more receptive mental state.

For live lectures, a good lecturer will speak at about a rate of 125 words per minute, but the average person processes information at a rate equivalent to 400 to 500 words a

## TABLE 5-2 Basic Lecture/Discussion Components and Their Effects on Learning

| Lecture/Discussion Components | Learning Process Affected |
|---|---|
| 1. Orientation<br>Presenting information so that trainees understand the direction the lecture is headed and the organization for getting there. | Attention |
| 2. Enthusiasm<br>Presenting information in a manner that conveys the topic's importance and inherent value. | Attention |
| 3. Variety<br>Using voice, gestures, various components listed in this table, and audiovisual aids. For printed lectures this component is minimized. | Attention<br>Retention:<br>    Symbolic coding |
| 4. Logical organization<br>Presenting information in a logical order and providing logical transitions between topic areas | Retention:<br>    Cognitive organization |
| 5. Explanations<br>Describing facts, concepts, and principles in a clear and easily understood manner. | Retention:<br>    Symbolic coding.<br>    Cognitive organization |
| 6. Directions<br>Providing instructions in a manner that allows trainees to understand what they are to do and how to do it. | Retention:<br>    Cognitive organization.<br>    Symbolic rehearsal |
| 7. Illustrations<br>Providing clear, interesting, and relevant examples of how information can or has been applied (both correctly and incorrectly). | Attention<br>Retention:<br>    Cognitive Organization |
| 8. Compare and contrast<br>Articulating the similarities and differences, advantages and disadvantages, of relevant topic areas. | Attention<br>Retention:<br>    All areas |
| 9. Questions and discussion<br>Seeking information from the trainees regarding their comprehension and their content-related ideas, and stimulating the trainees' thought processes (e.g., Socratic questioning). This component is not possible in printed lectures. | Attention<br>Retention:<br>    All areas |
| 10. Summarize<br>Highlighting important concepts covered in a manner that links the topics/ideas together. | Retention:<br>    Cognitive organization |

minute. Thus, a trainee's attention can fluctuate dramatically over the course of a one-hour lecture. Attention begins to decline after 15 to 20 minutes and begins to pick up again only near the end.[6] This phenomenon is a primary reason for the use of lecturettes. Likewise, demonstrations should be short enough to maintain trainee attention while providing the necessary information about how to complete the task. Discussion, if properly managed by the trainer, acts to heighten attention and refocus thought processes.

***Retention.*** Retention involves the processes of symbolic coding, cognitive organization, and symbolic rehearsal. The lecture's strongest link in the retention process is the first step of symbolic coding. A symbolic coding system is provided during the lecture while the trainer is describing, explaining, and illustrating the learning points. The trainer is symbolically coding the material by using the appropriate words and images. Likewise, in the demonstration, the actions of the trainer are symbolic coding. The learners translate the trainer's words and actions into their individual

## TABLE 5-3 Basic Demonstration Components and Their Effects on Learning

| Demonstration Components | Areas of Learning Affected* |
|---|---|
| Present | |
| • Tell | Attention |
| • Demonstrate | Retention: |
| • Explain |   Symbolic coding |
| |   Cognitive organization |
| Try Out | |
| • Trainees talk through the task | Retention: |
| • Trainees do task while describing what they are doing and why |   Symbolic rehearsal |
| | Behavioural reproduction |
| • Trainer provides positive/negative feedback | |
| • Trainees practise | |

*Source:* Adapted from Gold, L. (1981). Job instruction: Four steps to success. *Training and Development Journal,* September, pp. 28–32.

*From social learning theory as illustrated in Figure 2-5.

symbolic coding schemes. The challenge for the trainer is to present the material in a way that ensures the trainer's and learner's symbolic codes hold the same meaning. Discussions and questions help align the trainee's symbolic coding with the training objectives. Putting the lecture into print or creating a video for a demonstration facilitates the trainee's symbolic coding process by allowing the trainee more time to adjust her coding to that used by the text or video. This adjustment increases recall of the information at a later date (e.g., back on the job). Using visual aids, such as graphics in a text or projections in a live lecture, will facilitate the trainee's coding process by providing additional cues. The more varied the stimuli used to present the same material, the more accurately the information is coded.

Organizing the coded information into already existing or new cognitive structures is what social learning theorists call cognitive organization. The organization of information determines the ease of recall and its appropriate use when recalled. When trainees become actively engaged in integrating concepts and principles into their cognitive structures, the cognitive organization process is facilitated. Thus, demonstrations allow more opportunity for cognitive organization than does straight lecture. Discussion and questioning allows trainees to clarify their understanding of the lecture and organize it appropriately. Better cognitive organization occurs when the trainees are free to discuss various aspects of the new knowledge and its relationship to already existing knowledge and to question the trainer about actual or hypothetical situations in which they might use the knowledge.

Demonstrations, by their very nature, stimulate symbolic rehearsal. By simply watching the trainer demonstrate the task, the learner is encouraged to think about doing it, especially if the learner knows he will be asked to do the task when the trainer is finished. Lectures present greater difficulty in this area. The lecturer can and should stimulate symbolic rehearsal by making suggestions about how the knowledge could be applied. However, these suggestions are not as powerful as the trainee seeing how the knowledge is applicable to her specific situation.

Properly managed, a lecture/discussion session can facilitate this symbolic rehearsal. For example, as a trainer you might ask the trainees to think about ways in which the knowledge could be used in their work area and write their ideas on a flip chart. Trainees could then be organized into small groups and each individual encouraged to report his or her thoughts to the group. You might say to the group members, "As you listen to others describe how they could apply this knowledge, imagine you were applying it that way in your work area. When the person is finished, discuss the application idea and how it would apply in your area." This process would not only bring misunderstandings to the surface and possibly clarify them but would assist in the cognitive organization of the information. The primary value, however, would be that each trainee was getting a chance to practise mentally (i.e., symbolic rehearsal) using the new knowledge in a variety of ways and situations.

*Behavioural Reproduction.* The lecture/discussion approach does not provide for practising actual behaviours, so it is not appropriate for skill development objectives. Conversely, the demonstration incorporates behavioural reproduction into the training through practice. Remember, however, that it is important for the trainer to monitor the learner's performance, providing appropriate feedback to ensure that the correct behaviour is learned.

## Training Group Characteristics

*The Trainees.* For any type of lecture to be effective, trainees should be at about the same general level of intellectual ability and possess about the same level of related content knowledge. If the trainee group is widely divergent in either of these areas, it is difficult to aim the lecture at the appropriate level of understanding. If the lecture is in other respects an appropriate method, the best approach then is to train such groups separately.

Discussions allow more diversity in a training group because the discussion period provides an opportunity for more active learning. Trainees who learn better in a more active mode have the opportunity to do so. Trainees also have the opportunity to learn from their peers as they participate in the discussion and ask questions.

The training group can be fairly diverse for demonstrations. However, the trainer must be able to observe each trainee performing the task. As with lecture/discussion, the trainees in a demonstration are able to learn not only by observing the trainer but also by observing other trainees performing the task and attending to the instructor's feedback.

*Size of Training Group.* Lectures or lecturettes can be given to groups ranging from just a few to hundreds of trainees. This is not true of the lecture/discussion method. In general, class size should be small enough to allow all trainees ample opportunity to participate in discussions and questioning. The appropriate size depends on the complexity of the material and the amount of time allocated. More complicated material requires more time for more questions, so fewer trainees can be accommodated in a given amount of time. The dynamics of large groups make it difficult or impossible for all to participate in a meaningful way. When trainees cannot participate meaningfully, they will inevitably become less involved and withdraw their attention. So when utilizing lecture/discussions in training, it is necessary to make sure groups are small enough to allow all to participate within the time constraints of the training.

As with lecture/discussion, many of the advantages of the demonstration are lost when the group is too large. To capture all the advantages of a demonstration, it should be limited to small groups. A way to allow for larger groups is to provide additional trainers to monitor trainee practice on the task and provide feedback. A good rule of thumb is to have no more than five trainees per trainer when the demonstration involves hands-on practice by the trainees.

# GAMES AND SIMULATIONS

Training games and simulations are designed to reproduce or simulate processes, events, and circumstances that occur in the trainee's job. Thus, trainees can experience these events in a controlled setting where they can develop their skills or discover concepts that will improve their performance. Equipment simulators, business games, in-basket exercises, case studies, role-plays, and behaviour modelling are the primary examples of this method. We discuss each of these separately and then describe the strengths and limitations of simulations in general.

# EQUIPMENT SIMULATORS

If technical skills in the operation or maintenance of equipment are the focus of training, one of the best instructional methods is the equipment simulator. **Equipment simulators** are mechanical devices that require trainees to use the same procedures, movements, or decision processes they would use with equipment back on the job. Simulators train airline pilots,[7] air traffic controllers,[8] military officers,[9] taxi drivers,[10] maintenance workers,[11] telephone operators,[12] ship navigators,[13] and product development engineers.[14]

It is important that the simulators be designed to replicate, as closely as possible, the physical aspects of the equipment and operating environment trainees will find at their job site. This resemblance is referred to as the **physical fidelity** of the simulation. In addition, psychological conditions under which the equipment is operated (such as time pressures and conflicting demands) must also be closely matched to what the trainees experience on the job. This similarity is called **psychological fidelity**. Training in Action 5-1 describes what can happen when the match between simulation and work setting is less than adequate. The events described in this example were reported by one of the new sales clerk trainees.

**Equipment Simulators** mechanical devices that require trainees to use the same procedures, movements, or decision processes they would use with equipment back on the job.

**Physical Fidelity** the degree to which the simulation replicates, as closely as possible, the physical aspects of the equipment and operating environment trainees will find at their job site.

**Psychological Fidelity** the degree to which the simulation replicates, as closely as possible, the psychological conditions under which the equipment is operated (such as time pressures and conflicting demands).

## Training in Action 5-1

### Sales Simulation

Twenty-five retail sales clerk trainees were learning how to operate the company's electronic sales register system. The trainees each stood in front of a sales register that was actually an older model sales register refitted to serve as a training device. On a screen facing each trainee, a video depicted a customer waiting to make a purchase. The items this customer wanted to purchase were automatically brought on a conveyer belt to the trainee. The trainee entered specific keystrokes to activate the register for a new sale, picked up each item and scanned it into the register. When all the items were entered, the trainee entered more keystrokes to total the sale. When the sale was totalled, the conveyer brought forward cash, a cheque, or a credit card, simulating the customer's payment choice. The trainee entered different keystrokes denoting a cheque, credit, or cash sale. If cash was used, the cash drawer opened. The clerk was to deposit the customer's payment and remove the correct amount of change, if any. Credit cards were scanned and automatically debited for the total of the purchase. Payment by credit card or cheque also required the customer's identification to be documented. Once payment was received, any change and the receipt were to be given to the customer. This was simulated by placing the change in a bin on the counter. The purchased items were then bagged and given to the customer (again placed in the bin).

This simulation might be fairly good. Unfortunately, when the trainees were placed at the real registers the next day things were quite different from their training experiences. First, the registers they used were a newer model than those used in training, so some of the keys were in different places. Second, people were standing impatiently in line. Some wanted to purchase items and others needed help with merchandise or wanted to know the location of items in the store. The clerks couldn't concentrate only on working the register; they also had to interact with the customers. The scanner wouldn't read some customers' credit cards. Some customers argued about the price of items, insisting it was on sale for a lower price, though the scanner indicated a higher price. Some customers had their items totalled up and then decided they did not want one of the items or that they wanted additional items. Needless to say, the simulation training proved less than helpful, and many considered it to have lowered their capabilities. They felt they made many keystroke errors because of the training. If they just were allowed to learn on the job, they would not now be unlearning portions of the previous day's training.

The organizational development literature provides guidelines for the design/redesign of equipment.[15] HRD professionals engaged in the design of simulators and their pre-testing should involve those who will be using the equipment and their supervisors. Their input helps reduce potential resistance to the equipment and, more importantly, increases the degree of fidelity between the simulation and the work setting. In Training in Action 5-1, if trainers had brought in experienced sales clerks or their supervisors to pilot the simulation, they might have identified the fidelity problems, which could have then been corrected.

## How to Use the Equipment Simulation Effectively

When the simulator is used, it often occupies the bulk of the training time. Tasks are attempted on the simulator, feedback is provided, and then more simulator time is taken. Learning by doing is the major focus. At the same time, the instructor is available to provide feedback.

In the development of a simulation there may be a temptation to use out-of-date machinery to reduce costs. Why use a brand-new piece of machinery for training when it could be on the shop floor and have a direct impact on productivity? This issue was part of the problem in Training in Action 5-1. What must be taken into account is the reduction in transfer of training that is created by reducing the fidelity of the simulation. After all, productivity is lost and training time and costs are wasted if the appropriate skills do not transfer back to the job.

Psychological fidelity is just as important as physical fidelity. Imagine a pilot learning how to fly a simulator that did not have a wind factor built in. Suppose in landing a real plane, the pilot lines up with the runway and heads straight in, as taught, when suddenly a 50-kilometre-per-hour crosswind appears. This type of thing happened in Training in Action 5-1, when customers suddenly appeared with different requests and events occurred that had not been part of the simulation.

The simulation should first be designed to allow the learning of the job skills without complications from other factors, such as wind in the case of the pilot and customers in the case of the clerks. Once the trainee acquires these basic skills, outside factors can be introduced in the training. Increasing levels of complication are added to the simulation until the trainee reaches the appropriate levels of physical and psychological fidelity.

# BUSINESS GAMES

Decades ago, the University of Washington debuted a board game, *Top Management Decision Game,* as a way for business students to see the theories in their textbooks put into action.[16] Since then, trainers have moved to computer-based simulations that use interactive multimedia and virtual reality. **Business games** are simulations that attempt to represent the way an industry, company, or unit of a company functions. Typically, they are based on a set of relationships, rules, and principles derived from theory or research. However, they can also reflect the actual operations of a particular department in a specific company. Trainees are provided with information describing a situation and are asked to make decisions about what to do. The system then provides feedback about the impact of their decisions, after which trainees are asked to make another decision. This process continues until some predefined state of the organization is reached or a specified number of trials are completed.

Depending on the objectives, you will choose either an inter-company or an intra-company game. The inter-company games require trainees to compete in a marketplace. The more complex games require decisions about where to build factories, what product to advertise, the quality to be built into the product, how many

**Business Games** simulations that attempt to represent the way an industry, company, or unit of a company functions.

salespeople to hire, how to pay them, and so on. Trainees are assigned to teams that compete against one another in the simulation game. As a result, the decisions made by each team affect the environment they all share.

These business games involve an element of competition, either against other players or against the game itself. Some of the purposes for which business games have been developed and used are listed below:[17]

- Strengthen executive and upper-management skills,

- Improve decision-making skills at all levels,

- Demonstrate principles and concepts,

- Integrate separate components of training into an integrated whole,

- Explore and solve complex problems in a safe, simulated setting,

- Develop leadership skills,

- Improve application of total quality principles and develop skill in using quality tools.

Games that simulate entire companies or industries provide a far better systems perspective than do other training methods. They allow trainees to see how their decisions and actions influence not only their immediate target but also related areas. Training in Action 5-2 describes one such simulation.

Intra-company business games require teams or individuals to represent different functional areas in a single company. The process is similar to that of the inter-company but without the competition. In fact, cooperation is usually required for success in the game.

If it is decided to use a business game, first find one that meets the training objectives. A wide variety of business games and simulations are available and cover a wide

## Training in Action 5-2

### *The People's Express Simulator*

People's Express (PE) is an airline company that made quite a splash in the business news for a while during the 1980s, but was eventually acquired by a competitor. As a start-up passenger airline, it managed to capture a significant market share in just a few years. It was one of the first airlines to offer deep-discount air travel, with friendly but no-frills service.

A simulation based on PE can be played individually or by several people adopting different top management decision-making roles within the company. The game begins with the decisions to be made after the company's first year in business. The player(s) must decide how much money to invest in new aircraft, new employees, quality, services, and marketing. The game utilizes industry and economic statistics from the time periods involved to determine the effect of the players' decisions in these areas. The game is played for a specified number of years or until specified financial criteria are reached (positive or negative).

If only a single player is involved, the game can be used to demonstrate the integrated nature of decision-making in this business. Too much money invested in new aircraft means not enough trained staff to work the aircraft, higher payroll and training costs, and lower service levels. Too much investment in marketing, and demand may outstrip capacity, wasting a portion of the marketing investment, creating unnecessarily high costs, and resulting in lower demand in the future (due to turning away customers and having lower service). The player must find the right balance among investments in these four critical areas. When multiple players are involved, the learning can also focus on how to reach consensus decisions and the importance of sharing information and strategies across functional areas.

range of topics such as marketing, accounting, finance, and general management. A good source for exploring new games and learning how to develop your own games is the Association for Business Simulations and Experiential Learning. Its publication *Developments in Business Simulation and Experiential Learning* describes new business games and simulations. The association also sponsors an annual conference where new exercises, games, and simulations are demonstrated and discussed.

### How to Use the Business Game Effectively
Business games should not be used as a standalone training method. A typical training program would alternate methods (such as readings, lecture, discussion) with trials on the simulation, continuing in this way to the end of the game, at which point a general discussion would take place. Initial interest needs to be created in the game. However, as the game progresses, trainees often become quite involved, spending a great deal of time determining their strategies and plotting moves.

Business games can take between a few hours and a number of weeks to complete. Unless the training objectives are fairly simple, expect to need at least a few days for trainees to complete the game. Prior to beginning the game and at its conclusion, point out to the trainees what the learning objectives are and how the game relates to the objectives. These briefings will help keep trainees focused on the key learning points. Prior to beginning the game, trainees will need to read the manual. Once trainees are familiar with the objectives of the game and its rules and procedures, they meet in teams to make decisions about strategy, roles, and such. Once the game begins, the team decisions are transferred to the trainer (game administrator) or computer. Results are tabulated and fed back to the teams. Teams examine the feedback and any new information in light of the previous decisions and then make another decision. This process continues over a number of decisions. Dr. Tony Faria, an expert in the field, suggests that a minimum of 12 decisions need to be made in order for trainees to benefit from the exercise. The first four decisions provide trainees with a general understanding of the game and how the various factors interact; the second four provide a framework for competing; and in the final four, strategic decisions are made with enough knowledge to be meaningful.[18] After the final decisions are in and results tabulated, trainees meet to discuss the results, as well as the logic and criteria they used in making their decisions. These discussions regarding how and why decisions were made, and their consequences, are a very important part of the training, as this is where a great deal of the learning takes place.

## IN-BASKET TECHNIQUE

**In-Basket Technique** a simulation that provides trainees with a packet of written information and requests, such as memos, messages, and reports, that would typically be handled in a given position.

The **in-basket technique** provides trainees with a packet of written information and requests, such as memos, messages, and reports, that would typically be handled in a given position such as sales manager, staff administrator, or engineer. This popular quasi-simulation focuses primarily on decision-making and allows an opportunity for both assessing and developing decision-making KSAs. This technique is most often used when preparing employees for promotion or transfer to a new work environment.

Typically, the trainee's decisions are simply written down rather than carried out. Thus, the technique is good at teaching trainees what decision to make but not at developing the skills needed to carry out the decision. A few in-basket exercises require the trainee to "call" someone and communicate the decision or request additional information. In these cases, interpersonal skills can also be developed.

In-baskets are not as readily available commercially as simulations. One reason is that they are relatively easy to develop. Simply examine current job-holders' in-baskets for the material. Take papers from the in-basket, including filler material that requires no action (flyers, memos copied to the person) and follow the scenario from Training in Action 5-3. Use the trainee's current position as the position in the scenario. To provide the stress of real-life management, the amount of information that needs attention should be more than can be expected to be completed in the allotted time. To determine the appropriate actions that should be taken, choose high performers from the job in question and ask them what they would do. The attraction of the in-basket is that it is developed from real information from the trainees' organization.

<u>How to Use the In-Basket Effectively</u> Typically, trainees are given a type of job to role-play. They receive a description of their role and general information about the context in which the role is being carried out. See Training in Action 5-3 for an example. Trainees are then given the packet of materials that make up the in-basket and asked to respond to the materials within a certain time period. After all the trainees complete the in-basket, a group discussion with the trainer follows in which the trainees describe the rationale for their decisions. For example, as a trainer you might ask about what strategies the trainees used to prioritize the information, asking questions such as, "What criteria did you use to determine which person to contact first when you arrived on the job?" "How did you determine the order in which you addressed the issues?" The discussion will gradually become more specific and address how trainees responded to specific items, such as "What did you do about the complaint that was three weeks old?"

The advantages and disadvantages of different approaches are highlighted in the group discussion. This allows trainees to see different strategies and approaches to

## Training in Action 5-3

### *Typical Instructions for an In-Basket Exercise*

**Salesperson In-Basket Instructions**

Your name is Lee. You have been with Bennett Corporation for 1½ years as a salesperson in the business machines marketing force on the east coast. A position opened up in the Midwest region a few weeks ago when the salesman, John Quitt, left the company and his customers without notice. The other salespeople in your new office tried to cover the calls coming in from the accounts you are to be assuming but were not able to handle all the calls, so you must do some catching up. Your transfer is still a week away, but the company flies you out to the Midwest office to go through your predecessor's overflowing in-basket. It is Sunday evening, April 13, and no one else is in the office. In 75 minutes, you must leave to catch a plane to the Training Centre and you will not be able to be contacted for the week you are there.

Read through the items and decide on a course of action. It is imperative that you respond immediately because you will not be back for a week. All responses must be in writing so you can leave them for the other office personnel. Responses may include letter writing, writing memos to others

or yourself, scheduling meetings, making phone calls (outline what is to be discussed), and so on. You may write your responses on the same memo you received or on the memo pad provided. Writing paper is also provided if you wish to write a letter. Be sure to attach any memos or letters to the appropriate item. It is your first trip to the Midwest, and you have not yet met any of your new co-workers.

An organizational chart and calendar are provided for your reference.

Remember, every action you take or plan to take must be in writing. If you don't write it down, the assessor will have no way of assessing your performance.

It is advisable to read through the entire in-basket before taking any action.

#### Timetable

5 minutes          Read instructions.
75 minutes         Read and respond to in-basket items.

***Please do not proceed until told to do so.***

the same set of issues. During or immediately following the discussion, the trainer provides a summary of the alternative approaches to making the various types of decisions. The training concludes with a discussion of the lessons learned and how these can be applied on the job.

The majority of the learning with the in-basket technique occurs during the discussion session. It can take a half-day or more to complete the in-basket and the discussion that follows. If the training objectives allow trainees to complete the in-basket materials prior to the start of the training session (perhaps the evening before), the actual time spent in training can be reduced. In such cases the time constraint on the trainee to complete the in-basket is removed. If you are able to create the in-basket electronically, then the time limit can be retained. The extra time you gain could be used to provide individual feedback on each trainee's decisions before the discussion session. This will help focus the trainees' attention on the areas most important to their individual development. It will also allow you to develop more targeted and effective questions to ask during the group discussion.

A variation on the technique is to run multiple, simultaneous in-baskets in which each trainee receives a different but interrelated set of information. The trainees must interact with one another to gather all the information necessary to make an appropriate decision. This activity allows development of communication, as well as decision-making skills. It also includes elements of role-play and business games training.

# CASE STUDIES

**Case Study** a simulation that attempts to simulate decision-making situations that trainees might find on the job.

**Case studies** attempt to simulate decision-making situations that trainees might find on the job. The trainee is usually presented with a written (or videotaped) history, key elements, and the issues faced by a real or imaginary organization or organizational unit. The trainer should convey that no single solution is right or wrong and that many solutions are possible.[19] The learning objective is to get trainees to apply known concepts and principles and discover new ones. The solutions are not as important as is trainees' understanding of the advantages and disadvantages that go along with the solutions.

The written case study can range in length from a few pages to 100 or more. A series of questions usually appears at the end of the case. Longer ones provide a great deal of information to be examined and assessed for its relevance to the decisions being made. Others require the trainee to conduct research to gather the appropriate information. Based on the information available, the trainee must analyze the situation, identify the key issues, and then identify ways to address the issues. Typically the issues revolve around threats and opportunities to the organization in relation to its strengths and weaknesses.

**Incident Process** a simulation in which trainees are given only a brief description of the problem and must gather additional information from the trainer (and perhaps others) by asking specific questions.

A variation of the case study is the **incident process**, in which trainees are given only a brief description of the problem[20] and must gather additional information from the trainer (and perhaps others) by asking specific questions. Since managers gather most of their information from questioning and interacting with others, this activity is meant to simulate a manager's work more closely. In all case study methods, the information sorting and gathering process can be as much a learning focus as the nature of the problem being worked on. In such instances, the focus is on understanding the criteria that separate relevant from irrelevant information and learning where and how to gather relevant information.

If the decision is to use a case, it is necessary to find or develop one that will achieve the objectives. Harvard University and the University of Western Ontario are good sources. Their cases are based on real organizations' experiences. The advantage of "real" cases is that they can be enriched with up-to-date information from the organization, as well as describing "what the outcome of the case really was," and how it affected the company.

Writing a case requires a special skill, and if one that fulfills your objectives can be located, it is probably preferable to use it. However, there are inherent advantages in writing a case about your own company. The case can be written with the learning objectives in mind and therefore be truly focused on the company's needs. Additionally, trainee interest and transfer of training will be high because it is about the trainees' own organization.[21] The issues will be relevant to the training objectives and to the trainees personally. If you do decide to write a case, refer to guides such as the *Handbook of Creative Learning*.[22]

### How to Use the Case Study Effectively
Cases reflect the typical situation faced by most managers—incomplete information about many of the factors that influence how an organization should move forward. For most cases the trainees are given time to digest the information provided individually. If time permits, they may be allowed to collect additional information and integrate it into their strategy and action plan. Once individuals complete their case write-up, they may meet in small groups to discuss the different analyses, issues, strategies, and action plans. Then the trainees meet with the trainer, who facilitates and directs further discussion.

The trainer guides the trainees in examining the possible alternatives and consequences without actually stating what they are. The guided discovery method is especially important in this situation. The trainer's analysis of the case and action plan to address the issues is irrelevant to that process; in fact, it hinders it. The trainer must also direct the discussion of the case toward achieving the training objectives. Suppose problem analysis is the objective of the training. Here you allow the case to go in the direction the trainees wish it to go, as long as they are pursuing a problem and analyzing it.

The role of trainer also requires facilitation of group discussion, keeping the communication climate open while ensuring that the focus remains on important learning points. The trainer becomes the catalyst for discussion by calling on trainees for opinions and encouraging others to confront aspects of a position they do not support. In this role the trainer must remember to deflect requests from trainees to give her own "solution" to the case. Instead, use relay or reverse questioning techniques.

One major concern for trainers when using the case method is making sure individuals read the case and prepare for the discussion. Using training time for case reading and preparation ensures that work will be done, but it cuts into discussion time. If several training days are to be used, especially if the training is off-site and trainees are staying at a hotel, structured assignments can be built into the evenings. This option reduces the downtime of the training day. Of course, with a one-day training period, you can always provide the case and ask that trainees read it and answer questions ahead of time. However, this technique is advisable only when you can be sure everyone will in fact read it ahead of time. Trainees are more likely to read the case if they realize they will be required to meet in small groups to discuss it.

# ROLE-PLAY

Role-play is an enactment (or simulation) of a scenario in which each participant is given a part to act out. Trainees are provided with a description of the context—usually a topic area, a general description of a situation, a description of their roles (e.g., their

**Role-Play** an enactment (or simulation) of a scenario in which each participant is given a part to act out.

objectives, emotions, concerns), and the problem they each face. For example, the topic area could be managing conflict and the situation might revolve around scheduling vacation days, with the two parties in conflict being the supervisor and subordinate. The problem could be that the subordinate wants to take a vacation during the first week of August and the supervisor knows that a big project comes due on that date. Once the participants read their role descriptions, they act out their roles by interacting with one another.

The degree to which a scenario is structured will depend on what the learning objectives are. **Structured role-plays** provide trainees with more detail about the situation as well as more detailed descriptions of each character's attitudes, needs, opinions, and so on. Sometimes, structured role-plays even include a scripted dialogue. This type of role-play is used primarily to develop interpersonal skills such as communication, conflict resolution, and group decision-making.

**Spontaneous role-plays** are loosely constructed interactions in which one of the participants plays himself while the other(s) play people with whom the first trainee interacted in the past, or will in the future. This type of role-play focuses on attitudes and is typically used to develop insight into our own behaviour and its impact on others, rather than to develop specific skills.

In a **single role-play**, one group of trainees role-plays for the rest, providing a visual demonstration of some learning point. Other trainees observe the role-play, analyzing the interactions and identifying learning points. Although this format provides a single focus for trainees and feedback from a skilled observer (the trainer), it does have some disadvantages. Those chosen to act as the characters may experience acute embarrassment at being the centre of attention. They also do not have the advantage of watching others perform the roles. In addition, they may not play the roles in a manner that clearly portrays the behaviours that are the focus of training. Having people other than trainees act out the role-play eliminates these problems but adds some cost to the training.

A **multiple role-play** is the same as a single role-play except that all trainees are in groups, with each group acting out the role-play simultaneously. Following the role-play, each group analyzes the interactions and identifies learning points among themselves. Each group may report a summary of its analysis and learning to the others. This format allows a rich discussion of the issues because each group will play the roles somewhat differently. It also reduces the amount of time required to complete the process, but may reduce the quality of feedback as well. Trainees are generally reluctant to provide negative feedback to peers. Even if they are willing, they may not have the experience or expertise to provide constructive feedback. Videotaping the role-play is another option. The trainee uses the tape for self-evaluation and the trainer can examine the tapes between sessions and provide individual feedback.

The **role rotation** method begins as a single role-play. After the characters interact for a period of time, the trainer will stop the role-play and discuss what happened so far, as well as what can be learned from it. Then different trainees are asked to exchange places with some or all of the characters. These trainees then pick up where the others left off. This format allows both a common focus for all trainees (except those in the role-play) and demonstrates a variety of ways to approach the roles. It keeps trainees more active than the single role-play and allows for feedback from a skilled observer. However, it requires the progress of the role-play to be frequently interrupted, creating additional artificiality. Again, trainees may be inhibited from publicly critiquing the behaviour of their fellow trainees and may be embarrassed to play a role in front of everyone else.

**Structured Role-Play** a role-play that provides trainees with more detail about the situation as well as more detailed descriptions of each character's attitudes, needs, opinions, and so on.

**Spontaneous Role-Play** loosely constructed role-plays in which one of the participants plays himself while the other(s) play people with whom the first trainee interacted in the past, or will in the future.

**Single Role-Play** one group of trainees role-plays for the rest, providing a visual demonstration of some learning point.

**Multiple Role-Play** the same as a single role-play except that all trainees are in groups, with each group acting out the role-play simultaneously.

**Role Rotation** similar to a single role-play, but after the characters interact for a period of time, the trainer will stop the role-play and discuss what happened so far, as well as what can be learned from it, then continue with other trainees.

## How to Use the Role-Play Effectively

Role-plays are available in many textbooks and from other sources, but they are also reasonably easy to write. The advantage of writing a role-play is that it can be tailored to the trainee population. Role-plays can be strategically placed throughout the training to provide not only the skills practice but also a change of pace.

Feedback is an important component in the role-play. The decision as to how it will be given is a function of the amount of time available. Training is more effective when the trainer can provide individual feedback. However, time and financial constraints may limit the degree to which this is possible. When time is limited, trainees may be asked to provide feedback to other trainees. One way to do this is by putting the trainees into groups of three: the person creating the situation (initiator), the person who will respond using the skills (responder), and the person who will provide feedback (observer). Provide three sets of role-plays that are different but contain the same learning points. Also, provide sheets of "learning points to look for" regarding the three role-plays. Now each of the trainees is given the opportunity to be in each position. The advantage is that this approach reduces the amount of time required to complete the process. The disadvantage is in the quality of feedback. Trainees are generally reluctant to provide negative feedback to peers, and even if they are willing, they are not experts, so feedback may not be accurate. Nevertheless, if it is set up with clear instructions and an understanding of the requirements, it can be an excellent learning tool. Each trainee is able to practise the skills, see how the skills work on them (as the initiator), and watch and provide feedback (as the observer). It may be useful to have the instructor and two volunteers run through exactly what is required (using a different role-play) before starting. Another option is to videotape the role-play. The trainee can use the tape for self-evaluation, peers in small groups can use it to evaluate each other, or the trainer can use it between sessions to provide individual feedback.

It is important to avoid the following problems when selecting or writing a role-play:[23]

1. Reduced level of generalizability to the job; this results from problems addressed in the role-play that are not generally handled at the trainees' level in the organization,

2. Confusion that results from incomplete information or too much or misleading information,

3. Confusion about how to behave in the role-play because the interrelationships are too complex,

4. Conflicts left unresolved because the script creates more than can be resolved in the allotted time, and

5. Unrealistic or trivial scripts.

Some concerns may arise about the trainees' involvement in the role-play. For some trainees the role-play can be considered "fun" but not real, which lessens the generalizability to the job. Others find it stressful to act out a role with others watching. Table 5-4 provides tips on how to develop and present a role-play.

Depending on the method used in providing feedback, the time frame for completing a set of role-plays could be from one hour to one day. Considering that just the preparation of trainees for the role-play (along with a demonstration) could take 20 to 30 minutes, the complete session could take a whole day if everyone were to role-play in front of everyone else.

## TABLE 5-4 Tips for Developing and Presenting Role-Plays

**Developing**

- Create your characters carefully to prove your point. Provide two characters who are going to clash in exactly the way you want. For example, use one player to force another either to use the skills taught or to illustrate what happens when those skills are not used. Do not write a script (unless you are teaching rote responses), but provide detailed background on characters' habits, attitudes, goals, personalities, and mood; as well as on the business restrictions that motivate or restrain them.

- Use role-playing to illustrate one key problem. Do not try for more than one topic or you will diffuse the impact and distract the learners with too much information.

**Presenting**

- Take the time to introduce the situation. Give trainees enough background to understand what's at stake, then assign the roles.

- Both the role-plays and the discussions can get off topic. To prevent digression, make sure participants understand your instructions. For example, tell them, "The customer service representative must (1) use the customer's name three times; (2) organize, clarify, and confirm the nature of the customer's problem; (3) empathize with the customer; and (4) offer to do something for the customer." If you plan to use observers to provide feedback, have each of them use an observation sheet to look for key behaviours and to respond to key aspects of the performance.

- If the role-play gets off topic, stop the performance and ask, "What are the problems here? Why isn't the conversation moving in the right direction?" Be assertive to ensure that they stay in character and on topic.

- After the performance, always discuss what happened. This is how learning takes place. Ask questions of each player, and have the group advise the players. Encourage discussion. Challenge them with alternatives: "What would have happened if...?"

*Source:* Adapted from Mitchell, G. (1993). *The Trainer's Handbook*. New York: AMACOM.

# BEHAVIOUR MODELLING

**Behaviour Modelling** learning through watching and then imitating a model who provides an example of the behaviour to be learned.

**Behaviour modelling** uses the natural tendency of people to observe others in order to learn how to do something new. This technique is most frequently used in combination with some other technique. For example, the modelled behaviour is typically videotaped and then watched by the trainees. We include it in the games and simulation section because once the trainees observe the model, they typically practise the behaviour in some form of simulation or role-play. However, the behavioural modelling process itself is distinctly different from these methods. Only minor differences exist among the various descriptions of behaviour modelling in the literature.[24] The behaviour modelling process can be summarized as follows:

1. Define the key skill deficiencies;

2. Provide a brief overview of relevant theory;

3. Specify key learning points and critical behaviours to watch for;

4. Use an expert to model the appropriate behaviours;

5. Encourage trainees to practise the appropriate behaviours in a structured role-play;

6. Provide opportunities for the trainer and other trainees to give reinforcement for appropriate imitation of the model's behaviour; and

7. Ensure that the trainee's supervisor reinforces appropriate demonstration of behaviour on the job.

A training module comprising all seven steps is developed for each skill to be learned. An overview module should also be provided, as well as a separate workshop for those who supervise the trainees back on the job.

Behaviour modelling differs from both role-plays and simulations by first providing the trainee with an understanding of what the desired skill level looks like. This method is based on Bandura's social learning theory and is focused on developing behavioural skills. However, steps two and three reflect the cognitively oriented learning features of the technique, and steps five to seven reflect behaviourist/reinforcement theory features.

Behaviour modelling is useful for almost any type of skill training. It can be used to provide interpersonal skills, sales skills, interviewee and interviewer skills, safety skills, and skills in many other areas.[25] One method of behaviour modelling makes extensive use of video modelling and feedback. The trainee first observes the behaviour being performed by a model and then attempts to reproduce the behaviour (step 5) while being videotaped. Through split-screen devices, the model and the trainee can be shown side by side, and the trainee can see exactly where his performance does or does not match the model's.

### How to Use Behaviour Modelling Effectively Although a live model can be used, a video is better for two reasons. First, it will be an accurate, standardized depiction of the required behaviour. The action can be redone until it is exact. Using a live model leaves room for variations or inappropriate behaviours. Second, scripted learning points and steps being followed can be inserted into the video. These descriptions allow the trainee to see the behaviour and the specific point being highlighted at the same time.

One difficulty is finding or developing a video for the desired behaviour. A number of videos are available, but the quality varies considerably.[26] Also, it is important to preview them before purchase, because the video must match the learning objectives. Videos developed for general resale typically do not provide the behaviour modelled exactly the way the company would like it done. Developing a video is also a possibility, but cost, ability to make a professional product, and the time needed may rule out that option. Table 5-5 provides a number of suggestions if the decision is made to use behaviour modelling.

A behaviour modelling training session starts with trainees watching a video of the modelled behaviour. Trainees would then perform the behaviour and watch a videotape of their performance. Finally, trainees would receive feedback on their behaviour. If videotaping is used, the number of video cameras and VCRs available limits the number of concurrent sessions that can take place. This method is highly dependent on effective feedback; thus a sufficient number of trainers must be available to provide feedback.

## STRENGTHS AND LIMITATIONS OF GAMES AND SIMULATIONS

Even though games and simulations come in a variety of formats, they share many common strengths and limitations. When a specific format differs from others in this regard, we discuss it separately; otherwise our discussion of strengths and limitations applies to all formats.

Knowledge for Business Training and Instruction; Modelling and Simulation *www.tm.tno.nl/research/perception.html*

### Costs The development costs of games and simulations vary from format to format. In general, equipment simulators are the most expensive to develop, but cost will depend on the nature of the equipment that is simulated. For example, millions of dollars are spent on aircraft simulators used to train commercial and military flight officers. Conversely, retail clerks and bank tellers can be trained on the actual equipment they will use on the job. The equipment can be moved back and forth from

## TABLE 5-5 Things to Consider When Implementing Behaviour Modelling

- Use care in selecting the trainer/program administrator who will set up and conduct the sessions. This person must be skilled and experienced with this technique.
- Consider carefully whether this technique will meet your needs within your constraints of time and money. Unless you can accomplish the following, you probably should not use this technique:
  - identify specific skill deficiencies,
  - present a positive model of the appropriate behaviour,
  - provide the time for each trainee to practice the behaviour under the watchful eye of the trainer, and
  - arrange for reinforcement from the manager of each trainee back on the job.
- Identify real skill deficiencies in advance of training and involve the potential trainees and their bosses in this process. This activity will gain the key peoples' attention and their ownership of the objectives of the training sessions.
- Break the skills into small behaviours. Build a module around each small behaviour and progress one step at a time, starting with a simple behavioural element, in order to gain confidence.
- Do not emphasize more than seven learning points during any one training module.
- Ensure models used to demonstrate the correct way of behaving/handling a certain situation have sufficient status to be credible yet easy for the trainees to identify with.
- Use a videotape of a model performing the correct behaviour to ensure all groups of trainees will see a positive example. It may reduce costs because it is reusable. However, this advantage may be negated because it is difficult to find a model and a situation likely to be highly relevant and identifiable across diverse groups of trainees.
- Ask trainees to verbalize the behavioural cues demonstrated by the model and then to visualize their pending performance before they actually practice the desired behaviour. Verbalization may help improve generalization and use of the behaviours in new situations.
- Establish a supportive climate that encourages experimentation for the practice sessions. Emphasis on positive reinforcement rather than criticism increases self-confidence and learning.
- Provide a wallet-sized card that outlines the key learning points and critical steps, after each session. This reminder acts as a security blanket for the trainees to reassure them that they will know the crucial features as they attempt to apply the training back to their jobs.
- Conduct a review session after the completion of several modules in order to reinforce the learning points and to demonstrate the progress attained by the trainees.
- Manage the consequences of attempting the newly trained behaviours in the actual job situation. Work with the managers of the trainees to ensure that they set attainable goals for their subordinates, remove obstacles that may prevent trainees from attempting the new behaviours, and provide incentives for such attempts.

*Source:* Camp R., Blanchard, P., & Huszczo, G. (1986). *Toward a More Organizationally Effective Training Strategy and Practice.* Upper Saddle River, NJ: Prentice Hall.

training to the job site. Even if the development costs of equipment simulators are high, they are often the best alternative. For example, pilot trainees taking test flights in an airplane will not be exposed to all the possible situations they might encounter in flying thousands of hours a year, so the trainees would not learn from this method as much as they could from a simulator. Also, pilots will need to know how to respond in dangerous situations, which are best practised in the safety of the simulator. In addition, the cost of "flying" a simulator is a small fraction of the cost of flying an actual aircraft. The total costs of using the simulation can be lower than alternative methods, even when the development cost is quite high.

At the low end of development costs are role-plays. A wide range of role-plays are already developed and published and include instructions and suggestions for their use. Many of these publications are free. However, a role-play tailored to the company's needs can be done at little cost.

Business games are somewhat more complicated and thus usually more expensive than role-plays. Multimedia or computer-based games or simulations will be more expensive but have the advantage of being reusable, so the cost can be amortized across the number of trainees. Behaviour modelling costs can range from moderately low to high, depending on the format used. Using an expert to model the desired behaviour live (e.g., welding two plates together) simply involves the cost of the model. Since the model is typically an employee of the company, the cost is just the lost production while the expert is modelling. Using professional actors as models for interpersonal skills training, for example, will add to the cost but may be worth it in terms of improved quality. The use of live models is more expensive than using video-taped models because the cost is incurred each time the model is used. Videotaping the model allows the videotape to be used again but adds the cost of creating it. Professionally developed videos can be fairly expensive and will be discussed more fully in the audiovisual section of this chapter.

Two things to consider when examining cost of a game or simulation are

- The degree of flexibility built into the simulation or game, and
- The cost of making mistakes while in training must be factored into the cost/benefit decision when comparing various methods.

Regarding flexibility, the cockpit simulator that is programmable to reflect the characteristics of many different aircraft will be more cost effective than one that can simulate only one type of aircraft. The same is true of business games and other types of simulations. A business game that is programmed to create different economic situations and business conditions will have a wider audience base and a longer useful life than one that does not.

One of the primary strengths of games and simulations is that they allow trainees to develop and practise skills in a safe setting. Mistakes in business decisions can be financially disastrous. Mistakes in equipment operation can cause damage to the equipment and physical harm to the operator and others. Mistakes in interpersonal behaviour can also result in financial losses to the company through lost customers, resentful employees, and misinterpreted instructions. Mistakes may result in psychological harm to the trainee, such as lowered self-esteem and confidence or increased defensiveness. Simulations and games allow trainees the opportunity to develop their skills in a situation where the costs of making a mistake are low or nonexistent.

## Control of Content and Process
When games and simulations are used, both the trainer and the trainee influence the content of what is learned and the processes used in learning. The game or simulation provides a set of information that focuses on a particular content area. The People's Express Simulator (Training in Action 5-2), for example, focuses on integrating business decisions across functional areas to improve company profitability and growth. Games and simulations also provide instructions and guidelines that strongly influence the learning process. By selecting an existing game or simulation or developing a new one, the trainer exerts control over the learning content and process. Many games and simulations are structured so that situations occur in a predetermined order, providing the trainer with greater control over both content and process. This control is desirable if all trainees will be exposed to the same situations back on the job. Arrest procedures for police or machine maintenance and troubleshooting for equipment operators are examples of such jobs. Other games and simulations allow the situation to change according to how trainees respond, enabling the trainee to exercise greater influence on what is learned and how. These types of games and simulations are useful when trainees must

learn how to deal with a wide range of situations and how to apply general principles, in areas such as business and financial planning, decision-making, and military battle tactics.

The format providing the least built-in structure is the unstructured role-play in which only a general set of guidelines is given to the participants beforehand. How the trainees interact while playing out their roles is under their own control. Although the trainer controls the choice of situation and roles, the trainees control how they are carried out. By asking the role-players to focus on certain steps in the learning process, such as saying, "First try to identify the cause of the conflict, and then try to generate win-win alternatives," the trainer exerts more influence. In the case of role-plays, reduced structure allows the trainees to imagine the situation as it might occur on the job. The potential danger is that it may be so unstructured that they do not take their roles seriously or they are unable to imagine how it could possibly apply to their job.

Cases provide more structure, particularly in setting the situation (i.e., characteristics of the organization). However, the trainees' process of analyzing the case is largely internal or influenced by the interaction within the training group. Through the manner in which trainers facilitate discussion of the case, they are able to exert more or less control over what trainees learn and how.

Equipment simulators generally provide the most structure. They must replicate the physical and psychological characteristics of the equipment and the environment in which it is operated. The simulator itself controls the content and process of learning. To the extent that the simulation is programmable, the trainer can manipulate the content.

**Learning Objectives (KSAs)** Games and simulations provide opportunities to learn through concrete experiences that require both theory and application. Theory provides the general principles that guide action. Application provides the opportunity to test those principles and understand them at a behavioural level, not just as abstract intellectual knowledge. As the philosopher Confucius said, "I hear and I forget. I see and I remember. I do and I understand."

Some types of knowledge enhancement and attitude change are achievable through games and simulations, but usually supplemental methods are required. Games and simulations generally require some background knowledge and provide a context in which this knowledge is applied. For example, a business game in which several teams of trainees compete for product market share makes some assumptions about the knowledge that trainees have about basic marketing strategies (e.g., product, pricing, promotions, and location). It allows them to apply their knowledge and see the consequences of that strategy.

For these and numerous other reasons, games and simulations do a good job of developing skills. First, they simulate the important conditions and situations that occur on the job. Second, they allow the trainees to practise the skill. Finally, they provide feedback about the appropriateness of the trainees' actions. Each of the formats is most appropriate for particular types of skills.

- Equipment simulators are best at teaching people how to work with equipment;
- Business games are best for developing business decision-making skills (both day-to-day and more strategic) and for exploring and solving complex problems;
- The in-basket technique is best suited to development of strategic knowledge used in making day-to-day decisions;
- Case studies are most appropriate for developing analytic skills, higher-level principles, and complex problem-solving strategies. As trainees do not actually

implement their decision/solution, its focus is more on the "what to do" (strategic knowledge) than on the "how to get it done" (skills); and

- Role-plays provide a good vehicle for developing interpersonal skills and personal insight, allowing trainees to practise interacting with others and receiving feedback.

Role-playing is an especially effective technique for creating attitude change.[27] It allows trainees to act out behaviour that reflects their attitudes and to experience others' reactions as well as their own feelings about the behaviour. The experience and feedback allow the trainee to make appropriate attitudinal adjustments. The role reversal is even more powerful, as it requires the trainee to take a position opposite to their attitude. It allows the trainee to better understand why others may hold differing attitudes. One such situation would be the supervisor with a negative attitude about union officials being asked to play the role of union steward defending an employee who had been treated unfairly. As an old role-playing saying goes: "Seeing is believing, but feeling is the truth." Although trainees may see the logic of a principle through a lecture and see its application in a video, they are able to feel its personal value only when they use it themselves.

## Learning Process

*Attention.* One of the strengths of games and simulations is their ability to gain the attention of the learner. The active learning process used by these training methods is generally more compelling to trainees than is sitting through a lecture or reading a text. In most games and many simulations, the aspect of competition against ourself or others increases attention and enthusiasm. Many also use clever gimmicks that capture trainees' interest, but these aspects can also distract trainees from the real learning objectives of the training. Sometimes trainees get so engrossed in the competition or "figuring out" the gimmick, they fail to learn the principles or develop the skills the game/simulation was intended to produce. It is important for trainers to build modules into the training that prepare trainees to use the game or simulation by identifying the desired learning outcomes. Modules might also be planned for breaks during the simulation to capture learning that occurred and to refocus trainees on the learning objectives. In general, a debriefing module should always be included so that trainees can reflect and elaborate on what they have learned.

Another important factor affecting trainee attention is the credibility of the game or simulation. When it does not realistically represent the key characteristics of the trainees' job, trainees will not take it seriously and will give it less attention. Consider a role-play or simulation designed to improve union–management problem solving. It asks trainees who are members of union–management committees to work on resolving certain issues. If these issues are, in reality, already contractually mandated in the company, both sides must pretend that part of the labour contract does not exist. When this happens, trainees are likely to consider the training irrelevant and not take it seriously.

*Retention.* Games and simulations are best at developing trainees' skills in applying or using knowledge. This approach assumes that the knowledge needed to play the game or use the simulation was already learned. This information exists as symbolic codes in the trainees' cognitive structure. Games or simulations do not do a good job of teaching facts or procedures, but they are especially good at enhancing this knowledge through the repeated recall and use of the information during the training. Thus they serve to refine and reinforce symbolic coding. Games and simulations focus primarily on the cognitive organization and symbolic rehearsal processes. Since the trainee must use many different areas of knowledge to complete the game or simulation, the trainee is able to see the connections and relationships between the different areas. Learning these new connections and relationships allows trainees to solve problems and develop strategies for achieving goals. Most games and simulations require trainees to engage in symbolic rehearsal by having them plan their action steps and anticipate their consequences.

*Behavioural Reproduction.* Of course, the real strength of games and simulations is their focus on learning by doing. Creating realistic situations in which trainees can apply their knowledge to goal-directed actions and receive fairly immediate feedback is critical for skill development. Behavioural reproduction is a significant part of the learning process when games and simulations are used. In order for the desired learning to occur, the training design must include feedback to the trainees about their actions. This requirement follows from the principles of reinforcement and shaping discussed in Chapter 2.

### Training Group Characteristics
Only one person at a time can use an equipment simulator, so to some extent differences in trainee readiness are addressed. As with all games and simulations, however, trainees must possess the prerequisite knowledge and skill to make effective use of the method. Since equipment simulators do limit the number of trainees who can be trained, this becomes a problem when a large number of trainees must be trained in a short period of time.

Business games and simulations, including behaviour modelling, typically use small groups ranging in size from three to eight trainees. Differences in trainee characteristics can be both an advantage and a disadvantage, depending on the goals of the training. Differences in content knowledge or experience can be an advantage if one of the goals of training is to increase the awareness of how different people approach the situation. In a business game or simulation, for example, constructing a group of trainees from different functional areas of the business allows each trainee to learn how decisions in their area affect other areas. Thus, all trainees learn a more integrative framework for decision-making. However, such groups generate more conflict and require more time for discussion and decision-making. Other differences in content knowledge can be more troublesome. When some trainees in the group are more knowledgeable in basic business concepts than are others, they can become irritated at having to educate the rest of the group. In general, it is best to make sure that groups are formed so that everyone shares relatively the same level of basic knowledge, unless, of course, the goal is to have more-knowledgeable trainees educate those less knowledgeable. The point is that the trainer must take care to identify how trainee group composition matches the training objectives.

# ON-THE-JOB TRAINING

**On-the-Job Training (OJT)** using more-experienced and skilled employees, whether co-workers or supervisors, to train less-skilled or less-experienced employees.

The most frequently used training method, especially in smaller businesses, is **on-the-job training (OJT)**. OJT uses more-experienced and skilled employees, whether co-workers or supervisors, to train less-skilled or less-experienced employees. OJT takes many forms and can be supplemented with classroom training. However, many organizations do not follow a structured approach.[28] Instruction by co-workers or supervisors at the job site often occurs on an informal basis and is characterized by the following:

- It has not been carefully thought out or prepared;
- It is done on an ad hoc basis with no predetermined content or process;
- No objectives or goals have been developed or referred to during training;
- The trainers are chosen on the basis of technical expertise, not training ability; and
- Trainers have no formal training in how to train.

Formal OJT programs are quite different. Those chosen to be the trainers for OJT are not necessarily the ones with the best technical knowledge and skills. These trainers need to have a solid understanding of the job and be able to use one-on-one instructional techniques effectively. One-on-one training is not a skill most people develop on their own, so organizations with formal OJT programs provide "train the trainer" training for these employees.

Formal OJT programs should follow a carefully developed sequence of learning events. Learning is usually achieved through the following steps:

1. The trainee observes a more experienced and skilled employee (the trainer) performing job-related tasks;

2. The procedures and techniques used are discussed before, during, and after the trainer has demonstrated how the job tasks are performed;

3. The trainee begins performing the job tasks when the trainer determines that the trainee is ready;

4. The trainer provides continuing guidance and feedback; and

5. The trainee is gradually given more and more of the job to perform until he can adequately perform the entire job on his own.

The generalized instructional process just described is formalized in more detail as the job instruction technique.

## JOB INSTRUCTION TECHNIQUE (JIT)

**Job instruction technique (JIT)** uses a behavioural strategy with a focus on skill development. However, as with most jobs, some knowledge objectives are usually involved as well. JIT[29] was developed during World War II and continues to be a standard in evaluating OJT programs. JIT consists of four steps—prepare, present, try out, and follow-up—as shown in Table 5-6.

**Prepare** Preparation and follow-up are the two areas most often ignored in OJT programs. Preparation should include a written breakdown of the job. The person responsible for the OJT may believe that, because of a familiarity with the job, written documentation is unnecessary. To ignore this step, however, is to miss seeing the job through the eyes of the trainee. A trainer who knows the job well is likely to be able to do a number of things without thinking, and these tasks may be overlooked in training. A systematic analysis and documentation of the job tasks will ensure that all the points are covered in the training.

The next step is to prepare an instructional plan. As a trainer, first determine what the trainee already knows. The person analysis portion of a needs assessment provides this information (see Chapter 3). Next, review any data available from a completed TNA. If no TNA is available, checking personnel records and interviewing the trainee are ways for you to find out what the trainee knows and what training should focus on.

Finally, putting the trainee at ease is just as important in OJT as it is in the classroom. Care must be taken to create a comfortable learning atmosphere. One way to create such an environment is to provide the trainee with an orientation to the OJT/JIT learning process. This orientation may or may not be provided by the JIT trainer. In this orientation, help trainees understand their role and the role of the trainer in the process. The importance of trainee listening and questioning should be emphasized. Familiarizing trainees with the steps in the JIT process will reduce their anxiety because they will know what to expect.

**Present** The four activities of this stage are tell, show, demonstrate, and explain.[30] First, tell and show. As the trainer, provide an overview of the job while showing the

**Job Instruction Technique (JIT)** a structured approach to on-the-job training that uses a behavioural strategy with a focus on skill development. It consists of four steps—prepare, present, try out, and follow-up.

Knowledge management *www.cio.com/forums/knowledge*

## TABLE 5-6 JIT Instruction/Learning Sequence

| Basics of Instruction | Areas of Learning Affected |
|---|---|
| **Prepare** | Attention and Motivation |
| • Break down the job. | |
| • Prepare an instruction plan. | |
| • Put the learner at ease. | |
| **Present** | Retention: |
| • Tell. | Symbolic coding |
| • Show. | Cognitive organization |
| • Demonstrate. | |
| • Explain. | |
| **Try Out** | Retention: |
| • Have the learner "talk through" the job. | Symbolic rehearsal |
| • Have the learner instruct the supervisor on how the job is done. | Behavioural reproduction |
| • Let the learner do the job. | |
| • Provide feedback, both positive and negative. | |
| • Let the learner practice. | |
| **Follow-Up** | Behavioural reproduction |
| • Check progress frequently at first. | |
| • Tell the learner whom to go to for help. | |
| • Gradually taper off progress checks. | |

*Source:* Gold, L. (1981). Job instruction: Four steps to success. *Training and Development Journal*, September, pp. 28–32.

trainee the different aspects of the job. You are not actually doing the job but pointing out where buttons are pushed, where materials are located, where to stand, and so on. When finished, demonstrate how to do the job and explain why it is done in that manner. If the job involves many components or is complex, cover only one segment at a time, in the same order in which segments occur when the job is performed. During the demonstration, indicate why the procedure is performed in that particular way, emphasizing key learning points and important safety instructions.

**Try Out** Before actually trying the behaviours, the trainee describes to the trainer how to do the job. This step provides a safe transition from watching and listening to doing (symbolic rehearsal). The trainee then attempts to perform the job and the trainer is able to provide instant feedback. Any errors that take place are probably a function of the training, and not the fault of the trainee. With this in mind, the focus will be on improving the method of instruction rather than on the inability of the trainee to comprehend. In any case, it is useful to allow the trainee to learn from mistakes, provided they are not too costly. Allowing the trainee to see the consequences of using an incorrect procedure (such as having to scrap the product) reinforces the use of the correct procedures. Such an occurrence becomes a form of negative reinforcement because using the correct procedures avoids the scrap. Questioning the trainee about her actions while she is performing the job and guiding her in identifying the correct procedures will help.

**Follow-Up** There is a tendency for informal OJT programs to consider training completed after the previous step. That is not correct. The trainer must check the trainees' work often enough to prevent incorrect or bad work habits from developing.

It is important that trainees feel comfortable asking for help during these initial solo efforts. Every opportunity should be taken to reinforce trainees in areas where they are performing well. As trainees demonstrate proficiency on the job, progress checks can taper off until they are eventually eliminated.

**How to Use JIT Effectively** Since trainers are chosen from those already knowledgeable about the job, these trainers often see the first step, preparation, as unnecessary. Ignoring the preparation step may result in missing something important because for the trainer it is automatic. Table 5-7 provides an example of the preparation step for the job of press feeder. If it looks similar to the operational analysis in the chapter on needs assessment, it is. If an operational analysis was previously completed, the majority of the work outlined in Table 5-7 is already done.

The follow-up step may also be ignored because it is not considered important. This step, however, is critical to ensure that the trained skills continue as they were

## TABLE 5-7 Job Breakdown Sheet for OJT

Dept: Metal Decorating  Prepared by J. Smith
Job: Feeder Pressman  Date: June 8

| Main Steps | Key Points | Tools/Equipment Material | Safety Factors |
|---|---|---|---|
| **Part I (Start of shift)** | | | |
| 1. Check level of fountain solution and refill if necessary. | Ask pressman which solution to use. Scratch mark shows minimum and maximum capacities. | All solutions kept in metal containers in storeroom | Do not spill on walkway. |
| 2. Check level of varnish in wet varnish machine and refill if necessary. | Check card for type of material being used and determine amount of thinner necessary to obtain proper viscosity. | Same as #1 | Very volatile and flammable. |
| 3. Wash sponges, bucket, and gum containers. | Use same thinner as in #2. | Same as #1 | Do not wash in enclosed area because of fumes. |
| **Part II (Start a new bundle in press)** | | | |
| 1. Request lift driver to bring over new bundle. | Do not wait until bundle on press is almost finished. | | |
| 2. Check new bundle to be sure it is the correct one and is in good condition. | Pull the job ticket and check order number; examine top sheets and sides and corners of bundle. | Leather-palmed gloves | Always wear gloves when handling sheets to prevent cuts. |
| **Part III (Whenever press is stopped)** | | | |
| 1. Lower elevator with bundle on it and cover with master sheet. | Lower only until top of bundle is at a convenient height. | Leather-palmed gloves | Wear gloves. |
| 2. Unless otherwise instructed by pressman, wet plate on front unit. | Be sure entire plate is wet; dry spots can oxidize and damage plate. | Sponges and clear water | Be sure press is clear before wetting plate. |

*Source*: Adapted from Gold, L. (1981). Job instruction: Four steps to success. *Training and Development Journal*, September, pp. 28–32.

taught. During the try-out step the trainee may demonstrate her capabilities in doing the job, but as with anything freshly learned, short cuts, poor work habits, and incorrect procedures can creep into performance. Periodically dropping by to follow up can catch such performance gaps and correct them before they become habitual. Following up becomes less important as the trainee's performance becomes consistently acceptable.

Structured OJT is effective when done properly and supported by the organization. The seven steps provided in Table 5-8 help ensure successful OJT. This process can be advantageous to small business, as shown in Focus on Small Business.

## Focus on Small Business

### What About Small Business?

Although any of the training methods described in this chapter are appropriate, OJT is the training method of choice for the small business. Many small businesses use peer training because they lack a budget for any formal training. The value of following the procedures outlined in the job instruction technique (JIT), whether the supervisor or a peer is to be the trainer, cannot be over-empha-sized. An up-front investment of time to train the OJT instructor and prepare the proper plan will ensure an optimal return on investment. Research suggests that structured OJT such as that described in JIT can get workers up-to-speed on their jobs in half the time regular training takes.[31]

## APPRENTICESHIP TRAINING

**Apprenticeship Training** a formal type of on-the-job-training in which trainees receive training from journeymen and knowledge through classroom instruction.

**Apprenticeship training**, another form of OJT, is one of the oldest forms of training. Its roots date back to the Middle Ages, when skilled crafts- and tradespeople passed on their knowledge to others as a way of preserving the guilds (similar to unions) they belonged to. Many similarities characterize today's North American apprenticeship programs. Apprenticeship programs are partnerships among labour unions, employers, schools, and the government. Most apprenticeships are in skilled trade and professional unions such as boiler engineers, electrical workers, pipe fitters, and carpenters. In general, an apprenticeship program requires about two years of on-the-job experience and 180 hours of classroom instruction, though requirements vary from program to program.[32] According to the Ontario Training and Adjustment Board, an apprentice cook, for example, requires one year of OJT and a week of classroom training, whereas a moldmaker requires four years of OJT with three eight-week classroom sessions.[33]

Journeymen provide the training on the job, and adult education centres and community colleges typically provide the classroom training. An apprentice must be able to demonstrate mastery of all required skills and knowledge before being allowed to graduate to journeyman status. These programs are regulated by governmental agencies, which also set standards and provide services.

### How to Use Apprenticeship Training Effectively
Although formal apprenticeship programs are strictly controlled by the Ministry of Labour, nothing would stop an organization from setting up its own informal apprenticeship programs. The journeyman rank provided to employees upon successful completion will not be transferable to other organizations, but it is possible to take advantage of the process nonetheless.

## TABLE 5-8 Steps to Follow for Better OJT

1. Establish policy.

   Prepare a written description that puts the organization "on the record" as supporting structured OJT and makes a commitment to it. Make sure that the purpose of structured OJT is spelled out and is related to the company's other HRD efforts.

2. Establish accountability.

   Make clear who is primarily responsible for OJT. Write it into their job descriptions. Then ensure that part of their performance evaluation is based on how well they carry out this responsibility.

3. Review precedents.

   Make a few calls to find out what other organizations in your industry are doing about structured OJT. Do they provide training on the subject? If so, to whom? For how long? What is the course content? What cost savings can be traced to it? Use this information in efforts to design your program. It will also be useful in case your attempts to improve structured OJT in your organization come under attack. Nothing quiets critics faster than pointing out that "our competitors—or other excellent firms in the industry—are doing it!"

4. Design and routinely conduct training on the principles of structured OJT.

   Supervisors and experienced workers are the most likely ones to conduct structured OJT in the workplace. In most organizations, they do not know how to do it. Teach them how and then sit back and take credit for the fantastic results!

5. Provide specialized support for line managers who use structured OJT.

   In most organizations, certain jobs are common entry points for employees. Design off-the-shelf lesson plans, job aids (checklists, procedures manuals, and training manuals), individualized learning contracts, and individualized training progress report forms for those jobs. They will save time and effort while improving the quality of structured OJT. Making that kind of support available enhances OJT by providing users with the tools to do it—and makes the HRD department a real partner with line management in improving structured OJT.

6. Avoid turf battles.

   Begin efforts to improve OJT on a small scale in work units where supervisors or managers are supportive. Use your successes there as a springboard to other units and to additional resources.

7. Consider literacy skills.

   Do not assume that employees—or, for that matter, supervisors—are highly literate. Indeed, take advantage of efforts to improve OJT to assess performance problems that can be traced to literacy issues.

*Source:* Adapted from Rothwell, W., & Kazanas, H. (1990). Planned OJT is productive OJT. *Training and Development Journal,* October, pp. 53–56.

One way to do this is to find and examine a comparable job with an apprenticeship program and use it as a model. The classroom training could take place at a local community college, school of technology, or similar institution. Apprentices are usually off the job for their classroom training, but in designing a program it might be possible to arrange night-school classes, classes on the weekend, or some combination of the two. Correspondence school training is sometimes substituted for classroom training.

Before venturing out to develop an apprenticeship program, check with local government agencies regarding the programs available. Given that government is usually willing to help pay for the classroom training part of the apprenticeship program, it may be advantageous to make the program official.

# COACHING

**Coaching** is the process of providing one-on-one guidance and instruction to improve knowledge, skills, and work performance. Coaching is usually directed at employees with KSA deficiencies, but it can also be used as a motivational tool for

**Coaching** the process of providing one-on-one guidance and instruction to improve knowledge, skills, and work performance.

those performing adequately. Although co-workers can be coaches, especially in team-based organizations, more typically it is the supervisor who acts as coach. One analysis suggests that in the past supervisors spent, on the average, only about 10 percent of their time coaching subordinates. In today's organizations supervisors typically spend more than 50 percent of their time in such activities.[34] The following outline looks at the process from the coach's perspective:

1. Understand the trainee's job, the KSAs, the resources required to meet performance expectations, and the trainee's current level of performance.

2. Meet with the trainee and mutually agree on the performance objectives to be achieved.

3. Arrive at a mutual plan and schedule for achieving the performance objectives.

4. Show the trainee how to achieve the objectives, observe the trainee perform, and provide feedback. This process is similar to JIT and is conducted at the work site.

5. Repeat step 4 until performance improves.

The main difference between coaching and traditional OJT is that in coaching, the supervisor continues to analyze the subordinate's performance, plan mutually acceptable action, create a supportive climate, and motivate the subordinate to improve.[34] Effective coaching requires a relationship between the coach (supervisor, peer) and player (employee) that motivates the employee to seek help from the coach in order to become a better performer.[35] Therefore the role of the supervisor must change from controlling to collaborating.

Even though coaching is clearly a skill-focused method, it can also be used for knowledge development, although other methods are better for transmitting knowledge. Like the OJT trainer, the coach must be skilled both in how to do the tasks and in how to train others to do them. HRD professionals typically do not perform the role of coach (unless they are coaching other HRD professionals). Rather, they train supervisors in the coaching process and develop the supervisors' interpersonal skills to make them more effective.

In most cases, the coach is the supervisor or peer responsible for improving specific performance problems. However, in recent years a significant increase occurred in the use of consultants as coaches for upper-level managers.[36] We discuss this trend in greater detail in Chapter 10.

### How to Use Coaching Effectively

For coaching to be effective, a needs assessment should be conducted. Figure 5-1 outlines the basic questions that the supervisor should ask. Note the similarity to Figure 3-1 (page 74) in the discussion of needs analysis.

Once it is decided that coaching is necessary, follow the five steps laid out above. Skills required to be an effective coach are similar to those for an effective trainer. Good questioning techniques, active listening skills, and good feedback skills are all essential when coaching.

## MENTORING

**Mentoring** a form of coaching in which an ongoing relationship is developed between a senior and junior employee.

**Mentoring** is considered to be a form of coaching in which an ongoing relationship is developed between a senior and junior employee. The purpose of mentoring is to provide the more junior employee with guidance and a clear understanding of how the organization goes about its business. Whereas coaching focuses on the technical aspects of the job, mentoring focuses more on improving the employee's fit within the organization. Thus, coaching emphasizes skill development, and mentoring emphasizes

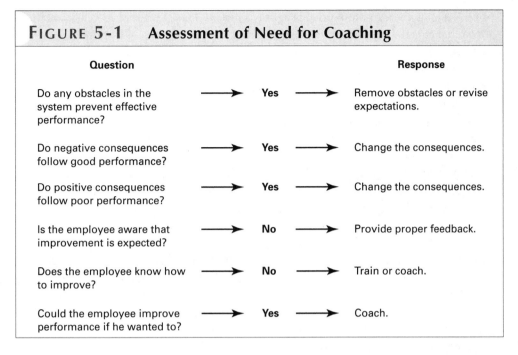

**FIGURE 5-1   Assessment of Need for Coaching**

| Question | | Response |
|---|---|---|
| Do any obstacles in the system prevent effective performance? | Yes | Remove obstacles or revise expectations. |
| Do negative consequences follow good performance? | Yes | Change the consequences. |
| Do positive consequences follow poor performance? | Yes | Change the consequences. |
| Is the employee aware that improvement is expected? | No | Provide proper feedback. |
| Does the employee know how to improve? | No | Train or coach. |
| Could the employee improve performance if he wanted to? | Yes | Coach. |

attitude development. Generally, mentoring is conducted only for management-level employees, though in some cases it is applied at lower levels. In the past, mentoring was mostly informal, but more recently some organizations have formalized the process.[37] The concerns about untrained OJT trainers discussed earlier apply to mentoring as well.

**How to Use Mentoring Effectively** A number of features characterize successful mentoring programs, all of which should be considered if mentoring is to be effective. These features include the following:[38]

- Top management support,
- Integration into the career development process,
- Voluntary involvement,
- Assignment of mentees to mentors,
- Relatively short phases to the program,
- An established orientation, and
- Monitoring of the process.

As in any organizational intervention, top management support is essential. Allowing mentoring activities to take place on company time is one way of sending the signal that these activities are important. Providing rewards to successful mentors is also a way of indicating that it is a valued behaviour.

Also, mentoring needs to be integrated into the overall career development process. It must be seen as an extension of the mentee's development process. Internal access to training is needed, along with development programs and materials to supplement mentor/mentee activities. The mentor program needs to be voluntary. Forcing managers to take part in mentoring activities will do more harm than good. A reluctant mentor cannot provide the interest and motivation needed to assist someone in the organization.

It is helpful to assign mentors to mentees. Most formal mentor programs require a nominating procedure. Mentees are nominated by their supervisor and matched by the director of training to a mentor. It is a good idea to allow for switching, particularly if a match does not seem to be working.

Keeping each phase of the program short will help prevent potential mentors from being reluctant to take on mentoring responsibilities. Six-month cycles are enough time for a mentor to help a mentee in a significant manner while not being tied indefinitely to him. Mentors who find the process successful will sign up for another stint.

Provide an orientation for mentors and mentees. This is a formal process by which they can meet and hear about what worked in the past and the role expectations for both parties in the mentoring relationship. The mentors should be allowed to do their mentoring in a manner congruent with their style and not be forced to follow a strict format. The orientation can feature successful past mentors who can describe how they took on and carried out the role. Presenting a few different approaches will reinforce the idea that it is not necessary to follow a specific process.

Finally, it is important to monitor the mentoring process, as this is critical to its success. At specific checkpoints, both parties can be surveyed about the progress of the mentee. This survey could take the form of a meeting to discuss what has happened, a request for mini-reports on progress, or simply phone calls to ask how the process is working. Use this information to highlight successful mentoring relationships in company newsletters and other communications. This publicity will keep individuals motivated and keep the program visible. Plotting the career paths of mentees is another method of showing the success of the program.

## STRENGTHS AND LIMITATIONS OF OJT

OJT is clearly a useful method for skill enhancement. Trainees learn their KSAs in the actual job situation; thus, transfer of training occurs naturally. An additional benefit is that the OJT process will provide new employees with a rapid orientation to how the company operates. It also has the potential to develop a more positive relationship among older and newer employees and between supervisors and their subordinates.

A major concern in OJT is the competency of the trainer. The trainer must possess the technical competence, training competence, and motivation to train. Without all these characteristics, training is not likely to be successful. In addition, the organization must provide the trainer with enough time away from her regular job to do the training. This accommodation not only leads to better training but also demonstrates the organization's commitment to its OJT program.

**Cost** OJT offers some clear cost advantages if it is done effectively. Trainees and trainers are both at the job site performing job activities. Though neither the trainee nor the trainer will be producing at full capacity, they are at least producing something. With other techniques, neither the trainer nor the trainee is engaged in producing the organization's products or services while training is going on. Also, OJT does not require the purchase of expensive training materials such as simulators, games, or computer-based training modules. All the materials are part of the normal work equipment.

OJT also speeds up the learning process. No delay separates training from its application to the work situation. In addition, some evidence indicates that one-on-one training produces faster learning that is more resistant to forgetting.[39] The more efficient the training, the less costly it is.

One cost concern in implementing OJT is the cost of training the trainers. Unlike other methods, for a start-up OJT system most, if not all, of the trainers will need training. In addition, while other methods have one trainer for many trainees, this method uses one-on-one training. The drop in productivity from having the more-skilled employees conducting training must be added into the cost. In addition, companies should expect some increased waste, breakage, and downtime because of inexperienced trainees operating the equipment. More will be said about training trainers in Chapter 7.

**Control of Content and Process** The trainer primarily controls the content and process of learning in OJT during the "prepare" and "present" stages of training. As training progresses to the "try out" and "follow-up" stages, the trainee and trainer jointly control the content and process because it is the trainee's actions that determine what the next learning module will be. The training moves as quickly or as slowly as necessary for the trainee to master the learning. Thus, if the trainee is in the "talk through" portion of trying it out and misses some steps, the trainer might again demonstrate how the job is done. If the trainee is able to "talk through" the steps correctly, the trainer might be ready to move to the "instruct the trainee" portion. However, if the trainee said, "You know, I was just guessing on some of those steps," the trainer might repeat the "talk through" portion until the trainee felt confident of knowing all the steps.

**Learning Objectives (KSAs)** The primary focus of OJT is skill development, but OJT can also enhance the knowledge base of trainees and influence their attitudes. Through discussions with the trainer and through questioning and restating of techniques, the trainee can learn facts and procedures that are required on the job. However, classroom techniques and individual reading assignments are more efficient at this type of learning.

The attitudes that new employees hold about their jobs and their company come from observing and interacting with others. OJT provides a great opportunity to get employees off on the right foot by clarifying the norms, expectations, and culture of the work unit. Of course, accomplishing this task will depend on the ability of the OJT trainer to convey these appropriately to the trainee.

On a final note, if knowledge acquisition is required to perform the job, OJT techniques should be supplemented with other techniques—such as apprenticeship training—that are more suited to knowledge acquisition. For skilled trades, it is important to develop the skills of the trade; however, certain knowledge is a prerequisite for that skill development. For that reason, a significant amount of classroom training is also required as a part of the training. Computer-based training, role-playing, reading of texts and manuals, and other techniques can all be combined successfully with OJT.

**Learning Process** Trainees are likely to be relatively more attentive and more motivated during OJT, because it is easier to see a direct relationship between the training and job performance. Verbal and visual stimuli direct attention to key learning points. Periods of active practice require the trainees to attend to what they are doing and what is being said, thus increasing the learning potential.

The visual, auditory, and tactile cues in OJT assist in the symbolic coding process, providing many relationships among objects and actions in the work environment. Through observation, practice, and discussion, the trainee cognitively organizes these relationships into easily recalled patterns of behaviour.

By asking the trainee to describe the steps in the operation (before letting the trainee perform the operation), the trainer is facilitating the symbolic rehearsal process. The trainee must imagine himself going through the operations as he describes the procedures.

Behavioural reproduction, of course, is a strong point of this method. The trainee practises small portions of the operation until they are mastered. The trainee then moves on to larger portions until command over all the tasks that make up the job reaches the level needed to perform the job alone.

# AUDIOVISUAL ENHANCEMENTS TO TRAINING

**Audiovisual Aids** any physical, mechanical, or electronic media used to provide or assist instruction.

Audiovisuals (AVs) can be useful enhancements for meeting all three types of training objectives (knowledge, skills, and attitudes) and are easily applied to any of the other methods discussed. **Audiovisual aids** consist of any physical, mechanical, or electronic media used to provide or assist instruction. Typically they are used as a supplement to other methods of training rather than as a standalone means of instruction, though some are effective training devices by themselves.

The range of AV alternatives is quite large, from simple chalkboard or whiteboard text and images to interactive multimedia presentations. They can be grouped under the headings of static or dynamic media. **Static media** are presentations of fixed (stationary) text or images such as printed matter, overhead transparencies, pictures/slides, and computer-generated projections. An AV is considered static if the material presented is stationary. **Dynamic media** create sequentially moving stimuli, where the information is presented in a continuously moving progression from beginning to end, as with audiotapes and videotapes, computer-generated presentations, and moving film.

**Static Media** presentations of fixed text or images such as printed matter, overhead transparencies, pictures/slides, and computer-generated projections.

**Dynamic Media** sequentially moving stimuli, where the information is presented in a continuously moving progression from beginning to end.

## STATIC MEDIA

Static media are generally not suitable for training as a standalone method. Rather, they are used to augment and enhance other methods, in particular the lecture method, but they are adaptable to other training techniques as well.

### Newsprint, Charts, and Posters

Newsprint, charts, and posters display information through words or images. They range from handmade, with felt markers and newsprint, to professionally prepared glossy prints. An advantage of these presentations is that they can be posted on walls or other vertical surfaces so the information is visible to trainees while other training methods are in use (e.g., lecture, role-plays, video). For example, these media are frequently used to post an outline of the day's training and to display procedural steps related to the training material. They allow trainees to place the material that is presented at any time into the context of the total program. Figure 5-2 shows a poster that could be used during conflict resolution training. It might be left up during the entire training so that trainees are constantly reminded of the six steps the training focuses on. Posters and charts that the trainer knows will be used during training should be prepared before training and checked for accuracy. The credibility of the training and the trainer will suffer if errors exist.

### Projected Text and Images

One of the older methods of projecting material is the overhead transparency. Today digital camera projectors and computer-generated projections are also used.

Creating overhead transparencies requires text and images to be transferred to the transparency material (generally clear acetate). It can be done by hand with transparency markers, but the result is not usually professional-looking and can damage the credibility of the training. Computer-generated text and images, as well as those copied from printed matter, can be pasted together to create attention-getting and informative overheads. Although overheads can be created through a variety of mechanical devices, usually a computer system and an image scanner are required.

## FIGURE 5-2 Example of a Conflict Resolution Training Poster

**SIX STEPS TO CONFLICT RESOLUTION**

**Solutions**
- Actively Listen
- Indicate Respect
- Be Assertive
- Provide Information
- Reconsider Problem
- Brainstorm Possible Solutions

Computer-generated projections are more sophisticated. Many popular office software packages, such as those produced by Microsoft and Corel, contain presentation software components that create projections, discussion notes, and other training aids that can be integrated into the presentation. Once the projections are created and placed in proper order, they can be downloaded onto a floppy disk or stored on the hard drive. During the training, the trainer will require a computer (typically a laptop or notebook) and a high-intensity digital projector. The computer communicates the image to be projected to the projector, which projects an enlarged image onto a screen. Most projectors will also project video images from a VCR, CD, or DVD player. The presenter can control the display of the projections with a mouse, clicking to move from one projection to the next, or time the presentation so that the image automatically advances to the next projection after a specified period of time.

Each of these methods fulfills the same purpose—to focus trainees' attention on specific content. In addition to displaying information, projections can aid the trainer in moving systematically through the components of the training. This feature is especially useful in training methods where the interaction between trainer and trainees may cause the trainer to stray from the training outline; the trainer can simply look to the projection being displayed to get back on track.

## Effective Use of Static Visuals

Trainers tend to put too much information on transparencies. This is also true for computer-generated projections. Guidelines to follow are:

- Present one idea or concept.
- Print in large letters (6–12 mm type), larger if handmade.
- Limit to six or seven lines with six to eight words per line.
- Use colour for impact.
- Place the pointer on the overhead rather than pointing at the screen; this allows you to keep your focus on the trainees.
- Turn off the projector when it is not in use.

- Keep the line of sight to visual aids clear by placing the aid in a strategic location.

- Do not talk to the visual aid; instead face the trainees. Turn to the visual aid to identify a point, and then turn back to the trainees.

- When a visual aid is no longer being discussed, remove it.

- When writing on newsprint, try as much as possible to continue to face the trainees; do not stand in front of the easel or face it.

For effective static visuals, the room set-up must allow easy viewing by all trainees. Seating should be arranged to allow a clear path for the projector's beam, and the projector should not block the trainees' view of the screen. Line of sight should also be clear for newsprint information. Here are some additional considerations:

1. Rehearse the presentation using the static visuals on the equipment in the room where training will occur. Doing so will reveal all the things forgotten about as well as the things not known (e.g., the circuit breaker for the outlet won't handle the computer projection unit and the video equipment at the same time).

2. Bring extra equipment accessories such as extra projector bulbs, cables, extension cords, and easels to the training facility before training begins. Remember, Murphy's Law applies to trainers too. In fact, trainers face the following addendum: The more important the event, the more likely it is that things will go wrong. Extra precautions are always wise.

3. Arrive at the training site early and check that all equipment is in working order. Make sure visuals are ready to operate when training starts (overheads are in the correct order, right side up, computer-generated projections are ready, etc.).

4. Bring along a set of traditional overheads (transparencies) for emergencies if using computer-generated projections.

## DYNAMIC AUDIOVISUAL METHODS

Dynamic AVs include audiotapes, moving picture film, videos, and computer-generated presentations. Dynamic visuals can also serve as aids to enhance other methods of training. However, unlike static visuals, these methods can be, and frequently are, used as the sole method of training.

**Audiotapes** The audiotape has the same characteristics as the straight lecture. The only differences are that the audiotape is exactly the same each time it is used and provides no accompanying visual stimulus. Even while advances in video and computer-generated presentations reduce the popularity of audiotapes as training tools, they have an advantage in some situations. They are effective when the content of the training is primarily auditory recognition or auditory response. Almost 50 percent of companies with more than 50 employees use audiocassettes in their training.[40] One obvious instance is if the material to be learned requires specific responses to auditory cues. Telephone and radio operators of all types (e.g., 911 emergency operators, taxi dispatchers, and customer-service line operators) can receive beneficial training through audiotape playback that closely simulates the work environment. Learning a foreign language is also a fairly common use of audiotapes.

Audiotapes are also useful when other forms of training are not available. For example, audiotape training can be a productive use of the long hours sales representatives spend in their cars.

Advantages of the audiotape over the lecture are its portability and its ability to be reused both for training additional people and for easy review and clarification by trainees. Also, if it is important that all trainees receive exactly the same information, an audiotape will be better than a lecture.

<u>Videos</u> Videos are good ways of both showing and telling trainees how to do something. They can present conceptual or factual information by integrating narration with visual illustrations, graphics, and animated depictions. This medium is relatively portable and generally can be made available to trainees at their convenience. The many advantages offered by videos make it clear why 96 percent of companies with 50 or more employees used videotapes for training, second only to classroom instruction.[41]

Videos are used as a standalone training technique. A video, like a lecture, is a one-way communication system, with the disadvantage of not allowing discussion/question opportunities. A number of firms use video to enhance training in ways similar to those described in Training in Action 5-4.

The advent of widespread video recording and playback capability effectively eliminated the use of film. Many of the most frequently viewed training films have been transferred to the video format. The ease of use, both in developing the product and presenting it during the training, makes video superior to film in almost every instance. However, if a film that can be of value in training already exists, by all means use it (if a projector can be found).

<u>Computer-Generated Dynamic Presentations</u> With the ability to project computer screen images onto a large screen and the increasing ability to digitize sound and image electronically, the computer is rapidly becoming a critical training tool. Multimedia software allows computers to store, modify, and reconfigure sound and image as well as text, to create nearly any combination of audio and visual presentation. Developing a computer-generated dynamic presentation (CGDP) does require considerably more hardware and software knowledge than do the presentation software packages discussed earlier. The development process is similar to that of producing a video but also includes converting all the components into digital media. As with video productions, it is advisable to use professionals to ensure the quality of the presentation.

## Training in Action 5-4

### Using Video in Catalogue Sales Training

Following are two examples of how videos are being used to train employees working in the catalogue department of two different types of organizations.

The Boston Museum of Fine Arts mails out a catalogue of museum reproductions on a seasonal basis. The museum uses seasonal and temporary labour to help keep costs low, but this practice requires constant training of new personnel. To meet this need the museum commissioned Creative Video Design to produce a training video for their telephone order takers. The video demonstrates how to greet the customer, use the phone system, log on to the computer, enter the order, and so on. Another video was developed for the warehouse personnel demonstrating how to read and interpret inventory and shipping slips.

Talbots is a women's fashion merchandiser with hundreds of stores and a large catalogue sales department. To make sure catalogue employees understand Talbots' total operations, particularly the way the catalogue department works, Talbots developed a series of videos. One video provides a video tour of the catalogue and store distribution centre to new employees. Another video traces how a piece of clothing listed in the catalogue makes its journey from the customer's order to delivery at the customer's home. A full understanding of the operations helps catalogue salespeople give better service and advice to their customers.

*Source:* Adapted from *Catalog Age*, January 1994, p. 59.

**<u>Effective Use of Dynamic Media</u>** How close to the AV equipment should trainees sit in order to adequately view the material? A rule of thumb (whether static or dynamic visuals are used) is one foot (0.3 m) of trainee distance from the screen for every inch (2.5 cm) of screen size. Thus for a 32-inch TV screen, the maximum distance that trainees should be from the screen is about 32 feet (10 m). Sound can be a problem if the room is not wired and the TV not adaptable to external speakers. Adequate volume for those who are seven feet (2 m) from the TV will be too low for those who are 32 feet (10 m) away, and making the sound adequate for those who are furthest away can make it too loud for those in the front. One solution is to create a semicircle around the TV, although this arrangement limits the number of people who can be comfortably seated. Learning to operate the equipment is also more difficult than with the other methods. Little skill is required to operate an overhead or slide projector. Significantly more skill is required to operate a computer- or image-projection equipment. Finally, most projection equipment built prior to 1995 requires dimming the lights so low that the atmosphere is more conducive to sleeping than learning. However, new technology has solved that problem.

As with anything mechanical, it is important to try the system before training begins. Arrive early to check out all the equipment. Be sure that remote controls for lights, video, and so on are operating and that you understand how they work. Put the equipment through a trial run. Have a backup for any video or disk that will be used. Video machines do eat tapes and disks do crash. Most training facilities have more than one VCR and computer, which are critical if an important part of training requires their use. Find out where the extra VCR is kept, carry a portable computer as a spare, or arrange for backup overheads. Breakdowns do happen. When you are using dynamic visual aids, keep these points in mind:

- Turn off the TV/computer or other visual aids when not in use.

- Keep the line of sight to visual aids unblocked. If the group is large, use two TVs placed in strategic locations, connected to the single VCR.

- Turn the lighting up when talking about or discussing an issue (even for a short time) between film clips. Do not attempt to discuss issues in a darkened room.

## STRENGTHS AND LIMITATIONS OF AUDIOVISUALS

Static AVs are one-way communication techniques and should rarely, if ever, be used as standalone training tools. The only exception is printed material, such as books or pamphlets, which can be used alone if the material is simple and straightforward. This use typically occurs as self-study materials and not as part of a formalized training program. Since static media cannot demonstrate how to use the material, answer questions, or allow for interaction between the trainee and trainer, their value is greatest as a supplement to other methods. As they are generally not appropriate as a standalone training method, we will compare static visuals with each other and with dynamic audiovisual methods.

### <u>Cost</u>

***Static Audiovisuals.*** An advantage of static audiovisuals is their lower development costs. Costs range from low (overhead transparencies, flip charts, and computer-generated projections) to moderate (photographic slides and professionally prepared posters). Implementation costs range from low (flip charts and overhead transparencies) to high (computer-generated projections). The high implementation cost is entirely a result of the cost of equipment. Overhead projectors are relatively inexpensive (several hundred dollars), slide projectors are slightly more, and computer image projectors (requiring a relatively sophisticated system) can range from $3500 to $10 000. Of course, all this equipment is amortized across the training sessions in which it is used, so even the most expensive projection devices may be only a minor factor in the total cost of training.

Static visuals are reusable, so a trainee who did not understand something the first time can look at it again and again. It is not necessary, however, for the trainee to use the original materials. For a minimal cost, overhead transparencies and computer-generated projections can be copied to paper and given as handouts; slides are more expensive to convert. Providing these handouts will help to address any moderate-to-small differences in learning readiness among trainees.

Computer-generated overhead transparencies and projections provide a unique advantage because they are stored electronically. Any given display can be modified easily by adding or removing text and images. This reduces the cost of program modifications or adaptations. Slides, on the other hand, would need to be completely redone. For example, assume that 30 photographic slides are produced for training human resource clerks in the proper procedure for processing a worker's compensation claim. It is not likely that these slides would be much use in training supervisors about how to handle a workplace accident, even though worker's compensation claims are closely related. If computer-generated overheads or projections had been used, the original projections could be easily modified to delete irrelevant material and include the new material. Likewise, if six months later the government rewrites the worker's compensation laws, it will probably be necessary to replace most of the slides for the HR clerks rather than modifying the existing slides. Technological advances in computer imaging and projection make slides less and less viable as static visual aids.

***Dynamic Audiovisuals.*** Using a professional video production company is expensive. A completed video can cost from $700 to $1200 per minute[42] or more, but it is often worth the cost because of the professional appearance of the video. Even developing in-house videos is fairly expensive, given the cost of labour, equipment, and so on. Developing an original CGDP can require even greater up-front costs than producing a video, because each component of the multimedia package must be developed, then digitized and integrated into a coherent, logically flowing package. The cost of development is reduced if the training components can be developed digitally in the first place.

Although the up-front cost is high, the per-person cost of producing a video can be low if the trainee population is large enough. Videos, film, and CGDP are portable and reusable. Videos and computer-generated dynamic presentations are easily and cheaply duplicated, enabling many trainees in different places to see them at any time, or one trainee to see them many times. This capability is valuable for refresher courses or for trainees who learn at a slower pace. Because of their reusability, the development cost can be spread over a large number of trainees, thus reducing the per-trainee costs.

When they are used for standalone training, the biggest advantage of videos and CGDPs is that trainees can view or study at their convenience. This capability can have significant cost and time savings because the trainees and trainers do not have to travel to the presentations. For example, ADC Communications estimated that it would cost about $150 000 to bring the company's 60 salespeople to the Minneapolis headquarters for a week of sales training.[43] By using standalone video training, this cost was eliminated. Since most employees can use VCRs and televisions in their homes, the company is not required to buy much equipment. The company should, however, provide on-site equipment to those employees who do not own the equipment or whose home environment is not conducive to learning. CGDP does not offer this equipment cost advantage, because the employees do not likely own the necessary hardware and software.

Finally, if employees view the tape at home or during free time at work, the productivity savings are substantial. If trainees must travel more than 320 kilometres to reach a centralized training location, they lose not only their productivity for the time at training but also one or two days of travel time.

One way to cut the cost of video training is to rent or buy a video from commercial producers. A large number of commercially available training videos cover a wide variety of topics. Also, some videos and films produced primarily for entertainment can be used effectively in training. We used segments of the classic film *Twelve Angry Men* (a film about a jury's deliberations during a criminal trial) to illustrate the problems and benefits of consensus decision-making. Small portions of the movie *Falling Down* can illustrate various risk factors and warning signs for workplace violence. Television broadcasts can be used in a similar fashion. For example, textbook publishers now provide, as accompaniments to their textbooks, videocassettes containing segments of news programs and TV specials that relate to the content of the text.

Equipment costs vary across the media used. A film requires a projector and screen for presentation, and a video requires a VCR and television. Videos can also be projected onto large screens with a video projector. The technology is rapidly improving, and state-of-the-art projectors (costing about $4000) can display large-screen images. This capability overcomes one of the disadvantages of the TV video, which is that only a small group of trainees can easily see it at the same time.

## Control of Material and Process

*Static Audiovisuals.* Generally computer-generated projections are more easily controlled by the trainer than are other static visuals. The sequence of projections can be structured so that material is displayed only when the presenter begins to discuss it. Text can be programmed to fade into and out of the projection with a click of the mouse. The mouse can also be used to point to or highlight particular parts of the projection. Finally, worry about slides or overheads getting out of order, being upside down, and the like is eliminated. Since the whole visual presentation is contained on a single floppy disk, it is more easily transportable than slides or overheads.

Although computer-generated projection offers many advantages, it also comes with a major disadvantage—it suffers all the potential problems of computer technology. Hard drives crash at inopportune times, floppy disks are not readable by the operating system, viruses abound, and software and disk-formatting compatibility issues must be solved. To avoid most of these problems, take a portable computer to the training site, but make sure a compatible backup is available. Of course, carrying a laptop reduces the convenience of having to carry only a single floppy disk.

*Dynamic Audiovisuals.* The disadvantage of acquiring a commercially made video is that the information may not be specific to the company or the training content, but rather must appeal to the largest audience. Such videos will likely need to be augmented with additional training relevant to the trainees. You can control the content and process of learning by selecting the appropriate video and creating the supplemental materials yourself.

The portability of dynamic audiovisuals means that trainees can take them off the shelf and use them when convenient. To this extent, the trainee controls the learning process. However, many distractions may disrupt watching a training video or multimedia presentation at home. Here the training process is completely in the hands of the trainee, who can stop the presentation at any point and do something else. The desired level of learning may not be attained.

When video and CGDP are used as standalone techniques, the content and presentation format are controlled, but not the manner in which the trainee goes through the material. Especially with video, trainees may fast-forward over parts they do not understand or find boring, making evaluating learning particularly important when this training technique is used.

## Learning Objectives (KSAs)

Appropriately prepared and displayed audiovisuals will enhance almost any training and are especially effective for techniques in which the trainee is less active, such as lecture/discussion and some types of CBT. However, the nature of the learning objective will determine which type of audiovisual is most appropriate.

*Knowledge.* Both static and dynamic AVs facilitate the trainee's knowledge development through their ability to activate or enhance learning processes. AVs focus trainee attention and provide visual stimuli that aid symbolic coding and cognitive organization. They are also useful for highlighting cues that will stimulate appropriate recall. AVs are most effective at enhancing declarative knowledge but can also be useful in developing procedural knowledge. Dynamic audiovisuals are more suited than are static AVs for developing procedural knowledge, because they are able to model the steps required to perform the task and display a variety of situations in which the task is appropriate.

*Skills.* Static presentation of information is not especially useful for skill building because it does not lend itself to facilitating development or the practice of skills. Dynamic presentations, however, can be useful in skill development and practice, and foreign language audiotapes use this approach. Dynamic audiovisuals can also make it easier to simulate the work environment. Police departments might use a film or video to place the trainee in the position of searching a building for an armed and dangerous suspect. The trainee must make decisions about what to do in a variety of situations, such as the sudden appearance of objects and people, or entering a room that has a closed door.

Another audiovisual technique increasingly being used is videotaping the trainee's performance during practice and using the video as feedback for skill improvement. Even though dynamic AVs can provide good models and instructions for skill development, they usually are not capable of providing feedback, so they should not be used as standalone methods. Interactive videos and CGDP provide the exceptions to this rule.

*Attitudes.* Static and dynamic AVs, used in conjunction with other techniques, can facilitate attitude change by visually clarifying the relationships among objects and events that are the basis of trainee opinions and evaluations. For example, the Domtar plant in southern California used static visuals to display the consequences of not following correct safety procedures. This manufacturer of construction products used graphic displays of eye injuries in a safety-training program to develop positive attitudes about wearing safety goggles. It also used pictures of employees working on various equipment, with some wearing and some not wearing safety goggles; trainees were asked to identify the potential hazards to the individual in each picture. The process allowed the trainees to make the proper links between wearing the goggles and protecting themselves from injury. It is interesting to note that this plant won many safety awards from both the company and the state. The ability to provide visual documentation of the relationship between objects and events is a powerful source of learning and attitude change. Beliefs such as "wearing goggles is uncomfortable and unnecessary" are often reinforced by cognitive distortions and rationalization. Statements such as "If you're careful, you don't need goggles" and "I'm too experienced to get an eye injury" are examples of the kind of rationalizations heard at the Domtar plant before training. The trainer's words alone may not be sufficient to change attitudes. Visual displays allow the trainees to see that their distortions and rationalizations are inaccurate, making a change in attitudes easier to accomplish. Dynamic AVs can produce even more powerful images, because the connection among objects, actions, and consequences can be made even more explicit.

## Learning Process

*Attention.* The saying "a picture is worth a thousand words" reflects the importance of visual representation in the learning process. Static visuals provide the trainee with a visually based message, even if the image is simply enlarged text. Visual stimuli focus the trainee's attention when they represent a change in the environment. No matter how professional a trainer's voice and image are, they may become familiar to the trainees after a period of time. When familiarity occurs it becomes easier for the trainee's attention to wander. The periodic presentation of new visual stimuli activates the attention process. If the visuals are consistently similar in format (e.g., all text, black print, same font size), they too will lose their ability to attract attention. Combining graphic images, charts, and text as well as varying colour to highlight key learning points will add zest to the training and maintain trainee attention. With dynamic audiovisuals, the dynamic nature of the presentation itself attracts attention because it is constantly changing.

The trainer should be careful that all AVs are integrated with the content of the training. When they show little relationship to the content, they become distracting and can actually reduce learning. This distraction can also occur if the trainer fails to manage the presentation of the visuals properly, such as incorrectly placing transparencies on the projector, standing in front of the screen, or otherwise interfering with the normal viewing of the visual. Trainees often begin to pay attention to the trainer's management of the presentation rather than to the content of the presentation, thus reducing learning.

*Retention.* Since different trainees learn more or less effectively through different media, the use of AVs provides additional modalities for learning. When several media are used to convey the same message, the message is more easily coded for storage and contributes more reference points. In general, visual communications are absorbed more quickly and retained for a longer time than are auditory messages. Visual images are also more readily coded symbolically and recalled in their original form.[44]

The symbolic coding process is enhanced when pictures or graphic images provide visual cues that supplement or complement auditory or written cues. Combining cues from different senses results in more accurate symbolic coding and thus better retention.[45] Showing a variety of images all pertaining to the same issue presents trainees with a wider base of common cues to use in storing the information. Audiovisuals are also extremely good for demonstrating events and effects not usually observable or noticed. For example, enlarged images of tiny or microscopic objects are useful in many training settings. In the safety training example discussed earlier, trainees were able to see the effects of not wearing goggles. Eye injuries are often not easily observable, but the visual projections used in the training allowed the trainees to see what actually happened to the eye and what damage tiny bits of material can do. By making objects and effects visible, symbolic encoding becomes much easier.

Cognitive organization can be facilitated by graphic images that demonstrate how the training relates to familiar concepts. Pictorially representing these relationships makes integrating the new with the old easier than does using verbal descriptions alone. Integration is likely to be easier and faster if the trainer is able to represent visually both the old cognitive organization and the new, showing the changes required. To the degree that the trainees' cognitive structures are different from one another, creating visual representations of them all is difficult. However, it can be accomplished by asking trainees to develop pictorial representations of their cognitive organization on flip charts. They can then compare these representations with the new organization being presented. For example, suppose jobs in a work group were redesigned because of a change in how the product is produced. During training, trainees could map out how the old job was performed. Then, after presenting the new work procedures, the trainer could compare the old with the new and identify the areas for which the new KSAs provided by the training will be needed.

Using AVs in training provides a common reference for all trainees. When you ask the trainees to "picture this" or "imagine you are...," each trainee may hold a different image, but when you provide the image, they all receive the same sensory cues. When the trainees later recall the image, the frame of reference will be similar for all. Though a differential loss of information and detail is likely to occur across trainees, the basis of the recalled information is the initial image that is provided.

AVs can be somewhat useful in aiding symbolic rehearsal. They provide visual cues that trainees can use to practise hypothetical applications of the training material. This process works in much the same manner as behavioural reproduction (described next). The difference is that in symbolic rehearsal, the trainees are only imagining themselves applying the new learning. The AVs can help to create the context in which the symbolic rehearsal takes place as well as provide cues to assist in the symbolic rehearsal (as in guided discovery).

*Behavioural Reproduction.* AVs can be used to enhance the learning of a new behaviour. By illustrating what to do, AVs can provide a model of how to perform. This modelling is usually accomplished best with dynamic AVs. Static or dynamic AVs can also be used to provide the appropriate cues for when to perform. For example, sometimes cue cards are given to trainees when they are practising new behaviours. These aids need to be present and visible when the new behaviour is first being practised. In the training facility, supplying these cues shouldn't pose a problem. However, to allow opportunities for reproduction outside the training environment, the visual images must be easily portable. Many training programs provide pocket- or wallet-sized cards (static visual aid) to help trainees practise the new material back on the job. As we mentioned earlier, videos and CGDPs are portable but require equipment that may not be compatible with the trainee's workstation (particularly line employees). What AVs are not able to do is observe the trainee's performance and provide appropriate feedback. Thus, although AVs can enhance behavioural reproduction, they are limited as standalone tools for this type of learning.

The big advantage of CGDPs is that each component of the training can provide the audiovisual format best suited for meeting the objectives of that component. Some of these multimedia packages are now interactive, allowing the trainee to respond to and even pose questions, thereby partially eliminating the one-way communication limitation of standard videos and static AVs. With interactivity comes two-way communication, though the limitations discussed earlier about the quality and type of interaction should be kept in mind.

*Limitations for Learning.* The principal limitation of static visuals is that they are typically not standalone learning tools. They are best used as enhancements to other methods. Since they are static, they cannot capture the full range of material that is dynamic. Even though it is possible to capture the essence of some types of dynamic material, such as the "steps in conflict resolution" or "tips for providing constructive feedback," dynamic audiovisual media will generally perform this task more easily and with higher quality. Except for the most sophisticated dynamic AVs (i.e., interactive CGDP), they are unable to adapt to differing characteristics of the trainees or the situation. It is a "one-size-fits-all" technique. If trainees do not have the KSAs to learn from the AV, they will not learn no matter how many times they reuse it.

### Trainee Characteristics

Obviously the trainees must be able to understand the AVs. This point may sound fairly trivial, but it is often overlooked. For example, the poster in Figure 5-2 assumes the trainees can read. If the trainees are managers, it is a pretty safe assumption. However, if they are line employees in an assembly plant, problems may arise. Not only must trainees be able to read, but they must also be able to understand the terms. Even all managers may not know what the trainer means by "actively listen," "be assertive," or "reconsider the problem." Displaying this poster without defining all the terms might create confusion for the trainees. The issue of understandability applies to all AVs, both static and dynamic.

When wide differences in trainee readiness levels are present, AVs aimed at the highest level of KSAs may not be understandable to those at the lower level. If they are aimed at the lowest level, they will seem unnecessary and boring to those at higher levels. If a dynamic AV is being used as a standalone program, it is probably best to provide separate training AVs customized to the readiness levels of each group.

### Summary

This chapter focused on non-computer-based training methods. We described the process of using the method effectively and the method's ability to meet knowledge, skills, and attitudes learning objectives. These methods are included in a summary (Table 7-1) at the beginning of Chapter 7. Please note that this table represents a general guide. More specific information is provided in the relevant sections of this chapter and Chapter 6.

Learning objectives are a critical factor in designing a training program, but other factors such as cost, control of training content, and learning processes also need to be taken into account. This chapter discussed the non-computer-based training methods in terms of their advantages and disadvantages as they relate to the above factors. In most cases, organizations need to make trade-offs between effectiveness at meeting the learning objective and the cost of the method or the time required to develop it into a usable training program.

## Implications for Practice

**1.** For adult learning, the use of various types of questioning will increase trainee interest and provide the trainer with important information on how much learning is taking place.

**2.** When using a simulation for training, do not use old or dated equipment. Training needs to be on current equipment so to achieve maximum transfer.

**3.** When there are time constraints, a useful method for allowing everyone to practise skills is the use of triads. Each person in the triad gets to practise the skill, watch someone else practise the skill and provide feedback, and have the skill used on them to experience the effect it has.

**4.** When using OJT, be aware that you need to consider carefully the skills being taught and that some level of JIT should be followed. Also, you need to train the person doing OJT in the appropriate skills for training. Finally, you need to provide incentives for the trainer to do a good job, one of which should have to do with a reduction in expected performance in his regular job.

**5.** To be a proper coach the supervisor must be more of a collaborator than a controller, so that the subordinate is not deterred from asking for assistance when it is needed.

## Key Terms

## Questions for Review

1. Supervisors often resist taking on the role of coach. What can organizations do to encourage supervisors to be effective coaches?

2. Go through the different instructional methods and sort them into those that you think would be most useful in training someone on the technical aspects of the job and those that would be most useful in the more-social aspects of the job. Provide the rationale for your decisions.

3. Why are classroom-based training programs (lecture/discussion, role-play, games, etc.) used so much more than individualized approaches to training? Do you think that this choice is appropriate?

## Exercises

1. Your instructor will assign you (or your group) to one of the methods from the chapter. Contact the HRD department of a local business. Indicate that you are learning about training and would like to know whether the department uses the method in its training programs. If so, ask if you can schedule a time to observe the method being used. If the method isn't used or if you are unable to observe it, try another company until you are successful. While observing the method, take careful notes on how it is used. On a date specified by your instructor, the class members will report their observations.

2. In small groups, develop a role-play. First determine the objective of the role-play, a limited one that can be achieved in 15 to 20 minutes. Then develop all aspects of a role-play that will achieve your objective.

3. Take ten minutes to think about your best classroom-based learning experience and list the things that made it such a good experience. When the ten minutes are up, use ten additional minutes to think of your worst classroom-based learning experience and list the factors that made it such a bad experience. At the end of this time, the instructor will ask you to share your experiences.

## Web Research

1. Use the Internet to identify the types of games and business simulations that are available. From your research, select four that list different learning content objectives. Prepare a one-to-two paragraph description for each.

# CASE ANALYSIS

## Training for Customer Service Specialists

As a part of the president's initiative to remove "barriers to learning" at a regional midwestern university, an analysis of student services operations was conducted. That analysis revealed that the barriers deemed most important by students were those that would delay or prevent them from registering for classes. These barriers fell into three areas:

1. Resolving issues relating to fines accrued over the previous terms (e.g., library, parking, late fees),

2. Completing forms accurately and meeting processing deadlines for financial aid in time to enroll in classes, and

3. Acquiring appropriate advice so that they enrolled in the right classes (avoiding the problems associated with drops and adds).

As a result of this analysis, the university decided to create a new position called customer service specialist (CSS). The job description is presented here.

## CLASSIFICATION SPECIFICATION

### SUPERSEDES: NEW CLASSIFICATION

### Title: Customer Service Specialist
### Specialist Grade: PT08

**General Summary** Supervise, support, monitor, and assist with the continuous improvement of the work unit's customer service functions and related operational activities. Ensure quality customer service, both in person and over the telephone. These activities require a working knowledge of the work unit's program policies, procedures, and regulations, as well as an understanding of other departments and systems that interface with the work unit's activities.

**Essential Duties** Personally provide and ensure that customer support staff provide positive customer service practices throughout the work unit, including greeting departmental customers in person or over the telephone, identifying their needs, obtaining necessary and appropriate information, and processing customer requests in a manner that will best meet the needs of the customer.

Monitor staff and ensure that customers perceive customer service support staff as treating them with courtesy, respect, tact, and a sincere desire to meet their needs.

Provide mediation and resolution to customer complaints and requests within delegated authority limits and consistent with departmental policies.

Communicate to customers the departmental policies and procedures related to their needs, and provide customers with the appropriate forms and instructions.

Design and implement systems to ensure that forms turned in by customers are the appropriate forms for their service request and that they are complete and as accurate as possible.

Work with the appropriate departmental administrator to identify the training needs of designated support staff in the work unit who provide direct customer service. Where appropriate, provide on-the-job training and coaching. Work with the designated department administrator to identify appropriate training experiences for customer service support staff.

Recruit, interview, and make recommendations in the hiring of customer support staff.

Identify processes and procedures in the department that are causing problems for groups of customers (not individuals) and work with department management toward their improvement. Where authorized, implement improvements in systems, processes, and procedures that will increase the customer satisfaction capability of the department.

Develop and maintain a network of contacts with other university departments that commonly interface with the work unit.

Interact with other university departments to resolve a customer's problem or meet the customer's needs.

Interpret and reconcile account records related to area of assignment.

Receive, read, and interpret correspondence and determine proper handling.

Perform other related duties as assigned.

**Supervision Received** Supervision is received from the designated departmental administrator.

**Supervision Exercised** Supervision may be exercised, as determined by the appropriate departmental administrator, over customer service representatives, clerical support staff, and student support staff in the work unit who provide direct customer service.

**Qualifications** Ability to read, write, interpret instructions, perform basic arithmetic, and communicate orally and in writing at a level typically acquired through the completion of a college degree is necessary.

Personal computing skills sufficient to utilize word processing and spreadsheet applications, and to perform file management and data input/retrieval functions are necessary. Knowledge of specific software applications and university information systems utilized in the work unit assigned is desirable.

Supervisory skills needed to provide direction to subordinates, monitor and manage subordinate performance, and to plan, organize, and coordinate the customer service activities are required, and supervisory experience is desirable.

Preference is given to those who master basic customer service and problem-solving skills as listed:

- The ability to communicate accurately and pleasantly with customers (across a wide diversity of cultural backgrounds) is necessary in order to identify customer needs and solve customer problems.

- The ability to communicate moderately to highly complex policies, procedures, and regulations and to ensure understanding of these while working under pressure (e.g., handling several requests at the same time) is required.

- Effective problem-solving abilities are required to (1) identify and prioritize customer service problems, (2) conduct a root cause analysis to determine the cause(s) of a problem, (3) develop a range of alternatives that will remove the cause(s) of a problem, (4) identify the alternatives that are most effective, and (5) develop an implementation plan for carrying out the alternative selected.

- Effective conflict management skills are required (e.g., defuse emotionally charged situations, clearly identify issues, and clearly communicate procedures for resolving the issue, working with the customer to develop a resolution acceptable to the customer and the work unit).

- Knowledge and understanding of university, state, and federal policies, systems, procedures, and regulations as they pertain to the work unit's ability to meet customer needs and to areas of the university that interface with the work unit in meeting those needs.

Those hired without the preceding competencies will undergo training prior to assuming job responsibilities. During the training period, these individuals will be considered temporary employees. Upon successful completion of the training, the classification will be changed to permanent. Failure to complete training successfully will result in termination of employment or reassignment to another position, at the discretion of the university.

**Working Conditions** Work is performed in a typical office environment.

After the position was posted and advertised, 25 applicants were selected. Unfortunately only seven applicants were assessed as demonstrating the desired level of problem-solving and customer service knowledge and skills.

### Case Questions

You are assigned the challenge of designing the training program for the temporary CSS employees who must complete training before they become permanent CSS employees.

1. What are the training objectives for the CSS training program? Indicate how these objectives are tied to the KSA requirements. Assume that all trainees have college degrees but need KSAs in all other areas listed in the qualifications section.

2. Based on the training objectives, provide a training agenda and indicate the time allocated and order of modules in your program.

3. For each module, describe the goals of the module and the training methods you will use to accomplish it. Provide your rationale.

4. How will you evaluate whether each person in your training program has mastered the knowledge and skill levels needed to perform as a CSS? Describe the types of questions you would ask of those supervising the CSS employees graduating from your program.

# 6

## COMPUTER-BASED TRAINING METHODS

*640k should be enough for anybody.*

Unknown, 1981

### CHAPTER OBJECTIVES

After reading this chapter, you should be able to:

- Describe the relationship between computer-based training (CBT) and e-learning.

- Identify the components required to develop and deliver CBT.

- Describe the various formats, procedures, strengths, and limitations of the following computer-based training methods:

    - Programmed instruction,

    - Intelligent tutoring systems,

    - Interactive multimedia, and

    - Virtual reality.

- Describe the types of learning objectives for which CBT is most suited and indicate to what degree each method is applicable.

- Indicate the impact of each CBT method on the learning process.

- Evaluate CBT as standalone training.

- Identify resources small business can use to access CBT while minimizing costs.

## CASE

### *Evolution of Training at Mr. Lube*

In 1979 Clifford Giese had become so frustrated with the amount of time it took to get his fleet of vehicles serviced that he created a drive-through oil change system. His first store opened that year in the town of Pickering, Ontario. By 1984 there were 45 stores and Mr. Giese sold the Canadian rights to the Mr. Lube trademark to Imperial Oil Limited (Esso). By 2003, the number of corporate stores and franchised outlets had grown to 87 across the nation. However, this growth has created new challenges for maintaining the consistent high quality and customer-focused service across the widely distributed network.

The success of Mr. Lube Canada, Inc. depends on a high level of competence from a relatively young and geographically dispersed workforce. The technical aspects of the industry are becoming increasingly sophisticated, making training a key component in Mr. Lube's strategic thinking. In 2002, Senior Vice-President Bill Tickner did not feel that the paper-based training system that had developed over the history of the company could meet the demands of the current workforce and company configuration. The training manuals contained all the correct information about how to service a vehicle properly, but he didn't feel that employees were actually reading the voluminous training manuals and technical bulletins distributed to each of the stores and franchises. Additionally, there was no reliable and easy way to ensure that the employee actually understood and retained the information. How could he ensure that every employee across the country had the competencies needed to meet Mr. Lube's standards, while keeping the cost within reasonable limits?

# OVERVIEW OF THE CHAPTER

The material in this chapter will provide you with an understanding of the various **computer-based training (CBT)** methods, how to use them effectively, their strengths and limitations in terms of cost, suitable learning objectives, and other factors related to their effectiveness. Following that, we will examine the various delivery methods available for use with these methods.

**Computer-Based Training (CBT)** training that uses a computer to provide instruction.

# OVERVIEW OF COMPUTER-BASED TRAINING (CBT)

Today's competitive business environment requires more knowledge and skill from employees than ever before. This translates into more training for more employees than ever before. At the same time, business success requires companies to lower costs, so companies are looking for ways to provide low-cost training to their employees. Compared with the training methods in Chapter 5, CBT offers this potential to do the following reasons:[1]

- Reduce trainee learning time,

- Reduce the cost of training,

- Provide instructional consistency,

- Afford privacy of learning (errors can be made without embarrassment),

- Track trainees' learning progress with ease,

- Allow the trainee to master learning,

- Provide a safe method for learning hazardous tasks, and

- Increase employee access to training.

CBT utilizes many of the methods described in Chapter 5 but converts those methods into electronic form and delivers the training through the computer. CBT is so varied in its forms and applications that it is difficult to describe in concise terms. We stay with convention and use the term CBT to refer to any training that occurs through the use of a computer.[2] It is distinguished by the fact that face-to-face interaction with a human trainer is not required. Under this definition, CBT may include many different techniques and processes for providing the training experience. Table 6-1 lists and briefly describes some of these in order of technological sophistication.

The growth of electronic technology and connectivity has made the use of CBT feasible for most companies. By 2001 about 75 percent of organizations surveyed indicated that they provided training to employees through the Internet or an intranet (accessible only to those in the particular organization).[3] A more recent survey showed, however, that most companies are in the early stages of developing their CBT programs.[4]

# E-LEARNING AND DELIVERY SYSTEMS

Often, CBT and the systems used to deliver CBT are used interchangeably. They are two distinct systems and require different types of expertise to create, manage, and

Justice Institute of British Columbia Simulation Training
*www.jibc.bc.ca/Libraryfiles/ Main/Find/Links/Simulation_ Training.htm*

| TABLE 6-1 | Names and Descriptions Used for Computer-Based Training Approaches |
|---|---|
| CBT | Training provided in part or whole through the use of a computer. *Computer-based training* is the term most often used in private industry or government for training employees using computer-assisted instruction. |
| PI | *Programmed instruction* (PI) is used in computer-based programs consisting of text, graphics, and multimedia enhancements that are stored in memory and connected to one another electronically. Material to be learned is grouped into chunks of closely related information. Typically, the trainees are presented with a chunk of information and then tested on their retention of that information. If the trainees have not retained the material, they are referred back to the original information. If they have retained the information, they are referred to the next chunk of information to be learned. PI may be computer-based but is also found in printed material and interactive videos. |
| ICAI | When the computer-based training system is able to provide some of the primary characteristics of a human tutor, it is often referred to as an *intelligent computer-assisted instruction* (ICAI) system. It is a more advanced form of PI. Expert systems are used to run the tutoring aspect of the training, monitor trainee knowledge within a programmed knowledge model, and provide adaptive tutoring based on trainee responses. |
| ITS | *Intelligent tutoring systems* (ITS) make use of artificial intelligence to provide tutoring that is more advanced than ICAI type tutoring. ITS "learns" the best methods of facilitating the trainee's learning based on how the trainee is responding. |
| Simulations | Computer *simulations* provide a representation of a situation and the tasks to be performed in the situation. The representation can range from identical (e.g., word processing training) to fairly abstract (e.g., conflict resolution). Trainees perform the tasks presented to them by the computer program and the computer program monitors their performance. |
| *Virtual Reality* | Virtual reality is an advanced form of computer simulation, placing the trainee in a simulated environment that is "virtually" the same as the physical environment. In this simulation, the trainee wears special equipment, such as head gear or gloves that control what the trainee is able to see, feel, and otherwise sense. The trainee learns to achieve some goal by interacting with objects in the electronic environment. |

maintain. Innovation in CBT and associated learning management and delivery systems occurs so rapidly that confusion often exists regarding terms and their usage. In this section we provide a description of the process used in creating a CBT program and delivering it to trainees. This will clarify our use of terms throughout the rest of the chapter.

Figure 6-1 shows the basic components for creating and delivering a CBT program. E-learning is often used as a synonym for CBT. In practice, however, **e-learning** refers to the delivery of training or education through electronic media. The training itself is distinct from the **delivery system**. The Internet and intranets are common means of delivering training, but they are not learning systems or training programs. As Figure 6-1 shows, the training content is developed from a **knowledge base** created by subject matter experts. Once the content is developed, it is translated into some type of electronic format through the use of authoring and learning development tools. The design of the training is discussed in more detail in the sections on CBT methods. In the late 1990s some predicted that e-learning would become the primary delivery method for training within five years. That has not yet happened but e-learning is gathering momentum. In a recent survey, almost all large firms had an e-learning capability. Almost 80 percent had developed their first e-learning systems within the last four years. Cost, employee resistance, and lack of management buy-in were the top reasons for the limited adoption and use of e-learning. Additionally, companies are trying to figure out how to best position e-learning within the training portfolio.[5]

**E-learning** the delivery of training through electronic media.

**Delivery System** The method chosen to deliver computer based training.

**Knowledge Base** The things that the trainee will need to know for a particular training program

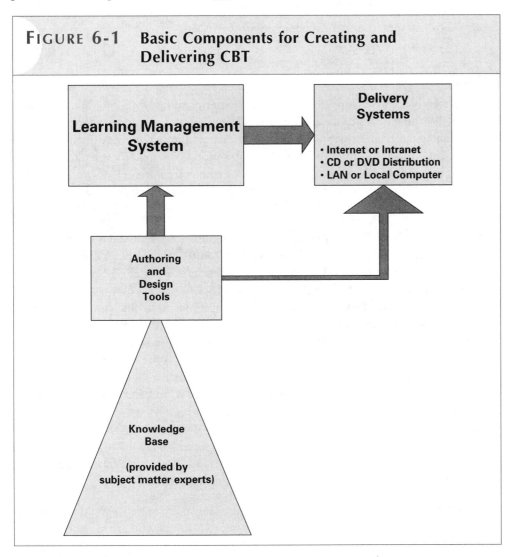

**FIGURE 6-1 Basic Components for Creating and Delivering CBT**

**Learning Management System (LMS)** software of varying degrees of sophistication that manages the delivery of training content and monitors and records trainee activity.

Once developed, it may or may not be integrated into a **learning management system (LMS)**, depending on the sophistication of company's e-learning systems. An LMS is software that manages the content of the training and records the progress of trainees. Learning management systems vary in their level of sophistication and may or may not include features such as

- Authoring,
- Class management,
- Competency management,
- Knowledge management,
- Certification or compliance management,
- Mentoring,
- Chat,
- Threaded discussion, and
- Video conferencing.

A set of standards called the Sharable Content Object Referenced Model (SCORM) has been created to encourage the standardization of learning management systems.

As Figure 6-1 indicates, the final step is delivering the CBT to the trainees. The most common delivery methods are:

- Local computers and local area networks (LANs),
- CD-ROM, DVD, and
- Internet and intranet.

Recently some companies have been experimenting with "mobile learning." Mobile learning refers to the use of wireless devices, such as the telephone, to deliver the training material. British Columbia Hydro has embarked on transitioning its training to an e-learning solution that incorporates mobile devices.[6] This makes sense for a company that has 1800 employees, many of whom are in remote locations. Mobile learning may or may not catch on, but it's something training professionals need to keep an eye on.

**Off-Line Delivery Systems** Local computers are individual computers that are available to the trainees. The CBT is loaded onto each computer's hard drive and can be accessed by the trainee. This is not a very efficient delivery method if more than a few trainees are to be trained. A more efficient process is to use the organization's **local area network (LAN)**. A LAN is simply the electronic connection among the various computers and a central server. With a LAN, the CBT is loaded into the server where it becomes accessible from any authorized computer on the network. This saves memory in the individual computers, as well as the time and inconvenience of trainees loading the program onto their own computers.

**Local Area Network (LAN)** the electronic connection among the various computers and a central server.

The CBT can be reproduced on CDs or DVDs and delivered to individual trainees. This method of delivery allows trainees to access the training outside the LAN and without downloading the program onto the computer. The development of small, portable DVD players allows trainees to access the training even in remote locations where computer connections do not exist. CDs and DVDs are small, easy to package, and inexpensive to reproduce and distribute.

**Internet and Intranet** The Internet and intranets are also rapidly becoming methods for transmitting standardized training to trainees who are in many different locations.

Companies using an **intranet** provide access to training through a company portal. The portal allows only authorized employees access to training. Training over the Internet or intranet will require the use of an LMS to monitor who is accessing the training, record trainee progress, and perform other training management functions. An advantage to this delivery approach is that the time trainees spend on the training and any evaluation of trainee learning can be recorded in a central location.

**Intranet** similar to the Internet, but accessible only to a specific company's employees.

# COMPUTER-BASED TRAINING METHODS

## PROGRAMMED INSTRUCTION

**Programmed instruction (PI)** is a method of self-paced learning managed by both the trainee and the learning system. **Self-paced learning** means the trainees move through the training as fast as they are able to learn the material. The program determines the trainees' learning through trainee responses to questions. PI began many years ago, long before computers were around. However, with the coming of the computer age, it was only natural that PI would become computerized. Although PI can also be used without a computer, today its principal use is in CBT. Higher forms of CBT, such as intelligent tutoring, are much more than PI, but the principles of PI are the basis on which these other techniques operate. PI is the process of leading a trainee systematically through new information in a way that facilitates the most-efficient learning. At its most basic level, PI provides the trainee with information, asks a question, and, based on the response, goes to the next bit of information. Table 6-2 describes the PI principles while at the same time providing an example of the PI approach. Working sequentially through the questions shows how this method works and what principles of learning are used.

**Programmed Instruction (PI)** a method of self-paced learning managed by both the trainee and the learning system (e.g., computer program or text).

**Self-Paced Learning** trainess move through the training as fast as they are able to learn the material.

## TABLE 6-2    Programmed Instruction for Programmed Instruction

| Learning Stem | Questions | Instructions |
|---|---|---|
| 1. Many people think it is impossible to learn without making a large number of errors. Because *trial and error learning* is time consuming and creates frustration in the learner, most people don't like this method. After making a large number of errors, people begin to *lose their desire* to learn.<br><br>   Many trainers feel that if learning is carefully *programmed* to occur in a specific manner, people can learn without making a large number of errors. | 1a. Learning by making a number of errors until the right response is discovered is called:<br><br>1b. What is likely to happen to people's desire to learn when they must use the trial and error method?<br><br>1c. When the material to be learned is prepared so that the trainee makes few errors, it is said to have been carefully: | Compare your answers with those below:<br>1a. Trial and error learning.<br>1b. It decreases.<br>1c. Programmed<br>If your answers closely match those above go on to section 2. If not, reread section 1, paying close attention to the italicized concepts. Then answer the questions again. |
| 2. Programmed instruction (PI) operates on the principle that if *learning is programmed to occur in small steps,* few errors will occur. Another principle of PI is that if | 2a. If the goal is to reduce the number of trainee errors before the material is learned, how | Compare your answers with those below:<br>2a. In small steps.<br>2b. Immediately.<br>If your answers closely |

## TABLE 6-2 (Continued )

| Learning Stem | Questions | Instructions |
|---|---|---|
| trainees are *given immediate feed-back* regarding the appropriate ness of their response, they will learn more quickly and complete a greater amount of material. | should learning be programmed?<br>2b. To increase the amount learned and the speed of learning, when should feedback be given? | match those above go on to section 3. If not, reread section 2, paying close attention to the italicized concepts. Then answer the questions again. |
| 3. Trainee learning is enhanced if the trainee is active in the learning process. PI asks trainees to *respond to questions, putting the trainee in an active learning mode.* Because trainees learn at different rates, *they will learn best if they can move through the material at their own pace.* PI allows people to learn at their own pace. Finally, *frequent review of material helps trainees retain* the material for longer periods of time. | 3a. Programming questions into the material enhances learning because it places trainees into a(n) _____ mode of learning.<br>3b. At what pace should trainees move through the material to be learned?<br>3c. Frequent review of material results in: | Compare your answers with those below:<br>3a. Active.<br>3b. Their own pace.<br>3c. Longer retention of the material.<br>If your answers closely match those above go on to section 4. If not, reread section 3, paying close attention to the italicized concepts. Then answer the questions again. |
| 4. In summary, PI allows trainees to learn more material, quicker, and retain it longer with less frustration by 1) programming small learning steps resulting in fewer response errors, 2) requiring frequent active responses by the trainees, 3) providing immediate feedback to trainee responses, 4) allowing trainees to move through the material at their own pace, and 5) reviewing the material frequently. | 4a. What are five principles that PI uses to improve the ease, amount, speed, and retention of learning?<br>4b. PI increases the trainees' desire to learn by reducing the number of _____ the trainee is likely to make. | Compare your answers with those below:<br>4a. 1) Small learning steps, 2) Frequent and active response by the trainee, 3) Immediate feedback, 4) Self-paced learning, and 5) Frequent review.<br>4b. Response errors.<br>If your answers closely match those above you have successfully com pleted the section on PI. If not, review section 4 again. |

In its most sophisticated form, PI consists of a set of branches that might be activated depending on the answer provided to a question. If the trainee provides a correct answer, one branch moves the trainee forward to new information. If the answer is incorrect, a different branch is activated, taking the trainee back to review relevant information in more detail. This format allows trainees to move through the material as rapidly as they are capable. Trainees who show a better grasp of the material (based on their responses) move rapidly through the material. The branches taken by those for whom the material is more difficult are different and will depend on the types of errors they make.

CBT applies PI techniques within a computerized format to create the learning experience. However, PI can also come in book, tape, interactive video, or other formats. We will focus on the computerized application, but keep in mind that the principles are the same regardless of format.

## How to Use PI Effectively
Development of PI is a difficult and expensive process and may not justify the cost and effort needed. However, when a large number

of people require training, especially if they are geographically dispersed, it can be a viable option. Once developed, PI can be transferred to whatever media is appropriate for the training (printed, floppy disks, CD-ROM, DVD, or website). Trainees are then able to complete the training at their own pace, on their own time (if desirable), and from different locations around the world. PI can automate the less-interactive components of training.[7] In a blended approach, you can use PI to provide the required knowledge base, and then use classroom and on-the-job training for the hands-on practice. PI can be used to teach some skills (e.g., computer) as well as knowledge. PI can be a stand-alone type of training or it can be integrated into a multi-method training program.

# INTELLIGENT TUTORING SYSTEMS

An **intelligent tutoring system** (ITS) is a more-sophisticated form of programmed instruction. It uses artificial intelligence to assist in tutoring or coaching the trainee. ITS provides guidance and selects the appropriate level of instruction for the trainee. In addition, an ITS can learn from its own process what worked and did not work in the training process. Based on this information, the ITS improves its methods of teaching the trainee. Intelligent tutoring can be a text-based system or a combination of text with graphics and other types of audiovisual aids.

ITSs consist of five components: an expert knowledge base, a trainee model, a training session manager, a scenario generator, and a user interface.[8] The **expert knowledge base** is the set of knowledge about what is correct (e.g., the best way to perform a task, the knowledge needed to be effective). This corresponds to the "knowledge base" triangle in Figure 6-1. The **trainee model** component stores information about how the trainees are performing during training and what they seem to know. As the trainees respond to items, the information is used to tutor or coach them. The **training session manager** is the component that interprets the trainees' responses and responds either with more information, coaching (helping the trainee explore the topic), or tutoring (guiding the trainee toward the correct answer). This component also determines how and when to send the trainee back to more basic material and what strategy to use in the remedial work. For example, the session manager may act simply as a reference source (providing sources for the trainee to look up needed information), or possibly a tutor or coach (suggesting an appropriate response). The session manager might decide to provide a demonstration.[9] The **training scenario generator** is the component that determines the order and level of difficulty of the problems that are presented to the trainee. Lastly, the **user interface** is the equipment that allows the trainee to interact with the ITS. It commonly includes a computer keyboard, mouse, or joystick. ITS sets itself apart from simple programmed instruction because it is able to do the following:[10]

- Generate instruction that matches the individual trainee's needs,

- Communicate and respond to trainee questions,

- Model the trainee's learning processes (assess current level of knowledge; identify misconceptions, learning problems, and needs),

- Determine what information should follow based on previous trainee responses,

- Determine the trainee's level of understanding of the topic, and

- Improve its strategies for teaching the trainee based on the trainee's responses.

An examination of Figure 6-2 illustrates how trainee responses allow the system to interpret the response and provide the trainee with specific training to address the problem.[11] Note that the three trainees depicted in Figure 6-2 all provided the wrong

**Intelligent Tutoring System (ITS)** a sophisticated form of programmed instruction.

**Expert Knowledge Base** a component of an intelligent tutoring system that stores the correct answers to the knowledge being taught.

**Trainee Model** a component of an intelligent tutoring system that stores the information about how the trainee is responding and what the trainee seems to know.

**Training Session Manager** a component of an intelligent tutoring system that interprets trainees' responses and responds with either more information, coaching, or tutoring.

**Training Scenario Generator** a component of an intelligent tutoring system that determines the order and level of difficulty of the problems that are presented to the trainee.

**User Interface** the equipment that allows the trainee to interact with the intelligent tutoring system.

---

## FIGURE 6-2 Trainee Modelling Example

| | | |
|---|---|---|
| Trainee A | $\begin{array}{r}22\\+\,39\\\hline 51\end{array}$ | $\begin{array}{r}46\\+\,39\\\hline 75\end{array}$ |
| Trainee B | $\begin{array}{r}22\\+\,39\\\hline 161\end{array}$ | $\begin{array}{r}46\\+\,39\\\hline 185\end{array}$ |
| Trainee C | $\begin{array}{r}22\\+\,39\\\hline 62\end{array}$ | $\begin{array}{r}46\\+\,39\\\hline 83\end{array}$ |

---

answer to the addition questions, but each made different errors. The intelligent tutor determines that trainee A never carries over, trainee B carries over but sometimes inappropriately, and trainee C has trouble with simple single-digit addition. The tutor will then provide a different type of instruction to each of the trainees based on the diagnosis of the errors. This process continues, with the tutor constantly re-evaluating and providing new instruction until the learning objectives are achieved.

**How to Use ITS Effectively** ITS is even more expensive to develop than PI and requires specific expertise not likely found in the organization. With electronic training technology changing so fast, however, it is difficult to make recommendations that will hold even a short time into the future. ITS is definitely worth considering, given the enormous advantages over simple PI. Numerous vendors offer relevant PI and ITS training that is available for purchase. Whether to buy off the shelf or to develop one will depend on a cost/benefit analysis.

## INTERACTIVE MULTIMEDIA

**Interactive Multimedia Training** integrates the use of video, graphics, photos, animation, and sound to produce a complex training environment with which trainess can interact.

**Interactive multimedia training** integrates the use of text, video, graphics, photos, animation, and sound to produce a complex training environment with which the trainee interacts. Typically, PI methodology is applied to learning chunks that are converted into a multimedia format to facilitate learning. For example, the trainee is put into a real-life job situation and asked to solve a specific problem. Once the trainee interacts with the program to solve the problem, he can receive immediate feedback as to the effectiveness of his decision.[12] Typically, trainees become very engaged in this type of learning because they are immersed psychologically into the situation.

The development of CD, DVD, and networking technology has allowed interactive multimedia to grow rapidly over the last few years. In the early 1990s few firms used this technology for training. By 2003 about 45 percent of those responding to a training survey indicated that they used IM often for training. Only 8 percent indicated never using the technology.[13]

**Examples of IM Usage** Interactive multimedia training systems are capable of providing training related to almost any training objective. It can be as simple as providing some basic knowledge, or as complex as teaching how to diagnose heart disorders or improve communication skills. Companies across a variety of industries are using this technology for training in widely differing content areas. Below are some examples of the types of training for which IM is used.

Nugget Brand Distributors developed a Certificate in Food Safety Training, which it markets to restaurants.[14] Jackson Hewitt Tax Service, with its huge number of part-time workers (in the tax season), needed a way to bring employees up-to-speed regarding tax changes. CD-ROM technology allowed them to distribute the information more easily and cheaply than did printed material. It provides training just when the new employee needs it and a trainer does not have to be there.[15] Training in Action 6-1 describes the success of Aeronett, a British Columbia–based company that specializes in the development of IM training for the airline industry.

IM technology is also used to provide medical training.[16] This training, delivered via Internet, allows a medical student to take the medical history of a hypothetical patient, conduct an examination, and run lab tests. For example, as part of the examination the medical student may choose to examine the patient's chest. The student clicks the "examine chest" button and is then asked to choose a type of examination to conduct (visual inspection, palpation, or auscultation). The trainee might click on auscultate (listen to sounds made by the lungs) and hear the chest sounds that would be made by a particular patient. Based on the interpretation of the sounds, the trainee would make a diagnosis and click the button that represented a diagnosis. The trainee would then be informed of the accuracy of the diagnosis. If the diagnosis were incorrect, the trainee would be given an explanation and moved to supplementary materials designed to provide the knowledge needed to make a correct diagnosis.

The previous examples show how useful IM can be in developing knowledge, psychomotor, and decision-making skills. What about improving interpersonal skills? Training in Action 6-2 describes a training program developed by Marriott

## Training in Action 6-1

### *Aeronett Corners Airline Training*

Aeronett Technologies Limited, based in British Columbia, is in the business of developing courseware for a new generation of aviation training. Development of courseware comes from their team of subject matter experts, instructional designers, graphic designers, 3D animators, multimedia programmers, and sound engineers. Air Canada, Pan Am International Flight Academy, Jetway Aeronautics, and Star Airlines have selected Aeronett's CBT for their employees.

Training packages for Air Canada can be delivered over the Internet and include initial pilot training as well as transitional and recurrent ground school training. Other CBT training packages for pilots include flying dangerous goods, cold weather/winter operations, Pacific operations, and minimum equipment. But Web-based training has been developed for more than just pilots. Aeronett has developed training for maintenance personnel and flight and cabin crews. Pan Am International Flight Academy's (PAIFA) Gary LaGuardia indicates that Aeronett's course will enable PAIFA to offer state-of-the-art training "that is specifically designed to meet

the needs of our commercial airline clients who come to our training from around the world." Air Canada selected Aeronett because its integration of 3D simulation, 2D digital images, and interactivity provides a realistic portrayal of the flight deck. The courses motivate the learner, improve retention of new information, and allow for effective transfer of knowledge, skills, and attitudes to aircraft operation.

As a result of their advances in CBT, Aeronett was named the 2001 Leading Edge Training Innovator by the Aerospace Industry Association of British Columbia. Training times have dropped 50 percent to 70 percent from previous methods. Their technology-based training programs have lowered costs associated with travel and time spent in training centres. Since the system provides learners with the ability to study anytime and anywhere, trainees are enjoying the flexibility this training provides.

*Source*: This case was developed from information contained in the following Aeronett website: www.aeronett.com.

## Training in Action 6-2

### Marriott International Uses Multimedia Training for Soft Skills

Marriott International, a widely recognized name in the lodging industry, is noted for their people-oriented, high-touch culture, so their strategic plan indicating a commitment to growing from 900 properties to 2000 in only a few years raised a concern regarding their ability to train such large numbers. Analysis indicated that in the next five years, Marriott would be hiring about a million employees, and all would need training.

A training transformation team was struck to study the problem and find a solution. The solution that made the most sense was a set of multimedia training packages that use CD-ROM technology and operate from a traditional PC computer. One of these, Front Desk Quest, provides soft-skills training. To begin the training, the trainee logs on with an ID and a password. An on-screen person greets the trainee, walks her through the training, and is always available for help (by pressing the Help button). The trainee is presented with a series of different training modules, the culmination of which is a simulation in which where the trainee plays an active role in combining the skills and knowledge learned earlier. In the simulation, trainees are presented with a situation in which they are required to determine, from a set of choices, what is the correct thing to say or do. They then click on what they believe to be the correct response, and the computer program responds by playing out the scenario to show the student what happens if they make a correct or incorrect decision. If the trainee was correct, the trainee sees the customer on the screen saying something positive. If the choice was not correct, the video may show an angry customer responding. The trainee is able to make alternative responses and see the customer reaction.

Trainees are able to sign on to the training at any time and start up where they left off in the previous session. They are able to go over previous exercises as often as they want, as well as track their progress. Management can also sign on and note the progress of employees.

Do employees like the new training format? Reactions are consistently positive, so the answer must be yes. Even those with minimal skill in the use of a computer find it easy to use and are going full speed in only a few minutes. As Starr Shafer, a manager at Marriott says, "They immediately give better service with greater self-assurance. And they say, "Wow, I felt so comfortable doing it."

*Sources:* Stauffer, D. 1999. High-tech training a huge win in Marriott's high-touch culture. Available from www.traininguniversity .com; Jensen, E. (Personal communication, January 31, 2002).

International to develop their employees' interpersonal skills. Another application, Virtual Leader was developed by SimuLearn Inc. It utilizes artificial intelligence (fuzzy logic) to render graphics and dialogue dynamically to give the user a simulated real-life environment for learning and practising persuasive leadership skills. In this example of high-end IM, the system is able to simulate realistic situations, interpret trainee responses within the logic of the leadership model, and show how trainee interactions will influence employees to behave. The simulation's intent is to teach people to monitor and balance power, tension, and ideas appropriately in order to align the work of others with business goals (financial performance, customer satisfaction, and employee morale). The authors received training in the use of the simulation and found it to be challenging and engaging. As with any off-the-shelf training product, the trainer will need to carefully evaluate the product's fit with the firm's training objectives.

## How to Use Interactive Multimedia Effectively

As always, the effectiveness of the program will depend on how closely it meets the learning objectives. With IM, trainees are likely to enjoy their experience and give the training high marks because it is so much fun, even if many of the training objectives are not met. Thus, it is especially important to verify the match between the IM program's outcomes and the training objectives. Although this sounds logical and straightforward, our discussions with Nina Adams, president of Adams I Solutions (a firm that designs IM training), suggests it is often not the case. She told us,

If I had one message to give people considering the use of IM training, it is this: Understand the goals of the program you're going to develop before you do anything else. I recently worked on a project where the client was converting a live presentation to multimedia. The major problem was pulling out of the client what they wanted to accomplish ... what they wanted people who went through the training program to think, do, or feel. It's amazing how many people develop a program without knowing what they're trying to accomplish. How do you know the program is "successful" if you don't know what you're trying to do?

To be most effective, your IM should accommodate multiple learning styles and make it easy for trainees to organize the new KSAs into their existing knowledge base (cognitive organization). Any target group of trainees is likely to have a variety of learning styles and cognitive organization systems. Thus it is necessary to ensure that the IM uses a variety of audio and visual cues to communicate the information and the many ways of connecting new KSAs to old. Attention to self-pacing, interactivity, and the sophistication of the multimedia will address these issues and improve its effectiveness.[17]

Self-pacing allows trainees to learn based upon what they already know. It is important that the self-pacing is designed to accommodate multiple ways of organizing and using information (cognitive organization). The better the design in this area, the better the learning that will be realized by trainees. Interactivity is the program's ability to allow trainees to respond to situations and to receive feedback. The more interactive the CBT, the greater the trainees' retention of the training. It is important to make sure the CBT has a sufficient level of interactivity for trainees to retain the learning. The sophistication of the multimedia, in this context, refers to audio/visual integration and realism of the program. The more ways the same information is communicated, the easier it will be for trainees to learn it. At the same time, the various ways of presenting the information must be connected realistically and reinforce each other. A good IM program should rate high on all three factors. Table 6-3 provides points to consider when evaluating IM training.

The degree to which the IM training will result in the transfer of new KSAs back to the job will depend on the physical and psychological fidelity the programming creates. This fidelity can be accomplished by having the program developers visit the operational areas that will be involved in the training and by having a representative from these areas consult with the development team. The more closely the IM program reflects the kinds of situations faced on the job, the more the KSAs will transfer back to the job.

It is a good idea to consider blending IM with other methods. This blending allows each method to provide unique learning opportunities while reinforcing learning from other methods. Blending has been shown to improve the transfer of the training to the job.[18] Instructor-guided discussion will generally be helpful as a supplement to IM. One thing that was evident after going through the SimuLearn leadership training was the energy it creates for discussing the experience. Some of our conversation focused on the balance of realism and artificiality, some on the relation of the leadership model to other models in the literature, and some on our rationale for our personal scores. All of these topics, guided appropriately by a trainer, can provide valuable insight to the trainees. Other advantages to blending guided discussion with IM include the following:

- The trainer's enthusiasm for the training content encourages learning;

- The trainer provides assessment and accountability that is missing in IM alone;

- Trainees' questions and comments raise issues not addressed in the IM programming; and

- Trainees acquire a deeper understanding through social interaction.

**TABLE 6-3    Points to Consider in Development of Interactive Multimedia**

| Factor | High If | Low If |
|---|---|---|
| Self-Pacing | • The pace of the program is entirely controlled by the learner.<br>• Trainees can select menu options to determine the order of modules.<br>• Trainees can skip lessons or segments at will and can exit the program from any screen.<br>• Additional practice and more in-depth material are available upon request. | • The only way to control the pace of the presentation is by using a special key.<br>• It is not menu-driven, i.e., the trainee can't select a particular lesson segment or skip segments.<br>• Trainees can exit the program only at certain points. |
| Interactivity | • Trainees' responses follow instructional segments.<br>• The program tests skills and judgments, not just facts.<br>• The orderly sequence of topics is apparent to the learner. | • The program has long, uninterrupted lesson segments that offer no chance for the trainee to ask or answer questions.<br>• The program tests recall instead of skills.<br>• Segments do not build on one another.<br>• The learner's answers are tagged right or wrong with no further explanation. |
| Multimedia Sophistication | • The voices are distinct and natural.<br>• A voice provides program instructions so that the trainee doesn't have to read them.<br>• Sound and visuals reinforce one another.<br>• Visuals use color and motion to reinforce the audio message and illustrate the idea presented. | • The sound or visuals are of poor quality.<br>• There is no direct connection between the audio and visual material (the sound is limited to irrelevant music, for example).<br>• The sound is restricted to a voice saying, "You are correct," or "Try again."<br>• The visuals don't reinforce instructional points. |

*Source:* Put SPIMM in your CBT. (1993). *Training,* Feb. pp. 12, 14.

Although significant learning can occur without it, guided discussion can lead to additional learning and greater understanding. Another approach is to supplement the IM with manuals and other material. This was Duracell's approach, as described in Training in Action 6-3. This method also seems to increase learning beyond what was gained in the IM training.

# VIRTUAL REALITY

**Virtual Reality (VR) Training** training in which an artificial, three-dimensional environment is used to simulate real situations.

Virtual reality (VR) training is the next best thing to being there. It allows training for dangerous situations (police car chases, hostage situations) and situations for which using the real thing is very expensive (flying, operating heavy equipment). VR puts the trainee in an artificial three-dimensional environment that simulates events and situations that might be experienced on the job. The trainee interacts with these

## Training in Action 6-3

### Duracell's Integrated Approach to Training in China

Duracell's battery manufacturing plant in China was to serve the growing Asian market demand for its product. The company wanted to create a highly visual training process that would rely on graphics, animation, digitized photos, video, and Chinese text. The key component was the multimedia presentation. It was supplemented with manuals that trainees could take with them to use as a reference, printed job aids to assist with recalling more complex processes, and of course "hands-on" practice. It was felt that these backup methods were necessary to aid the trainee in retention and transfer.

The training was comprehensive and included health and safety, operations, quality, and faultfinding. The goal was to create a standardized training process that would promote a safe work environment and facilitate the workforce in becoming as productive as possible, as fast as possible. How successful was this training? Well, we know motivation was high. From the moment the programs were installed, a crowd immediately formed around the workstations. Employees were anxious to be next to get their personalized training session. As motivation is a critical component of successful training, this program was off to a positive start.

*Source*: Marquardt, M. (1999). *Technology-Based Learning: Maximizing Human Performance and Corporate Success.* Boca Raton, FL: CRC Press.

images to accomplish specific goals. In these respects VR is not much different from the more advanced forms of IM. The difference is in how the trainee experiences the simulation. In VR, the trainee experiences a physical involvement with and a presence in the simulated environment.[19] That is, the trainee psychologically experiences the environment as real. To experience a computerized VR, the trainee must wear devices that provide sensory input. Such devices include a headset that provides visual and audio information, gloves that give tactile information, and treadmills or other types of motion platforms for creating the sense of movement. Some even have the ability to supply olfactory information.

Many advanced forms of IM use artificial intelligence to portray situations more realistically and manage interactions with the trainee. They do not, however, reach the level of creating a sense of physical presence. The creators of these advanced IM programs wish to distinguish themselves from the less-advanced IM training and have taken to referring incorrectly to their products as VR. So when reading about VR in trade journals, you must to be aware that much of what is called VR is in reality IM. For some good reasons that are discussed later, few actual VR training systems exist.

VR provides trainees with an understanding of the consequences of their actions in the work environment by interpreting and responding to the trainees' actions in the simulation. Sensory devices transmit to the computer how the trainee is responding in the virtual workplace, allowing the VR program to respond by changing the environment appropriately. For example, a police academy trainee sitting in a simulated driver's seat of a police car can see the speedometer and all the gauges on the dashboard; looking to the right, the trainee sees an empty seat; when the trainee turns the steering wheel, the view out the windshield provides a visual representation of the car turning a corner. VR has been used to train police officers how to stop a speeding car safely, without the danger of using real people and automobiles. To date, VR has been used for training complex and dangerous skills, such as flying outside the earth's atmosphere[20] and more traditional skills, such as teaching someone to speak in front of large audiences.[21]

**Using Virtual Reality Effectively** The points raised for effective use of IM apply even more strongly to VR. A concern unique to virtual reality training, "simulator sickness," has limited the growth of VR. Prolonged immersion in the VR environment has caused some people to experience vertigo and general motion sickness. Because people show different tolerances in terms of how long they can last in such an environment, and because of the cost and long lead-time, VR training is a risk not many companies are willing to take. For the most part, VR remains in the entertainment industry.[22] If it is being used, a number of organizations are available to provide assistance, but expect a long lead-time and possible problems when trainees are using it. It is necessary to do extensive pilot testing, as the complexity of this type of programming leads to bugs in the program that are not readily apparent.[23]

## STRENGTHS AND LIMITATIONS OF CBT METHODS

**Costs** Arguments are made both supporting and criticizing the cost effectiveness of CBT. The costs of developing and implementing a CBT program are related to the following factors:

- Number of trainees taking the course per year,
- Cost of wages per hour for trainees while they are taking the course,
- Cost of wages per hour for course developer,
- Amortized cost of hardware to support the CBT,
- Amortized cost of software used in the CBT,
- Hours needed to complete the CBT program,
- Hours needed to develop CBT course content,
- Stability of the course content, and
- Cost of not addressing the training need sooner with some other method.

The development cost of CBT is not usually justified for a small number of trainees. On average, an hour of CBT instruction is reported to require about 200 hours of development time.[24] This estimate is probably conservative for multimedia and virtual reality development and is excessive for simple PI. In situations where the training is not likely to change, and where a large number of people need training, CBT can be a cost-effective alternative to instructor-led training.

Intelligent tutoring systems consist of shells that house a learning management system (LMS) and a knowledge base. The LMS is the engine that delivers the knowledge to the trainee. The knowledge base is the information that needs to be learned. Development of the LMS is fairly expensive, while the development of the knowledge base is less so.[25] Using the same shell, a knowledge base that is used for one application (training a salesperson to sell the automobile), can be quickly and easily changed to fit another application (training the HR manager to explain why a grievance cannot be allowed).[26] Thus the shell engine, once developed, can be used across many training programs. Many e-learning companies have developed very sophisticated shell engines that they lease or license. Many companies acquire access to a shell engine and develop the knowledge base in-house to keep the cost of ITS and IM down.

Multimedia training is also initially costly to develop but is easy to deliver and convenient to use. CDs or DVDs are inexpensive to reproduce and distribute to trainees across geographically dispersed locations. If the topic to be trained is generic, various programs are available at a reasonable cost. Consider the health and safety training programs offered by Comprehensive Loss Management of Minneapolis presented in Table 6-4. They offer a number of reasonably priced canned CD-ROM training programs in safety. Likewise, companies can share in the development costs for common types of training, as was the case with Learnshare (see Training in Action 6-4). Its charter members can access more than 500 000 online development courses.[27] This concept is a great idea for small companies to consider in the pursuit of all types of training, but particularly the more expensive types of CBT.

Unless there is access in the organization to a technology unit with specific skills related to the development of IM, it will probably be more cost-effective to use outside vendors. The more sophisticated and complex the material, the more likely it is that it will be necessary to contract with an outside provider. Although many generic "off the shelf" programs can be useful, many vendors will customize the content to fit the objectives of the company. In addition to the organizations discussed previously, Michelin, IBM, Motorola, Volvo Heavy Truck, and Duracell make use of IM training. Applications range from the start-up and shut-down of a production line, to verbal interaction skills.[28] Some of these programs are developed in-house while others are purchased.

A virtual reality unit can cost as little as $20 000 and even with the cost of designing, the training could make the total cost reasonable compared with something like an equipment simulator.[29] Keep in mind the time to build a VR program can be eight months or longer. The potential health risks will also need to be weighed when using VR.

Although all CBT technologies generally involve more expensive start-up costs than does classroom training, they offer a major advantage: CBT delivery systems

## Training in Action 6-4

### The High Cost of Multimedia Training

The software developer was extolling the virtues of multimedia training. "It will alter the learning landscape for the next millennium," he said to 200 training executives at a Boston conference. Rick Corry, newly appointed training executive from Owens Corning, listened with mild annoyance. He was recently told by one of these people that they would develop a nice CD-ROM training program for Corning for $150 000. The software developer went on to say that Corry's division would not be able to share the program with other business units in Owens Corning. In fact, the corporation would not even own the copyright on the program for two years, during which time the developer could sell it to anyone else who was interested.

When the speaker asked if there were any questions, Corry looked at all the others in the audience and said, "I'm just wondering, why don't we get together and share what we have and fund what we need? After all, most companies have similar training needs in a number of areas: basic sales skills, time management, leadership skills, and interpersonal skills." The room went silent. The speaker did not say a word. As the session ended, Corry was surrounded by training executives and collected 27 business cards from people who

wanted to explore the idea. From that encounter came a consortium of nine large non-competing manufacturing companies; it is called LearnShare. One of its goals is to develop partnerships with vendors of multimedia training, "but in a manner that is as good for us as it is for them," said Corry. With the consortium's combined revenues of more than $100 billion and 2.2 million employees, they are likely to carry some real clout with vendors.

One of LearnShare's first objectives was to determine similarities in the training needs across the different companies. LearnShare conducted a survey in all nine companies of the training material that was not related to processes or products. The result: 74 percent of the training was addressing the same needs. In other words, diversity training is diversity training, no matter where it is taught.

The companies are already sharing non-multimedia training information and programs. Furthermore, they are sharing training space. Motorola, for example, allows managers at Owens Corning who are stationed in the Pacific Rim to sit in on some training Motorola is conducting in its facility there.

*Source:* Adapted from Blumfield, M. (1997). Learning to share. *Training 34*: 38–42.

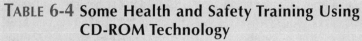

## TABLE 6-4 Some Health and Safety Training Using CD-ROM Technology

St. John Ambulance Canada
Health and Safety Training
*www.sja.ca/english/health_saf
ety_training/cbt/index.asp*

*Accident Investigation*

Prevents costly accidents from recurring by investigating to find causes and implementing steps to prevent them.

Training time 30–60 minutes. Price $695

*Basics of Ergonomics*

Helps workers understand injuries caused by repetitive motion and how to prevent them.

Training time 30–45 minutes. Price $695

*Blood-Borne Pathogens*

Helps workers understand the cause of Hepatitis B and HIV, the virus that causes AIDS. This course uses 30 interactions to teach workers what blood-borne pathogens are and the precautions to take to prevent being infected.

Training time 20–40 minutes. Price $695

*Confined Space Entry*

This training teaches workers concepts essential for a safe work environment when in a confined space. Twenty-nine interactive activities assess the level of understanding of the key learning objectives and let trainees apply what they learned in a safe environment.

Training time 30–45 minutes. Price $695

*WHMIS: Learning the System*

This training covers the Canadian regulations related to workplace safety as it relates to hazardous material.

Training time 45–75 minutes. Price $695

**Minimum Hardware Requirements**

*Stand-Alone Training Station*

Pentium 100 mhz

8 MB RAM, 10MB hard disk per course

Windows 95 or better

Soundblaster-compatible soundcard

4X CD-ROM

*Networked Training Station*

486/25 computer

8 MB RAM, 10MB hard disk per course

Windows 95 or better

Soundblaster-compatible soundcard

*Source:* Information available at www.clmi-training.com/cdrom_training.htm.

make it possible to eliminate many of the costs incurred with other methods, such as trainers, facilities, and trainee travel and lodging.

Research shows that CBT reduces training time and in most cases travel and lodging costs related to training. A number of studies examining various types of CBT (programmed instruction and multimedia) indicate that CBT learning takes less time.[30] In a more recent study, Air Force trainees were taught troubleshooting of the hydraulic subsystems of F-15 aircraft using ITS and CBT using programmed instruction. Evaluation of the two teaching methods indicated ITS not only results in faster training time but more is learned.[31]

As mentioned earlier, there is typically a significant lag time between the point at which a training need is identified and completion of a relevant CBT program. The cost of not immediately addressing the training need through some other method must be factored into the cost of developing the CBT. Focus on Small Business provides some other alternatives.

## Focus on Small Business

We have already indicated options available to small business in terms of collaborating to obtain a common set of training practices. Many Web-based training packages are also available. These packages can vary from simple PowerPoint presentations online, to animated graphics, interactive exercises, and simulations.[32] The Canada Business Service Centres website (www.cbsc.org) offers a number of online training packages for small business. Among these are "Online Small Business Workshop," "Interactive Business Planner," and "Business Start-up Assistant." This site also links to the Aboriginal Business Service Network.

**Control of Material and Process** CBT software determines the content and process of the training. Perhaps the most important advantage of CBT is its control over the content of the material, method of presentation, and movement of the trainee through sequentially structured learning episodes based on previous trainee responses.[33] The pace of learning is controlled by the interaction between the software and the trainee.

The above features are both strengths and weaknesses of various CBT compared with instructor-based training. The advantages are that CBT ensures consistency of topic coverage and topic mastery across all trainees. Sometimes, however, learning opportunities are lost if trainees cannot diverge from prescribed topic areas to clarify understanding. A live trainer can identify when such divergence is necessary. CBT programs have tried to address this issue by providing instant messaging and other communication tools that allow trainees to communicate with one another and a live trainer. Of course, this adds to the cost of training. Pilot testing of the CBT can attempt to identify these issues ahead of time and incorporate appropriate segments to deal with them.

CBT has the advantage of being portable, allowing the trainee to learn at times and places that are most convenient, as well as to control the pace of learning. Trainees can stop and start training whenever they wish. Unfortunately, we were not able to find any studies that looked at the effects of such interrupted learning. It may be that frequent interruptions in the learning process lead to increased time to learn the material, as trainees must go back and review previously covered material to catch up to where they left off when the training was stopped. In Chapter 5 we cited research showing that whole rather than part learning is more effective when the task to be learned is highly organized but not complex. Spaced practice of the learning is more effective than when done all at once. It is important then for CBT to provide guidance to the trainees about when and when not to interrupt their learning.

Most CBT programs lack control over who is actually taking the training. A few years ago, a professor of an introductory MBA accounting course decided to use an online learning program to teach basic accounting principles. Each student was provided with a personal password to sign on to the system. Students could complete lessons at their convenience, as long as they completed the ten modules within a three-week period. The modules were linked so that the students were required to complete module one before they could begin module two, and so on. According to the records generated by the program, everyone completed all the modules by the end of the third week. At this point the professor began his lectures and discussions about contemporary accounting practices. It soon became clear that many of the students did not understand the basic principles covered in the CBT. Further investigation revealed that a number of students recruited others to use their password and complete their CBT modules. The professor abandoned the CBT approach the following year.

This could also happen when training is mandated (e.g., safety, sexual harassment) and the trainees are not particularly motivated to complete it, or when rewards are attached to completing the training, but not to actually using the KSA on the job. For example, employees in "pay for knowledge" systems have been known to divide the training among the members of the group so that one or two people complete the training for all the other members. When it is important to ensure that the target population is completing the training, it is necessary to develop appropriate control mechanisms for the CBT.

## Learning Objectives (KSAs)

CBT is a useful method for enhancing trainees' knowledge base. It can do so through repeated presentation of facts in a variety of formats and presentation styles. It can do an excellent job of describing when and how to apply the knowledge to situations relevant to the training objectives. CBT can document the appropriateness of the trainee's application and provide additional practice modules to improve areas of weakness.

Skill development is also possible with CBT when task simulations are highly consistent with the actual job. For example, CBT software training employees in the use of word processing, spreadsheet, and other computer-based programs can easily replicate situations they will face when back on the job. Evidence exists that even more complex skills that require the use of natural language (e.g., interpersonal or conflict resolution skills) or psychomotor development (driving a forklift) can be developed through IM and VR, though not to the level of mastery. Recall the Marriott hotel chain in Training in Action 6-2. Although Eric Jensen, director at Marriott headquarters, was initially hesitant about the ability of multimedia to train soft skills, he changed his mind. The Marriott soft skills focus on improving the interaction between two or more people. Developing these skills requires trainees to engage in the interaction and receive immediate feedback about their performance. It is extremely difficult for computers to simulate these situations in a fully realistic manner. That is why we recommend a blended approach, combining CBT with instructor-led training that allows the trainee to practise with the feedback and guidance of an expert. As Eric Jensen noted regarding the training at Marriott, "There is no 'intelligent tutoring' in terms of the system 'knowing' what kind of tutoring an individual needs. The program simply branches in certain areas, but the branching is also limited, because of the enormous cost in trying to take many different options into account."[34] Although the interaction is far from perfect, it does provide one-on-one feedback, and learning does occur.

What about training of psychomotor skills? The National Guard trains its members on how to troubleshoot and repair Bradley tanks. In many situations the tanks are not available: Having members train in an IM-simulated environment is less expensive and still effective. Of course, the Aeronett example (see Training in Action 6-1) also demonstrated that CBT can improve psychomotor and decision-making skills for pilots, flight crew, and aircraft maintenance personnel.

What do all these examples mean? CBT can be a useful tool in developing skills, including more complex skills such as those that can be simulated electronically. However, other methods are required to develop those skills to higher levels. For instance, unless a virtual reality program is highly sophisticated, it will not be able to observe the person and provide feedback on such things as standing too close when talking to someone or not maintaining good eye contact.

Attitudes and motivation can be positively or negatively influenced through CBT by showing connections among objects, events, and outcomes. The opportunity to experience or interact personally with the objects and events, however, is limited by the CBT's ability to simulate reality. As a result, the emotional or affective side of attitudes may not be strongly activated. This may partially explain why most adult learners prefer CBT when it is blended with some form of instructor-based training.[35]

## Learning Process

*Attention.* CBT is generally seen as more interesting and motivating than instructor-based training such as the lecture. Trainees cite reasons for this such as feeling less threatened by the machine and having more control over the pace of instruction. In addition, CBT can integrate audio and visual effects that draw the learner's attention to the material. For these reasons, CBT is good at capturing and retaining trainee attention.

*Retention-Symbolic Coding.* CBT can provide multiple cues that can be used in the symbolic coding process. Textual, auditory, and oral cues can be integrated to allow trainees to use those that fit best with their learning style to code the content of the training. Audiovisuals (AVs) are also effective in facilitating trainees' cognitive organization. The programming of the CBT creates a specific organization of the material, with each learning segment broken down into small steps. This makes it easier to integrate with the trainee's existing cognitive organization. Through the accumulation of these small steps and their repetition, CBT is able to shape the cognitive organization of the trainee in the desired manner. The ease with which the trainee is able to do this will depend on how closely the organization of the CBT matches the cognitive organization of the trainee. The more self-paced the CBT, the more it facilitates cognitive organization.

*Retention-Symbolic Rehearsal.* Symbolic rehearsal is a strong feature of the CBT approach, especially IM and VR. The trainees are first moved through mastery of the facts, and then provided application segments in which to apply the facts to specific situations. For example, suppose trainees were learning to take photographs. The CBT would provide a simulated situation such as the inside of a room with artificial lighting, objects that are closer or farther away, and a description of what should be photographed. The trainees would then indicate the camera settings for taking the picture. The CBT could even provide feedback that shows what would happen in a real situation. Using the photography example, the CBT program could show what kind of photograph would be produced. It allows each trainee to continue to practise while providing immediate feedback, until the trainee masters the simulation. This type of symbolic rehearsal borders on behavioural reproduction and is valuable for retaining the material.

*Behavioural Reproduction.* CBT is effective at modelling appropriate behaviour and providing simulations in which the trainee can apply knowledge. These components facilitate the development of skills but do not provide the opportunities to actually reproduce the desired behaviour and receive feedback. For example, CBT can be used to learn a foreign language. The trainee can learn the meaning of words, correct usage, and appropriate pronunciation, but the trainee will not master the language conversationally until actually interacting with an expert and receiving feedback. Likewise, the photography example is not true behavioural reproduction, because the trainee is not using a real camera or a real scene. Pilots do not complete their training until they spend time flying under the guidance of experts. Physicians are not certified to practise until they have spent time training under the guidance of experts. Blending CBT with some form of on-the-job training will allow trainees to master the more complex skills.

## Training Group Characteristics
Typically, only one trainee can use a computer at a time, so the number of computers limits the number of trainees who can be trained at the same time. However, because training is available virtually all the time, this is usually not much of a problem. If the CBT is online or on a CD, then trainees can take it anywhere they have access to a computer and, in the case of online situations, the Internet.

Because CBT can take into account many differences in trainee readiness, there are few trainee limitations. As with most methods, trainees must be able to read and understand the text and AV components presented. Trainees must also have basic computer skills. If you are considering CBT as a training method, it will be necessary to assess the trainees' reading levels, computer literacy, and attitude toward CBT. Some type of pre-training orientation or preparation program can address these issues. It may also be possible to build the considerations into the design of the CBT program.

## Blending CBT and Other Methods

Although each type of CBT can stand alone and in some cases be sufficient, you should consider integrating CBT with other methods when possible. For example, training supervisors in active listening skills through an interactive video would provide the trainee with some level of skill. Coupling the video with some instructor-led, active listening role-plays with real people, followed by trainee-instructor discussions of the experience, will lead to a much richer learning experience. Remember, all the previously discussed advantages related to guided discussion apply to any training conducted by an instructor. Combining CBT with these other methods, therefore, can only enhance the learning experience.

## Summary

CBT is delivered to trainees through e-learning systems such as LANs, CDs, DVDs, intranets, and the Internet. CBT methods integrate the content to be learned (knowledge base) into a training design such as programmed instruction (PI), intelligent tutoring system (ITS), interactive multimedia (IM) or virtual reality (VR). The content and design are transformed into electronic media through the use of authoring and design tools. A learning management system (LMS) is sometimes used to integrate training management functions and learning tools with the training program.

PI is a method of self-paced learning managed by both the trainee and the program software. Although typically delivered electronically, this training can also be delivered in paper, multimedia, or other formats. ITS utilize PI and artificial intelligence to diagnose and deliver the kind of training the trainee needs. Interactive multimedia training integrates the use of text, video, graphics, photos, animation, and sound to produce a complex training environment with which the trainee interacts. Typically, PI or ITS methodology is applied to learning chunks that are converted into a multimedia format to facilitate learning. VR puts the trainee in an artificial three-dimensional environment that simulates events and situations that might be experienced on the job. The trainee experiences a physical involvement with and a presence in the simulated environment. To experience a computerized VR, you must wear devices that provide sensory input. This method is relatively new and has not caught on as rapidly as some had predicted. This method also raises some health concerns.

CBT can provide training to more employees, in more locations, and at a lower cost than other training methods. However, development costs for CBT are typically higher than for other methods, so a careful cost/benefit analysis is necessary to determine whether a CBT method is appropriate. The more sophisticated the CBT, the higher the development costs and the longer the time it will take to develop the training. CBT maintains very good control of the learning process. In most cases this is an advantage, but it can become a disadvantage when the software does not allow needed clarification or discussion that addresses trainee concerns. Because CBT can take into account many differences in trainee readiness, there are few trainee characteristics that would limit its use. CBT can do an excellent job of activating the learning processes of attention, symbolic coding, cognitive organization, and symbolic rehearsal, making it a good method for addressing knowledge and attitude training objectives. It does a fairly good job of developing skills up to, but not including, the mastery level. It is recommended that where possible, CBT be blended with other training methods to maximize learning.

# CASE

## Conclusion of Opening Case: Evolution of Training at Mr. Lube

Senior VP Bill Tickner had decided that his paper-based training system was not an effective tool for ensuring that the geographically dispersed workforce had the competencies required by Mr. Lube Canada, Inc. After investigating many alternatives, Mr. Tickner found his solution in partnering with the Ottawa based e-learning company Acerra Learning Inc., and Q9, a provider of outsourced Internet infrastructure and managed hosting services. Mr. Lube now conducts its training over the Internet, using a learning management system (LMS) developed by Acerra. Mr. Tickner says he is sure the system is working because employees are completing oil changes and safety checks more quickly now that they are being coached with an LMS. For Mr. Lube, e-learning presents a compelling business proposition. It provides training on a just-in-time basis to employees anywhere in the world. It allows on-the-job training and self-paced learning. For Mr. Lube, an important component is that the LMS can monitor the progress

of each employee and administer and score online tests to ensure that each employee has the required competencies. Mr. Lube blends computer-based training with worksite mentors assigned to the trainees. The LMS data are complemented by online progress reports from these worksite mentors.

Mr. Lube plans to eventually integrate its LMS with other corporate information systems such as payroll and human resources. Mr. Tickner sees an advantage to having all employee information stored in one place. This would allow the mining of these data to improve systems and make better decisions. For example, he believes such a system would allow Mr. Lube to get a better understanding of how new recruits respond to the training programs.

*Sources*: This case is based on information contained in the following websites: www.globeandmail.com/servlet/story/RTGAM.20030710. welearn.0710BNStory/Technology/; www.mrlube.ca; www. newswire.ca/en/releases/archive/july2002/.

## Implications for Practice

**1.** When using CBT to train employees in areas they may not be interested in (e.g., sexual harassment, safety), it may be necessary to develop a method for tracking their progress and ensuring the person who is online receiving the training is the person who is supposed to be getting the training.

**2.** No matter what the skill to be learned, it is quite likely that interactive multimedia training could at some level provide some of the training.

**3.** No matter how sophisticated the interactive multimedia training is, consider some level of instructor-guided discussion, as it will greatly enhance the learning that takes place.

## Key Terms

Computer-based training (CBT)   *209*

Delivery system   *211*

E-learning   *211*

Expert knowledge base   *215*

Intelligent tutoring systems (ITS)   *215*

Interactive multimedia training   *216*

Intranet   *213*

Learning management system (LMS)   *212*

Local area network (LAN)   *212*

Knowledge base   *211*

Programmed instruction (PI)   *213*

Self-paced learning   *213*

Trainee model   *215*

Training scenario generator   *215*

Training session manager   *215*

User interface   *215*

Virtual reality (VR) training   *220*

## Questions for Review

1. How is CBT different from e-learning?

2. What are the basic components of CBT and its delivery?

3. How does programmed instruction allow the trainee to work at his or her own pace?

4. How does ITS differ from programmed instruction?

5. What learning processes are most influenced by interactive multimedia? Which are influenced the least?

6. What is the most expensive part of developing a CBT?

7. What are the factors associated with calculating the cost of CBT?

8. How effective is CBT in maintaining control over learning processes and training content? Provide your rationale.

9. What is the purpose of an LMS?

10. How are ITS and LMS related to each other?

11. What resources might small businesses use to gain access to CBT while keeping cost to a minimum?

## Exercises

1. Your instructor will assign you (or your group) to one of the CBT methods from the chapter. Conduct an Internet search to find a company in your area that uses the method. Contact the HRD department, and indicate that you are learning about training and would like to know how they use the method in their training programs. Schedule an interview with your contact person, meet with him or her, and find out the following information:

   a. How long has he or she been using this method?

   b. Approximately how many people get training with this method each year? What are the advantages of using this over other methods?

   c. What are the disadvantages of using this over other methods?

   d. Does he or she blend this type of training with other methods? If so, why?

   e. Does he or she have any evidence of whether trainees are responding positively or negatively to the method?

   f. How is the method delivered to the trainees (e.g., LAN, Internet)?

## Web Research

Use the Internet to identify two companies that provide some type of CBT service (e.g., develops training, learning management, training delivery, etc). For each service that is provided, identify where it fits in Figure 6-1.

## CASE ANALYSIS

Science and Technology Inc (STI) is a high-tech consulting firm. The core business is helping firms and individual scientists transfer basic scientific discoveries into practical applications. Their forty consultants provide consulting and training services in the development of strategies and implementation processes for the commercialization of new technologies. These employees are grouped into teams that operate from offices in Quebec (Montreal), Ontario (Toronto), British Columbia (Richmond), and Alberta (Edmonton). These teams are frequently on the road and individual employees often work from home.

In addition to its work with private companies and individual scientists, SCI recently was awarded a grant by the government to provide training to 150 small-business owners awarded governmental grants to pursue the development of businesses based on new technology. Each of these business owners has a different set of circumstances that must be addressed in making the business a success. Also, there are widely differing types of technology that need to be commercialized. The basic training has already been developed by STI, but the consulting will require the expertise of different STI consultants, based on the small business owners' needs and situations.

STI has several challenges to overcome in order to fulfill the government grant and successfully move its core business forward. Your task is to

- Provide basic technology commercialization training to the 150 small-business owners and ensure that they have learned the material.

- Provide customized consulting to each of the 150 small-business owners.

- Develop a method for small-business owners to be able to get the appropriate consultation and be able to document that the consultation was provided.

- Develop a system that would capture the learning provided by each of the STI consultants and make that available to all STI consultants. This would allow SCI to develop their consultants' knowledge base.

- Ensure whatever is developed is as cost-effective as possible because government grants leave little room for profit.

### Case Question

Develop a business solution for STI that addresses all of the challenges they face. Indicate any assumptions you are making that are not directly addressed by the case.

# DEVELOPMENT AND IMPLEMENTATION OF TRAINING

*Good teaching is one-fourth preparation and three-fourths theater.*

Gail Godwin, American novelist, short story writer

## Development Phase

| Input | Process | Output |
|-------|---------|--------|

**Program Development Plan**

- Instructional Material
- Instructional Equipment
- Trainee and Trainer Manuals
- Facilities
- Trainer

Determine Factors That Facilitate Learning and Transfer → Instructional Strategy → 

Alternative Instructional Methods →

## CHAPTER OBJECTIVES

After reading this chapter, you should be able to:

- Describe how to develop and implement the following methods of training in a manner that facilitates adult learning and meets training objectives:

  - Lecture/discussion,

  - Computer-based,

  - Games and simulations,

  - Role-plays and behavioural modelling, and

  - On-the-job training.

- Choose the most effective seating arrangement based on the nature of the training.

- Examine a room and determine whether it meets training requirements.

- Describe the mechanisms that should be put in place to assist in the transfer of training.

- Explain how you would deal with each of the four types of difficult trainee.

## CASE

### Jack Goes to Training

Jack, a 43-year-old machinist, had worked for Scanton Industries for 23 years. It seemed that the need to learn something new was constant, and Jack was getting nervous about his job. The nervousness grew last week when he saw a new batch of equipment arrive. It looked something like the machinery he uses now, but it was hooked up to computers. Bill, his foreman, said, "It looks like you'll be going back to school for a couple of days, Jack. You're going to have to learn how to program your work into the computer." Jack smiled but felt sick to his stomach. He was always good with his hands, but he had never done well in school.

All Jack thought about that weekend was the training he would be going to. He fell asleep Sunday night thinking about it. The phone awakened him at 7:00 the next morning. It was Bill telling him that training had been switched from the local training centre downtown to the local school because of a sudden strike at the training centre. The school was the only place available on short notice.

As Jack walked up the steps of the local school, he felt sick to his stomach again. He entered the hall and then the classroom. Everything was similar to what he remembered about school, except now a computer was on each desk. Even the smell was the same, and it brought back memories. Some were good (the guys getting together between classes), but most were bad (being yelled at, taking tests, and doing poorly). As he sat in the wooden chair in the back where he used to sit, he looked out the window and began to daydream, just as in high school.

The other 20 trainees were sitting quietly at their desks. All of them seemed as nervous as Jack. Suddenly someone burst through the door. "Hi, my name is Jason Reston. I'm your instructor for this course. You're here to learn some basic computer skills and how to program the machines that you will be using at work. I realize that you come from different companies and will operate different machines, but the process for all of them is similar. First, I am going to show you how to get signed on and into the program you will be running. . . ." Jack was back from his daydream. Well, here we go, he thought.

At lunch Jack and his classmate Murray went to a local deli. "Are you keeping up?" Jack asked.

"Are you kidding? Are we going to be tested on this stuff?" asked Murray.

"I have no idea. If we are, I'm dead," said Jack.

The afternoon went slowly. The trainer simply gave an instruction and the trainees entered the information into the computer. Then he gave another and they entered that as well. "How are we supposed to remember all this?" Murray whispered. The second day was worse. On a few occasions Jack was jolted out of his daydream while staring out the window. "Jack," yelled Jason, "Are you with us?" It was 3:00 P.M .on the second afternoon when Jason announced that they would be tested to see what they had learned. Jack looked at the test questions. Was he that stupid? He did not even understand many of the questions. Would he lose his job if he failed this test? He could almost hear his boss yelling at him, "You are fired, get out, get out!"

This case is an example of how not to conduct training. The training room and the training itself exacerbated the anxiety that Jack felt about going to training. As we go through the chapter, think about what you would do to make the training more conducive to adult learning.

# DEVELOPMENT OF TRAINING

An examination of the model for the development phase of training shows two inputs: alternative methods of instruction and factors that facilitate learning and transfer. The former was presented in Chapters 5 and 6, and the latter was discussed in Chapter 4.

In Chapters 5 and 6, we discussed a variety of training methods. Our discussion included the strengths and weaknesses of each method. Many of them, such as role-play, behaviour modelling, and case study, are not meant to be stand-alone methods, but rather facilitate learning by providing alternative mechanisms for providing practice. A summary of these methods and their effectiveness in developing KSAs is presented in Table 7-1.

Canadian Society for Training and Development
*www.cstd.ca*

## TABLE 7-1 Training Method Effectiveness at Meeting KSA Objectives

| | OBJECTIVES OF TRAINING | | | |
| | Skills | | Training Methods | |
| | Knowledge | Technical | Interpersonal | Attitudes |
|---|---|---|---|---|
| **Lecture** | | | | |
| Straight[a] | 2 | 1 | 1 | 3 |
| Discussion | 3 | 1 | 1 | 4 |
| **Demonstration** | 2.5 | 4 | 4 | 3 |
| **Computer-Based** | | | | |
| Programmed Instruction | 3 | 2 | 1 | 2 |
| Intelligent Tutoring | 5 | 3 | 2 | 3 |
| Interactive Multimedia | 5 | 4 | 4 | 4 |
| Virtual Reality | 2 | 5 | 4 | 4 |
| **Simulations/Games** | | | | |
| Equipment | 2 | 5 | 1 | 2 |
| Case Studies | 3 | 2 | 2 | 3 |
| Business Games | 3.5 | 2 | 2[b] | 2 |
| In-Basket | 3 | 1 | 2[c] | 2 |
| Role-Play | 2 | 2 | 4 | 5[d] |
| Behaviour Modelling | 3 | 4 | 5 | 3 |
| **OJT** | | | | |
| JIT | 4 | 4 | 2 | 5 |
| Apprentice | 5 | 5 | 2 | 5 |
| Coaching | 4 | 4 | 4 | 5 |

Scale:  1 = Not effective
2 = Mildly effective
3 = Moderately effective
4 = Effective
5 = Very effective

[a] This rating is for lectures delivered orally; printed lectures would be one point higher in each knowledge category.
[b] If the business game is designed for interpersonal skills, this rating would be a 4.
[c] If multiple in-baskets were used, this rating would be 3.
[d] This rating applies specifically to role reversal.

Centre for Organization and
Human Resource
Effectiveness
*http://socrates.berkeley.edu/~iir/
cohre/cohre.html*

Although the method's effectiveness in meeting the learning objective should be the major criterion for selection, other considerations are costs, time needed to develop the material, and time allotted for the training session. For example, if cost prevents you from using the best method, then choose a different method that meets the budget but still provides the necessary KSAs. The workforce's literacy is another issue to consider. Methods such as programmed instruction and computer-based instruction rely on trainees' ability to read and understand. If they are not skilled in these areas, alternative approaches are necessary, particularly if reading is not an important skill for the job.

The knowledge gained from Chapter 4 provides an awareness of the factors that facilitate learning and transfer, one of the inputs into development of the instructional strategy.

## INSTRUCTIONAL STRATEGY

The information presented earlier in this text comes together in the instructional strategy used for a training program. The strategy is compiled in a written document, often called a **program development plan**. This plan details the methods, materials, equipment, facilities, and trainers for the training program. A variety of systems guide the documentation of the plan (e.g., program management timing charts, technical reports). Our purpose is to indicate what should be included in the documentation, rather than the form that it should take. Important issues to address in the development of the instructional strategy are discussed next.

**Program Development Plan** a detailed plan that outlines the methods, material, equipment, facilities, and trainers for a training program.

**Learning Point** an important piece of information that a trainee must acquire in order to accomplish the learning objective.

### Content: Learning Points  A **learning point** is an important piece of information that a trainee must acquire in order to accomplish the learning objective. Each objective provides specific information as to what needs to be learned. Consider this learning objective: "Solder six metres of half-inch copper pipe, using elbows and unions, in 20 minutes or less with no leaks." In order to ensure that there are no leaks, the trainee must pay specific attention to the cleaning of the copper pipe, the proper heating of the pipe, and the correct application of the solder. These factors would be learning points, which the trainer would need to be sure the trainee has mastered.

For each objective, a number of things are identified: facilities and configuration, learning points, methodology for training, and equipment and material required. Table 7-2 can serve as a guide for developing instructional strategy. It will help you systematically examine what is required and what sequence (in the case of more than one objective) makes the most sense. As each learning objective is considered (along with its learning points), the most effective configuration of methods, material and equipment, facilities, and trainers is determined. In Table 7-2, the lecture method provides the cognitive information; the simulation provides the actual practice. If the training is to teach supervisors how to deal effectively with conflict, the methodology might be lecture or discussion to provide information, depending on the sophistication of the group, and role-play or behaviour modelling to provide practice. Once the methods to be used and the sequencing of the training are established, it is necessary to determine time frames for each of these activities. In most cases time is limited, and the inexperienced training developer tends to overload the material to be covered. Always allow for a reasonable amount of time for discussion and interaction, which is where much of the learning occurs.

Based on the type of training, the next step is to decide on the training facility and the seating configuration. Clearly documenting this information reduces the likelihood of mistakes. A problem may develop if the training requires a great deal of face-to-face interaction among the trainees but the training facilities are too small to accommodate those interactions.

Mechanisms used to ensure transfer must be documented so it is clear what will occur once training is completed. It is generally expected that transfer of training will

## TABLE 7-2 Components of Instructional Strategy

**PROGRAM DEVELOPMENT PLAN**

*Name of Program: Pipe Fitting I*

Target Population: Apprentices who successfully passed the gas fitters exam

Overall Training Objective: Trainees will be able to examine a work project and with appropriate tools measure, cut, thread, and install the piping according to standards outlined in the gas code.

| Learning Objective | Learning Points | Method | Material and AV |
|---|---|---|---|
| 1. Using a tape measure, determine the length of and number of pipes necessary to connect the furnace to the gas meter in a manner that meets the gas code | 1. The extra length necessary because of threading<br><br>2. That length is reduced by different fittings, e.g., street elbow, union elbow, etc.<br><br>3. Method for constructing appropriate drop for furnace | Lecture and simulation | Training manual<br>Overhead projector<br>Assortment of 1-inch and 3/4-inch fittings, elbows, street elbows, and unions<br>Mock meter and furnace setup<br>Tape measure, note pads |
| 2. Using a threading machine, cut and thread length of pipe required | 1. Length of thread required<br><br>2. Importance of cutting and reaming, measuring, and use of threading machine oil | Lecture and simulation | Trainee manual<br>VCR and TV<br>Threading tape<br>Threading machine<br>Steel pipe<br>Oil<br>Tape measure |

Facility and configuration:
Trainer:
Measures to assist transfer:
Method of evaluation:

occur, but often little is done to ensure that it does. When no one person is responsible, the feeling of responsibility is diffused and transfer is soon forgotten.

Similarly, it is important to indicate the methods used in evaluating the training, along with time frames. Once again, clearly outlining this information helps to ensure that evaluation happens.

After the program development plan is carefully constructed and agreed on, the next step is to obtain or develop the instructional material, instructional media, and equipment. This is also the time to choose a trainer.

The output from the development phase is the program development plan. Components of the plan include material, equipment, trainee and trainer manuals, facilities, and the trainer(s).

A program development plan is critical to the success of the training. By methodically completing the program development plan and using it as a guide, it should be possible to identify and develop everything required for training. The development phase of our training model depicts this process.

## MATERIALS AND EQUIPMENT

Document all the necessary material such as text, overheads, and the like, as well as the time frames for their completion. If material is being developed, allow sufficient time to prepare it properly. Order equipment and anything else provided by others at off-site locations well in advance. Important charts, posters, and easel sheets can be professionally printed if they are affordable and time is available.

# TRAINEE'S MANUAL

The trainee's manual is an important learning tool for training. To keep the trainees' interest and their complete involvement in discussions, provide notes on all the information that will be presented. The trainees will then be able to pay more attention to what is being said and done, rather than being concerned about taking notes. The manual often includes all lecture materials, learning points, and supplemental readings. It may also include exercises and some blank sheets for jotting down notes and lists in small group meetings.

A good choice for holding the manual's material is a three-ring binder because the trainee can add information as the training continues. It is sometimes better to hold back certain information—e.g., exercises—from the trainees until it is time to use it. Trainees should not be distracted from the current topic by trying to figure out various problems ahead of time.

# INSTRUCTOR'S MANUAL

The instructor's manual provides all the information in the trainees' manual, as well as information on what the trainer needs to do and how to do it. It is a visual aid for the trainer. One format is to have the lecture notes on the right-hand side of the page, and the instructions for the trainer on the left-hand side. These instructions range from indicating when to generate lists on newsprint, to what some of the expected information on the list might be and how the trainer may want to respond. A well-prepared instructor's manual will provide everything a trainer needs to know to conduct the training.

# FACILITIES

If training is taking place in the company's facility, be sure the room is available by reserving it. If training will be off-site, be selective as to the design of the room. Be sure that the site can accommodate breakout rooms if they are needed and that the seating arrangements are appropriate. If movable dividers separate the room from others, inquire about the events scheduled next door. Attending a training session when a motivational speaker or sales rally is next door can be distracting. If nothing is scheduled, get assurance that the booking office will be sensitive to your concerns if they book the rooms next door. Check the soundproofing of the panels that separate the rooms. Avoid booking rooms that lead directly to the kitchen unless it is certain that the walls are soundproofed.

**The Training Room** Whether you are designing a training facility or going off-site to train, many factors contribute to making the training room a learner-friendly environment. The following describes the type of training room that is ideal for most types of training.

A windowless room is best. Windows can distract the trainees, as was evident in the case at the start of the chapter. Jack was easily distracted from the training for many reasons, but the window gave him a way to avoid the training. If the room does contain windows, be sure that they are fitted with shades or curtains you can close. Light coming through the windows can create glare and also be distracting. The walls should be blank—not decorated with pictures or brightly painted—and a nice neutral colour, such as beige. Lighting should be adjustable so it can be dimmed for over-heads or video presentations and can be made brighter for the lecture, discussions, and exercises. The room should be close to square in shape. Rectangular rooms limit the type of seating arrangements possible. A rule of thumb is to avoid a training room where its length exceeds its width by more than 50 percent.[1] The room should be carpeted and have a sound-absorbing ceiling. As noted earlier, a soundproof facility, whether on premises or off-site, is very important.

The room should be equipped with its own temperature control and quiet heating/cooling fans. This point may sound trivial—after all, who would build a training room with noisy fans? The problem is that contractors are good at building buildings but do not specialize in any particular type. When the University of Windsor Business School was being built, a team of faculty members provided input into the design of the classrooms. This input helped tremendously in the development of user-friendly classrooms, but the team did not think about fan noise. The result: one of the few complaints about the building is fan noise. When the fans are on, it becomes difficult to hear the questions being asked.

Under the heading "nice to have," consider the following for a multipurpose training room:

- Have tracks built onto the walls with a slot into which newsprint can be pushed, allowing for the hanging of charts and posters anywhere in the room.

- Have whiteboards built into the walls at strategic locations to allow easy access to large writing surfaces.

- Have built-in consoles that control lighting, audiovisuals, and computers, to provide easy access to the operation of these training aids.

- Have a working remote control so trainers can operate the lights and AVs from anywhere in the room.

- Have a smart board for developing models or listing points generated in discussions and providing copies to trainees easily.

If AVs are built into the facility, make sure they are situated so that all trainees are able to view and hear them. Also make sure AVs are not built into places where the equipment itself blocks sight lines.

*Furniture.* Choose tables and chairs rather than classroom desk-chairs. Tables should be movable so they can be set up in any configuration. An ideal table size is 1.5 metres long and 0.75 metres wide, as this allows two people to sit comfortably on one side. Many configurations are possible by arranging the tables. Putting two of these tables together makes a 1.5-metre square where eight people can hold a group discussion.

Obtain padded swivel chairs that are cloth covered (not vinyl) and have castors and armrests. Trainees will be required to sit for extended periods of time, and comfort is important. In addition to providing overall comfort, the swivel and castors allow for ease of movement when trainees must form small groups or turn to work with another trainee. Being able to lean back and rest your arms creates a relaxing environment, conducive to learning.

*Furniture Set-Up.* Seating arrangements depend on the type of training being conducted. The typical configurations are classroom, U-shape, conference, and circle. The arrangement determines the degree of formality, focus of attention, and level of two-way communication.[2] To appreciate this point, consider the two extremes, circle and classroom (A and B in Figure 7-1). The classroom style (B) places the focus on the trainer and limits two-way communication between trainees because the trainees are all facing one direction. If no tables are used, more trainees can be accommodated. This arrangement is called theatre style. When a trainee sees such a set-up, her role is clearly defined in her mind: she is there to listen. In the circle set-up (A), the focus is evenly distributed; no single person is being looked at. A trainee sees this style and his role is also defined: he will be a part of the discussion. Furthermore, this lack of focus makes it easier for trainees to debate and discuss issues among themselves.

To provide employees with information on the company's position regarding sexual harassment, for example, the classroom configuration is appropriate. Here the goal is to provide information and the focus should be on the trainer. Most two-way communication involves question-and-answer exchanges between the trainer and trainee. Suppose the goal is to train managers to deal with sexual harassment. A circle is chosen because the goal is to generate discussion about managers' experiences and ways of handling them. In the circle, trainees face one another and the trainer is just one of the members of the circle; focus on all members of the group is equal. Another obvious difference between these two configurations is that a larger number of trainees can be accommodated in the classroom setup.

Various modifications of these two extremes can also be used. The semicircle (Figure 7-1C) encourages trainee discussion, allowing trainees to be face-to-face

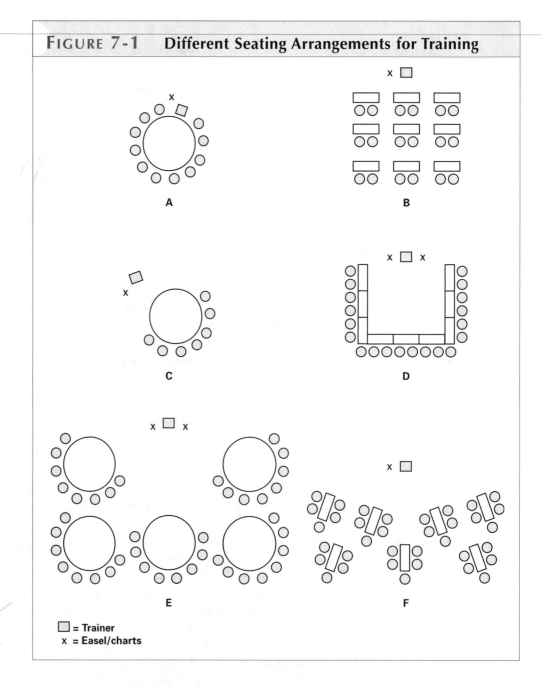

**FIGURE 7-1     Different Seating Arrangements for Training**

☐ = Trainer
x = Easel/charts

when the trainer is not talking. In this situation, the trainer stands when presenting information and sits with the trainees when encouraging discussion.

Perhaps the configuration used most often is the U-shape (Figure 7-1D). It is similar to the semicircle, but allows for a larger group of trainees. The U-shape places the main focus on the instructor allows a fair amount of face-to-face discussion among the group members and can accommodate a reasonably large group (30 to 35 trainees). However, the U itself can become too large. The trainer must be careful not to move too deeply into the U and cut off those at the end. Also, if flip charts are used, two sets may be needed to make reading them easy for all participants, particularly if the number exceeds thirty. Placing the charts slightly inside the open end of the U (see Figure 7-1D) ensures they are not blocked and all participants can easily see the material.

Another alternative is to have trainees sit at round tables in a semicircle (Figure 7-1E). This arrangement facilitates easy switching from lecturette to small group exercises or discussions. Figure 7-1F is similar but with rectangular tables. The other advantage of these configurations is that they set up small groups where members can interact, making the training less threatening at the beginning.

### Off-Site Training Facilities

Although a certain pride can come from having your own training facilities, they can be expensive. Off-site training offers several advantages.

First, being off-site provides more assurance that trainees will not be interrupted. It is simply too easy to contact the trainee if he is on the same floor or even in the next building.

Another advantage is the change of pace off-site training offers. Going to a hotel or conference centre is not the same as going to work. Many trainees will associate staying in a hotel with a vacation (unless they are travelling salespersons). This change of pace is even more important if a great deal of stress is associated with the job. Recall the discussion of classical conditioning. Regular pairing of work with stress will result in a feeling of stress upon arrival at the workplace. Off-site training in this situation might be more suited to the learning process. However, choose the off-site facility with care. Remember Jack and his training at the old school?

Going off-site also allows the trainer to choose a facility compatible with the needs of the particular training event. If breakout rooms, a classroom, U-shaped set-up, or all three are required, you can choose the location that best fits the requirements.

## THE TRAINER

How is the trainer chosen? One of the most commonly cited reasons for training not being effective is its lack of relevance to the trainee's situation. Comments such as "The training is great but it will not work in our plant," "You do not understand the problems we have," "My boss is the one who should be here, because the boss makes the decisions," indicate the concern trainees perceive as to the transferability of the training to their job.

One way to handle these concerns is to use middle managers as trainers.[3] Their involvement alleviates most of the preceding concerns, but some other problems may arise. If the middle manager also supervises some of the trainees, his presence could dampen these trainees' enthusiasm for training.

Larger organizations can overcome this issue by not involving managers in training people who report directly to them. Smaller organizations need to assure such trainees that they will be treated the same as others. As long as trainees do not perceive any different treatment, the word would get out that this system was okay.

Another concern is the potential that the middle manager may spend too much time dealing with organizational issues rather than on the training topics. Solid training objectives would help prevent this conflict.

Using a seasoned trainer (e.g., outside or internal consultant) and a manager to team-teach the training program is another way to develop a successful training program. The two could work from each other's strengths. An advantage of this approach is that the manager receives good on-the-job training on how to be an effective trainer. The disadvantage, cost, is a reason this alternative is not often chosen.

**Trainer KSAs** The KSAs of an effective trainer are presented in Table 7-3. Note that many of the requirements are similar to those suggested for an effective lecturer. This is important because almost all training includes a lecture component.

Just how much knowledge of the subject matter does the trainer need? The level of knowledge required depends on the complexity of the subject matter. Highly technical subject matter requires a high level of such knowledge. Is the high level of knowledge more important than being a skilled trainer? Perhaps that question is not the correct focus, because both subject matter knowledge and trainer skills are important. We know that trainer skills are critical to effective training, so the better question is, "Which is more advisable, to train the trainer in the technical skills or to train the expert in training skills?" The answer, especially if the subject matter is highly technical or complex, is the latter. In the short term, it may be necessary to pair a technical expert with a training specialist until the technical expert acquires sufficient training skill.

The trainer should possess a reasonable knowledge of the organization and trainees. Such knowledge increases the credibility of the trainer and helps her answer questions that come up regarding integrating the training back into the workplace.

Although most of the knowledge and many of the skills required of a trainer are trainable, it would be best to be able to begin with individuals who already possess the attitudes identified in Table 7-3 because attitudes are more difficult to change.

---

**TABLE 7-3  Knowledge, Skills, and Attitudes Required of an Effective Trainer**

**Knowledge**

Subject matter

Organization   *relate it to the org.*

Adult learning process  *+learning style, adjust training to meet standard needs*

Instructional methods

**Skills**

Interpersonal communication skills

Verbal skills (ability to explain clearly)

*most difficult*

- Active listening
- Questioning
- Providing feedback

Platform skills (ability to speak with inflection, gesture appropriately, and maintain eye contact)

Organization skills (ability to present information in logical order and stay on point)

**Attitudes**

Commitment to the organization

Commitment to helping others

High level of self-efficacy

**Experience** How important is it to have experience related to the training topic? Such a credential (depth of experience) would provide a high level of credibility for the trainer. Consider, for example, one successful trainer's early run-in with trainees because of a seeming lack of experience. He was part of a corporate training staff. The course he was asked to teach was called "Non-financial Motivation Techniques." The trainees were first-line supervisors with an average of six years' experience in their positions and more than ten years with the company. Ten minutes into the first training component (the lecture), one of the older trainees raised his hand and said, "Sonny, have you ever supervised a group of unskilled labourers?" The answer, of course, was no, but he qualified it with the fact that he had supervised white-collar employees. Several knowing smirks around the room made it clear that the trainer's credibility had been destroyed. Throughout the rest of the program, trainees were inattentive, lethargic, and occasionally rude. This trainer learned early on that trainer credibility is a key factor in the effectiveness of classroom training.

How could the trainer handle such a situation more effectively? One approach would be to set the context of the training at the beginning. He might say something like the following: "I will be presenting a number of non-financial techniques that you might be able to use to motivate your employees. These techniques worked for other supervisors in a variety of situations. First, I will explain the technique, and then we will discuss how it might work for you or how it might be adapted to work for you. You know your work units better than anyone else, so I'm counting on everyone to help identify ways that these techniques can be applied."

A trainer does not need to have the same work experience as the trainees to be effective. However, a trainer needs to be seen as having something worthwhile to offer. Here the trainer is offering some new ideas and expertise in facilitating the discussion of these ideas, but—and this point is important—the trainer does not dismiss or diminish the expertise of the audience. In effect the trainer says, "Let's merge our separate areas of expertise to arrive at something we both want—more motivated employees."

Acknowledging the differences in experience at the beginning of training is also important. It allows the trainees to see that the trainer is aware of the differences and is taking them into account. For example, in the previous situation the trainer might say, "My experience has been supervising white-collar employees. How do you think the motivations of these employees differ from those you supervise?" After some differences are noted, the trainer might then ask, "At one time, most of you were unskilled workers. What were the things that motivated you when you were an unskilled worker?" This question would allow the supervisors to see that while individuals may differ in the things that motivate them, general categories of motivators apply for all individuals. The questioning process allows the trainees to test their assumptions and learn through self-discovery.

**OJT Trainers** On-the-job trainers are different from the traditional trainer. OJT trainers are usually classified as a jobholder or supervisor for the job for which they are providing training. As a result, there are some unique issues to consider. For OJT programs to be effective, the trainers need to[4]

- know the job to be trained,
- be knowledgeable in the interpersonal skills necessary to interact effectively with those they train,
- be skilled as trainers, and
- be motivated to be trainers.

OJT in general uses co-workers and supervisors as trainers. None of these people started out to be a trainer and likely none has formal training in how to be an effective trainer. The OJT trainer does need to know the job to be trained, but the best trainer is not necessarily the person who can best do the job. The OJT trainer should have a solid understanding of how the job is performed, as well as an ability to interact effectively with others. But given that they did not sign on as trainers, it should not be expected that they would understand specifics related to teaching others how to do the job. To be effective, therefore, such training is necessary and should include[5]

- The company's formal OJT process (e.g., JIT), as well as the policies and support provided by the organization,
- Interpersonal skills and feedback techniques, and
- Principles of adult learning.

Motivating the OJT trainer is also a key factor in making the OJT method effective. Trainers need to observe the trainee closely to ensure adequate skill development and to prevent the trainee from causing damage to equipment and property or injury to self or others. For this to happen, OJT trainers must be rewarded for spending their time training as well as for doing their job. This can be done in a number of ways, but there are several things to keep in mind. Someone who is training another employee as well as performing his own job should not be expected to perform at the same level of productivity as someone who is not engaged in training others. Rewards must be provided for giving effective training. Think back to the proper process of OJT. It requires the trainer to go through the steps of particular tasks methodically and then observe as the trainee does the same. This process requires time, which will take away from the productivity that would be possible if the trainer were doing nothing but his own job.

One way to motivate the OJT trainer would be to institute a different (higher) classification for someone who was capable of training other employees. This designation would provide prestige (and perhaps more money) for the position. At the same time, the measure of performance for the trainer could be how well the trainee performs at the end of the formal OJT. Here the motivation would be to turn out good trainees. If this is not done, and trainers are expected to perform their regular job at a similar level as non-trainers, then the result might well be similar to what happened in the following example. A food service and vending company used experienced vending machine service route drivers to train new route drivers. The company attributed a history of high turnover among trainee drivers to the nature of the job, the low starting wage, and the hours required. The arrival of a new human resources manager led to a re-examination of this problem. Discussions with current trainees and trainees who had voluntarily terminated their employment in the recent past revealed that many of the trainers would do all the easy work (restocking the machines) and make the trainees do the "dirty" work (performing maintenance on the machines). Others would not let the trainees do any of the work because it "slowed them down." As the drivers were paid on the basis of the number of machines they serviced, rather than on an hourly rate, they were essentially doing the training for free.

## THE ALTERNATIVE TO DEVELOPMENT

For a number of reasons, an organization may choose not to develop its own training. A small business may not have the resources; a large company may not have many individuals to train or may simply have too many other projects in the works.

In such situations, alternatives are available. It may be possible to hire a consultant and use one of their pre-packaged programs or look to outside training seminars. The option to hire a consultant to do all the work is an expensive alternative but would result in a program tailored to the company's needs, much as if the organization did it all itself.

**The Consultant** If the training required is not specific to the organization but more generic (e.g., conflict management, interviewing skills, or computer skills), find a consultant with a training package that can be adapted to fit the company's needs. Using the consultant's pre-packaged program without any alterations would reduce the overall cost.

The advantage to pre-packaged programs is that they are ready to go. The disadvantage is that they are not specific to a company. This trade-off may be more acceptable for a session on conflict resolution than for a session on team development. In fact, many pre-packaged programs can be used to supplement a company's own program. They can be less costly than hiring a consultant, but some are still expensive. Some consulting firms offer pre-packaged programs and also provide training for the trainers. This option adds to the cost, but the training is usually quite good. If a great deal of training will be taking place in the organization, this option may be worth the extra expense if it is amortized over a number of sessions.

In deciding whether to use a consultant, consider questions such as the following:

- How many employees are to be trained, and will they need constant retraining?
- Can advantages be realized from involving a neutral third party (e.g., union–management cooperative ventures)?
- Is there a rush to get the training done?
- Is there in-house expertise?

If the decision is to use a consultant, consider the following:

- Ask for references, ask who they have trained, and be sure to follow up on this information (consultants vary in their expertise).
- Determine how much the consultant knows about the industry.
- Review some of the training objectives in his or her training packages.
- Find out how the consultant evaluates success in training.
- Make sure you know who will be doing the work. Often you meet the salesperson, not the trainer.

**Outside Seminars** The outside seminar is training offered from time to time at local hotels, conference centres, and universities. These seminars are the least expensive and best alternative if only a few employees need training. For a sufficient number of attendees, these seminars may be brought to your site. On-site seminars can be tailored to the organization for a moderate extra cost. They can also include an evaluation component.

When choosing a seminar, consider the following questions:

- What are the training objectives? Skills require practice, and seminars often are too large to include practice sessions.
- Is any form of evaluation used? (Seldom is evaluation done.)
- How focused is the content based on the training objectives?
- Can someone be sent to preview the seminar and report back on its potential value?

If the decision is to purchase training, assess how it fits into the overall training strategy. Many companies have implemented team training in the past because it was "the thing to do." Spending money on team training simply because others were doing it wasted money. Training should be seen as a mechanism to support the organization's mission and goals. Other mechanisms must also be in place to support the training if it is to transfer effectively.

## ALTERNATIVES FOR THE SMALL BUSINESS

A recent study of small businesses (under 100 employees) in Canada indicated most (83%) had some form of formal training.[6] This is important because a study in Britain indicates that training provides positive benefits for small business. Organizations with fewer than 100 employees reported a 25 percent increase in training with about 60 percent reporting financial benefits from the training.[7] The cost of this training is unknown, but knowing how important costs are for the small business, it is useful to consider options that could reduce these training costs. To achieve the benefits of formalized training, the small business may find it advantageous to hire a consultant or purchase pre-packaged training. If so, it is important that they follow the same suggestions mentioned previously when choosing a consultant or packaged training.

Small businesses should also examine the feasibility of developing a consortium of small businesses that could all use the same training. LearnShare (see Training in Action 6-4) discovered that 74 percent of their training is not specific to a particular organization's process or products.[8] The same is likely true for small companies. Why not take advantage of this commonality and work together to identify training needs and share in the cost of developing or purchasing relevant training? This is what LearnShare does. LearnShare recently developed an online training program called the Leader Survival Kit.[9] The total cost of the program was $285 000, but by sharing the cost among companies it was only about $22 000 each. If this shared development expense can be done for e-learning, it can also be done for any type of training development, thus becoming affordable for smaller businesses. Also, given the increasing number of small businesses, the expense could be shared among more, making the cost of development even less.

E-learning is now an option for the small business. Numerous businesses are providing a template for developing online learning. This way, the small business gets affordable training that can be tailored to its needs. There are a number of e-learning opportunities now available. Quelsys is a company that allows trainers from other companies to use their authoring tools to build training programs. No cost is charged until employees begin to take the course, and then the cost is on a per-employee basis.[10] Some companies are even more adventuresome and develop an online learning university (see Training in Action 7-1).

Small businesses often belong to industry-specific associations that can provide a venue for discussing this idea to determine the level of interest. The associations themselves could develop a consortium for their constituents. If a consortium is too complex a project to consider, why not simply purchase a few pre-packaged training programs? If a small business located three other companies with similar training interests, it would save 75 percent of the cost.

Western Learning Systems of California is a variation on the consortium idea. It develops courses for larger companies but retains the copyright. It then markets these courses to small companies at a more affordable rate. They offer a one-year membership for $5000 that entitles a company to 75 classes at the rate of $195 per class.[11]

Another inexpensive way to train in some areas is to require trainees to read a particular book, and then participate in a discussion group on the topic. The person most

## Training in Action 7-1

### *What a Small Company Can Do*

Walker and Associates, a telecommunications equipment distributor, has just under 300 employees. A new president came on board who strongly believed in the training and development of employees. He formed a partnership with GeoLearning Inc., a Web-based learning provider, to create the Walker Institute of Training and Development, an online corporate university.

To facilitate using the Internet for training, Walker's president offered employees an interest-free loan to purchase a home computer. At the same time, he purchased a number of laptops for employees to check out for home or travel. Some employees were still a bit reluctant to use the Internet for fear of misusing it.

To help encourage e-learning, Frank Russell, president of GeoLearning, provided some much needed advice to

Walker's president. "Start small, with a pilot program of a few employees, and get feedback from the naysayers," was his advice. This approach helped to launch the program. To further encourage its use, supervisors made its use one of the goals for employees in their performance review. They also integrated e-learning and its use into their orientation.

Note that these practices, starting with a pilot program integrating the use of the Web training into an employee's first experience in the organization (orientation), and building it into performance appraisal, are all practices for any effective training, Web-based or not.

*Source:* Adapted from Tyler, K. (2001). E-Learning: Not just for e-normous companies anymore. *HR Magazine* 46: 82–88.

knowledgeable about the subject leads the group. A company preparing for ISO certification asked a group of employees to read a book written by one of the quality gurus, Philip Crosby. After they read each chapter, they met to discuss it. The manager prepared questions in advance to keep the discussion going.[12] Earlier we indicated how important trainee involvement is for adult learning. These discussion groups are the epitome

## Training in Action 7-2

### *Training in a Small Business: Different Approaches*

Brenda Schissler, president of Staffmasters, a small temporary service provider in Louisville, has 10 permanent employees. Each of them specializes in a topic (e.g., safety) and attends outside seminars to gain relevant knowledge. Upon return, each is responsible for teaching the others about the particular issue.

Kevin O'Brian is responsible for ISO standards at Rivait Machine Tools Inc., a 14-person operation in Windsor, Ontario. One basic type of work is done at Rivait Machine, so instead of providing training in the procedures required, [the company] developed a "job aid," which is a checklist of tasks. The employee goes through the list, checking off each task as completed, then moving to the next task. This means training, except at the basic level, is not necessary.

You do not have to be big to win prestigious awards, but you do need training. Custom Research Inc. is a market research company based in Minneapolis. Each of its 105 employees received a minimum of 130 hours of training in

1995. In 1996, it became the first professional service company and the smallest company ever to win the Malcolm Baldrige National Quality Award.

Steve Braccini, president of Profastener, a small business in California with about 150 employees, suggests that it is a good idea to send two rather than only one employee to a specific type of training. A single trainee might return with a skewed view of what took place. Sending two, who discuss the training with each other, ensures a common understanding. Braccini believes that this system results in a better overall product. Braccini makes one other important point: He always sends these employees to attend a "train the trainer" course before going on any training.

*Sources:* Excerpted from O'Brien, K. (1997). Personal communication. Rivait Machine and Tool, Oldcastle, Ontario, July 24; Zemke, R. (1997). The little company that could. *Training*, January, pp. 59–64; Filipczak, B. (1996). Training on the cheap. *Training*, May, pp. 28–34.

of involvement. The informal training in this company became more formal after this initial orientation.

Although this method does not follow all the criteria that we suggest for an effective training program, it might more than compensate for this by motivating participants. No single best way to train has been established, especially when the variations in cost benefit for different training alternatives are considered. Training in Action 7-2 (see previous page) provides examples of various methods being used by small businesses.

# IMPLEMENTATION

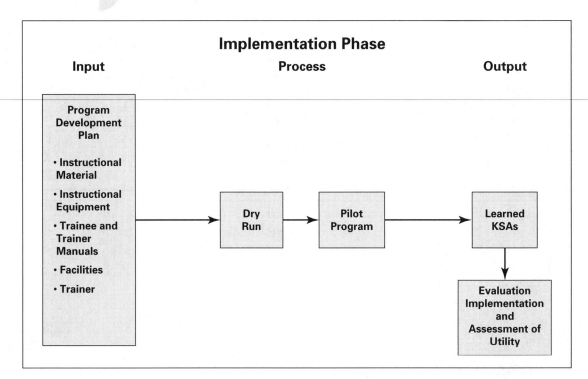

At this point you are ready to implement your instructional strategy. This phase of the training model is depicted above. Note the outputs from the development phase are brought together and become the inputs for the implementation stage. Next, the "process" phase contains two steps that are important to take before your training is ready for general use.[13] They are first, a dry run, and then a pilot program. The former is a "first test" of new material; here, the training package may not be presented in its entirety. The latter is the first full-blown presentation of the training using finished materials.

The output of the development phase is the program development plan, which is the input to the implementation phase. The next step in the model is the dry run, followed by the pilot program, and finally the output, which is the actual training provided.

Before discussing the dry run and pilot program, let us examine some ideas to consider in the implementation of training, first in terms of the structure of training, and then in terms of what the trainer should do.

## IMPLEMENTATION IDEAS FOR TRAINING

There are a number of things you can do in the training to ensure trainees become, and remain, interested in training.

<u>Icebreaker</u> Have an **icebreaker** to start the training. An icebreaker is a game or exercise that prompts trainees to get involved in meeting and talking with others. It is designed to be fun but at the same time generate energy that will transfer to the rest of the training. Would an icebreaker have been a useful way for Jason Reston to start his training? We believe so. The major reason given for not using an icebreaker is that it takes up too much time; but this assumption is a mistake.[14] Without the icebreaker, training starts off fast, but because of the lack of "getting to know others" and making discussion a legitimate part of training, it soon slows down and loses the race.[15] The choice of icebreaker depends on the size of the group. One approach, if the class is not too large and trainees do not know one another, is to group trainees into triads. If possible, set up these groups ahead of time so that group members do not know each other. Each trainee interviews one member of the triad, with the third as an observer. The questions should be simple but should help in getting to know the person. For example, ask for the following information:

- The person's name (for obvious reasons),
- Organization the person is from and title (learn about the type of work he or she does),
- Length of time in present job (learn about his or her experience),
- Best aspects of the job (learn about work person), and
- The person's hobbies (learn about home person).

Once the interviews are complete, each trainee in turn introduces the interviewed person to the total group. This activity gets everyone talking to the entire group, provides information on trainees, and releases a great deal of tension. If one of the objectives of training is to increase listening and communication skills, this icebreaker pays double dividends.

## Learning Objectives
Another useful step at the beginning of training is to review the learning objectives. This will help provide focus for the training, and, if the needs analysis was successful, it will mean all trainees will understand the need to learn the KSAs.

## Provide Variety
Provide variety during training to maintain interest. Recall from Chapter 5 that trainees' attention begins to decline after 15 to 20 minutes of lecture,[16] so be sure to provide breaks, activities, and the like to keep trainees interested in what you are saying. Keep a watchful eye on the trainees to signal time for a break. Even a five-minute stretch can help.

## Exercises or Games
Exercises or games (not to be confused with business games) are also valuable for gaining and maintaining interest, assuming the games are relevant. They are especially useful if they provide an entree to, or an example of, the training objective. These tools need to be used with a clear and definite purpose. We emphasize this point because of the experience of a colleague at a training workshop a few years ago (see Training in Action 7-3).

A number of models incorporate exercises into the learning process.[17] One such model is exhibited in Figure 7-2. This modification of an earlier model from Pfeiffer and Jones[18] allows trainees to experience first-hand a process related to the current training, and then hear some information about the topic for comparison with what they did. Then they process the new information, generalize it to their situation, and attempt to apply it in a more relevant situation. Let's examine this process more closely.

# Training in Action 7-3

## Using Games in Training

A few years ago, Helen went to Amelia Island for a seminar that was heralded as an Advanced Seminar in Process Consultation. She even called the instructor to be sure that it would be advanced, not "an introduction to."

At the seminar Helen soon realized that although the other 11 attendees possessed a great deal of experience as trainers, they were not at an advanced stage of process consultation. It was also evident that the trainees were from a number of prominent companies across the United States. About halfway through the five-day seminar they were put in two groups to learn about the different ways of intervening in a team's process. After receiving the information, the two groups were told to go off separately and develop a game for training the other group.

Each of the participants in Helen's group told of a game that was used in previous training and how much everyone liked it. Helen suggested developing a role-play whereby they could demonstrate the various components of process intervention. One of the other trainees said, "No one likes role-plays." "That's right," agreed another, and the group moved on to the more enjoyable games they were discussing. When they finally decided they would play the spider web game, Helen asked how they would tie the training into the game. Unanimously, they said that it was not necessary.

"The professor did not say we needed to do that," was the reply. "The game is to get the group interested in training. We'll move to the training after the game is finished," was another reply. Helen insisted that they somehow tie the game to the process consultation training they had been given, and reluctantly two of the group worked with her to accomplish this connection.

Back in the training room, the other group went first, getting Helen's group to play a game. After the game was completed, the professor asked, "But how does this activity tie into the training?" They all looked puzzled, and everyone in Helen's group looked at her rather sheepishly. When it was their turn, Helen's group did tie the training to the game but the professor commented, "It looks like you first decided on what game you wanted to play, then tried to fit the training into the game; it should be the other way around. First think what are you trying to accomplish, then find a game to meet that requirement."

The point of this story is that exercises and games that do not tie into the training objective are a waste of valuable training time. Although games are fun, their main value lies in their ability to reinforce the learning while providing a break in the routine.

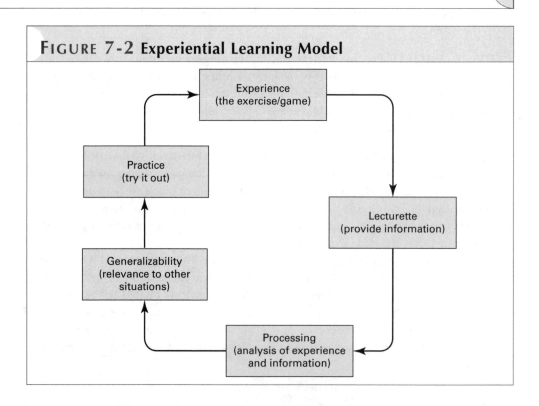

## FIGURE 7-2 Experiential Learning Model

Experience (the exercise/game)

Lecturette (provide information)

Processing (analysis of experience and information)

Generalizability (relevance to other situations)

Practice (try it out)

*Step 1: The Experience.* The learning experience begins with some sort of activity that ties into the training topic. In this way, all trainees begin by sharing a common experience. This first experience should not be related too closely to the actual work setting.

For example, when managers are being trained to be better interviewers, one of the objectives is to teach them how to develop appropriate interview questions. The first thing to realize is that most managers already believe they are good interviewers. So how does the trainer convince them training is necessary? To emphasize the importance of sound question development, the exercise (experience) is for them to help a committee select the new leader of a scout troop. Trainees take ten minutes to develop their own interview questions. Then they meet in small groups and develop an overall list of questions and the rationale for each. This list is posted on newsprint and discussed.

*Step 2: The Lecturette.* After the experience, the trainer provides information (e.g., concepts and principles) related to the topic at hand. This can be a lecture, a video, or some other form. In our example, a lecture would describe how to develop interview questions related to job requirements. Here the trainer shows how important it is to examine the job to determine what is needed, rather than simply making up questions that sound good.

*Step 3: Processing the Information and Experience.* After the experience and lecturette, trainees work in small groups to discuss their experience, based on the information they just received. In our example, the trainer might ask the groups to analyze the questions they developed and answer the question, "What criteria did we use to develop these questions?" Another question might be, "How are these questions related to the job of scout leader?" Then each of the small groups could report to the entire group what they discovered about how they developed interview questions.

*Step 4: Generalizability.* At this point it is important for the trainees to see how the learning is relevant to situations outside the training. According to Pfeiffer and Jones, the key question here is "So what?"[19] The goal is to have trainees consider how this new information fits with the things they do back on the job. From the analysis and learning that took place, trainees should infer that scout leader interview questions can be developed in a better way and be able to generalize this to other similar situations. In our example, the trainees should decide that the use of job-related information for developing interview questions is appropriate for all jobs. This point would be an opportunity to provide another lecturette on how to examine a job to determine the relevant questions to ask.

*Step 5: Practice.* The trainees receive another task similar in nature to the first so that they are able to practise the newly found skill. Note that in this step the task should be more closely related to the actual job. In our example, the trainees could be asked to develop interview questions for selecting someone for a job in the area they manage.

## IMPLEMENTATION IDEAS FOR TRAINERS

Trainers need to consider a number of issues for training to be effective. They must ensure that everything is ready on time, that they provide an initial positive impression, and that they gain and maintain trainee interest. Below are some things to consider in that regard.

### Preparation
As a trainer, you need to arrive at the training site early enough to ensure everything is in order. Check seating arrangements and make sure materials have arrived. Before trainees begin arriving, ensure all equipment is working and you

know how to operate it. Do not assume you can; turn it on and find out. Check the overhead projector to see that a spare bulb is stored inside. If not, find a spare (if you don't, you are tempting the fates). If a video will be used, try out the remote control to ensure that it works and you know how it operates. Ensure there is enough newsprint and markers available. As the trainer, you need to be sure that everything is ready to go before the trainees arrive; otherwise you can lose your credibility before you get started.

**First Impression** Typically, the favourable (or unfavourable) impression that a job candidate makes in a selection interview is made in the first few minutes. The same could be said of the impression that the trainer makes on trainees. Since this issue is so critical to effective training, the first few minutes need to be managed well. In the case at the beginning of the chapter, what kind of first impression do you think Jason Reston made? Did he establish any credibility with the trainees? Did he demonstrate a concern for their needs? Did he seem approachable?

What should a trainer wear? The answer is: know the audience. If unsure, ask. In many situations, a business suit is a safe bet. Training accountants, who all come to work in conservative business attire, suggests a business suit is a good idea. This same attire, however, could create distance from some other groups. Training line workers from a manufacturing plant, for example, might require more casual dress, not wearing the uniform of management. Remember, the trainees should perceive the trainer as someone able to help them in their job. To gain this credibility, the trainer needs to dress appropriately. Appropriate dress for training line workers might be casual dress—tasteful casual, but casual nevertheless.

What is equally important is that the clothes fit well, shoes are shined, and accessories match the outfit. This first impression will help establish your credibility.

If the dress code is a suit, it is always possible to loosen up after the training gets underway. Trainees need to feel comfortable, and if many show up wearing suits, the trainer can signal a more relaxed nature by removing his jacket or loosening his tie. The trainer might say, "I think I need to loosen up a bit; please feel free to do the same." For training spread over several days, at some point on the first day ask the trainees to decide on an appropriate dress code.

**The Start of Training** When trainees begin to arrive, greet them individually. Small talk with individual trainees before the session helps make them comfortable and, in turn, will facilitate discussion once the training begins.

Starting on time is important. Recall reinforcement theory as discussed in Chapter 2. If those who arrive late discover that training has not begun, the belief is reinforced that showing up on time is not necessary. A late start also punishes those who do arrive on time. For the rule of starting on time to be effective, however, it is necessary to obtain commitment from the trainees.

Starting on time is important, but few trainers we know start exactly on time the first day. Most allow for some tardiness the first day, when trainees may not know exactly where the training room is or simply did not give themselves enough time to get to the location. A good practice is to start training with an icebreaker—an exercise that allows for those who arrive a little late to fit right in with little disruption.

Trainees may come with different expectations about what the training will be about, and they also come for various reasons. After an icebreaker, it is useful to ask trainees what they expect to get from the training. Simply ask each person or ask small groups to develop lists to present to the larger group. These expectations are written on newsprint for future reference. Indicate to the trainees which of the points mentioned are a part of the training. For any points that are not part of the training design, offer to try to fit them in if they are appropriate. If not, explain why they are not appropriate for this training session. Also promise to go back to the list periodically to be sure all the things that were promised to be covered were in fact covered.

Following or concurrent with this introductory step, go through the agenda to indicate what will be happening over the duration of the training. Explain how breaks will be distributed and how messages for the trainees will be handled. One way to determine these things is to ask for a short discussion regarding the rules that will be set down for the training period. In this way, the trainees abide by these rules because they helped to develop them. To expedite the process, prepare a set of suggested rules and explain why they are useful. Then ask the trainees for any suggestions to modify, add, or delete from the list. At this point, the rule of starting on time can be discussed and decided upon. Involving the trainees in setting the rule builds their commitment to the rule.

<u>The Podium</u> One of the authors was hired to assist a consultant in training automobile workers in a new plant. The consultant hired a number of local people because of the size of the project. Concurrent training sessions allowed opportunities for the trainers to observe one another. One trainer was in the habit of sitting behind a table while talking to the trainees, another stood behind a podium, and the rest stood and moved around, going back to their notes only occasionally. Which procedure is best? Again, it depends. Standing behind the podium or sitting at a desk is acceptable for one-way communication, but it is not the most effective style for training adults, for whom two-way communication is important. In these cases, any barriers (desk, podium) present nonverbal impediments to the communication process. Additionally, seeing someone sitting behind a desk who is teaching them might remind some trainees of unpleasant school experiences. Being out in front of a desk or podium and moving around helps make the trainer look more accessible and open to input. In any event, two-way communication is much more important in the lecture/discussion method, whereas for the straight lecture a podium is perfectly acceptable. A skilled trainer will use the podium to signal to trainees when interruptions and comments are appropriate and when they are not.

<u>Communication Tips</u> As training generally has a lecture component, it is important to consider how effective your communication skills are. Below are some things to consider.

*Listening and Questioning.* What separates good trainers from average or poor trainers are their listening and questioning skills. This statement is not to demean presentation skills, but rather to stress the importance of listening and questioning. The techniques discussed earlier cannot be emphasized too strongly. If you are using the lecture/discussion method, use the experience and information provided by the trainees. Control the urge to tell them continually about your experiences. Remember that trainees relate to one another and their experiences more often than to yours. In the beginning, it may be helpful to share your relevant experiences to establish credibility and to show that sharing of experiences is desirable and useful. As training moves on, you will want to encourage trainees to begin sharing their experiences that are related to the training.

This requires being a good listener. Good listening is difficult, for several reasons, including:

- We are able to process information much faster than someone speaks, which gives us opportunities to do or think of other things;
- We often believe we know what the person is going to say, so we interrupt to respond; and
- We believe that speaking, not listening, is where the power and control are.

Therefore, listening requires practice. Active listening, originally developed for clinical counselling, involves three steps:

1. Listen carefully to what is said.

2. Summarize in your mind what was said.

3. Feed the summary back to the individual.

Following this process helps to keep us focused but, more importantly, confirms to the speaker (and all other trainees) what has been said, leaving little room for misunderstandings. Training in Action 7-4 provides an example of active listening.

***Providing Instructions.*** It is important to provide clear instructions with each exercise used. Many role-play exercises are wasted because trainees do not understand exactly what is expected. Oral instructions certainly need to be provided, but a handout containing the same information is also a useful resource for trainees. Even then, it is helpful to provide an example of what is expected. Once the exercise has begun, it is too late. It is discouraging both to the trainer and to the trainees if the trainees are confused and embarrassed because they misunderstood what they were supposed to be doing.

***Moving Around While Talking.*** This technique does not imply methodically pacing back and forth, but rather moving out from behind the podium. If a podium must be used, step away from it at times. If possible, stay away from it altogether. Moving around while lecturing shows knowledge of, and comfort with, the material. Approaching trainees from time to time, and talking specifically to them, sets up a friendly atmosphere. The movement also requires trainees to follow the trainer with their eyes, preventing the "glazed stare" that can occur if the trainer is stationary.

**Nonverbal Cues** the body language used when interacting with others.

***Using Nonverbal Communication.*** Everyone is always sending out **nonverbal cues**, so it is important that these cues are the correct ones. Keep eye contact on a trainee who is asking a question; do not turn and walk away while the trainee is talking. Give a head nod when a trainee answers a question, and hold eye contact. Also, maintain eye contact with the trainee group as a whole while talking to them. Avoid talking to the overhead projector, the image on the screen, or the lecture notes. Avoid folding your arms, as it can suggest displeasure or that the discussion is over. If writing on the board or flip chart, turn your head to the trainees while talking.

The key to nonverbal behaviour is to convey enthusiasm about the information being discussed. If the enthusiasm is real rather than feigned, it will show in nonverbal expressions. Think of someone passionately arguing a point of view. Are her arms

## Training in Action 7-4

### *Active Listening*

Dialogue between trainer and trainee at the training workshop on decision making:

**Trainee:** This is training in decision-making but I am in sales. What I want to know is how will this training help me?

**Trainer:** You want to know how this training will help you improve your sales?

**Trainee:** No, not necessarily in sales... Just help me do my job better.

**Trainer:** So you would like to know what the benefits of this training are and how these benefits will help you do your job.

**Trainee:** Yes, that's right.

out in front her and her palms up? Perhaps she is moving her hands up and down in short gestures. In any case, it is unlikely her arms are folded across her chest.

What if the trainer is not enthusiastic about the material that must be presented? This lack of energy can happen after presenting the same material a number of times. What to do? First, realize how important enthusiasm is to effective training. Recall training sessions in which you were the trainee. It is easy to distinguish the good from the not-so-good traineis. The good one was enthusiastic. So the trainer needs to psych himself up to generate enthusiasm. The trainer needs to give himself reasons to be enthusiastic about the material. Remember, the trainees are not as familiar with the material as the trainers. Starting off enthusiastically will be infectious, for both the trainees and the trainer.

*Getting Rid of Dysfluencies.* **Dysfluencies** are those "and uh," "like," "um" space fillers injected into speech. Everyone uses them occasionally, but some use them far too often. This tendency is usually more prominent when a trainer is nervous or unsure. It becomes immediately noticeable, and trainees tend to focus on these utterances rather than on the material. Videotaping lectures, or simply asking others to inform you when you use dysfluencies, can help you to get rid of them.

**Dysfluencies** the fillers used when talking, such as um, uh, etc.

## Tips on Dealing with Different Trainees

A successful trainer needs to understand how to deal with the various types of trainees that might be encountered. Some will need to be encouraged to become more involved in discussion, while others are far too involved.

*Quiet Trainee.* In Chapter 5 we discussed methods for encouraging quiet trainees to become more involved (small group discussions, writing their answers first), and these approaches are usually successful. What if they do not work? If there are a number of small groups for discussion sessions, one way to encourage the quiet trainee is to ask each group to rotate the person who is responsible for reporting back to the larger group. The quiet trainee will then take a turn reporting to the larger group, thus increasing his participation. However, too much pressure to become involved is not a good idea. If a quiet person is speaking up during the small group sessions, he is providing input. Do not attempt to get these trainees to participate at a level equal to others if they are not so inclined. Doing so can create too much tension in the environment. If all these methods are tried with little change in the quiet trainee's behaviour, do not push any further. Further attempts will only create barriers to the trainee's learning.

*Talkative Trainee.* The talkative trainee is usually far more of a problem than the quiet one. No matter what question is asked, this trainee wants to answer. Usually the answer involves a long story, and soon other trainees are rolling their eyes and tuning out. The trainer loses the trainees' attention, and valuable training time is wasted on irrelevant stories. It is important to tone down that trainee's input but not embarrass anyone. One approach is to ask others for their opinion. Say something like, "We have been making Lex do all the work here so far—how about someone else responding?" Or use the direct questioning technique to get the focus away from the talkative trainee. It may be helpful to speak to the talkative trainee in private, suggesting that her comments are appreciated, but there is a concern that others are not participating as much as they should. In this context, asking the talkative trainee to hold back on participation usually works.

*Angry Trainee.* Some trainees who come to training simply do not want to be there. They set out to ruin the session for everyone. Such trainees must be dealt with early on before they disrupt the class. One of the authors was training line workers in team concepts and although the union executive and most union members were supportive of the training, some were violently opposed. In the first session one of these trainees said, "I really do not want to be here; this training is management propaganda designed to weaken the union." The author's response was, "I have heard that said before; how do others feel about the training?" At that point, a number of others indicated support for the training and although the angry trainee did not participate much in the rest of the training, he did not disrupt it either.

If in such a situation most trainees felt the same way, it would be wise to spend some time discussing the issue because such an attitude will certainly affect training. The important point is to focus on how training can benefit them. One way to accomplish this task is to ask trainees to identify ways they would be able to use the training.

*The Comedian.*  These trainees are a gift and a curse. They are a gift because when their jokes work, and if they are not put forth too often, they will do wonders to set a positive tone. Laughter is good medicine, and a comedian is able to provide it. The potential curse is in the nature and frequency of the jokes. Some jokes are clearly inappropriate. In other cases it is difficult to know what is offensive. However, it is not productive for even a small number of trainees to feel that a particular joke was offensive. Also, if the comedians do get a lot of laughs, they are likely to continue to joke around. This behaviour can disrupt the timing of the sessions and put the trainer behind.

What to do? If the joking gets out of hand or some jokes are inappropriate, you can talk with the comedian at a break. Indicate a concern that some of the humour is offensive to some of the other trainees or is distracting from the focus of training. In taking this approach, you need to indicate appreciation of the comedian's intention to contribute to the training, but reach an agreement about how often the jokes can be offered and what types of jokes are acceptable. This conversation should be enough to curb such behaviour. Sometimes the comedian's jokes are directed at the trainer. In these cases the trainer must have a tough skin and be willing to laugh without taking it personally. This reaction will defuse any tension that may have been created, reduce the amount of distraction, and show that the trainer is not "too full of herself." It is only when the jokes become distracting or offensive that action needs to be taken.

# DRY RUN

In the training model, the process component of the implementation phase contains two important steps that should be completed before training is ready for general use:[20] the dry run and pilot program. The former is a first test of new material; here, the training package may not be presented in its entirety. The latter is the first full-blown presentation of the training using finished materials.

**Dry Run** a step prior to piloting the training where developers of the training determine the value and clarity of the various pieces of the training program in a controlled setting.

The **dry run** is not designed to actually train the participants. Instead, it is designed to determine the value and clarity of the various pieces of the training program in a controlled setting. To assess its value it is necessary to get as many key perspectives as possible to view the training. The trainer should be someone involved in the training design and development. For an effective dry run, use some potential trainees but choose them carefully, according to their diverse backgrounds, their general supportiveness of the value of training, and their willingness to provide feedback. More seasoned employees will be able to help evaluate the transferability of the training back to the job. Include some content experts who can provide feedback on the validity of the material and its usage. Some members of the training design and development team should also participate in the dry run. They can provide feedback as to how well the various pieces of the design fit together.

The dry run may not require that all the training modules in the program be tested. If a previously used specific exercise, case, or role-play is used with similar participants, the dry run for this exercise may simply involve the participants reading the exercise and providing feedback as to its relevance. Working through the exercise and a full discussion may not be necessary. Other exercises, particularly newly developed ones, probably require the participants to go through the full process.

It is important to ask participants a list of questions after each exercise or module that is tested. For example, after participants complete a role-play, you ask:

- Is the situation realistic for this organization? If it is not, future trainees may dismiss the training as being irrelevant.

- Is the information and direction for the exercise clear enough for trainees to do the exercise?

- Is the time allocation too long or too short?

After the dry run is completed, examine the feedback carefully and revise the training where applicable. Then it is time for the pilot program.

## PILOT PROGRAM

The **pilot program** is different from the dry run in that trainees are there to be trained. It will be a full-fledged training program. The dry run refines the training to eliminate any major glitches. In the pilot, trainees are again carefully chosen, as you want people who are generally supportive of training and who are not likely to be disruptive. Trainees will spread the word about training to others in the organization quickly. That word should be as positive as possible, so that when new trainees come into the program, they bring positive expectations. The pilot program will provide additional input to further refine the training (if necessary) and disruptions are not conducive to this process. To evaluate how the training comes across to different groups, it is desirable to have a good cross-section of those who will be in the later training sessions.

The main goals of the pilot program are:

- to provide the trainees with the relevant training;

- to assess further the timing and relevance of modules and various training components; and

- to determine the appropriateness, clarity, and flow of material.

The pilot program provides valuable responses and viewpoints that are inserted in the trainer's manual. These inputs will help guide new trainers in what to expect. Another goal of the pilot is to provide an opportunity for future instructors to attend the training and experience what takes place firsthand. Finally, the pilot program will provide valuable feedback to designers regarding the effectiveness of the training.

After the pilot, any further revisions are implemented. One final note: Although this pilot program will help to improve the program, examination and appropriate revisions should not stop here. Training evaluation goes on continuously. The primary objective of training is the transfer of the training to the job to positively affect organizational results. Training should continue to be modified until desirable outcomes can be reliably achieved.

**Pilot Program** training in a controlled setting, provided to specially selected trainees so as to get feedback for any possible program development plan refinements.

# TRANSFER OF TRAINING

After a training session, it is useful to evaluate the training to assess the level of learning that took place; this is explained in detail in Chapter 8. Assuming learning occurred, it does not do much good unless the new KSAs are transferred to the job. Transfer of training to the job can be simple and easy, or, at the other extreme, complex and next to impossible. Consider training on how to complete a new requisition form. Once training is complete and the form is available, transfer of the new behaviour should be relatively easy. However, consider the supervisor training that teaches a supervisor to take time to use conflict resolution skills to deal with subordinates. Back on the job the supervisor is measured by the units his subordinates produce. In the past, being angry and yelling at them resulted in high productivity. Here transfer of the new behaviours is less likely. Let us examine this more difficult type of transfer in more detail.

There are two parts to the transfer of training. First, because the behaviours are more difficult and not part of the trainee's regular behaviour, he will need to practise these new behaviours on the job. Examining Figure 7-3, there are two inputs that specifically deal with this: trainer support and relapse prevention/goal setting. It is hoped that, in the design of the training it was possible to obtain the trainer's commitment to do a sit-in. Recall from Chapter 4 that in a sit-in the trainer follows the supervisor around for a while noting how well he is using the skills and then provides feedback to him. Also, providing the trainee with the relapse prevention/goal setting process to help him when relapses do happen will help increase the likelihood that transfer will occur.

Other inputs into the transfer of training, such as supervisor and peer support will provide an incentive for the trainee to practise the new behaviours. The supervisor and peers should also continue to support these new behaviours once they are fully transferred. The supervisor in particular needs to help the trainee by providing support and feedback as to how the trainee is doing. Trainers hope for supportive climate and culture, as they will increase the likelihood that the new behaviours will be

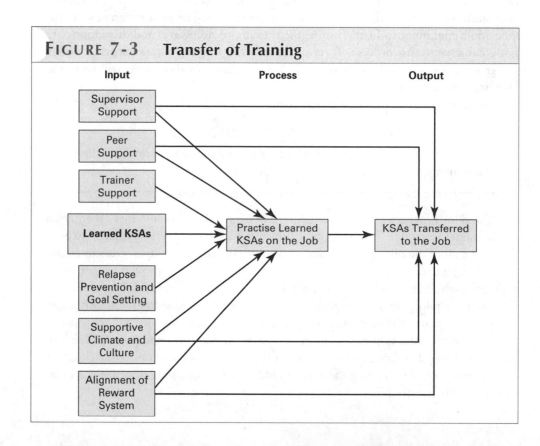

## FIGURE 7-3     Transfer of Training

practised and maintained after transfer has taken place fully. Finally, alignment of the reward systems to encourage the new behaviours will add to the likelihood that the transfer will take place and be lasting.

From the training needs analysis, any reward systems that were not aligned, or supervisor and peer attitudes toward the training that were dysfunctional, should have been identified. Plans to make needed changes in these areas should have been addressed in the design phase and implemented prior to training. All those forces in the input phase of the transfer of training should be pushing the trainee to use the new behaviours when he returns to work. The more this is true, the more likely it is that the behaviours will transfer.

Of all the forces that are important to ensure transfer, peer support can be problematic. Peer pressure from those who have been around for a long time and who are comfortable doing things the "old way" can do a great deal to inhibit a trainee's ability to change, even if she wants to. In many cases this peer pressure for the status quo is very difficult to change. Training in Action 7-5 provides an example where Ford was successful in dealing with potential peer pressure. However, this involved a new plant, new relationships, and training focused on changing attitudes. It is very different in an older plant where employees are set in their ways and there are strong relationships among the workers. In cases like this, OD skills are required to help employees see the advantages of new ways and obtain their support. A review of Training in Action 4-2 is a reminder of just how much can and should be done to ensure transfer of training takes place. After all, without it, the training was a waste of money.

## Training in Action 7-5

### *Peer Pressure and New Skills*

Ford needed a new plant and was determined to implement a more flexible work system that included teamwork in this new plant. So, before agreeing to build the plant in Windsor, Ford management insisted that the Canadian Auto Workers union sign a "special operating agreement" to allow such changes. However, the union was strong, and many of those who transferred to the new plant were strong union members who believed in the old way of working. They laughed at the idea of teamwork. Peer pressure in such a situation was a concern. It could derail any effort to institute this major change to the way work was done. If peers on the shop floor were making fun of the idea of teamwork, it would be difficult to get others interested and willing to be involved.

At the opening of the plant, all workers who had transferred to the new plant were required to attend a week of training. To deal with this potential negative impact of peer pressure, Ford incorporated information designed to change attitudes toward this more flexible system of working into this training program. In the beginning, some trainees were openly hostile to the training. One said: "The company pays me to come here, but they cannot force me to learn this stuff." Others, by their lack of participation, were likely feeling the same but were not as vocal. However, by the end of the week, many were actively involved and, when asked at the end of training what they thought of the more flexible work systems, most indicated a positive response. Was there transfer to the job? There was no formal evaluation but most did become actively involved back on the job. Although there were still those actively opposed to it who did not get involved, there were not enough of them to create the pressure on peers to stay uninvolved.

## CASE

### Jack Goes to Training... (Continued from beginning of chapter)

"Get up. Get up, you're going to be late for the training!"

"Huh," grunted Jack. "What time is it?"

"It's 7:30 and you have to go downtown to the training centre today, remember?" said his wife.

Wow, what a dream, thought Jack as he walked up the steps of the training centre, feeling a little nervous. The training room was not at all like a schoolroom. No windows, no blackboards. As he entered the room, a nicely dressed man approached him and said, "Hi, my name is Doug, welcome to the training centre. Have you ever been here before?" The nametag indicated Doug was the trainer. He seems like a nice guy, thought Jack.

"There's some coffee and doughnuts over there—help yourself," said Doug. This might even be enjoyable, thought Jack, although he still felt a little apprehensive.

With introductions out of the way and the objectives and agenda explained, Doug summed up by saying, "So, at the end of the two days you will be expected to take a set of specifications and program them into the machine. Are there any questions?"

"So there are no tests?" asked Jack.

"Well," responded Doug, "that is the test."

Jack was a bit confused, "But that is what we do at work—I don't see it as a test. A test is where I have to write down an answer to some question you pose about all this stuff."

"There are no paper-and-pencil tests, just behavioural tests," said Doug.

Suddenly it was lunchtime. Jack thought, "It was true, time does go fast when you are having fun. This sure isn't like school." All 23 trainees went to another room where lunch was served.

"I can't believe it. This is nothing like I expected," said Ron. Ron was the fellow whom Jack had to interview and introduce to the group in what was called an icebreaker. That icebreaker sure did a lot to get me relaxed and actually interested in the training, thought Jack.

Ron continued, "I always did poorly in school and was petrified about coming here." Jack responded, "Me too."

Ron said, "I like the idea of his periodically giving us mini-tests. Gives us an idea of how we are doing and provides us with extra help if we are falling behind."

"Tests. . . oh, yeah, I find it hard to consider them tests. They're hands-on, exactly what we will do on the job," said Jack.

Later Jack thought, "Wow, it's already over."

"Nice job, Jack. You are now certified on this piece of equipment," said Doug.

"Hey, Ron," said Jack, "do you believe how much fun learning can be?"

Ron agreed, "Doug was great. He kept getting our input and tying our experiences to the new stuff we had to learn. I never thought I would say this, but I would like to get more training like this."

"You bet," said Jack. "I still can't believe how great this was—especially after the dream I had."

## Summary

First, we discussed the development of training. At this stage, creating a program development plan is crucial to ensure everything that needs to be done is done. This plan outlines everything that must be done to prepare for training, from material and equipment to trainee and trainer manuals. Content learning points from each learning objective need to be highlighted to clearly identify what needs to be learned.

The type of training facility chosen is also important. Arrangement of the seating and closeness of the trainer to the trainees should be a function of the objectives of the training, not the design of the room. Also, noise levels from adjoining rooms or from outside the room need to be determined before choosing a training room. The proper training facility then allows the seating to be arranged in a manner that best reflects what type of training will be taking place.

We examined the factors to consider when choosing a trainer, and specifically an OJT trainer, because of the unique issues that revolve around on-the-job trainers.

Alternatives to development of the training were examined. After all, sometimes it is simply not viable to develop training. In cases like this, the use of consultants, prepackaged training, and outside seminars can provide a solution. This is especially true for the small business.

In the implementation of training, we first focused on some practical issues related to keeping trainees' interest in training. Use of icebreakers, learning objectives, variety and an example of a type of exercise to keep training interesting were discussed. Next we provided some tips for trainers in the execution of the training program. Preparation, importance of the first impression, what to consider at the start of training, and how to use the podium were all discussed. Finally, some tips on communication and how to deal with certain types of trainees were provided.

The dry run and pilot program were discussed. Before implementation of a large training program, it is useful to have a dry run in which the material is tested to see how effective it is. This dry run is not an actual training session but a process of going through the material and determining whether it is doing what you expect it to. The next step is a pilot program in which the first trainees go through the training, but with selected supportive trainees, so they can spread the word about the training program in a positive manner. Also, constructive feedback from the trainees is solicited in order to put the finishing touches on the program before it is formally launched.

## Implications for Practice

**1.** If there will be more than one trainer teaching training, and it will be taught many times, consider development of an instructor's manual to help ensure consistency and provide assistance to trainers.

**2.** Knowledge of the job is an important criterion in choosing OJT trainers, but more important than choosing the *most* knowledgeable is choosing someone who would be supportive and is likely to be able to make the trainee feel comfortable. Be sure to provide the person with training in how to be effective as a trainer and do not expect the same level of productivity while he is training. In fact rewards need to be based on the skill as a trainer, not on production.

**3.** When examining a consultant as a possible provider of training, do not assume higher cost is equal to better product. There are often effective consultants with low overhead who can offer good service. Do ask (a) if they are the person who will actually be doing the training, (b) to see their learning objectives, (c) if they evaluate, and (d) to provide previous customers' names for reference.

**4.** Small businesses can consider contacting (through a Chamber of Commerce or other such institutions) other companies that are not their competition, to see if they would be interested in sharing costs of some types of training.

**5.** For any training to be successful it is useful to have peers of the trainee want the trainee to use the new skills. If the opposite is true, it will be difficult to get transfer of training to occur. Getting peers to buy into the training is sometimes not easy, but unless it is accomplished, it will severely diminish the likelihood of transfer of training.

## Key Terms

Dry run    *254*

Dysfluencies    *253*

Icebreaker    *247*

Learning point    *234*

Nonverbal cues    *252*

Program development plan    *234*

Pilot program    *255*

## Questions for Review

1. You are asked to deliver a two-day workshop for managers on effective feedback skills. It is focused primarily on performance reviews. Approximately 100 managers need to be trained. Describe what the content of the training would entail, the methods you would use (e.g., lecture, case study, role-play), and the instructional media and equipment you would want and why. Also, what type of room set-up would you want, and why? Indicate how many sessions you would need for this number of managers and explain why.

2. Describe how the experiential learning model relates to the social learning model.

3. What are some typical difficult trainers and how would you deal with them?

4. How do the dry run and pilot training differ? Why?

## Exercises

1. Check the room where your class meets. Does it meet the requirements of a good training room? What additions would make it more amenable to effective training?

2. Assume you are in training on conflict resolution. Think of a situation in which you got in an argument with someone, and write up the role of the person with whom you were in conflict. Follow the instructions in the chapter. Do not forget that you need to write the role of the other person, not you, because you will play yourself. Show the role to a classmate and ask him or her to play it. As you play your part, try to behave differently from the way you did in the original confrontation. Although you

do not have any training in the area of conflict resolution, simply try to remain calm and not turn the situation into a confrontation. Now debrief. How did it go? Was the role-play useful in helping you practise being calm? Ask the classmate whether the role you wrote could be better in terms of providing information as to how the classmate is to act.

3. In a small group, each person takes a turn giving a three-minute impromptu speech (on anything). Have someone designated as the bell ringer. Each time the speaker uses a dysfluency (uh, and uh, um, etc.), the bell ringer will hit a glass with a spoon (or make some other sound). Keep score for each person. Over the next few weeks, ask friends to tell you when you use these dysfluencies and try to reduce them. Then get together with your group and redo the exercise. Do you note any improvement?

4. In small groups, choose someone who worked in a particular job. Interview the person to determine the job requirements, and develop a procedure for providing OJT for the job.

## Web Research

Conduct a search of the Internet to identify tips for trainers in dealing with difficult trainees. Compare the types you find with the types identified in the text. If different, compare those you found with those in the text and offer an explanation as to why you think they were not included. If types are similar, compare how the text and Internet suggest handling these types, noting any differences and explaining which method you prefer.

## CASE ANALYSIS

Jim worked as a labourer for a gas utility in Winnipeg, Manitoba. When the opportunity came to apply for a backhoe/front-end-loader operator job, he was excited. Three people applied. To select the one who would get the job, the company asked each of them to go out and actually work on the backhoe for a day. Jim felt his chance for the job disappear because he had never even driven a tractor, let alone used a backhoe. When he went out, he did not know how to start the tractor. One of the other backhoe operators had to show him. He managed through the day, and to his surprise, did better than the others. He was given the job.

On his first day at the new job, one of the other backhoe operators showed him where to check the hydraulic fluid and said, "These old Massey's are foolproof. You will be okay." Jim taught himself how to dig a hole by trial and error. He initially believed that the best way was to fill the bucket as much as possible before lifting it out of the hole and emptying it. He would wiggle the bucket back and forth until it was submerged and then curl it. When it came out of the hole, the earth would be falling off the sides. This job was not so difficult after all, he thought.

He cut through his first water line about two weeks after starting his new job. Going into a deep, muddy hole did not make the crew happy. After Jim cut through his third water line, the crew chief pulled him aside and said, "You are taking too much earth out with each bucket, so you don't feel the bucket hitting the water line; ease up a bit." Water lines were usually two to two-and-a-half metres down, so Jim would dig until about one-and-a-half metres and then try to be more careful. It was then he pulled up some telephone lines that were only about one metre deep.

Realizing more was involved in operating a backhoe than he first thought, he sought out Bill Granger, who was known to have broken a water line only twice in his 15 years. It was said that he was so good he could dig underneath the gas lines—a claim that Jim doubted. Bill said, "You need to be able to feel any restriction. The way to do that is to have more than one of your levers open at the same time. Operating the bucket lever and the boom lever at the same time reduces the power and causes the machine to stop rather than cut through a line of any type." Jim began to use this method but still broke water lines. The difference now was that he knew immediately when he broke a line. He could feel the extra pull, whereas in the past he found out either by seeing water gushing up or by hearing the crew chief swearing at him. He was getting better. Jim never did become as good as Bill Granger. In fact two years later he applied for another job as gas repairperson and was promoted, but the training as a gas repairperson was not much better.

### Case Questions

1. What are the potential costs to this lack of training? Why do you think the company operated in this manner?

2. What type of training would you recommend: OJT, classroom, or a combination? Describe what the training might entail.

3. What type of training environment would you provide?

4. Who would you get to do the training and why?

5. Would you consider purchasing a training program for backhoe operators? Provide your rationale.

# 8

# EVALUATION OF TRAINING

*What we see depends mainly on what we look for.*

Sir John Lubbock

**EVALUATION PHASE**

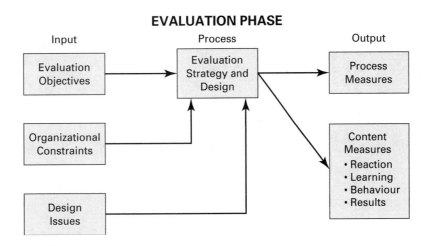

## CHAPTER OBJECTIVES

After reading this chapter, you should be able to:

- Describe the pros and cons of evaluation and indicate which way to go on the issue.

- Explain what process evaluation is, and why it is important.

- Describe the interrelationships among the various levels of outcome evaluation.

- Describe the costs and benefits of evaluating training.

- Differentiate between the two types of cost-effectiveness evaluation (cost savings and utility analysis).

- Describe the various designs that are possible for evaluation, and their advantages and disadvantages.

- Define and explain the importance of internal and external validity.

## CASE

### Training Designed to Change Behaviour and Attitudes

The city of Palm Desert, California, decided to provide training to improve employees' attitudes toward their work and to provide them with the skills to be more effective on the job. The two-day seminar involved a number of teaching methods including a lecture, films, role-plays, and group interaction. Among the topics covered were conflict control, listening, communicating, telephone etiquette, body language, delegation, and taking orders. Throughout the two days, the value of teamwork, creativity, and rational decision-making was stressed and integrated into the training.

Before the training was instituted, all 55 non-management employees completed a paper-and-pencil questionnaire to measure both their attitudes toward the job and their perception of their job behaviours. Supervisors also completed the job behaviour questionnaire (a type of assessment) for each of their employees. All 55 employees were told they would be receiving the same two-day seminar. The first set of 34 employees was chosen at random.

The 21 employees who did not take the training immediately became a comparison group for evaluating the training. While the first group of employees were sent to the training, the others were pulled off the job, ostensibly to receive training, but they simply took part in exercises not related to any training. Thus, both groups were treated similarly in every way except for the training. Both groups completed attitude surveys immediately after the trained group finished training. Six months later both groups completed self-report surveys to measure changes in their job behaviour. Their supervisors were asked to complete a similar behaviour measure at the six-month mark as well.

The data provided some revealing information. For the trained group, no changes in attitude or behaviour were indicated, either by the self-report or by supervisor-reported surveys. This result was also true (but expected) for the group not trained.

*Source:* Adapted from Miller, S. (1990). Effects of municipal training on employee attitudes and behaviour. Public Personnel Management 19:429–40.

Was training a failure in the Palm Desert case? Would the training manager be pleased with these results? Was the evaluation process flawed? These types of issues will be addressed in this chapter. We will refer back to the case from time to time to answer these and other questions.

## RATIONALE FOR EVALUATION

Network for the Evaluation of Education and Training Technologies
*http://socserv2.mmaster.ca/ srnet/evnet.htm*

Imagine a business that decided it would not look at its profitability, return on investment, or productivity. You are a supervisor with this company, but you never look at how well or poorly your subordinates are performing their jobs. This is what training is like when no evaluation is conducted. Good management practice dictates that organizational activities are routinely examined to ensure that they are occurring as planned and are producing the anticipated results. Otherwise people, processes, and products or services that stray "off track" are provided with no means of getting back on.

Nonetheless, many rationalizations for not evaluating training continue to exist, and evaluation of training is not done. For example, a survey of Canadian organizations in the early 1990s revealed only 30 percent evaluate learning, 16 percent evaluate behavioural change, and 5 percent evaluate the impact of training on organizational outcomes.[1] But this is changing. More recent data indicate that for non-management training, 31 percent of Canadian organizations evaluated learning, 47 percent evaluated behavioural change, and 36 percent evaluated organizational results.[2] An increase in accountability for everyone is a major reason for this change. Top management is demanding evidence that training departments are contributing positively to the bottom line.[3] Dave Palm, training director of LensCrafters, knows first-hand about this trend. A frantic regional manager called Dave and told him that executives were looking to improve the bottom line and could not find enough evidence that training programs were providing a quantifiable return on the company's investment. Yes, they knew that trainees were satisfied with training, but were they getting the bang for their buck? The conversation ended with the regional manager saying, "So, Dave, what are you going to do about it?" Dave got his wake-up call.[4] Evaluation of training at all levels is becoming more commonplace. Nevertheless, there are still a number of reasons many resist evaluation of training.

# RESISTANCE TO TRAINING EVALUATION

Training managers can come up with a surprising number of reasons for not evaluating training, including:

- There's nothing to evaluate.
- No one really cares about it.
- Evaluation is a threat to my job.

## THERE'S NOTHING TO EVALUATE

For some companies, training is a luxury provided as a reward for good performance, or simply something mandated so everyone must take his or her turn.[5] The argument here is that training is not expected to accomplish anything, so there is nothing to evaluate.

*The Counterargument.* Even in cases where training is a reward, it is designed with some goals or objectives in mind. Some type of KSA change is expected from the trainees, even if it is just that they feel more positive about their job or the company. Once this goal or objective is identified, you can measure it. Evaluation is simply measuring the degree to which objectives are achieved.

## NO ONE REALLY CARES ABOUT EVALUATING TRAINING

The most common rationale for not conducting training evaluations is that "formal evaluation procedures are too expensive and time-consuming and no one really cares anyway." This explanation usually means that no one specifically asked for, demanded, or otherwise indicated a need for assessment of training outcomes.

*The Counterargument.* If an evaluation is not specifically required, this does not mean training is not evaluated. Important organizational decisions (e.g., budget, staffing, performance evaluations) are made with or without formal data on the effectiveness of training or its contribution toward organizational objectives. If no formal evaluations of training have taken place, decisions will be based upon the decision-makers' impressions of training. Even in good economic times, the competition for organizational budget allocations is strong. Departments that can document their contributions to the organization and the return that can be expected on the investment of new budget dollars are more likely to be granted their budget requests. The question, then, is not whether training should be evaluated, but rather who will do it, how it will be done, and what data will be used.

## EVALUATION IS A THREAT TO MY JOB

Think about it. In North America, tens of billions of dollars are spent every year on training. So why are companies not evaluating this training? Fear of the result is one reason. Football coach Woody Hays, back in the 1950s, once said that he never liked to throw the forward pass because three things could happen and two of them were bad. The same could be said for evaluation. If time and money are spent on training and an evaluation determines that no learning occurred, or worse, job performance declined, tough questions will be asked. Although most managers are not likely to admit this concern publicly, it is perhaps the real problem. When we use the term *evaluation*, we too often think of a single final outcome at a particular point that represents success or failure—like a report card. This type of evaluation is called summative or outcome evaluation. When the focus is on this type of evaluation, managers are naturally concerned about how documenting the failure of their programs will affect their careers. Consider Training in Action 8-1. It provides an example of an evaluation designed to provide feedback so that improvement (through training and practice) can take place. But when the focus shifted from "helping to improve" (**formative evaluation**) to a "measurement of success or failure" (**summative evaluation**), the desire to participate in the process disappeared and the airline threatened to discontinue it.

**Summative Evaluation** evaluation to determine success or failure of the training program.
**Formative Evaluation** evaluation to determine areas that need improvement in order to make the training program more effective.

## Training in Action 8-1

### *Evaluation: What It Is Used for Matters*

For 30 years, British Airways maintained a system in all its aircraft that monitors everything an aircraft and its pilot does. This information is examined continuously to determine any faulty aircraft mechanisms and to constantly assess the skill level of the pilots. When a pilot is flagged as having done "steep climbs" or "hard" or "fast landings" for example, [the pilot is] targeted for training to alleviate the skill deficiency. The training is used, therefore, as a developmental tool to continuously improve the performance of pilots. The evaluation is not used as summative, as a measure of performance upon which disciplinary measures might be taken. The result for British Airways, one of the largest airlines in the world, is one of the best safety records in the world.

In the past, one of the major ways of determining problems in the airline industry in North America was to wait until an accident occurred and then examine the black box to find the causes. The findings might indicate pilot error or some problem with the aircraft. This information was then sent to all the major airlines for their information. This form of sum-mative evaluation met with disastrous results. Recently, six major American airlines began a program similar to the one discussed above. After all, it makes sense to track incidents and make changes (in aircraft design or pilot skill level) as soon as it is noticed. In this way, major incidents are more likely to be avoided. In fact, [airlines] are using the evaluation information gathered as a feedback mechanism to ensure the continuous improvement of performance and not as a summative evaluation of "failure."

This seemingly effective way of assuring high performance is about to come to an end in the United States. The Federal Aviation Administration (FAA) wants access to this information for possible use as a measure of summative evaluation of pilots. The airlines fear that the information given to the FAA could be used to punish airlines and pilots for certain types of behaviour. As a result, they are considering dropping the program.

*Source:* Orr, B. (2001). Toward safer skies. Available at BSnews.com/now/story/0,1597,277042-412,00.shtml.

*The Counterargument.* Can the airline in Training in Action 8-1 be blamed for wanting to opt out of the program? No, it is difficult to imagine anyone wanting to participate in a program where the information can be used against them. This type of summative evaluation is a legitimate reason for not wanting to evaluate. The main purpose of evaluation should not be an after-the-fact measure of accountability (summative evaluation), but a feedback mechanism to guide efforts toward success.[6] While trying to convince a client that the company's training should be evaluated, one trainer decided not to use the term *evaluation*. Instead, he chose the term *data tracking*. He emphasized tracking attitudes and behaviours over time and supplying feedback based on the findings to the training designers and presenters. This feedback could then be used to modify training and organizational systems and processes to facilitate the training's success. The term *data tracking* did not imply the same connotation of finality as *evaluation*. Hence, managers saw it as a tool for improving the likelihood of a successful intervention rather than as a pass/fail grade.

Was the evaluation in the Palm Desert case seen as summative or formative? It is difficult to say without actually talking to those involved. If it was used for continuous improvement, assessment of learning at the end of training could be helpful in determining the reason transfer did not take place. Based on this information, the city could design additional interventions in order to achieve desired outcomes.

# SO WE MUST EVALUATE

On the surface, the arguments for ignoring evaluation of training make some sense. But they are easily countered when more carefully analyzed. However, perhaps the biggest reason for abandoning the resistance to evaluation is its benefit, especially today when more and more organizations are demanding accountability at all levels. Managers are increasingly demanding of training what they demand of other departments: provide evidence of the value to the organization.[7]

Other factors influencing the need to evaluate training are the quality movement, focus on continuous improvement, and organizational cost cutting.[8]

The image of the training function, especially by many line managers, is sometimes poor. By using the same process line managers use to demonstrate accountability, it is possible to improve the image of training. Furthermore, the technology for evaluating and placing dollar amounts on the value of training has improved in the last several years. The caveat here is that we do not advocate a comprehensive evaluation of all training, because the value of the information must be worth the cost. Sometimes, the cost of evaluation is simply too high.

# TYPES OF EVALUATION DATA COLLECTED

Let's go back to the evaluation phase figure at the beginning of the chapter. Recall from Chapter 4 that one of the outputs from the design phase is evaluation considerations. These considerations, or more specifically what is determined important to evaluate, are inputs, along with organizational constraints and design issues, to the evaluation phase of the training model. Remember that at the time of obtaining the design output, evaluation processes and outcome measures should be developed concurrently. The types of outputs from the evaluation phase are process and outcome evaluation. **Process evaluation** compares the developed training to what actually takes place in the training program. **Outcome evaluation** determines how well training has accomplished its objectives.

**Process Evaluation** an examination of the developed training program compared with what actually takes place in the training program.

**Outcome Evaluation** evaluation to determine how well training has accomplished its objectives.

# PROCESS DATA

One of the authors has a cottage near a lake, and he often sees people trying unsuccessfully to start their outboard motors. In going to their assistance, he never starts by suggesting they pull the plugs to check for ignition or disconnect the float to see whether gas is reaching the carburetor. Instead, he asks if the gas line is connected firmly, if the ball is pumped up, if the gear shift is in neutral (many will not start in gear), and if the throttle is at the correct position, all of which are process issues. He evaluates the "process" of starting the engine to see whether it was followed correctly. If he assumed it was followed and tried to diagnose the "problem with the engine," he might never find it.

It is the same with training. If learning objectives were not achieved, it is pointless to tear the training design apart in trying to fix it. It might simply be a process issue—the training was not set up or presented the way it was intended. By examining the process, it is possible to see all the places where the training might have gone wrong. In the examination of the process, you determine whether the training that was done reflected what was proposed, designed, and contained in the training manual. If it was and the objectives are not being achieved, it is the design that must be changed. Or did the trainer or others in the organization make some ad hoc modifications? If this information were available in the Palm Desert case, an analysis might provide information as to why the training was not successful.

Imagine, for example, that the Palm Desert training required the use of behaviour modelling to provide practice in the skills being taught. The evaluation of outcomes shows that learning of the new behaviours did not occur. If no process data were gathered, the conclusion could be that the behaviour modelling approach was not effective. However, what if examination of the process revealed that trainees were threatened by the behaviour modelling technique and the trainer allowed them to spend time discussing behaviour modelling, which left less time for doing the modelling? As a result, it is quite plausible that it is not the design of the training that is a problem, but the implementation of the training as it was designed. Without the process evaluation, this information would remain unknown, and the inference might be that behaviour modelling was not effective.

Examples of implementation issues to examine are depicted in Table 8-1. Here, it is up to the evaluator to determine whether all the techniques that were designed into the program actually took place. It is not good enough simply to determine that the amount of time allotted was spent on the topic or skill development. It must also be determined whether trainees actually were involved in the learning activities as prescribed by the design. As in the previous behaviour modelling example, the time allotted might be used for something other than behaviour modelling.

**Putting It All Together** Actual training is compared with the expected (as designed) training to provide an assessment of the effectiveness of the training implementation. Much of the necessary information for the expected training can be obtained from records and reports developed in the process of setting up the training program. A manual would provide an excellent source of information about what should be covered in the training. Someone can monitor the training to determine what actually was covered. Another method is to ask trainees to complete evaluations of process issues for each module. Videotape, instructors' notes, and surveys or interviews with trainees can also be used. Keep in mind that when you are gathering any data, the more methods used to gather information, the better.

**When to Use It** Table 8-2 depicts those interested in process data. Clearly the training department is primarily concerned with this information to assess how they

---

### TABLE 8-1    Potential Questions to Be Addressed in a Process Analysis

- Were the trainer, training techniques, and learning objectives well matched?
- Were lecture portions of the training effective?
  Was involvement encouraged or solicited?
  Were questions used effectively?
- Did the trainer conduct the various training methodologies (case, role-play, etc.) appropriately?
  Were they explained well?
  Did the trainer use the allotted time for activities?
  Was enough time allotted?
  Did trainees follow instructions?
  Was there effective debriefing following the exercises?
- Did the trainer follow the training design and lesson plans?
  Was enough time given for each of the requirements?
  Was time allowed for questions?

*Source:* Adapted from Camp, R. P., Blanchard, P. N., & Huszczo, G. E. (1986). *Towards a More Organizationally Effective Training Strategy and Practice.* Upper Saddle River, NJ: Prentice Hall.

---

are doing. The customers of training (defined as anyone with a vested interest in the training department's work) usually are more interested in outcome data than they are in process data.

Providing some process data is important, even if it is only the trainer's documentation and the trainees' reactions. The trainer can use this information to assess what seems to work and what does not. Sometimes more detailed process data will be required, such as when training will be used many times, or the training outcomes have a significant impact on the bottom line. If, however, it is only a half-day seminar on the new computer software, collecting process information may not be worth the cost.

Once training and trainers are evaluated a number of times, the value of additional evaluations decreases. If you are conducting training done numerous times before, such as training new hires to work on a piece of equipment, and the trainer is one of your most experienced, then process analysis is probably not necessary. If the trainer was fairly new or had not previously conducted this particular session, it might be beneficial to gather process data through a senior trainer's direct observation.

---

### TABLE 8-2    Who Is Interested in the Process Data

#### Training Department

| Training Department | |
|---|---|
| Trainer | Yes, it helps determine what works well and what does not |
| Other trainers | Yes, to the extent the process is generalizable |
| Training manager | Only if training is not successful or if a problem is present with a particular trainer |
| **Customers** | |
| Trainees | No |
| Trainees' supervisor | No |
| Upper management | No |

*Source:* Adapted from Camp, R. P., Blanchard, P. N., & Huszczo, G. E. (1986). *Towards a More Organizationally Effective Training Strategy and Practice.* Upper Saddle River, NJ: Prentice Hall.

# OUTCOME DATA

To be most effective, we believe that evaluations should be formative and focused on providing information to improve training, not summative or designed only to determine whether training is successful. Some disagree with this approach and suggest that formative evaluation ends when the training program is launched.[9] We suggest, however, that the focus should always be on formative evaluation for these reasons:

- It removes the connotation of pass/fail, making evaluation more likely.
- It facilitates continuous improvement, a desirable goal even when training is deemed successful.[10]

To determine how well the training met or is meeting its goals, it is necessary to examine various outcomes measures. The four outcomes measures that are probably the best known are reaction, learning, behaviour, and organizational results.[11] These outcomes are ordered:

- Reaction outcomes come first and will influence how much can be learned;
- Learning outcomes influence how much behaviour can change back on the job;
- Behaviour outcomes are the changes of behaviour on the job that will influence organizational results; and
- Organizational results are the changes in the bottom line related to the reason for training in the first place, such as high grievance rate, low productivity, etc.

This description is a simplified version of what actually happens, and critics argue that no empirical evidence indicates that these relationships between these outcomes exist.[12] We discuss this argument in more detail later.

**Reaction Outcomes** a determination of the trainee's perceptions, emotions, and subjective evaluations of the training experience.

## Reaction
Reaction outcomes are measures of the trainee's perceptions, emotions, and subjective evaluations of the training experience. They represent the first level of evaluation and are important because favourable reactions create motivation to learn. Learning may also occur even if the training is boring, or alternatively, may not occur even if it is interesting.[13] However, if training is boring it will be difficult to attend to what is being taught. As a result, the trainee may not learn as much as he would if he found the training interesting and exciting. High reaction scores from trainees, therefore, assure the designers that attention was obtained and maintained, which, as you recall from social learning theory, is the first part of learning—getting their attention.

**Learning Outcomes** a determination of the degree to which the learning objectives were met.

## Learning
Learning outcomes are measured by how well the learning objectives and the overall training objective were achieved. The type of measurement used will depend on the measurement technology available to the evaluator and the type of learning being evaluated. Note the critical relationship between the needs analysis and evaluation. If the training process progressed according to the model presented in this text, how to measure learning has already been identified during the training needs analysis (TNA). At that time, the employee's KSAs were measured to determine whether they were adequate for job performance. The evaluation of learning should use the same measurement techniques as in the TNA. Thus, the needs analysis is actually the "pre-test." A similar measure at the end of training would show the "gain" in learning.

**Job Behaviour Outcomes** a determination of the degree to which the learned behaviours are transferred to the job.

## Job Behaviour
Job behaviour outcomes are measures of the degree to which the learned behaviour has transferred to the job. During the training needs analysis (TNA) performance gaps were identified and traced to areas in which employees were

behaving in a manner that was creating the gap. The methods used for measuring job behaviour in the TNA should be used in measuring job behaviour after the completion of training. Once again, the link between needs analysis and evaluation is evident. The degree to which job behaviour improves places a cap on how much training can improve organizational results.

### Organizational Results

**Organizational results** occupy the highest level in the hierarchy and reflect the performance gap identified in the TNA. It is the organizational result that often triggers reactive (as opposed to proactive) training. Here are some examples:

> **Organizational Results** a determination of the degree to which there are improvements in related organizational functioning as a result of the training.

- High levels of scrap are being produced;

- Employees are quitting in record numbers;

- Sales figures dropped over the last two quarters;

- Grievances are on the increase; and

- Number of rejects from quality control are rising.

Once again, if one of these organizational results triggered the training, it can be used as the baseline for assessing improvement after training. This process of integrating the TNA and evaluation also shows potential as a means of streamlining both processes, thereby making the integration more cost effective.[14]

### Putting It All Together

If each level of the hierarchy is evaluated, it is possible to have a better understanding of the full effects of training.[15] Let's examine one of the items in the preceding list—a high grievance rate—as it relates to the training process and the four levels of evaluation.

The needs analysis determines that the high grievance rate is a function of supervisors not managing conflict well. Their knowledge is adequate, but their skills are deficient. From the needs analysis, data are obtained for later comparison with skill levels after training has been completed. Tools for evaluation are developed at this time, if they are not already available from the needs analysis. Training is provided, and then participants fill out a reaction questionnaire. This tool measures the degree to which trainees feel positive about the time and effort they have invested in the program and each of its components. Assume the responses are favourable. However, even though the trainees feel good about the training and believe that they learned valuable things, the trainer recognizes that the intended learning may not have occurred. A test of conflict management skill is administered and the results are compared with pre-training data. If the results show that the trainees acquired the conflict management skills and can use them appropriately, the learning objectives were achieved. Will these skills then transfer to the job so that the employees are using them in conflict situations? If we show that employees are using the skills, then the learning was transferred to the job. The next step is to examine the grievance rate. If it has declined, it is possible, with some level of confidence, to suggest that training is the cause of the decline. If it is determined that learning did not take place after training, it would not make sense to examine behaviour or results, because learning is a prerequisite.

Let's examine each of these four levels of evaluation more closely.

## Reaction Questionnaire

***What It Is.*** The data collected at this level are used to determine what the trainees thought about the training. Reaction questionnaires are often criticized, not because of their lack of value, but because they are often the only type of evaluation undertaken.[16]

Affective and utility are two types of reaction questionnaire.[17] An **affective questionnaire** measures general feeling about training ("I found this training enjoyable"), whereas the **utility questionnaire** reflects beliefs about the value of training ("This training was of practical value"). We focus here on the latter type because we believe that specific utility statements on reaction questionnaires are more valuable for making changes.

Training reaction questionnaires do not assess learning, but rather the trainees' attitudes about and perceptions of the training. A number of categories should be considered in developing a reaction questionnaire, including the training relevance, training content, materials, exercises, trainer(s) behaviour, and facilities.

**Training Relevance.** Asking trainees about the relevance (utility) of the training they experienced provides the organization with a measure of the perceived value of the training. If most participants do not see any value in it, they will experience difficulty remaining interested (much less consider applying it back on the job). Furthermore, this perceived lack of value can contaminate the program's image. Those who do not see its value will talk to others who have not yet attended training and will perhaps suggest that it is a waste of time. The self-fulfilling prophecy proposes that if you come to training believing that it will be a waste of time, it will be. Even if the training is of great importance to the organization, participants who do not believe it is important are not likely to work to achieve its objectives.

Once trainees' attitudes are known, steps can be taken to change the beliefs, either through a socialization process or a change in the training itself. Think about the Palm Desert case. What do you think the trainees' reactions to the training were? Might this source of information help to explain why no change in behaviour occurred?

**Training Materials and Exercises.** Any written materials, videos, exercises, and other instructional tools should be assessed along with an overall evaluation of the training experience. On the basis of responses from participants, it is possible to introduce modifications to the training to make it more relevant to participants. Making suggested modifications follows the organizational development principle of involving trainees in the process.

**Reactions to the Trainer.** Reaction questionnaires are also useful in determining how the trainees evaluated the trainer's actions. Care should be taken to develop statements that specifically address the trainer's actions. General statements tend to reflect trainees' feelings about how friendly or entertaining the trainer was (halo error) rather than how well the training was carried out. Simply presenting an affective statement such as "The trainer was entertaining," would likely elicit a halo response. For this reason, it is useful to identify specific aspects of trainer behaviour that need to be rated.

Asking about a number of factors important to effective instruction causes the trainees to consider how effective the instructor was in these areas. When the final question, "Overall, how effective was the instructor?" is asked, the trainees can draw upon their responses to a number of factors related to effective instruction. This consideration will result in a more accurate response as to the overall effectiveness of the instructor. There will be less halo error. Note that the questionnaire in Figure 8-1 asks the trainee to consider several aspects of the trainer's teaching behaviour before asking a more general question regarding effectiveness.

**Facilities and Procedures.** The reaction questionnaire can also contain items related to the facilities and procedures to determine whether any element impeded the training process. Noise, temperature, seating arrangements, and even the freshness of the

## FIGURE 8-1 Reaction Questionnaire for the Trainer

**Please circle the number that reflects the degree to which you agree or disagree with the following statements.**

1 = Strongly disagree
2 = Disagree
3 = Neither agree nor disagree
4 = Agree
5 = Strongly agree

| | | | | | |
|---|---|---|---|---|---|
| 1. The trainer did a good job of stating the objectives at the beginning of training. | 1 | 2 | 3 | 4 | 5 |
| 2. The trainer made good use of visual aids (easel, white board) when making the presentations. | 1 | 2 | 3 | 4 | 5 |
| 3. The trainer was good at keeping everyone interested in the topics. | 1 | 2 | 3 | 4 | 5 |
| 4. The trainer encouraged questions and participation from trainees. | 1 | 2 | 3 | 4 | 5 |
| 5. The trainer made sure everyone understood the concepts before moving on to the next topic. | 1 | 2 | 3 | 4 | 5 |
| 6. The trainer summarized important concepts before moving to the next module. | 1 | 2 | 3 | 4 | 5 |

7. Overall, how would you rate this trainer? (check one)

_____ 1. Poor—I would not recommend this trainer to others.
_____ 2. Adequate—I would recommend this trainer only if no others were available.
_____ 3. Average
_____ 4. Good—I would recommend this trainer above most others.
_____ 5. Excellent—This trainer is among the best I've ever worked with.

doughnuts are potential areas that can cause discontent. One way to approach these issues is to use open-ended questions, such as the following:

- Please describe any aspects of the facility that enhanced the training or created problems for you during training (identify the problem and the aspect of the facility).

- Please indicate how you felt about the following:

- Refreshments provided,

- Ability to hear the trainer and other trainees clearly, and

- Number and length of breaks.

Facility questions are most appropriate if the results can be used to configure training facilities in the future. The more things working in the trainer's favour, the more effective training is likely to be.

The data from a reaction questionnaire provide important information that can be used to make the training more relevant, the trainers more sensitive to their strengths and shortcomings, and the facilities more conducive to a positive training atmosphere. The feedback the questionnaire provides is more immediate than with the other levels of evaluation; therefore, modifications to training can be made much sooner.

***Timing of Reaction Assessment.*** The timing and type of questions asked on a reaction questionnaire should be based on the information needed for evaluating and improving the training, the trainer(s), the processes, or the facility. Most reaction questionnaires are given to participants at the conclusion of training, while the training is still fresh and the audience is captive. However, a problem with giving them at this time is that the participant may be anxious to leave and may give incomplete or less-than-valid data. Also, trainees may not know whether the training is useful on the job until they go back to the job and try it.

An alternative is to send out a reaction questionnaire at some point after training. This delay gives the trainee time to see how training works in the actual job setting. However, the trainee may forget the specifics of the training. Also, there is no longer a captive audience so response rate may be poor.

Another approach is to provide reaction questionnaires after segments of a training program or after each day in a multi-day training session. In such situations, it may be possible to modify training that is in progress on the basis of trainees' responses. Of course, this system is more costly and requires a quicker turnaround time for analysis and feedback of the data.

Regardless of how often reaction evaluation takes place, the trainer should specify at the beginning that trainees will be asked to evaluate the training and state when this evaluation will occur. It not only helps to clarify trainee expectations about what will happen during training but also acknowledges the organization's concern for how the trainees feel about the training. It is also important that the data gathered be used. Trainees and the rest of the organization will quickly find out if the trainer is simply gathering data only to give the impression of concern about their reactions. Figure 8-2 provides a list of steps to consider when developing a reaction questionnaire.

***Caution in Using Reaction Measures.*** A caution is in order regarding reaction questionnaires sent out to trainees some time after training querying them about the amount of transfer of training that has occurred on the job. Trainees tend to indicate that transfer has occurred when other measures suggest it did not.[18] Therefore reaction measures should not be the only evaluation method used to determine transfer of training.

Reaction questionnaires are not meant to measure learning or transfer to the job. They do, however, provide the trainees with the opportunity to indicate how they felt about the learning. How interesting the training is found to be will affect their level

---

**FIGURE 8-2    Steps to Consider in Developing a Reaction Questionnaire**

1. Determine what needs to be found out (consider learning objectives).
2. Develop a written set of questions to obtain the information.
3. Develop a scale to quantify respondents' data.
4. Make forms anonymous so participants will feel free to respond honestly.
5. Ask for information that might be useful in determining differences in reactions by subgroups taking the training (e.g., young vs. old; minority vs. non-minority). This could be valuable in determining effectiveness of training by different cultures, for example, which may be lost in an overall assessment. Note: Care must be taken when asking for this information. If you ask too many questions about race, gender, age, tenure, and so on, participants will begin to feel that they can be identified without their name on the questionnaire.
6. Allow space for "Additional Comments" in order to allow participants the opportunity to mention things you did not consider.
7. Decide the best time to give the questionnaire to get the information you want.
   a. If right after training, ask someone other than the instructor to administer and pick up the information.
   b. If some time later, develop a mechanism for obtaining a high response rate (e.g., encourage the supervisor to allow trainees to complete the questionnaire on company time).

of attention and motivation. What the trainees perceive the trainer to be doing well and not so well is also useful feedback for the trainer. This information can be used to make decisions about modifications to the training program.

**Learning** Learning objectives are developed from the TNA. The difference between the individual's KSAs and the KSAs required for acceptable job performance define the learning that must occur. The person analysis serves as the pre-training measure of the person's KSAs. These results can be compared with a post-training measure to determine whether learning has occurred and whether those changes can be attributed to training. The various ways of making such attributions will be discussed later in the chapter. As we noted, training can focus on three types of learning outcomes: knowledge, skills, and attitudes.

*Knowledge Outcomes.* If the goal of the training is to impart some sort of factual knowledge, such as "rules covering search and seizure" or "understanding the type of question that cannot be asked in an interview," a test can be developed to determine whether trainees acquired this knowledge. Paper-and-pencil tests such as the multiple-choice test are often used. Multiple-choice tests offer many advantages. They are easy to administer and score and, when skilfully developed, can accurately measure knowledge.[19] Some trainees indicate that they are not good at taking multiple-choice tests. However, evidence suggests that such tests consistently correlate highly with other forms of testing. A big advantage of multiple-choice tests is their reliability. Also, because of the number of questions that can be asked, it is possible to cover a broader range of the content than with other methods.

The major difficulty with this type of test is in the construction of the items. A complete discussion on how to write good multiple-choice questions is beyond the scope of this text, but some general rules to consider in constructing questions are found in Figure 8-3. More comprehensive information can be found in *Evaluating Training Programs,* a book published by the American Society for Training and Development.[20] It may be wise to contact a local university and discuss the project with someone who has the appropriate background. Even small companies with limited budgets should be able to obtain such help from a supervised graduate student eager to get some real-world experience.

*Skill-Based Outcomes.* Determining whether a skill or set of behaviours was learned is not the same as measuring whether it is used on the job. Obviously, if it is used on the job, it was learned. However, it may be learned but not used on the job.

---

## FIGURE 8-3    Procedures for Developing a Multiple-Choice Test

1. Examine objectives to gain a clear understanding of the content area you wish to test.
2. Write the questions in a clear manner. Shorter is better.
3. Choose alternatives to the correct response from typical errors made during training. Make alternatives realistic.
4. Do not consistently make the correct response longer than the incorrect responses.
5. Provide four options. More than four takes longer to read, and it is difficult enough to write three reasonable alternatives along with the correct answer.
6. Pre-test items by giving the test to those expected to know the material. Ask them for feedback on clarity. Note any questions that many of them get wrong.
7. Give revised items to a group of fully trained (experienced) employees and a group of untrained (inexperienced) employees. The former should score well and the latter should do poorly.

Knowing that the skill was learned is important, particularly if it does not transfer to the job. In this situation, the focus is on lack of transfer to the job and not a learning problem.

If the training being evaluated was in swimming, it is obvious that a paper-and-pencil test to determine the learning that has occurred is not appropriate. Similarly, if you wanted to evaluate the training of supervisors in interpersonal skills, a paper-and-pencil test could provide information regarding what the trainee understands about interpersonal skills, but it will not identify the trainee's actual interpersonal skills.

Developing behavioural tests and standards for scoring such tests can be difficult. A number of situations need to be created in which the trainee is required to demonstrate the target skill(s). The difficulty lies in developing scoring standards. Consider a study that examined the training of machinists.[21] It was noted that passing the training was more a function of the trainer who was running the course than of the trainees. Different trainers used different standards for passing.

To address this problem, a standardized method was needed to provide points based on criteria outlined in the training objectives. These criteria were based on tolerance requirements and finished specifications. These criteria, once developed, gave the trainers clear standards from which to evaluate, thereby eliminating trainer differences. For skills that have a specific output, such as a widget, assessment simply compares what was produced with what was required. For other skills, such as those required for conflict resolution, assessment could occur through the use of a structured scenario in which a person acts in an angry and aggressive manner and the trainee responds using the skills taught. These types of tests can be scored using multiple raters or standardized forms. Achieving inter-rater agreement is important in developing such tests. This consistency is accomplished through standardized methods of rating that are clear to the trainer or whoever is required to conduct the testing.

***Attitudes.*** As noted earlier, attitudes are an important outcome of training. At the conclusion of training, it is useful to assess any changes in attitudes that were learning objectives. Numerous attitude scales are available through journals (*Personnel*

## FIGURE 8-4    Example of an Attitudinal Measure

Attitudes Toward Empowerment
Please indicate the degree to which you agree or disagree with the following statements.

1 = Strongly disagree
2 = Disagree
3 = Neither agree nor disagree
4 = Agree
5 = Strongly agree

| | | | | | |
|---|---|---|---|---|---|
| 1. Empowering employees is just another way to get more work done with fewer people. [reverse scored] | 1 | 2 | 3 | 4 | 5 |
| 2. Empowering employees allows everyone to contribute their ideas for the betterment of the company. | 1 | 2 | 3 | 4 | 5 |
| 3. The empowerment program improved my relationship with my supervisor. | 1 | 2 | 3 | 4 | 5 |
| 4. Empowerment brought more meaning to my life at this company. | 1 | 2 | 3 | 4 | 5 |
| 5. Empowerment interventions should be introduced in other plants in this company. | 1 | 2 | 3 | 4 | 5 |
| 6. The empowerment process provided a positive influence in labour-management relations. | 1 | 2 | 3 | 4 | 5 |

*Psychology, Journal of Applied Psychology, Academy of Management Journal, Academy of Management Review, Academy of Management Executive*) and books (*Assessing Organizational Change, The Experience of Work, Buros Book of Mental Measurements*). Developing attitude scales requires care, and you should use existing scales whenever possible, rather than attempting to develop one yourself. However, items in the survey may need to be reworded to reflect the specific training being done.

Assessing true attitude change is difficult. The primary assessment tool is a pre/post-measure of responses on an attitude scale. A scale measuring "attitude toward empowerment" is depicted in Figure 8-4. A comparison of responses before and after training that indicates an increase in positive attitude toward empowerment would suggest successful training. However, some doubts arise about such self-report measures, particularly if the trainees are identified. The new employee might see the wisdom in hiding a dislike of team-based work after a concentrated orientation espousing the value of teams. Going to great lengths to assure respondents of their anonymity encourages honesty in trainee self-reports.

*Timing of Assessment of Learning.* Depending on the duration of training, it might be desirable to assess learning periodically to determine how trainees are progressing. Periodic assessment would allow training to be modified if learning is not progressing as expected.

Assessment should also take place at the conclusion of training. If learning is not evaluated until sometime later, it is impossible to know how much was learned and then forgotten.

In the Palm Desert case, the measures they took six months after training created a dilemma. Was the behaviour ever learned, learned but forgotten, or learned but not transferred to the job?

## Job Behaviour Data

Once it is determined that learning took place, the next step is to determine whether the training transferred to the job. Assessment at this step is certainly more complex and is often ignored because of the difficulties of measurement.

A number of methods can be used to assess job behaviour. These methods were covered in depth in the discussion of TNA in Chapter 3 and, in fact, the instrument used when conducting the needs assessment should serve well as the post-test evaluation tool. The primary sources of data are interviews, questionnaires, direct observation, and archival records of performance. Questionnaires are often preferred, for several reasons including:

- Opinions can be obtained about specific behaviours from a large number of employees;

- Information can be tabulated to yield a numerical response;

- Respondents are anonymous, so it is more likely that they will be honest; and

- Time to gather data is relatively short.

Since this method of evaluation is so common, it is important to understand how to develop effective questionnaires. Figure 8-5 provides some guidelines.

Performance appraisals can also be used to document job and performance changes. As was noted in Chapter 3, one useful technique is the 360-degree performance review. If a 360-degree appraisal is used annually, then trainees can examine their results after they receive training. Trainees can determine if they have improved by comparing their pre- and post-training results.

*Scripted Situations.* Some recent research indicates that scripted situations may provide a better format for evaluating transfer of training than the more traditional behavioural questionnaires.[22] Scripted situations help the rater to recall actual

The University of British Columbia School of Library, Archival and Information Studies: Research Methods on the WWW - Questionnaires *www.slais.ubc.ca/resources/ research_methods/ questions.htm*

---

## FIGURE 8-5    Guidelines for Writing an Effective Questionnaire

1. Write simply and clearly, and make the meaning obvious.
   **Bad:** To what extent do supervisors provide information regarding the quality of performance of people at your level?
   **Good:** How often does your boss give you feedback on your job?
2. Ask one question at a time.
   **Bad:** Both the organization's goals and my role within the organization are clear.
   **Good:** The organization's goals are clear.
   My role within the organization is clear.
3. Provide discrete response options.
   **Bad:** During the past three months how often did you receive feedback on your work?

   | 1 | 2 | 3 | 4 | 5 |
   |---|---|---|---|---|
   | Rarely | | Occasionally | | Frequently |

   **Good:** During the past three months how often did you receive feedback on your work?

   | 1 | 2 | 3 | 4 | 5 |
   |---|---|---|---|---|
   | Not once | 1–3 times | About once a week | More than once a week | Once a day or more |

4. Limit the number of response options.
   **Bad:** What percentage of the time are you sure of what your compensation will be?

   | 1 | 2 | 3 | 4 | 5 | 6 | 7 | 8 | 9 | 10 |
   |---|---|---|---|---|---|---|---|---|---|
   | 0%–10% | 11%–20% | 21%–30% | 31%–40% | 41%–50% | 51%–60% | 61%–70% | 71%–80% | 81%–90% | 91%–100% |

   **Good:** What percentage of the time are you sure of what your compensation will be?

   | 1 | 2 | 3 | 4 | 5 |
   |---|---|---|---|---|
   | 0%–20% | 21%–40% | 41%–60% | 61%–80% | 81%–100% |

5. Match the response mode to the question.
   **Bad:** To what extent are you satisfied with your job?

   | 1 | 2 | 3 | 4 | 5 |
   |---|---|---|---|---|
   | Strongly disagree | Disagree | | Agree | Strongly agree |

   **Good:** To what extent are you satisfied with your job?

   | 1 | 2 | 3 | 4 | 5 |
   |---|---|---|---|---|
   | Not at all | A little bit | | Quite a lot | Very much |

---

situations and the behaviours related to them, rather than attempting to recall specific behaviours without the context provided. The rater is provided with a number of responses that might be elicited from the script and is asked to choose the one that describes the ratee's behaviour. Research suggests that this method is useful in decreasing rating errors and improving validity.[23] An example of this method is depicted in Figure 8-6.

Finally, the trainer who includes coaching as a later part of training can observe on-the-job performance of the trainee. As was discussed in Chapter 4, these sit-ins facilitate transfer[24] and also help the trainer to determine the effectiveness of the training in facilitating the transfer of training to the job.

***Attitudes.*** If attitudinal change is a goal of training, the success of transfer and duration of the attitudinal change once the trainee is back on the job should be assessed. As discussed earlier, such attitudinal change can be assessed through attitude surveys. The same instruments used in the needs analysis and learning assessment can be used. If respondents' anonymity is ensured in such surveys, responses are more likely to reflect true attitudes.

## FIGURE 8-6 Scripted Situation Item for Evaluation of a School Superintendent

The following is a scenario regarding a school superintendent. To rate your superintendent, read the scenario and place an X next to the behaviour you believe your superintendent would follow.

The administrator receives a letter from a parent objecting to the content of the science section on reproduction. The parent strongly objects to his daughter being exposed to such materials and demands something be done. The administrator would most likely: (check one)

____ Ask the teacher to provide handouts, materials, and curriculum content for review.

____ Check the science curriculum for the board-approved approach to reproduction, and compare board guidelines with course content.

____ Ask the head of the science department for his or her opinion about the teacher's lesson plan.

____ Check to see whether the parent made similar complaints in the past.

A study of steward training provides an example of the assessment of an attitude back on the job.[25] Training was designed to make union stewards more accessible to the rank and file by teaching them listening skills and how to interact more with the rank and file. Results indicated that when factors such as tenure as a union official and age were controlled, stewards who received the training behaved in a more participative manner and were more loyal to the union. For the union, loyalty is important because it translates into important behaviours that might not be measured directly, such as supporting the union's political candidates and attending union functions.[26]

*Timing of Job Behaviour Assessment.* The wait time for assessing transfer of training depends on the training objectives. If the objective is to learn how to complete certain forms, simply auditing the work on the job before and after training would determine whether transfer took place. This could be done soon after training was complete. When learning objectives are more complex, such as learning how to problem solve or resolve conflict, wait time before assessment should be longer. The trainee will first need to become comfortable enough with the new behaviour to exhibit it on a regular basis; then it will take more time for others to notice that the behaviour has changed.

To understand this point, consider a more concrete change. Jack loses ten kilograms. First, the weight loss is gradual and often goes unnoticed. Even after Jack lost the weight, for some time people will say, "Gee, haven't you lost weight?" or "What is it that's different about you?" If this uncertainty about specific changes happens with a concrete visual stimulus, imagine what happens when the stimuli are less concrete and not consistent. Some types of behavioural change may take a long time to be noticed.

To help get employees to notice the change in behaviour, you can ask them to assess whether certain behaviours have changed. In our example, if asked, "Did Jack lose weight?" and he had lost ten kilograms, you would more than likely notice it then, even if you did not notice it before.

## Organizational Results

Training objectives, whether proactive or reactive, are developed to solve an organizational problem—perhaps an expected increase in demand for new customer services in the proactive case, or too many grievances in the reactive case. The fact that a problem was identified (too many grievances) indicates a measurement of the "organizational result." This measurement would be used to determine any change after the training was completed. If it was initially determined that too many defective parts were being produced, the measurement of the "number of defective parts per 100 produced" would be used again after training to assess whether training was successful. This assessment is your organizational result.

It is important to assess this final level because it is the reason for doing the training in the first place. In one sense, it is easier to measure than job behaviour. Did the grievances go down? Did quality go up? Did customer satisfaction go up? Did attitudes in the annual survey get more positive? Did subordinates' satisfaction with supervision improve? Such questions are relatively easily answered. The difficult question is "Are the changes a result of training?" Perhaps the grievance rate dropped because of recent successful negotiations and signing of a contract the union liked. Or if attitudes toward supervision improved but everyone recently received a large bonus, the improvement might be spill-off from the bonus and not the training. These examples explain why it is so important to gather information on all levels of the evaluation.

The links among organizational results, job behaviour, and trainee KSAs should be clearly articulated in the TNA. This creates a model that specifies that if certain KSAs are developed and the employees use them on the job, then certain organizational results will occur. The occurrence of these things validates the model and provides some confidence that training caused these results. Thus, the difficult task of specifying how training should affect the results of the organization is already delineated before evaluation begins. Since TNAs are not always as thorough as they should be, it often falls to the evaluator to clarify the relationship among training, learning, job behaviour, and organizational outcomes. For this reason, it is probably best to focus on organizational results as close to the trainee's work unit as possible. Results such as increased work unit productivity, quality, and decreased costs are more appropriate than increased organizational profitability, market share, and the like. Quantifying organizational results is not as onerous as it might seem at first glance.

*Timing of Assessment of Organizational Results.* Consistent tracking of the organizational performance gaps such as high scrap, number of grievances, or poor quality should take place at intervals throughout the training and beyond. At some point after the behaviour is transferred to the job, it is reasonable to expect improvement. Consistently tracking performance indices provides information as to whether or not improvements have taken place at some point after training is complete.

## Relationship Among Levels of Outcomes
As suggested earlier, research has not generally supported a relationship among these four levels of evaluation. For example, some studies show reaction and learning outcomes to be strongly related to each other.[27] Others indicate little correlation between results of reaction questionnaires and measures of learning.[28] As noted earlier, a good response to the reaction questionnaire may simply mean the trainer obtained the trainees' attention. This factor is only one of many in the learning process. The findings also indicate that the more removed from the actual training the outcome is, the smaller the relationship between higher- and lower-level outcomes. Figure 8-7 illustrates the hierarchical nature of the outcomes and the factors that can influence these outcomes.

The research showing no relationship between the levels makes sense if we remember that organizational outcomes generally are the result of multiple causes.[29] For example, productivity is affected not only by the employees' KSAs but also by the technology they work with, supplier reliability, interdependencies among work groups, and many other factors. Although improvements can occur in one area, declines can occur in another. When learning takes place but does not transfer to the job, the issues to be concerned with do not involve learning, but transfer. What structural constraints are being placed on trainees so they do not behave appropriately? Beverly Geber, special

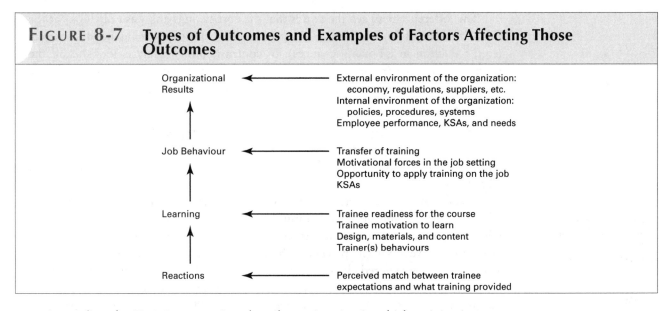

**FIGURE 8-7    Types of Outcomes and Examples of Factors Affecting Those Outcomes**

| | |
|---|---|
| Organizational Results ← | External environment of the organization: economy, regulations, suppliers, etc. Internal environment of the organization: policies, procedures, systems Employee performance, KSAs, and needs |
| Job Behaviour ← | Transfer of training Motivational forces in the job setting Opportunity to apply training on the job KSAs |
| Learning ← | Trainee readiness for the course Trainee motivation to learn Design, materials, and content Trainer(s) behaviours |
| Reactions ← | Perceived match between trainee expectations and what training provided |

projects editor for *Training* magazine, describes a situation in which training in communication skills at Hutchinson Technologies, a computer component manufacturer, was not transferring to the job for some of the employees.[30] An examination of the issue (through worker focus groups) disclosed that some employees were required to work in cramped space with poor lighting. These conditions made them irritable and unhappy. Did this situation affect their ability to communicate to their customers in a pleasant and upbeat manner? "You bet," said their human resource representative.

**Evaluating the Costs of Training** Looking at the outcomes of training is only half the battle in evaluating its effectiveness. The other half is determining whether the results were worth the cost. If the number of grievances goes down, the new behaviours are exhibited, and the skills were learned, then training might be considered the cause of the reduction, although cause-and-effect relationships are never a sure thing. The examination of all four levels of evaluation provides evidence of cause and effect, and appropriate designs enhance the level of confidence in cause and effect, but not to an absolute certainty. Many managers today still might ask, "So what? Was the training cost worth it?" This question can be answered in either of the following two ways:[31]

- Cost/benefit evaluation
- Cost-effectiveness evaluation

*Cost/Benefit Evaluation.* A **cost/benefit evaluation** of training compares the monetary cost of training with the non-monetary benefits. It is difficult to place a value on these benefits, which include attitudes and working relationships. The labour peace brought about by the reduction in grievances is difficult to assess but rates high in value compared with the cost of training. The conflict resolution skills learned by supervisors provide the non-monetary benefit of better relationships between supervisors and union officials, and this is important. However, it is also possible to assess the reduction in grievances (for example) in a way that directly answers the cost-effectiveness question.

**Cost/Benefit Evaluation** a method of evaluation that compares the actual costs of training with non-monetary benefits, such as a better relationship between management and non-management.

*Cost-Effectiveness Evaluation.* A **cost-effectiveness evaluation** compares the monetary costs of training with the financial benefits accrued from training. Two approaches can be used to assess cost effectiveness:

1. Cost savings, a calculation of the actual *cost savings*, based on the change in "results," and

2. Utility analysis, an examination of value of overall improvement in the performance of the trained employees.

**Cost-Effectiveness Evaluation** a method of evaluation that compares the monetary cost of training with the financial benefits accrued from training.

The difference between the two is that the cost savings analysis only looks at the financial value of improvement in the problem that training was intended to correct (e.g., reduction in labour grievances). In contrast, utility analysis looks at all the ways in which the trainee's improved job performance will financially benefit the organization (e.g., reduced grievances, improved relations with labour force, less turnover).

**Cost Savings Analysis (Results Focus).** The common types of costs associated with training programs were presented in Chapter 4, Table 4-4. These costs are compared with the savings that can be attributed to training. Let's look at Table 4-4 in Chapter 4.

**Cost Savings Analysis** a method of evaluation that compares the monetary cost of training with the financial benefits accrued from training, using only factors that training focused on correcting.

Recall that the cost of training was $32 430. Now, determine how much is saved when training is completed. To perform this **cost savings analysis,** we must first determine the cost of the current situation (see Table 8-3). The company averaged 90 grievances per year. Seventy percent of these (63) go to the third step before settlement. The average time required by management (including HR managers, operational supervisors, etc.) to deal with a grievance that goes to the third step is ten hours. The management wages ($50 per hour on average) add $500 to the cost of each grievance ($50 × 10). In addition, union representatives spend an average of 7.5 hours at $25 per hour and cost $187.50 for each grievance. This is because union representative wages are considered paid time as stipulated in the collective agreement. The total cost of wages to the company per grievance is $687.50. The total cost for those 63 grievances that go to the third step is $43 312.50. The cost of training is $32 430.00.

The data show a $37 812. 50 return on a $32 430 investment. Therefore, in the first year cost saving is $5382.50. Dividing the return by the investment produces a return-on-investment ratio of 1.16. If the ratio is exactly 1.0, the training broke even. If it is below that, it costs more than it returns to the company. In this case we calculate a 16 percent return on investment for the first year. Most companies would be delighted if all their investments achieved this level of return. In addition, the non-monetary benefits described earlier are also realized. Presenting this type of data to the corporate decision-makers at budget preparation time is certainly more compelling than stating, "Thirty supervisors were given a five-day grievance reduction workshop."

## TABLE 8-3  Cost Savings for Grievance Reduction Training

|  | Pre-training | Post-training |
|---|---|---|
| **Management Time** | | |
| (for those going to third step) 10 h per grievance | 10 h × 63 grievances = 630 h | 10 h. × 8 grievances = 80 h |
| **Union Reps Time** | | |
| (paid by management) 7.5 h per grievance | 7.65 h × 63 grievances = 472 h | 7.65 × 8 grievances = 60 h |
| **Total Cost** | | |
| Management time | 630 h × $50 per h = $31 500 | 80 h × $50 per h = $4 000 |
| Union reps time | 472 h × $25 per h = $11 812.50 | 60 h × $25 per h = $1 500 |
| Total | $43 312.50 | $5 500.00 |
| Reduction in cost of grievances going to the third step | | $43 312.50 – $5500.00 = $37 812.50 |
| Cost of training | | 32 430.00 |
| Cost saving for the first year | | $5 382.50 |

Many training departments are beginning to see the importance of placing a monetary value on their training for a number of reasons:[32]

- HRD budgets are more easily justified and even expanded when HR can demonstrate that it is contributing to the profit;

- HRD specialists are more successful in containing costs; and

- The image of the training department is improved by showing dollar value for training.

Recall Dave Palm from LensCrafters. Top management told him to demonstrate what they were getting in the way of "bang for the buck." Well, he did, and the result was that his training budget was doubled.[33] Training in Action 8-2 is a similar example. Here, Alberta Bell demonstrated the value of the training that prompted management not only to restore funding for the original training but also to consider increasing it.

Because of the time and effort required to calculate the value of training, many small business managers simply do not do it. However, assessing the value of training is not an exact science and can be done more easily by means of estimates. Table 8-4 on page 282 provides a simplified approach for small business.[34] When estimates are necessary in completing this form, it is useful to obtain them from those who will receive the report (usually top management). If you use their estimates, it is more likely that your final report will have credibility. Of course, larger organizations can also use this method.

**Utility Analysis.** In the previous example, training supervisors in grievance handling reduced the total number of grievances by 50 percent and the number going to the third step from 63 to 8. In this example we calculated only the cost savings related to the change in third-step grievances. **Utility analysis** permits us to estimate the overall value to the organization of the supervisors' changes in behaviour. In other words, if those trained are better performers, on average, and better performers are worth more in dollar terms, utility analysis allows us to estimate that increased worth. A general approach to utility is presented next:[35]

**Utility Analysis** a method of evaluation that compares the monetary cost of training with all the financial benefits accrued from the resulting change in behaviour.

$$\Delta U = (N)(T)(D_T)(SD_Y) - C$$

## Training in Action 8-2

### Reduction in Training Time: The Value of Demonstrating Value

Alberta Bell of Edmonton, Alberta, was looking for ways to reduce the cost of its operations. Downsizing and cost cutting were necessary to meet the new competitive environment. One of the decisions made was to reduce the entry-level training program for their customer service representatives from two weeks to one week. This would save a great deal of money by reducing the cost of training and getting service representatives out "earning their keep" sooner.

The manager of training decided to assess the value of this decision. By gathering information from data already available, he calculated the average time necessary to complete a service call for those who attended the two-week and one-week training program. Those from the two-week program completed a call on average in 11.4 minutes. Those in the one-week program took 14.5 minutes. This difference alone represented $50 000 in lost productivity for the first six weeks of work. He further analyzed the differences in increased errors, increased collectables, and service order errors. This difference was calculated at more than $50 000. The total loss exceeded $100 000.

He presented this information to upper management, who quickly restored the two-week training program and is considering making it longer.

*Source:* Adapted from Fitz-Enz, J. (1994). Yes you can weigh training's value. *Training,* July, pp. 54–58.

where

$\Delta U$ = dollar value of improved performance

$N$ = number of trainees

$T$ = time the benefits will last

$D_T$ = difference in performance between trained and untrained groups (in standard deviation units)

$SD_Y$ = dollar value of untrained group's performance (in standard deviation units)

$C$ = total cost of training the trained group

## TABLE 8-4    Training Investment Analysis Work Sheet

Objective: _____

Audience: _____

Returns measured over:_____ One year: _____

Other: _____

---

Part 1: Calculating the Revenue Produced by Training

Option A—Itemized Analysis

| Increased sales: | _____ | Additional sales per employee |
|---|---|---|
| × | _____ | Revenues (or margin) per sale |
| × | _____ | Number of employees |
| = | _____ | Revenue Produced by Training |

| Higher productivity: | _____ | Percent increase in productivity |
|---|---|---|
| × | _____ | Cost per employee (salary plus benefits plus overhead) |
| × | _____ | Number of employees |
| = | _____ | Revenue Produced by Training |

| Reduced errors: | _____ | Average cost per error |
|---|---|---|
| × | _____ | Number of errors avoided per employee |
| × | _____ | Number of employees |
| = | _____ | Revenue Produced by Training |

| Client retention: | _____ | Average revenue per client |
|---|---|---|
| × | _____ | Number of clients retained |
| = | _____ | Revenue Produced by Training |

| Employee retention: | _____ | Average cost of a new employee (training plus lost productivity) |
|---|---|---|
| × | _____ | Number of employees retained |
| = | _____ | Revenue Produced by Training |

Other: _____    _____

Total Revenue Produced by Training:

$_____

Option B—Summary Analysis

_____  −  _____  =  _____

Revenue          Revenue          Revenue

After            Without          Produced

Training         Training         by Training

Part 2: Calculating the Return

_____  −  _____  =  _____

Revenue          Cost of          Total Return

Produced         Training         on Training

by Training                       Investment

*Source:* Adapted from Hassett, J. (1992). Simplifying ROI. *Training,* September, pp. 53–57.

Some of the variables in the equation can be measured directly, whereas others must be estimated. For example, $N$, $C$, and $D_T$ can be determined objectively. However, determining how long the benefits will last is really an estimate that will be more or less accurate depending on the estimator's experience with training and the types of employees involved. Calculating the dollar value of the untrained group's performance falls somewhere in between. It is relatively easy to determine the compensation costs. However, it is often more difficult to translate their actual performance into dollar amounts. Recall our third-step grievance example. Even though we know what a third-step grievance costs in management labour compensation, we do not know the impact of those third-step grievances on the productivity of the work unit or the quality of the product/service. What is included in determining the dollar value of performance becomes a subjective decision. The final result will be an estimate of the value of the increased performance in dollars. Using the same example, an analysis of the possible utility is presented in Table 8-5.

Utility analysis is complex and beyond the scope of this text; what has been presented here is just a taste of the complexity. More-complex models account for even more factors that may affect the true financial value of training outcomes.[36] The purpose here is to demonstrate the difficulties of getting a true picture of the total financial benefits associated with training outcomes. However, these complexities exist for any area of the business when you try to determine the effects of change. By becoming more quantitative in the assessment and description of training outcomes, training managers can put themselves on an equal footing with other managers in the organization.

One important note regarding the use of utility methods for gaining support for the training program being promoted: Some recent research has indicated that utility is not an effective method for garnering support for human resource policies. In fact, the research concluded that using utility analysis to bolster the claim

## TABLE 8-5  Calculation of the Utility of the Grievance Training

Formula:    $\Delta U = (N)(T)(D_T)(SD_Y) - C$

$N = 30$

$T$ = 1 year (an overly conservative estimate)

$$D_T = 0.2 D_T = \frac{X_t - X_u}{SD(r_{yy})}$$

   $X_t$ = average job performance of the trained supervisors

   $X_u$ = average job performance of the untrained supervisors

   $SD$ = standard deviation of job performance for the untrained supervisors

   $r_{yy}$ = reliability of job performance measure

$D_T$ is a measure of the improvement (in standard deviation units) in performance that trained supervisors will exhibit. Although obtaining the data is time-consuming (collecting the performance appraisal data for supervisors, trained and untrained), the calculations can be done easily on using a computer.

$$SD_Y = \$14\,000 = 0.40 \times \$35\,000$$

The equation assumes average salary of \$35 000. The 0.40 comes from the 40% rule, which is a calculation based on 40% of the average salary of trainees. This rule comes from the Schmidt and Hunter research. This and other methods to calculate $SD_Y$ can be found in Cascio (1991). According to the preceding information, the utility of the training based on this formula is

$$(30)(1)(0.2)(14\,000) - 32\,020 = \$51\,980$$

*Sources:* Cascio, W. (1991). *Applied Psychology in Personnel Management*, 4th ed. Upper Saddle River, NJ: Prentice Hall; Schmidt, F., & Hunter, J. (1983). Individual differences in productivity: An empirical test of estimates derived from studies of selection procedure utility. *Journal of Applied Psychology* 68:407–14.

as to the value of a project actually decreased managerial support for the project.[37] Until it is clear why this tendency is the case, it may not be wise to use this particular type of analysis to sell a project. It may still be useful for showing the benefits after the fact.

**When to Use It** So do we compute a comprehensive evaluation at all four levels as well as a cost/benefit analysis for all training programs? No. To determine what evaluation should take place, ask the question "Who is interested in these data?" The different levels of outcome evaluation are designed for different constituencies or customers. Note in Table 8-6 that the trainer is interested in the first three levels, because they reflect most directly on the training. Other trainers may be interested in these data as well if the results show some relation to their training programs. Training managers are interested in all the information. Both reaction and learning data, when positive, can be used to evaluate the trainer and also promote the program to others. When the data are not positive, the training manager should be aware of this fact because it gives the trainer information to use to intervene and turn the program around. The training manager's interest in the transfer of training is to evaluate the trainer's ability to promote the transfer. Care must be taken in using this information because many other factors may be present and operating to prevent transfer. Also, if transfer is favourable, the information is valuable in promoting the training program. These generalizations are also true for the organizational results. If the training manager is able to demonstrate positive results affecting the financial health of the company, the training department will be seen as a worthy part of the organization.

Trainees are interested in knowing whether others felt the same as they did during training. They are also interested in feedback on what they accomplished (learning) as well as how useful it is to all trainees back on the job (behaviour). A trainee's supervisor is interested in behaviour and results, which is the main reason for sending subordinates to training in the first place. Upper management is interested in the results, although in cases where the results may not be forthcoming, behaviour may be the focus.

Does the interest in different levels of evaluation by different customers mean that you need to gather information at all levels every time? Not at all. First, a considerable amount of work is required to evaluate every program offered. As with process data, it makes sense to gather the outcome data in some situations and not in others.

### TABLE 8-6  Who Is Interested in the Outcome Data

| | Outcome Data | | | |
|---|---|---|---|---|
| | *Reaction* | *Learning* | *Behaviour* | *Results* |
| **Training Department** | | | | |
| Trainer | yes | yes | yes | no |
| Other Trainers | perhaps | perhaps | perhaps | no |
| Training Manager | yes | yes | yes | yes |
| **Customers** | | | | |
| Trainees | yes | yes | yes | perhaps |
| Trainees' Supervisor | not really | only if no transfer | yes | yes |
| Upper Management | no | no | perhaps | yes |

*Source:* Adapted from Camp, R. P., Blanchard, P. N., & Huszczo, G. E. (1986). *Toward a More Organizationally Effective Training Strategy and Practice.* Upper Saddle River, NJ: Prentice Hall.

Again, the obvious question to ask in this regard is, "What customer (if any) is interested in the information?' Although one of the major arguments for gathering the outcome data is to demonstrate the worth of the training department, some organizations go beyond that idea. In an examination of "companies with the best training evaluation practices," it was noted that none of these companies (IBM, Motorola, Arthur Andersen, etc.) were evaluating training primarily to justify it or maintain a training budget.[38] They evaluated (particularly at the behaviour and results levels) when requested to do so by the customer (top management or the particular department). This selectivity is a function of the cost in developing such evaluations because these type of evaluations:[39]

- Need to be customized for each situation,

- Are costly and time consuming, and

- Require cooperation from the customer.

Motorola, for example, evaluates only at the behavioural level, and not the results level. Executives at Motorola are willing to assume that if the employee is exhibiting the appropriate behaviour, the effect on the bottom line will be positive.[40] Training in Action 8-3 shows how various companies are dealing with evaluation, particularly behaviour and results.

Certainly all levels of data gathering are important at different times, and the training professional must be able to conduct an evaluation at every level. So, what and when should the trainer evaluate? The answer is that it depends on the organization and the attitudes and beliefs of upper management. If they perceive the training department as an effective tool of the organization and require only behaviour-level evaluation, that is the evaluation to do.

# Training in Action 8-3

## *Evaluation: What Companies Are Doing*

Motorola developed a 360-degree performance appraisal process that they used as their behaviour measure of leadership skills. The appraisal form is sent to the supervisors, their subordinates, and their bosses four times a year for two years and asks them to rate how frequently the supervisors display certain behaviours related to the leadership training (Geber, 1995).

Texas Instruments noted that once trainees left training, it was difficult to obtain transfer of training information from them. It was generally ignored because of the time and expense of gathering this information. Then an automated e-mail system was developed through which trainees, after being back on the job for 90 days, were contacted and asked to complete a survey related to transfer. This system increased the use of evaluations, reduced the time necessary to gather information, and provided a standardized process. Texas Instruments noted

an improvement in the quantity and quality of participant feedback. It would seem easy enough to include an e-mail to the trainees' supervisors for the same purpose (Overmyer-Day and Benson, 1996).

FPL Nuclear uses testing to assess learning. First, however, the testing serves as the needs analysis to determine who needs the training. Second, it is used as a post-test to be compared with the pre-test to assess learning. Finally, the test is administered a few months after training to assess the degree of retention. If trainees do not do well on the retention test, they are provided with refresher training (Dixon, 1996).

*Sources:* Dixon, N. (1996). New routes to evaluation. *Training and Development,* May, pp. 82–85; Geber, B. (1995). Does your training make a difference? *Training,* March, pp. 27–34; Overmyer-Day, D., & Benson, G. (1996). Training success stories. *Training and Development,* June, pp. 24–29.

However, this level may still require vigilance at the learning and reaction levels to ensure positive results. Darryl Jinkerson, director of evaluation services at Arthur Andersen, looks at the size and impact of the training before deciding how to evaluate it. Only those that are high profile, or for which the customer requests it, will be evaluated at the results level.[41] What if training is a one-time event and no desire is indicated to assess individual competence (e.g., a workshop on managing your career)? Such a situation provides simply no reason to evaluate.[42]

# EVALUATION: THE VALIDITY ISSUES

Once it is decided to evaluate training, it is important to be reasonably sure that the findings on the effectiveness of training will be valid. After all, evaluation is both time-consuming and costly.

Let's say Sue is sent to a one-week training seminar on the operation of Windows. According to the needs analysis, she clearly did not know much about how to operate a computer in a Windows environment. After training, she is tested and it is determined that she learned a great deal. Training was effective. Perhaps—but a number of other factors could also result in her learning how to operate in a Windows environment. Her own interest in Windows might lead her to learn it on her own. The question is: "How certain is it that the improvement was a function of the training that you provided?" In other words, does the evaluation exhibit internal validity? Once internal validity is ensured, the next question is "Will the training be effective for other groups who go through the same training?" That is, does training show external validity? We will deal with internal and external validity separately. These "threats" are not specific to training evaluation, but relate to evaluation in general. When we discuss each of the threats, we will indicate when it is not a serious threat in the training context.

## INTERNAL VALIDITY

**Internal Validity** the confidence that the results of the evaluation are, in fact, correct.

**Internal validity** refers to confidence that the results of the evaluation are in fact correct. Even when an improvement is demonstrated after training, the concern is that perhaps the change occurred for reasons other than training. To address this problem, it is necessary to examine factors that might compromise the findings; these are called threats to internal validity.

**History** changes noted in the evaluation of training could be because of other factors that took place concurrent with the training.

**History** History refers to events other than training that take place concurrently with the training program. The argument is that those other events caused learning to occur. Consider the example of Sue's computer training. Sue is eager to learn about computers so she buys some books and works extra hard at home, as well as attending the training. At the end of training she demonstrates that she has learned a great deal, but is this learning a function of training? It might just as well be that all her hard work at home caused her to learn so much.

In a half-day training seminar, is history likely to be a concern? Not really. What about a one-day seminar or a one-week seminar? The more that training is spread across time, the more likely history could be a factor in the learning that takes place.

**Maturation** changes noted in the evaluation of training could be because of other factors related to the passage of time, such as growing older, hungrier, fatigued, bored.

**Maturation** Maturation refers to changes that occur because of the passage of time (e.g., growing older, hungrier, fatigued, bored). If Sue's one-week training program was so intense that she became tired, when it came time to take the post-training test her performance would not reflect how much she has learned. Making sure that the testing is done when trainees are fresh reduces this threat. Other maturation threats can usually be handled in a similar manner, by being sure that training and testing are not so intense as to create physical or mental fatigue.

## Testing

What is the influence of **testing** on learning? Suppose the pre-test and post-test of the KSAs are the same test. The questions on the pre-test could sensitize trainees to pay particular attention to certain issues. Furthermore, the questions might generate interest, and the trainees might later discuss many of them and work out the answers before or during training. Thus, learning demonstrated in the post-test may be a function not of the training, but of the pre-test. In Sue's case, the needs analysis that served as the pre-test for evaluation got her thinking about all the material contained in the test. Then she focused on these issues in training. This situation presents less of a validity problem if pre-tests are given in every case and if they are comprehensive enough to cover all of the material taught. Comprehensive testing will also make it difficult for trainees to recall specific questions.

**Testing** changes noted in the evaluation of training could be because of the pre-test providing clues as to what to look for in training.

## Instrumentation

The problem arising if the same test is used in the pre-test and post-test was already noted. If a different but equivalent test is used, however, the question becomes "Is it really equivalent?" Differences in **instrumentation** used could cause differences in the two scores. Also, if the rating requires judgments, the differences between pre- and post-test scores could be a function of different people doing the rating.

For Sue, the post-test was more difficult than the pre-test, and even though she learned a great deal in the computer training, her post-test score was actually lower than the pre-test, suggesting that she did not learn anything. If the test items for both tests were chosen randomly from a large population of items, it would not be much of a concern. For behavioural tests where raters make subjective decisions, this discrepancy may be more of a concern, but careful criteria development can help to deal with it.

**Instrumentation** changes noted in the evaluation of training could occur because the post-test is not really the same as the pre-test; they are not equivalent.

## Statistical Regression

The tendency is for those who score either very high or very low on a test to "regress to the middle" when taking the test again. This phenomenon, known as regression to the mean, occurs because no test is perfect and differences result as a function of measurement error. Those who are going to training will, by definition, score low for the KSAs to be covered in training and so will score low on their pre-test. The tendency, therefore, will be for them to regress to the mean and improve their scores, irrespective of training. In the earlier example, Sue did not know much about computers. Imagine that she got all the questions on the pre-test wrong. The likelihood of that happening twice is very low, so on another test she is bound to do better.

This threat to internal validity can be controlled through various evaluation designs that we will discuss later. In addition, the use of control groups and random assignment (when possible) goes a long way toward resolving **statistical regression**.

**Statistical Regression** changes noted in the evaluation of training could occur because trainees had such low scores in the pre-test that they improved, simply because getting worse was almost impossible; they regressed to the mean.

## Initial Group Differences (Selection)

In some cases, in order to provide an effective evaluation, a comparison is made between the trainees and a similar group of employees who were not trained—known as the control group. It is important that the control group be similar in every way to the training group. Otherwise, the inherent differences between the groups may be the cause of differences after the training. Suppose that those selected for training are the up-and-coming stars of the department. After training, they may in fact perform much better than those not considered up and coming, but the problem is that they were better from the start and more motivated to improve. So if Sue is one of the highly motivated trainees, as are all her cohorts in training, they would potentially perform better even without training.

This problem does not arise if everyone is to be trained. The solution is simply to mix the two types so both the group to be trained and the control group contain both types.

## Loss of Group Members (Mortality)

In this situation, those who did poorly on the pre-test are demoralized because of their low score and soon drop out of training. The control group remains intact. As a result, the trained group does better in the post-test than the control group because the poorer-scoring members left the trained group, artificially raising the average score. The opposite could occur if, for some reason, members of the control group dropped out.

This situation becomes more of a problem when the groups are made up of volunteers. In an organizational setting, those who go to training are unlikely to drop out. Also, all department members who agree to be in the control group are a captive audience and are unlikely to refuse to take the post-test. Although some transfers and terminations do occur to affect the numbers of participants, they are usually not significant.

## Diffusion of Training

When trainees interact with the control group in the workplace, they may share the knowledge or skill they are learning. For example, when Sue is back in the office, she shows a few of the other administrative assistants what she has learned. They are in the control group. When the post-test is given, they do as well as the trained group because they were exposed to much of what went on in training. In this case, training would be seen as ineffective, when in fact it was effective. This would be especially true if certain quotas of trainees were selected from each department. When such sharing of information reduces differences between the groups in this way, determining the effectiveness of the training could be difficult.

## Compensating Treatments

When the control group and training group come from different departments, administrators may be concerned that the control group is at an unfair disadvantage. Comments such as "Why do they receive the new training?" or "We are all expected to perform the same, but they get the help" would suggest that the control group feels slighted. To compensate for this inequity, the managers of the control group's department might offer special assistance or make special arrangements to help their group. For example, let's look at trainees who are learning how to install telephones more efficiently. Their productivity begins to rise, but because the supervisors of the control group feel sorry for the control group, they help them to get their work done, thereby increasing their productivity. The evaluation would show no difference in productivity between the two groups after training is complete.

## Compensatory Rivalry

If the training is being given to one particular intact work group, the other intact work group may see this situation as a challenge and compete for higher productivity. Although the trained group is working smarter and improving its productivity, the control group works harder still and perhaps equals the productivity of the trainees. The result is that although the training is effective, it will not show up in the evaluation.

## Demoralized Control Group

The control group could believe that it was made the control group because it was not as good as the training group. Rather than rivalry, the response could be to give up and actually reduce productivity. As a result, a difference between the two groups would be identified, but it would be a function of the drop in productivity and not the training. Even if training were effective, the test results would be exaggerated.

These threats to validity indicate the importance of tracking the process in the evaluation. Just as data are gathered about what is occurring in the training, it is also useful to gather data about what is going on with the control group.

# EXTERNAL VALIDITY

The evaluation must be internally valid before it can be externally valid. If evaluation indicated that training was successful, and threats to internal validity were minimal, you would believe that the training was successful for that particular group. The next question is "Will the training be effective for the rest of the employees slated to attend training?" **External validity** is the confidence that these findings will generalize to others who undergo the training. A number of factors threaten external validity.

**External Validity** the confidence that the results of the evaluation are generalizable to other groups of trainees.

<u>Testing</u> If the training is evaluated initially by means of pre- and post-tests, and if future training does not use the pre-test, it can be difficult to conclude that future training would be as effective. Perhaps those in the initial training focused on particular material because it was highlighted in the pre-test. If the pre-test is then not used, other trainees will not have the same cues. The solution is simple: Pre-test everyone taking the training. Remember that pre-test data can be gathered during the needs analysis.

<u>Selection</u> Suppose that a particular program designed to teach communication skills is highly effective with middle-level managers, but when a program with the same design is given to shop-floor workers, it does not work. Why? It may be differences in motivation or in entering KSAs, but the important thing to remember is that you cannot be sure a training program that was successful with one group of trainees will be successful with all groups. Once it is successful with middle managers, it can be assumed that it will be successful with other, similar middle managers, but if it is to be used to train entry-level accountants, you could not say with confidence that it would be successful (that it had external validity) until it was evaluated.

One of the authors was hired to assist in providing team skills to a large number of employees in a large manufacturing plant. The first few sessions with managers went reasonably well; the managers seemed to be involved and learned a great deal. After about a month, training began for the blue-collar workers, using the identical processes that included a fair amount of theory. It soon became evident that trainees were bored, confused, and uninterested. In a discussion about the problem, the project leader commented, "I'm not surprised—this program was designed for executives." In retrospect, it is surprising that lower-level managers received the training so well, given that it was designed for executives.

<u>Reaction to Evaluation</u> In many situations, once the training is determined to be effective, the need for further evaluation is deemed unnecessary. Thus, some of the trainees who went through the program were evaluated and some were not. The very nature of evaluation causes more attention to be given to those who are evaluated. Recall the Hawthorne Studies that indicated the power of evaluation in an intervention. The Hawthorne Effect is explained by the following:[43]

- The trainees perceived the training as a novelty;
- The trainees felt themselves to be special because of being singled out for training;
- The trainees received specific feedback on how they were doing;
- The trainees knew they were being observed, so they wanted to perform to the best of their ability; and
- The enthusiasm of the instructor inspired the trainees to perform at a high level.

Whatever the mechanism, those who receive more attention may respond better as a function of that attention. As with the other threats to external validity, when the way groups are treated is changed, the training's external validity is jeopardized.

**Multiple Techniques** In clinical studies, a patient receives Dose A. It does not have an effect, so a month later she receives Dose B, which does not have an effect, so she receives Dose C and is cured. Did Dose C cure her? Perhaps, but it could also be that it was the combination of A, B, and C that resulted in the required effect. The use of multiple techniques could influence training when some component of the training is changed from one group to the next. For example, a group received one-on-one coaching and then video instruction. The members did poorly after receiving the coaching but excelled after receiving the video instruction, so video instruction became the method used to train future employees. It was not successful, however, because it was the combination of coaching and video instruction that resulted in the initial success.

## WHAT DOES IT ALL MEAN?

It is useful to have an understanding of the preceding issues in order to recognize why it is difficult ever to suggest with certainty that training or any other intervention is the cause of any improvement. We cannot be absolutely certain about the internal or external validity when measuring things such as learning, behaviour, and organizational results. Careful consideration of these issues, however, and the use of well-thought-out designs for the evaluation can improve the likelihood that training, when shown to be effective, is in fact effective (internal validity) and will be effective in the future (external validity). This information is useful for assessing training and, equally important, helps assess evaluations of outside vendors.

# EVALUATION DESIGN ISSUES

A number of texts provide excellent information on appropriate designs for conducting evaluations.[44] Unfortunately, many of their recommended designs are impractical in most organizational settings. Finding the time or resources to create a control group is difficult at best. Getting approval to do pre-tests on control groups takes away from productivity time and is difficult to justify.

Scientifically valid research designs are difficult to implement, so organizations often use evaluation designs that are generally not acceptable to the scientific community.[45] However, it is still possible to have some confidence in the results with less-rigorous designs. Some research designs are less than perfect, but it is possible to find ways of improving them. The two designs most often used, and most criticized by scientists, are the post-test only and the pre-test/post-test methods.[46]

## BASIC DESIGNS

**Post-Test Only** The post-test-only method occurs if training is provided (represented by X) and then a post-test is given (represented by $T_2$). The design is represented as $X\ T_2$.

Some problems with the post-test-only design mean that in certain instances, it is not a recommended choice. At other times, however, the method is completely acceptable.[47] The two possible goals of evaluation are

1. To determine whether change took place; and
2. To determine whether a level of competence was reached.

If the goal of the training is the latter, a post-test-only design should suffice. If, for example, legal requirements state that everyone in the company who handles hazardous waste be trained to understand what to do in an emergency, then presumably any training developed need only provide a test at the end to confirm that all trainees reached the required level of knowledge. As more companies are required to be ISO 9000 (or equivalent) certified, it will be increasingly important to prove that employees possess the required skills. As a result, certification will become the goal of employee training, and in that case the post-test only will suffice.

We frequently mention the value in doing a needs analysis. Conducting a needs analysis provides pre-test data, making the post-test-only design moot. Giving the post-test automatically applies a pre-test/post-test design. Furthermore, in the absence of a TNA, archival data may serve as the pre-test. Performance appraisals, measures of quality, and the like, might allow for some pre/post comparison. Although such historical data may not be ideal, it could provide some information as to the effectiveness of training. Alternatively, it is possible to identify an equivalent group and provide its members with the same post-test, thereby turning the design into a post-test only with control group. Suddenly, a much more meaningful design is created.

The post-test-only design as it stands is problematic for assessing change. A number of other competing causes could be responsible for the change, as noted in Table 8-7. Nevertheless, we would agree with other professionals that any evaluation is better than none.[48] Gathering any pre-training information that might suggest that the level of KSAs prior to training was lower than in the post-test would help to bolster the conclusion that training was effective.

## Pre-Test/Post-Test

The pre-test/post-test design is the other method organizations frequently use. Here, a pre-test is given $(T_1)$, training is provided $(X)$, and then a post-test is given $(T_2)$. This design is expressed as $T_1 \, X \, T_2$.

This design can demonstrate that change has occurred. But even though it can be demonstrated that KSAs have changed, it is not possible to say that training is responsible for those changes. There are a number of threats to validity (see Table 8-7). For example, you may have been training a group of machine operators to operate new drill-press machines. Pre-testing the trainees revealed that none knew how to operate the machine. After a three-day training session, a post-test showed that, on average, the trainees were able to operate the machine correctly 85 percent of the time. A big success? Not if the supervisor of the work group says that the ones without training can operate the machines correctly 95 percent of the time by just reading the manuals and practising on their own. A variety of reasons might explain why those who did not go to training are performing better on the job. Perhaps they already knew how to operate the machine. Perhaps a manufacturer's representative came and provided on-the-floor training to them. Or it could be that your training somehow slowed down the learning process. Therefore, it would be useful to have a control group.

In many instances, using a control group is simply not an option. Does that mean that the trainer should not bother to do anything? Absolutely not. In fact, it is better to do something than nothing. We tend to focus on the negative aspects of the pre-experimental designs rather than to examine ways of using them most effectively when other options do not exist.[49] The pre/post-no-control group at least establishes that changes did take place. History can be examined through some detective work. Recall that Sue had learned a great deal about operating in a Windows environment according to the pre/post-test. Did she do extra reading at home? Did she practise on her own irrespective of training expectations? Did she get some help from someone at the office or elsewhere? Simply asking her might indicate that none of those factors occurred, suggesting that it was in fact the training. This process may be particularly relevant for the small business, where size makes it easier to identify potential threats.

## TABLE 8-7 Sources of Invalidity

| Techniques | Internal | | | | | | | | External | | | |
|---|---|---|---|---|---|---|---|---|---|---|---|---|
| | History | Maturation | Testing | Instrumentation | Regression | Selection | Mortality | Interaction of Selection and Maturation | Testing | Selection | Relative to Evaluation | Multiple Techniques |
| Post-test Only (no control group) | – | – | | | | – | – | | | – | | |
| Pre-test/Post-test (no control group) | – | – | – | – | ? | + | + | – | – | – | ? | |
| Post-test Only (with control group) | + | + | + | + | + | + | + | + | + | ? | ? | |
| Pre-test/Post-test (with control group) | + | + | + | + | + | + | + | + | – | ? | ? | |
| Time Series Design | – | + | + | ? | + | + | + | + | – | ? | ? | |

*Note:* In the tables, a minus indicates a definite weakness, a plus indicates that the factor is controlled, a question mark indicates a possible source of concern, and a blank indicates that the factor is not relevant.

It is with extreme reluctance that these summary tables are presented because they are apt to be "too helpful" and to be depended upon in place of the more complex and qualified presentation in the text. No + or – indicator should be respected unless the reader comprehends why it is placed there. In particular, it is against the spirit of this presentation to create uncomprehended fears of, or confidence in, specific designs. These tables are based on random assignment and we suggest that representative sampling is more appropriate when the small numbers are used as in organizational training. So for each of these designs, assume the representative sampling results in true equivalence of the group.

*Source:* Adapted from Campbell, D. T., & Stanley, J. C. (1963). *Experimental and Quasi-Experimental Designs for Research.* Chicago: Rand McNally.

<u>**Internal Referencing Strategy**</u> Another way of dealing with the lack of a control group is to use the **internal referencing strategy (IRS)**.[50] With this method, include both relevant and non-relevant test questions in the pre- and post-test. Here's how it works.

Both pre-tests and post-tests contain questions that deal with the training content as well as questions that deal with related content not in the training. In the pre-test, trainees will do poorly on both sets of questions. In the post-test, if training is effective, improvement should only be shown for the trained items. The non-relevant items serve as a control. In their research on the IRS, Haccoun and Hamtiaux noted that the results obtained from the IRS design were identical to those obtained when a control group was used.[51] This method deals with many of the concerns that arise when a control group is used, as well as several other concerns. Many of the threats to internal validity do not exist with the IRS because with no control group to react in an inappropriate manner, issues such as diffusion of training, compensatory treatment, and compensatory rivalry are not a concern. The only threats are history, maturation, testing, statistical regression, and instrumentation.

As previously noted, history can be investigated through examination of the time frame in which training has occurred. Any events that potentially affected the trainees could be assessed as to their impact. Also, given that the relevant and non-relevant items are similar in nature in the IRS, any historical event should affect both types of items in a similar manner. Maturation issues can be dealt with by ensuring that the training is designed to keep trainees interested and motivated, and to prevent them from becoming tired or fatigued. The reactive effect of testing can be dealt with if parallel tests are used. Parallel tests cover the same content but do not use identical questions. This technique does lead to another potential problem (instrumentation) that can be addressed. If all trainees receive a comprehensive pre-test, then instrumentation is not an issue.

Instrumentation is a concern if two different tests are used. If a large pool of items is developed from which test items can be chosen at random, the result should be equivalent tests. Once again, it is important to note that in any evaluation, we can never be 100 percent sure that training has caused the improvement. We are not suggesting that this design take the place of more stringent designs when they are practical. It is appropriate, however, when the alternative is post-test only or nothing. Again, some control is better than none at all.

One final note: The IRS design can be used to determine improvement in KSAs, but research indicates that it tends to show that training is not effective when, in fact, it is.[52] In other words, the training must provide a substantial improvement from pre-test to post-test in order for it to be detected by this design.

## MORE COMPLEX DESIGNS

Two factors need to be considered when developing a sound evaluation design:

1. Control groups
2. Random assignment

The **control group** is a group of similar employees who do not receive the training. The control group is used to determine whether changes that take place in trainees also take place for those who do not receive training. If change occurs only in the trainees, it is probably a result of training. If it occurs in both trained and untrained groups, it is probably a result of some other factor.

**Internal Referencing Strategy (IRS)** a way of dealing with the lack of a control group, in which both relevant and non-relevant test questions in the pre- and post-tests are included.

**Control Group** a group of similar employees who do not receive the training.

**Random Assignment** placement
of employees in either the control
group or the training group by
chance in order to ensure that the
groups are equivalent.

**Representative Sampling**
matching employees in the control group and training group on a
number of factors such as age,
tenure, and education to make the
groups as equivalent as possible.

**Random assignment** is the placement of employees in either the control group or the training group by chance in order to ensure that the groups are equivalent. Random assignment is more applicable to experimental laboratories than to applied settings (such as in training) for two reasons. First, given the small number of employees placed in one group or the other, the theory of randomness is not likely to hold true. When we split a group of 60 employees into two groups of 30, it is quite likely that real differences will be present within the two groups. Random assignment works well when multiple groups of 30 are used, or when the total number of subjects is quite large (e.g., 500).

Second, it is unlikely that the organization can afford the luxury of randomly assigning employees to each group. The work still needs to be done, and managers would want some control over who will be in training at a specific time. For this reason, finding the best match of employees is important so that the control group contains a representative sample of employees who are in the training group. **Representative sampling** is matching employees in the control group and training group on a number of factors such as age, tenure, and education to make the groups as equivalent as possible. The following discussion covers a number of designs that use control groups. We believe that assigning trainees through representative sampling is a more effective way of obtaining equivalent groups.

## Post-Test Only with Control Group

The following represents post-testing only with a control group:

Trainee Group (representative sampling) X $T_2$

Control Group (representative sampling)    $T_2$

This design and the following one are equivalent in terms of internal validity (see Table 8-7).

If for some reason a pre-test was not conducted or if the trainer did not provide a pre-test to a control group at the beginning of training, the trainees can be compared with a control group using a post-test-only design. Differences in test scores noted between the groups, if trainees do better, provide evidence of the success of the training. The tendency is to downplay the effectiveness of this design because no pre-test assessed the equivalence of the groups before training. But if representative sampling has resulted in the groups being equivalent, there is no need to have a pre-test. Of course there is greater confidence regarding the equivalence of the groups if there was a pre-test.

## Pre-Test/Post-Test with Control Group

The expression for pre-test/post-test with a control group is:

Trainee Group (representative sampling) $T_1$ X $T_2$

Control Group (representative sampling) $T_1$    $T_2$

This design is one of the more favourable for eliminating threats to internal validity (see Table 8-7). Recall that we do not use random assignment in dividing the groups. So how equivalent are they? A pre-test can determine their level of equivalence. Equivalent pre-tests in both groups provide you with one more piece of evidence that the groups are equal, and post-test differences (if the trained group obtains higher scores) will suggest that training was successful.

## Time Series Design

The time series design is represented by:

Trainee Group    $T_1$  $T_2$  $T_3$  $T_4$  X  $T_5$  $T_6$  $T_7$  $T_8$

This design uses a series of measurements before and after training. In this way, the likelihood of internal validity threats such as testing or regression to the mean is minimized. Also, when everyone attends training at the same time (a one-shot training program), this design can be used whether the number is large or small. In such a case it could still be argued that with no control group, there are alternative reasons for any change. But in an applied setting the goal is to be as sure as possible about the results, given organizational constraints. If enough measures are taken pre- and post-training to deal with fluctuations in performance, changes after training are certainly suggestive of learning. Remember that in an applied setting there will never be absolute certainty regarding the impact of training, but taking care to use the best possible design (considering constraints) is still better than doing nothing at all.

To make this design more powerful, consider adding a control group, expressed by:

Trainee Group    $T_1$  $T_2$  $T_3$  $T_4$  X  $T_5$  $T_6$  $T_7$  $T_8$

Control Group    $T_1$  $T_2$  $T_3$  $T_4$     $T_5$  $T_6$  $T_7$  $T_8$

## Multiple Baseline Design
Multiple baseline design is represented by:

Trainee Group A    $T_1$  $T_2$  $T_3$  X  $T_4$  $T_5$  $T_6$  $T_7$  $T_8$  $T_9$  $T_{10}$

Trainee Group B    $T_1$  $T_2$  $T_3$  $T_4$  $T_5$  X  $T_6$  $T_7$  $T_8$  $T_9$  $T_{10}$

Trainee Group C    $T_1$  $T_2$  $T_3$  $T_4$  $T_5$  $T_6$  $T_7$  X  $T_8$  $T_9$  $T_{10}$

Trainee Group D    $T_1$  $T_2$  $T_3$  $T_4$  $T_5$  $T_6$  $T_7$  $T_8$  $T_9$  X  $T_{10}$

In this design, multiple measures are taken much as in time series, but each group receives the training at a different time. Each untrained group serves as a control for the trained groups. This approach deals with many of the concerns when no control group is used. Here the ability to say that changes measured by the test are a result of the training is strong. If each group improves after training, it is difficult to argue that something else caused the change.

## WHAT DESIGN TO USE

Determining the true impact of training requires an investigation into the validity of evaluation results. A number of methods are available, and the more complex the design, the more valid the results. Other considerations need to be taken into account when you are deciding on an evaluation design. Innovation can provide good substitutes when the best is not possible. Consider the multiple baseline design. It is a powerful design and certainly is a possibility if a number of employees need to receive the training over time.

However, what if multiple measures are not possible? The following design would address many of the same concerns, and although it is not as elaborate, it certainly deals with many of the concerns regarding outside influences causing the change. If pre-test scores are all comparable, and post-test scores indicate an improvement, these results are a strong argument for showing that training was responsible.

Trainee Group A   $T_1$ X $T_2$

Trainee Group B            $T_1$ X $T_2$

Trainee Group C                     $T_1$ X $T_2$

Trainee Group D                              $T_1$ X $T_2$

We have already mentioned that most organizations do not evaluate all training at all levels. Furthermore, even when evaluating training, many organizations do not use pre-test/post-test or control groups in a manner that would eliminate concerns about the validity of the results.

Dr. Dixon of George Washington University indicated that, of the companies she investigated in her article "New Routes to Evaluation," only one used designs that would deal with many of the validity issues. Other companies, including IBM and Johnson Controls, follow such procedures only when asked by particular departments or higher-level management, or when they can defray some of the high cost of developing reliable and valid tests by marketing the final product to other organizations.[53] The demand for certification in some skills (primarily because of ISO and others' requirements) created a need for these types of tests.

When you are evaluating training, if using control groups or pre-testing is not possible, remember that other investigative methods can be used for assessing the likelihood that factors other than training account for any change in KSAs.

# WHAT ABOUT SMALL BUSINESS?

For the small-business owner, sending employees to training that is not effective could significantly affect the company's financial health. Consider the owner who is constantly terminating employees because they are unable (or unwilling) to do the job properly. They all receive training and most, but not all, turn out to be ineffective. Why? If training is not evaluated, it is not possible to know whether employees are lost because the training is not effective or because of some other factor that is blocking effective performance.

The small-business owner might think it is not necessary to evaluate training because whether or not it was effective will be obvious by changes observed on the job after training. Actually, this assessment is probably true; in a small business, it would soon be evident if recently trained employees were performing at the expected level. However, if training is a significant cost to the owner, evaluating learning before and after training can still be of value. After all, the trainees may be learning on the job and the training may not be adding anything to their KSAs.

Much of the training in a small business is done on the job. In such cases, evaluation is often simply an assessment of the trainee's ability to learn. Examining the training process is not considered. As we discussed in the previous chapter, on-the-job training requires trainer skills just like any other training. Simply placing a new employee with an experienced employee and expecting the experienced one to train is not wise. It can be worthwhile to evaluate the process of training that goes on, as well as the outcomes, especially if the position is at a lower level where, because of turnover or promotion, a rather high number of employees receive training.

Since a small business may have one or two employees who need training, using a training design to determine training success may be difficult.

## SINGLE-CASE DESIGNS

Single-case designs are often used to evaluate the training provided to professional counsellors. But managers can also use this method when the number of employees is small.[54]

**Single-Case Design** a method of evaluation in which a single person is measured pre- and post-training and inferences are made as to the learning that took place.

The **single-case design** uses data from one individual and makes inferences based on that information. To increase confidence in the results, use the multiple baseline approach. Suppose two supervisors need to be trained in active listening skills. Because the business is small, both cannot attend training at the same time. Using a predetermined checklist developed for evaluating the training, count the number of active listening phrases each of them uses in conversations with you. Take several measures over three or four weeks, then send one supervisor to training. Continue monitoring the active listening after the person returns. Did the number of active listening phrases increase for the trained supervisor and not the other supervisor? Now give the second supervisor training, and afterward, continue monitoring the conversations. If both employees improved after training, it can be inferred that the training was effective. Although this approach is suggested for the small business, it is also useful in any-sized organization with few trainees.

The movement to quality standards, such as ISO 9000, creates a need for certification in a number of areas. Although the standards do not suggest how to evaluate training, they do specify that the organization must maintain training records and periodically evaluate training. The following excerpt comes from the QS 9000 requirements manual.

> Training records can be diplomas, certificates, licenses, experience, résumés. . . . The standard does not suggest any specific method for evaluating training effectiveness. A popular method is an annual review of training. . . . Results of the review are recorded and are used as feedback for revising and updating the training program. Another method is a periodic assessment of individual employees.[55]

Certification can become both the documentation and evaluation of training, something that might explain why certification is so popular.

David Alcock of Canadian Plastics Training Centre in the Toronto area says that even though few of the centre's clients request an evaluation of training, such requests are on the increase. Most of the centre's clients are small injection molding businesses. The need for certification seems to be the driving force behind the necessity to evaluate. Canadian Plastics Training conducts standardized injection molding training on its own site and provides a skill-based evaluation. A trainee who passes the skill-based test becomes certified as an injection molder. Generally the company sends its employees for this training; however, some employees pay their own way to improve themselves.

One reason that these small companies do not evaluate is the cost. For in-house training done by Canadian Plastics Training, a late-1997 cost of evaluation for 20 employees to be trained to a higher-level classification was $25 000. Many small companies simply do not have those resources. Another issue noted by Alcock involves what the evaluation would be used for. For example, suppose a unionized shop wants to upgrade the skills of the workforce. Sending them to training would carry with it the union's blessing. Evaluating the learning, however, might be met with a great deal of resistance. The union leadership and rank and file might be concerned about the company knowing how well the employees did on a test. They might believe that the company's goal is to get rid of some employees based on how they did on the test. Otherwise, why evaluate? Convincing the union that evaluation is a way of assessing the effectiveness of training might be difficult to do, depending on the relationship between union and management. Focus on Small Business shows what one small company is doing.

Much of the preceding discussion relates to the evaluation of learning. What about organizational results in this case? After publishing the article on Scepter Manufacturing,[56] Villers was asked how he knew the drop in scrap and defective parts (results) was a function of training. His reply: "We are a small company, and it is the only thing that we changed." He makes an important point related to the examination of results in small businesses. When a small business does training, evidence of the impact can be much clearer and faster. Also, it should be easier to rule out alternative explanations for the change, without the need for the more complex designs.

## Focus on Small Business

### *Training and Evaluation at scepter Manufacturing*

"ISO makes training mandatory," says Don Villers, plant manager of the 160-employee Scepter Manufacturing plant in Scarborough, Ontario. "We train everyone from the shop floor to the front office." The plant was ISO 9002 certified in 1994 and since then has moved beyond the ISO training requirements.

In the company's rating system, supervisors are required to rate each of their employees on a scale from 1 to 10. An employee must reach 10 to be certified at that level and to be eligible for promotion. The rating system is not seen as punitive, but developmental. It is used as a needs analysis to identify skill deficiencies, then as a learning measure, and finally as a transfer of training measure.

What about results? According to Villers, "Defective parts dropped from 5 percent to 0.1 percent. Scrap also dropped 50 percent." He attributes this success primarily to training. As a result of the success, the training budget is ten times the $6000 per year that the company spent three years ago.

*Source:* Adapted from LeGault, M. (1997). In-house training that gets results. *Canadian Plastics*, February, pp. 14–18.

## CASE

### *Palm Desert continued*

The Palm Desert case at the beginning of the chapter provides an example of an effort to evaluate using a control group and pre/post design. Even here, however, problems arose in the way the evaluation was managed. One issue is that learning was not assessed. Only behavioural change was assessed six months after training. We know that the training did not transfer, but we do not know why. If it did not transfer because it was never learned in the first place, what was the reason? Perhaps there was just too much material to learn in a one-day seminar? Examining the process of developing the training might reveal this problem, and the training could be revised before being implemented. For a small organization, the training was obviously a major undertaking, and a more comprehensive training evaluation might be more advisable.

### Summary

We began this chapter by discussing the importance of a comprehensive evaluation. We end it by suggesting that a comprehensive evaluation is not always necessary. With the understanding of validity and design issues, it is now possible to realize the difficulties that surround evaluation.

It can be complex, and in many cases, costly. For this reason, we suggested throughout this chapter that evaluation is useful and important but not necessary at all levels all the time. Furthermore, good detective work can, in some cases, replace complex designs in assessing the validity of evaluation.

The decision as to what training should be evaluated, and at what levels, will be easier if the organization is proactive. By examining the strategic plan, it is possible to identify those areas of training that require evaluation and the extent to which evaluating is necessary. Without such direction, the training department will need to identify its mission and goals as best as it can and work from there to determine the training that needs to be evaluated. Even for a large organization, it is simply not practical to evaluate everything. All organizations need to determine what training they want to evaluate and how they will do so.

## Implications for Practice

**1.** To obtain commitment from those whose training you are evaluating, emphasize that the focus is not on a summative approach (pass/fail) but rather a formative approach (data tracking to improve the product). This will ensure everyone wants the evaluation, as it provides a means of improving the training.

**2.** When evaluating training, always remember to keep track of the process; otherwise, if training was not effective, you will not be sure if the reason was that (a) the training design was problematic, or (b) the design was not followed for unknown reasons.

**3.** Although you may believe evaluation of the training is not important as no one is specifically asking for it, understand that when it is time to fund various department projects, top management determines in some way the value added by these projects. If you have no idea of the value of your training, neither does top management. That likely means it will not consider the training of managers as a top priority. If you have evidence of cost savings, top management is likely to pay more attention to your requests.

**4.** If you simply do not have the time to do a full-blown evaluation, consider that some level of evaluation is better than nothing.

## Key Terms

Affective questionnaire    *270*

Control group    *293*

Cost/benefit evaluation    *279*

Cost-effectiveness evaluation    *279*

Cost savings analysis    *280*

External validity    *289*

Formative evaluation    *264*

History    *286*

Internal referencing strategy (IRS)    *293*

Internal validity    *286*

Instrumentation    *287*

Job behaviour outcomes    *268*

Learning outcomes    *268*

Maturation    *286*

Organizational results    *269*

Outcome evaluation    *265*

Process evaluation    *265*

Random assignment    *294*

Reaction outcomes    *268*

Representative sampling    *294*

Single-case design    *296*

Statistical regression    *287*

Summative evaluation    *264*

Testing    *287*

Utility analysis    *281*

Utility questionnaire    *270*

## Questions for Review

1. What is the relationship among the four levels of evaluation? Would you argue for examining all four levels if your boss suggested you should look only at the last one (results) and that if it improved, you would know that training had an impact?

2. What is the difference between cost/benefit evaluation and cost-effectiveness evaluation? When would you use each and why?

3. What is the difference between cost-effectiveness evaluation and utility analysis? When, if ever, would you use utility rather than cost effectiveness? Why?

4. Assume you were the training manager in the Westcan case (in Chapter 3). How would you suggest evaluating the training, assuming they were about to conduct it as suggested in the case? Be as specific as you can.

5. Of all the designs presented, which one would you consider to be most effective while also being practical enough to convince an organization to adopt it? If your design involved representative sampling, how would you accomplish it?

## Exercises

1. Examine the reaction questionnaire that your school uses. Is it designed to rate the course content or the instructors? Does it meet the requirements of a sound reaction questionnaire?

Why or why not? Explain how you would improve it (if possible).

2. Break into small groups, with each group containing at least one member who previously received

some type of training in an organization. Interview that person on what the training was designed to teach, and how it was evaluated. Did the evaluation cover all the levels of outcomes? How did the trainee feel about the evaluation? Devise your own methods for evaluating each of the levels based on the person's description of the training.

3. Go to the role-play for active listening in the Fabrics Inc. example. In groups of five or six choose someone to be the initiator and someone to be the trainee. Have them go through the role-play while the rest evaluate the trainee's response on a scale of 1 to 7 (1 being poor, and 7 being excellent). Now share your scores. Were they all exactly the same? If not, how could you make the instrument more reliable? If they were all the same, why was that? Is there anything you would suggest to make the evaluation process easier?

## Web Research

Conduct a search of the Internet to identify eight distinct reasons for conducting an evaluation of training.

Document the source of these reasons and compare the list with reasons cited in the chapter.

## CASE ANALYSIS

You run Tricky Nicky's Carpet Cleaning Co. that cleans carpets for businesses. On average, one carpet cleaner can clean six offices per shift (work hours are 6:00 p.m. to 3:00 a.m.) Currently, 100 cleaners work for you and they work 250 days per year. A supervisor inspects carpets when the cleaner notifies him or her that the carpet is done. Because of Nicky's "Satisfaction Guarantee," when a carpet does not meet the standard, it is redone immediately at no extra cost to the client. A recent analysis of the rework required found that, on average, one in every six carpets cleaned does not meet Nicky's standards.

The profit averages $20 a cleaning. You pay your cleaners $15 per hour. When you re-clean a carpet, you lose, on average, $20 in employee time. You still receive the same amount from the client, but, on average, your profit is gone.

Your training manager conducted a needs assessment regarding this issue at your request. He reported that half the employees are not reaching the standard one in nine times, and the other half are not meeting the standard two in nine times, for an overall average of one in six [(1/9 + 2/9)/2 = 1/6]. The needs assessment also indicated that the cause was a lack of KSAs in both cases.

The training manager proposes a training program that he estimates will reduce the re-cleaning by half, to one carpet in twelve. The training would take four hours and could handle 20 employees per session.

Costs associated with the training (assuming five training sessions and 250 working days in a year) are as follows:

**Developmental Costs**

| | |
|---|---|
| 20 days of training manager's time for development at $40 000 per year | $ 3 200 |
| Miscellaneous | $ 800 |

**Direct Costs**

| | |
|---|---|
| 4 hours per session at $40 000 per year (trainer) | $ 400 |
| Training facility and equipment | $ 500 |
| Materials | $ 2 000 |
| Refreshments | $ 600 |
| Employee salaries at $20 per hour per employee (Nicky decides to do training on a Saturday and pay employees an extra $5 per hour as overtime) | $ 8 000 |
| Lost profit (none because training done on overtime) | 0 |

**Indirect Costs**

| | |
|---|---|
| Evaluation of training 10 days of training manager's time at $40 000 per year | $1 600 |
| Material and equipment | $ 600 |
| Clerical support—20 hours at $10 per hour | $ 200 |

## Case Questions

1. How much does the re-cleaning cost Nicky per year? Show all mathematical calculations.

2. If everyone is trained, how much will the training cost? How much if only the group with the most errors is trained? Show all mathematical calculations.

3. If everyone is trained, what is the cost savings for the first year? If only the group with the highest re-cleaning requirements is trained, what is the cost savings for the first year? Show all mathematical calculations.

4. What is your recommendation? Should both groups be trained or just the one with the most re-cleanings? Provide a rationale for your recommendation. Show any mathematical calculations used.

5. Let's back up and assume we are still at the needs analysis stage. Assume that employees had the KSAs needed to clean the offices effectively. What other factors might you look at as potential causes of the re-cleaning problem?

## The Training Program (Fabrics Inc.) Continued

We are now ready to examine the evaluation phase of the Fabrics Inc. training. We presented the training, and it is time to do the evaluation. In the design phase of the training process, one of the outcomes was development of evaluation objectives. Although we developed and implemented the training, it is critical to remember that the development of the tools for evaluation need to be done concurrently with development of the training, not after it.

Examination of the output of the evaluation phase of training indicated two types of evaluation: process and outcome. The process evaluation will consist of the trainer, during training, documenting the content phases and times taken in each of the training modules. These results will then be compared with the actual expectations regarding training content and times allotted.

For the outcome evaluation, four types are identified. The reaction questionnaire for trainers will model the one presented in Figure 8-1 of the text. For the training itself, the reaction questionnaire is shown in Fabrics Reaction 1 below.

**Fabrics Reaction 1**

Rate the following questions using the following scale anchors:

1 = Strongly disagree
2 = Disagree
3 = Neither agree nor disagree
4 = Agree
5 = Strongly agree

**Active Listening Skills:**

| | |
|---|---|
| The training met the stated objectives. | 1 2 3 4 5 |
| The information provided was enough for me to understand the concepts being taught. | 1 2 3 4 5 |
| The practice sessions provided were sufficient to give me an idea of how to perform the skill. | 1 2 3 4 5 |
| The feedback provided was useful in helping me understand how to improve. | 1 2 3 4 5 |
| The training session kept my interest throughout. | 1 2 3 4 5 |

The pace of this part of the training session was

1. Way too fast
2. A bit fast
3. Just right
4. A bit slow
5. Way too slow

What did you like best about this part of the training?

What would you change?

Comments:

*Note: A similar scale would be used for each of the other components of training that were taught.*

For learning, we need to revisit the learning objectives to determine what is required. We need a paper-and-pencil test for measuring knowledge (objectives 1 and 2 below), and two behavioural tests to measure active listening and conflict resolution skills (objectives 3 and 4). More specifically, the first two learning objectives (and the others related to the training but not developed here) are accommodated using the paper-and-pencil test. The content of this test is partially represented in <u>Fabrics Paper-and-Pencil Test</u>.

The trainee will, <u>with no errors</u>, **present in writing the four types of active listening, along with examples of each of the types**, *without using reference materials*.

The trainee will, <u>with 100 percent accuracy</u>, **provide in writing each step of the conflict resolution model, along with a relevant example**, *without help from any reference material*.

*After watching a role-play of an angry person and an employee using the conflict resolution model*, **the trainee will**, *without using reference materials*, immediately **provide feedback as to the effectiveness of the person using the conflict resolution model**. <u>The trainee must identify four of the six errors.</u>

## FABRICS PAPER-AND-PENCIL TEST

# Evaluation of Learning

No specific time limit is set for this test, but you should be able to finish in about one hour.

Answers to the questions should be written in the booklet provided.

**Please read each question carefully. Some of the questions contain more than one part.**

1.  List four types of active listening and provide an example for each.

2.  List the steps in the conflict resolution model. After each step, provide a relevant example of a phrase that could be used to represent that step.

3.  And so forth . . . .

The next objective is partly related to skill development. Below are a number of standardized scenarios and guidelines to evaluate them. See <u>Fabrics Scenarios, Active Listening</u> for an example of this.

*When, in a role-play, the trainee is presented with an angry comment,* **the trainee will respond** <u>immediately</u> **using one of the active listening types**. The trainee will **then explain orally the technique used and why**, *with no help from reference material*. <u>The trainee will be presented with five of these situations and be expected to correctly respond and explain a minimum of four techniques.</u>

## FABRICS SCENARIO: ACTIVE LISTENING

**This is read to the trainee:** The following set of scenarios is designed to determine how well you, the trainee, have learned the active listening skills. There are three roles here: initiator, active listener (you, the trainee), and evaluator. The initiator is a non-trainee who speaks a conflict-provoking statement to you (the active listener). You, the trainee, listen to the statement then respond using active listening skills. The evaluator, who is trained in evaluating active listening, listens to your response and evaluates it based on the use of effective active listening skills.

**Note:** The following forms (initiator's role, active listener's role, evaluator's role) are given to the respective people, with the active listener's role being given to you, the trainee.

*The sheet below (separated by dotted lines) is for the person playing the initiator.*

........................................................................................................................

 **INITIATOR'S ROLE (The initiator is to be played by the same actor for all trainees.)**

**Instructions for the initiator:** Read the sentence describing the scenario carefully, wait until the trainee indicates he or she is ready, then read the comment in bold under Scenario 1 angrily.
Wait until you are told by the evaluator to move to the next scenario and repeat the above.

### Test Scenario 1
You were just asked by your supervisor (the trainee) to serve on the same committee again. You are angry that they always ask you.

→ You start. Say angrily: **"OH, NO YOU DON'T. I'VE BEEN ON THAT COMMITTEE THREE YEARS IN A ROW AND IT TAKES UP TOO MUCH TIME!"**

### Test Scenario 2
Your supervisor just talked to you about following procedures. You think, Why me?, After all, no one follows procedures.

→ You start. Say angrily: **"WHY ARE YOU PICKING ON ME ALL THE TIME? I'M NOT THE ONLY ONE WHO DOESN'T FOLLOW THESE STUPID PROCEDURES!"**

### Test Scenario 3
You were just asked by your supervisor for a second time today whether you will be attending the weekly meeting.

→ You say angrily: **"I ALREADY TOLD YOU, I CAN'T ATTEND THE WEEKLY MEETING BECAUSE I HAVE TO COMPLETE THE STAFF REPORTS FOR TOMORROW!"**

...................................................................................................................

And so forth (for a total of 5).

*The next sheet (separated by dotted lines) is for the trainee.*

...................................................................................................................

### TRAINEE'S (ACTIVE LISTENER) ROLE

**Instructions for the trainee:** This test will require you to respond to five different short scenarios in which you are a supervisor and you say something to a subordinate that elicits an angry response. You will be expected to respond using the skills of active listening. The description of each of the scenarios provides what you initially said to the subordinate. When you are ready for each of the scenarios to begin, nod your head to the initiator. At that time, the initiator will say something. You need to respond to the comment, and when complete, explain to the evaluator the rationale for your response.

### Scenario 1
You asked a subordinate to continue working on a particular committee for another year. Listen; then respond using active listening. Nod your head when ready . . .

### Scenario 2
You just talked to a subordinate regarding the importance of following procedures. Listen; then respond using active listening. Nod your head when ready . . .

### Scenario 3
Today is the day of your weekly meeting. You asked your subordinate if he or she would be attending the meeting; they said no. It is now time for the meeting and you call once more to check to see whether he or she can make the meeting. Listen; then respond using active listening. Nod your head when ready . . .

...................................................................................................................

And so forth (for a total of 5).

*The next sheet (separated by dotted lines) is for the evaluator.*

...................................................................................................................

### EVALUATOR'S ROLE

**Instructions to evaluator for scoring trainee responses:** Trainee fails the scenario if the response is focused on the issue instead of reflecting what the initiator says. For example, a poor (fail) response to the first scenario would be something where the trainee responds to the concern by dealing with the issue **"But you are my best person for the job"** or **"You have to do it; I have no one else"** or "**Look, I am asking you as a favour to me.**"

Appropriate responses reflect what the person is saying, as in the first scenario: **"So, you're saying that being on the committee interferes with your doing your job"** or "**You feel you have done your share regarding committee work.**"

It is also important that the response does not sound like a mimic of what the person said. Although at this time we do not expect perfection regarding responses, the responses must, at a minimum, sound sincere. Refer to the tape recordings provided to understand the difference between what we consider mimicking and acceptable.

For each of the five scenarios, there is an example of a poor (fail) response and an acceptable response. When the trainee explains his or her response, we expect the trainee to be able to identify the type of active listening response used (paraphrasing, decode and feedback, summarizing) and why it was chosen. Answers to why it was chosen are intended to show that they understand the different methods, and thus almost any answer is acceptable.

## Scenario 1

The supervisor (trainee being tested) asked the subordinate to continue working on a particular committee for another year, and the subordinate responds. Listen to the supervisor's response and grade according to guidelines.

→ Unacceptable response: **"I am willing to talk about reducing the work you have to do if you will be on it."**

→ Acceptable response: **"YOU DON'T WANT TO BE ON THAT COMMITTEE AGAIN BECAUSE IT INTERFERES WITH YOUR WORK AND YOU FEEL YOU HAVE DONE YOUR SHARE."**

## Scenario 2

The supervisor (trainee being tested) just talked to a subordinate regarding the importance of following procedures, and the subordinate responds. Listen to the supervisor's response and grade according to guidelines.

→ Unacceptable response: **"You are not the only one I have talked to about this."**

→ Acceptable response: **"YOU BELIEVE THAT YOU'RE THE ONLY ONE THAT I AM SINGLING OUT FOR NOT FOLLOWING PROCEDURES."**

## Scenario 3

The supervisor (trainee being tested) called first thing in the morning and asked the subordinate if he or she would be attending the weekly meeting; the subordinate said no, he or she was busy. The supervisor just called again at meeting time to check to see whether he or she could make the meeting, and the subordinate responds. Listen to the supervisor's response and grade.

→ Unacceptable response: **"The meeting will only be an hour."**

→ Acceptable response: **"YOU'RE NOT ABLE TO ATTEND THE MEETING BECAUSE YOU ARE COMPLETING STAFF REPORTS THAT ARE DUE TOMORROW."**

And so forth (for a total of 5).

Note that we do not present the test for determining the knowledge part of this objective, where the trainee is asked to explain their response orally.

The next objective is skill related and has to do with conflict resolution. See Fabrics Role-Play Conflict Resolution for an example of this. The objective is:

*In a role-play of an angry employee,* the trainee **will calm the person, using the steps in the conflict resolution model,** with help from an easel sheet that lists the steps.

## FABRICS ROLE-PLAY CONFLICT RESOLUTION

**Read this to the trainee**: The following role-play is designed to determine how well you, the trainee, have learned the conflict resolution skills. There are three roles here: initiator, active listener (you, the trainee), and evaluator. The initiator is a non-trainee who starts off very angry at something you did. You, the trainee, listen to what is said, and respond using the conflict resolution model. The evaluator, who is trained in evaluating effective conflict resolution, listens to your response and evaluates it based on your effectiveness. The following forms (initiator's role, active listener's role, evaluator's role) are given to the respective people, with the active listener's role being given to you, the trainee.

*The sheet below (separated by dotted lines) is for the person playing the initiator.*

## INITIATOR'S ROLE (The initiator to be played by the same actor for all trainees.)

### Instructions for the Initiator

- Read the role a couple of times and get in the mood suggested.

- Be sure you understand the issues so you can present them without referring to the role.

- Once into the role, allow your own feelings to take over; if what the supervisor is saying makes you less angry, then act that way, and vice versa.

- Do not refer back to the role after the role-play begins; simply act the way you normally would do in such circumstances.

- Begin the role-play by presenting the points at the end of the role-play with anger.

- To elicit an assertive response, interrupt the trainee at least once after the trainee begins to present his or her point of view. If the trainee allows the interruption, interrupt again until the trainee becomes assertive and asks you not to interrupt (maximum of four interruptions).

### The Role of the Initiator

Your name is Pat. You are the longest-working machinist in the plant, with 25 years service. You taught many of those who are presently there, including most of those who were made supervisor recently. The company has been busy for the last number of years, and you have been called upon many times to provide the extra boost to get some projects out. You worked hard all your life and are starting to feel it in your bones. The work is getting harder and harder to complete, especially with the older lathes. With only three years to retirement, you are wishing you could afford to retire now. You are really worn out, that is, until you heard the news that the company just purchased one of those new computer-operated lathes. You feel confident that once you get to use the new machine you will be rejuvenated. In fact, the thought of getting to work on one of these new machines gives you goosebumps. You have not felt this excited in years. Actually, the thought of going back to school to learn about it is the most exciting thing, as it is making you feel young again. You are sorry that you missed today's meeting at which they were going to talk about the new equipment, but your car would not start.

"Hey, did you hear the news?" your friend Bill called out.

"I don't think so, what is it?" you replied.

"They just announced that Fred is going for training on the new computer-operated lathe. I guess he will be the one operating it."

"Are you sure?" you ask.

"Yep, it was announced at the circle meeting this morning. He was selected to operate it and will be going for a two-week training course next week."

You are furious. Fred was only just hired and is just a kid. You deserve first crack at the new machine, given your loyal service. Well, that is it. Your supervisor (the young guy you taught how to run a lathe before he got promoted) never did get along with you, and now this. Well, you are not going to take it. You walk into the supervisor's office and in a loud voice start off by saying:

**"What do you think you are doing? How can you give the new lathe to Fred, after all the years I have been here? This is not fair and I am not going to sit still for it."**

Be sure to continue the anger and bring up all the points mentioned in the role-play. Go over them again and again until the trainee calms you down.

........................................................................................................................................................................

*The next sheet (separated by dotted lines) is for the trainee.*

........................................................................................................................................................................

## TRAINEE'S ROLE

### Instructions for the Trainee

- Read the role a few times and be sure you understand the issues so you can present them without referring to the role.

- Do not refer back to the role after the role-play begins, but you can jot down a few points for reference.

- Use the conflict resolution model to deal with the issue.

- Nod at the initiator when you wish to begin.

### The Role for the Trainee

You are the supervisor of a manufacturing firm and have about ten subordinates. They are all lathe operators, and you were also one until you recently got promoted. Your subordinates are all good people, and with the exception of Pat, who has been here 25 years and is a few years away from retirement, all are fairly young and have at most ten years' service. Pat is a great machinist, knowing more than everyone put together. He taught you the job when you had just started and although you never really hit it off with him, you do respect his ability.

You are pretty excited these last few days because the company just purchased a new computer-operated lathe. It is your understanding that you will be getting a new lathe each year until all are replaced. You are moving into the new age. Choosing only one of your machinists to go to training and be the first one on the new machine was a difficult decision. All were likely candidates, with the exception of Pat, who was too old to learn the new machine, computer stuff and all. Furthermore, why train Pat on a new machine when he will only be here a short time? It makes more sense to train those who will be able to use the new skills for the longest time. Anyway, Pat really knows how to operate the older machine better than anyone, so why move him? Finally, you came up with the perfect solution. The new guy, Fred, has not been trained on any machine yet, so training him on the new lathe would mean that no one else needed training for the time being. Putting anyone else on the new machine would mean training Fred on the old machine, then when they are phased out, retraining him on the computer-operated lathe. So you announced it today at your circle meeting. Everyone was pretty quiet, but they will get over it. Too bad Pat wasn't there. Wonder if he is sick?

*The next sheet (separated by dotted lines) is for the evaluator.*

## EVALUATOR'S ROLE

**Instructions for the Evaluator:** The trainee fails the scenario if the initial response is focused on the issue instead of reflecting what the initiator says. For example, a poor (fail) response would be if the first comment to Pat was **"I did not think you wanted it"** or **"It is probably too complicated for you"** or **"We value your contribution "** or **"You're the best we've got on the old machine, and we need you there**."

Keys to successfully passing this exercise are to:

- Actively listen to Pat (using the active listening skills);

- Question to obtain as much information as possible before dealing with the issue.

To be successful, it is expected that the trainee will use active listening and questions at least four to six times (preferably more) before moving to the trainee's point of view. The key is to note how much the initiator has calmed down.

- Be sure the trainee indicates respect (must have at least one phrase such as **"I can appreciate why you feel you should have the opportunity to receive the training. It makes sense that you believe after such long and loyal service you should receive some reward)".**

- Be assertive, not aggressive, if necessary to present points.

When interrupted, the trainee must use the proper assertive response to inhibit interruptions. The trainee is given four opportunities to be assertive, since the role requires interruptions until an assertive response given (up to four). Note how that interruption is handled; the trainee needs to be assertive (for example, **"I have carefully listened to everything you have had to say; I think it only fair that now you give me a chance to respond, okay?"**)

- Provide the supervisor's points as "point of view" not *correct* point of view.

The role-play will begin with the initiator being angry. Response can be a summary of these points, paraphrase of one of them, or decode and feedback regarding emotion expressed, but not anything dealing with the specific issue. Below is a form to assist in the evaluation of the trainee.

**Evaluator Report Form**
Put a mark next to each of the responses in terms of their type. Try to jot down the words used in some of the cases to enable you to provide specific feedback.

## ACTIVE LISTENING

Nonverbal behaviour

Say more responses

Paraphrase

Decode and feedback

Summarize

## INDICATE RESPECT

Use of active listening

Questioning

Show acceptance of other's point of view

## BE ASSERTIVE

Needs to be phrased in terms of YOUR POINT OF VIEW

My perception is . . .

It seems to me that. . .

It is my belief that. . . and so forth.

## PROVIDE INFORMATION

Use collaboration (problem solving) or compromise (negotiate). Note: Although this response is a part of the conflict resolution model, it is not part of the learning objectives for this training; hence, it is not evaluated in this training program.

You will note that a standardized scoring key, examples of acceptable and unacceptable behaviour of the trainee, and a checklist for different responses are provided for the evaluator.

The above are evaluations related to learning, but we still need to consider behaviour (transfer of training) and organizational results. In the Fabrics Inc. case the owner is not interested in doing any of this type of evaluation. Recall that we indicated that an evaluation using elaborate designs is nice but seldom happens in reality.

The owner of Fabrics Inc. does not want us to assess any transfer of behaviours to the job. His argument is that his primary interest is in getting fewer complaints from employees and customers. He notes that in a small organization such as his, these changes (lowering of complaints) are proof enough that training was successful. We agree, so the evaluation will consist of gathering weekly archival information on complaints from customers and subordinates as a baseline (gathering it for two months prior to the training) and tracking it for six months after training is complete.

# 9

# TRAINING IN CANADIAN ORGANIZATIONS

*You have to learn to treat people as a resource ... you have to ask not what do they cost, but what is the yield, what can they produce.*

Peter Drucker

## CHAPTER OBJECTIVES

After reading this chapter, you should be able to:

- Describe what organizations are doing in the following key areas of training and why this training is important:
  - Orientation training,
  - Diversity training,
  - Sexual harassment training, and
  - Team training.
- Explain equity issues as they relate to training, specifically related to females in non-traditional jobs, the glass ceiling, and people with disabilities.
- Describe issues that organizations need to consider related to basic skills training and safety training.
- Describe HRD's role in a learning organization.

# CASE

## The Competent Employee

Schrader-Bridgeport International (SBI) is a large manufacturing company with plants in Canada, England, Brazil, Japan, the United States, France, and Northern Ireland. It is a world leader in the design and manufacturing of innovative engineered solutions to meet system, sub-module, and component needs for industrial and automotive applications. Its sophistication in the engineering field, however, does not translate to sophistication in its management system. But perhaps you should judge for yourself.

A few years ago, nine males and one female—Ms. Conner—were hired at the same time for the position of "craftsmen." They were all graduates of a community college with a degree related to the job they had applied for. Their job was to operate multi-spindle machines.

On joining SBI, the men were sent to Department 767 where special one-on-one, hands-on training took place for six months. This training taught them how to operate the machinery used at SBI, including how to load metal bars properly into the machines. Then they were transferred to Department 710, where they began operating the machines. Ms. Conner was placed directly into Department 710, and did not receive the training.

On numerous occasions, George Schaefer, SBI's General Supervisor in Department 710, stated explicitly that, in his view, women did not belong in the workplace at all. However, he admitted that Ms. Conner had "excellent mechanical ability," and estimated that of the 10 persons hired from the community college training program, Ms. Conner was "probably number three from the top."

When one of the men's machines malfunctioned, supervisor Bruce Boyd would explain and demonstrate to the operator how to fix the machine and permit the employee to assist, to learn how to get it going again. If Ms. Conner's machine malfunctioned, however, Boyd simply fixed it without showing or explaining what he did. When she asked to participate in order to learn he "rolled his eyes" at her and refused. Ms. Conner then specifically asked General Supervisor Schaefer to see that she was provided with comparable training. He dismissed her request by responding that she had a high rate of absenteeism.

The machines all 10 employees operated were idiosyncratic—each required its own particular techniques for it to perform well. New machine operators were typically assigned to a specific machine for a long period so they could learn how to keep that particular machine operating effectively. An inexperienced machine operator would advance to learning machine set-up and unplanned tool setting only after gaining basic operating skills on a single machine. As a result, the machine operator's efficiency and productivity were greater.

Mr. Schaefer, however, repeatedly moved Ms. Conner from one machine to another. These machine changes caused her to spend a much greater proportion of her time on machine set-up and unplanned tool setting than on production. She was always learning the idiosyncrasies of a new machine. For the period from October through April, Ms. Conner spent 139.3 hours on machine set-up and unplanned tool setting. The male operator who spent the most time on this task during that time period spent 82.5 hours. The male operator with the least amount of set-up and unplanned tool-setting time in the same period spent 12.1 hours.

Ms. Conner put up with a number of other things, such as being ridiculed, being forced to "mop up" the place, not receiving the same pay raise as the men, and so forth. She finally went to the personnel manager to complain. SBI had an anti-harassment policy. The policy required investigation of employee complaints "thoroughly and promptly to the fullest extent practicable." However, the investigation conducted by the personnel manager consisted of asking supervisors Schaefer and Boyd about Ms. Conner. It is not surprising that the findings indicated no problem.[1]

# OVERVIEW

In this chapter we will explore four key areas of training, indicate why they are important, and discuss what organizations are doing. These areas are orientation training, diversity training, sexual harassment training, and team training. We will then describe some other types of training programs and issues that organizations need to be aware of. Finally, we will examine a type of organization that has training as its main focus—the learning organization.

Corporate Training and Development Issues
*www.bpubs.com/Human_Resources/Training_and_Development/more3.html*

Yes, the case described on page 309 really happened. No, it was not something from the 1950s or 1960s, before we were more enlightened. It occurred in 1993. Was the company that "out of touch"? Perhaps, even though it did have an anti-harassment policy. So what went wrong?

A number of possible reasons might explain why this company was unable to align the behaviour of its employees with its policy. From an orientation perspective, none of the employees went through a formal orientation to the workplace when hired. Orientations provide new employees with information about rules, policies, procedures, and the workplace.[2] A well-designed orientation program for supervisors should help them understand the importance of treating everyone on the basis of ability and not gender. An orientation for employees that introduced them to the procedures to follow if they wished to air a concern could help employees, such as Ms. Conner, deal with an issue early on, before something serious occurs.

Let's examine this issue from a diversity training focus. Diversity training for managers would expose managers to the differences people from various cultures bring to the organization and why these differences should be valued. Gender differences would be a part of this discussion. Such a training topic would emphasize the value the organization put on these differences. Messages of this kind from upper management, if sincere, do affect how gender and ethnic differences are treated in an organization.

This problem can also be viewed from a sexual harassment training perspective. Some of the things Ms. Conner endured were clearly sexual harassment. Given that an anti-harassment policy was in place, harassment training was perhaps conducted. If so, the training was not taken seriously. Furthermore, the policy on investigating harassment was clearly flawed. The HR Manager talked only to the two supervisors, which clearly was not of much value, considering they both seemed to be part of the problem.

From a team training perspective, you would probably uncover the negative attitude toward females during the needs analysis phase. The section on team training shows that attitudes among and toward team members are a vital factor in developing effective teams. Training can be designed to provide a forum for dealing with the issue.

In any event, no effective training took place at SBI in any of these areas, so the harassment continued. We return to the case at the end of the chapter, but for now let's examine each of these key training areas in terms of why they are important and what organizations are currently doing.

# ORIENTATION TRAINING

**Orientation Training**
introduces new employees to
the organization, the job, and
their co-workers.

**Orientation training** introduces new employees to the organization, the job, and their co-workers. It is often done on the employee's first day or soon thereafter. The orientation begins the socialization process for new employees, helping them to learn about the way the organization works and what it values. New employees eventually learn about these aspects whether an orientation program exists or not. So, why spend the time and money on an orientation program?

## WHY IT IS IMPORTANT

From a learning theory perspective, we know that new learning is based upon previous learning. New information is interpreted and understood in the context of what is already known. The best companies recognize that providing new employees with the information they need to understand the company and its expectations is a good investment. On the first day, the new employee is anxious to impress, nervous about what this new job is all about, and excited about what is in store. It is the new employee's first entry to the organization, so what happens on that first day and the next few days is critical. The first impression of the organization will be lasting, and it is important to orchestrate it in a manner that creates all the images and impressions that will enhance the effectiveness of the company and the employee.

Research shows that employees who attend orientation programs are more willing to adopt the organization's goals and values than those who do not.[3] Orientations also provide guidance to the new employee regarding management's expectations and inform the employee about job expectations. Effective orientations result in a number of positive outcomes for the organization, as depicted in Table 9-1. Higher commitment to the organization, increased job satisfaction, more job involvement, clear role understanding, as well as increased tenure are all outcomes of an effective orientation.[4]

# WHAT ORGANIZATIONS ARE DOING

The orientation is one of the most common types of training programs.[5] It is also one of the most neglected.[6] It is often done haphazardly with little thought to what should be included. In some organizations it lasts a few hours; in others it can be a few days. Large organizations often develop orientation packages but forget about revising them until they are far out of date. Small organizations frequently develop them with little thought, if they do them at all.[7] The positive outcomes identified by research suggest that the design and development of effective orientations is a good investment for most organizations.

| TABLE 9-1 Positive Outcomes Possible from an Effective Orientation | |
| --- | --- |
| **Reduced anxiety** | A better understanding of expectations and formalized meeting of co-workers results in the new employee not feeling the higher level of anxiety associated with the first few days on the job. |
| **Reduced role ambiguity** | A structured opportunity to determine what is required on the job and a comfortable feeling about approaching the supervisor and co-workers to ask questions about the job provides an opportunity to clear up any misunderstandings about job requirements. |
| **Reduced turnover** | Substantial evidence indicates that effective orientations reduce turnover. |
| **Improved job performance** | A better understanding of job requirements and the willingness to ask for assistance results in fewer errors and the ability to get up to top production levels sooner; all of which translates to improved performance. |
| **Higher level of commitment** | Evidence suggests those who receive effective orientations are more committed, more involved in their job, and more likely to take on the values of the organization. |
| **More effective/efficient organization** | The organization with more employees achieving optimal performance quicker, operating at a higher level of performance, showing a clearer understanding of their responsibilities, staying with the organization for a longer time, and being more committed to the values and objectives of the organization is definitely going to be more efficient, effective, and valuable to its shareholders. |

Orientations do not require a long, drawn-out process to provide positive outcomes. Training in Action 9-1 provides an example of what can be done in a day. A well-designed and implemented one-day orientation will be more effective than a poorly designed or outdated program that spans a year. Bison Transport of Pine Falls, Manitoba, is a good example of how important orientation training can be. BT grew from about 35 employees in the early 1990s to more than 600 employees by 1999. To experience such growth and still be effective (twice chosen as one of the top 50 best-managed companies in Canada), it focuses on choosing only the best drivers. Bison relies on its four-day orientation to ensure a good match between company expectations and the new employee's expectations. The orientation is a method of continuing to screen new drivers to be sure of the "fit."[8]

For larger, more-complex companies or higher-level jobs, it is useful to spread the orientation out over a longer time period. This approach minimizes the problem of information overload. It also ensures that opportunities for behaviours that management wants to encourage are practised and feedback given. So, given the importance

## Training in Action 9-1

### *Even a One-Day Orientation Can Have an Impact*

Texas Instrument's HR department put on a two-hour orientation for its new assemblers. The new employees were told about the company, their job, and the performance requirements. Then they were introduced to their supervisor, and after he gave the employees a short introduction to their job, they were on their own.

Management at Texas Instruments noted a high rate of tardiness and turnover in the assembly department. Management conducted a TNA and discovered that new hires experienced a high level of anxiety when they started the job, and this anxiety increased for the following reasons:

- New employees worried they would not be able to meet production requirements.

- Old employees would tell new employees they would never be able to reach performance requirements. This bit of hazing was considered a rite of passage.

- They were afraid to ask supervisors questions for fear of being seen as stupid.

Anxiety resulted in three important outcomes: low job satisfaction, tardiness, and high turnover.

Texas Instruments decided to see what could be done to affect these outcomes. They designed an additional six hours of orientation, which consisted of four specific points. New hires were told the following:

1. They were highly likely to succeed, based on statistics that indicated 99 percent of new employees met expectations. The new hires also viewed the learning curves for production so they would understand that productivity would not be at the appropriate level at first. Throughout the six hours the new hires were constantly told they all would succeed.

2. They needed to disregard the hazing (being told they would never make it). They were told to take it in good humour, but not to believe it.

3. They should take the initiative in talking with their supervisors, because the supervisors are busy and would probably not come to see how each of them is doing. Supervisors are open to questions, new workers are expected to ask questions, and no question is considered stupid.

4. They were told a bit about their supervisor (hobbies, personality, likes, and dislikes) to give the new employees a view of the supervisor as an approachable person.

The HR department wanted to be reasonably sure that any changes in turnover or tardiness could be attributed to the orientation. So, the next batch of new hires was separated into two groups: a control group (that received the typical two-hour orientation) and the experimental group (that received the two-hour along with the extra six hours of orientation).

The result was better than expected. The experimental group showed 50 percent less tardiness and absenteeism, 80 percent less waste, and a 50 percent reduction in overall training time during the first year.

*Source:* Ivancevich, J. (1995). *Human Resource Management.* New York: Richard D. Irwin.

of the orientation, how long should it be? Having read to this point in the book, the anticipated answer is, "It all depends." The orientation is like any other training effort. Go back to the model for developing training, and work through the TNA, design, development, implementation and evaluation phases.

# DIVERSITY TRAINING

Currently about 55 percent of Canadian immigration comes from Asia and the Pacific Rim, with another 16 percent from Africa and the Middle East.[9] Almost 60 percent of women are in the workforce, compared with only 35 percent in 1966,[10] and more members of the 65-and-older population are working than ever before, at about 13 percent, and it is expected to top 21 percent in 20 years.[11]

This diversity creates tension and conflicts in the workplace. One of the reasons is that supervisors (and people in general) tend to make decisions that favour those who are similar to themselves.[12] Thus, ratings of performance, promotion recommendations, and such are often biased in favour of those who are most similar to the person making the evaluation or recommendation. When employees perceive that decisions affecting their pay or status are biased by factors such as race or gender, they become upset. A recent study found that this similarity bias is directly related to a personal characteristic called "openness to dissimilarity."[13] People who are less open to differences between themselves and others are more likely to evaluate those who are different (in terms of ethnicity, gender, age, etc.) more harshly and those who are similar more favourably.

## WHY IT IS IMPORTANT

Consider the case at the beginning of the chapter. Ms. Conner, who was identified by her boss, George Schaffer, as "one of the best new hires," was continually thwarted when she tried to get help in order to be more effective. Even though Mr. Schaffer acknowledged she was one of the best, he did nothing to assist her in being a productive employee. In fact, his attitude was that women did not belong in the workplace. Here is a motivated and talented worker who is being prevented from being as productive as she is capable. Is this practice good for the organization? Clearly not, and something needs to be done to ensure that all employees are nurtured to become highly effective employees.

Lack of acceptance by co-workers and management of those "different from themselves" leads to tension and biased treatment. Those "different" workers who are treated unfairly often quit, which can be costly to the organization if the numbers are high. The fact that the turnover of women in salaried jobs is double that of men and the rate for black people is two-and-a-half times that of white males supports the notion that being different is too often a disadvantage for those employees.[14] The costs to the organization for this type of turnover include the following:

- Loss of a productive employee who could end up at a competitor,
- Cost of recruiting a replacement,
- Cost of retraining the replacement, and
- Loss of productivity during the preceding items.

Furthermore, the resulting loss of reputation in the community entails its own costs (especially in metropolitan areas):

- Minorities and women will stop applying for jobs, reducing the pool from which to hire;
- Minorities and women will stop being customers or boycott the company; and
- Stock price may drop.[15]

Finally, costs are associated with having legal action taken by such employees. These costs go beyond the cost of the settlement if you are found guilty and include:

- The hiring of legal staff to deal with the case,
- Managers' time gathering the required information for a hearing,
- Managers' time preparing to testify, and
- Managers' time testifying.

Considering all of these costs as well as settlement costs, providing training to prevent such problems would seem the wise move. This is especially true considering that, if the company loses, it will incur not only all the costs indicated but also face the cost of training that is likely to be ordered by the human rights tribunal or the courts. Not all companies provide diversity training to their employees, however. A survey of more than 1600 companies in North America that employ 100 or more people found that 25 percent did not provide diversity training. Another 24 percent provided this training on an as-needed basis, and the other 51 percent provided diversity training on a regular basis.[16]

**Diversity Training** focuses on understanding the differences that are found among people of different backgrounds (race, age, ethnicity, gender).

**Diversity training** focuses on understanding the differences that are found among people of different backgrounds (race, age, ethnicity, gender). Diversity in organizations is a fact of life. Diversity training can help everyone in the company understand how differences can be useful to an organization. With the changing demographics in North America, organizations need to be effective in attracting, promoting, and retaining a diverse workforce in order to be competitive.[17] Advantages to an effective diverse workforce are noted in Table 9-2. Effective organizations that recognize the issues revolving around employing a diverse workforce do something to capitalize on the advantages and at the same time deal appropriately with any negative aspects of diversity.

## WHAT ORGANIZATIONS ARE DOING

Think about the opening case. Would providing a formal training program in diversity help to prevent the way Ms. Conner was treated? Would it put a company in a better position if it faces discrimination charges? An early and serious investment by companies in diversity training may help avoid time-consuming and costly fights with the human rights commission or the courts. However, just having a program is not enough.

Many North American companies implement policy and training programs to deal with diversity issues, but these efforts often simply do not change anything.[18] Why? Like any intervention, training is only a part of it. General Motors certainly provides training on this subject. Yet in July of 2000 an employee walked into a GM plant wearing a mock KKK robe and hood. The company immediately held meetings to tell employees this behaviour was not acceptable.[19] Was this action sufficient? GM articulates its employee guidelines in manuals, videos, and has a hotline to deal with the diverse workplace and inappropriate behaviour. Still, as one black man in the plant put it, "Sometimes it feels like this plant is run by white supremacists, but it is really worse for the women. They complain and are told to shut up, this is a man's job."[20]

| TABLE 9-2 | **Advantages of an Effective Diverse Workforce** |
|---|---|
| **Larger applicant pool** | Maintaining an effective and diverse workforce will contribute to a good reputation, and more individuals will want to join the organization. It will mean more people will apply for jobs, giving the organization a better likelihood of selecting better employees, which will translate into a more effective workforce. |
| **Reduced costs** | An effective diverse workforce will result in fewer turnovers, which will translate into less rehiring because of quits. |
| | Also, the tension created in organizations that do not deal with diversity will not be present and the outcomes of such tension (lower productivity, absenteeism, fighting, refusing to cooperate on projects, etc.) will not be present. |
| | Those organizations with effective diverse workforces will not incur the costs associated with paying for legal representation and settling lawsuits for discrimination. |
| **Access to more markets** | The North American population is more diverse. The more your organization reflects this diversity the more likely a diverse customer base will be cultivated. Minorities and females will be attracted to an organization that employs a diverse workforce. |
| | As we become an international community with more international business, those organizations whose employees understand the culture of these international markets will do better. |
| **Creative problem solving** | The more diverse the group, the more diverse the ideas that are generated. Employees with different backgrounds are more likely to see issues from different perspectives, resulting in more creative ideas (other things being equal), which can result in better products and service. |

*Sources:* Loudin, A. (2000). Diversity pays. *Warehousing Management*, April, pp. 30–33; Diversity: A new tool for retention.(2000). *HR Focus*, June, pp. 1–14; Hunsaker, P. (2001). *Training in Management Skills*. Upper Saddle River, NJ: Prentice Hall.

Many of the above problems may result from lack of support from top management. Consider the Conference Board of Canada survey of 466 organizations. The survey revealed only 6 percent had reference to diversity in their mission statement. Eighty-six percent indicated diversity was the responsibility of the Human Resource Department.[21] Clearly, without top management support, many diversity efforts are not likely to be very successful. Similar results are found in a United States survey of 785 organizations. In that survey, only 11 percent of the organizations had diversity training initiated by the CEO. Another 50 percent indicated their CEO was only minimally involved in the implementation of diversity training.[22] We indicated elsewhere the importance of upper management support in any successful intervention. This involvement is probably more important for diversity training. Without strong support from upper management, many will see the training and policy as something the company requires from a legal standpoint, but not something that is really valued.

Which organizations have successful programs? The Bank of Montreal won the prestigious Catalyst Award for their effective diversity programs, promoted vigorously by their senior management.[23] Then there is IBM. They developed a diversity program that resulted in an increase in black executives (from 62 to 115) and female minority executives (from 17 to 54) in about two years.[24] Carrier Corp. formed diversity councils in all business units. They develop diversity business cases to assist in training and successfully increased the percentage of black people in executive positions.[25] What

**TABLE 9-3    Agenda for Ensuring Diversity Remains an Important Part of the Organization**

Develop a broad diversity refresher training session and implement throughout the plant.

Cover holidays that reflect diversity and publish throughout the plant.

Create a diversity council and maintain its image by sharing what it does throughout the plant.

Write articles about diversity in the plant newsletter.

Set up a booth on diversity at the company picnic.

Invite non-member managers to diversity council meetings.

Ask plant managers, on a monthly basis, to share information on what is going on in the way of diversity issues within their department.

Establish a mentoring program to provide employees with a source for help.

Continue to address the guidelines supervisors need to be aware of when appraising and making training and development decisions.

Address, in a timely manner, any concerns regarding diversity and report back to the person affected.

Monitor the impact of diversity efforts, praise successes, and investigate the failures.

the successful companies have in common is their understanding that training alone is not enough. Two key additional elements are required:[26]

1. Top management commitment/involvement, and

2. Tying diversity success to performance appraisals.

Both these ideas are utilized in the new Texaco training initiative on diversity. In response to a court order,[27] they trained 14 930 of their U.S. workforce (about 93 percent).[28] The training includes input from top management on the importance of diversity to their goal of excellence. They also tied managers' ability to promote diversity and equal opportunity within their departments to an incentive bonus plan.

So what does it take to see that diversity training is effective and results in a positive climate for everyone? Table 9-3 provides information about what one successful company did.[29]

# SEXUAL HARASSMENT TRAINING

Feminist Majority Foundation: working for women's equality *www.feminist.org/911/harass. html*

**Sexual Harassment** an unwelcome advance of a sexual nature.

**Quid Pro Quo Harassment** an employee higher in the organization makes an offer of some job perq or raise to a subordinate, in return for sexual favours.

Sexual harassment is one specific type of behaviour that diversity training attempts to eliminate. It deserves special attention because, although it has likely been going on for years, there were relatively few complaints in the past. About a decade ago, however, law clerk Anita Hill filed a sexual harassment complaint in the United States against Supreme Court Justice nominee Clarence Thomas. Since then, it has become acceptable to file such complaints. In Canada, 16 percent of the complaints filed with the Canadian Human Rights Commission in 2002 and 2003 were related to sexual harassment.[30]

**Sexual harassment** is an unwelcome advance of a sexual nature. It is prohibited under human rights legislation in Canada. It can take one of two forms: quid pro quo and hostile environment.

**Quid pro quo harassment** occurs if an employee higher in the organization makes an offer to a subordinate of some job perk (raise, promotion, easier job) in return for sexual favours. If a supervisor sexually harasses a subordinate, the company can be considered liable, even if no one else was aware of the harassment.[31] If an employee is harassed by someone other than a supervisor (such as a co-worker or customer) the employer can still be liable if evidence shows that the employer was aware or should have been aware of the harassment.

When words, gestures, and/or behaviours make someone feel uncomfortable based on their gender, the result is a **hostile work environment**. The term comes from the U.S. Supreme Court ruling in *Meritor Savings Bank v. Vinson*.[32] In this case, Vinson was abused verbally and sexually over a number of years by her boss, but she was making good career progress. The court ruled that in this case the verbal and sexual abuse was "unwelcome" and sufficiently severe and pervasive to be abusive. This was subsequently reiterated in a Canadian Human Rights ruling.[33]

**Hostile Work Environment**
words, gestures, and/or behaviours that make someone feel uncomfortable based on their gender.

The ruling broadened the definition of sexual harassment to include verbal or physical conduct that creates an intimidating, hostile, or offensive work environment or interferes with an employee's job performance. Thus, if an employee is touched in some inappropriate and unwelcome manner, such as being pinched or slapped on the buttocks, it is illegal. Even the use of foul language, telling sexually oriented jokes, or hanging sexually provocative pictures on the wall can be found to be sexual harassment. This notion of a "hostile work environment" is complex in terms of what is and is not considered sexual harassment. Sexual harassment training needs to define these concepts in ways that fit the specific workplace.

## WHY IT IS IMPORTANT

More than 90 percent of *Fortune 500* companies field sexual harassment complaints and more than one-third were sued for sexual harassment.[34] Just like diversity, not paying attention to sexual harassment can be expensive. Irrespective of the damages awarded, preparation and attendance at hearings, as well as legal expenses, all take away from the bottom line for a company. Furthermore, it is estimated that the damage to a company's reputation from a sexual harassment charge can decrease the firm's market value on the stock exchange by 5 percent to 30 percent.[35]

Just how many employees are sexually harassed? Some data suggest that sexual harassment is fairly common in the workplace. One survey in the United States reported 42 percent of the females and 15 percent of the males indicated being sexually harassed on the job.[36] In Canada, a survey showed that 48 percent indicated being sexually harassed in the previous year, with only 3 percent indicating the harassment was of the quid pro quo type.[37]

To win a harassment suit in which the supervisor sexually harassed someone, the organization must prove that the supervisor's harassment was against the company's harassment policy. Therefore, maintaining such a policy is critical. The courts accept training supervisors in the use of these policies as compelling evidence of the company's concern regarding the issue.[38] In fact, the court previously held that if a company does not provide some kind of sexual harassment training to its employees, the company will be liable.[39] Although these court rulings are from U.S. courts, Canadian decisions often use U.S. case law in the development of Canadian rulings.

But there are more than just the obvious costs associated with sexual harassment. Sexually harassed employees experience psychological distress and in some cases post-traumatic stress disorder, both of which interfere with productivity.[40] A more direct impact on productivity is that these employees experience higher levels of absenteeism and turnover.[41] What is of real concern is the evidence that these outcomes manifest themselves in employees who, although they experience sexual harassment, do not define it as such and therefore do not report it.[42] This troubling tendency suggests that vigilance on the part of management is critical to stamp out such behaviours.

None of the preceding points address the ethical issues. Allowing an employee to be sexually harassed by others in the company is morally and ethically reprehensible. It is a part of a company's responsibility to the employees to protect their physical and psychological health while at the workplace.

# WHAT ORGANIZATIONS ARE DOING

A survey of U.S. organizations indicated that more than 80 percent provided some type of sexual harassment training.[43] For many companies it is effective. A survey of 663 human resource practitioners indicated that in 500 of the responding organizations, sexual harassment complaints declined after initiating training. Based on the information from these organizations, an effective strategy for dealing with sexual harassment was developed and is depicted in Table 9-4.[44]

However, many organizations are not doing a good job in this area. For that reason, we continue to hear of flagrant violations of the various human rights codes. Consider IMP group in Halifax, Nova Scotia. Although it was the action of a manager that led to the complaint, failure of the company to show up at the hearing

| TABLE 9-4 | Effective Strategies for Dealing with Sexual Harassment |
|---|---|
| Set an example at the top | Get top management's support for training and their support through their behaviour at the office. |
| Provide training | Everyone needs to know what is acceptable and what is not, which can only be provided in information sessions. Also examples and role-plays are useful to make it clear what is not appropriate. |
| Check for understanding | Labour lawyers strongly recommend a written exam to determine (and demonstrate in the case of a suit) whether everyone understood the information provided. This indicates the importance of evaluating training at the learning level. |
| Refresher training | The executives in the study suggested refreshers once a year to keep everyone sensitized to the topic and current on the issues. |
| Investigate complaints quickly | Be sure an adequate complaint procedure is in place that does not involve a person's supervisor. Often it is the supervisor who is the problem. Also respond quickly to not only determine the merits of the case but also to stop the behaviour immediately if it exists. |
| Keep information confidential | Only those directly involved should know about the investigation. You do not want someone being intimidated because they filed a complaint. You may also want to remove the person from the workplace during the complaint (with pay) just to demonstrate you take all such complaints seriously. |
| Provide equal and effective punishment | Guidelines regarding sexual harassment should be clear and penalties for violation severe. Those who violate the guidelines need to be dealt with no matter who they are in the organization. It must be made clear that no one is free to take such liberties with any employee. |

*Source:* Adapted from Moore, H., Gatlin-Watts, R., & Cangelosi, R. (1998). Eight steps to sexual harassment free workplace. *Training & Development*, April, pp. 12–13.

indicated a general lack of concern by upper management regarding the harassment complaint. The result was an award of more than $27 000 to the complainant and an order by the Human Rights Commission that all employees at IMP receive mandatory sensitivity training, including top management. Going back to the SBI case, we note that a procedure was in place for dealing with harassment. This procedure was correct in that it did not expect the harassed employee to report the allegation to the supervisor (who was the offender) but instead to the supervisor's boss. The problem was that the boss apparently lacked training and failed to take the complaint seriously. In fact, many companies conduct minimal training and even less evaluation of the outcomes of the training.[45]

As noted earlier, sexual harassment of the quid pro quo type is most obvious, and its definition is relatively clear. Defining sexual harassment when it relates to a hostile environment is difficult, and care in determining what is enforceable is important. Those who develop and conduct the training must not bring their own values into the training. Rather, they must present the company's guidelines and their application. It is important that the training not create situations that are irrelevant and could quite likely lead to a backlash. For example, swearing on the shop floor may not be considered harassment.[46] However, the same behaviour at the management level might be. The preceding should not be interpreted as implying fixed and absolute guidelines. For example, the company may set a policy that is more stringent than the law requires. If policy bans the use of foul language or the use of derogatory names, appropriate consequences for violating the policy can be enforced. However, what is being enforced is company policy, not sexual harassment as defined by the courts.

For the small business, the costs associated with development of an effective sexual harassment policy need not be high, as Focus on Small Business indicates.

## Focus on Small Business

Controlling sexual harassment does not have to be costly for the small business. There are also software programs retailing for about a $100 that can help create a manual, such as Employee Manual Maker 3.0 by JIAN Tools for Sale Inc. in Mountain View, Calif. The program, designed for companies with 100 or fewer employees, also has a sexual harassment questionnaire and discussion guide. Cheaper still, try networking with other companies and cutting and pasting from their policies.

After developing a policy, you should begin training. Brumberg Publications Inc., of Brookline, Mass., sells a $95 training video aimed at companies with 15 or fewer employees. Interactive Media of New York has a $425 interactive CD-ROM about harassment for supervisors at companies with fewer than 100 employees.

Judith Nitsch, a civil engineer at a small company, saw how to react effectively to offensive conduct. The same day her firm's chief engineer heard of a harassing remark, he sent a memo to all 35 employees that such conduct wouldn't be tolerated. It stopped.

When Nitsch opened her own firm in 1989, which now has 54 employees and $3.6 million in annual revenues, she also took a hard line. She not only created a sexual harassment policy but also named a male and a female employee to whom workers can report complaints directly. She says this has worked well.

Ultimately, however, the best defence isn't a board game, video, or strongly worded policy. To talk the talk, experts say, the boss must walk the walk. "If the senior people behave appropriately, that's the message that's communicated, irrespective of what's in the policy," says training consultant Lynn Revo-Cohen. Best of all, it doesn't cost a thing.

*Source*: Donovan, K. (1997, Oct. 13). Avoiding a Time Bomb: Sexual Harassment: From videos to Web sites, new resources are available for small businesses. *Business Week Magazine, October 1, 1997*, p. 20.

# TEAM TRAINING

Teamwork is a pervasive part of organizational functioning in North America. A survey of *Fortune* 1000 organizations in the United States indicates about 70 percent of them use teams.[47] A survey of Canadian organizations indicates a similar percentage (76 percent) use teams.[48]

## WHY IT IS IMPORTANT

Use of teams seems to make a difference in the effectiveness of an organization. A common characteristic of North America's 100 best organizations is the effective use of teams.[49] A great deal of evidence indicates that effective teams can significantly improve the effectiveness of an organization. For example:

- The Campbell soup plant in Toronto reduced its costs to produce soup by $3.55 per case;[50]
- Westinghouse Furniture Systems increased its productivity 74 percent in three years;[51]
- FedEx cut service errors by 13 percent;[52]
- Volvo's Kalamar plant reduced defects by 90 percent;[53] and
- Corning Cellular Ceramics decreased defect rates from 1800 per million to 9 parts per million.[54]

In today's highly competitive environment, organizations are looking for ways to obtain an advantage. Effectively implementing the right kind of team concept can make the organization more responsive to customer needs, reduce the workforce by requiring fewer levels of management, reduce waste, improve quality and productivity, and make the company more competitive in other ways.

Work teams are also a benefit to employees who are given the opportunity to be involved in more meaningful work.[55] More meaningful work leads to other positive organizational outcomes such as

- Improved employee satisfaction and commitment,
- Lower absenteeism and turnover, and
- Improved performance.

Organizations see a reason to be moving toward this style of management in ever-increasing numbers.

## WHAT ORGANIZATIONS ARE DOING

The use of teams began in earnest a few decades ago under names such as *quality of work life, quality circles, employee involvement,* and so forth.[56] They all centred on getting workers more involved in their work and helping in a manner beyond what was traditionally expected. These efforts were met with skepticism, particularly by some unions that believed it was simply a way for management to co-opt workers and reduce the workforce.[57] In some cases this assessment was probably true. In these early years many of these efforts failed.[58] The main reasons for failure were that, after initial team training, there was no[59]

- Refresher training,
- Evaluation and feedback of team efforts,

- Alignment of systems, procedures, and organizational design to the team approach, and

- Training of new members brought into the team.

From a transfer-of-training perspective, maintaining support from the top, removing roadblocks, and creating systems and practices that support the team process (performance appraisals, compensation systems, and so forth) are critical to the success of the program.[60]

Today, there are a number of successful team efforts, and Training in Action 9-2 is but one of these.[61] The transition from a hierarchical system to a flatter, more inclusive system is not easy, and training is one of the important ingredients for success. Coca-Cola's Baltimore syrup operation, for example, was a plant with high turnover, absenteeism, worn-out equipment, and an old-style management.[62] Mr. Bentley, the new plant manager, decided to change that. He promised to run the business competitively and provide the employees with the KSAs to do it now and in the future. Four years later it emerged as a highly successful plant with cost savings at $1 million. This transformation was accomplished primarily through the use of teams. For a team to be effective, however, it must receive training. Training was the second part of Mr. Bentley's promise and he came through on it.

The Coca-Cola training came in three categories: technical, interpersonal, and team. For the technical training, employees were encouraged to learn four different jobs to provide for flexibility in the organization. This increased knowledge also provided employees with a greater understanding of the operation of the plant, making them more valuable team members.

Interpersonal skills training was also provided, because of the belief that, before anything can be done effectively, employees need to be able to interact effectively with others. All shop floor employees, supervisors, and managers were trained together. This way everyone was seen as regular human beings, not supervisor or worker. This approach helped employees work together as a team without necessarily seeing the other person as a boss or supervisor. The training included listening, handling conflict, and negotiation skills.

Team training included leadership, managing meetings, group dynamics, and problem solving. As members are provided with these skills, they are also provided

## Training in Action 9-2

### *Teamwork Saves $1 Billion at Chrysler*

Don Callahan, an hourly assembly worker, and Brian Large, a production engineer, were trying to determine why the warning light on the Dodge Intrepid was on when the system was working fine. Was this unique? If Dodge built the Intrepid like most American cars, the problem would not have been fixed, because the two workers would never meet. Brian would be too busy to contact anyone about the problem and Don would say it was not his problem. For this car, however, the manufacturing process depended on a team of workers, designers, and engineers collaborating on all stages of the car's development.

The collaboration resulted in the car reaching production a full year earlier than the average production cycle for Chrysler. It also required 40 percent fewer engineers. The total cost for the car from its inception was just over $1 billion, less than half of the cost of two other well-known team efforts, the Ford Taurus at $3 billion and the GM Saturn at $3.5 billion.

*Source:* Hunsaker, P. (2001). *Training in Management Skills.* Upper Saddle River, NJ: Prentice Hall.

with additional skills to explore future career or retirement options. Self-assessment, résumé writing, and interview skills are all part of preparing employees for the future at Coke or anywhere else they decide to go. When people work for a company because they want to, rather than because they see no other options, it ensures that they stay because they enjoy their work and want to be part of the Coke team.

# OTHER TRAINING PROGRAMS AND ISSUES

The types of training provided and the way they are managed affect almost every aspect of organizational life. Training can assist an employee in doing a job more effectively, as well as provide opportunities for promotion, transfers, increased pay, and employee well being. It also prepares employees for dealing with emergencies and in some cases even saving lives. Let's examine a few of these types and the issues organizations need to consider.

## TRAINING AND EQUITY

**Training Equity** providing equal access to training for all employees.

In the section on diversity training we deal with ways the organization can improve the ability of a diverse group of employees to work together effectively. **Training equity** means providing equal access to training for all employees. Like hiring and promotion, training is a personnel decision that is subject to legal proscriptions and prescriptions. Even though we would hope the ethics of treating everyone equitably would predominate the world of business, unfortunately many lawsuits are filed each year because an individual or group feels it has been treated inequitably. A large number of these suits are based on an employee not being selected for a particular position. It may seem like a selection issue, but many times the organization's training practices played an important part in the outcome of the suit.

The majority of selection decisions within an organization involve current employees (transfers and promotions). Even if the promotion or transfer is based on who has the best set of KSAs for the new job, the company can be found guilty of unfair discrimination. This situation happens when one group of employees (e.g., minorities) are not provided with the same opportunities for training as another group (e.g., non-minorities).

Consider the female technician who worked for the Canadian Broadcasting Company (CBC).[63] She wanted to go on remote location assignments but was refused because many took place at night and were not safe. When promotions came up at the CBC, she was not considered because one of the qualifications was a broad-based understanding of the types of assignments technicians go on. She never received the on-the-job training that going on remote assignments provided. The CBC's good intentions, which were meant to protect her, prevented her from developing important KSAs. This in turn inhibited her advancement. Training is an important part of the development of employees, whether they want transfers, promotions, or simply to be better at what they do. It is the manager's responsibility to ensure that all employees are given opportunities to improve themselves and prepare for advancement.

**Developmental Review** the opportunity for the employee and supervisor to discuss career goals, areas of strength and weakness, and the opportunities for development that are open to the employee.

In addition to the traditional performance review for the purpose of compensation and promotion decisions, many companies conduct a separate **developmental review**. This review provides the opportunity for the employee and supervisor to discuss career goals, areas of strength and weakness, and the opportunities for development that are open to the employee. This discussion benefits the organization because it helps develop employees for higher-level positions in the company. It benefits the employee because it provides opportunities to grow and develop. In addition to traditional types of training programs, development plans may include off-site seminars, on-the-job training, being put on a task force, being given a temporary assignment, or other ways the employee can develop the appropriate KSAs. The key is making sure all supervisors understand the importance of providing all employees with opportunities based on their current capabilities and developmental readiness, not on their gender, race, age, or other irrelevant criteria. Training in Action 9-3 provides an excellent example of an organization doing everything possible to provide opportunities for employees.

# THE GLASS CEILING

The **glass ceiling** is a metaphor for an invisible barrier that prevents minorities and women from moving up the corporate ladder. It is an example of how training and development opportunities can limit the ability of employees to advance in the company. Let's examine the glass ceiling for women. In the late 1980s, only about 2 percent of the corporate offices of the *Fortune* 500 companies were filled by women.[64] That proportion improved and passed 12 percent in 2000, but considering the number of females in the workforce, it still seems rather low,[65] especially compared with Kraft Foods, one of the *Fortune* 500. Kraft Foods takes equity seriously, with more than 26 percent of its corporate positions filled by women.[66] What is the difference between Kraft and many others? One difference seems to be in the area of training. One of the main points, suggested by Kraft Foods Executive Vice-President Mary Kay Haben, is the company's commitment to personal development and career advancement, both of which focus on training.

**Glass Ceiling** an invisible barrier that prevents minorities and women from moving up the corporate ladder.

# Training in Action 9-3

## *Providing Training for Success*

Many women at Bell Telephone wanted to transfer from the operator's job to the more interesting and lucrative installation and repair jobs. When they applied, however, they failed to pass one of the required tests. Bell Telephone and the Communication Workers of Canada got together to work out a way the women could be more successful.

When women applied to the installation and repair department, they often were not accepted because they did not pass the electronics test. It was an important criterion for acceptance, because much of the work involves understanding and working on the components of a telephone and its accessories. Women did poorly on the test because they usually did not take such courses in high school or follow it as a hobby as men seemed to do. Management and the union worked out an agreement in which operators could apply for a limited number of special training slots created in installation and repair. Successful candidates were required to be able to climb a ladder, have a valid driver's licence, and pass a colour vision test. Those who were successful were chosen on the basis of their seniority as operators.

Once accepted into a training slot, the operators received six months of on-the-job training in installation and repair. After training they returned to their operator job until an opening became available. Then they applied like anyone else. The training the women received prepared them for the test and resulted in many operators being selected into the position.

*Source:* Martin, D. (1993). Personal communication. Communication Workers of Canada, Toronto.

At Kraft, employees meet with their supervisor once a year (formally) to discuss performance, developmental progress, and career aspirations. They meet again (informally) six months later to review how things are going. At Kraft, executives seldom hire from the outside for management positions, so opportunities for moving up are available. When they do lose a senior manager to the competition, they are able to fill the position within minutes.[67] To accomplish this level of preparedness, Kraft developed an extensive human resource planning process with a heavy focus on preparing (training) employees for promotion. Part of this program takes place through an extensive mentoring program. Kraft also formed a high-level committee that monitors how the company is doing regarding women and minorities at each level in the organization. When the committee identifies a problem in any area, it goes about solving it immediately. This example illustrates how a company can tie training to changes in the organizational environment to ensure equitable treatment for all employees.

## PEOPLE WITH DISABILITIES

Legislation in Canada makes it unlawful, when hiring or training, to discriminate on the basis of a person's disability, whether physical or mental, if it does not prevent the person from doing the job. Basically, a job analysis describes the critical KSAs. Based on that information, it is possible to assess whether the disability will negatively affect job performance. If not, then the candidate must be provided with the same opportunity to be hired, promoted, or trained as anyone else.

Consider Mary, who is hearing impaired but able to speak and read lips. She applies for the job of accounting clerk. The job analysis identifies all the critical tasks and KSAs, and she meets all of them. However, although not a critical task, the job requires using the phone from time to time. Can the employer refuse to hire her based on her inability to use a phone? Although each case needs to be examined on its merit, it would seem that such a refusal to hire her for the job would be illegal. According to the law, the company faces a **duty to accommodate**. It would require the company to purchase a special phone used by the hearing impaired.

**Duty to Accommodate** adjustments to working conditions and/or requirements of the job expected to be taken by the employer in order to allow a person with a disability, who is protected by the Human Rights Code, to do the job.

Duty to accommodate requires the employer to help people with disabilities to do their job. Remember, these employees possess the necessary KSAs to do the job but require some help in certain areas. Accommodation may come in the form of special desks for wheelchairs, large computer monitors for the visually impaired, removal of an unimportant task from a job (that the employee with a disability is not able to do), and so forth. Whether an employer needs to accommodate a person with a disability depends on whether it will result in **undue hardship** for the employer. Undue hardship is determined by a number of factors such as cost of the accommodation, financial resources of the organization, number of employees, and impact of the accommodations on the operation of the company.

**Undue Hardship** an argument that is allowed by the Human Rights Commission regarding duty to accommodate. The employer provides evidence that accommodating the particular employee will place undue hardship on the organization.

Irrespective of the legislation, when considering the nearly 3.8 million workers with disabilities in Canada,[68] it makes financial sense to include as many competent applicants in the selection pool as possible, with a disability or without. After all, with more qualified applicants, the likelihood of selecting a strong candidate is higher. If the job analysis indicates that the job of operator requires answering phones and directing calls, someone who is legally blind can be considered. The main accommodation required in this situation is a phone in Braille. Training, however, may also require some changes in order to accommodate the special needs of someone who is blind. We return to that issue later.

So, let us return to Mary, the hearing-impaired accounting clerk. She moved up to the highest level in non-management accounting. Six years later when she applied for the accounting manager position, she is turned down because she does not possess the requisite KSAs. Frank does demonstrate the required KSAs and gets the job, even though he worked there three years less. However, Frank got those skills through training courses offered by the company. Mary was never told about those training opportunities. If the skills Mary is lacking were available through training and she was not told, the company failed to provide her with the same opportunities as others in the company. This failure puts the company in a vulnerable legal position. Perhaps more important, the organization potentially missed out on a competent supervisor and instead faces an extremely angry accounting clerk.

**The Training Dimension** For people with disabilities, it is not only accommodation in the workplace that needs to be considered but also the implications for accommodation in training as well. Treating someone with special needs equitably in your training requires preparation. Proper furniture and accessibility to the training facility need to be considered. The trainer may require additional training for talking to someone who is hearing impaired. Perhaps the organization may accommodate by providing a certified sign language interpreter. The best way to deal with this issue is to meet with those who have disabilities and ask them what they need.

**Summing up Training and Equity** Whether it involves not promoting a female to the job of technician, a minority or female to an executive position, or a hearing-impaired person to supervisor, the issue is the same: The organization is losing out on potential. The career and personal development of everyone in the organization needs to be a top priority. Although this point seems intuitive, a recent survey of organizations noted that about one-third provided no mentoring or coaching for employees, and 16 percent did not provide personal or developmental planning.[69] How many of the remaining companies are just "going through the motions" rather than doing it properly is also unknown. It is clear, however, that effort needs to go into helping all employees do their best if a company is going to compete. It makes good economic sense. To be sure it happens, organizations need to consider the following:

- Obtain support from the top that identifies the importance of the issue of equity for all employees;
- Write clear descriptions of job requirements and make them the focus of personnel decisions;
- Focus part of every manager's appraisal on the equitable treatment of employees;
- Assemble a steering committee that examines the issue and reports on progress each year;
- Establish a liaison and reporting procedure for dealing with issues of inequity; and
- Provide extensive training to managers on issues related to equity at all levels.

What it comes down to is considering the implementation of an equity program as an intervention that will require training and changes in policies and procedures to ensure that the forces pushing in the direction of equity for all are stronger than those pushing against.

# BASIC SKILLS TRAINING

**Literacy training** generally includes training in reading, writing, and basic arithmetic. The functionally illiterate are unable to use those skills even at the most basic level

**Literacy Training** training in the basic skills of reading, writing, and arithmetic.

(reading instructions, writing a report, balancing a chequebook, etc.). The problem may be getting worse as a result of the following factors:

- Lower standards in many high schools today,

- More minorities and non-English-speaking immigrants entering the workforce, and

- An increase in skill requirements for most jobs.

In Canada, about 22 percent of adults struggle with a severe literacy problem.[70] This translates into a productivity loss of about $4 billion (Canadian) per year.[71] Organizations find that, even when hiring high school graduates, they need to provide remedial skills training to get them ready for the job. In addition to issues within the school system, immigration from non-English-speaking countries continues to increase. In Canada, only 21 percent of immigrants are from Europe or the United States.[72] As immigration increases, new employees with English as a second language will be more prevalent, making reading and writing in English more problematic.

At the same time as skill levels were dropping, most jobs began to require more skills. A machinist now needs computer skills to operate the computerized machinery; truck drivers need to understand logistics, inventory control, and flow analysis from the computer in their truck. Even parcel delivery requires data entry into a computer. Furthermore, many organizations are becoming ISO certified, requiring a new list of skills for the shop floor. Teamwork, which for years was the purview of management, is now also down on the shop floor, demanding that workers understand charts and know how to interact effectively with others.

It is necessary, then, for organizations to upgrade their employees' skills. Before they can, however, employees need to possess the basics. Just providing the basics can result in a positive financial impact. A survey of workplaces in Canada where literacy programs were installed revealed a drop in error rate in employees' work, improved morale, and a general improvement in health and safety.[73] Another positive outcome of such training is the improvement of employees' self-efficacy. Recall the importance of self-efficacy for training. Those with poor literacy skills will likely show a low self-efficacy. Providing employees with these skills will definitely lead to positive effects.

Developing basic skills (or literacy) training is similar to developing any other training program. The first step is a TNA. Here, more than in other TNAs, the need to ensure confidentiality is critical.[74] Workers who are illiterate generally take great pains to hide it out of embarrassment and shame. It may be advisable to use an outside vendor in this case to ensure that few in the organization would know who requires literacy skills training. One company hired a consultant to provide outside assessment over a long period of time in order to encourage everyone who thought they might have a problem to go for assessment outside the workplace.

Outside vendors need not be the answer. Sea World did it itself and was successful through the use of company tutors. Trainees are given the option of a non-company tutor, but most preferred someone from within the company. As with most things, no single way is always best.[75] The key is to keep the training relevant by using material that the employee uses every day. So for reading, use the memos received and typical instructions. This tie-in to actual work makes the success and value immediate. Some tips for improving employees' self-efficacy in literacy training are shown in Table 9-5.

**TABLE 9-5 Tips for Improving Self-Efficacy of Those Requiring Literacy Training**

Assure trainees that they are being asked to upgrade because of their importance to the company.

Do not call it "literacy training" or "basic skills training," as both can sound demeaning. Use a positive name that stresses job training.

Make participation rewarding, not punishing. Pay them for the time or conduct it on company time.

Talk about "improving reading" rather than learning how to read.

Indicate the problem is widespread and that many similar employees have successfully completed the training.

Provide early success stories so trainees can see they are able to do it.

Use company-related examples to make sure it is not only meaningful and therefore easier to learn but also useful right away.

*Source:* Tyler, K. (1996). Tips for structuring workplace literacy programs. *HR Magazine* 41:112–16.

# TRAINING WORKERS FROM DIFFERENT CULTURES*

Increased globalization and new technologies available for training have resulted in more training for more people in more countries. As noted in Chapter 6, there are many types of distance learning methods available to provide organizational training. Consequently, the question arises: Do you simply send North American–style training abroad, or do you need to be sensitive to cultural differences?

Training in North America often contains

- Games, exercises, and role-plays to make it interesting; and

- A large interactive component requiring trainees to be involved through questioning and providing their experiences. Listening to trainees' experiences, and having other trainees discuss the relevance of these experiences facilitates retention.

These two design aspects of North American training can be problematic for some cultures. In Russia, for example, trainees see training as an opportunity to get ahead and are already motivated to learn.[76] Maintaining interest is not important, and games are unheard of. In Europe, trainees want the training, not things such as games and exercises that could be seen as a waste of time.[77]

A trainer in Norway noted that trainees were reluctant to become involved in discussions during the training. They preferred a highly structured training atmosphere.[78] In Russia, trainees respond better to self-study, especially if it is structured.[79] Chinese trainees expect a very formal lecture, with little interaction or questioning by trainees.[80]

So is it important to consider the culture when transferring your training to other countries? The answer seems to be yes and no. First, according to Mike Davis, General Manager of Oracle Corporation, North American training does have too much of an entertainment component and toning it down may be beneficial. He says his European clients just want the nuts and bolts of training, not the flash.[81] They are already highly motivated to learn the material. This is particularly true of sales training, where cheerleading and giving prizes to trainees like a game show takes place.

What about involvement? In Asia, Alan Chute, the Chief Learning Strategist for Lucent Technologies, says he asks the senior management for questions. If others have a question they send it to the senior manager so he can ask it. This ensures that a junior person does not ask a better question than a senior manager.[82]

But, as we have emphasized in this text, involvement by trainees ensures understanding and improves retention. So what to do? It seems that those who do try to

*Adapted from the article "Think Locally, Train Globally" by Bob Filipczak in Training Magazine, 34, January 1, 1997, p. 40-46.

include a high level of interaction in their training abroad are successful. In Russia, for example, the discussions are received positively but need to be highly structured. Even icebreakers, role-plays, and exercises, which are viewed as taboo, seem to be enjoyed once they are tried, and trainees expect them in the future.[83] In China questioning of instructors is simply not done. When Chuck Greenwood from Drake University in Iowa was teaching students in China, he suggested they "act like Americans" for the class and ask lots of questions. He found them eager to participate.[84] A trainer from England asked a student in Korea if the training he was attending might not be Americanizing him. He answered: Of course, that is the whole point.[85] It seems that prolonged exposure to trainers that have an interactive style is infectious; given the advantages of the interactive style for adult learning, that is a positive thing.

So, it would seem that more entertaining training methods might initially be more difficult to sell abroad. Note, however, that we do not adhere to the idea that entertainment per se is a good thing. We suggest that the use of games and other means to make training more interesting is a good idea but that it needs to be relevant to the topic being taught. As for the interactive component, given its importance to learning, and given that it seems to be something other cultures can get used to and even enjoy, it should be considered as an important component of any learning. The implementation strategy, however, needs to be carefully developed to address the cultural issues of the group being trained.

What about training in Canada, where organizations have multiple cultures to contend with in their training? Given the information above, it seems that games and interactive methods can be effective across many cultures. To increase acceptance, trainers should consider an orientation to training before those from different cultures attend their first regular training session. This would involve trainees learning the value of the novel training methods for retention and transfer back to the job. From the information above, this acceptance may not be all that difficult to generate.

So what is the conclusion? First, there are many factors that may need to be considered when training is developed by one culture and provided to another. Here, we have addressed only two important components of North American training. There seems to be an acceptance of exercises that make the training interesting and get trainees involved in interactions with the trainer. But culture still needs to be considered in training those in other countries. In China, because it would be embarrassing to have a junior manager ask a better question than the senior manager, it may make sense to train one level in the organization at a time. As well, providing some type of orientation to training methods that are novel for the culture will increase the level of acceptance.

## SAFETY TRAINING

In Canada, on average, one Canadian worker out of 16 was injured at work in 1997. It is estimated that the total cost of workplace injuries to the Canadian economy is about 9 billion dollars a year,[86] in spite of legislation dealing with safety in the workplace. Clearly, there must be a large number of organizations that see safety efforts as a cost rather than as an investment. Otherwise why would an organization have a forklift with three safety devices bypassed so they were not working? That is what was found at Nu-Gro of Brantford, Ontario, and it resulted in the death of an employee. They were fined $200 000. Don Dickie of the Construction Safety Association of Ontario indicates that there is a direct correlation between the number of government safety inspections and workplace safety.[87] This suggests there are still organizations that will be lax when it comes to safety if they think they can get away with it.

For many other organizations, a culture of safety is a requirement to be competitive in a global marketplace. In a survey of organizations considered to be on the cutting edge of safety training, it was noted that they developed this "culture of safety" rather than a number of different training courses on safety.[88] In such an organization, safety training is not considered a cost, but an investment. This distinction may seem minor, but it changes the focus by looking at the benefits of safety training—it is viewed as a cost savings—rather than seeing it as forced compliance with provincial or territorial health and safety legislation. Evaluating training at the "results" level and identifying the cost savings in fewer accidents, less machine wear, lower compensation costs, and so forth, provides continued support for this proactive approach to safety.

During years of consulting and training in organizations, we noted that most discussions with employees about safety training reveal how boring it is. From what has been presented so far, it is safe to conclude that this impression does not bode well for learning. Valerie Overheul, president of Summit Training Source, suggests a number of ways to make training interesting.[89] She indicates that in many years of training employees in various safety skills, the one comment consistently made over the years is how interesting employees find the training, which is not like previous safety training. Valerie's recipe for increasing trainee motivation in safety training it to "jazz it up." Get trainees' attention through the use of humour, familiar music, action clips, and dynamic graphics. Be sure the trainer is upbeat and interested in the topic. In a recent survey of the pulp and paper industry, where safety is a critical component of the job, one of the questions dealt with "obstacles to effective training." Fifty-two percent of the respondents indicated "boredom." The next closest response was scheduling, which only 22 percent indicated as an obstacle. These statistics reiterate a common theme in the text: Motivate trainees by making training interesting.

# THE LEARNING ORGANIZATION

No training text would be complete without addressing training in the context of a learning organization. The learning organization is a term used to describe an internal strategy for improving the competency base of the organization. The goal of a learning organization is to stimulate and capture individual learning in ways that allow the learning to be retained and spread across the organization.

## DEFINING THE LEARNING ORGANIZATION

Many definitions explain the essence of the learning organization.[90] Our definition attempts to combine the common elements among them. The **learning organization** builds a sense of common understanding among individuals and enhances their capacity to create desired results through continually learning how to learn. Its systems support employees in creating, acquiring, and transferring knowledge to others. In a learning organization, employees modify their behaviour to reflect new knowledge. It is part of an overall competitive strategy in which knowledge is the competitive advantage. It requires large investments in time, energy, and people.

Even though it is an obvious fit with a market leader strategy, in which innovation separates winners from losers, it also has applications to every organization, including those that adopt cost leader strategies. Creating a learning organization is a challenging process. Its components are listed in Table 9-6. Organizational learning requires a focused support system and an infrastructure that can capture and deploy learning to those who seek it. Upper management must provide the appropriate climate and

**Learning Organization** has a sense of common understanding among individuals and an enhanced capacity to create desired results through continually learning how to learn.

## TABLE 9-6 Components of a Learning Organization

| | |
|---|---|
| **Personal mastery** | This involves the continual clarification and deepening of our personal vision. It connects personal learning with organizational learning. |
| **Mental models** | These are the deeply ingrained assumptions and generalizations that influence how we understand the world. Until these are brought to the surface, little learning takes place that does not conform to these models. |
| **Building a shared vision** | This sets up a creative tension that pulls individual's visions into a common future that all employees desire, thus galvanizing a group toward goal accomplishment. |
| **Team learning** | Teams are the learning blocks of the organization; if the team does not learn, the organization does not learn. |
| **Systems learning** | This framework enables an understanding of interrelationships rather than simply seeing things that are related. |
| **Systematic problem solving** | This is a reliance on the scientific method rather than on guesses or hunches. Data, rather than assumptions, are used for decision-making. People are skilled in the use of basic statistical techniques for analysis. |
| **Experimentation** | This is distinguished from problem solving in that its focus is on expanding knowledge rather than responding to current difficulties. Failure of experiments is accepted as a way of gaining knowledge. |
| **Learning from experience** | The lessons of experience are documented in a form that employees find accessible and understandable. |
| **Learning from others** | Knowledge is gained from what others do and how they do it, rather than from the results they have achieved. Benchmarking and similar practices are encouraged. |
| **Transference of knowledge** | For the organization, rather than just individuals, to learn, knowledge must be documented and made transferable quickly and easily. |

reinforcement, demonstrating commitment to the strategy even through the difficult initial stages of implementation.

The primary responsibility of management, and the focus of management practices in a learning organization, is to create and foster a climate that promotes learning. Management's task is not to control or be a corporate cheerleader or crisis handler; it is to encourage experimentation and open communication, promote constructive dialogue, and facilitate the processing of experience.[91]

# HRD's Role in the Learning Organization

HRD systems and employees are critical to the success of the learning organization strategy. They must not only know their field and craft well but must also fully understand the organization and its strategic direction. They must be able to fashion learning experiences for employees that fit the culture, systems, and values of the organization. Learning organizations often require fewer employees because line managers are able to integrate many of the staff functions into their daily routine, especially the HR function.

For example, the selection process is traditionally an HR activity, but in learning organizations this process might be handled by an autonomous work team that learned how to perform this activity. HR staff in such organizations learn how to improve HR processes so that fewer dull, routine tasks are required, thus reducing staff and clerical support needs. However, because HRD professionals are doing less stand-up training, and instead creating more learning situations, opportunities, and systems, the number of HRD personnel increases dramatically. James DeVito, Vice-President of Educational Research and Services for Johnson & Johnson, described HRD's former role as learning stonemasons and their new role as learning architects.[92] As stonemasons, they were responsible for providing the content and the process of learning; as architects they are designing systems that allow individuals and groups to identify what they need to know and the best way of learning it. The learning organization radically changes the focus and core competencies required of HRD professionals. They now meet the responsibility of empowering employees to identify and meet their training needs.

Electronic information systems are critical to the success of this strategy. No organizational learning can occur without the capacity to store learning compactly and cheaply and to transmit it quickly and easily. Self-directed training delivery systems such as satellite broadcast systems, video discs, and networked learning libraries make it possible for people to learn what they need to know when they need to know it. This capability changes the paradigm for how the training function meets the training needs of the organization. Rather than directing the learning experiences of employees, training entails helping employees learn how to learn on their own and also developing the means for that learning to happen. Xerox, Samsung, and Corning implemented these systems with much success some time ago. Corning, for example, set a company-wide goal that 5 percent of each employee's annual workload would be spent in job-related training. A few years later, in 1991, *Business Week* recognized Corning as a prime example of an effective competitor.[93] Corning attributes its success to a commitment to employee and organizational learning.

At this point you might be wondering, "If this strategy is so difficult to implement and requires so much time, money, and commitment, why would a company decide to do it? Doesn't it face a fairly high risk of failure?" The answer is that the potential advantages are so large that companies are willing to take the risk. Let's assume the learning organization strategy is successful and allows a company to jump ahead of its competitors who are using a traditional training system. By the time this fact becomes apparent, the company has already gained a substantial knowledge lead on the competition. Because of the difficulties in moving to a learning organization strategy, it will take the competitors some time to put this strategy into place. Meanwhile, the company is continuing to improve the competencies of its employees and increasing its competitive advantage. Since it has a head start, competitors will probably require substantial time to catch up; perhaps some never will.

Although the learning organization strategy is still young, it shows great promise. It also presents a significant threat to traditional training organizations and training professionals. If the preceding scenario proves correct, the focus and technology of HRD and training professionals will shift dramatically. Those who fail to keep up will go the way of buggy whips and computer punch cards.

## CASE

### The Competent Employee (Continued)

Recall that Ms. Conner requested that the personnel manager investigate her complaints, and he found no merit to her complaint. As a result, she filed a civil action against SBI based on the treatment she endured. The judgment was in her favour, awarding her more than $500 000 in damages.[94] Clearly much of this award was based on the hostile environment created by her managers and co-workers. It might be argued that such settlements are not likely in Canada but will be more like the award paid by IMP in Nova Scotia (this case is presented later in this chapter). However, consider the costs of simply going to court: time required for managers to get records together, preparations for trial, and the cost of legal representation. This potential expense alone is reason enough to motivate organizations to pay attention to such issues and provide appropriate training to see it does not happen. But even more important are the ethics of fair treatment and the potential loss of a productive employee.

## Summary

This chapter examines in depth four of the more prevalent training practices taking place in organizations today: orientation, diversity, sexual harassment, and team training. Orientation training seems to be done haphazardly in many organizations, with little thought to the desired outcomes. The value of an effective orientation in terms of performance and turnover is clear. We discuss the importance of each and what is going on in organizations. With orientation training we provide some ideas on how to approach the development of orientation training.

Additional issues and training programs were discussed more generally and briefly. Equity was discussed in relationship to employment and training opportunities; employees are more often selected from within the organization than not. Even when promotions and transfers are based on the person's skills and potential, all employees, regardless of their race, gender, or disability, must be provided access to training and development opportunities. The importance of equitable access in preventing costly litigation is understood, but it is more important in terms of fair treatment and obtaining the best employees in all positions.

The need for highly skilled, continually learning employees requires a solid foundation of basic reading, writing, and arithmetic skills. More and more companies are taking it upon themselves to provide these skills. However, employees experiencing functional illiteracy are unlikely to admit it unless organizations take the time to develop and market training that addresses these skills.

Many companies see safety training as a significant cost savings tool. In the past it was generally presented in an uninteresting manner, leading to poor learning and transfer to the job. If safety training is to achieve its cost avoidance potential, it needs to be designed to arouse the interest of the trainees.

Finally, the learning organization is an organization that has learning and transfer of information as a major strategy focus. Such a focus dramatically changes the role of HRD. Fewer administrative employees are needed and many more professionals are required to provide the support required in a learning organization.

## Implications for Practice

**1.** New employees are very impressionable in the first few days on the job. Many organizations miss out on the value of orientating these new employees in a manner that benefits the organization. Instead they allow the employees to learn operating procedures from others who may or may not hold the values the company wishes the new employees to have.

**2.** Although there are numerous advantages to a diverse workforce, there is a downside that can lead to very dysfunctional behaviour in the organization. Top management needs to be aware of this and develop processes and procedures for dealing with these behaviours and, more importantly, provide training to minimize such behaviours.

**3.** Most human rights complaints arise in organizations that have policies and procedures in place, because policies and procedures alone are not enough. Management must understand the ramifications of such behaviour and take it seriously. This often requires changes in attitudes, which usually requires training.

**4.** One reason to examine the KSA requirements of jobs carefully is that otherwise we might assume some types of disabilities automatically disqualify a person from the job. We are less likely to make that mistake if we have a clear understanding of what KSAs are required for the job. Doing this is good for the organization, as it results in less likelihood of a human rights complaint. But more importantly it likely gives the organization a highly committed and productive employee.

**5.** Finding a way to determine the level of literacy in your organization and doing something about helping those with problems is good for morale and good for productivity in the long run.

## Key Terms

Developmental review    *322*

Diversity training    *314*

Duty to accommodate    *324*

Glass ceiling    *323*

Hostile work environment    *317*

Learning Organization    *329*

Literacy training    *325*

Orientation training    *310*

Quid pro quo harassment    *316*

Sexual harassment    *316*

Training equity    *322*

Undue hardship    *324*

## Questions for Review

1. What is an orientation designed to do? What are the characteristics of an effective orientation?

2. How are organizations dealing with diversity? Are the methods effective? Why or why not?

3. What are the important components of an effective sexual harassment strategy?

4. Why is team training necessary? What are the seven components of effective teams? What are some of the KSAs required of team members in effective teams?

5. How can training affect the selection of competent candidates for vacant positions? What would you recommend an organization do to ensure that everyone receives equitable opportunities for promotions?

6. In today's environment, why is it important for organizations to focus on training of basic literacy skills?

7. Why is safety training an important component of the training mix in so many companies? What is the biggest concern regarding safety training that was noted in the survey referenced in the chapter? Is it fixable, and if so how?

8. What is a Learning Organization? How is HRD different in a learning organization than in a traditional organization?

## Exercises

1. Over the next few days, watch the instructor in the various classes you attend. Jot down notes about any differences you see in terms of how the instructor treats males, females, minorities, or people with disabilities. Share this information with a group and generate a list of what differences exist and how you would deal with them. If you found no differences, indicate what specific things the instructor does to be sure everyone in the class is treated equitably.

2. Break into small groups. Have each person think about a current job or one held in the past for which orientation training was provided.

- If you never held a job that provided orientation training, just think of a job you held. Describe four things that good orientation training would include to make breaking into the job easier. Post these activities on an easel under the heading "Wish they had done."

- If you went through an orientation training, think about the orientation and list two things that were good about the experience and two things you thought were a waste of time or boring. Post these activities on an easel, with the positive under the heading "Glad they did" and the negative under the heading "Wish they hadn't done."

- After everyone contributes, discuss how the "Glad they did" and the "Wish they had done" tie into the training model in terms of what you need to do right. Do the same for the "Wish they hadn't done" in terms of what to avoid.

3. Think about your role as a student in this class. Now think trainees who are visually impaired, paraplegic, or hearing impaired. What kind(s) of accommodation(s) to the training facilities (classroom) would need to be made for each to be successful? What changes (if any) should the teacher make to be sure the person is getting full value of the training/education?

4. Break into small groups to discuss the following situation. The vice-president of human resources asked you, the director of training, to develop a sexual harassment training program for the company. During your needs analysis you discover that most of the executives do not believe they need this training and do not plan to

attend. You identify a couple of instances in which an executive's behaviour seems bordering on sexual harassment. You discuss your findings with the VP, who asks you to come back with a strategy for dealing with the resistance to training. Develop your response and be prepared to present it to the rest of the class.

## Web Research

Go on the Web and identify two organizations not used as examples in the chapter that are using orientation training to good advantage. Describe your reasons for picking these organizations, based on concepts presented in the orientation section.

# CASE ANALYSIS

## All It Takes Is for Good Men to Do Nothing

In 1987, Ms. Dillman was hired by IMP to work in Hanger 3 at the Halifax International Airport as a seamstress in their fabric shop. After six months, the workload dropped, so Ms. Dillman approached her supervisor and asked for additional responsibilities. He sent her to the sheet metal shop. A number of months passed and she approached the supervisor and asked if her classification could be changed from fabric worker to sheet metal technician; he complied.

At 20 years of age, she was the only woman out of about 100 employees working in Hanger 3. She often received special attention in terms of help and guidance, which she indicated she appreciated. But it was a male-dominated environment, and the language was crude and vulgar. Having pictures of naked women in the locker room was prohibited, but such pictures were posted and little was done about it. There was also evidence that in apprenticeship programs men received extensive training, whereas women in the same programs received minimal training.

Mr. Pettipas was a long-time employee at IMP. In 1989, Ms. Dillman was assigned to work for him, and he was to provide her with on-the-job training. The first problem arose when Ms. Dillman made a mistake. Mr. Pettipas erupted in a torrent of verbal abuse directed at her. No one had ever heard him act so inappropriately. The incident caused Ms. Dillman to ask if she could be reassigned; the request was granted. When Mr. Pettipas was working in other hangers, things went fine. But when Mr. Pettipas was in her vicinity, he always made snide comments and insinuations. On one occasion he screamed at her, calling her a tramp and troublemaker. He said she was not welcome in the workplace. Whenever he went by her, he would say something derogatory. By 1990, everyone in Hanger 3 knew of the situation between the two employees.

In late 1990, a series of meetings between Pettipas, Dillman, a company representative, and a union representative were held, in attempts to diffuse the situation. But Mr. Pettipas refused to admit he had done anything wrong. The union representative and manager involved agreed that a warning letter would be placed in Mr. Pettipas' file relating to his treatment of Ms. Dillman, and it would remain there for two years. In response, Mr. Pettipas went to see Mr. Rowe, the President and CEO of IMP, and convinced him to remove the letter. Mr. Pettipas then went around the hanger bragging to everyone that he had won.

All this had a devastating effect on Ms. Dillman, and in early May of 1991, she went on long-term disability for a few months. When she returned, she met with the HR manager to discuss the difficulty with Mr. Pettipas. He suggested she take more time off, which she did.

In January of 1992, Ms. Dillman was transferred to another hanger, where she was involved with airframe construction. In the following nine months she was there, the supervisor often complimented her on the quality of her work. None of her work was ever rejected. Then she received word that she was being transferred back to Hanger 3. Even though her own supervisor had nothing but praise for her work, the Director, of Aircraft Maintenance had given the order because "her work was not up to standard." When she questioned the Director, he gave no specifics. When she indicated the problem regarding going back to Hanger 3, he promised to look into it. Nothing happened and she was sent back to Hanger 3.

She filed a complaint with the Nova Scotia Human Rights Commission. As a result of the commission's findings, IMP had to pay Ms. Dillman about $30 000. IMP was also ordered to provide training to all employees, on company time.

*Source: I.M.P. Group Ltd. v. Dillman (1994), 24 C.H.R.R. D/322 (N.S. Bd.Inq.)*

### Case Questions

Answer the following questions, assuming you have been contacted to provide this training.

1. Would a TNA be needed in this situation? Why or why not? If yes, who would you want to talk to?

2. Based on the case as presented above, what KSAs need to be trained?

3. Why has the commission insisted on training for the whole company when the problem is clearly only Mr. Pettipas? Elaborate.

4. In order for the training to be effective, what other things do you think need attention?

5. What would you suggest in the way of evaluation of the training? How would you convince top management that it would be worth it?

# 10

## MANAGEMENT DEVELOPMENT

*A good manager is a man who isn't worried about his own career but rather the careers of those who work for him.*

H. S. M. Burns, President, Shell Oil

### CHAPTER OBJECTIVES

After reading this chapter, you should be able to:

- Identify and describe the roles and responsibilities of managers at different levels in the organization.

- Describe the general competencies and characteristics of effective managers.

- List the important organizational factors that determine which managerial characteristics are desirable at a given time and situation.

- Explain how management training needs can be influenced by changes in organizational strategy.

- Identify the various sources and types of training related to management development.

- Identify the specific problems associated with training executives and some of the methods that can be used to deal with these problems.

- Describe why development of executives is so critical to effective organizational functioning and the most effective way to deal with executive development.

In 1986 Linda Wachner took over as CEO of Warnaco, a manufacturer of women's lingerie, which was experiencing financial difficulty. Wachner's goal was to take the company public and ensure its profitability in a hostile, competitive market and fairly stagnant economy. She knew radical changes were needed to restore the company to competitiveness. Since then, the company went public, the stock rose 75 percent above its initial offering, the debt was cut by 40 percent, sales increased by 30 percent, earnings before taxes increased by 140 percent, and operating cash flow almost doubled. Wachner pursued an unrelenting focus on the company's performance, which is closely tied to her personal financial situation since she owns 10 percent of the stock.

As the only female CEO of a *Fortune* 500 company at the time, her leadership was subject to careful scrutiny. Wachner continues to combine energy, drive, and enthusiasm with hard-core fiscal management. She maintains a focus on the customer and has high demands for her employees. Her employees view her as a tough boss, and often feel that she expects too much. Although her "do it now" philosophy focuses on responding to customer preferences in the short and long run, she also managed to reap considerable savings from cost cutting. For example, she reduced the corporate staff from 200 to 7. Some say that Wachner does not do a good job of managing people because of her single-minded focus on company profitability. She is unrelenting in getting to the point and requiring her colleagues to do the same.

"Have I yelled at meetings? No question. Do I think I've ever hurt anybody? I hope not. Look, I just want people to be good and I put enormous pressure on everyone to get this company moving in the right direction," she says. "I know I push very hard, but I do not push anybody harder than I push myself. Last year I travelled 200 days visiting stores, plants, and so on."

At the same time, she motivates her workers with her praise of their work. She visits the stitch room almost daily, picking up and examining the fabric, lace, and trim the stitchers are working on. "These are to die for," Wachner declares with a supremely satisfied smile as she holds up a garment. "Beautiful. Just beautiful." Maintaining the gruelling schedule may be difficult for employees, but Wachner emphasizes creating an environment to which employees bring a high energy level and a focus on a common goal. Her determination created a hard-as-nails image, but it's a style that gets the job done.

# WHY FOCUS ON MANAGEMENT DEVELOPMENT?

We have discussed the training process and a great many training techniques in detail, so why single out managers for special consideration? Do the processes and techniques already presented not apply to them? The answer is of course they do. However, several reasons prompt us to examine this part of the organizational community in more detail. Perhaps foremost is how important management development is in today's environment. Evidence indicates that those companies that align their management development with their strategic planning are generally more competitive.[1] So, we need to thoroughly understand such an important part of organizational competitiveness. Other related reasons include the following:

- Managers get a lot of training;
- Managers are accountable for success; and
- Managers have complex jobs.

## MANAGERS GET A LOT OF TRAINING

One of the most frequent types of training provided by companies over the last several years is management development and executive leadership.[2] This is true across every industry from financial and banking institutions to manufacturing to communications

The Leadership Network
*http://leadership.gc.ca/menu_e.
asp*

to utilities. Management training is more important as the organization increases in size, but not dramatically. Eighty-eight percent of firms report management development programs, compared with 90 percent that provide executive leadership training.[3] For companies of all sizes approximately 37 percent of all training budgets go toward management and executive training. Thus, whether large or small, and regardless of the industry, management training is seen as a vital part of improving organizational performance. A training professional needs to understand a part of the business that is in such demand.

## MANAGERS ARE ACCOUNTABLE FOR SUCCESS

Managers carry a different and more complex burden for ensuring the success of the enterprise than do non-managers. Think back to the opening case. How much responsibility does Ms. Wachner assume for the success of Warnaco relative to other employees? The business environment over the next decade is expected to place even more demands on management. Consider the following responsibilities of the manager of the new millennium:[4]

- Managers face a shrinking labour pool in terms of the skilled and educated. It is management's responsibility to grow and keep the talent necessary to be competitive.

- At the same time, more technologically sophisticated systems are being implemented, and management is responsible for ensuring that employees obtain the knowledge and skills required to perform their jobs.

- Managers must also deal with a more diverse workforce, see that diversity as a strength, and not allow it to become a focus of divisiveness.

- Mergers, acquisitions, downsizing, and fast-paced changes must all be managed effectively.

In fact, it is management's responsibility to ensure that all systems and resources are appropriately integrated so the organization can achieve its objectives. No wonder companies place a high priority on developing the KSAs of their managers.

## MANAGERS HAVE COMPLEX JOBS

Perhaps the most important reason to closely examine management development lies in the nature of managerial effectiveness. What makes a manager effective is more complex and difficult to ascertain than are most other targets of training and development. Thus, it is more difficult to assess needs, to develop training content and methods and, most certainly, to evaluate the effects of training. Is Ms. Wachner a good manager at Warnaco? What criteria are being used to decide this? Would everyone agree with those criteria?

Effective training requires an understanding of the employees' training needs before a training program can be designed. For management development this is not easy. Typically, a manager's effectiveness is determined by how well his unit meets its objectives. However, determining his training needs from the performance of the unit is problematic. A complex alignment of many factors influences the unit's performance, and the manager can affect these factors in many ways. For example, Ms. Wachner's organization is successful. Would she be just as successful in a different company in a different industry? To understand a manager's development needs, the context in which the manager and the unit operate must be first under-stood. This context includes the strategic direction of the organization, the technology of the manager's unit, the human and financial resources available to the unit, and how the unit relates to the rest of the organization.

Information about the context in which the manager must operate is collected from an organizational analysis, as discussed in Chapter 3. The operational analysis, also discussed in Chapter 3, identifies the managerial competencies required to create the appropriate match between the organization's strategy and the unit's structure, resources, and technology so the unit is able to achieve its objectives. To identify the manager's developmental needs, her knowledge, skills, attitudes, and behavioural styles are compared with the competencies required for the job. The job in this case is the management position in a particular unit. Determining all these factors is diffi-cult enough, but it becomes even more difficult when we realize how many different ways a manager may go about achieving the unit's objectives. Just identifying a man-ager's developmental needs is a complex task filled with ambiguities. Identifying or developing a training program to meet those needs is just as difficult and ambiguous.

# OUR APPROACH TO MANAGEMENT DEVELOPMENT

An appropriate needs analysis can only take place when the managerial process is understood. This understanding is also required for the trainer to be able to select the instructional strategy that will best meet the manager's developmental needs. Although we identify some sources from which training programs can be acquired or developed, they are not the focus of this chapter. Thousands of programs are avail-able, and new management development programs are developed frequently, as older ones fall out of favour and then many years later suddenly re-emerge as a "favoured" approach. Instead, the focus of this chapter is on increasing your ability to determine management development needs. Our philosophy is that the educated consumer makes wiser choices. Understanding the match required between managers and their organizational context provides the following two long-lasting benefits to the train-ing professional:

Canada School of the Public Service, including the Canadian Centre for Management Development *www.myschool-monecole.gc.ca/main_e.html*

1. An increased ability to determine a manager's development needs, and

2. An increased ability to assess accurately the appropriateness of a particular train-ing program for meeting those needs.

Thus, we provide an integrated framework (a model) for assessing managerial behaviour within the organizational context. Again, doing so takes a systems per-spective in which we look at the manager within both the unit and the organization.

# GENERAL OVERVIEW OF THE MANAGERIAL JOB

A well-established principle of management holds that the effectiveness of a particu-lar managerial style is contingent on other organizational variables.[5] That is, a successful managerial approach in one situation can be unsuccessful in another. How, then, can general statements be made about managerial duties and responsibilities across industries? Actually, no real contradiction arises here. The general activities carried out by managers seem to show more similarities than differences.[6] However, the frequency, the relative importance, and the manner in which these behaviours are performed differ greatly between organizations, even within the same industry. The first task is to understand the general makeup of the managerial job. With that understanding, we can turn our attention to some of the contextual factors that determine the frequency and style in which these activities are performed.

## MANAGERIAL ROLES

Research on managerial activity is integrated into general roles that are "customized" to fit into a particular management position in a particular organization.[7] Figure 10-1 illustrates the relationships among these roles, which form an integrated whole in which each role affects the others. One implication of this model is that managers must not only demonstrate the KSAs required to perform each role but also the KSAs required for their integration. Although individual managers may give more or less importance to a particular role, eliminating or neglecting one role results in direct consequences on the performance of other roles and hence on managerial effectiveness.

Mintzberg defines a manager as anyone who is in charge of an organization or one of its subunits. The manager's roles derive directly or indirectly from the formal authority and status granted to the position. The nature of the activities required of each role is described in Table 10-1.

Managers operate in a dynamic internal environment where they must constantly act to meet the challenges of new circumstances. Managers of subunits must not only adapt to new circumstances themselves but also must coordinate their actions with other subunits that are also adapting. Typically little time is available for careful planning and reflection. When careful planning occurs, it often will not reflect new circumstances that arose after the plan was developed.

Managers must be able to get their hands on the knowledge and skills necessary to meet these challenges as soon as they arise. This is not to say that careful planning and reflective analysis are not important in organizations. Managers, however, often cannot take much time for this important activity. For that reason, many organizations maintain staff units whose job it is to provide the manager with recommendations based on careful planning and thoughtful reflection. A typical manager, however, must quickly diagnose a situation, develop an appropriate response, see that it is implemented, and move on to the next task. This process requires that the manager understand the organization, its strategies and capabilities, how his unit fits into the puzzle, and how his behaviour will influence events. The next section addresses many of these issues.

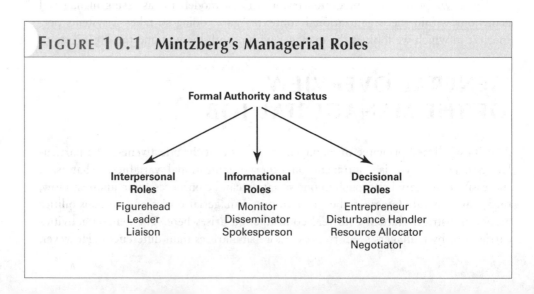

### FIGURE 10.1  Mintzberg's Managerial Roles

Formal Authority and Status

| Interpersonal Roles | Informational Roles | Decisional Roles |
|---|---|---|
| Figurehead | Monitor | Entrepreneur |
| Leader | Disseminator | Disturbance Handler |
| Liaison | Spokesperson | Resource Allocator |
| | | Negotiator |

## TABLE 10-1    Description of Managerial Roles

| Roles | Activities |
|---|---|
| **Interpersonal** | |
| Figurehead | Meets the routine, obligatory, social, and legal duties required of the head of a unit (examples: attendance at social functions, meeting with politicians, buyers, or suppliers). |
| Leader | Maintains, develops, and motivates the human resources necessary to meet the needs of the unit. |
| Liaison | Develops and maintains a network of individuals outside the unit to acquire information and action of benefit to the unit. |
| **Informational** | |
| Monitor | Searches for and acquires information about the unit and its environment so the manager becomes an information centre for the unit and the organization; derives from liaison and leader roles. |
| Disseminator | Distributes selected information to others within the unit or organization, some of which is transformed through integration with other information. |
| Spokesperson | Distributes selected information to others outside the unit regarding plans, values, activities, and other elements of the unit, and conveys the appropriate image of the unit. |
| **Decisional** | |
| Entrepreneur | Adjusts and proactively develops the unit to take advantage of existing opportunities or meet anticipated threats in the environment; acts based on inferences and conclusions drawn from the evaluation and integration of information gathered in the monitor role. |
| Disturbance Handler | Reacts to meet the immediate demands of the unit (examples: a wildcat strike, loss of a major customer). |
| Resource Allocator | Evaluates and chooses among proposals; integrates and authorizes activities and resource utilization. |
| Negotiator | Bargains to acquire the resources to meet the needs of the unit and organization. |

# ORGANIZATIONAL FACTORS

**Managerial context** refers to the alignment of an organization's environment, strategy, structure, and technology as described in Chapter 1. These factors play a significant role in determining which managerial KSAs are necessary. Although many of the KSA requirements may be the same across organizations, different organizational contexts will require the KSAs to be used more or less frequently and in varying manners (or styles). The organizational analysis portion of a managerial needs analysis should carefully consider the factors discussed here and their relation to managerial requirements.

**Managerial Context** the alignment of an organization's environment, strategy, structure, and technology.

# INTEGRATING STRATEGY, STRUCTURE, AND TECHNOLOGY

Organizations seek to maximize the integration of strategy, technology, structure, and human resources through their design. Managers must monitor and manage these interactions within their unit to ensure their unit's activities are integrated with the strategic direction and technological base of the organization. This integration is depicted in Table 10-2.

As discussed in Chapter 1, the market leader organization will be subject to a more uncertain environment and thus require more non-routine technologies. Rapid changes

**TABLE 10-2   Strategy, Technology, and Structure Integration**

|  | *Market Leader* | *Cost Leader* |
| --- | --- | --- |
| **Technology** | Non-routine | Routine |
| **Structure** | | |
| **Design** | Organic | Mechanistic |
| **Decision-Making** | Decentralized | Centralized |

in technology create high levels of complexity in organizations that are driven by technology, which market leaders typically are. In these organizations, interactions among the factors that affect efficiency and effectiveness create ambiguity and uncertainty. As a result, less job specialization, more coordination, and more decentralized decision-making are the strategy. Convrsely, recall from Chapter 1 that the cost leader strategy is more effective in environments with greater certainty. This type of strategy calls for more routinized technology, more centralized decision-making, and reduced organizational complexity. These various strategies have direct implications for the skills, traits, and styles of managers within these different organizations.

Whereas a corporation or strategic business unit faces an array of environmental forces, the individual subunit will face only a portion of those forces directly and must respond appropriately to these direct forces. Even though the subunits must support the organization's strategy, effective management practice for a subunit varies according to its own environment and its role in the overall strategy. However, on a general level, the environment of the subunits tends to reflect the organization's strategic environment.

# GENERAL CHARACTERISTICS OF MANAGERS

In the discussion of needs assessment in Chapter 3, we noted that an employee's duties and responsibilities must be understood to determine the KSAs required to perform those tasks. Unfortunately much of the management development literature suggests that evidence of managerial effectiveness in one organization can be applied to other organizations. Whether this application is possible depends on the similarity of the organizational context. Remember our caution about copying other organizations without understanding the theory behind their practice. Nevertheless, the literature does identify many managerial characteristics that seem to be necessary for most managers.

The characteristics we discuss below are, like managerial roles, general in nature and thought to be applicable across most organizations. Later we provide a model that can be used to integrate these general characteristics into various organizational contexts. As we review the empirical literature on managerial characteristics that are predictive of success, remember that the criteria used to determine "effectiveness" or "success" vary considerably across studies. However, some aspect of effectiveness or success is associated with these characteristics. Certainly, the frequency with which they are reported in the literature gives support to their organizational utility in certain contexts.

## MANAGEMENT STYLES

A number of management theories attempt to demonstrate the relationship between managerial behaviour and the situation in which that behaviour occurs.[8] Although we will not explore each of these theories, there is a common thread running through most of them. **Managerial style** seems to be related to two dimensions of leader behaviour: employee-oriented and task-oriented behaviours.[9] Research on path-goal theory further differentiates these two styles. The **employee-oriented style** has two types: participative and supportive. The **task-oriented style** also has two types: directive or achievement-oriented.[10]

Employee-oriented styles require higher levels of interpersonal skills (discussed in the next section). The **participative style** emphasizes involving subordinates in decision making, particularly in how they go about achieving their task. A **supportive style** is characterized by friendliness, empathy, and concern for meeting employees' needs.

Task-oriented styles require fewer human and more technical skills. In the **directive style**, subordinates are given instructions about what to do, how to do it, and when it should be done. The **achievement style** emphasizes goal setting and high performance expectations for subordinates.

## CATEGORIES OF MANAGEMENT CHARACTERISTICS

In addition to a manager's style, which represents her actual behaviour, factors related to the manager's cognitive makeup also affect her effectiveness. The research we examined[11] is organized into four major categories: conceptual knowledge/skill, technical knowledge/skill, interpersonal knowledge/skill, and personal traits. These categories are not independent of one another. Personal traits influence interpersonal skills, and both will affect how technical and conceptual activities are carried out. Most likely it is the integration of all four categories into a whole that determines the degree of a manager's success. Unfortunately, little research is available to tell us about how successful managers integrate these characteristics. For now, we will consider them separately.

### Conceptual Knowledge and Skills
Conceptual knowledge and skills refer to the mental abilities required to analyze and diagnose complex situations and make appropriate decisions. They are essential and common to all (or nearly all) management positions. Listed here are some of the more frequently cited examples of the requirements in this category:

#### Planning and Decision-Making

- Being aware of decision-making alternatives and being skilled in their use,
- Setting priorities,
- Forecasting events,
- Integrating organizational policies, procedures, and objectives, and
- Adapting to legal, social, and political environments.

#### Organizing

- Developing appropriate organizational structures,
- Coordinating separate but interrelated activities,
- Scheduling activities to reach time, efficiency, and quality goals, and
- Allocating resources to maximize return on investment.

**Managerial Style** two dimensions of leader behaviour: employee-oriented and task-oriented behaviours.

**Employee-Oriented Style** behaviour that focuses on the subordinate as a person; made up of two types: participative and supportive.

**Task-Oriented Style** behaviour that focuses on the work the subordinate does; made up of two types: directive or achievement-oriented.

**Participative Style** involvement of subordinates in decision making, particularly in how they go about achieving their task.

**Supportive Style** characterized by friendliness, empathy, and concern for meeting employees' needs.

**Directive Style** subordinates are given instructions about what to do, how to do it, and when it should be done.

**Achievement Style** emphasizes goal setting and high-performance expectations for subordinates.

**Conceptual Knowledge and Skills** the mental abilities required to analyze and diagnose complex situations and make appropriate decisions.

**Controlling**

- Knowing how to apply various control systems,

- Developing control systems,

- Developing and supporting initiatives, and

- Developing policy, procedures, and objectives.

## Technical Knowledge and Skills

**Technical Knowledge and Skills** the knowledge and skills needed to perform the functional and general management aspects of the organizational unit.

Technical knowledge and skills are necessary to carry out the operations of a particular functional area (e.g., marketing, engineering, human resources). For example, a marketing manager will find advertising, direct sales, and consumer psychology are areas in which technical knowledge and skills are expected. Also included in this category are general technical knowledge and skills required for managing any organizational unit. The most frequently mentioned are financial analysis, budgeting, managerial accounting, and marketing goods and services.

## Interpersonal Knowledge and Skills

**Interpersonal Knowledge and Skills** the ability to work with, understand, and motivate others.

Interpersonal knowledge and skills, often called "human" skills, refer to the ability to work with, understand, and motivate others, both individually and in groups. As Mintzberg's research indicates, managers spend most of their time interacting with others. It is primarily the manager's interpersonal skills and knowledge of human behaviour that determine her success in influencing others and developing information networks. Examples of knowledge and skill elements in this category include the following:

- Understanding individual differences,

- Motivating subordinates,

- Developing subordinates,

- Building a work team and providing team leadership,

- Managing conflict constructively,

- Adjusting behaviour to fit situational demands (behavioural flexibility),

- Presenting a position in a compelling fashion (persuasion),

- Listening effectively,

- Showing awareness of social cues, and

- Maintaining objectivity in social situations.

## Personal Traits

**Personal Traits** a relatively permanent predisposition to behave in a particular way.

Personal traits are not knowledge and skills, but rather qualities of the manager as a person. In some ways personal traits could be thought of as attitudes, but they are more complex. A personal trait is a relatively permanent predisposition to behave in a particular way. Early leadership studies consistently failed to identify personality traits that predict successful leaders[12] but research over the last 15 years found certain measurable characteristics that seem to be predictive of future success as a manager. It is important to remember that personal traits may change markedly over the course of a manager's career. The traits discussed here were characteristic of early career stages and were associated with managers' success over the long term. However, the causal relationship is far from clear.

**nAch** a strong desire to assume personal responsibility, to receive concrete feedback on task performance, and to single-mindedly pursue task accomplishment.

Early work by McClelland and his colleagues identified four need states that are predictive of effective managers. We focus on three: need for achievement (nAch), need for power (nPow), and need for autonomy (nAut). Those high in **nAch** possess a strong desire to assume personal responsibility, wish to receive concrete feedback on task performance, and demonstrate a single-minded preoccupation with task accomplishment.[13] Those high in **nAut** show a strong desire to work independently. For situations in which those with high nAut work alone, they prefer to control their own pace and procedure and not to be hampered by excessive rules.[14] These individuals tend to resist working in groups and indicate their need to be personally responsible for outcomes. Those high in **nPow** desire to lead, influence, and control the people and things around them.[15]

Recent research describes these need states in terms of two general characteristics: drive and leadership motivation.[16] **Drive** includes nAch as well as ambition, energy, and tenacity.[17] **Leadership motivation** relates primarily to nPow and distinguishes between a need for institutional power, which is directed toward organizational goals, and a need for personal power, which is focused on personal goals.[18] Institutional power needs are related to more-successful managers and personal power to less-successful managers and non-managers. The research also shows that those with high nPow (institutional), moderately high nAch, and moderate to low nAut are generally the most effective managers.[19] In addition, likeableness, resistance to stress, and career orientation are generally found to be predictive of future success.

Recall that a common thread running through the management style literature is the existence of two general styles of management. A second common thread is that leaders/managers must adapt their style to fit the situations. A manager's ability to be flexible or adaptable with respect to style of management is also highly predictive of success.[20] This adaptability/flexibility characteristic is found in the literature as both a personal trait and a skill, and it is clearly a necessary component for long-term success as a manager. However, it may be required more in certain kinds of organizations than in others.

## INTEGRATING MANAGERIAL ROLES AND CHARACTERISTICS

When examining the roles that managers must perform and the characteristics needed for effective managers, it becomes possible to match characteristics with roles. Table 10-3 depicts such integration. For example, performing obligatory ceremonial duties (figurehead) will almost certainly require awareness of social cues, oral communication skills, and behavioural flexibility. The manager's personal traits, particularly likeableness and resistance to stress, are likely to influence how they respond to those situations; conversely, it is not likely that a manager's technical or conceptual knowledge/skill will be much of a factor in this role. Using similar logic, we matched the other characteristics with roles.

Table 10-3 serves as a heuristic device, relating a manager's knowledge, skills, and traits to various aspects of the managers' job. It is important to remember, however, that the precise nature of the roles and requisite managerial characteristics differ from organization to organization and even within the same organization. In particular, the evidence is reasonably conclusive that the importance of the various roles, and consequently the associated knowledge and skills, differs from level to level within the organization's hierarchy.

## ROLES, KSAs, AND MANAGEMENT LEVEL

Lower-level managers primarily supervise and coordinate the work of non-managers. They are usually in daily contact with their subordinates and peers and are responsible

**nAut** a strong desire to work independently.

**nPow** a desire to lead, influence, and control people and things.

**Drive** combination of nAch, ambition, energy, and tenacity.

**Leadership Motivation** a nPow relationship that distinguishes between a need for institutional power, which is directed toward organizational goals, and a need for personal power, which is focused on personal goals.

**TABLE 10-3    Managerial Roles and Associated Management Characteristics**

| Managerial Role | Knowledge and Skills | | | |
| | Conceptual | Technical | Interpersonal | Personal Traits |
| --- | --- | --- | --- | --- |
| **Interpersonal** | | | | |
| Figurehead | | | yes | yes |
| Leader | yes | | yes | yes |
| Liaison | yes | | yes | yes |
| **Informational** | | | | |
| Monitor | yes | yes | | yes |
| Disseminator | yes | yes | yes | |
| Spokesperson | yes | yes | yes | |
| **Decisional** | | | | |
| Entrepreneur | yes | yes | yes | yes |
| Disturbance Handler | yes | yes | yes | yes |
| Resource Allocator | yes | yes | yes | yes |
| Negotiator | yes | | yes | yes |

for the day-to-day operations of their unit. They depend primarily on interpersonal and technical skills to get the job done.[21] Their roles are primarily leader, monitor, disseminator, disturbance handler, and negotiator. Usually other roles, requiring greater levels of conceptual skills, are unnecessary, with rules, policies, procedures, and upper management decisions taking their place.

Middle managers co-ordinate the activities of lower-level managers. The manager in the middle (or sometimes "in the muddle," as they like to say) performs the role of liaison, spokesperson, resource allocator, and entrepreneur as well as most of the roles performed by the lower-level manager. Interpersonal skills remain important, but technical skills decrease in importance. Conceptual skills are somewhat more important.

Top managers coordinate the activities of the organization through their middle managers. Conceptual skills are of primary importance at this level, particularly the entrepreneurial role. Leader behaviour is also important here, as it instills a sense of direction and motivates those who report directly to them as well as employees in general. Informational, liaison, and figurehead roles are predominant, and the focus of the other roles changes from inside to outside the organization.

Organizations in general place higher priority on certain types of managerial KSAs at different levels in the organization, but the preceding discussion is not especially helpful in identifying the job requirements of managers in a specific organization. Each organization has its own context and specific expectations of managers within that context. Thus, even though it is generally helpful to know that supervisors typically are expected to rely on their technical knowledge and skills more than on their conceptual knowledge and skills, the relative importance will depend on the organizational context.

# INTEGRATION: STRATEGIES AND MANAGEMENT CHARACTERISTICS

Combining research on organizational environment, strategy, structure, and technology with the research on leadership provides some general prescriptions for effective managerial characteristics at each extreme of the strategy continuum. In the most general sense, effective managers possess technical, interpersonal, and conceptual skills.[22] Leadership research adds the concepts of personal traits and style. We examine these factors and assess the degree to which each is more or less relevant in market and cost leader organizations. Table 10-4 provides a summary of this.

## TECHNICAL COMPETENCE AND CONTEXT

Research indicates that technical competence is an important foundation for effective management.[23] Both market leader and cost leader strategies require managers with high levels of technical competence, but the technical sophistication required of market leaders is much greater because they operate on the leading edge of technology. Many technologies capable of significant flexibility in application are also required, making the environment more complex and less predictable. Thus, market leader organizations are rated higher in the need for managers with technical skills, as noted in Table 10-4.

## INTERPERSONAL COMPETENCE AND CONTEXT

The market leader strategy uses a more organic, less formalized design that requires the manager to interact more with higher-level managers, subordinates, and peers. These interactions are critical to coordinating activities within and between units. In cost leader organizations, the centralization of decision-making and the formalization of rules, procedures, and policies decrease the importance of many of the interpersonal skills. These characterizations reflect a relative difference in the two types of organizations and should not be construed in an all-or-none fashion. Effectiveness in these "human skills" generally differentiates between successful and unsuccessful managers,[24] but logic suggests this is more likely in market leader organizations, where considerably more interaction is required (see Table 10-4).

## CONCEPTUAL COMPETENCE AND CONTEXT

Again, the cost leader organization, by design, reduces the importance of managerial conceptual skills except at the higher levels of the organization, because of the routine

## TABLE 10-4  Strategy and Managerial Characteristics Integration

|  | Market Leader | Cost Leader |
|---|---|---|
| **Skills** | | |
| Technical | More sophisticated and non-routine | Less sophisticated and routine |
| Interpersonal | Higher | Lower |
| Conceptual | Higher | Lower |
| **Traits** | | |
| Drive | High | High |
| Flexibility | Higher | Lower |
| Leader motive | High | High |
| **Style** | | |
| Participative | Higher | Lower |
| Supportive | No difference | No difference |
| Achievement | Higher | Lower |
| Directive | Lower | Higher |

technology, mechanistic design, centralized decision making, and formalized coordination systems. Market leader organizations, conversely, require managers with greater conceptual skills at all levels because of their more complex organization and the need to reduce barriers to creativity. In other words, conceptual skills are more important at all levels in the market leader compared with the cost leader organization. There is agreement that technical skills are more important at lower-level management positions, conceptual skills more important at higher levels, and human skills important at all levels.

Studies support the idea that interpersonal and conceptual skills are more predictive of managerial success than are technical skills.[25] This conclusion, of course, makes sense if technical activities decrease in frequency as a person moves from lower to higher management positions. The more effective managers are those who are able to handle the increasing demands of human and conceptual problems. In addition, individuals are typically hired or promoted to management positions on the basis of their technical competence at lower levels, so these skills are less likely to differentiate effective from ineffective performers. Particularly in technical units, new employees are rarely hired on the basis of interpersonal skills or ability to conceptualize complex organizational systems. When they are promoted to managerial positions, they are likely to need development in these areas.

## PERSONAL TRAITS AND CONTEXT

For nearly all of the traits examined, no compelling evidence or logic suggests that managers high in these traits will be more or less effective in any particular organizational context. The only trait likely to be more useful in one organization than the other is flexibility. Because market leader organizations face more ambiguity and change than do cost leaders, the manager with higher levels of adaptability would likely be more effective than one who was less flexible. This point is reflected in Table 10-4.

## MANAGEMENT STYLE AND CONTEXT

Of the two employee-oriented styles, only the participative style is expected to show differences in effectiveness based on strategy. Logic suggests that participative styles are more effective in market leader organizations. Obviously, a decentralized structure promotes higher levels of participation in decision-making. In the technical units of the market leader organization, this issue is especially important, because innovation and creativity are facilitated by multiple inputs and synergistic (working together) outcomes. In addition, because of the non-routine nature of the technology, decisions relating to a particular area of that technology require the input of those most familiar with it.

We can expect the participative style to be less effective in the cost leader organization for several compelling reasons. For one, decisions are more centralized. The jobs are well defined by the routine technology, policies, procedures, and structure. Few reasons or opportunities arise that would promote the participation of employees in decisions that would meaningfully affect their job. Remember, we are talking about an organization at the extreme end of the continuum. Even here, we are not saying no participation would take place, only that it would be of less value to the organization.

We find no logic to support the notion that a supportive style is more or less effective in either organizational context. Although employees are likely to be somewhat different in organizations at opposite ends of the strategy continuum, there is no justification for postulating differences in the need for friendliness, empathy, or concern from their managers. In other words, this style is effective in nearly all organizations.

For the task-oriented styles, clear structural reasons suggest differences in the effectiveness of the achievement versus directive styles. The achievement style is more effective for the market leader. Market leaders require managers to reduce some of the ambiguities of their unit's task, ambiguities created by the market leader's need to quickly identify and place new products or significant modifications of old products in the market. So, the achievement-oriented manager clarifies goals, parameters, and performance expectations. For the cost leader, goals and expectations are well understood and standardized, leaving little need for the manager to exert effort in this area. In fact, subordinates are likely to see such behaviour as redundant and negative.

Some amount of directive behaviour will be useful in the market leader organization to the extent that it clarifies responsibilities and expectations. However, the detailed direction of who will do what, how, and when is contrary to the structural and technological systems of the market leader. For the cost leader, however, it is clearly important for the manager to monitor and ensure that the right people are doing the right things at the right time. In addition, the cost leader's design uses a centralized system in which operations are driven from the top. It is the manager's responsibility to ensure that changes in expectations are conveyed accurately to subordinates and that subordinates comply with the direction in a specific manner. We view the directive style as being more effective in the cost leader organization. Still, managers in such organizations must be discriminating in how it is applied. High- or adequately performing employees in this organization may find additional direction from the manager irritating. Conversely, in the market leader organization employees may come to desire direction from their managers because of the absence of well-defined structure in their jobs. Nevertheless, the design of this organization favours the achievement style over the directive, providing employees with goals and objectives and giving them the autonomy to figure out the best way to achieve them (see Table 10-4).

The relationships described here between strategy and manager characteristics are generalizations, as are the relationships described among strategy, structure, and technology. Any given organization that adopts a market leader strategy will require some routine as well as non-routine technologies. The point is that they will experience a greater preponderance of non-routine technologies than if they followed a cost leader strategy. Likewise, the managerial characteristics related here to organizational strategy point to those characteristics that will be most effective with the particular structural and technology characteristics of that strategy. Perhaps the most appropriate use of Table 10-4 is at the organizational subunit level. If the subunit is structured in ways consistent with the strategy, the managerial characteristics associated with the strategy are likely to be more effective. Consideration could be given to using this table in developing a managerial needs assessment where the organizational context of the manager's unit can be measured.

# MANAGEMENT DEVELOPMENT IMPLICATIONS

The preceding model suggests that the first key to effective management is for managers to know and understand the context in which they are operating. Then, based on that knowledge, they have to know the effective skills, traits, and styles that will be effective in that context. Finally, they must determine which of the KSAs they feel they are deficient in and who get relevant training. All of these steps are important if a company is going to have managers who are effective in the environment they are placed. Management development needs to address the following:

- Understanding context,

- Self-awareness and diagnostic skills, and

- Managerial person analysis.

## UNDERSTANDING CONTEXT

The most obvious implication of the context/management characteristics model is that effective managers must be able to adapt themselves and their unit to the needs of the organization. To do so, they need a clear understanding of the organization's strategy and their unit's part in that strategy. It is only with this understanding that managers can use their personal characteristics most effectively. Thus, the following are important parts of all developmental programs:

- The clarification of the organization's situation,

- Its strategy for coping with the situation,

- How the various units fit into the strategy, and

- How the training program relates to these things.

Organizations that develop their managers in this manner get a competitive advantage.[26] Too often, however, management development programs try to provide managers with skills, knowledge, styles, and traits without an understanding of the context in which they are to be applied. In the worst case, the development is inappropriate for some units; in the best case, in those units for which the development is appropriate, managers do not understand why it is appropriate.

## SELF-AWARENESS AND DIAGNOSTIC SKILLS

Once managers understand what is needed from their unit and why, it is important that they understand how their own characteristics influence the activities within their unit and their unit's interaction with other units. This understanding requires self-awareness and diagnostic skills. To increase self-awareness, managers need to be able to access basic data required to diagnose cause-and-effect relationships between their behaviour and others' actions.

Diagnostic skills are necessary to identify why gaps exist between what is expected of the unit and what actually occurs. Managers must be able to create the appropriate match between their behaviour and

a) The structure/design of the unit, and

b) The characteristics of the subordinates.

Creating these matches requires the ability to diagnose the existence and cause of mismatches. Self-awareness and diagnostic skills are the basic requirements for managerial adaptability to changing conditions.

Once a manager understands the organizational context within which his unit operates and acquires the adaptability skills of self-awareness and diagnosis, he is ready for the appropriate development of knowledge, skills, and styles. For this, a managerial person analysis is required.

## MANAGERIAL PERSON ANALYSIS

Identifying the required KSAs for a managerial job is difficult. Assume this identification is completed and now it must be determined whether the managers in unit A possess the required KSAs. How do you go about determining a manager's style, traits, and ability to interact with peers, subordinates, and superiors? One method gaining considerable popularity is the 360-degree feedback (360-DF) described in Chapter 3. This approach requires a sample of those with whom the manager interacts to fill out an anonymous questionnaire about the manager. Responses are then analyzed and graphed to provide feedback to the manager. The results show where general agreement lies among subordinates, peers, and superiors concerning how the manager "comes across." These data, combined with the data from the unit's operations and other measurement tools, can be used to identify areas of development for each manager. It can also be used during training to help the manager identify the cause-and-effect relationships between her behaviour and others' reactions. The manager, of course, should be involved in identifying her areas of strength and weakness.

This multiple-source feedback should be used only for development purposes, not for formal performance evaluations or for pay, promotion, or termination decisions.[27] If it is used for the latter purpose, the responses of those filling out the questionnaire are likely to change. Respondents who are friends will inflate the manager's score, rivals (peers and some of the superiors) will lower their ratings somewhat, and the staff support person the manager complained about would cut him to the bone. However, the research shows that when assessment occurs for developmental purposes, the validity of personal characteristics measurement is enhanced by the inclusion of supervisor, co-worker, subordinate, and customer ratings.[28]

Though 360-DF often results in positive comments about the manager, it can also provide powerful, uncomfortable, and surprising information. In addition to the characteristics discussed in this chapter, 360-DF provides feedback about a number of other personal characteristics that typically do not show up in the research on management effectiveness. For example, one manager learned that he stood too close to people when talking to them and that little bits of saliva would fly out of his mouth when he spoke—not a good combination for a manager looking to advance his career. After feedback, he stood farther back and started speech therapy. Another manager, the head of Nestlé's Perrier operation, found out that when he moved from Head of Sales and Marketing to the CEO position, people changed their interpretation of his behaviour. His temper and occasional "public whippings" of senior managers that was previously tolerated and seen as demonstrating forceful management became frightening after he became CEO with the authority to fire anyone, and managers stopped coming to him with problems and ideas.[29]

Because of the sensitive nature of the data, feedback must be carefully handled by the training professional to ensure that the manager sees it as "legitimate" and constructive. The most difficult comments to accept are those about interpersonal skills, such as "untrustworthy," "poor listener," "uses poor judgment." These characteristics are seen as core competency skills and nearly every manager assumes she is strong in these areas. The Centre for Creative Leadership estimates that only about one-third of all managers accurately predict how others view them. Another third hold inflated views of their talents. The most surprises await these managers, because subordinates almost always rate them the least effective.[30] For some hard-core control-oriented managers it sometimes takes massive doses of feedback before the message finally sinks in. Many will attempt to dismiss the results as inaccurate, inappropriate, or irrelevant. The training professional's job is to help the manager come to terms with and accept the results. When results are consistent (e.g., most people rate the manager in the same way), it is more difficult for the manager to explain them away. The most important part of the feedback agent's job is helping the manager understand that her intentions are not the same as other people's interpretation of her behaviour. Once the manager makes this association, she can then begin to explore what she might do differently to achieve the desired results.

# SOURCES OF KNOWLEDGE/SKILL ACQUISITION

The most obvious source of management training is the organization itself. However, most companies use a combination of internal and external sources to provide their managers with the appropriate mix of developmental opportunities. A survey of training managers[31] showed 93 percent of the surveyed companies providing both internal and external training to supervisors and middle managers, and 63 percent providing such training for executives. Only about 15 percent of the firms said they developed internal courses for executives, while more than 60 percent did so for middle managers and supervisors. These numbers tell us that few firms rely only on internal training resources, especially for upper-level managers and executives. Those involved in management development must be familiar with training and development opportunities outside their organization as well as being able to develop useful programs internally.

The following sections explore some of the more frequently discussed alternatives in the literature. This does not imply an endorsement of any particular source. Rather we present them to demonstrate the variety of sources that are available.

## EXTERNALLY BASED TRAINING

**Executive/management education programs** university programs that cover the range of management issues from traditional MBA programs to building strategically effective organizations.

Executive/management education programs at universities provide knowledge and skills of a general nature. These programs cover the range of management issues from traditional MBA programs to building strategically effective organizations. Other sources of management development activities are training companies, consultants, and professional associations. They supply a wide variety of training activities ranging from broad-based, general-application programs to those that are narrowly focused on limited areas of skill and knowledge. When the education is narrowly focused, dealing with specific topics such as project management, team building, financial analysis, or effective communication, the managers typically stay in residence at the training site for a few days to several weeks. When the focus is broader, dealing with general management domains (e.g., executive MBA programs), the manager likely attends training for a few hours to a few days periodically over periods up to 24 months. Typically, the goal of broad-based programs is generic skill or content learning rather than job-specific skills. Personal insight is generally not a goal; classroom-based methods tend to be used rather than games and simulations.[32] Personal insight and job-specific KSAs are more typically addressed in the narrow-focus programs.

The principal advantages of externally based programs are:

- They expose managers to the current thinking and theory in management;
- They remove organizational constraints in exploring new approaches;

- They allow interchange of ideas among managers from different organizational backgrounds; and

- They cost less per person than internally developed programs.

Problems that may arise with externally based programs include:

- Inability to relate content to company-specific approaches,

- Inconsistency of instructor effectiveness (some are excellent, others poor) and the inability of the contractor to choose the right instructor (more typical with executive MBA programs than with residential programs),

- Inability to specify expected company outcomes as a result of the training,

- Extended time away from the job,

- Failure of the manager's company to provide on-the-job reinforcement of concepts and skills, and

- Inability to control the content of the training (the company can choose the course or program, but not the content).

Despite these concerns, most companies see externally based management programs as valuable tools. Enrolment in traditional MBA education is up, and enrolment in the growth of "for-profit" universities is up even more.[33] About 49 percent of companies utilize university-based residential or executive MBA programs, and most of these companies use some form of external short courses.[34] The primary reasons for utilizing these programs are the credibility of the organization offering the program, the nature of the program topic areas, and the managers' belief that it will meet their needs.

## CORPORATE UNIVERSITIES

The growth of **corporate universities** is even greater than the growth of for-profit universities.[35] In an attempt to overcome some of the deficiencies of university-based education while maintaining many of its advantages, large corporations create their own internal "universities." Phillips Petroleum, General Electric, IBM, Motorola, McDonald's, and Xerox are just a few of the companies that have developed their own university-type education. According to Jeanne Meister, President of Corporate University Exchange, about 1600 corporate universities exist in the United States.[36] The reason organizations are exploring this approach is that after examining the characteristics of university-based versus external, non-university-based formal educational programs for managers, they determined they could do better internally.[37] The primary reasons are as follows:

**Corporate Universities** universities created by corporations in an attempt to overcome some of the deficiencies of university-based education while maintaining many of its advantages.

- The organization understands its own approach to management and can convey it better to its managers;

- Managers can obtain job-specific knowledge and skills;

- The company can ensure quality instruction; and

- The courses are cost-effective because of the organization's size.

Dr. Bill Lee explains why American Airlines developed its own university in Training in Action 10-1.

Public and private universities draw a wide range of managers to their management development programs. The diversity of backgrounds and interests requires that the concepts and methods taught must be general in nature so as to be applicable

## Training in Action 10-1

### Why American Airlines Developed Its Own Corporate University

American Airlines decided to develop a Corporate University (CU) because training was fragmented and many departments operated as cottage industries. Departments were hiring their own outside consultants, vendors, and so forth. Dr. Lee said, "We found that in many departments, the local management had contracts with the same off-the-shelf course providers and were all paying premium price." Other departments were hiring consultants to provide custom programs already developed by other departments. Before the CU was developed, this money came out of the operations budget, and no one was really tracking it.

"The CU is becoming a central clearinghouse for all material in the company, and is able to negotiate a better price with vendors and off-the-shelf providers as more and more departments come under the CU mantle," says Dr. Lee, "but there are still some groups that develop and provide their own training. We have reached out to them and offered to share what we have rather than trying to take them over. They have viewed that very positively and some groups have agreed to turn over their training to the CU because it is one less thing they have to manage. In many areas, such as publishing materials, we have saved thousands of dollars. In the area of government compliance we have saved literally millions by providing quality programs with consistent delivery."

Dr. Lee reports, "We are currently pursuing relationships with similar industries that are non-competitive but have some of the same needs to reduce costs and maximize benefit."

*Source:* Personal communication with Dr. Bill Lee, Director of Measurement and Performance Analysis, American Airlines Corporate FlagShip University, Fort Worth Texas, September, 2002.

across most situations. Although students are usually encouraged to apply these concepts and methods to their own organization, faculty can do only a limited amount to facilitate the transfer of this knowledge back to students' jobs.

The corporate university, conversely, can integrate the technical, conceptual, and interpersonal skills within the context of the organization's strategy, structure, and technology. The company can control and shape the curriculum to meet its own needs and values, provide the same content to everyone, and schedule instruction to be convenient for the organization and the trainee.

Some problems, however, exist with the corporate university approach. Matching the curriculum to the needs of the organization remains a difficult task. Pressures within the organization may discourage training in some areas or the use of certain methods, while encouraging others. Although this situation reflects the political reality of the organization, it limits the organization's ability to develop new and more-effective approaches. In addition, costs may actually be higher than for externally developed programs. Phillips, for example, found its costs to be about 50 percent more than for similar external training and education.[38]

This approach is possible only for large organizations. It is neither practical nor feasible for small- to moderate-sized businesses to create their own university that includes faculty and attendance requirements. Smaller organizations must rely on public and private universities as well as other external training and development suppliers.

Regardless of whether training is provided internally or through external sources, the training department needs to match the content of the training with the context within which the managers are to use it. Before adopting a management development program, the following questions are useful in assessing the match of a particular program to managers' needs.

1. Do the program outcomes meet an identified need?
2. Will the learning that results from the training be supported on the job?

3. Will behaviour resulting from the training conform to the organization's policies, procedures, and norms?

4. Will the individuals receive any personal benefit from the training?

5. What is the cost/benefit ratio of the approach compared with that of alternative approaches?

Another important point is the evaluation of such training. It is one thing to train managers and discover that the training is of little or no value. It is quite another to continue to do so, wasting training dollars and credibility year after year.

## TYPES OF MANAGEMENT DEVELOPMENT PROGRAMS

A description of the full diversity of management development approaches and techniques is beyond the scope of this chapter. However, the following descriptions cover a variety of programs and techniques associated with the competencies of effective management described earlier. We are not necessarily advocating the use of any of them but are simply providing a glimpse of the diversity available. Those wishing to probe deeper into this area might begin with the references provided.

**Knowledge/Skills Development: Conceptual** A variety of ways to develop conceptual skills in managers include the following:

1. Management/business games, simulations, and case studies.

2. On-the-job training: Included in this are mentoring, coaching, action learning, job rotation, understudy training, and junior boards. Mentoring and understudy training are similar in that the manager works closely with a senior manager to develop or improve skills. Understudy training occurs when the manager is assigned as an assistant or adjunct to the senior manager; she learns by observing the senior manager and completing assignments of gradually increasing complexity and responsibility. Junior boards combine simulation and on-the-job training techniques. A junior board of directors is created, comprising promising middle-level executives who are given critical issues relating to the company's business and asked to provide senior management with recommendations.[39]

3. Decision making: Situations are diagnosed to determine the appropriate approach to making a decision. For example, Vroom and Yetton provide a model in which the manager learns the relevant situational variables that determine whether the decision should be made by the manager alone, delegated to a group of subordinates, or handled somewhere in between.[40] Another approach to decision making is rational manager training, which uses simulations to develop managers' problem-solving and decision-making skills. A unique feature of this approach is the use of actual situations in the company for analysis, identification, and elimination of potential problems.

4. Managerial roles: This approach, based on Mintzberg's model discussed earlier, is aimed at providing managers with an understanding of what they are doing and why. Through self-observation and understanding of our roles, effectiveness is increased.[41] A related approach, the incident technique, utilizes critical incidents from the organization, asking managers to identify the facts needed to address the incident.[42] Doing so develops the skills especially needed to perform the monitoring and disturbance-handler roles.

### <u>Knowledge/Skills Development: Technical</u> Technical training, especially professional skills training, is often purchased from outside sources.

1. Degree and certification programs: Degree programs in business and technical disciplines provide the technical foundation for most managers. In addition, technical knowledge and skills specific to a particular discipline are developed through external suppliers such as professional associations and through certificate training programs. For example, the Human Resources Professionals Association of Ontario provides training programs that prepare human resource managers to take the certification exam. Other professional disciplines (e.g., accounting, finance, engineering) provide similar types of programs.

2. Workshops and seminars: These are offered on a wide range of topics and by a wide range of providers (e.g., universities, professional associations, consultants, training companies). Larger companies that prefer internally developed workshops and seminars possess the resources to acquire high-level instructors and develop the appropriate training materials. These programs are also more easily tailored to fit the specific needs of the company.

### <u>Interpersonal and Management Style</u> We combined these approaches because it is difficult to separate management style from interpersonal skills. In fact, management styles are often addressed in training through emphasizing one or more interpersonal skills.

1. Interactive skills training: This approach uses simulations and feedback from observers to provide trainees with ways of interacting more effectively with others. It is an approach that makes managers more aware of how their behaviour influences the way others perceive and react to them.[43]

2. Grid management: The two most important managerial characteristics in this approach are the manager's concern for work outcomes and her concern for people (note the parallel here with "employee and task orientation"). The proposition here is that managers who have strong concerns in both of these areas are the best managers. Training focuses on developing the manager's ability to display these characteristics simultaneously. Even though the manager must respond to different situations with the appropriate behaviour, it is the value orientation associated with both a strong concern for people and task that guides the manager's behaviour.[44]

3. Workshops and seminars: Again, these are offered on a wide range of topics and by a wide range of providers. These programs typically focus on a particular skill area, such as communication, managerial style, or team facilitation.

### *Developing Personal Traits.* Development of personal traits can be a part of many management development programs. A few programs that focus specifically on trait development are listed below.

1. Role motivation: The object of this program is to develop six motivational states in managers: favourable attitude toward authority, desire to compete, assertiveness, desire to exercise power, desire for distinctiveness, and a sense of responsibility. These motives help managers deal with employee work deficiencies and meet organizational criteria for effectiveness (primarily in large organizations). It includes development of interpersonal skills but focuses primarily on self-examination and development of internal values.[45]

2. Need for achievement: This program of self-study, goal setting, and case analysis is designed to provide managers with an understanding of their need for achievement and development of that need so that it is focused on constructive behaviour. This approach yielded the best results for small business owners, particularly at the early stages of their careers.[46]

# TRAINING FOR EXECUTIVE-LEVEL MANAGEMENT

One of the reasons cited earlier for providing a chapter on management training is that "managers are accountable for success"; this is *especially* true at the senior level, as the success of the whole company is at stake here. Furthermore, at this level it is absolutely critical to align training needs to the overall strategy, yet it is surprising how many companies still do not do it.[47] Consider the company that goes international. What do they do when they discover that their executives do not possess the KSAs necessary for such a venture? There are numerous examples of this.[48] So, before any development takes place at this level, a thorough examination of the strategic direction needs to be undertaken. Once the direction is set, the KSAs required to meet the strategic direction (operational analysis) can be determined. These KSAs are then compared with each of the executive's performance capabilities (person analysis), and developmental plans for each executive can be determined.

## SKILLS, TRAITS, AND LEADERSHIP STYLE

An important duty for executives is to help formulate the strategic direction of the organization, plan for effective implementation of the plan, create mechanisms for ensuring the strategic direction is followed, and track the progress of the change. These activities require strong conceptual skills in the entrepreneurial role, and conceptual and interpersonal skills in the leader role.

**President/CEO** The top executive must be effective in her role as entrepreneur (able to analyze the situation and choose the proper direction for the organization) and as leader (able to implement the plan through others). Although both of these roles are important, the more important one is leadership. The literature is full of examples of top executives coming in and revamping the organization, making it into what they view it should be, and more importantly, getting the employees to buy into that vision. In fact is that not what happened at Domtar?

Even CEOs who are promoted from within need to examine the current environment and determine what changes in direction (if any) need to be taken. The important point is that the employees need to feel confident in the CEO's ability and buy into the executive's decisions regarding the direction the organization is taking. To inspire this kind of loyalty requires sound leadership skills. Of course, the importance of these skills will depend on the strategic direction being taken. The leadership skills for a CEO in a cost leader organization that is not making substantial changes in its strategic direction will not be as important as those for the CEO in a market leader that is beginning to move in a different direction.

**Executives in General** One of the reasons for grooming internal higher-level managers to become executives is that they are already part of the organizational culture and possess many of the skills that are important to the type of organization they are in, whether market leader, cost leader, or somewhere in between. This reasoning is especially applicable if management performance is based on a set of competencies. As long as promotion is based on sound appraisals and development continues, managers should continue to be effective when they are promoted to the executive level. However, there still must be a process for preparing them for the move.

## STRATEGIES FOR DEVELOPMENT OF EXECUTIVES AND FUTURE EXECUTIVES (MANAGERS)

Note we are discussing two different levels of management here: development of executives and development of managers (preparing them for the executive level). Certain problems are specifically associated with training executives:

- These people are at the top of the organization, making it difficult for them to ask for help or even be aware they need it.

- Who is capable of helping them, or at least has the credibility to be listened to by these executives?

- These busy individuals work long hours and do not have much time for development.

Because of these issues, some strategies are better for executives and others are more likely to be used for developing managers (to be future executives).[49]

**Coaching** Not long ago coaching was considered a corrective method for inadequate performance.[50] Not anymore. When Bob Peters was promoted to Vice-President of Sales and Marketing for American Science and Engineering, one of his perks was an executive coach.[51] An advantage of using a personal coach is that the coach can fit into the busy schedule of the executive. The credibility factor is also dealt with, as coaches are often experts from outside the organization. In a survey conducted by the International Coach Federation, more than 4000 companies were using coaches for their executives.[52] For the CEO, a coach is the ideal training format. It can be done at the CEO's convenience; it is one-on-one; and it provides an opportunity for feedback from a professional. "It gets lonely at the top, and it's difficult to find someone to talk to about my concerns," says Mr. Venners, chairman of KFx, a high-tech company in Denver.[53]

An advantage of this method is it can be done in short meetings, phone conversations, and Internet communications, when the executive has the time. It also focuses on specific areas identified as needing improvement. Again, the important first step is identifying the executive's specific developmental needs, which can be determined through 360-degree performance reviews.[54] The coach and executive mutually determine an action plan, followed by successive meetings and counselling by the coach.

For the manager, it is much more likely that any coaching would be done by her supervisor, although outside consultants are sometimes used for up-and-coming managers. Again, the personalized approach helps the manager focus on specific needs and improvements.

**Mentoring** Coaching and mentoring are different in that mentoring is generally more of an ongoing relationship, and coaching is often for a shorter, more specific length of time. Also, meetings between a coach and the employee are generally more structured and regular than in mentoring.[55] Another difference for executives is that someone inside the company generally does the mentoring and an outside consultant often does the coaching.[56]

For the executive, "being a mentor" is an important developmental tool, from which he can learn a great deal. By dealing with different mentees, the executive is given the opportunity to grow professionally by honing leadership skills and learning how to work with various personality types and backgrounds.[57] Executives sometimes also have mentors. In cases where the executive is new to the organization, a senior executive could be assigned as a mentor to help get the new executive settled into his new role.

For managers who are potential executive material, being mentored is a valuable method for preparing them to be future executives. This one-on-one interaction allows the mentor to determine what is required to improve the mentee's effectiveness. Once the mentor identifies an area or competency that requires work, she can suggest relevant training. Also the mentor can provide opportunities to work on special projects that require use of the competency. One real advantage of a mentoring program is that it keeps your talent at home.[58] In a study conducted by the Centre for Creative Leadership, 77 percent of companies indicated development of a mentoring program improved their retention rate.

### Executive Development Programs/Executive MBAs
This type of training can take place at the organization's leadership centre or at a university (public or corporate). It mixes classroom learning with real-life problem solving. In such environments the mix often includes both executives and middle managers. The training generally follows the boot camp philosophy, as championed by Noel Tichy, or the less intense approach championed by Mintzberg.[59] The boot camp approach is designed to be stressful; which is generally what the executive's job is all about. Trainees are pushed to their limit, much like Navy SEAL or Special Forces training. Noel Tichy's point is that managers need to know how to operate in a stressful environment, so one is provided for them. Mintzberg does not agree. He says, "these managers live boot camp every day. The last thing in the world they need is more boot camp." Either way, both agree that the classroom is only a small part of the learning. Most programs offer some sort of action learning to accompany the classroom work. Action learning provides trainees with real company problems to solve. For example, GE managers are in a classroom in the morning, then given a real problem from GE to work on in a team for the rest of the day (and often into the wee hours of the morning). Sometimes these real-world projects provide a bonus for the company, as described in Training in Action 10-2.

### Action Learning
Although often a part of executive training programs, action learning can also stand alone. It is effective because it focuses on exactly what managers and executives need to do—come up with effective solutions to complex problems, then implement and evaluate them. It requires working in teams (to problem solve) and on their own (researching the issue and gathering relevant data), both of which are important for effective managers and executives. The difference between traditional meetings to solve problems and action learning is the focus on the learning that takes place. To ensure this learning happens, a facilitator is assigned to assist the team. The facilitator helps the team through debriefing after the meetings are over. Her focus would be on how members communicated with each other, how they provide feedback, and how well they are following their plan of action. She also gets them to reflect on how they are approaching the problem and how their basic assumptions might affect their view regarding the selection of a solution to the problem.[60] Once the group determines what specific training is required to help the team be more effective, "just-in-time" training is provided.[61]

The result: Not only do organizations get solutions to problems, but the team members develop skills necessary to be effective managers. And just as important, they learn how to continuously learn from the process.[62]

### Job Rotation
For the executive, the job rotation takes on a different perspective. The executive is usually not simply going to another department. In some vertically integrated organizations (e.g., where the supplier is actually part of the same organization or a subsidiary), the job rotation might be to the supplier to see how the business operates from the supplier's point of view. Learning how the organization is

## Training in Action 10-2

### U.S. Postal Service Gets a Bonus

At the U.S. Postal Services' Advanced Leadership Program, one of the requirements is working on real Postal Service problems. At the end of week three of the training, a Postal Executive meets with each of the work teams that were formed at the beginning of training. The executive gives each of the teams a business problem. These problems are chosen from those submitted by executives from all across the country.

Over the course of the next three months the team works on the problem. When they return for the last week of the training, they present their solution to a panel of executives from the Postal Service. Generally, the solution is immaterial; it is the process that is important and where the learning takes place. So where is the bonus?

It turns out that even though the important part of the exercise is the process of working out a solution, the solutions are often so innovative that they are implemented, and they save the company money.

A team from California was given the problem of workplace violence. The team determined a common link to much of the violence was related to money problems. They recommended development of a four-hour workshop on how to manage money. This recommendation was implemented in California and the workplace environment there improved.

Another group was challenged to increase retail income or reduce expenses in post offices. The group decided to put advertisements on the rolls of receipt paper they used. In that way they could advertise their own products for free and hopefully increase revenue. Or, they could sell the advertisement space to others, decreasing their cost for receipt paper. Although neither of these options has been adopted yet, it is estimated that the use of external advertising to defray the expenses of receipt rolls would save about $13 million per year.

*Source:* Delahoussaye, M. (2002). Licking the leadership crisis. *Training*, January, pp. 24–29.

perceived from the outside broadens the executive's perspective on its operation. A rotation to a foreign office would provide an international perspective.

For managers being developed for executive roles, rotating to different departments in the organization is common practice. This approach allows the manager to operate in different roles and understand the different issues that arise. If someone is to be a corporate leader, they need this type of understanding. After interviewing the company's top 120 leaders, Jerry Yelverton, Executive Vice-President of Entergy, indicated that the single most important factor that led to these leaders' success was the variety of their experiences in different functions, business units, and even countries.[63] The other point these leaders made was that the earlier these opportunities started, the better.

### Special Job Assignments

Special job assignments are a useful tool for both the executive and the manager, and are more likely an outcome of coaching or mentoring. The coach helps the executive identify needs to improve his feedback skills. They decide that he will increase the number of feedback meetings with direct reports to improve these skills. These typically short-term assignments address specific skill deficiencies.

### Team Building/Outward Bound

Whenever a team is formed, or a number of team members are replaced (especially if one is the CEO), some sort of team building is useful. Skills to operate effectively in a team are critical to effective executive functioning. For more in-depth team building, companies often send managers to Outward Bound programs such as the one discussed in Chapter 3. Here they are able to learn the importance of teams and how to operate effectively in one.

**Summary** Developing managers and executives requires some combination of these methods in order to provide the experiences necessary to become effective executives. Methods not mentioned here may also be used from time to time in certain circumstances. To get an idea of what a developmental process in a large organization looks like, see Training in Action 10-3.

## SUCCESSION PLANNING

Succession planning is a systematic and effective way to develop talent for the executive level of management. Recall that **succession planning** is the process of preparing employees at a lower level to replace someone at the next level. It is usually done for the positions critical to the effective functioning of the organization.

**Succession Planning** the process of preparing employees at a lower level to replace someone at the next level.

**For the President/CEO** It is surprising how many organizations do not develop succession plans for replacing their top person. Two reasons for this are that more immediate and important things need doing, and the belief that it is always a good idea to go "outside" for a new CEO.[64] As for the first reason, it does take a great deal of time to implement and keep a succession plan up to date, but do the costs outweigh the benefits? The answer in most cases is no. As for the second reason, going outside for a new CEO should only be done when no talent can be found within the organization or when a major shift in thinking is required. As Philip Caldwell of Ford Motors said, "The best source of CEO candidates is the company itself. There are times when it makes sense to look outside, but in general you want successors to emerge from within the company."[65] After all, they know the organization and understand its culture and direction. Most important, if there is a good succession plan, knowing the potential candidate's skill set makes the likelihood of success is much higher. Furthermore, without this option, many of the best employees will be looking outside for their promotion.

## Training in Action 10-3

### From Oshawa to Warren to Singapore: The Developmental Process at General Motors

Steve Carlisle, a middle manager at GM, is being sent to Singapore as Vice-President of Planning for their Asia Pacific region. This three-to-five-year assignment is part of his ongoing development at GM. The developmental process for Steve started some time ago when he was a manager in Oshawa, Ontario.

As part of his development, he was given a temporary assignment in Warren, Michigan. This temporary job assignment later turned into a permanent one at the tech centre in Warren.

Obtaining an advanced degree also played an important part in steve's development. After a few years at the Warren plant, he was told that, to enhance his chances of continuing to move up at GM, he would need to go back to school. He was one of only a few who were sent by GM to MIT to receive an MBA. Steve received his full salary for the year it took to obtain the degree.

Upon return, Steve was promoted to Group Director of Planning for the GM truck group in Warren. Then, in 2002, he got the news that he was going to the Asia Pacific region as part of his continued development.

Before leaving for Singapore, several alternative future assignments were discussed in preparing him for the current job rotation. Although no firm commitments could be made, general agreement pointed to future possibilities in his continued development upon his return.

The process of succession planning for the top position should entail

- Identification of the KSAs or competencies required for the CEO position,
- Assessment of individuals who have potential for filling the position,
- Identification of areas where development is necessary, and
- A plan to provide the individual with opportunities to develop the areas identified as requiring improvement.

The job at the top is more difficult to assess in terms of KSAs and is, to a certain extent, based on the strategic direction of the organization. If a major change in direction is required, the CEO needs the KSAs to manage change more so than if the focus is to increase market sales. Think back to Domtar. Why was it in such poor shape financially when Royer took over? Why was Royer able to turn it around? Clearly the KSAs Royer possessed had some relationship to the eventual success of Domtar.

Next, assessment of executives needs to be done and decisions regarding how to prepare and make the final choice for a replacement need to be made. Is it possible that Royer would have different expectations of those he considers potential replacements for himself?

Once developmental needs are determined, examine training delivery. A human resource planning system makes succession planning much easier, and a good succession plan prepares organizations to deal with sudden and even planned personnel changes with minimal disruption. So, with a succession plan, the assessment of the vice-presidents (for the position of president) is an ongoing process of performance review. From the review, developmental activities to hone the executive's skills would be worked out with the CEO (the vice-president's boss). In such scenarios, the change from one CEO to another is often smooth and immediate. The downside must also be considered. When more than one candidate is working toward the promotion, those who are not moved up may not only be disappointed but also angry, as Training in Action 10-4 indicates.

So, as Training in Action 10-4 shows, in an effective succession planning process, where the best are constantly being groomed to become better, it is likely that when a promotion is made, those who do not get the promotion may leave. Good talent is lost. However, because the company is "growing the talent," two important things happen. First, the company gets first choice of the talent it has grown, which should translate into the best person. Second, the critical position is filled immediately, which is a real advantage.

## Training in Action 10-4

### *The Downside of an Effective Succession Planning Process*

GE is widely known for its ability to grow executive talent. Recent CEO Jack Welch fortified this commitment to the development of high-level talent. His strong dedication to developing effective leaders is carried out through a comprehensive succession planning process. It is so effective that other companies, such as Polaris, emulate it. Each year top executives at GE meet to review the talent requirements and discuss plans for developing its managers. In looking for his own replacement, Jack Welch, working with his board of directors, had some great talent to choose from.

When Jeff Immelt was chosen to succeed Jack Welch, Bob Nardelli was surprised and hurt. His record at GE was one of the best, and he simply did not understand why he did not get the job. As a result, Nardelli accepted a job as CEO of Home Depot, and one of the other candidates in the running, Jim McNerney, accepted the CEO position at 3M.

*Source:* Gale, S. (2001). Bringing good leaders to light. *Training,* June, pp. 38–42; Tyler, J. (2002). Succession planning: Charting a course for the future. *Trustee* 55:24–28.

<u>**For Executives in General**</u> With all the money spent on management training, it is surprising that so little is spent on leadership development. A recent survey indicated more than half the organizations either did not have executive development programs or only supplied them when needed.[66] Forty percent rate their approach to leadership development as low, or very low.[67] This statistic is problematic for a number of reasons:[68]

- The pool of available managers to fill executive positions continues to shrink;

- The cost of recruiting outside talent is increasing at a high rate; and

- The average company expects a 33 percent turnover of executives in the next five years.

This failure to prepare future executives is surprising given the importance of having effective executives. One reason for this problem is continued downsizing in U.S. corporations.[69] Little attention is paid to succession planning when an organization is reducing employee numbers, and succession planning is the backbone of preparing relevant talent. Many of the middle managers let go in the job cuts were potential future executives. This trend does not bode well for many organizations in North America, but those that are paying attention to the issue will be the winners in the long run.

All of *Training* magazine's "top 50 training organizations" are constantly developing possible successors for their top positions through succession planning.[70] GE Lighting is one of those companies. In its succession planning process, executives meet twice a year to focus on the company's future needs, and then determine the developmental needs of managers targeted for advancement.[71]

Of course, many of these ideas are okay for the large organization that has the resources to fund them, but what about the small company? Focus on Small Business provides some insight into this issue.

## Focus on Small Business

For the small company, the senior manager/CEO or owner of the firm needs to take responsibility for the development of her managers. Some options include:[72]

- Clearly articulate a vision and goals for the organization and what these managers need to do to help you reach them,

- Help managers understand themselves and their shortcomings through feedback from the senior manager's own observations and the observations of others,

- Be sure the assignments provided to these managers are in line with their developmental needs,

- Provide managers with opportunities to learn the total organization through job rotation or different projects,

- Be a positive role model and coach, and

- Let them shadow an executive for a week or so to fully understand what the responsibilities are for senior management.

Some real advantages are available to the small business leader when it comes to training future executives. Because the company is small, it is likely that doing all possible jobs and experiencing many of the issues that will arise is much more likely. Furthermore, under the guidance of the CEO, the manager surely will be learning what the CEO deems as important because the CEO is the one who designs and implements the development program. Morgan McCall, Professor of Management from the University of Southern California, says that leaders grow better under good tutelage than in a classroom.[73] The key is for the CEO to take the development of managers seriously and be that role model.

## Summary

All managers take on certain general roles, but the importance of these roles varies depending on the level of the manager and the type of strategy followed by the organization. Therefore, the development of managers needs to take these situations into account when determining what types of training to provide. The three main roles identified by Mintzberg are interpersonal, informational, and decisional. Within each of these roles are more specific roles: (1) figurehead, leader, and liaison are part of the interpersonal role; (2) monitor, disseminator, and spokesperson are part of the informational role; and (3) entrepreneurial, disturbance handler, resource allocator, and negotiator are part of the decisional role. For each of these specific roles, certain skills (conceptual, technical, and interpersonal) and traits are required. The key to effective management development is to determine the roles required for the position, and from these roles the relevant KSAs (operational analysis). Then, as in a traditional needs analysis, it is possible to assess the current KSAs of the managers (person analysis). The 360-DF, when used properly, is an effective tool for determining the managers' current KSA levels.

A number of methods can be used to obtain the relevant training for managers, from externally based programs to corporate universities. Depending on the needs—conceptual, technical, interpersonal, or even development of personal traits—all of these can be provided through various programs.

Development of executives is critical to organizational functioning, but again it is often ignored. Special attention needs to be focused here because executives are already at the top and likely feel competent or at least do not like to ask for help. It is difficult for someone who is a peer or lower to be credible enough to offer advice. Executives are also busy, often working long hours, making it difficult to find the time to receive any training. Executive coaching is one way to deal with these issues, and its use has grown at a tremendous rate over the last few years. Other methods are also available, and the key to smooth development is succession planning. An effective succession plan will allow all executives and high-level managers to be appraised constantly and provided with opportunities to develop using many of the methods mentioned, such as coaching, action learning, executive MBAs, and so forth.

## Implications for Practice

**1.** Managers carry a large and complex burden for ensuring the success of the business. It is important for the future success of the organization that top management invest in developing managers to their fullest potential.

**2.** To be effective, managers must monitor and manage the strategy, structure, and technology of the organization in order to meet the demands of the business environment. Management development programs must develop the managerial competencies in these important areas.

**3.** Multiple sources exist for developing managerial competencies. Internal, university-based, and consultant-developed programs are available. In creating a management development portfolio, an organization needs to match the training it makes available to managers with its strategic direction.

**4.** Top executives have different development needs from other managers. Developmental experiences that involve coaching and mentoring seem most appropriate for meeting these needs.

**5.** Management no longer looks negatively on having a coach. Coaching has become a critical component in the development of high-level executives.

## Key Terms

Achievement style     *343*

Conceptual knowledge and skills     *343*

Corporate universities     *353*

Directive style     *343*

Drive     *345*

Employee-oriented style     *343*

## Questions for Review

1. Why is it necessary to have a special chapter on management training?

2. Compare and contrast the skills, traits, and management style for the manager in a cost leader vs. market leader organization.

3. Why are corporations setting up their own universities? Explain in detail, indicating some disadvantages of this approach as well.

4. Why is it difficult to train executives? Explain five training methods and why they are useful for training executives.

## Exercises

1. Bring a recent article (no more than a year old) that identifies KSAs that will be critical for managers in the immediate future. Be prepared to discuss the article and its management development implications in small groups or with the entire class.

2. Interview two managers with at least two years of management experience. One manager should come from a company whose strategy is toward the cost leader side, the other toward the market leader side. If possible they should both be in the same functional area. Determine what management development they received from their company. Determine how satisfied they are with the development they have received so far. Provide an analysis of how consistent these two experiences are with what the text proposes. Bring the information back to class and be prepared to share it with others.

3. How does management education prepare a manager for her role? What are the ways in which management education occurs? Do some seem better to you than others? Why or why not? Can other forms of training substitute for management education? Why or why not?

4. Interview a manager with five or more years of experience. Record the manager's current position, previous positions, and education. Identify the

manager's roles and responsibilities. Afterward, answer the following:

a. How do the roles and responsibilities compare with those described in the text?

b. Identify the KSAs required to meet this manager's roles and responsibilities.

c. How did the manager's previous experience and education prepare that manager for current roles and responsibilities?

5. Interview an HR person from a company and ask how its executives are developed. Find out how managers are prepared for executive positions. If the company uses a succession planning process, ask how it works and how often it is reviewed. If the company does not, ask how it determines who to promote to executive positions when one becomes available. From the interview, answer the following questions:

a. How many different methods does the company use for developing executives? For developing managers?

b. If the company does use a succession plan, how does it work? Do you think it prepares the managers for the higher-level management positions? If the company does not use a succession plan, how does it fill higher-level positions?

## Web Research

Research the Internet to find companies noted for Best Practices in Canada. See what these best companies do in management development. What are the similarities? Describe any major differences. Be prepared to discuss this information in class.

## CASE ANALYSIS

### Will Teams Work?

An automobile parts manufacturer (APM) was attempting to institute employee problem-solving teams to improve quality. This action was strongly encouraged by its biggest customer, a major automobile manufacturer. The competition in the original equipment manufacturing (OEM) business is especially fierce. The major automobile manufacturers (Ford, GM, DaimlerChrysler, Toyota, Honda, etc.) now demand high-quality parts at extremely low costs, and they often play one supplier against the other in order to force the OEM industry to meet their standards.

A training needs analysis of middle- and first-level production managers was conducted. These managers were responsible for the operation of the parts production system, a system that is highly mechanized and somewhat automated. The labour force in this area is primarily high-school graduates, but many have less education. The managers' responsibility prior to the change was to ensure that the hourly workers did their jobs in the proper manner and that the right amount and type of parts were produced to meet the production schedule.

The TNA showed low technical knowledge among these managers because they had been hired to monitor the hourly employees. They did not really understand the machinery and equipment and had never operated it. Most of them use a confrontational style in dealing with their subordinates because they feel that if they took a gentler approach, the unionized workforce would take advantage of them. The managers were all selected on the basis of their high need to control their environment, high need to achieve, and willingness to work with others to get the job done. These traits still characterize this group of managers.

### Case Questions

1. What is the managerial context in which these managers will be operating? Do you think training designed to help managers understand the context they will be operating in will be helpful? Why or why not?

2. What types of competencies should be developed in the management training? Give your rationale.

3. What types of training should be used to provide the different competencies? How long will it take to provide this training? Give your rationale.

4. What are the alternatives to management development? Do you think one of these alternatives should be used? Why or why not?

# ENDNOTES

## Chapter 1

1. Katz, D., and R. L. Khan. 1978. *The Social Psychology of Organizations*. New York: Wiley.

2. 2002 Industry report. Training budgets: How much do U.S. organizations spend on employee training? *Training*, October 2002, pp. 24–73.

3. Brown, D. 2002. Ottawa unveils national training and development strategy. *Canadian HR Reporter*, March 11, pp. 3, 6.

4. McMurrer, D., and M. VanBuren. 1999. The Japanese training scene. *Training and Development*, August, pp. 43–46.

5. Cooney, J. Cohen, A. 2003. Training and development outlook for 2003: Canadian organizations continue to under-invest. Conference Board of Canada; www.conferenceboard.ca.

6. Bassi, L. J., and D. P. McMurrer. 1998. Training investment can mean financial performance. *Training & Development*, May, pp. 40–42.

7. Brown, D. 2002. Legislated training, questionable results. *Canadian HR Reporter*, May 26, pp. 1–2.

8. Le Gault, M. 1997. In-house training that gets results. *Canadian Plastics*, February, pp. 14–18.

9. Peirce, J. 2003. *Canadian Industrial Relations*. Toronto: Prentice Hall; p. 130.

10. Fattal, T. 1996. Quality is what ISO 9000 is all about. *Computing Canada* 22: 30.

11. Dolack, P. 1996. ISO 9000 comes of age. *Chemical Marketing Reporter* 249: 7–8.

12. Williamson, D. 1997. ISO rating the sign of the times. *Windsor Star*, July 16, p. F1.

13. Fleishman, E. 1972. On the relation between abilities, learning, and human performance. *American Psychologist* 27: 1017–32.

14. Dunnette, M. 1976. Aptitudes, abilities, and skills. In *The Handbook of Industrial and Organizational Psychology*, edited by M. Dunnette. Chicago: Rand McNally.

15. Oskamp, S. 1991. *Attitudes and Opinions*, 2d ed. Upper Saddle River, NJ: Prentice Hall.

16. Webster's Universal Dictionary and Thesaurus. 1993 Toronto: Tormont Publications.

17. Op. cit. Dunnette, 1976.

18. Op. cit. Oskamp, 1991.

19. Chuvala, J., J. Gilmere, and T. Gillette. 1992. The new kid on the training block. *Security Management*, August, pp. 65–72.

20. Mintzberg, H. 1987. Crafting strategy. *Harvard Business Review*, July/August.

21. Gutpa, A., and V. Govindarajan. 1984. Business unit strategy, managerial characteristics, and business unit effectiveness at strategy implementation. *Academy of Management Journal* 27:25–41; Jackson, S., R. Schuler, and J. C. Rivero. 1989. Organizational characteristics as predictors of personnel practices. *Personnel Psychology* 42: 727–86.

22. Miles, R., and C. Snow. 1978. *Organizational Strategy, Structure and Process*. New York: McGraw-Hill.

23. Miller, D. 1987. The structural and environmental correlates of business strategy. *Strategic Management Journal*, January/February, pp. 55–76.

24. Porter, M. 1980. *Competitive Strategy: Techniques for Analyzing Industries and Competitors*. New York: Free Press.

25. Op. cit. Miles and Snow, 1978.

26. Perrow, C. 1970. *Organizational Analysis: A Sociological View*. Belmont, CA: Wadsworth; Thompson, J. D. 1967. *Organization in Action*. New York: McGraw-Hill; Woodward, J. 1965. *Industrial Organization: Theory and Practice*. London: Oxford University.

27. Burns, T., and G. Stalker. 1961. *The Management of Innovation*. London: Tavistock.

28. David, F., J. Pearce, and W. Randolf. 1989. Linking technology and structure to enhance group performance. *Journal of Applied Psychology*, April 10, p. 233–41.

29. Op. cit. Perrow, 1970.

30. Mintzberg, H. 1979. *The Structuring of Organizations*. Upper Saddle River, NJ: Prentice Hall, pp. 272–85; McDonough E. and R. Leifer, 1983. Using simultaneous structures to cope with uncertainty. *Academy of Management Journal*, December. pp. 727–35.

31. Becker, B., and Huselid, M. 1999. Overview: Strategic human resource management in five leading firms. *Human Resource Management*, Winter, pp. 287–301.

32. Tichey, N. 1983. *Managing Strategic Change: Technical, Political and Cultural Dynamics*. New York: Wiley; Op. cit. Tichey, Fombrun, and Devanna, 1992.

33. Rossett, A. 1996. Training and organizational development: Separated at birth? *Training*, April, pp. 53–59.

34. Golembiewski, R., C. Proehl, and D. Sink. 1982. Estimating the success of OD applications. *Training and Development Journal*, April, pp. 86–95; Nicholas, J. 1982. The comparative impact of organizational development interventions on hard criteria measures. *Academy of Management Review*, October, pp. 531–42.

35. Goodman, P., and J. Dean. 1983. Why productivity efforts fail. In *Organizational Development: Theory, Practice, and Research*, edited by W. French, C. Bell, and R. Zawacki. Plano, TX: Business Publications.

36. Schuler, R., and S. Jackson. 1987. Linking competitive strategies with human resource management practices. *Academy of Management Executive* 1(3): 207–19.

37. Op cit. Rossett, 1996.

38. Ibid.

39. Griffin, R., and R. Ebert. 1996. *Business*, 4th ed. Upper Saddle River, NJ: Prentice Hall.

40. Industry Canada, "Canada's Small Business Community," http://strategis.ic.gc.ca/epic/internet/insbrp-rppe.nsf/vwGeneratedInterE/re00022e.html. [accessed March 16, 2004].

# Chapter 2

1. Demming, W. E. 1986. *Out of the Crisis*. Massachusetts Institute of Technology.

2. Dobyns, L., and C. Crawford-Mason. 1991. *Quality or Else*. Boston: Houghton Mifflin.

3. Lawler, E. E., S. A. Mohrman, and G. E. Ledford. 1995. *Creating High Performance Organizations: Practices and Results of Employee Involvement and Total Quality Management in Fortune 1000 Companies*. San Francisco: Jossey-Bass.

4. Maslow, A. H. 1954. *Motivation and Personality*. New York: Harper & Row; Maslow, A. 1968. *Toward a Psychology of Being*, 2d ed. New York: Van Nostrand Reinhold.

5. Alderfer, C. 1969. An empirical test of a new theory of human needs. *Organizational Behaviour and Human Performance* 4(2): 142–75.

6. Ibid.; Schneider, C. P., and C. Alderfer. 1973. Three studies of measures of need satisfaction in organizations. *Administrative Science Quarterly*, December, pp. 489–505.

7. Pavlov, I. P. 1897. *Lectures on the Principal Digestive Glands*. St. Petersburg, Russia: Kushnereff; and Pavlov, I. P. 1912. Principal laws of the activity of the central nervous system as they find expression in conditioned reflexes. As reported by G. Murphy and J. Kovach in *Historical Introduction to Modern Psychology*. New York: Harcourt Brace Jovanovich.

8. Thorndike, E. L. 1905. *The Elements of Psychology*. New York: Seiler; Thorndike, E. L. 1913. The psychology of learning. *Educational Psychology*, vol. 2. New York: Teachers College, Columbia University Press; Thorndike, E. L. 1932. *Purposive Behaviour in Animals and Men*. New York: Appleton-Century-Crofts.

9. Skinner, B. F. 1953. *Science and Human Behaviour*. New York: Macmillan; Skinner, B. F. 1968. *The Technology of Teaching*. New York: Appleton-Century-Crofts.

10. Ibid.

11. Grote, D. 1995. *Discipline Without Punishment*. New York: AMACOM.

12. Vroom, V. 1964. *Work and Motivation*. New York: Wiley.

13. Bandura, A. 1977a. Self-efficacy: Toward a unifying theory of behavioural change. *Psychological Review* 84:191–215.

14. Gecas, V. 1989. The social psychology of self-efficacy. In *Annual Review of Sociology*, edited by W. R. Scott and J. Blake. Palo Alto: Annual Reviews, Inc., 15: 291–316; Gist, M. 1987. Self-efficacy: Implications for organizational behaviour and human resource management. *Academy of Management Review*, July, pp. 472–85; and Manz, C. C., and H. P. Simms. 1981. Vicarious learning: The influence of modeling on organizational behaviour. *Academy of Management Review* 6: 105–13.

15. Ford, J., E. Smith, D. Weissbein, S. Gully, and E. Salas. 1998. Relationships of goal orientation, metacognitive activity, and practice strategies with learning outcomes and transfer. *Journal of Applied Psychology* 83: 218–33; Locke, E. A., E. F. Lee, and P. Bobko. 1984. Effect of self-efficacy, goals, and task strategies of task performance. *Journal of Applied Psychology*, May, pp. 241–51.

16. Kozlowski, S., S. Gully, K. Brown, E. Salas, E. Smith, and E. Nason, 2001. Effects of training goals and goal orientation traits on multidimensional training outcomes and performance adaptability. *Organizational Behaviour and Human Decision Processes* 85: 1–31; Colquitt, J., J. Lepine, and R. Noe. 2000. Toward an integrative theory of training motivation: A meta-analytic path analysis of 20 years of research. *Journal of Applied Psychology* 85: 678–707.

17. Ibid.; Op. cit. Ford et al., 1998.

18. Ibid.; Kraiger, K., J. Ford, and E. Salas. 1993. Application of cognitive, skill-based, and affective theories of learning outcomes to new methods of training evaluation. *Journal of Applied Psychology* 78(2): 311–28.

19. Schacter, D. 1996. *Searching for Memory: The Brain, the Mind and the Past*. New York: Basic Books; Squire, L., A. Shimamura, and P. Graf. 1985. Independence of recognition memory and priming effects: A neuropsychological analysis. *Journal of Experimental Psychology* 11: 34–44; and Squire, L., and S. Zola-Morgan. 1991. The medial temporal lobe memory system. *Science* 253: 1380–86.

20. Bruner, J. S. 1966. *Toward a Theory of Instruction*. New York: Norton.

21. Gagné, R. M. 1965. *The Conditions of Learning*. New York: Holt, Rinehart, and Winston.

22. Piaget, J. 1954. *The Construction of Reality in the Child*. New York: Basic Books.

23. Skinner, B. F. 1971. *Beyond Freedom and Dignity*. New York: Bantam/Vintage.

24. Knowles, M. F. 1984. Adult learning: Theory and practice. In *The Handbook of Human Resource Development*, edited by D. A. Nadler. New York: Wiley; Knowles, M. F. 1989. *The Making of an Adult Educator*. San Francisco: Jossey-Bass.

25. Bandura, A. 1977b. *Social Learning Theory*. Upper Saddle River, NJ: Prentice Hall; op. cit. Bandura, 1977a; and Kraut, A. J. 1976. Behavior modeling symposium: Developing managerial skills via modeling techniques. *Personnel Psychology* 29: 325–28.

26. Gagné, R. M., L. Briggs, and W. Wager. 1992. *Principles of Instructional Design*. Fort Worth: Harcourt Brace Jovanovich.

27. Ibid.

28. Ibid; p.90.

29. Based on an example from Gagné et al. 1992.

30. Baltes, P. B., and S. L. Willis. 1976. Toward psychological theories of aging. In *Handbook on the Psychology of Aging*, edited by J. E. Birren and K. W. Schaie. New York: Van Nostrand Reinhold; Griffin, G., A. Tough, W. Barnard, and D. Brundage. 1980. *The Design of Self-Directed Learning*. Toronto: Ontario Institute for Studies in Education; Knowles, M. S. 1978. *The Adult Learner: A Neglected Species*. Houston: Gulf Publishing; and Pierce, J., D. Gardner, L. Cummings, and R. Dunham. 1989. Organization-based self-esteem: Construct definition, measurement, and validation. *Academy of Management Journal*, September, pp. 622–48.

31. Geddie, C., and B. Strickland. 1984. From plateaus to progress: A model for career development. *Training*, June, pp. 56–61; and Leibowitz, Z. B., C. Farren, and B. L. Kaye. 1986. *Designing Career Development Systems*. San Francisco: Jossey-Bass.

32. Blum, M., and J. Naylor. 1956. *Industrial Psychology*. New York: Harper Row.

33. Facteau, J., G. Dobbins, J. Russell, R. Ladd, and J. Kudisch. 1995. The influence of general perceptions of the training environment on pretraining motivation and perceived training transfer. *Journal of Management* 21: 1–5; Tracey, J., S. Tannenbaum, and M. Kavanaugh. 1995. Applying trained skills on the job: The importance of the work environment 80: 239–52.

34. Coch, L., and J. French. 1948. Overcoming resistance to change. *Human Relations* 1: 512–32.

35. Op. cit. Facteau et al., 1995.

36. Smith-Jentsch, K., E. Salas, and M. Brannick. 2001. To transfer or not to transfer? Investigating the combined effects of trainee

characteristics, team leader support, and team climate. *Journal of Applied Psychology* 86: 279–92.

37. Op. cit. Knowles, 1978; Knowles. 1984; and Tough, A. 1979. New conclusions on why and how adults learn. *Training*, January, pp. 8–10.

38. Op. cit. Knowles, 1984.

39. Westmeyer, P. 1988. *Effective Teaching in Adult and Higher Education*. Springfield, IL: Charles C. Thomas.

40. Belmont, J., and E. Butterfield. 1971. Learning strategies as determinants of memory deficiencies. *Cognitive Psychology* 2: 411–20; and Brown, A., and A. Palicsar. 1982. Inducing strategic learning from texts by means of informed, self-control training. *Learning and Learning Disabilities*, April, pp. 1–17.

41. Borkowski, J. 1985. Sign of intelligence: Strategy generalization and metacognition. In *The Growth of Reflection*, edited by S. R. Yussen. New York: Academic Press; Kendall, C., J. Borkowski, and J. Cavanaugh. 1980. Metamemory and the transfer of an interrogative strategy by EMR children. *Intelligence* 4: 255–70; and Walker, C. 1987. Relative importance of domain knowledge and overall aptitude on acquisition of domain-related information. *Cognition and Instruction* 4: 25–42.

42. Brookfield, S. 1987. *Developing Critical Thinkers*. San Francisco: Jossey-Bass; op. cit. Knowles, 1984; Marsick, V. 1987. *Learning in the Workplace: Theory and practice*. London: Croom Helm.

43. Kanfer, R., and P. Ackerman. 1989. Motivation and cognitive abilities: An integrative aptitude/treatment interaction approach to skill acquisition. *Journal of Applied Psychology* 74: 657–89.

44. Newstrom, J. W., and M. L. Lengnick-Hall. 1991. One size does not fit all. *Training and Development Journal* 45(6): 43–48.

45. Adapted from Gordon, E., R. Morgan, and J. Ponticell. 1995. The individualized training alternative. *Training and Development*, September, pp. 52–60.

# Chapter 3

1. Rummler, G. 1987. Determining needs. In T*raining and Development Handbook*, edited by R. L. Craig. New York: McGraw-Hill.

2. Cascio, W. 1989. Using utility analysis to assess training outcomes. In *Training and Development in Organizations*, edited by I. L. Goldstein. San Francisco: Jossey-Bass; Cascio, W. 1991a. *Costing Human Resources: The Financial Impact of Behavior in Organizations*. Boston: PWS Kent.

3. Galagan, P. A. 1999. Training isn't the point. *Training and Development*, May, pp. 28–29.

4. Korth, S. 2001. Consolidating needs assessment and evaluation. *Performance Improvement* 40: 38–43.

5. McGehee, W., and P. W. Thayer. 1961. T*raining In Business And Industry*. New York: Wiley.

6. Op. cit. McGehee and Thayer, 1961.

7. Tannenbaum, S., and G. Yukl. 1992. Training and development in work organizations. *American Review of Psychology* 43: 399–441.

8. Das, H. 2003. *Performance management*. PH series in Human Resource Management, Toronto: Pearson Education.

9. Blanchard, P.N. & Thacker, J.W. 2004. *Effective training: systems strategies and practices*. Upper Saddle River, Prentice Hall.

10. Dayal, I., and J. Thomas. 1968. Operation KPE: Developing a new organization. *Journal of Behavioral Science* 4: 473–506.

11. McCormick, E. 1979. *Job Analysis*. New York: AMACOM.

12. Shippmann, J., et al. 2000. The practice of competency modeling. *Personnel Psychology* 53: 703–40.

13. Parry, S. 1998 Just what is a competency? *Training*, pp. 59–64.

14. http://www.pao.gov.ab.ca/learning/competencies/apscomp/index.html

15. Miller, L. 1999. Editorial. *International Journal of Training and Development* 3: 82–89.

16. Op cit. Shippmann, J., et al. 2000.

17. Rothwell, W., and Lindholm, J. 1999. Competency identification, modeling and assessment in the USA. *International Journal of Training and Development* 3: 90–105. Op. cit. Shippmann etal., 2000.

18. Op. Cit. Shippmann et al., 2000.

19. Op. Cit. Rothwell, 1999; Mirabile, R. 1997. Everything you wanted to know about competency modeling. *Training and Development Journal*, August, pp. 73–77.

20. Dalton, M. 1997. Are competency models a waste? *Training and Development*, October, pp. 46–49.

21. Ibid.

22. Thorndike, R. L. 1949. *Personnel Selection: Test and Measurement Technique*. New York: Wiley.

23. Blum, M. L., and J. C. Naylor. 1968. *Industrial Psychology: Its Theoretical and Social Foundation*. New York: Harper & Row.

24. Ibid.

25. Ibid.

26. Nunnally, J. 1978. *Psychometric Theory*. New York: McGraw-Hill.

27. Op. cit. Blum and Naylor, 1968.

28. Bernardin, H. J., and R. Beatty. 1984. *Performance Appraisal: Assessing Human Behavior at Work*. Boston: Kent.

29. Benedict, M. E., and E. L. Levine. 1988. Delay and distortion: Tacit influences on performance appraisal. *Journal of Applied Psychology* 73: 507–14; Longenecker, C. O., H. P. Sims, and D. A. Gioia. 1987. Behind the mask: The politics of employee appraisal. *Academy of Management Executive* 1: 183–93.

30. Payne, R., and D. Pugh. 1976. Organizational Structure and Climate. In *Handbook of Industrial and Organizational Psychology*, edited by M. Dunnette. Chicago: Rand McNally, pp. 1125–73.

31. Cascio, W. 1991b. *Applied Psychology in Personnel Management*. Upper Saddle River, NJ: Prentice Hall.

32. Herbert, G., and D. Doverspike. 1990. Performance appraisal in the training needs analysis process: A review and critique. *Public Personnel Management* 19: 253–70.

33. Murphy, K. R., and J. N. Cleveland. 1991. *Performance Appraisal: An Organizational Perspective*. Boston: Allyn & Bacon.

34. Thorndike, E. L. 1920. A constant error in psychological ratings. *Journal Of Applied Psychology* 4: 25–29.

35. Bass, B. 1956. Reducing leniency in merit ratings. *Personnel Psychology* 9: 359–69. Harris, M. M., and J. Schaubroek. 1988. A meta-analysis of self–supervisor, self–peer, and peer–supervisor ratings. *Personnel Psychology* 41: 43–62.

36. Farh, J., and G. Dobbins. 1989. Effects of self-esteem on leniency bias in self-reports of performance: A structural equation analysis. *Personnel Psychology* 42: 835–50.

37. Williams, J., and P. Levy. 1992. The effects of perceived system knowledge on the agreement between self-ratings and supervisor ratings. *Personnel Psychology* 45: 835–47.

38. McEnery, J., and J. McEnery. 1987. Self-ratings in management training: A neglected opportunity? *Journal of Occupational Psychology* 60: 49–60.

39. Cheung, G. 1999. Multifaceted conceptions of self–other ratings disagreement. *Personnel Psychology* 52: 1–35.

40. London, M., and R. Beatty. 1993. 360-degree feedback as a competitive advantage. *Human Resource Management* 32: 353–72.

41. Brutus, S., M. London, and J. Martineau. 1999. The impact of 360-degree feedback on planning for career development. *Journal of Management Development* 18: 676–93.

42. Pfau, B., I. Kay, K. Nowack, and J. Ghorpade. 2000. Does 360-degree feedback negatively affect company performance? *HR Magazine* 47: 54–60.

43. Maurer, T., D. Mitchell, and F. Barbeite. 2002. Predictors of attitudes toward a 360-degree feedback system and involvement in post-feedback development activity. *Journal of Occupational and Organizational Psychology* 75: 87–107.

44. Seashore, S., E. Lawler, P. Mirvis, and C. Cammann. 1983. *Assessing Organizational Change*. New York: Wiley.

45. Cook, J., S. Hepworth, T. Wall, J. Toby, and P. Warr. 1981. *The Experience of Work: A Compendium and Review of 249 Measures and Their Use*. New York: Academic Press.

46. Robinson, J., R. Athanasiou, and K. Head. 1976. *Measuring of Occupational Attitudes and Occupational Characteristics*. Ann Arbor: Institute for Social Research.

47. Ford, J. K., and R. A. Noe. 1987. Self-assessed training needs: The effects of attitudes toward training, managerial level, and function. *Personnel Psychology* 40: 39–53.

48. Fisher, C. 1979. Transmission of negative and positive feedback to subordinates: A laboratory investigation. *Journal of Psychology* 64: 533–40.

49. Carrol, S., and C. Schneier. 1982. *Performance Appraisal and Review Systems*. Glenview, IL: Scott Foresman.

50. Michalak, D. F., and E. G. Yager. 1979. *Making the Training Process Work*. New York: Harper & Row.

51. Schneider, B., and A. Konz. 1989. Strategic job analysis. *Human Resource Management* 28: 51–63.

52. Ibid.

53. Casner, J. 1989. *Successful Training Strategies*. San Francisco: Jossey-Bass.

54. Burns, T., and G. M. Stalker. 1961. *The Management Of Innovation*. London: Tavistock.

55. Mintzberg, H. 1987. Crafting strategy. *Harvard Business Review*, July/August, pp. 66–75.

56. Keats, B., and J. Bracker. 1988. Toward a theory of small firm performance. *American Journal of Small Business* 4: 35–43.

57. Banks, M., A. Bures, and D. Champion. 1987. Decision-making factors in small business: training and development. *Journal of Small Business Management*, January, pp. 19–26.

58. Fairfield-Sonn, J. 1987. A strategic process model for small business training and development. *Journal of Small Business Management*, January, pp. 11–18.

59. Lee, W., and D. Owens. 2001. Rapid analysis model. *Performance Improvement Quarterly* 40: 13–18; Rossett, A. 1998. *First Things Fast: A Handbook For Performance Analysis*. New York: Pfeiffer.

60. The list is partially based on Rossett, 1998.

# Chapter 4

1. Harris-Lalonde, S. 2001. *Training and development outlook*. Conference Board of Canada, Ottawa.

2. *Baylis-Flannery v. DeWilde* (No. 2) (2003), 48 C.H.R.R. D/197, 2003 HRTO 28; *Bobbitt v. Royal Canadian Legion*, Branch 19 (2003), 47 C.H.R.R. D/185 (N.S. Bd.Inq.); *Turnbull v. Famous Players Inc.* (No. 2) (2003), 46 C.H.R.R. D/334, 2003 HRTO 10.

3. Perlman, S. (1996) Dignity and respect for all. *CA Magazine*, October, 129(8); pp. 29–31.

4. Marquardt, M., N. Nissley, R. Ozag, and T. Taylor. 2000. International briefing 6; Training and development in the United States. *International Journal of Training and Development* 4: 138–49.

5. Mager, R. 1975. *Preparing Instructional Objectives*. Belmont, CA: Pitman Learning.

6. Langdon, D. 1999. Objectives? Get over them. *Training and Development*, February, pp. 54–58; Stoneall, L. 1992. The case for more flexible objectives. *Training and Development*, August, pp. 67–69.

7. Op. cit. Stoneall, 1992.

8. Op. cit. Langdon, 1999.

9. Colquitt, J., J. LePine, and R. Noe. 2000. Toward an integrative theory of training motivation: A meta-analytic path analysis of 20 years of research. *Journal of Applied Psychology* 85: 678–707.

10. Lewis, J. 1981. Answers to twenty questions on behavioral objectives. *Educational Technology*, March, pp. 27–31.

11. Locke, E., K. Shaw, L. Saari, and G. Latham. 1981. Goal setting and task performance. *Psychological Bulletin* 90: 125–52.

12. Latham, G. P., and G. A. Yukl. 1975. A review of research on the application of goal setting in organizations. *Academy of Management Journal* 18: 824–45.

13. Op. cit. Lewis, 1981.

14. Filipczak, B. 1998. Old dogs, new tricks. *Training* 35: 50–58.

15. *A Stronger Canada*. (1998). Employment and Immigration Canada. Ottawa, October 23.

16. Cronbach, L., and R. Snow. 1977. *Aptitude and Instructional Methods*. New York: Irvington.

17. Goldstein, I. 1980. Training in work organizations. *Annual Review of Psychology* 39: 229–72.

18. Ryman, D., and R. Biersner. 1975. Attitudes predictive of diving training success. *Personnel Psychology* 28: 181–88.

19. Op. cit. Colquitt et al., 2000.

20. Camp, R., P. N. Blanchard, and G. Huszczo. 1986. *Toward a More Organizationally Effective Training Strategy and Practice*. Upper Saddle River, NJ: Prentice Hall.

21. Latham, G. P., and E. A. Locke. 1979. Goal setting: A motivational technique that works. *Organizational Dynamics* 8: 68–80; Op. cit. Locke et al., 1981.

22. Ibid.

23. Reigeluth, C. 1999a. What is instructional design theory and how is it changing? In *Instructional Design Theories and Models: An Overview of Their Current Status*, vol. 2, edited by C. Reigeluth. Mahwah, NJ: Laurence Erlbaum Associates, pp. 5–29.

24. Op. cit. Latham and Locke, 1979; Op. cit. Locke et al., 1981.

25. Klatzky, R. 1975. *Human Memory: Structures and Processes.* San Francisco: Freeman.; Lindsay, P., and D. Norman. 1972. *Human Information Processing: An Introduction to Psychology.* New York: Academic Press.

26. Anderson, J. R., and G. H. Bower. 1972. Recognition and retrieval processes in free recall. *Psychological Review* 79: 97–123; Bandura, A. 1977. Social Learning Theory. Upper Saddle River, NJ: Prentice Hall; Melton, A., and E. Martin. 1972. *Coding Process in Human Memory.* Washington, DC: Winston.

27. Anderson, J. R., and G. H. Bower. 1973. *Human Associative Memory.* Washington, DC: Winston.

28. Cascio, W. 1995. *Managing Human Resources.* New York: McGraw-Hill Ryerson.

29. Demster, F. 1990. The spacing effect: A case study in the failure to apply the results of psychological research. *American Psychologist* 43: 627–34.

30. Dipboye, R. 1997. Organizational barriers to implementing a rational model of training. In *Training for a Rapidly Changing Workplace*, edited by M. Quinones and Ehrenstein. Washington, DC: American Psychological Association.

31. Donovan, J., and D. Radosevich. 1999. A meta-analytic review of the distribution of practice effect: Now you see it, now you do not. *Journal of Applied Psychology* 84: 795–804.

32. Ibid.

33. Baldwin, T., and K. Ford. 1988. Transfer of training: A review and directions for future research. *Personnel Psychology* 41: 63–105.

34. Adams, J. 1987. Historical review and appraisal of research on the learning, retention, and transfer of human motor skills. *Psychological Bulletin* 101: 41–74.

35. Naylor, J., and G. Briggs. 1963. Effects of rehearsal of temporal and spatial aspects on the long-term retention of a procedural skill. *Journal of Applied Psychology* 47: 120–26.

36. Blum, M., and J. Naylor. 1968. *Industrial Psychology, Its Theoretical and Social Foundations.* New York: Harper & Row.

37. McGehee, W., and P. W. Thayer. 1961. *Training in Business and Industry.* New York: Wiley.

38. Atwater, S. 1953. Proactive inhibition and associative facilitation as affected by the degree of prior learning. *Journal of Experimental Psychology* 46: 400–4; Hagman, J. D., and A. M. Rose. 1983. Retention of military tasks: A review. *Human Factors* 25: 199–214; Mandler, G. 1954. Transfer of training as a response to overlearning. *Journal of Experimental Psychology* 47: 411–17.

39. Schendel, J. D., and J. D. Hagman. 1982. On sustaining procedural skills over a prolonged retention interval. *Journal of Applied Psychology* 67: 605–10.

40. May, L., and W. Kahnweiler. 2000. The effect of a mastery practice design on learning and transfer in behavior modeling training. *Personnel Psychology* 53: 353–73.

41. Thorndike, E. L., and R. S. Woodworth. 1901. The influence of improvement in one mental function upon the efficiency of other functions. Functions involving attention, observation, and discrimination. *Psychological Review* 8: 553–64.

42. Op. cit. Camp, Blanchard, and Husczco, 1986.

43. Locke, E., and G. Latham. 1990. *A Theory of Goal Setting and Task Performance.* Upper Saddle River, NJ: Prentice Hall.

44. Martocchio, J. J., and J. Dulebohn. 1994. Performance feedback effects in training: The role of perceived controllability. *Personnel Psychology* 47: 357–73.

45. Bandura, A. 1991. Social cognitive theory of self-regulation. *Organizational Behavior and Human Decision* 50: 248–87.

46. Marx, R. D. 1982. Relapse prevention for managerial training: A model for maintenance of behavior change. *Academy of Management Review* 7: 433–41.

47. Brownell, K. D., G. Marlatt, E. Lichenstein, and G. Wilson. 1986. Understanding and preventing relapse. *American Psychologist* 41: 765–82.

48. Feldman, M. 1981. Successful post-training skill application. *Training and Development Journal* 35: 72–75; Op. cit. Wexley and Baldwin, 1986.

49. Wexley, K., and T. Baldwin. 1986. Post-training strategies for facilitating positive transfer: An empirical exploration. *Academy of Management Journal* 29: 503–20.

50. Marx, R. 1986. Improving management development through relapse prevention strategies. *Journal of Management Development* 5: 27–40.

51. Op. cit. Wexley and Baldwin, 1986.

52. Burke, L., and T. Baldwin. 1999. Workforce training transfer: A study of the effect of relapse prevention training and transfer climate. *Human Resource Management* 38: 227–42.

53. Seyler, D., E. Holton, R. Bates, R. M. Burnett, and M. Carvalho. 1998. Factors affecting motivation to transfer. *International Journal of Training and Development* 2: 2–16; Op. cit. Baldwin and Ford, 1988.

54. Orpen, C. 1999. The influence of the training environment on trainee motivation and perceived training quality. *International Journal of Training and Development* 3: 34–43.

55. Noe, R. A., and S. L. Wilk. 1993. Investigation of the factors that influence employees' participation in developmental activities. *Journal of Applied Psychology* 78: 291–302.

56. Hicks, W. D., and R. J. Klimoski. 1987. Entry into training programs and its effect on training outcomes: A field experiment. *Academy of Management Journal* 30: 542–52.

57. Ibid.

58. Op. cit. Sayler et al., 1998.

59. Bergman, T. 1993. Job performance learning: A comprehensive approach to high-performance training design. *Employment Relations Today*, Winter, pp. 399–409.

60. Op. cit. Wexley and Baldwin, 1986.

61. Stark, C. 1986. Ensuring skills transfer: A sensitive approach. *Training and Development Journal*, March, pp. 50–51.

62. Ibid.

63. Op. cit. Orpen, 1999.

64. Tracey, B., S. Tannenbaum, and M. Kavanaugh. 1995. Applying trained skills on the job: The importance of the work environment. *Journal of Applied Psychology* 80: 239–51.

65. Schneider, B. 1990. *Organizational Climate and Culture.* San Francisco: Jossey-Bass.

66. Op. cit. Orpen, 1999.

67. Op. cit. Burke and Baldwin, 1999.

68. Olsen, J. 1998. The evaluation and enhancement of training transfer. International. *Journal of Training and Development* 2: 61–75.

69. Schein, E. H. 1985. *Organizational Culture and Leadership.* San Francisco: Jossey-Bass.

70. Op. cit. Tracey, Tannenbaum, and Kavanaugh, 1995.

71. Op. cit. Cascio, 1995.

72. Thacker, J., and J. Cattaneo. 1992. *Survey of personnel practices in Canadian organizations.* Working paper series W92-04, ISSN 07146191.

73. Gagné, R., L. Briggs, and W. Wager. 1988. *Principles of Instructional Design.* New York: Holt, Rinehart, and Winston.

74. Ibid.

75. Hornsby, J., and D. Kuratko. 1990. Human resource management in small business: Critical issues for the 1990s. *Journal of Small Business Management,* July, pp. 9–19.

76. Deshpande, S., and D. Golhar. 1994. HRM practices in large and small manufacturing firms: A comparative study. *Journal of Small Business Management,* April, pp. 49–56.

77. Ahire, S., and D. Golhar. 1996. Quality management in large vs. small firms. *Journal of Small Business Management,* April, pp. 1–13.

78. McRae, C., A. Banks, A. Bures, and D. Champion. 1987. Decision-making factors in small business: Training and development. *Journal of Small Business Management,* January, pp. 19–25.

# Chapter 5

1. Broadwell, M. 1980. *The Lecture Method of Instruction.* Englewood Cliffs, NJ: Educational Technology Publications.

2. Brown, G. 1978. *Lecturing and Explaining.* London: Methuen and Co. Also see Bligh, D. 1974. *What's the Use of Lectures?* Middlesex, England: Penguin Education.

3. Op. cit. Broadwell, 980.

4. Broadwell, M., and C. Dietrich. 1996. How to get trainees into the action. *Training,* February, pp. 52–56.

5. Ibid.

6. Johnstone, A., and F. Percival. 1976. Attention breaks in lectures. *Education in Chemistry* 13: 273–304; Lloyd, D. 1968. A concept of improvement of learning response in the taught lesson. *Visual Education,* Winter, pp. 23–25; Maddox, H., and E. Hook. 1975. Performance decrement in the lecture. *Educational Research* 28: 17–30.

7. Killian, D. 1976. *The Impact of Flight Simulators on U.S. Airlines.* Fort Worth, TX: American Airlines Flight Academy: Mecham, M. 1994. Cathay refines approach to simulator training. *Aviation Week and Space Technology,* January 17, pp. 35–37.

8. Op. cit. Killian, 1976; Parsons, H. M. 1972. *Man–Machine System Experiment.* Baltimore: Johns Hopkins Press.

9. Erwin, D. E. 1978. Psychological fidelity in simulated work environments. Proceedings of the American Psychological Association, Toronto, Canada.

10. Edwards, D., C. Hahn, and E. Fleishman. 1980. Evaluation of laboratory methods for the study of driver behavior: Relations between simulator and street performance. *Journal of Applied Psychology* 62: 559–66.

11. Fink, C. D., and E. L. Shriver. 1978. Simulators for maintenance training: Some issues, problems, and areas for future research. *AFHRL Technical Report,* Brooks Air Force Base, Texas, 78–127.

12. Barrett, G., T. Benko, and G. Riddle. 1981. Programmable simulator speeds operator training. *Bell Laboratories Record* 59(7): 213–16.

13. Paffet, J. A. 1978. Ships' officers use simulators to learn vessel operation. *Minicomputer News* 4(8): 11–13.

14. Slack, K. 1993. Training for the real thing. *Training and Development,* May, pp. 79–89.

15. Davis, L. 1973. Evolving alternative organizational designs: Their sociotechnical bases. *Human Relations* 30: 261–71; Walton, R. 1975. From Hawthorne to Topeka and Kalmar. In *Man and Work in Society,* edited by E. Cass and F. Zimmer. New York: Van Nostrand Reinhold Co.

16. Barbian, J. 2001. Get Simulated. *Training,* February, pp. 67–70.

17. Dakin, S., and G. Wood. 1995. Learn TQM principles using jumbled proverbs. *Quality Progress,* October, pp. 92–95; Kaplan, R., M. Lombardo, and M. Mazique. 1985. A mirror for managers: Using simulation to develop management teams. *Journal of Applied Behavioral Science* 21: 241–53; Goudy, R. 1981. Two years of management experience in two challenging weeks. *ABA Banking Journal* 73(6): 74–77; Groth, J., and C. Phillips. 1978. What would you do if a crisis hit your firm? *Management World* 7(3): 12–16; Zemke, R. 1982. Can games and simulations improve your training power? *Training* 19(2): 24–31.

18. Faria, T. 2002. Personal communication.

19. Argyris, C. 1980. Some limitations of the case method: Experiences in a management development program. *Academy of Management Review* 5: 291–98.

20. Pigors, P., and F. Pigors. 1987. The case method. In *Training and Development Handbook: A Guide to Human Resource Development,* edited by R. Craig. New York: McGraw-Hill, pp. 414–29.

21. Argyris, C. 1980. Some limitations to the case method: Experience in a management development program. *Academy of Management Review* 5: 291–98.

22. Engel, H. 1973. *Handbook of Creative Learning Exercises.* Houston: Gulf.

23. Wohlking, W. 1976. Role playing. In *Training and Development Handbook,* edited by R. L. Craig. New York: McGraw-Hill.

24. Huegli, J., and H. Tschirgi. 1980. Preparing the student for the initial job interview: Skills and methods. *American Business Communication Association Bulletin* 42(4): 10–13; Op. cit. Goldstein, 1993; Wexley, K., and G. Latham. 1991. *Developing and Training Human Resources in Organizations,* 2d ed. New York: HarperCollins, pp. 88–90; Sims, H., and C. Manz. 1982. Modeling influences on employee behavior. *Personnel Journal* 61(1): 58–65.

25. Burke, M., and R. Day. 1986. A cumulative study of the effectiveness of managerial training. *Journal of Applied Psychology* 71: 232–45; Decker, P., and B. Nathen. 1985. *Behavior Modeling Training: Principles and Applications.* New York: Praeger; Op. cit. Huegli and Tschirgi, 1980; Latham, G., and C. Frayne. 1989. Self-management training for increased job attendance: A follow-up and replication. *Journal of Applied Psychology* 74: 411–16; Smith, P. 1976. Management modeling training to improve morale and customer satisfaction. *Personnel Psychology* 29: 251–59.

26. Hequet, M. 1996. Video shakeout. *Training,* September, pp. 46–50.

27. Solem, A. R. 1960. Human relations training: A comparison of case studies. *Personnel Administration* 23: 29–37; Fazio, R., and M. Zanna. 1981. Direct experience and attitude–behavior consistency. In *Advances in Experimental Social Psychology,* edited by L. Berkowitz. New York: Academic Press.

28. Suzik, H. 1999. On-the-job training: Do it right. *Quality* 38: 84–85.

29. Gold, L. 1981. Job instruction: Four steps to success. *Training and Development Journal*, September, pp. 28–32.

30. Ibid.

31. *National Apprenticeship Training Program*. 1987. Washington, DC: Employment and Training Administration: Department of Labor.

32. *Apprentice Information*. 1995. Ontario Training and Adjustment Board. Toronto: Queens' Printer.

33. Finnerty, M. 1996. Coaching for growth and development. In *The Training and Development Handbook*, edited by R. Craig. New York: McGraw-Hill.

34. Orth, C. D., H. E. Wilkinson, and R. C. Benfari. 1987. The manager's role as coach and mentor. *Organizational Dynamics* 15(4): 66–74.

35. Evered, R., and J. Selman. 1989. Coaching and the art of management. *Organizational Dynamics* 18(2): 16–32.

36. Feldman, D. 2001. Career coaching: What HR professional and managers need to know. *Human Resource Planning* 24: 26–35.

37. Kram, K. 1985. Improving the mentoring process. *Training and Development Journal*, April, pp. 40–43.

38. Phillips-Jones, L. 1983. Establishing a formalized mentoring program. *Training and Development Journal*, February, pp. 38–42.

39. Gordon, E. E., R. Morgan, and J. Ponticell. 1995. The individualized training alternative. *Training and Development*, September, pp. 52–60.

40. Filipczak, B. 1996. Training on the cheap. *Training*, May, pp. 28–34.

41. Van Buren, M. 2001. *The 2001 ASTD State of the Industry Report*. February, pp. 19–20.

42. Ibid.

43. Honeycutt, E. Jr., T. McCarty, and V. Howe. 1993. Sales technology applications: Self-paced video enhanced training: A case study. *Journal of Personal Selling and Sales Management* 13(1): 73–79.

44. Ibid.

45. Gagné, R. 1977. *The Conditions of Learning*. New York: Holt, Rinehart, and Winston.

46. Ibid.

## Chapter 6

1. Interaction has its attraction. 1995. *Personnel Journal*. July, pp. 27–28.

2. Gordon, S. E. 1994. *Systematic Training Program Design*. Upper Saddle River, NJ: Prentice Hall, p. 197.

3. Van Buren, M. 2001. The 2001 ASTD State of the Industry Report. *Training and Development*, February, pp. 19–20.

4. Hequet, M. 2003. The State of the E-Learning Market. *Training*, September, pp. 24–29.

5. Op. Cit. Hequet, 2003.

6. Ellis, K. 2003. Moving into M-Learning. *Training*, November, pp. 57–59.

7. Forlenza, D. 1995. Computer-based training. *Professional Safety*, May, pp. 27–29.

8. Steel-Johnson, D., and B. Hyde. 1997. Advanced technologies in training: Intelligent tutoring systems and virtual reality. In *Training for a Rapidly Changing Workplace*, edited by M. Quinones and A. Ehrenstein. Washington, DC: American Psychological Association.

9. Ibid.

10. Seidel, R., O. Park, and R. Perez. 1988. Expertise of ICAI: Development requirements. *Computers in Human Behavior* 4: 235–56.

11. Ong, J., and S. Ramachandran. 2000. Intelligent tutoring systems: The what and the how. ASTD Learning Circuits. Available at www.learningcircuits.orgfeb2000/org.html.

12. Ibid.

13. Galvin, T. 2003. Industry Report. *Training*. October, pp. 21–45.

14. Nugget introduces food safety training & certification through CD-ROM. 1999. *Restaurant Hospitality* 83: S6–7.

15. Grunberg, D. 1999. Multimedia Training. *Franchising World* 31: 50.

16. 2004. www.medtrng.com.

17. Put SPIMM in your CBT. 1993. *Training* February, pp. 12, 14.

18. Johnson, G. 2003. Brewing the Perfect Blend. *Training*, pp. 31–34.

19. Marquardt, M. 1999. *Technology-based learning*. Boca Raton Fl. CRC Press.

20. Steel-Johnson, D. Hyde, B. 1997. Advanced technologies in training: Intelligent tutoring systems and virtual reality. In *Training for a Rapidly Changing Workplace*, edited by M. Quinones, A. Ehrenstein. Washington. American Psychological Association.

21. Fister, S. 1999. Tech trends. *Training*, Aug. pp. 24–26.

22. Field, S. 2002. Personal Communication. RTI International.

23. Lee, W. 2000. *Multimedia-Based Instructional Design: Computer-Based Training, Web-Based Training, Distance Broadcast Training*. San Fransisco, Jossey-Bass.

24. Hequet, M. 1996. Video shakeout. *Training*, September, pp. 46–50.

25. Blumenthal, R. L. Meiskey, S. Dooley R. Sparks. 1996. Reducing developmental costs with intelligent tutoring system shells. Paper presented at the Workshop on Architectures and Methods for Designing Cost-Effective and Reusable ITSs. Montreal, June 26.

26. Ibid.

27. Baynton, D. 2001. Cyber learning fortunes. *Training*. 38, pp. 22–23.

28. Release of the Virtual Reality Training Decision Tool. 1997. News Release, www. rti.org/news/news.

29. Ibid.

30. Nash, N. J., and Muczykf Vettori. 1971. The relative practical effectiveness of programmed instruction. *Personnel Psychology*, 24, pp. 397–418; Burns, T. 1997. Multimedia and quality. *Quality Progress*, February, pp. 77–84; Stauffer, D. 1999. High-tech training a huge win in Marriottís high-touch culture. 7, www.traininguniversity.com. Fletcher, D. 1999. Intelligent Tutoring Systems: Then and Now, Workshop on Advanced Training Technologies and Learning Environments held at NASA,Langley Research Center, March NASA/CP-1999-209339.

31. Op Cit. Fletcher, D., 1999.

32. Training flexes small firms' competitive muscle. 2001. *Management Services*. 45, p. 6.

33. Kearsley, G. 1984. *Training and Technology*. Reading, MA: Addison-Wesley.

34. Jensen, E. Personal communication, Jan. 31, 2002.

35. Op. Cit. Johnson, 2003.

# Chapter 7

1. Davis, I. K., and J. Hagman. 1976. What is right and wrong with your training room environment. *Training*, July, p. 28.

2. Chaddock, P. 1971. How do your trainers grow? *Training and Development Journal*, March, pp. 2–7.

3. Curry, T. 1977. Why not use your line managers as management trainers? *Training and Development Journal*, November, pp. 43–47.

4. Rothwell, W., and H. Kazanas. 1994. *Improving On-the-Job Training*. San Francisco, Jossey-Bass.

5. Ibid.

6. Kerr, G., S. Way, and J. W. Thacker, 2004. Performance, HR practices and the HR manager in small, entrepreneurial firms. Proceedings of the Administrative Science Association of Canada, June 5–8; Quebec City, Quebec.

7. Training flexes small firm's competitive muscle. 2001. *Management Services* 45: 6–7.

8. Blumfield, M. 1997. Learning to share. *Training*, April, pp. 38–42.

9. Anfuso, D. 1999. Trainers prove many heads are greater than one. *Workforce* 78: 60–65.

10. Tyler, K. 2001. E-Learning: Not just for e-normous companies anymore. *HRMagazine* 46: 82–88.

11. Leeds, L. 2002. Personal communication, Western Learning Systems.

12. Filipczak, B. 1996. Training on the cheap. *Training*, May, pp. 28–34.

13. Abella, K. 1986. *Building Successful Training Programs*. Reading, MA: Addison-Wesley.

14. Jolles, R. 1993. *How to Run Seminars and Workshops*. New York: Wiley.

15. Ibid.

16. Johnstone, A. H., and F. Percival. 1976. Attention breaks in lectures. *Education in Chemistry* 13: 273–304; Lloyd, D. H. 1968. A concept of improvement of learning in the taught lesson. *Visual Education*, pp. 23–25; Maddox, H., and E. Hook. 1975. Performance decrement in the lecture. *Educational Research*, 28: 17–30.

17. Palmer, A. 1981. Models of behavioral change. In *The 1981 Annual Handbook for Group Facilitators*, edited by J. E. Jones and J. W. Pfeiffer. San Diego: University Associates Press.

18. Pfeiffer, J. W., and J. E. Jones. 1980. *The 1980 Annual Handbook for Group Facilitators*. San Diego: University Associates Press.

19. Ibid.

20. Op. cit. Abella, 1986.

# Chapter 8

1. McIntyre, D. 1994. *Training and Development 1993: Policies, Practices and Expenditures*. Toronto: The Conference Board of Canada.

2. Blanchard, N., J. Thacker, and S. Way. 2000. Training evaluation: Perspectives and evidence from Canada. *International Journal of Training and Development* 4: 295–304.

3. Goldwasser, D. 2001. Beyond ROI. *Training*, January, pp. 82–90; op. cit. Geber, 1995.

4. Purcell, A. 2000. 20/20 ROI. *Training and Development*, July, pp. 28–33.

5. Meals, D., and J. W. Rogers. 1986. Matching human resource management to strategy. In *Strategic Human Resource Management*, edited by F. K. Folkes. Upper Saddle River, NJ: Prentice Hall.

6. Spitzer, D. 1999. Embracing evaluation. *Training*, June, pp. 42–47.

7. Geber, B. 1995. Does your training make a difference? Prove it! *Training*, March, pp. 27–34.

8. Ibid.

9. Geis, G. 1987. Formative evaluation: Developmental testing and expert review. *Performance and Instruction*, May, pp. 1–7.

10. Ibid.

11. Kirkpatrick, D. L. 1979. Techniques for evaluating training programs. *Training and Development Journal* 33(6): 78–92.

12. Alliger, G., S. Tannenbaum, W. Bennett, H. Traver, and A. Shortland. 1997. A meta-analysis of the relationship among training outcomes. *Personnel Psychology* 50: 341–58; Alliger, G., and E. Janak. 1989. Kirkpatrick's levels of training criteria: Thirty years later. *Personnel Psychology* 42: 331–42.

13. Blanchard, P. N., and J. W. Thacker. 1998. Organizational Strategy and Management Development. Paper presented at the Global Business Trends Conference of the Academy of Business Administration, Acapulco, Mexico.

14. Korth, S. 2001. Consolidating needs assessment and evaluation. *Performance Improvement* 40: 38–43.

15. Hamblin, A. C. 1974. *Evaluation and Control of Training*. New York: McGraw-Hill.

16. Saari, L., T. Johnson, S. McLaughlin, and D. Zimmerlie. 1988. A survey of management training and education practices in U.S. companies. *Personnel Psychology* 41: 731–43; Yancey, G. B., and L. Kelly. 1990. The inappropriateness of using participants' reactions to evaluate effectiveness of training. *Psychological Reports* 66: 937–38; Wexley, K., and G. Yukl. 1975. *Organizational Behavior and Industrial Psychology: Readings with Commentary*. New York: Oxford University Press.

17. Op. cit. Alliger et al., 1997.

18. Conroy, M., and M. Ross. 1984. Getting what you want by revising what you had. *Journal of Personality and Social Psychology* 47: 738–48; Dixon, N. 1990. The relationship between training responses on participant reaction forms and post test scores. *Human Resource Development Quarterly* 1(2): 129–37.

19. Nunnally, J. C. 1978. *Psychometric Theory*. New York: McGraw-Hill.

20. Kropp, R., and E. Hankin. 1975. Paper-and-pencil tests for evaluating instruction. In *Evaluating Training Programs*, edited by D. Kirkpatrick. Madison, WI: American Society of Training and Development.

21. Gordon, M. E., and J. F. Isenberg. 1975. Validation of an experimental training criterion for machinists. *Journal of Industrial Teacher Education* 12: 72–78.

22. Ostroff, C. 1991. Training effectiveness measures and scoring schemes: A comparison. *Personnel Psychology* 44: 353–74.

23. Bernardin, H., and J. Carlyle. 1979. The effects of forced choice methodology on psychometric characteristics of resultant scales. Paper presented at the annual meeting of the Southern Society of Philosophy and Psychology; King, L., J. Hunter, and F. Schmidt. 1980. Halo in a multidimensional forced choice performance evaluation scale. *Journal of Applied Psychology* 65: 507–16.

24. Stark, C. 1986. Ensuring skills transfer: A sensitive approach. *Training and Development Journal*, March, pp. 50–51.

25. Thacker, J. W., and M. Fields. 1992. Evaluation of steward training: Did it do what you wanted it to? Published in Proceedings of the 44th Annual Meeting of the Industrial Relations Research Association. New Orleans, January.

26. Thacker, J. W., M. Fields, and L. Barclay. 1990. Union commitment: An examination of antecedent and outcome factors. *Journal of Occupational Psychology* 63: 17–20.

27. Clement, R. W. 1982. Testing the hierarchy theory of training evaluation: An expanded role for trainee reactions. *Public Personnel Management Journal* 11: 176–84.

28. Op. cit. Dixon, 1990.

29. Holton, E. 1996. The flawed four-level evaluation model. *Human Resource Development Quarterly* 7: 21; op. cit. Blanchard and Thacker, 1998.

30. Op. cit. Geber, 1995.

31. Cascio, W. 1991. *Applied Psychology in Personnel Management*, 4th ed. Upper Saddle River, NJ: Prentice Hall.

32. Op. cit. Geber, 1995.

33. Op. cit. Purcell, 2000.

34. Hassett, J. 1992. Simplifying ROI. *Training*, September, pp. 53–57.

35. Op. cit. Cascio, 1991.

36. Cascio, W. 1989. Using utility analysis to assess training outcomes. In *Training and Development in Organizations*, edited by I. Goldstein. San Francisco: Jossey-Bass.

37. Whyte, G., and G. Latham. 1997. The futility of utility analysis revisited: When even an expert fails. *Personnel Psychology* 50: 601–10; Latham, G., and G. Whyte. 1994. The futility of utility analysis. *Personnel Psychology* 47: 31–46.

38. Dixon, N. 1996. New routes to evaluation. *Training and Development*, May, pp. 82–85.

39. Ibid.

40. Op. cit. Blanchard, Thacker, and Way, 2000.

41. Op. cit. Geber, 1995.

42. Sackett, P. R., and E. J. Mullen. 1993. Beyond formal experimental design: Toward an expanded view of the training evaluation process. *Personnel Psychology* 46: 613–27.

43. Goldstein, I. L. 1991. Training in work organizations. In *Handbook of Industrial and Organizational Psychology*, 2d ed., edited by M. D. Dunnette and L. M. Hough. Palo Alto, CA: Consulting Psychologists Press.

44. Cook, T. D., D. T. Campbell, and L. Peracchio. 1990. Quasi-experimentation. In *Handbook of Industrial and Organizational Psychology*, 2d ed., edited by M. D. Dunnette and L. M. Hough, pp. 507–620. Palo Alto, CA: Consulting Psychologists Press; Cook, T. D., and D. T. Campbell. 1979. *Quasi-Experimentation: Design and Analysis Issues for Field Settings*. Chicago: Rand McNally; Campbell, D. T., and J. C. Stanley. 1963. *Experimental and Quasi-experimental Designs for Research*, Chicago: Rand McNally.

45. Camp, R. P., P. N. Blanchard, and G. E. Huszczo. 1986. *Toward a More Organizationally Effective Training Strategy and Practice*. Upper Saddle River, NJ: Prentice Hall.

46. Wexley, K. N., and G. P. Latham. 1981. *Developing and Training Human Resources in Organizations*. Glenview, IL: Scott, Foresman.

47. Op. cit. Sackett and Mullen, 1993.

48. Ibid.

49. Ibid.

50. Haccoun, R., and T. Hamtiaux. 1994. Optimizing knowledge tests for inferring learning acquisition levels in single group training evaluation designs: The internal referencing strategy. *Personnel Psychology* 47: 593–604.

51. Ibid.

52. Ibid.

53. Dixon, N. 1997. Personnel communication, July 9. Associate Professor, George Washington University, Department of Administrative Sciences.

54. White, L., D. Rosenthal, and C. Fleuridas. 1993. Accountable supervision through systematic data collection: Using single case designs. *Counselor Education and Supervision* 33: 32–37.

55. QS 9000 Requirements. 1995.

56. LeGault, M. 1997. In-house training that gets results. *Canadian Plastics*, February, pp. 14–18.

## Chapter 9

1. *Conner v. Schrader-Bridgeport International, Inc.* (2000). No. 98-2055 (4th Cir. 09/13/2000).

2. Fisher, C. 1986. Organizational socialization: An integrative review. *Research in Personnel and Human Resource Management* 4: 104–45.

3. Klein, H., and N. Weaver. 2000. The effectiveness of an organizational-level orientation training program in the socialization of new hires. *Personnel Psychology* 53: 47–66.

4. Allen, N., and J. Meyer. 1990. Organizational socialization tactics: A longitudinal analysis of links to newcomers' commitment and role orientation. *Academy of Management Journal* 33: 847–58; Bauer, T., E. Morrison, and R. Callister. 1998. Organizational socialization: A review and directions for future research. *Research in Personnel and Human Resource Management* 16: 149–214; Saks, A. 1996. The relationship between the amount of helpfulness of entry training and work outcomes. *Human Relations* 49: 429–51.

5. Bassi, L., and M. Van Buren. 1998. The 1998 ASTD state of the industry report. *Training and Development* 52: 21–43.

6. Tyler, K. 1998. Take new employee training off the back burner. *HR Magazine*, May, pp. 49–57.

7. Ibid.

8. Smyrlis, L. 1999. Trail Blazers: How Bison's executive team transformed a small regional operation into Canada's best-managed fleet. *Motor Truck* 68: 25–37.

9. *A Stronger Canada*. 1998. Ottawa: Employment and Immigration Canada.

10. Statistics Canada. 2001. *Labour force and participation rates in Canada by age and sex*. Ottawa: Queen's Printer

11. Statistics Canada. 2001. *Population projections*. CANSIM ll Table 052-0001.

12. Tsui, A. S., and C. A. O'Reilly. 1989. Beyond simple demographic effects: The importance of relational demography in superior-subordinate dyads. *Academy of Management Journal* 29: 586–99; Wayne, S. J., and R. C. Linden. 1995. Effects of impression management on performance ratings:

A longitudinal study. *Academy of Management Journal* 38: 232–60.

13. Hartel, C. E., S. S. Douthitt, G. Hartel, and S. Y. Douthitt. 1999. Equally qualified but unequally perceived: Openness to perceived dissimilarity as a predictor of race and sex discrimination in performance judgments. *Human Resource Development Quarterly* 10(1): 79–89.

14. Gilbert, J. 2000. An empirical examination of resources in a diverse environment. *Public Personnel Management*, pp. 175–84.

15. Wright, P., S. Ferris, J. S. Hiller, and M. Kroll. 1995. Competitiveness through management of diversity: Effects on stock price valuation. *Academy of Management Journal* 38: 272–87.

16. Galvin, T. 2001. 2001 industry report. *Training*, October, pp. 40–75.

17. Naisbitt, J., and P. Aburdene. 2000. *Megatrends*. New York: Avon.

18. Gilbert, J., and J. Ivancevich. 2000. Valuing diversity: A tale of two organizations. *Academy of Management Executive* 14: 93–105.

19. Lords, E. 2001. Sex, race charges hit GM in Pontiac. *Detroit Free Press*, August 23, pp. 1A, 11A.

20. Ibid.

21. Moyer, C. 1995. Diversity Management: The bottom line impact of an equitable employment system. *Human Resource Professional*, November, 21–22.

22. Rynes, S., and B. Rosen. 1995. A field survey of factors affecting the adoption and perceived success of diversity training. *Personnel Psychology* 48: 247–70.

23. Lilley, W. 1995. Banking on equity. *Report on Business Magazine*, April, 65, p. 69.

24. Grossman, R. 2000. Is diversity working? *HR Magazine*, March, pp. 46–50.

25. Ibid.

26. Ibid.

27. *Roberts et al. v. Texaco Inc.* (1994). Civ. 2015.

28. Texaco. 1999. Second annual report of the equity and fairness task force for year ending June 30, 1999.

29. Gilbert, J., and J. Ivancevich. 2000. Valuing diversity: A tale of two organizations. *Academy of Management Executive* 14: 93–105.

30. *Annual Report*. 2003. Canadian Human Rights Commission. Ottawa: Queen's Printer.

31. Court holds employer liable for harassment by supervisor. 1987. *Daily Labor Report*, June 1, pp. A1, D1–5.

32. *Meritor Savings Bank v. Vinson.* (1986). 477 U.S. 57.

33. *Bell and Korczak* v.Ladas and The Flaming Steer Steak House Cited: (1980), 1 C.H.R.R.D/155 (Ont. Bd. Inq.).

34. Fisher, A. B. 1993. Sexual harassment: What to do. *Fortune*, August 23, pp. 84–88; Yang, C. 1996. Getting justice no easy task. *Business Week*, May 13, p. 98.

35. Foy, N. 200. Sexual harassment can threaten your bottom line. *Financial Times*, Sept. 8, p.27.

36. Flynn, K. 1991. Preventative medicine for sexual harassment. *Personnel* 68: 17.

37. Study: Many employers unaware of subtle sexual harassment. 2001. *Halifax Daily News*, March 8, p. 12.

38. Johnson, M. 1999. Anti-harassment training to shelter yourself from suits. *HR Magazine* 44: 76–81.

39. Ganzel, R. 1998. What sexual harassment training really prevents. *Training*, October, pp. 86–94.

40. Magley, V., C. Hulin, L. Fitzgerald, and M. DeNardo. 1999. Outcomes of self-labeling sexual harassment. *Journal of Applied Psychology* 84: 390–402.

41. Ibid.

42. Ibid.

43. Industry report. 1999. *Training*, October, p. 57.

44. Moore, H., R. Gatlin-Watts, and J. Cangelosi. 1998. Eight steps to a sexual-harassment-free workplace. *Training and Development*, April, pp. 12–13.

45. Bingham, S., and L. Scherer. 2001. The unexpected effects of a sexual harassment educational program. *Journal of Applied Behavioral Science* 37: 125–53.

46. Op. cit. Ganzel, 1998.

47. Tata, J. 2000. Autonomous work teams: An examination of cultural and structural constraints. *Work Study* 49: 187–93.

48. Way, S., and J. Thacker. 2000. Trends in human resource management. *HR Professional: Research Forum*, August/September.

49. Hunsaker, P. 2001. *Training in Management Skills*. Upper Saddle River, NJ: Prentice Hall.

50. Cascio, W., and J. Thacker. 1994. *Managing Human Resources*. Toronto: McGraw Hill.

51. Whetten, D., and K. Cameron. 2002. *Developing Management Skills*. Upper Saddle River, NJ: Prentice Hall.

52. Ibid.

53. Ibid.

54. Ibid.

55. Neuman, G., and J. Wright. 1999. Team effectiveness: Beyond skills and ability. *Journal of Applied Psychology* 84: 376–89.

56. Cutcher-Gershenfeld, J., T. Kochan, and A. Verma. 1987. Recent developments in U.S. employee involvement initiatives: Erosion or diffusion. Paper presented at the Pacific Rim Labour Policy Conference, Vancouver, Canada, June 25–26.

57. Wells, D. 1986. *Soft Sell*. Ottawa: Canadian Centre for Policy Alternatives.

58. Op. cit. Cutcher-Gershenfeld et al., 1987; Greenberg, P., and E. Glaser. 1981. Viewpoints of labor leaders regarding quality of work life improvement programs. *International Review of Applied Psychology* 30: 157–74.

59. Goodman, P., and J. Dean. 1983. In *Organizational Development: Theory Practice and Research*, edited by W. French, C. Bell, and R. Zawacki. Plano, TX: Business Publications Inc.

60. Why teams don't work. 1993. *Sales and Marketing Management*, April, p. 12.

61. Hunsaker, P. 2001. *Training in Management Skills*. Upper Saddle River, NJ: Prentice Hall.

62. Phillips, S. 1996. Team training puts fizz in Coke plant's future. *Personnel Journal* 75: 87–94.

63. Pay for lost opportunities. 1988. *Canadian Human Rights Advocate* 4.

64. Haben, M. K. 2001. Shattering the glass ceiling. *Executive Speeches* 15: 4–10.

65. Scott, M. 2001. For women the glass ceiling still persists. *Black Enterprise* 32: 30.

66. Op. cit. Haben, 2001.

67. Ibid.

68. Facwett, G. 1996. Living with disability in Canada: An economic portrait. *Human Resources Canada*.

69. Salopek, J. 1998. Arrested development. *Training and Development* 52: 65–66.

70. Calamai, P. 1999. The literacy gap. *Toronto Star*, August 28, pp. J1–2.

71. Tyler, K. 1996. Tips for structuring workplace literacy. *HR Magazine* 41: 112–16.

72. *A Stronger Canada*. 1998. Employment and Immigration Canada. Ottawa.

73. Workplace literacy training pays off. 1998. *OH & S Canada* 14: 8.

74. Op. cit. Tyler, 1996.

75. Ibid.

76. Thach, L. 1996. Training in Russia. *Training and Development*, 50: 34-38.

77. ·Filpczak, B. 1997. Think Locally, Train Globally. *Training*, 34: 40-46.

78. Ibid.

79. Op. cit. Thach, L. 1996.

80. Op. cit. Filpczak, B. 1997.

81. Ibid.

82. Ibid.

83. Op. cit. Thach, L. 1996.

84. Op. cit Filpczak, B. 1997.

85. Ibid.

86. Human Resources and Skill Development Canada Website. www.hrsdc.gc.ca/asp/gateway.asp?hr=/en/lp/lo/ohs/statistics/oicc/lt022.shtml&hs=oxs

87. Livingston, G. 2004. Ontario to Hire 200 More Inspectors to Target Unsafe Workplaces. *OHS Canada*. Website: www.ohscanada.com.

88. Overheul, V. 2001. A cure for boredom. *Occupational Health and Safety* 70: 192–95.

89. Ibid.

90. Garvin, D. 1993. Building a learning organization. *Harvard Business Review*, July/August; Senge, P. 1990. *The Fifth Discipline*. New York: Doubleday Currency; Shaw, R., and D. Perkins. 1991. Teaching organizations to learn. *Organizational Development Journal*, Winter, pp. 1–12.

91. McGill, M., and J. Slocum. 1993. Unlearning the organization. *Organizational Dynamics* 22: 67–79.

92. DeVito, J. 1996. The learning organization. *The ASTD Training and Development Handbook*, 4th ed., pp. 77–103.

93. Marquardt, M., and A. Reynolds. 1994. *Global Learning Organization*. New York: Irwin.

94. Op. cit. Conner v. Schrader-Bridgeport International, Inc.

# Chapter 10

1. Burack, E., W. Hochwarter, and N. Mathys. 1997. The new management development paradigm. *Human Resource Planning* 20: 14–21.

2. Industry Report. 2002. *Training*, October; Industry Report. 2001. *Training*, October; Industry Report. 1996. *Training*; Industry Report. 1995. *Training*.

3. Op. cit. *Training*, 2002.

4. Cascio, W., and R. Zammuto. 1987. *Societal Trends and Staffing Policies*. Denver: University of Colorado Press; Offerman, L., and M. Gowing. 1990. Organizations of the future: Changes and challenges. *American Psychologist* 45: 95–108; Patel, D. 2002. Managing talent. *HR Magazine*, March, pp. 112–13; Pater, R. 2002. Leadership skills for the 21st century. *Occupational Health and Safety*, March, pp. 6–15.

5. Howell, J., P. Dorfman, and S. Kerr. 1986. Moderating variables in leadership research. *Academy of Management Review* 11: 88–102; Morden, T. 1997. Leadership as competence. *Management Decision* 35: 519–26.

6. Campbell, J., M. Dunnette, E. Lawler III, and K. Weick, Jr. 1970. *Managerial Behavior, Performance, and Effectiveness*. New York: McGraw-Hill.

7. Mintzberg, H. 1975. The manager's job: Folklore and fact. *Harvard Business Review* 53(4): 49–61.

8. Wexley, K., and G. Latham. 1991. *Developing and Training Human Resources in Organizations*, 2nd ed. New York: HarperCollins.

9. Karmel, B. 1978. Leadership: A challenge to traditional research methods and assumptions. *Academy of Management Review*, July, pp. 477–79; Schein, E. 1980. *Organizational Psychology*, 3rd ed. Upper Saddle River, NJ: Prentice Hall.

10. House, R. 1971. A path-goal theory of leadership. *Administrative Science Quarterly*, September, pp. 321–38; House, R., and T. Mitchell. 1974. Path-goal theory of leadership. *Journal of Contemporary Business*, Autumn, p. 83; Keller, R. 1989. A test of the path-goal theory of leadership with need for clarity as a moderator in research and development organizations. *Journal of Applied Psychology*, April, pp. 208–12; Mathieu, J. 1990. A test of subordinates' achievement and affiliation needs as moderators of a leader's path-goal relationships. *Basic and Applied Social Psychology*, June, pp. 179–89.

11. The primary and secondary research we examined that led us to the conclusions in this section are Andrews, J. 1967. The achievement motive and advancement in two types of organizations. *Journal of Personality and Social Psychology* 6: 163–68; Bass, B. 1990. *Handbook of Leadership*. New York: Free Press; Bennis, W., and B. Nanus. 1985. *Leaders: The Strategies for Taking Charge*. New York: Harper & Row; Birch, D., and J. Veroff. 1966. *Motivation: A Study of Action*. Monterey, CA: Brooks/Cole; Bray, D. 1973. New data from the management progress study. *Assessment and Development* 1: 3; Bray, D., R. Campbell, and D. Grant. 1974. *Formative Years in Business: A Long-Term AT&T Study of Managerial Lives*. New York: Wiley; Bray, D., and D. Grant. 1966. The assessment center in the measurement of potential for business management. *Psychological Monographs* 80: 1–27; Brown, W., and N. Karagozoglu. 1993. Leading the way to faster new product development. *The Executive* 7: 1; Byham, W. 1980. Starting an assessment center. *Personnel Administrator* 25(2): 27–32; Gutpa, A. 1984. Contingency linkages between strategy and general manager characteristics: A conceptual examination. *Academy of Management Review* 9: 399–412; Gutpa, A., and V. Govindarajan. 1984. Business unit strategy, managerial characteristics, and business unit effectiveness at strategy implementation. *Academy of Management Journal* 27: 25–41; Howard, A., and D. Bray. 1988. *Managerial Lives in Transition: Advancing Age and Changing Times*. New York: Guilford Press; Katz, R. 1974. Skills of an effective administrator. *Harvard Business Review*, September–October; Kirkpatrick, S., and E. Locke. 1991. Leadership: Do traits matter? *The Executive* 5: 2; Kouzes, J., and B. Posner. 1988. *The Leadership Challenge: How to Get Things*

*Done in Organizations.* San Francisco: Jossey-Bass; Luthans, F., R. Hodgetts, and S. Rosenkrantz. 1988. *Real Managers.* Cambridge, MA: Ballinger Press; McCauley, C., M. Lombardo, and C. Usher. 1989. Diagnosing management development needs: An instrument based on how managers develop. *Journal of Management* 15: 3; McClelland, D. 1961. *The Achieving Society.* New York: Van Nostrand; McClelland, D., and D. Burnham. 1976. Power is the great motivator. *Harvard Business Review* 54(2): 100–10; McClelland, D., and R. Boyatzis. 1982. Leadership motive pattern and long-term success in management. *Journal of Applied Psychology* 67: 737–43; Miner, J. 1978. Twenty years of research on role-motivation theory of managerial effectiveness. *Personnel Psychology* 31: 739–60; Niehoff, M., and M. Romans. 1982. Needs assessment as step one toward enhancing productivity. *Personnel Administrator*, May, pp. 35–39; Porter, L., and L. McKibbin. 1988. *Future of Management Education and Development: Drift or Thrust into the 21st Century?* New York: McGraw-Hill; Smith, K., and J. Harrison. 1986. In search of excellent leaders. In *The Handbook of Strategy*, edited by W. Guth. New York: Warren, Gorham & Lamont; Starcevich, M., and J. Sykes. 1982. Internal advanced management programs for executive development: The experience of Phillips Petroleum. *Personnel Administrator*, June, pp. 27–33; Tornton, G., and W. Byham. 1982. *Assessment Centers and Managerial Performance.* New York: Academic Press; Zaleznik, A. 1970. Power and politics in organizational life. *Harvard Business Review* 48: 47–60.

12. Bass, B. 1981. *Stogdill's Handbook of Leadership: A Survey of Theory and Research*, Revised and expanded. New York: Free Press.

13. McClelland, D. 1961. *The Achieving Society.* New York: Van Nostrand.

14. Birch, D., and J. Veroff. 1966. *Motivation: A Study of Action.* Monterey, CA: Brooks/Cole.

15. McClelland, D., and D. Burnham. 1976. Power is the great motivator. *Harvard Business Review* 54(2): 100–10.

16. Kirkpatrick, S., and E. Locke. 1991. Leadership: Do traits matter? *The Executive* 5: 2.

17. For ambition, see Howard, A., and D. Bray. 1988. *Managerial Lives in Transition: Advancing Age and Changing Times.* New York: Guilford Press; for energy see Kouzes, J., and B. Posner. 1988. *The Leadership Challenge: How to Get Things Done in Organizations.* San Francisco: Jossey-Bass; for tenacity, see Bass, B. 1990. *Handbook of Leadership.* New York: Free Press.

18. McClelland, D., and R. Boyatzis. 1982. Leadership motive pattern and long-term success in management. *Journal of Applied Psychology* 67: 737–43; Miner, J. 1978. Twenty years of research on role-motivation theory of managerial effectiveness. *Personnel Psychology* 31: 739–60.

19. Andrews, J. 1967. The achievement motive and advancement in two types of organizations. *Journal of Personality and Social Psychology* 6: 163–68; Zaleznik, A. 1970. Power and politics in organizational life. *Harvard Business Review* 48: 47–60.

20. McCauley, C., M. Lombardo, and C. Usher. 1989. Diagnosing management development needs: An instrument based on how managers develop. *Journal of Management* 15: 3; Smith, K., and J. Harrison. 1986. In search of excellent leaders. In *The Handbook of Strategy*, edited by W. Guth. New York: Warren, Gorham & Lamont; Weiss, W. 1999. Leadership. *Supervision* 60: 6–9.

21. Coleman, E., and M. Campbell. 1975. *Supervisors: A Corporate Resource.* New York: AMACOM

22. Katz, R. 1974. Skills of an effective administrator. *Harvard Business Review*, September–October.

23. Bennis, W., and B. Nanus. 1985. *Leaders: The Strategies for Taking Charge.* New York: Harper and Row; Smith, K., and Harrison. 1986. In search of excellent leaders. In *The Handbook of Strategy*, edited by W. Guth. New York: Warren, Gorham and Lamont.

24. Brown, W., and N. Karagozoglu. 1993. Leading the way to faster new product development. *The Executive* 7: 1; McCauley, C., M. Lombardo, and C. Usher. 1989. Diagnosing management development needs: An instrument based on how managers develop. *Journal of Management* 15: 3; Kirkpatrick, S., and E. Locke. 1991. Leadership: Do traits matter? *The Executive* 5: 2.

25. Luthans, F., R. Hodgetts, and S. Rosenkrantz. 1988. *Real Managers.* Cambridge, MA: Ballinger Press; Op. cit. McCauley, Lombardo, and Usher, 1989; McClelland, D., and D. Burnham. 1976. Power is the great motivator. *Harvard Business Review* 54(2): 100–10; Porter, L., and L. McKibbin. 1988. *Future of Management Education and Development: Drift or Thrust into the 21st Century?* New York: McGraw-Hill.

26. Op. cit. Bruack et al., 1997.

27. Frisch, M. 2001. Going around in circles with 360 tools: Have they grown too popular for their own good? *Human Resource Planning* 24: 7–8.

28. Waldman, D., F. Yammarino, and B. Avolio. 1990. A multiple level investigation of personnel ratings. *Personnel Psychology* 43: 811–35.

29. O'Reilly, B. 1994. 360-feedback can change your life. *Fortune*, October, p. 17.

30. Ibid.

31. State of the industry report. 1998. *Training and Development*, January, pp. 22–43.

32. Op. cit. Hall, 1986.

33. Schleede, J. 2002. The future of management education. *Mid American Journal of Business* 17: 5–8.

34. Op. cit. *Training and Development*, 1998.

35. Ibid.

36. Op. cit. Schleede, 2002.

37. Eurich, N. 1985. *Corporate Classroom: The Learning Process.* Princeton, NJ: Carnegie Foundation for the Advancement of Teaching; Starcevich, M., and J. Sykes. 1982. Internal advanced management programs for executive development: The experience of Phillips Petroleum. *Personnel Administrator*, June, pp. 27–33.

38. Camp, R., P. Blanchard., and G. Huszczo. 1986. *Toward a More Organizationally Effective Training Strategy and Practice.* Upper Saddle River, NJ: Prentice Hall, pp. 285–86.

39. Op. cit. Mintzberg, 1975; Roberts, T. 1974. *Developing Effective Managers.* Stratford-upon-Avon: Edward Fox and Son.

40. Vroom, V., and A. Jago. 1988. *The New Leadership: Managing Participation in Organizations.* Upper Saddle River, NJ: Prentice Hall; Vroom, V., and P. Yetton. 1973. *Leadership and Decision Making.* Pittsburgh: University of Pittsburgh Press.

41. Op. cit. Mintzberg, 1975.

42. Pigors, P., and F. Pigors. 1987. Case method. In *Training and Development Handbook: A Guide to Human Resource Development*, edited by R. Craig. New York: McGraw-Hill.

43. Rackham, N., and T. Morgan. 1977. *Behavior Analysis in Training.* Maidenhead, England: McGraw-Hill.

44. Blake, R., and J. Mouton. 1985. *The Managerial Grid III: The Key to Leader- ship Excellence.* Houston: Gulf Publishing; Yukl,

G. 1989. *Leadership in Organizations*. Upper Saddle River, NJ: Prentice Hall.

45. Minor, J. 1978. Twenty years of research on role motivation theory of managerial effectiveness. *Personnel Psychology* 31: 739–60.

46. Op. cit. McClelland, 1961; McClelland and Burnham, 1976; Miron and McClelland, 1979.

47. Wellins, R., and W. Byham. 2001. The leadership gap. *Training*, March, pp. 98–106.

48. Ibid.

49. Thach, E. 1998. 14 ways to groom executives. *Training*, August, pp. 52–55; Zemke, R., and S. Zemke. 2001. Where do leaders come from? *Training*, August, pp. 44–48.

50. Tomlinson, A. 2002. The coaching explosion. *Canadian HR Reporter* 15: 7.

51. Bolch, M. 2001. Proactive coaching. *Training*, May, pp. 58–66.

52. Ibid.

53. Ibid.

54. Caironi, P. 2002. Coaches coach, players play, and companies win. *TIP* 40: 37–44.

55. Feldman, D. Career coaching: What HR professionals and managers need to know. *Human Resource Planning* 24: 26–35.

56. Op. cit. Thach, 1998.

57. Op. cit. Thach, 1998.

58. Barbian, J. 2002. The road best traveled. *Training*, May, pp. 38–42.

59. Op. cit. Zemke and Zemke, 2001.

60. Op. cit. Zemke and Zemke, 2001.

61. Peters, J., and P. Smith. 1998. Action learning and the leadership development challenge. *Journal of Workplace Learning* 10: 284–91.

62. Ibid.

63. Yelverton, J. 1997. Adaptive skills: Seven keys to developing top managers. *Vital Speeches of the Day* 63: 725–27.

64. Tyler, L. 2002. Succession planning: Charting a course for the future. *Trustee* 55: 24–28.

65. Ibid.

66. Galvin, T. 2001. Industry report. *Training*, October pp. 40–75.

67. Op. cit. Wellins and Byham, 2001.

68. Grossman, R. 1999. Heirs unapparent. *HR Magazine*, February.

69. Ibid.

70. Galvin, T. 2001. Birds of a feather. *Training*, March, pp. 58–68.

71. Ibid.

72. Tarley, M. 2002. Leadership development for small organizations. *Training and Development* 56: 52–55; op. cit. Zemke and Zemke, 2001.

73. Op. cit. Zemke and Zemke, 2001.

# REQUIRED PROFESSIONAL CAPABILITIES—ENTRY LEVEL RPCs

## ORGANIZATIONAL LEARNING, DEVELOPMENT, AND TRAINING

Assesses and reports on the costs and benefits of engaging internal and external suppliers of development programs, given the organizational constraints and objectives.

- adult learning principles
- program design
- available programs
- cost-benefit analysis
- training and development program design and administration
- methods of training and development (games and simulations, case method, lecturing, on-the-job training, distance learning, role-play, videoconferencing, group discussion)
- training cost-benefit analysis (including the direct and indirect costs associated with conducting training and development programs, costing sheets for training or development programs, costs of alternative training and development programs, net cost-benefit estimation)

Ensures the application of appropriate development methods and techniques based upon generally accepted principles of adult learning.

- adult learning principles
- program design
- available programs
- training and development program design and administration
- methods of training and development (games and simulations, case method, lecturing, on-the-job training, distance learning, role-play, videoconferencing, group discussion
- domains and levels of learning
- effective learning objectives
- transfer of training issues
- training programs delivery techniques
- conditions necessary for training success

Using a variety of methods facilitates the delivery of development programs to groups and individual learners.

- adult learning principles
- program design
- facilitation techniques
- methods of training and development (games and simulations, case method, lecturing, on-the-job training, distance learning, role-play, videoconferencing, group discussion)
- domains and levels of learning

- training programs delivery techniques
- conditions necessary for training success

**Documents participant feedback to evaluate effectiveness of program delivery.**

- adult learning principles
- program design
- evaluation instruments and design
- HRIS
- statistical analysis
- training and development program evaluation methods
- rationale and process of program evaluation
- techniques to analyse and interpret training results
- training cost-benefit analysis (including the direct and indirect costs associated with conducting training and development programs, costing sheets for training or development programs, costs of alternative training and development programs, net cost-benefit estimation)
- evaluation issues (including behaviourally anchored rating scales and staffing tables)

**Conducts an evaluation of the program.**

- program evaluation techniques/theory
- statistics
- business math/accounting/budgeting
- program design and delivery
- training and development program evaluation methods
- rationale and process of program evaluation
- techniques to analyse and interpret training results
- training cost-benefit analysis (including the direct and indirect costs associated with conducting training and development programs, costing sheets for training or development programs, costs of alternative training and development programs, net cost-benefit estimation)
- research methods and designs (including measurement of HR)
- validity and reliability (conceptual definitions and assessment techniques)
- measurement tools and their limitations
- statistical analyses and evaluation
- objectives, processes, and conceptual foundations of financial and management accounting
- importance, criteria, and techniques of program evaluation
- cost-benefit analyses (including audits, utility analysis, and impact studies)
- evaluation issues (including behaviourally anchored rating scales and staffing tables)

**Compiles, analyzes, and documents evaluation data based on feedback.**

- program evaluation techniques/theory
- statistics
- business math/accounting/budgeting
- program design and delivery
- training and development program evaluation methods
- rationale and process of program evaluation
- techniques to analyse and interpret training results
- training cost-benefit analysis (including the direct and indirect costs associated with conducting training and development programs, costing sheets for training or development programs, costs of alternative training and development programs, net cost-benefit estimation)

- research methods and designs (including measurement of HR)
- validity and reliability (conceptual definitions and assessment techniques)
- measurement tools and their limitations
- statistical analyses and evaluation
- objectives, processes, and conceptual foundations of financial and management accounting
- importance, criteria, and techniques of program evaluation
- cost-benefit analyses (including audits, utility analysis, and impact studies)
- evaluation issues (including behaviourally anchored rating scales and staffing tables)

**Interprets results of development programs in terms of contribution to organizational objectives, and does a post-development follow-up.**

- program evaluation techniques/theory
- statistics
- business math/accounting/budgeting
- program design and delivery
- cost benefit analysis
- techniques to analyse and interpret training results
- training cost-benefit analysis (including the direct and indirect costs associated with conducting training and development programs, costing sheets for training or development programs, costs of alternative training and development programs, net cost-benefit estimation)
- research methods and designs (including measurement of HR)
- validity and reliability (conceptual definitions and assessment techniques)
- measurement tools and their limitations
- statistical analyses and evaluation
- importance, criteria, and techniques of program evaluation
- cost-benefit analyses (including audits, utility analysis, and impact studies)
- evaluation issues (including behaviourally anchored rating scales and staffing tables)

**Provides the appropriate assessment tools for determining career development options for employees.**

- career development/management principles
- assessment tools available
- training and development needs analysis techniques (i.e., skill assessment strategies and levels of training needs analysis)
- validity and reliability (conceptual definitions and assessment techniques)
- measurement tools and their limitations
- statistical analyses and evaluation
- employee competencies, training, and development
- career and succession planning and management

**Facilitates the implementation of cross-functional development work experiences for employees.**

- career development program within the organization with particular emphasis on: work experience program and cross-functional concept
- domains and levels of learning
- effective learning objectives
- employee competencies, training, and development
- career and succession planning and management

Monitors, documents, and reports on career development activities within the organization.

- data gathering techniques
- procedures for information collection, manipulation, and analysis
- the identification, assessment, development, implementation, maintenance, and monitoring processes of effective systems of managing HR information
- career and succession planning and management

Ensures legislated training obligations are met within the organization.

- training requirements due to employment legislation
- common and statutory law (e.g., employment standard: labour relations)
- roles of the federal and provincial governments in providing training and development
- roles of municipal governments, unions, and professional associations in training and development

Conducts training need assessments by identifying individual and corporate learning requirements.

- needs analysis methods and techniques
- organizational development principles
- instructional design
- training and development needs analysis techniques (i.e., skill assessment strategies and levels of training needs analysis)

Recommends the most appropriate way to meet identified learning needs (e.g., courses, secondments, and on-the-job activities).

- needs analysis methods and techniques
- organizational development principles
- instructional design
- training and development program design and administration
- methods of training and development (games and simulations, case method, lecturing, on-the-job training, distance learning, role-play, videoconferencing, group discussion)
- domains and levels of learning
- effective learning objectives
- training programs delivery techniques

Establishes priority of responses to needs assessment results.

- priority setting
- needs analysis methods and techniques
- organizational development principles
- instructional design
- training and development needs analysis techniques (i.e., skill assessment strategies and levels of training needs analysis)
- methods of matching skills and people
- stakeholders in training and development
- assessment and forecasting techniques for HR Requirements (including benefits and types of qualitative and quantitative forecasting methods)

Facilitates coaching and post training support activities to ensure transfer of learning to the workplace.

- situational leadership
- coaching

- interpersonal communications
- communication theories and techniques
- domains and levels of learning
- transfer of training issues
- training programs delivery techniques
- conditions necessary for training success

**Develops training budgets, monitors expenditures, and documents activities associated with training.**

- basic accounting
- budgeting process
- measurement bases and underlying methodologies used in finance departments
- methods of preparing operating budgets
- objectives, processes, and conceptual foundations of financial and management accounting
- procedures for, and issues pertaining to, budget preparation (including cost forecasting; operating budget; budgeted income statement; budgeted balance sheet; cash flow budget)

**Identifies and accesses external sources of training funding available to employees.**

- sources of available funding
- application procedures
- roles of the federal and provincial governments in providing training and development
- roles of municipal governments, unions, and professional associations in training and development

**Develops requests for proposals (RFP) and reviews submissions by third parties.**

- RFP writing
- RFP evaluation
- research methods and designs (including measurement of HR)
- validity and reliability (conceptual definitions and assessment techniques)
- measurement tools and their limitations
- statistical analyses and evaluation
- needs analysis

**Recommends the selection of external training consultants and contractors such as public education institutions.**

- local and other training, and development consultants
- contract administration
- methods of training and development (games and simulations, case method, lecturing, on-the-job training, distance learning, role-play, videoconferencing, group discussion)
- validation of selection and training decisions and measures
- measurement tools and their limitations
- statistical analyses and evaluation

**Participates in course design and selection/delivery of learning materials via various media.**

- adult learning principles
- instructional design and delivery
- facilitation techniques

- training and development program design and administration
- methods of training and development (games and simulations, case method, lecturing, on-the-job training, distance learning, role-play, videoconferencing, group discussion
- domains and levels of learning
- effective learning objectives
- transfer of training issues
- training programs delivery techniques

**Ensures arrangements are made for training schedules, facilities, trainers, participants, and equipment and course materials.**

- adult learning principles
- instructional design and delivery
- facilitation techniques
- project management
- contract administration
- history, function, and process of training and development
- training and development program design and administration
- training programs delivery techniques

**Ensures participant and organizational feedback is documented and evaluated.**

- evaluation techniques
- interpretation of results
- survey and basic statistical techniques
- procedures for information collection, manipulation, and analysis
- research methods and designs (including measurement of HR)
- validity and reliability (conceptual definitions and assessment techniques)
- measurement tools and their limitations
- statistical analyses and evaluation
- importance, criteria, and techniques of program evaluation
- evaluation issues (including behaviourally anchored rating scales and staffing tables)

# REQUIRED PROFESSIONAL CAPABILITIES—RPCs FOR EXPERIENCED PROFESSIONALS

## ORGANIZATIONAL LEARNING, DEVELOPMENT, AND TRAINING

- Monitors and evaluates HR effectiveness as it relates to business success and identifies areas that need improvement and development
- Determines the best learning approaches and human capital development initiatives required for continued organizational success
- Performs a cost-benefit analysis of developing existing staff versus acquiring new staff, or outsourcing
- Develops and delivers learning strategies to close the gap between current human capital capabilities and the future needs of the organization
- Monitors and reports on the results of HR development activities in terms of their effect on organizational performance

- Identifies, evaluates, and implements measurement systems for current and future job/team performance
- Ensures performance feedback is an integral part of the organization's HR information system
- Provides development information, support activities, and procedures for learners, supervisors, and managers to assist in achieving performance improvement (e.g., training, coaching, feedback, and techniques for setting objectives)
- Assists and coaches supervisors to help employees achieve required performance levels
- Develops, implements, and monitors the success of performance feedback and coaching
- Designs development programs, consistent with organizational performance requirements at varying stages of the employment cycle
- Establishes measurement tools and processes to evaluate development programs for effectiveness relative to the needs of the organization
- Helps supervisors/managers to identify career options for employees, which are consistent with the organizational needs
- Ensures performance management information is an integral component of employee development
- Assists employees in identifying career paths, establishing learning plans and activities required for achieving personal success

# INDEX